Track and Field Omnibook

Third Edition
Revised and Updated

Ken Doherty, Ph.D.

tafnews

**Book Division of
Track & Field News**

THIRD EDITION

Published by Tafnews Press
Book Division of Track & Field News, Inc.
P.O. Box 296, Los Altos, CA 94022 USA

Standard Book Number 0-911520-99-6

Printed in the United States of America.

Cover photo: Javelin thrower Bob Roggy.
Photograph by Dave Drennan.

Cover design by Ann Harris.

CONTENTS

DEDICATION

TO THOSE AMATEUR ATHLETES

WHO take part in track and field

Primarily as an exciting challenge
Worth doing for its own sake;

WHO do their best to win,

Not as the main goal so much as
The incentive for doing one's best
And for motivating the long striving despite

The self doubts of beginning,
The hurt-pain-agony of training, and
The adversities of competition
That lead to the true main goal--

The higher development of self and society;

WHO practice fair play on the field,

But also off the field,
By furthering equality of opportunity
For better training and performance
By all competitors;

WHO honor the agreements of amateur sportsmen

That other life commitments--vocation,
   studies, service--have first priority,

That sports are and should be avocational,
And act within the limitations of

Material rewards,
Time for preparation and competition, and
Self-commitment
That it requires; but

WHO, within those limitations,

Strive to their utmost
   To raise performance
   Higher, faster, farther,
   To the highest levels of their potential.

Ken Doherty
Swarthmore, Pa.
August, 1980

iv

PREFACE

These opening paragraphs, commonly called a Preface, are equally an Epilogue, since they are written last in preparing this textbook for coaches-in-training for track and field. First, this is an epilogue of a full century of track and field development in performance; performance at all levels as shown in the Tables of Outstanding Performances for each event--world, college, high school, but most clearly in the great Olympic Games--from 1896 Olympic championships won at 36 feet 9½ inches in putting the shot, 10 feet 9½ inches in pole jumping, or 20 feet 10 inches in the long jump, to the 1968 Olympic long jump of 29 feet 2½ inches that many consider a "human ultimate."

Second, this is an epilogue of a century-long development by trial-error-success in better techniques and training methods. This is just as exciting a story as that of performance--a story of new ways of increasing the time-distance through which power is applied to the projected instruments--the shot, discus, javelin, hammer, or the human body itself; a story of better ways to greater power--basic, related, and simulative in both its strength and its velocity aspects; a story of greater speed through mastery of skill, relaxation, speed-power, and speed-endurance; and lastly, a story of greater endurance by training more days per year and years per career with a balanced concern for both quantity and quality training.

Third, this is an epilogue of development--painfully slow during the early decades-- in the sciences as they relate to both athletes and athletics. At first such research tended to focus on implements and "safe" mechanics. Neither coaches nor scientists had much understanding or interest in the others' problems or viewpoints. Coaches refused to allow their athletes to be tested in "dangerous" ways; scientists denied such dangers and, in any case, felt that the need to know had priority over the need to win. Until about the 1950s, useable research was in short supply and of doubtful quality.

Fourth, if I may be personal, this is an epilogue of my own half-century involvement in track and field: (1) as a mere dual-meet place winner whom 10 years of effort developed to two National Decathlon Championships and an Olympic bronze-medal; (2) as a track coach for over 30 years in high school and the Universities of Princeton, Michigan and Pennsylvania; (3) as an organizer of track and field meets--the Pennsylvania Relay Carnival, *The Philadelphia Inquirer* Games, the first (1959) USA-USSR dual meet in this country, and--most exciting--the 1935 "Jesse Owens Meet" in Ann Arbor, Michigan when he broke three world records and tied a fourth; and (4) as a writer of track and field textbooks beginning with *MODERN TRACK AND FIELD* in 1954. In looking back, those 20 years or more of writing have had their special uses not obtainable in any other ways. Writing requires concentrated thinking and a discipline of distractions just as severe as training for competition, and forces both an analytic and holistic approach to problems quite different from, and in some ways, superior to that of coaching.

Fifth, this is an epilogue of development in the organization of track and field. Of the many possible examples, consider the development of the Pennsylvania Relay Carnival from an informal get-together in May 1893 of Pennsylvania-Princeton 440-men to run a relay team-race with each man touching-off the next runner, to today's gigantic Carnival with some 140 events, not counting sections within races, some 6000 individual athletes representing over 500 schools and colleges, and requiring four days of competition. Or consider the Olympic Games in 1896 at which eight nations were represented--some unofficially--in such varied activities as mountain climbing, choral singing, dumbbell swinging, still-fishing, as well as track and field. Now, within only 20 Olympiads of four years each, that Grecian festive picnic has evolved to our Modern Mammoth Extravaganza with some 125 nations, 10,000 athletes trained year-round by coaches, scientists, physicians, in a score or more of sports.

A PREFACE

But more importantly--for you this is a preface to your own involvement in the challenging but frustrating world of track and field coaching. Such coaching demands the very best of you; it demands that you believe in the worthwhileness of what you are doing, that you concentrate your energies in terms of it and the boys you are trying to help, and that you set aside 101 other activities you'd like to do, and that are worth doing. But, no matter how demanding the work, small the results, or unappreciative the team members, the coach that puts the best of himself into his sport will get a comparable satisfaction out of it.

Murray Halberg dedicated his autobiography to: "The man I have cursed most on cold, wet winter days and thanked most on the victory dais--the man who has been my inspiration, guide, mentor and friend--Arthur Lydiard." Few express themselves so cogently; most never do so in any verbal way. But a coach knows whether or not he's given his best, and if he's wise, that's enough.

Second, this is a preface to a changed world of motivation--from locally centered to internationally derived; from play--the game for the game's sake--to work, the game for the reward's sake; from winning as a motivating force for training and personal development to winning as the main, indeed, the only end worth the arduous striving.

Be prepared in reading this OMNIBOOK for a confusing two-mindedness toward the time-energy-commitment that can properly be given to amateur sport. On the one hand I am certain that the greatest fun-joy-satisfaction emerges from the highest levels of struggle and risk. That's true in every field of human endeavor, physical, mental or spiritual. It's implied in the Olympic slogan, "higher-faster-farther," and confirmed in the assumption that all world records are made to be broken.

On the other hand, it is equally certain that all sports are encircled, occur within limits as fixed by the rules. The challenge is not how far we can project a 16# shot, but is how far we can put it in a fixed way from the narrow limits of a seven-foot circle. Increase or remove those limits and performance will improve, *but we have reached agreement on such limits and all conform without dissent.* In all sports at the non-professional level, there must be similar limits on time-energy-commitment that full-time students or workers can give to sports preparation and competition, and a social climate of integrity in conforming to those limits. That's a dilemma that future sportsmen will struggle to solve, though unlikely to ever resolve.

Third, this is a preface to the book itself. Above all else, and despite the 400,000 or so words, this book emphasizes the actions of track and field, and a coaching insistence on "learning by your doing, not by my telling." But as will be repeated many times, the apparently simple and natural actions at the highest levels of performance always lie at the far end of complex preparation--thoughtful analysis, careful organization, persistent practice--all of which culminate in a simple, unthinking flow of movement. Track and field is an art, with all the concentration of training and effort that goes into any art, if it is to be mastered and so become artless. That applies to competitive performance; it applies to competence in coaching.

BASIC VIEWPOINTS
The most basic concept of this third edition of the OMNIBOOK relates to what I like to call "the human uses of our sport." Not the use of our sport for institutional or national glory; not the use of our sport for private or group profit--that social cancer we must somehow remove or we all perish together. But the use of our sport for the betterment of individuals and humanity. Such use, as described in Chapter 3, requires a VITAL BALANCE as between expertise in working with persons and expertise in the techniques and methods of track and field. If this OMNIBOOK fails in advancing that Vital Balance, it fails. Period.

The first edition of this OMNIBOOK used Abraham Maslow's term, "holistic-analytic" to indicate its underlying approach to the problems of track and field. It assumed that sound understanding is always a two-phased process of analysis and synthesis, of discovering "parts" and clarifying relationships among many wholes. As examples, the essentials of training for endurance running were analyzed into 22 aspects, and the concept of relaxation was seen as having at least 10 ways to better understanding. But analysis inward was but one means to better understanding. The other, equally necessary as indicated by the unifying hyphen, looked outward toward the many relationships that lay the foundation, establish the motivation, determine the means for track and field, just as they do for all human activities. Nothing in nature is separate--not things, not mankind, not individuals, and certainly not the games they play. Gardner Murphy's tenet was accepted that "the only valid organism is the universe itself."

Throughout the OMNIBOOK, concern is expressed for the inter-relationships of track and field. Chap. 4 gives thumb-nail sketches of coaches of widely-varied attitudes and relationships, within the team and team family and outward with the sponsoring institution, the local community, the national organization, and with the international Olympic Games. In 1976, Lord Killanin of the I.O.C. stated that to accede to Canada's demand for the exclusion of Taiwan as the Republic of China would ultimately lead to the dissolution of the Games as a whole. In 1980, President Carter, with, in my judgment, a pitiful lack of understanding of the Olympic movement or concern for the longtime effects of what he did, decided that the United States and its allies should boycott the Moscow Games. On overall balance, the effect of this myopic action may be beneficial--to slow down or even reverse Olympic expansion. In one century we've reached a level of excess in our Modern Olympics that it took the Ancient Greeks a thousand years to gain--or should I write "lose."

The basic viewpoint I wish to emphasize is that sport emerges out of its social system, and can be separated from it only in a make-believe or as-if way. Nothing unusual in that; in fact, most of what we humans believe and say and do is based on make-believe. Our words--and so our assumptions--separate mind from body, a tree from earth and sun, an individual from society, Man from Nature. If we all, West and East, agree to believe it and act it, a single century could produce a workable separation of the Olympic Games from National drives for glory, or of college sports from College drives for glory. It could be done. Throughout man's history, his "common sense" has allowed him to separate the inseparable; in fact, scientific method is based on so doing. I repeat--it could be done, but don't hold your breath.

ACKNOWLEDGEMENTS

Frankly, it's absurd that an author should attempt to acknowledge those that have been helpful in the writing of a book such as this. Often the greatest help comes from those who intend it least, who give without awareness of their giving, in fact, without knowledge or interest in track and field or even awareness of the author's existence. A cogent idea in some seemingly unrelated discipline, or a careless word of praise can feed a man for years and inspire him to do his utmost to live up to it, simply out of respect for the men that said it. But absurd and unfair as such words of indebtedness may be, the custom is a most heart-warming game.

Of the many books listed in the bibliography, these were among the most helpful in forming its basic viewpoints: Wendell Johnson, *PEOPLE IN QUANDARIES*; Kurt Goldstein, *THE ORGANISM AND HUMAN NATURE*; Abraham Maslow, *MOTIVATION AND PERSONALITY*; Roger J. Williams, *BIOCHEMICAL INDIVIDUALITY AND PERSONALITY*; Karl Menninger, *THE VITAL BALANCE*; and various writings of William James, John Dewey and Alan Watts. (What a juxtaposition that is!) For biomechanics, I leaned heavily on Geoffrey Dyson, *THE MECHANICS OF ATHLETICS*; for physiology, on Astrand and Rodahl, *TEXTBOOK OF WORK PHYSIOLOGY*; for mutually-supportive relationships in coaching on Douglas McGregor, *THE HUMAN SIDE OF ENTERPRISE*, and Rensis Likert, *NEW PATTERNS OF MANAGEMENT*.

But were these really more helpful than such heart-warming letters as this from A. B. Krishnaswamy, Madras, India?

Your book is my bible, a household name in my family. Every morning, when I get up from bed, my daughter will place your book by my side. I read two or three pages and then only start my daily physical exercise. I am fond of quoting from the beautiful and very high English by which you explain techniques.

So much for the heart. But the heart is soon lifeless without bones and muscles, and these were provided primarily by *Track and Field News*[1] and *Track Technique*[1] as an entity--

---

[1]*Track & Field News*, Ed Fox, Publisher, P.O. Box 296, Los Altos, CA, 94022. Pub. monthly.

by Ed Fox, publisher; by Bert Nelson, editor; by Fred Wilt, editor of *Track Technique*; by Jon Hendershott, features editor of *Track & Field News*; and by their excellent staff writers. Lacking their informative writings, this OMNIBOOK would be only half what it is, or more likely, not written at all. Just now, I quickly ran down the Name Index and counted over 100 references that could be attributed directly to their work. To them all, I place the palm of my right hand on my forehead and bow in a deep salaam.

But one more source of important help and encouragement--George Dales, good friend and editor of *T&FA/USA TRACK & FIELD QUARTERLY REVIEW*. If my most basic and cherished viewpoint is "the human uses of track and field," George has been primary prompter, and even gadfly. When I told him of my intention to write a chapter on amateurism, coaching ethics, certification of coaches, he swamped me with related material and urged its use. In fact, I wrote over 20 pages ready for printing; then had to discard them "for lack of space." It certainly wasn't for lack of personal concern. Sorry, George, but also thanks for sequence photos and stills and articles and books and hard pushing that, at age 75, I needed more than you knew.

DRAWINGS
The hundreds of line-drawings in this OMNIBOOK are one of its most valuable assets. Blame me for the sub-human figures, but credit Oren Lyons, now in Duluth, Minn., and Jessica Teti of Media, Pa., for the obviously professional ones. Several hundred black-shirted figures are the work of Russian artists from books published by the *Physical Culture and Sports* publishing house of the USSR government. Where available, more specific attributions to the book author are made on the pages where the drawings appear.

EDITING AND TYPING
The entire manuscript was edited and typed in final form ready for litho-photography by Mrs. Nancy D. Johnson of Swarthmore, Pa. The knowledge that the final product would be so well and cheerfully done, kept me sleeping quieter, rising earlier, and working later throughout the final months of writing during a hot and frustrating summer in suburban Philadelphia.

A MUTUALLY SUPPORTIVE SURROUND
But most and best of all, my wife Lucile who, living her own full life throughout our more than 50 years together, has moved in quiet but effective ways to encourage my writing despite its rigors, and to help me help myself. Our University of Michigan track men used to say it was all worth while--if only to enjoy one of Lucile's dinners, perhaps be privileged to wash her dishes, and then be invited back to talk over problems of--who knows what or what not. What a great track coach she would have made! And lest you doubt, that's high praise; I once knew Brutus Hamilton.

APOLOGIA
Some time after the retirement of Brutus Hamilton--probably America's most articulate track coach--I asked him, in fact urged him, to set about writing a track and field textbook. His answer was given quickly and decisively, "NO, I can't do that. I just wouldn't want to impose my ideas on others." At first I laughed it off as only half-serious, or perhaps an excuse to relax after so many years of stress. Then, it troubled me that he was entirely serious and that our sport would be deprived of his very real wisdom in coaching.

Now, after some years, it still troubles me, for now I have the same feeling and realize he was at least half right. This textbook does impose its ideas on others--on active coaches today, and during the next decade or so, on thousands of young coaches-in-training. In certain ways, it is ahead of its time--in its emphasis on the human uses of sport, on coaching as mutually-supportive relationships, on the values of semantic and holistic-analytic approaches to problems, perhaps a few more. But in the area of the physical sciences--biomechanics, physiology and the like--a textbook can only hope to maintain contact with the field, as we say in endurance running.

Related research, here and abroad, makes surges of new knowledge each year, not unlike those of Yifter, Kedir and Kotu of Ethiopia in the 10,000 meters at Moscow, 1980. They broke pace, took turns in leading, slowed down then spurted ahead in ways that cracked the nerve and resistance of even the great Lasse Viren of Finland. So with Science today, and with those that seek to follow its ever-changing surges of knowledge.

CONVERTING ENGLISH-METRIC MEASUREMENTS

Meters into Feet and Inches

M.	FT.	IN.	M.	FT.	IN.
1	3	3⅜	51	167	3⅞
2	6	6¾	52	170	7¼
3	9	10⅛	53	173	10⅝
4	13	1½	54	177	2
5	16	4⅞	55	180	5⅜
6	19	8¼	56	183	8¾
7	22	11⅝	57	187	0⅛
8	26	3	58	190	3½
9	29	6⅜	59	193	6⅞
10	32	9¾	60	196	10¼
11	36	1⅛	61	200	1⅝
12	39	4½	62	203	5
13	42	7¾	63	206	8⅜
14	45	11⅛	64	209	11¾
15	49	2½	65	213	3
16	52	5⅞	66	216	6⅜
17	55	9¼	67	219	9¾
18	59	0⅝	68	223	1⅛
19	62	4	69	226	4½
20	65	7⅜	70	229	7⅞
21	68	10¾	71	232	11¼
22	72	2⅛	72	236	2⅝
23	75	5½	73	239	6
24	78	8⅞	74	242	9⅜
25	82	0¼	75	246	0¾
26	85	3⅝	76	249	4⅛
27	88	7	77	252	7½
28	91	10⅜	78	255	10⅞
29	95	1¾	79	259	2¼
30	98	5⅛	80	262	5⅝
31	101	8½	81	265	9
32	104	11⅞	82	269	0⅜
33	108	3¼	83	272	3¾
34	111	6⅝	84	275	7⅛
35	114	10	85	278	10¼
36	118	1⅜	86	282	1⅝
37	121	4¾	87	285	5
38	124	8⅛	88	288	8⅜
39	127	11⅜	89	291	11¾
40	131	2¾	90	295	3⅛
41	134	6⅛	91	298	6½
42	137	9½	92	301	9⅞
43	141	0⅞	93	305	1¼
44	144	4¼	94	308	4⅝
45	147	7⅝	95	311	8
46	150	11	96	314	11⅜
47	154	2⅜	97	318	2¾
48	157	5¾	98	321	6⅛
49	160	9⅛	99	324	9½
50	164	0½	100	328	0⅞

Centimeters into Feet and Inches

CM.	FT.	IN.	CM.	FT.	IN.
1	0	⅜	51	1	8⅛
2	0	¾	52	1	8½
3		1⅛	53	1	8⅞
4		1⅝	54	1	9¼
5		2	55	1	9⅝
6		2⅜	56	1	10
7		2¾	57	1	10½
8		3⅛	58	1	10⅞
9		3½	59	1	11¼
10		3⅞	60	1	11⅝
11		4⅜	61	2	0
12		4¾	62	2	0⅜
13		5⅛	63	2	0¾
14		5½	64	2	1¼
15		5⅞	65	2	1⅝
16		6¼	66	2	2
17		6¾	67	2	2⅜
18		7⅛	68	2	2¾
19		7½	69	2	3⅛
20		7⅞	70	2	3⅝
21		8¼	71	2	4
22		8⅝	72	2	4⅜
23		9	73	2	4¾
24		9½	74	2	5⅛
25		9⅞	75	2	5½
26		10¼	76	2	5⅞
27		10⅝	77	2	6¼
28		11	78	2	6¾
29		11⅜	79	2	7⅛
30		11¾	80	2	7½
31	1	0¼	81	2	7⅞
32	1	0⅝	82	2	8¼
33	1	1	83	2	8⅝
34	1	1⅜	84	2	9⅛
35	1	1¾	85	2	9½
36	1	2⅛	86	2	9⅞
37	1	2⅝	87	2	10¼
38	1	3	88	2	10⅝
39	1	3⅜	89	2	11
40	1	3¾	90	2	11⅜
41	1	4⅛	91	2	11⅞
42	1	4½	92	3	0¼
43	1	4⅞	93	3	0⅝
44	1	5⅜	94	3	1
45	1	5¾	95	3	1⅜
46	1	6⅛	96	3	1¾
47	1	6½	97	3	2⅛
48	1	6⅞	98	3	2⅝
49	1	7¼	99	3	3
50	1	7⅝	100	3	3⅜

Feet into Meters

FT.	M.
1	.31
2	.61
3	.91
4	1.22
5	1.52
6	1.83
7	2.13
8	2.44
9	2.74
10	3.05
20	6.1
30	9.15
40	12.2
50	15.25
60	18.3
70	21.35
80	24.4
90	27.45
100	30.5
110	33.55
120	36.6
130	39.65
140	42.7
150	45.75
160	48.8
170	51.85
180	54.9
190	57.95
200	61
210	64.05
220	67.1
230	70.15
240	73.2
250	76.25
260	79.3
270	82.35
280	85.4
290	88.45
300	91.5
310	94.55
320	97.6
330	100.65
340	103.7
350	106.75
360	109.75
370	112.8
380	115.8
390	118.85
400	121.9

Inches into Centimeters

IN.	CM.
¼	.63
½	1.27
¾	1.9
1	2.54
1¼	3.17
1½	3.81
1¾	4.44
2	5.08
2¼	5.71
2½	6.35
2¾	6.98
3	7.62
3¼	8.25
3½	8.89
3¾	9.52
4	10.16
4¼	10.79
4½	11.43
4¾	12.06
5	12.7
5¼	13.33
5½	13.97
5¾	14.6
6	15.24
6¼	15.87
6½	16.51
6¾	17.14
7	17.78
7¼	18.41
7½	19.05
7¾	19.68
8	20.32
8¼	20.96
8½	21.59
8¾	22.26
9	22.86
9¼	23.5
9½	24.13
9¾	24.77
10	25.4
10¼	26.04
10½	26.67
10¾	27.31
11	27.94
11¼	28.58
11½	29.21
11¾	29.85
12	30.48

PART 1
The Human Side of Coaching

Brutus Hamilton (University of California at Berkeley, 1932-1965) was a coach of track and field but, much more, a coach of young men by way of track and field. Their personal development was his primary goal, not his personal record of success. He liked to win, was a tough competitor as an athlete and a coach. But winning was not an end in itself so much as a means of motivating the day-after-day training and anguish that lead to the primary goal of self-development. Such a view respects the off-the-track rules of sport, even though aware that they are often unenforceable and violated by one's rivals. We tend to think of most men as enclosed within the outline of their own skin. Hamilton's true skin was equally an inline of the many, many persons--in and outside of track and field, in and outside of sport, in and outside our national boundaries--with whom he established mutually supportive relationships. But most of all, his story is one of loyalty and respect for his boys and their almost mystical devotion to the man they still remember as "The Coach."

INTRODUCTION

A moment's thought makes clear that the expression "coaching track and field" has two aspects--persons and actions. Over the past half-century or more, coaches, and especially the writers of coaching textbooks, seem to have assumed that actions are our primary, if not only, concern. If one may judge by the contents of textbooks, we actually are coaches of some entity called "track and field," with its 20 or more events of widely varied techniques and training methods. That was complex enough some 50 years ago (even though we had only 15 events) when this OMNI-BOOK gained its first "muscle-nerve" learnings. We had almost no textbooks, no related scientific studies; in fact, almost no knowledge of what others were doing--in other countries or even our own. But today the repeated process of analysis-synthesis has created computerized biomechanics, telemetered heart rates, measurement of slow-twitch and fast-twitch muscle fibers; not to mention periodizations of training time into macrocycles, mesocycles and microcycles. Surely such complexities are more than enough for a struggling hope-to-be coach of the 1980s.

Fortunately for peace of mind, I'm reminded of the comment by Sebastian Coe's father-coach that, after studying all the related literature and training systems, he had discarded 95 percent of it and was now concentrating on the remaining 5 percent; result: three world records within a 41-day period by his son. But to argue on the other side, if Peter Coe's 5 percent had not been distilled out of the decades of experience of such coaches as Holmer, Gerschler, Lydiard or Bowerman; or out of the wide-ranging research of modern science, his results would have been much less impressive.

But all that relates to only one side of the coaching coin; the other relates to an even greater complexity, to what I have called "the human side of coaching"--persons. As with actions, 50 years ago, "persons" was a relatively simple word. Everything we did was low-level; demands on time-energy, techniques and training systems, motivations. Consider motivations then and now. In general, though we didn't realize it then, we played at running, jumping and throwing. We were 90 percent self-motivated, if by "self" we include the team, the coach, and its members. Of the remaining 10 percent, all but one percent of motivation came from the greater team-family--the student body, a few fans. We begged for newspaper space from a one or two-page sports section; there was no television and very little public awareness.

Today, Communist countries have adopted sports, including track and field, as an instrument of government policy, and we in the United States are finally waking up to a realization of the need to adopt similar policies, or to quit the Big Game entirely. Today, our motivations are more socially than individually oriented. That goal of placing an American flag on the center Olympic flagpole inspires not only Olympic team aspirants, but filters deeply into our community and grade-school field days. Today, our college track program is Olympic-centered, with 10,000-meter runs, 400-meter hurdles, and a decathlon, with relatively little concern for whether such events are best for full-time students of higher education.

That is to say, the human side of coaching is just as complex as the technical side, and needs to be given at least as much research and careful consideration. Today, the nature of leadership and its methods is at least as vital to effective coaching as is biomechanics or physiology.

For these reasons, this OMNIBOOK is divided into two Parts: Part 2--techniques and methods

1

of track and field; Part 1--the human side--the individual athlete, the coach, the team, the team-family. Not all of the successful coaches I have known have been effective teachers of techniques, but with no exceptions, all have been effective on this human side of the coaching coin. True, they have differed greatly as to how they analyzed and organized that side. Some worked only within the local community, on a friendly basis of mutual help; others conducted a business of national and even international scope. But each in his own way realized the importance of public and personal relationships that were mutually supportive.

Apparently the assumption of track and field textbook writers has been that this human side was adequately taught in the more general courses in educational psychology and social psychology. But usually the relatedness of such courses is suspect. It is my feeling that this aspect of coaching is so important that we in track and field need to create our own approaches, in ways peculiar to our particular sport and profession. Part 1 is a first effort in that direction. Chapter 2 seeks to analyze coaching function: first, in terms of personal charisma and the many traits related to it. This is the traditional view of authoritarian leadership in many field--military, religion, coaching, teaching, political. But Chapter 2 also views coaching leadership in terms of relationships with others within the immediate team family and also among the many individuals and groups outside that family that can be of great help in making team performance and coaching more effective. Such diverse relationships require the coach to assume many roles, and these are spelled out briefly: the coach as toiler, instructor, planner, executor, recruiter, salesman, father figure, and scapegoat--a multi-faceted person indeed.

Chapter 3 uses an organizational chart based on "A Managerial Grid" now used effectively in the development of business management. This chart helps to make clear the vital balance required in effective coaching between expertise in technology and in personal relations. Each of these is analyzed on a nine-point scale, with nine indicating highest competency. A 9-9 coach is one that balances at the highest levels these two concerns. That for persons is analyzed on a selective basis: coaching authority, goal-insight methods, motivation, managing conflicts, relationships.

Chapter 4 provides brief sketches of nine coaches whose coaching styles and methods have special significance for the purposes of this OMNIBOOK. They are not necessarily outstanding, successful or models of what coaches should be. They do indicate the wide range of personalities, of attitudes and relationships with team members, and of ways of handling the problems of developing and recruiting talent. The descriptions are not done systematically; they follow no pre-set outline; in fact, they tend to rely on whatever material written by others was available. Perhaps this is as it should be, as it is in life itself. We tend to know others by bits and pieces--an hour here, a brief impression there. We just do not know people systematically.

Chapter 5 seeks a summary of the human side, with an emphasis on the need for compatibility between the goals and methods of the coach as related to those of his community-institution-supporters, and closes with an advocacy of the certification of coaches--at first, as related only to competence in techniques and methods, and on a single-event basis. In summary of Part 1, it is my belief that the greatest progress in track and field during the next 50 years will occur through a more systematic study of the human side of our sport, with special emphasis on the nature of leadership.

Lao-tse (C. 565 B.C.) on Leadership.

A leader is best
    when people are least aware of his
    leadership;

Not so good
    when people acclaim and obey him blindly;
Worse
    when they despise him.

But of a good leader
    who talks little,
    when his work is done
    and his aim fulfilled,

They will say,
    "We did this thing
    ourselves."

Chapter 1
THE DEVELOPMENT OF TRACK KNOWLEDGE

The development of knowledge in United States track and field can be divided into three periods: (1) that prior to 1932; (2) 1932-1952--from the Olympic Games at Los Angeles to those at Helsinki, Finland; and (3) 1952 to the present, when the adoption of sports as an arm of government policy by the USSR and East Germany greatly increased related research and knowledge in those countries and, as a natural reaction, within our own.

The organization of this chapter will be based on this three-phased development of track knowledge. But it will focus on college courses for the education of coaches, with emphasis on related sciences--physiology, biomechanics, sports medicine, psychology, and social psychology as it relates to business management. This evolution was strongly influenced by the forces that grew out of the 1932 and 1952 Olympic Games as suggested above. A few brief comments may clarify that influence.

The Los Angeles Olympic Games. The 1932 Olympic Games not only multiplied American enthusiasm for track and field, they expanded our awareness of much higher potentials--in performance, in facilities and equipment, in time-energy required, and in the need for better education of coaches. Up to 1932, all these were centered in terms of local views and traditions with little interest or knowledge of what was being done in other sections of the United States or in Europe. For example, a group of Eastern Colleges founded (1876) the ICAAAA (Intercollegiate Amateur Athletics Association of America). It was very well organized--undoubtedly better than anywhere else in the entire world--trained its officials, conducted clinics for its coaches, published its own college track and field rules book. What happened elsewhere-- on the West Coast or Middle West--was of doubtful validity, not something to be learned or copied. It took 20 years for Horine's Western style high jump to be copied in the East; a decade for USC's built-up sawdust landing pits. Charley Paddock's many sprint records were alleged to be a product of Hollywood and the fast guns and watches of Western starters and timers.

But 1932 marked a growing mutual respect among coaches of the various sections of the country. For some years, a few Western schools--Stanford, California, USC, Michigan, Notre Dame-- had come to the ICAAAA Outdoor Championships. Since 1921, the National Collegiate Championships at Stagg Field, Chicago, had brought coaches and individual athletes together. (As a matter of interest, in its early years, the NCAA meet recorded only individual, not team championships.) These influences were greatly expanded when many coaches, including some from Europe, experienced the excitement and technical excellence of the 1932 Los Angeles Games. Coaching journals, newspapers, textbooks, coaches' bull sessions--all led to a sounder knowledge of our sport and to courses in education for our coaches.

Fig. 1.1. Minimal technique, facilities and performance in the shot put.

The Helsinki Olympic Games. But 20 years later, the 1952 Olympic Games marked a new stage in the development of track and field and its knowledge. For the first time, we caught a glimpse of the implications of Communist doctrine that all phases of society, including sports, should contribute to national goals, to what IOC president, Avery Brundage, liked to call "national aggrandizement." Communist countries recruited well-trained scientists for better sports knowledge, just as they did for space travel or military technology. Now the approach to sport by all nations moved to new levels of urgency and intensity. Even in amateur-oriented England, professional coaches were given grudging acceptance, somewhere above the janitor and provider of witchhazel-alcohol rubdowns! Today, in the United States--for better or worse is still unclear--we are only beginning a national effort in reaction to this challenge.

THE EARLY YEARS. During the early years, roughly 1870 to 1932, the local coaches had almost no ways of knowing what was being done, or what had been tried and discarded in other areas of the country. Performance was low-level, but knowledge of techniques or training methods was equally so. Today, it's impossible to comprehend how minimal these were. A few books had been published, such as ATHLETICS, London: The Badminton Library, 1904; or Michael Murphy, ATHLETIC TRAINING, New York, 1920, but there were no ways of publicizing these--no national magazines, no radio, no national meetings of any kind--so they had little influence.

Each coach had to experiment out of his own ingenuity. In many instances he repeated the errors that had been made at other schools, in other isolated areas, decades before. For example, I went to Western High School, Detroit, 1921-4. Our "coach" was excellent as a German Turnverein instructor. He knew much about high bars and horses and Indian clubs but he had never heard of a shift of the hands in the pole vault. I competed for the team in that event; best height, 7'6". Then I went to Detroit City College (now Wayne State). David L. Holmes was Director of Athletics and coach of four sports including football and basketball--all with but three assistant coaches, none for track. He had an avid thirst for better methods and encouraged us to try this, try that, and keep on trying. He later gained national recognition for his starting blocks and hurdles, for his booklet of drawings, TRACK AND FIELD MOVIES ON PAPER, taken from his own films of champions, and for his development of five Olympic placewinners. During my four years, 1924-1927, we tried as many as a half-dozen different techniques in some events. In the discus, for example, we tried facing to the front and to the side, holding the discus behind the back with palm and discus up, spinning with one foot on the ground throughout the spin, hopping up-then-down to a low crouch, crouching throughout the turn, weaving the discus in a wave-like motion, throwing the discus at various planes from 20 to 45 degrees, pulling across the discus at release to give it more spin, and probably other woeful methods I have forgotten.

Similar, almost random, trials were made in each of the other field events. We threw the javelin as would any baseball-oriented American boy, with five or six easy steps and a hop. In the pole vault, we landed on sandy loam, about 12 inches above ground level. No wonder our first concern at takeoff was on turning over to ensure a safe landing.

In general, performances were consistent with such minimal techniques. In 1925, these performances won NCAA Outdoor Championships: high jump--6'2"; pole vault--12'4"; broad jump--25' 10 7/8" (world record); shot--50'; discus--148'4"; javelin--201'11"; hammer--150'1½"; mile--4:18.8; 2-mile--9:32.8. Small college and high school performances were scaled down accordingly. In 1925, the Indiana Conference Championships (DePauw, Wabash, Butler, Earlham, etc.) achieved these marks: high jump--5'9½"; pole vault--11'; shot--40'4"; discus--129'7½". The Pennsylvania Interscholastic Championships, 1925, brought forth: 12# shot--45'2"; (no discus or javelin); high jump--5'8¼"; pole vault--10'9"; broad jump--20'8½". Needless to say, California performances at all levels were superior to those listed here.

Time-energy For Training. The time-energy given to training and competition was as minimal as was performance and knowledge. Indoor track had few competitions and lacked facilities. The Big 10 Indoor Championships were first held in 1911, but there were no fieldhouses and few gyms that could be used. All indoor sports shared the one gym that most schools provided--along with classes in physical education of course. If that gym had a track, it was about eight feet wide and designed for jogging, not racing. Track and field was mainly an outdoor sport and, east of California, that meant it began in late April and ended with the local Conference meet in late May--a six-week season. Few schools included the NCAA Championships (first meet, 1921) in their schedule. Is it any wonder that the number of hours per day, days per week, and weeks per season given to training were very, very limited. In brief, we practiced one to two hours a day, three to five days a week, and started perhaps six weeks prior to our first meet, depending on when the frost was out of the ground. Distance runners could start earlier, but rain or snow on dirt surfaces or sandyloam landing pits are not helpful to jumping or throwing. Add to this that, since performance was generally low-level, most men doubled or tripled. In my own case, I divided my time--in training and competition--among some six events, simply because 21 feet in the broad jump or 150 feet in the javelin might score a point or two in a dual meet.

But in addition to these minimums in the potentially positive factors, there was a climate of negative attitudes that held back school sports. European schools had no such program and strongly doubted their values in Education. English schools and colleges enjoyed sports, but at what we would call an extramural level--no paid coaches, no gate receipts, no school subsidies or facilities. Even as late as 1954, the Oxford University track, on which Bannister ran the first mile under four minutes, was financed and maintained by Oxford students and their friends. Bannister had no coach, being convinced that "the athlete could be sufficient unto himself."[1]

Many American educators agreed with this view, pointing out that coaches at certain schools--Steve Farrell, Michigan; Tom Keane, Syracuse; Keene Fitzpatrick, Princeton; Lawson Robertson, Pennsylvania, Jimmie Curran, Mercersburg Academy--had taken part in professional racing with its gambling, roping, fictitious names, and cheating in any way to ensure a purse. "Fine characters to teach American youth!" (I knew them all; four, personally; they were a joy to be with and no one who knew them questioned their integrity.)

Taboos Against Exertion. During the early years and continuing into the 1940s, when Coach Billy Hayes, Indiana, first brought us word of the hard training of the Swedish runners, Gunder Haegg and Arne Andersson, there was much greater concern for the dangers of overtraining and staleness than exists today, though today's training levels are two or three times as great in time and intensity. Each advancement in training methods or performance in distance running brought forth charges of "burning out," or of "cutting a boy's life short." The danger of developing an enlarged "athlete's heart" was assumed by most members of the medical profession. Certainly no one should train year-round. Three or four months of complete rest, along with two days of each week were mandatory. "Breaking training" was a much-hallowed custom. A respected physiology of exercise,[2] 1932, warned,

Too frequently the day of the last athletic contest of the season's schedule marks the beginning of a short period of jollification and riotous living....This has neither a physiological nor hygienic foundation....The detraining process should be as gradual as the training process if one wishes to avoid indigestion, constipation, faulty slouching posture and the other ills attendant upon a loss of muscular tonus.

Strength training was another taboo. Everyone knew that the greater one's strength, the lesser one's muscle quickness, and quickness was all-important. We had heard of Sandow and Hackenschmidt and knew what oxen they were. It wasn't merely weight-lifting that was taboo. Long canoe trips, bicycling, and heavy gymnastics were all discouraged. Swimming? It produced soft muscles. Hot showers? They sapped one's energies. Social dancing? Absolutely out! It distracted the mind, weakened the will, dissipated one's powers. Beer drinking? Unthinkable for college men--at least in the middle-west. I still remember my own sense of wrong-doing when, on coming to Princeton as assistant coach in 1929, I saw beer being served to team members, following the dual meet with Oxford-Cambridge.

COMMUNICATION IN THE EARLY YEARS. During the early years, only a few University and Club coaches had an acceptably sound understanding of training principles and techniques. But there were almost no ways by which such knowledge could be shared--almost no track clinics or publications. In the late 1920s, the New York Public School Athletic League did conduct and

---

[1]Roger Bannister, *THE FOUR MINUTE MILE*, New York: Dodd, Mead & Co., 1955, p. 208.

[2]A. G. Gould & J. A. Dye, *EXERCISE AND ITS PHYSIOLOGY*, 1932, New York: A. S. Barnes and Co., p. 388.

publish (hardcover) a series of lectures by coaches of the ICAAA, some of whom had competed as professionals in Europe and America in the 1880s and 90s. The Big Ten and other Conference coaches did get together at their championships for bull sessions following games of bridge or poker. But I know of no other meetings that could be called coaching clinics.

The very few meets at which coaches could observe better techniques tended to be local affairs. The Pennsylvania Relay Carnival began in 1895 and was a great aid to the spread of knowledge. But transportation was so time-consuming and fatiguing that it tended to be an Eastern college and school event. The ICAAAA (1876) looked on its championships as the National Championship, as its name (Intercollegiate Amateur Athletic Association of America) implies. Individuals and even teams from Southern Cal, Stanford, California, Michigan, Notre Dame and a few others did compete, and this provided some interchange of ideas. The NCAA Championships did not begin until 1922, at Stagg Field, Chicago. The National AAU Championships were of little interest to colleges and schools. Even the Olympic Games were of relatively little consequence; it's now hard to realize how little as compared with their present preeminence. Up to 1932, all Olympic Games had been held in Europe; only a few American coaches had seen them or learned from them. In fact, one could say that our National awareness of the Olympics did not really gain momentum until the 1932 Games at Los Angeles. Thousands of coaches and future coaches attended and derived a tremendous boost in knowledge and enthusiasm.

Perhaps an example of slow communications will help our understanding. In 1912 George Horine of Stanford set a world record of 6'7" in the high jump using a new technique that came to be known as the Western Roll. But a decade later, in the 1920s, Horine's style was little known nationally. Jumpers in the Eastern and Middle States were still using the 1895 Sweeney style or some variation of it. We heard rumors of the new Western style, that another Westerner, Beeson of California, had jumped 6'7¼". In 1923, Tom Poor of Kansas won the NCAA (6'3") with his own version of such a style. But not until Harold Osborne of Illinois cleared 6'8¼" and won the 1924 Olympic title did the style gain general acceptance. To make my point even stronger, Osborne claimed that he originated his own style with no knowledge of Horine or Beeson, having read only an article by Walter Camp on Alma Richards, the 1912 Olympic champion. Richards' "style" was to simply draw up his legs and hop over the bar, so that Osborne's claim to originality seems valid.[1] Even in the 1930s, some coaches were claiming technical superiority for the Eastern style as jumped by George Spitz (1933-6'8¼"), a full twenty years after Horine.

Now contrast this 20-year molasses-slow process with the explosive change that followed Fosbury's Olympic performance in 1968. Within a mere four years, his revolutionary Flop was known, analyzed, and largely adopted throughout the entire world. In 1973, only five years later, the International Track and Field Coaches Association, meeting in Madrid, devoted ten of a total of 23 technical papers to some aspect of the Fosbury Flop.

TRACK AND FIELD LITERATURE. In the 1920s, books on track and field were few in number, meager in content, and lacking the advertising means for making them known to the coaches of the country. I remember as an athlete and young coach having heard of books by such coaches as Mike Murphy (Pennsylvania), Ernie Hjertberg (Texas), Harry Gill (Illinois), and Tom Jones (Wisconsin). But the only ones I saw during the 1920s were the paperback series of nine books of about 200 pages each published by the American Sports Publishing Company. They were ghosted by Boyd Comstock, a respected San Francisco Club coach, and edited by such well-known coaches as Harry Hillman of Dartmouth, Dink Templeton of Stanford and Lawson Robertson of Pennsylvania. They included a few figure-drawings indicating proper techniques. Most important, every other page was a picture of champions in actual competition going back some 20 years or more. Still-pictures are of little value in showing technique but they did provide a strong feeling for the history of the sport. Captions gave names and related information.

COLLEGE COURSES FOR COACHES. It is important to remember that, traditionally, there have been hierarchies of respectability among faculties and curricula in American universities. The Liberal Arts came first, ranked highest, and located their buildings on-campus. The vocational

---

[1] Harold M. Osborne, "Championship Competition," in THE HIGH JUMP, R. L. Templeton, editor, New York: American Sports Publishing Company, p. 153.

or specialized schools (Engineering, Architecture, Business, Education) developed later, were accepted though of lesser ilk, and located on back-yard ground, preferably off-campus. With the exception of various teacher-training schools (Normal Schools), such as Springfield College (Mass.), 1891, or Columbia Teachers College, 1901, Schools of Education with majors in physical education were not established, generally speaking, until the 1920s. Even then, many considered their emphasis on teaching methods rather than on intellectual content as below the standards of Higher Education. Even lower on the totem pole was physical education, though it earned a modicum of acceptance through its roots in Swedish and German gymnastics. But sports had no such foundation, having been pushed into University life through the back door of town and student-club rowdyism with its Saturday afternoon "circus sideshows." Sports had no intellectual theory, no solid European background, no scientific or even verbal content. Physical educators were given faculty status and tenure; sports coaches neither.

As a matter of fact, many early track coaches never attended college. Their credentials related primarily to success as athletes. Some had actually competed as professionals in England and the United States at county fairs and circuses, had even hung out with gamblers and other persons of low repute! (One of the most enjoyable track "clinics" I ever attended was in the 1930s when Steve Farrell, Michigan, and Tom Keane, Syracuse, swapped stories of their professional days--false names, losing in unaccountable ways, being ridden on rails out of town; in short, swindling the yokels in any way they could.)

Small wonder that such coaches had little respect for academic courses in the improvement of track coaching. "Why waste time with that tripe? You want to be a shot-putter? Just pick it up, put it, and keep on putting it. Do it the way Ralph Rose did it back in 1909. He was the greatest." That was the sole basis for judgment; best performance assumes best technique.

In fact, there was justification for their low opinion of the courses then offered in Education and the related sciences, for 95 percent of the stuff was far from being useable. I remember a 1931 course in the psychology of motor learning in which we studied Pavlov's theory of the conditioned reflex based on salivating dogs, and Thorndike's stimulus-response theory based on the responses of cats, chicks and dogs. When I spoke one day to head coach Steve Farrell about it, he looked at me sidewise, spit copiously, but said not one word.

In summary, mutually low respect between the faculty and the sports coach. One of the practices that helped break down this estrangement was that of employing track coaches who could also serve as trainers for football--on the field and in the training room. Medical doctors were also used to supervise such work, and this led to an interchange of knowledge and a growing respect for each other's expertise. Trainers (track coaches) visited the hospital, and even sat in on the regular courses for medical students in anatomy, physiology or orthopedics. As the number of such visitors, including physical education students, increased, such courses were gradually modified, then separated so as to focus on the needs of physical educators and coaches.

Biomechanics and Track and Field. Gradually, from one decade to the next, coaches recognized the practical values of course work in the related sciences. In keeping with this, such courses were modified to relate more closely to coaches' needs. Biomechanics had a two-pronged origin. Anatomy and physiology for physicians gradually evolved into kinesiology. The term titled a few courses and fewer textbooks, but it never caught on and is missing from modern dictionaries. As the use of "kinesiology" waned, the concept of mechanics and its offspring, dynamics, developed out of engineering mechanics to become biomechanics (the science of mechanics as related to animal movement). From this, in turn, developed biomechanics of sport and, later, the biomechanics of track and field. To trace that evolution is beyond the scope of this book. But mention should be made of the collaboration in the 1930s of Iowa coach George T. Bresnahan and scientist W. W. Tuttle. They pioneered research on the mechanics of sprint starting, and co-authored the classic, TRACK AND FIELD ATHLETICS[1] that went through seven editions or more. Some 15 years passed before their work was re-appraised and extended by California (Berkeley) scientist, Franklin M. Henry, who related reaction times in the blocks to acceleration and

---

[1]George T. Bresnahan and W. W. Tuttle, TRACK AND FIELD ATHLETICS, St. Louis: The C. V. Mosby Co., 1937, 300 pages.

maximal velocity in the sprint.[1]

Beginnings are always doubtful but it is valid to say that the first textbook in this country to apply the laws of mechanics to sport techniques was by John Bunn,[2] *SCIENTIFIC PRINCIPLES OF COACHING*, 1955. Chapters focussed on each sport, including chapter 7, "Analysis of Track Techniques," and chapter 8, "Analysis of Field Techniques." In 1962, Geoffrey Dyson, English National Coach of Athletics, published his very influential *THE MECHANICS OF ATHLETICS*.[3] This book, augmented by Dyson's nation-wide lectures and "clinics-by-doing," stimulated the important work of Fred Wilt in conducting similar clinics and publishing related books.

Today, biomechanics is an important section of the research to improve sports performance being done in Human Performance Laboratories in various universities, as well as at U. S. Olympic Training Centers at Colorado Springs and elsewhere. In 1980, Gideon Ariel, Ph.D., was chairman of the Division of Biomechanics and Computer Sciences of the USO Sports Medicine Committee. In "Biomechanical Assessment of Athletic Performance," he wrote,[4]

Biomechanical analysis generally begins with high-speed cinematography which allows careful scrutiny of even the fastest of human movements. The films are traced and resulting data stored in a computer which analyzes the workings of the body according to the principles of physics and mechanical engineering. Tables and graphs are generated which give a precise profile of what actually occurs during the execution of a skill....Biomechanics is a science still in its adolescence, with many discoveries yet to be made.

Physiology of Endurance Exercise. The 1920s saw a great upsurge in research into the physiology of exercise, especially as related to circulo-respiratory endurance. A number of excellent textbooks were published: Bainbridge, 1923; McCurdy and McKenzie, 1928; and most influential, A. V. Hill--*MUSCULAR ACTIVITY*, 1926, and *MUSCULAR MOVEMENT IN MAN*, 1927--who used track men at Cornell University as subjects. Related, wide-ranging research at the Harvard Fatigue Laboratory under the leadership of D. B. Dill was helpful. For example, Sid Robinson did his doctoral work there, set up his own lab at Indiana University and became assistant coach to Billy Hayes, America's greatest distance coach in the 1930s and 40s. Gould and Dye,[5] *EXERCISE AND ITS PHYSIOLOGY*, 1932, included chapters on training, second wind, overtraining, and breaking training, all of practical use on the track but without reference to actual track performances.

Today, we have numerous physiologies of exercise, including Astrand and Rodahl's[6] *TEXTBOOK OF WORK PHYSIOLOGY*, to which our chapters on endurance running make repeated reference. And at long last, in 1979, David L. Costill's[7] *A SCIENTIFIC APPROACH TO DISTANCE RUNNING*, whose preface states the problem clearly :

---

[1]Franklin M. Henry, "Force-Time Characteristics of the Sprint Start," *Research Quarterly*, October 1952, pp. 301-318.

[2]John Bunn, *SCIENTIFIC PRINCIPLES OF COACHING*, New York: Prentice-Hall, Inc., 1955, 300 pp.

[3]Geoffrey H. G. Dyson, *THE MECHANICS OF ATHLETICS*, London: The University of London Press, Ltd., 1962, 225 pp.

[4]Gideon Ariel, Ph.D., "Biomechanical Assessment of Athletic Performance," *USOC: The Olympian*, January 1979, p. 13, and February 1979, p. 10.

[5]A. G. Gould and Joseph A. Dye, *EXERCISE AND ITS PHYSIOLOGY*, New York: A. S. Barnes and Co., 1932, 420 pp.

[6]Per-Olaf Astrand and Kaare Rodahl, M. D., *TEXTBOOK OF WORK PHYSIOLOGY*, New York: McGraw-Hill Book Co., 1970, 670 pp.

[7]David L. Costill, Ph.D., *A SCIENTIFIC APPROACH TO DISTANCE RUNNING*, Los Altos, Cal., Track & Field News, 1979.

Despite the rapid accumulation of scientific information during recent years, much of this new knowledge often remains too technical for practical application. The sciences of sport are no exception in this. There are many difficulties in bridging the gap between scientific observation and its assimilation into sports performance. One reason for this is that the scientist and the practitioner are often separated by a gulf in their perspectives. On the one hand the scientist views his or her research as an end in itself and attempts to describe the results of research in terms understandable to other scientists. The coach and athlete, on the other hand, frequently lack a basic scientific knowledge of their sport and are ill-equipped to interpret the research that comes their way and translate it into improved performance.

From which one might conclude that the problems of the 1980s are not so basically different from those of 50 years ago.

Physiology of Muscle Power. A similar lethargic acceptance can be traced for training programs for muscle power. Advocates of weight training for sports claim that heavy resistance exercises were used in Ancient Greece and Rome as well as in Mediaeval Europe, primarily for the training of the military. Elizabethan archers trained with dumbbells so as to bend heavier bows and gain greater distance for their arrows. Foot soldiers trained with overweight packs. But the most persistent of all such stories was that of the Greek Olympic champion, Milo of Crotona, who "invented" the first course in progressive strength training by lifting a bull calf each day until it was fully grown.

But around 1900, mail-order courses in muscle building for male vanity became popular, especially when they used less expensive five-pound dumbbells. The Great Sandow claimed they were his secret without revealing the heavy weights he actually used. To ensure even greater profits, rumors were spread that men using heavy weights became muscle-bound, slow and awkward, rumors that became firmly fixed in the sports-training psyche.

Murray and Karpovich[1] state that, in the middle 1930s, Bob Hoffman, publisher of *Strength and Health* magazine, "became the first man to widely publicize his belief--weight training could help athletes in other sports of their choice." But such ideas were not accepted until the 1950s. World War II stimulated research toward more rapid and effective rehabilitation of muscles weakened or atrophied by injury or surgery. In 1945, DeLorme[2] published research proving the values of heavy resistance exercises and introduced the concept of 10 R.M. (repetitions maximum) that is still used in therapy and sports. In 1948, I was privileged to coach Charles Fonville, world-record shot-putter at 58'¼". We had no knowledge of such research and did not even consider weight-lifting of any kind. But within five years, shot-putters Otis Chandler, Stan Lampert and Parry O'Brien gave final proof of its values. Without such a strength-training program, there is a serious doubt that the famous O'Brien shot-put method would have brought him such great success.

Today, strength training as related to heavy weight-lifting provokes few arguments. It is power with its varying emphasis on two components, strength and velocity, that is still controversial.

SPORTS MEDICINE AND TRACK AND FIELD. It is beyond the scope of this book to trace the history and uses of sports medicine as related to track and field. Its first emphasis as a movement and within the American College of Sports Medicine was on the medical aspects of sport--health and longevity effects, prevention and care of injuries, health effects of sports diets, drugs, training at altitude, and the like.

But growing awareness of the challenge from Communist countries, of their effective use of sports sciences, and of our need to greatly improve performance brought increasing pressures on sports medicine to broaden its scope and change its emphasis to more positive approaches.

---

[1] Jim Murray and Peter V. Karpovich, M.D., *WEIGHT TRAINING IN ATHLETICS*, Englewood Cliffs, N.J., Prentice-Hall, Inc., 1956, p. 14.

[2] Thomas L. DeLorme, "Restoration of Muscle Power by Heavy Resistance Exercises," *The Journal of Bone and Joint Surgery*, 27 (1945), pp. 645-667.

In 1976, the United States Olympic Committee (USOC) established a U. S. Olympic Training Center at Colorado Springs that included "a well appointed sports medicine complex." An M.D. with personal experience in track and field was out in overall charge of research. Respected scientists chaired various sections in such sciences as biomechanics, physiology, and psychology, all as they relate to improved performance in Olympic sports.

In the early stages of this program, athletes and coaches were brought to this Center for relatively brief periods for analysis of techniques, training condition, mental attitudes and the like. Follow-ups and return visits occurred. During Olympic years and in special cases, these could become extensive. A few individuals and teams could derive much of value.

But to make such a program fully effective among a dozen or more Olympic sports on a nation-wide basis is a very complex and expensive operation. Whatever program is developed at the National Training Center will be inadequate unless it becomes the means for coordinating research and training at universities and other Centers throughout the country. According to Charles Dillman, Ph.D., sports medicine coordinator for the 1980 Olympic ski team, the Soviet Union is 10 years ahead of the United States in its use of scientific sports research, spending some $8 million a year for that purpose. Only a great national effort can hope to overcome such a lead.

PSYCHOLOGY AND TRACK AND FIELD. In the 1920s, courses in the psychology of education were available at many colleges. I sat through ten such graduate courses at the University of Michigan School of Education--psychology of learning, psychology of motor learning, psychology of the self, psychology of character, group dynamics--but unfortunately their combined direct use for coaching track and field could have been better acquired through ten one-hour sessions, if properly employed.

In 1926, Coleman R. Griffith[1] published his *PSYCHOLOGY OF COACHING*, oriented toward the team sports. But few track coaches heard of it and, if they had, would have ignored it as being of little practical use. "Who needs that stuff"?

Such lack of interest created a lapse of 25 years before another such text in the psychology of coaching, that by Lawther,[2] 1951, also pointed toward the more popular team sports. But in 1966, Ogilvie and Tutko,[3] *PROBLEM ATHLETES AND HOW TO HANDLE THEM*, did focus attention on track and field, its individual athletes, and importantly, on the track coach himself. The authors state the book was organized "with the coaches' needs as our primary concern."

Psychological investigations must provide the reliable data that will enhance and complement coaching skill. The role of the psychological consultant should be the systematic study of the problems with which every coach must deal when applying his technical knowledge.

A similar direct application to our sport was made in 1970 by Vanek and Cratty[4] in *PSYCHOLOGY AND THE SUPERIOR ATHLETE*, with sections on the evaluation and psychological preparation of the superior athlete. Another related psychology was by Tutko and Richards,[5] 1971, *PSYCHOLOGY OF COACHING*, in which they analyze the personalities of both coaches and athletes.

Despite these advances, it seems clear that the coaches of other countries assume a much

---

[1]Coleman R. Griffith, *THE PSYCHOLOGY OF COACHING*, New York: Charles Scribner's Sons, 1926, 213 pps.

[2]John D. Lawther, *PSYCHOLOGY OF COACHING*, Englewood Cliffs, N.J., Prentice-Hall, Inc., 1951.

[3]Bruce Ogilvie, Ph.D. and Thomas A. Tutko, Ph.D., *PROBLEM ATHLETES AND HOW TO HANDLE THEM*, London: Pelham Books Ltd., 1966, p. 10.

[4]Miroslav Vanek and Bryant J. Cratty, *PSYCHOLOGY AND THE SUPERIOR ATHLETE*, New York: The Macmillan Company, 1970, 212 pps.

[5]T. A. Tutko, Ph.D. and Jack W. Richards, *PSYCHOLOGY OF COACHING*, Boston: Allyn & Bacon, 1971.

greater value for Sports Psychology than we do in the United States. In 1980, the International Society of Sport Psychology had a total world membership of over 1600, many of whom were coaches.

THE SOCIAL PSYCHOLOGY OF BUSINESS MANAGEMENT. At first glance, coaching in educational institutions and management in private-profit business seem to have little in common as to either goals or methods. But when writing the first edition of this *OMNIBOOK* I became aware of important similarities, especially if we equate production with sport performance and profit with winning.

Intrigued by these similarities, I spent some months studying leading textbooks in business management, especially those taking a research approach to problems. In brief, the various theories of management fall into four classes, commonly called Theory X and Theory Y as developed by Douglas McGregor,[1] Rensis Likert's[2] principle of supportive relationships, and a broad spectrum of concepts related to General Systems Theory[3].

THEORY X--MANAGEMENT AS PRODUCTION-CENTERED. McGregor describes management under Theory X as traditional, production-centered, and authoritarian,

If there is a single assumption that pervades conventional organizational theory it is that authority is the central, indispensable means of managerial control....

(Such authority under Theory X) tends to rely on such control devices as rewards, promises, incentives or threats, and other coercive means, methods that are of limited value in motivating people whose important needs are social and egoistic....

So long as the assumptions of Theory X continue to influence managerial strategy, we will fail to discover, let alone utilize, the potentialities of the average human being.

Under Theory X, authoritarian business leadership is understood in terms of personal qualities or traits. The great Captains of Industry are assumed to have magnetic personalities or some undefinable charisma akin to occult powers, quite independent of the situation and other relationships.

As late as 1958, Robert McMurry,[4] of the Harvard Business School, called for a view of business as a "benevolent autocracy," with a "great man" at its head. He assumed a basic human need for security and direction from others. Only at the top of organizational structure was there room for a few dynamic leaders to direct the organization and its workers.

Under such assumptions, understanding leadership becomes primarily a process of analysis and use of traits. R. M. Stogdill,[5] after an extensive survey of the literature, concluded that leadership is associated with: (1) intelligence including judgment and verbal facility, (2) a reputation for related achievement, (3) emotional maturity including persistence and a drive for achievement, (4) social competence, and (5) a desire for socio-economic status. Innumerable related studies have been made, of course, but Stogdill's work indicates the trend.

Since the authoritarian managers under Theory X are production-centered, they naturally concentrated their efforts toward greater efficiency in work methods. This culminated in the

---

[1]Douglas McGregor, *THE HUMAN SIDE OF ENTERPRISE*, New York: McGraw-Hill Book Company, 1960.

[2]Rensis Likert, *NEW PATTERNS OF MANAGEMENT*, New York: McGraw-Hill Book Company, 1961, 97-118.

[3]Richard A. Johnson et al., "Systems Theory and Management," in Max S. Wortman, *EMERGING CONCEPTS IN MANAGEMENT*, New York: The Macmillan Company, 1969, 331ff.

[4]Robert N. McMurry, "The Case for Benevolent Autocracy," *Harvard Business Review*, Vol. 36, No. 1, January 1958, pp. 82-90.

[5]R. M. Stogdill, "Personal Factors Associated with Leadership: A Survey of the Literature," *Journal of Psychology*, Vol. XXV, January 1948, pp. 35-64.

"Scientific-Management School," as presented by Frederick W. Taylor,[1] that urged a science-oriented approach in all aspects of business related to production and profit. Workmen must be "scientifically" selected and trained for maximum outputs. (No mention was made of their personal goals or needs.)

THEORY Y--MANAGEMENT AS PERSON-CENTERED. In reaction to this use of science for only the work or production aspects of the managerial function, McGregor proposed his "Theory Y: the integration of individual and organizational goals." Actually there existed a 100-year background for this view, as in Robert Owen's (1825) emphasis on workers as human beings ("Vital machines") not as cogs in a machine; or in the work (1923) of George Elton Mayo[2] at the Western Electric Hawthorne plant from which he concluded that social-psychological factors determined workers' production more than did economic factors.

McGregor's Theory Y with its emphasis on the human side of business was a great advance over traditional views. He tended to assume that production and profit are the main goals of business enterprise, goals that generally take precedence over those of the individual member. But he concluded that when individual goals and procedures are integrated with those of the enterprise, men work harder and better, assume greater responsibility, do a better job of policing rules infractions, and therefore, sweet to the ears of industry, production and profit are increased.

McGregor analyzed 111 research studies of the nature of leadership and concluded it to be a special quality as had been widely held, but also a complex of relationships among the leader-followers-institution-social milieu, all of which are unique in any given situation and vary from one generation or culture to another. When such relationships are in opposition, as is usually the case under authoritarian leadership, interest and energy wane or may even become destructive. Methods of leadership that are mutually supportive of the enterprise and its workers produce gains in cooperation, effort and effectiveness in work output. He concluded that, in contrast to the technological excellence sought by those of the scientific management schools, "the major industrial advances of the next half century will occur on the human side of enterprise."

MANAGEMENT AS MUTUALLY SUPPORTIVE RELATIONSHIPS. In his award-winning book[3] of research on the problems of business management, Rensis Likert confirmed the work of McGregor in concluding that works at all levels of the business enterprise, top to bottom, are more productive and tend to increase profits when they feel the enterprise is centered in and organized under "a principle of mutually supportive relationships."

The leadership and other processes of the organization must be such as to ensure a maximum probability that in all interactions and all relationships with the organization each member will, in the light of his background, values, and expectations, view the experience as supportive and one which builds and maintains his sense of personal worth and importance.

The two words "view" and "sense" are specially significant, for Likert emphasizes that "it is how he (the worker) sees things that counts, not objective reality." The worker should believe that the mission of the organization is genuinely important and that he "contributes in an indispensable manner to the organization's achievement of its objectives. He should see his role as difficult, important, and meaningful."

CREATIVE MANAGEMENT. These theories of McGregor and Likert are strongly supported by the success experienced by Shigeru Kobayashi, personnel manager of Japan's great SONY Corporation,

---

[1] Frederick W. Taylor, SCIENTIFIC MANAGEMENT, New York: Harper & Brothers, 1947.

[2] George Elton Mayo, THE SOCIAL PROBLEMS OF AN INDUSTRIAL CIVILIZATION, in H. F. Merrill (ed.) CLASSICS IN MANAGEMENT, New York: American Management Association, 1960, pp. 21-25.

[3] Rensis Likert, op. cit., 103ff.

as reported in his book, *CREATIVE MANAGEMENT*.[1] Here are some of his chapter heads--"More About the Joy of Work," "Everyone is a Manager," "True Education Within the Company," :Self-Imposed Rules and Regulations," "Work Can't Be Purchased with Wages," "Relationships Based on Trust."

As an example of procedures, Kobayashi says that SONY plants have no timeclocks to be punched or absentee reports controlled by management. If production falls off in a department, small "cells" of workers check on themselves for possible causes. Such viewpoints and methods seem amazing, feasible only where a climate of mutual trust and mutual respect between management and workers prevail.

As in American corporations, Kobayashi found that successful business leaders do possess "charisma." that he related to such personal qualities as courage (strong will, vitality, sense of responsibility and determination to complete assigned tasks), and what he called "gentleness," the capacity to understand and trust human beings even when they sometimes betray that trust.

I felt then that the Oriental way of thinking inherent in the Japanese mind might excel in creating a type of management centered about human beings; that the integration of this management with the scientific methodology we acquired from abroad might provide the basis for the management style of the future, not only in Japan but throughout the world.

Production and profit? Kobayashi agrees they are absolutely essential, but as the indispensable means to the end of greater service to the common good, not as the ultimate end of the enterprise on a purely economic basis. I have no way of knowing to what extent SONY practice corresponds with Kobayashi theory. But it is clear that his theory represents a new concept of the true ends of business enterprise, one that is in keeping with the gradually emerging General Systems Theory that is unifying so many areas of human knowledge.

THE MANAGERIAL GRID. In 1961, Robert R. Blake and Jane S. Mouton established Scientific Methods, Inc. as a means for improving business management methods and relationships. Their success has been remarkable. In 1975 over 75 of the top 100 industrial companies of the United States, as judged by *Fortune*, were clients; seminars were conducted in most of the States, as well as in some 40 other countries.

The key to this operation is the book, *THE MANAGERIAL GRID*,[2] an introductory study for managers prior to their attendance at a series of extended week-end seminars. In the first of these, managers of similar levels but from different companies study their common problems; in later sessions, managers of different levels from the same company seek mutual goals and helpful relationships. Many client companies have reported improved managerial effectiveness through these seminars and follow-up use of Grid methods.

In *THE MANAGERIAL GRID*, Blake and Mouton assign numerical values to various degrees of concern for (1) methods that are work-oriented (concern for production methods and profit), and (2) methods that are people oriented. A checkerboard grid was constructed, 9 x 9 squares in size, with "concern for people" rated on the vertical scale, and "concern for production" on the horizontal. Low concern was given a value of 1; high concern, 9. The authors identified five basic styles of managerial leadership:

9,1 The highly authoritarian manager with expertise and high concern for methods of production but little or no concern for people as persons.

1,9 The manager primarily concerned with getting along with people, though with little understanding or interest in their high-level capacities, and little

---

[1]Shigeru Kobayashi, *CREATIVE MANAGEMENT*, New York: American Management Association, Inc., 1971, p. 68.

[2]Robert R. Blake and Jane S. Mouton, *THE MANAGERIAL GRID*, Houston: Gulf Publishing Company, 1964, 338 pages.

concern for the problems of production.

9,9   The manager equally concerned and expert in the two areas of human relations and production. He seeks high output but through the medium of committed people having mutual respect, trust, and a realization of the interdependence of the enterprise and its workers.

5,5   The "compromiser," who balances moderate concern for production with moderate concern for human relations.

1,1   The manager who gets by with minimum effort and concern.

Of these five basic viewpoints, the 9,9 managerial style, with its integration of the goals and attitudes of business management with those of workers as both individuals and groups, was found to be most likely to ensure success of the enterprise, that is, highest-level production and profit.

SUMMARY. The job of coaching young men and women in the many events of track and field is both simple and very complex. It is simple in its sharp focus on doing--doing what needs to be done again and again, day after day; more running leads to better running. But it is very complex in several ways--complex, for example, in its need for up-to-date knowledge of modern techniques and training methods, as well as for understanding derived from the related sciences. It is also complex in its relationships with people--the individual athlete, the team, members of the sponsoring institution, alumni, local community groups, and the like.

Even today, a coach can get by--even do well--with simple tools and limited understanding. By recruiting high-level talent and working hard at the essentials for success, he can win even a national championship. But as with any art, the more one knows about its tools and methods, the greater one's chances for mastery and, most important, the greater one's satisfactions out of the work.

The development of track and field has followed such a gradual evolution. It began on a basis of local trial and error-success, with very limited knowledge of how others in other places had tried and succeeded. Such sciences as physics or physiology had no existence for the coach or athlete, just as "track and field" had no existence for the physicist or physiologist. The two disciplines of sport and science simply had no sense of relevance, one to the other. Around the 1920s, mutual awareness and co-operation flickered timorously here and there, but was largely ignored, if not scorned, by both sides.

As might be expected in a machine-minded society, first break-throughs came in the area of mechanical tools and methods--more scientifically designed starting blocks, hurdles, vaulting equipment, throwing implements. Following mechanics came biomechanics, then track-and-field mechanics. Physiology, as a more measureable and "respectable" science, came into relatively early use as compared with the "damn-fool fantasies" of psychology. Psychology evolved from arm-chair subjectivism through gestalt-organismic-field theories--always with considerable empirical tailoring to make them fit the practical situation. Branching out, psychology and its sister-science, social-psychology, became involved in the problems of business management with its theories of "X" and "Y" and "mutually-supportive relationships."

Business with its primary goal of personal profit seems far afield from coaching track and field. But its research into the basic problems of leadership has had far greater financial support as well as trained probing by superior intellects than could possibly be available to any sport, certainly to track and field. Such research has direct application to the problems of coaching-leadership in track and field, and leads to the conclusion that modern coaching requires scientific training on the human side of our sport at least as much as on the mechanical and "physical" side. Future progress in our sport demands mutual understanding, respect and cooperation between scientists and coaches. Gabe Korobkov, Chief National Coach for the USSR, plans to retire from coaching to do research at the National Sports Institute, Moscow, to help other scientists understand the facts of training and competition. Laboratory theories must be validated within the less controlled complex of practical sport situations, and if they stand the test, they safeguard the individual and improve performance. Otherwise they must be modified or discarded and more useful theories must be formed. Thus the spiral of sports knowledge and performance rises through cooperative efforts of theorists and practitioners.

Chapter 2
COACHING LEADERSHIP

Careful consideration of the many problems and social forces influencing future progress in United States track and field leads to the conclusion that major advances during the next half-century will occur through a better understanding and use of the human side of track and field coaching.

By this statement I do not suggest that the methods and technology of track and field events are likely to be less important to future progress. I sometimes feel we are only beginning to utilize the great potentials of the physical sciences--physiology, biomechanics, physics. Much greater use of these should and will be made.

But up to the 1980s we have almost entirely neglected the human-centered sciences--individual psychology, group dynamics, sociology, social psychology. We have claimed that their research has had little relevance for track and field, and it's true that directly useable research has fallen far short of our needs. But Chapter 1 sketched all too briefly their uses in the hard-headed world of business management, and raised the important question as to whether such research has direct relevance to the problems of coaching management in track and field. In the remaining chapters of Part I, I shall try to interpret these insights into track and field terminology.

COACHING LEADERSHIP AS CHARISMA

Traditional viewpoints have tended to view the leader as the crucial element in the leadership process, an element that often takes the form of benevolent autocracy in which the Great Man assumes full control and responsibility. We have assumed a very limited capacity of ordinary human beings to take effective action on their own without undergoing great stress and anxiety. Their need for security is more basic than the need for adventure and self-realization, so that they tend to turn to the leader for direction and for safety within the well-structured organization he provides.

In keeping with these viewpoints, we tend to accept the Great Coach theory of track success-- behind every great athlete there stands a great leader. I think of Percy Cerutty behind Herb Elliott, of Bob Timmons behind Jim Ryun, of Vladimir Dyatchkov behind Valeriy Brumel, and of Arthur Lydiard behind Peter Snell and Murray Halberg. For example, Murray Halberg wrote,

I quickly found Arthur the sort of man to be naturally followed and listened to. He was a leader. He talked like one and he acted like one. My first impression of him was of a guy who wouldn't go halfway....He talks sense. There is no airy theory or indecision about him....I know now that if I had not met him then, there isn't an atom of chance that I could have developed as I did.[1]

When the great English distance runner, Gordon Pirie, wrote of his first meeting with Woldemar Gerschler, German coach and developer of the interval-training system, he said, "I

---

[1]Murray Halberg and Garth Gilmour, *A CLEAN PAIR OF HEELS,* London: Harbert Jenkins Ltd., 1962, p. 25.

was immediately impressed with the quiet authority of the man, and soon I unreservedly put myself in his hands."

Because of its emphasis on the individual rather than on the team, coaching charisma in track and field is not as apparent as in the team sports. For example, Frank Dolson[1] quotes one of Notre Dame's football players as having this reaction to coach Ara Parseghian,

"You see him (the first time), you can't help but be impressed," this year's No. 1 quarterback, Rick Slager, said. "You know how he talks. It's a feeling he gives you. You knows who's boss right off the bat. He's super-friendly, but you walk in his office, he's got a pad and pencil there and he starts talking. And you say, 'Oh boy...' And you keep saying it. And thinking it. And feeling it.

"He was Ara Parseghian," Slager said. "He ran the team. There was a certain air about him that you'd have to say was hard to penetrate. And a certain excitement.

"He'd come into the locker room just before we came out. He'd become extremely, EXTREMELY, intense. He was super with his pre-game talks. Especially before the big games. You couldn't wait to play."

I can think of perhaps a score of such charismatic leaders among the track coaches I have known. But that's a surprisingly small number among the hundreds of other very successful coaches. These others, perhaps out of my own myopic viewpoint, just did not have the striking personal qualities implied by the word "charisma." Their style was of the quieter kind, more related to warm friendships and concerned teaching than to some magnetic drawing power. For example, Bob Giegengack, Yale coach for 30 years. One might say Bob had charisma--a constant need to verbalize eased by a delightful wit, self-confidence to the point of cockiness, a friendly and ready smile, and the respect of his peers that led to his selection as Head Track and Field Coach for the 1964 Olympic Team. Here is his attitude toward the training of Frank Shorter, 1972 Olympic Marathon Champion, while at Yale,

He really enjoyed those activities (skiing and a singing group), and that's the way it has to be with a kid at Yale....I'm certainly not permissive in workouts. But on the other hand I have to respect the right of someone else to disagree with me about the importance for him of doing this particular thing....Even if I had the power, I couldn't say, "Now this is what you're going to do. You're going to stop taking that course. You're going to be out here for practice...whether you like it or not, because you have a scholarship.[2]
Hardly the kind of attitude you'd expect from a strong leader, no matter how benevolent.

Under normal conditions, young men accept strong leadership eagerly. They want to believe in the coach and his program as long as certain goals are held in common. They expect and even seek discipline. Discipline is not a problem for disciples. When the Master demands training to the levels of hurt-pain-agony as does swimming authority Doc Counsilman of Indiana, they follow with few if any reservations, even take pride in having done so and in their "slave-driver" coach.

But during the past decade or so, conditions have not been normal. Endless disclosures of deceit, bribery and betrayal associated with the Vietnam War have made the younger generation suspicious of the Establishment, its institutions, its leaders, and all authority indiscriminately. In his autobiography[3] Vince Matthews, 1972 Olympic 400-meters champion, states their

---

[1]Frank Dolson, "And the Habit is Apparent at Notre Dame," *The Philadelphia Inquirer*, October 6, 1975

[2]John Parker, *THE FRANK SHORTER STORY*, Mountain View, Cal.: Runner's World Magazine, 1972, p. 34.

[3]Vince Matthews with Neil Amdur, *MY RACE BE WON*, New York: Charterhouse, 1974, p. 265.

view clearly,

One of the problems connected with organized sports in the United States is that it has become too coach-oriented. The coach has been pictured so often as a father figure that he has begun to believe in it himself. What he cannot rationalize is that society has changed many of its attitudes toward authority and sports and that athletes have changed as well. The athlete no longer accepts everything a coach says as instant fact and truth. He wants to know why he should accept it, why what one coach is demanding is any better than the doctrine preached by another coach.

Actually, once a coach demonstrated he was competent and could be trusted, Matthews was more than willing to follow his lead. Resentful of the AAU rule that each club must have a coach, he and his teammates of the BOHAA (Boys Over the Hill Athletic Association) reluctantly chose Charlie Turner as their coach, but later credited him for much of their improvement in training organization and performance.

CHARISMA AS ENTHUSIASM. The art of coaching is partly a transfusion of the coach's enthusiasm, energy, confidence with the life stream of his athletes. Almost without exception, the biographies of great athletes tell how their coach inspired them, put backbones into their wishbones, gave them courage to begin, and then to keep on trying despite so many discouragements.

But a coach is enthusiastic, not merely out of an effervescence of animal spirits, but from a deep knowledge and feeling for the many aspects of his sport--the men and the action. Such a coach lives track and field--thinks, feels, acts, talks it. The more he becomes involved and absorbed in the sport, the more it expands him, opens up new channels to knowing more, and-- our main point here--lends an enthusiasm to his teaching that is hard to resist.

We often hear that the student of track and field is likely to be an ineffective coach. If so, and we doubt it, such a man is only a student of the words and ideas--the cold facts of the sport. The cold facts are important, but they must be mixed with the warm-blooded facts of actual running and jumping and throwing--in competition. Then zest emerges out of the capillaries and muscle fibers as well as from the tongue.

I would be hard pressed to decide whether it's more vital that this book should give you the facts of field and track, or whether its words should fire your enthusiasm until it fires you to go on the field and find out for yourself. Actually, knowledge and enthusiasm are two aspects of one coaching essential; lacking either, effective coaching is diminished. Men fail in coaching because they do not know enough about the job but also because they are not sufficiently enthused about what they do know.

In 1965 I attended an NCAA coaching clinic at Indiana University where the assistant coach, Bill Perrin, presented the uses of his rubber tubing for strength training. He was highly skilled in ways of strengthening each muscle group. But above all, his enthusiasm was most infectious. I bought a set. But on returning home, lacking Bill's expertness, my enthusiasm waned and soon the tubing rested on the shelf. The device was everything Bill showed it to be; I simply lacked know-how and, with it, zest.

This occurs at so many coaching clinics. We catch the key words and ideas; we write them down and take them home. But we fail to take home the drudgery of hard work behind those ideas which enthusiasm inspires and out of which enthusiasm is ignited. This is happening right now as you read these words. You're feeling--I hope--a faint rise in interest. But you are missing, you can't possibly know, the dull doggedness of will-energy that has wrenched forth these words. How could you know that just now I spent five minutes mulling over what word might be more apt than "wrenched." And so you miss something of the heart of what I am trying to convey.

The obverse of this heading is that an effective coach is never indifferent, never personally unconcerned. He does not have to bubble openly. He can be matter-of-fact and even mildly sceptical, but he can never be a colorless, indifferent nonentity. Track and field does matter. The performances of these athletes are of deep personal concern.

The minute you become aware of a sense of dullness toward your coaching, take a sharp look--

not at what's wrong with the sport, but at yourself. It is you that are losing your shine, not the team members, not the sport. It is you that needs polishing, whether it be by way of a vacation, or more likely, from some new insight gained from seeing some record performance, or from exposing yourself to the enthusiasm of other coaches at a clinic, or from reading an inspirational book. But above all, remind yourself that enthusiasm and work grow on the same stalk, gain strength from each other. When enthusiasm lags, concentration on some new phase of your job may restore it.

CHARISMA AS AN OUTGROWTH OF HARD WORK. A coach that plans for success adopts a policy of persevering work--for his team members, but even more crucial, for himself. It takes a dauntless spirit of resolution to get up at 6 A.M., as Mihaly Igloi and so many other serious coaches have done throughout their coaching careers, just to ensure an early morning workout for a dozen or so boys. It takes tenacity to study the mechanics of field events with no background in the terminology. It requires strength of purpose to make the rounds, trying to discover vacation jobs for team members that allow them to run early mornings or late afternoons. Only diligence and patience can arrange team trips so that every detail is covered satisfactorily. It takes endless persistence to get top performance out of a boy who does many things well--in different sports, but also in social affairs, or in school dramatics or music, and enjoys doing all of them.

There are no elevators in the Track and Field Hall of Fame. To get to the top floor one has to step up each stair, one by one by one at a time. They're moving stairs, moving downward; when you stop climbing upward, you're on a down staircase. Some say that recruiting is an easy escalator to the top. Not today; the competition there is just as tough as on the field. And even after you get good prospects by recruiting, you've got to work hard to make them great.

If you want to be inspired by the genius of hard work, read Irving Stone's biography of Michelangelo, *The Agony and the Ecstasy*. Granted he was a genius, a superman, his supreme artistry was an outcome of serious study and dogged perseverance, of furious chipping away endlessly at a block of stone--one blow at a time. But even before the chipping, the months of frustrating search for a clear vision of the image hidden in the marble. Without question, the greater the genius, whether in sculpture, mathematics, or in coaching, the greater the acceptance of unremitting hard work.

Wait a moment. That's not quite right. Work is not really the right word. For when the whole man is absorbed, fully wrapped up in what he is doing, there is no work. Work implies exertion to produce an extrinsic outcome or reward, but when you're engrossed in interesting work, only the work itself matters, not the reward. It becomes play. I'm reminded of the comment attributed to Babe Ruth, though I can't imagine the Babe saying it, "What a fraud--to be paid for doing what I'd enjoy doing for nothing."

We wrote above of unremitting continuous work. We all get fired up to work hard at times. When 15 seniors leave the team, we really scurry to fill their places. But truly effective coaching is continuous. William James (1911, 3), America's greatest practical psychologist, explained in his essay, *The Energies of Men*, what every distance runner knows, that all demanding work brings us, sonner or later, to a fatigue point--usually physical and mental and either acute or chronic--at which we want to quit. Soon we're sure we can't go on any longer. "Anything but this." But we discover that if we keep on doggedly, with brief intervals of recovery and re-creation of course, we move up to a new level of energy. We discover untapped reservoirs of energy deeper than we had thought possible. Every coach knows this, but tends to know it only for his distance runners and weight men. Few realize it applies equally to his own coaching energies. A Kansas track man (Nelson, 1967, 178) described Coach Timmons, "He just plain cares about the guys, and if he drives us hard, if he cuts the blood out of us, why he cuts the blood out of himself too. You go by that Field House any night at 11, and you'll see the light on in his office. He's a hell of a little guy."

For the past 40 years or more, I've watched certain teams, college and high school, establish a high success record. They seem to have the secret for winning. But then things change; they're on the losing end. I've talked with their coaches, and often find a man who has lost his drive to succeed. He's lost his enthusiasm, his belief in what he's doing, or in his school or town. Perhaps these have really gone down hill, but often the real change is in the coach. He thought he had it made. "Anyway, life is too short. I'm missing so much. I'm going to enjoy things for a while." This is the same kind of talk that so many champions give out when they quit as their best years are just beginning. I could name hundreds. Each coach must realize it applies to himself as to his athletes.

COACHING LEADERSHIP AS TRAITS

If, for purposes of analysis and better understanding, we accept the concept of special leadership traits as related to coaching, what would be their nature? The following items are uneven in significance and form, but they should stimulate discussion:

1. Person: figure and face, voice and diction, manner, dress, overall charisma.

2. Energy: forcefulness under stress, persistence over the long run, enthusiasm despite discouragement and frustration.

3. Ability to inspire others: helps them help themselves, furthers self-esteem, has high expectations of performance.

4. Authority: of person, of past experience, of related knowledge, of past success, of commitment to excellence, of team agreements.

5. Decision-making: decisive quickly and firmly; cautious--considers carefully then decides: slow--vacillating, unsound judgment.

6. Fairness and integrity: to team members, to rules of sport on and off the field.

7. Self-control and tact: courteous and restrained; quickly angered or excited; blunt-severe-crusty.

8. Empathy: keenly sensitive to other's wishes or reactions, encourages- persuades- praises; insensitive-ridicules-bullies.

9. Attitude toward team members: enjoys their companionship; indifferent; feels aversion.

10. Develops team spirit: among team members; within related institution; within local community; among greater team family.

11. Competitive attitude: all out to win; competitive with but not against others; primarily self-competitive.

12. Reaction under stress: calm; rises to increasing challenge; anxious and overburdened.

13. Competence and expertise: in personal relationships, in methods and techniques of track and field.

14. Ability to teach.

15. Work habits: coaching is a 24-hour job; coaches one to six P.M. six days a week during season only; just enough to get by and satisfy others.

LEADERSHIP TRAITS AS TENDENCIES.

Any serious discussion of the leadership qualities of the preceding section must have made clear their illusory nature. These are words and not the actuality, words that can be defined or interpreted to suit the user. We shall be much clearer and sounder in our understanding if we think of the traits these words seek to describe as merely tendencies to action, or as indicating ranges of possible development. By effort and will a man can function quite adequately along any portion of such ranges.

That is, heredity does give us leadership qualities, helpful and otherwise, but within wide ranges of possible use, not as fixed traits. Just where within that range a coach operates is determined by a number of variables but especially by his understanding of the problem and his will and imagination in making the most of what he has.

I am suddenly reminded of the decathlon as an example of how this principle operates. We must compete in ten events in each of which we have a wide range of potential. We can accept our present low performance or train gradually to the highest levels of our potential. We can concentrate our efforts in the few events in which we have great talent or we can work for consistency in all ten events. The latter requires tough persistence, day-after-day. But it must be done if we are to be real decathloners.

In the decathlon, our performance is measureable, can be given a number value. Unfortunately it's not that simple as related to our character. Over the years we have erected strong defenses to protect our ego, especially in its areas of possible weakness. We believe in the adequacy of our present qualities, and are slow to attempt, or may even resent, change. Unconsciously, we fear possible failure if we attempt better ways of behavior that are not our ways and with which we do not feel comfortable. For example, we may agree that we tend to be cautious and even uncertain in making decisions. But we'd rather continue in that pattern than undergo the risk of pushing ourselves to faster and firmer decisions. The right way feels wrong to us; the wrong way, right. Why then seek improvement?

But that's like the straddle-style high jumper for whom the flop style feels wrong until he has practiced and practiced until it becomes his way and feels right. Of course he has a coach; you don't, and that makes a great difference.

Every beginning coach should make a critical assessment of his range of personality and coaching style. The crucial word in that sentence is "range." Each "trait" always has a + or - sign indicating a flexibility or range of educability or usefulness. This seems obvious as stated here but it's hard to apply to ourselves as coaches. We rarely ask clearly defined questions of this kind about ourselves. And when such questions are asked, we tend to give vague answers.

We might feel sure that "I like boys." If you think you do, try putting your attitudes to a critical test by checking your reaction to twelve types of athletes, as listed by Ogilvie and Tutko (1966, 18). They provide a four-degree scale including deeply resent, slightly resent, slightly unconcerned, and completely unconcerned. If you're honest, you'll find in each instance a range of possible reaction; if you're analytical, you'll often be unable to answer, at least in a reliable fashion. You'll feel a very wide range of possible response depending upon an infinite variety of situations and individual differences.

Despite such difficulties, you will undoubtedly conclude from such a test that you do tend to react favorably to one type of athlete and negatively to another. Note the "tend to." How narrow and fixed is that tendency? How wide and flexible? Here is the key to improvement of your coaching assets. Quite possibly your attitudes are the result of your home community attitudes, or of the attitudes of your parents, or of your own coach you admire so much. *But there is a range within which these can be improved.*

We have used attitudes toward boys as our example. But the same range-of-potential approach can be taken toward such coaching attributes as self-assuredness, knowledge of track and field, personal experience in track and field, level of energy and enthusiasm, sense of humor, speaking voice and diction, or level of expectancy of competitive performance.

COACHING LEADERSHIP AS RELATIONSHIPS.

A coach can be effective as a leader of others only as his relationships are effective, or as Likert found with business management, as his relationships are mutually supportive. A coach may have great leadership charisma, exhibit all the traits of great coaching, and know the most scientific methods and techniques of track and field, but these have no meaning except in relation to other people. To state a sound principle, the life history of any coach can be predicted or can be retold on the basis of the scope and kind of his relationships--with the team as a group or as individuals, with his institution and its members, with the local community, with "feeder" groups--schools, alumni, clubs, many others--with fellow-coaches, with track and field organizations--local, state, national and international.

Such relationships vary with the sponsoring institution. They tend to be local at the high school level; more widespread at the college level. They tend to be one-state-oriented at such universities as Oregon, Iowa, Western Michigan or Penn State. Others, such as Harvard, Princeton, Michigan or California at Berkeley, tend to relate to most of the States of the Union. Relationships within institutions can change from one decade to another. State universities that drew students from many states in the 1950s became more local as out-of-state tuitions skyrocketed.

The scope of coaching relationships therefore needs careful analysis before trying to set up a program. Contrast the kind of program organized by Bill Bowerman and Bob Newland in the State of Oregon (see Chapter 4) with that of Jumbo Elliott at Villanova. The former was almost exclusively Oregonian, and rightly so if the track team is to be validly representative of its institution. In contrast, other than being a Catholic school, Villanova is not easily identified; its relationships extend widely and loosely. Irish lads and English schoolboys seem as much at home as do the champions from a dozen Eastern States. Specially recruited? Yes, but within the scope of Villanova's relationships.

The kind of relationship is equally important--mutually supportive of course if it is to be long lasting. But with what degree of personal friendship? With whom? Does a college coach establish friendships with "bird-dogs" that flush out the quarry? Is his relationship with many high school coaches longtime and personally warm, or does he have their respect as a sound coach they can trust. Perhaps the college coach operates as does a salesman--exchanging products of value with the high school coach or directly with the athlete.

In summary, and it's impossible to over-emphasize the point, the extent and nature of relationships with others is at least as crucial to coaching success as is knowledge of track and field methods and techniques. It will therefore be the primary concern throughout the remainder of this and the following Chapters in Part I.

ROLES OF THE COACH

The actual roles of the track and field coach are so numerous and complex as to defy definite analysis, and certainly are beyond the scope of this book. But the following summary may stimulate thinking and discussion. Actually we should add to our heading the words "in our American society today," with emphasis on the word "today." Coaching roles are constantly changing, through influences from within and outside sport, along with our changing culture. In my generation, the role of the coach was about what he made it; few questioned his authority to do so. But not all cultures take such a view. I shall never forget my sense of being put down, even humiliated, when Lou Montgomery and I, as head coaches, attended the Penn-Cornell, Oxford-Cambridge banquet in London. We were seated at a rear table with the English coaches and were never recognized at any time during the evening. In contrast, in Finland and Europe generally, student coaches and athletes rise respectfully when the head coaches enter the lecture hall.

Today, in America, the traditional roles of the coach are being seriously questioned, just as are so many other aspects of the so-called Establishment. Tomorrow the coach may interpret his roles from quite a different frame of reference to that presented here.

OVER-EVALUATION. The real value of a coach for improved performance, especially at the individual level, is easily over-estimated and over-stated. As I have observed great athletes that have developed under other coaches as well as under my own teaching, I've often felt that we coaches merely create helpful situations and a few pushes toward self-development. What they accomplish emerges mainly out of themselves, out of their own powers of muscle and heart and self-discipline and persistence. After three or more years of coaching a great athlete, a coach tends to acquire an attitude that now he has the secret. Whatever the coach says is quickly understood and becomes effective. Only after the athlete is gone does the coach realize clearly that the secret went with him. Brutus Hamilton was a most effective coach. But he often insisted that his greatest value lay in not interfering with the normal progress of his boys.

THE COACH AS TOILER. The word "toiler" was chosen deliberately as meaning one who engages in fatiguing, emotionally stressful, and even arduous work for long hours day after day after day. The job has so many aspects, all of which contribute or are even essential to success, that the days are simply not long enough to do a fully effective job. How well I remember my own experiences as a first-year coach when, coming home on the train from Chicago after the end-of-the-year Conference Championships, we reviewed our losses through graduation, assessed our chances for the coming year, and made plans effective immediately to improve those chances. It's a year-round vocation, regardless of the school calendar or pay checks.

Over the years, I've heard so many comments, "One thing I'll say about Coach so-and-so, he may drive his men hard, harder than I think he should, but he drives himself just as hard; he's always on the job." When Ara Parseghian retired after 25 years as head football coach, he was quoted as saying, "I was physically and emotionally drained. I knew I had to get out. I also knew I won't be able to stay away for good. I'll want back. But I need some time to get myself back together, and time is one luxury our business doesn't provide."

Woody Hayes, Ohio State's winningest football coach, was known to everyone as a workaholic, one who worked on weekends of course but also on all holidays in and out of season. He was said to have originated the present vogue for delivery truck pads in which he could grab a quick nap when on his way to recruiting or speaking appointments. Even a heart attack reduced only a little his time on the road. At one interview he estimated he had been away from home over 200 nights during the past year.

Of course, that's football, and fortunately the public pressure on track coaches is not nearly so great as that on football coaches. But the inner urge to succeed is just as great, and the demand for work just as crucial for success.

Even in those high schools and small colleges where coaching is an extra assignment for which a few hundred dollars extra are paid, the self-respecting coach will find himself forced to study hard to gain the required knowledge, to use many off-the-job hours in getting to know his protégées better, to eat many a warmed-over supper in order to complete the workout of the late-lab athlete, and even slip out to the track during a free period to emphasize a point or two with a twice-a-day shot-putter.

THE COACH AS INSTRUCTOR. Traditionally, the word "coach" implied a trainer, one who disciplined potential athletes by regular exercise and restricted diet. At first, running was the primary activity, so one gained endurance by "training" for running. But this concept became confused when track coaches also acted as "trainers" for the football and basketball teams--one who supervised calisthenics and the conditioning of the team, along with giving rubdowns (an almost daily ritual with talented athletes) and caring for injuries. Such trainers had great power and prestige, sometimes taking players off the field when the head coach wanted them to stay.

Gradually this work became specialized and year-round. Perhaps Ducky Drake of UCLA was the last of the dual track-coach-trainers who in about 1972 retired from coaching to continue as fulltime trainer. In almost all other instances the training duties were dropped to serve the fulltime needs of coaching.

So today, a track coach is primarily an instructor, one who instructs in the methods and techniques of field events as well as in the best uses of the various systems of training for running. (Note how we still retain the "training" terminology.)

THE COACH AS PLANNER. The track coach tends to assume primary responsibility for making plans, both team and individual. He alone knows the entire set-up: training and competition, team and individual, on and off the track, at home and on trips, etc. Much as he may insist that he is but one member of the team, and that his plans are team plans, the necessity for getting the job done, and done well, tends to put major planning in the hands of the coach.

THE COACH AS EXECUTOR. The sources of basic team policy are many: tradition within the sport of track and field, school tradition, school administration, alumni and community enthusiasts, and then of course the team and the coach. Regardless of how team policies are reached, the paid coach in America tends to be the primary executor of policy. He is paid to get things done. It must be added that in America the coach is paid to get things done in such a way as to best ensure winning. As one educator said recently,

I have found that 99 percent of all communities want you to win. True, they also want you to build character, promote rules of amateurism and good sportsmanship, and be a worthy leader whom young Americans should follow, but they want you to win. They believe in character education; they employ guidance counselors, principals, teachers to build such character, and certainly they do not want the coach to tear it down, but they want him to win.

But each season and each team develops its own views and problems as related to basic policy. In trying to solve such problems, the coach must often tread lightly in executing policy and shift to the role of arbitrator-mediator. An arbitrator is empowered by others on both sides of the issue to analyze the facts and make a final decision. A mediator brings all related persons and facts together and by contrivance or toughness keeps them together until they reach agreement.

THE COACH AS RECRUITER. It's rather surprising that someone has not written a full-size book revealing the wide variety of methods and viewpoints of recruiting, with special emphasis on its positive aspects. For, contrary to common usage, recruitment as a means of ensuring a constant supply of fresh talent, can have a legitimate place in both school and college sports. Every effective coach must be a recruiter. Even such coaches as Arthur Lydiard or Bill Bowerman, who declare that they never seek the athlete, that the athlete must come to them for help, do recruit by means of the reputation that success has created, or perhaps by way of the disciples that follow them. No one could accuse Coach Ted Haydon of being a recruiter in the sense of seeking out and subsidizing talent for his Chicago Track Club, but he was an outstanding recruiter by way of the nation-wide reputation he slowly acquired as a sound coach unselfishly interested in the welfare of his boys.

What is basically wrong with the concept of hard-sell recruiting? First, within the institution, it reduces the opportunities of members of the regular student body to participate in sport and so gain the valuable developmental training and competitive experiences of sport. Second, among institutions organized into conferences of associations to provide fair play among individuals of comparable talent and attitudes toward sport, recruiting upsets the normal balance of winning and losing. Each recruiter assumes all others are at least bending the rules and so feels justified in bending them even further to make sure he's getting a fair shake. But even more fundamental, hard-sell recruiting adopts the goals of business management that production and profit are primary and so subverts the educational goals of higher education.

The most flagrant example of this in the entire history of college track and field occurred at the University of Texas at El Paso. In 1973, UTEP's coach was fired for excesses in recruiting and promotion. But in 1980, his successor, Ted Banks, won the NCAA Indoor Team Title by recruiting athletes from seven countries--Kenya, Sweden, Nigeria, South Africa, Jamaica, Bermuda and Tanzania. These men scored 64 of UTEP's winning total of 72. What's wrong with such a program? Two important things: First, the opportunity to participate had been taken from regular members of the UTEP student body; second, the principle of fair play had been violated--at least two of these men were over 28 years of age, and others were well over the usual age of college students.

It's hard to argue against the thesis that such hard-sell recruiting is inherent in our competitive industrial-military culture. Educational institutions are necessarily supportive of the ways and ethics of the culture that creates them. In a business-oriented society, "educational" becomes interpreted as vocational training; "ethics" as those of the business community. Small wonder that recruiting of the so-called student-athlete takes on the stench of automobile sales procedures with their emphasis on the bottom line of private profit.

But education in our society is not entirely vocational training within the business ethic. Some schools and colleges still emphasize a truly liberal education; and all have departments and faculties that try to inculcate broader horizons and an ethic somewhat higher than that of the marketplace. For such schools, the geographical radius of recruiting should be roughly that of the regular student body, not as a rule to be policed but as a common-sense approach to the problem. Even better, recruiting would occur at home, from within the regular student body. Intercollegiate sports programs would now become extramural.

Utopian? Unrealistic? Of course. But not because the idea is unsound; not because some rigid human nature makes our present system inevitable. On the contrary, these ideas are unrealistic only in a business culture that follows McGregor's Theory X--authoritarian, selfserving, profit-centered. To the extent that growing environmental and social problems force business and its training institutions to adopt a Theory Y approach, such ideas can gain common acceptance and usage. Now winning in sports, like profit in business, will still be essential, but winning, not as the only end, not as the main end, not as the end at all; rather as the means of motivating what Coubertin called, "the struggle of life"--the hard training, the sacrifice of ease and fun that are essential for both improvement and satisfaction in sports, as in any worthwhile work.

How would such a principle work in practice? Study the operation of the University of Chicago Track Club under Ted Haydon, as outlined in this OMNIBOOK. Their gate receipts and donations are the means to greater service to more track and field athletes of wide-ranging talents and backgrounds. Winning and record-breaking emerge out of numbers and opportunities for practice and competition, not out of recruitment or intense training directly related to winning. As a second example, the Board in Control of Athletics (faculty-controlled) at the University of Michigan has as a basic principle allocated gate receipts to improvement of inter-collegiate sports facilities but only if a like amount were spent on recreational facilities for all students.

But the most soundly-based example of this mutually-supportive principle of which I know is that at the city of Medford and the state of Oregon under the 30-year leadership of Bob Newland and Bill Bowerman, as outlined in this OMNIBOOK. In a nutshell, these two men assumed the many phases of the Medford Public Schools sports system and of the State of Oregon sports system were many phases of one system. To develop successful track and field at the State University level or at the Medford High School level required well-organized programs at all sublevels-- the junior high schools and elementary schools. Meetings were held to discuss common problems and goals. Out of those a track and field handbook was prepared under the leadership of the high school coach, Bob Newland, that provided (1) the gist of sound coaching methods, (2) track and field records at all levels from grade schools up, (3) selected textbook references, and (4) a free copy of a leading textbook. Clinics were held. High School (and later, University) coaches and athletes were available to help beginners at all levels. By such methods, not only was motivation increased, but commonly-held coaching procedures were ensured. Now the elemen-tary-school coach feels that his role is a challenge to him and of some importance to the entire Medford sports system. If the high school athlete wins, at least three coaches feel they were of some help, however small. In keeping with this attitude, their continuing card-file is of special value. As an athlete progressed in school, his personal file with all relevant infor-mation, including each coach's comments, progressed with him.

And as Bill Bowerman, the originator of the Medford system, moved up to the University at Eugene, these views and procedures tended to move with him. No wonder the city of Eugene is often called the distance-running and jogging capitol of the United States, and certainly its most enthusiastic track and field city. All-in-all, a sound grass-roots recruiting system mutually supportive of itself and all its subsystems.

If this soft-sell approach to recruiting is still not clear, try contrasting the Medford or Chicago approaches with that at any one of all too many Universities that pluck the athlete out of his home-school environment, transport him to a "foreign" milieu, exchange his talents for something of monetary value, with scarcely a nod to the home helpers. Even when they receive "first-class treatment throughout," as is claimed by the Villanova champions, one has an impres-sion of good-business procedures- not of a developmental educational system.

THE COACH AS SALESMAN. Every coach, if he is to be effective, must be a salesman. Some will protest this statement on the basis that selling implies an exchange of goods of monetary value. Unfortunately, this is what actually happens at some colleges. But my use of the word "salesman" was intended to imply persuasion, inducement, encouragement, cooperative exchange and the like. Such salesmanship is warranted in any situation.

Certain key questions arise. What is he selling? Himself or his program, institution, situation? What sales methods is he using? True, each coach-situation is unique and so each sales approach will be similarly unique. But there must be some answers that have broad impli-cations. I think of the head college coach who followed a two-step approach with all prospec-tive athletes. First, the assistant guided the prospect through all parts of the campus and student life that interested him. He thereby gained detailed answers to all questions. But most important, the head coach also spent some time alone with the prospect. Why? "Because I love this school. I believe in it and what it does for its individual students and all those associated with it. Somehow I must convey a portion of that love and belief to this prospect." Such a combination of selling the mind and the heart would be hard to improve.

Though written some 40 years ago, Dale Carnegie's HOW TO WIN FRIENDS AND INFLUENCE PEOPLE,[1] with its strong emphasis on cooperation is still relevant today and not far removed in its views from Rensis Likert's principle of mutually supportive relationships. Carnegie's pre-scription was simple--be like Charles Schwab, the genius in executive management selected by

---

[1] Dale Carnegie, HOW TO WIN FRIENDS AND INFLUENCE PEOPLE, New York: Simon & Schuster, 1936.

Andrew Carnegie to manage his financial empire. Schwab knew how to get men to do what he wanted them to do while thinking it was primarily their idea to do it. His secret, according to Dale Carnegie, was an enormously winning smile, a smile claimed to be "worth a million dollars." Schwab made men feel important, the "deepest urge in human nature," according to Carnegie. He extended lavish praise, offered hearty approbation, talked about things the listener was interested in, let them feel new ideas were their ideas, evidenced genuine interest in them as persons. All this made them feel important. And somehow this ennabled the smiler to sell his program and product.

The first question that arises relates to the sincerity and integrity of this approach. Does one smile out of sheer good spirits and good will, or is it an obvious mask related to the need to sell? An insincere grin doesn't fool anyone; in fact, we resent it. In a true salesman, the smile must come from within, from a deep-seated belief in the enterprise and the product, and from a genuine interest in the welfare of other people.

We must keep in mind that Dale Carnegie believed in the business enterprise he was selling; his was salesmanship within and for the system. Without such a genuine belief, his program was based merely on William James' teachings that we can acquire attitudes of mind by acting *as if* we actually feel a certain way. We can learn to feel happy simply by smiling *as if* we are happy. Furthermore, people are quite willing to believe in such smiles, if only out of their great need to be smiled at and so be made to feel important.

With whom does the coach have the relationship of salesman? To athletes of course--present, past, and future. Since future athletes are unknown individually, one must maintain close relationships with all the coaches, near and far, who will be developing them. On this point consider again the Medford, Oregon organization. But also mutually supportive relationships must be maintained with the school administration, with interested members of the community, with parents, even with rival coaches; in short with the entire track team family. The more broadly based, the more effective it will be.

I think of Joe Paterno, the Penn State football coach, who over the course of years has established a solid reputation for personal integrity, pride in his profession of coaching, and personal concern for the general betterment of his charges. Everyone--the communications media, other coaches, the man on the street--speaks well of him and his program. That's real salesmanship, and in the long run the most successful.

THE COACH AS FATHER FIGURE. Some coaches tend to elicit warm emotional feelings from their boys and to respond in kind. In fact, as I try to assess the many coaches I have known, a large percentage had this quality; some more, some less. Among the more outstanding were Tom Jones of Wisconsin, Emil Von Elling of NYU, Don Mollenauer of Mt. Lebanon High School, Pa., Billy Hayes of Indiana, Bob Giegengack of Yale, and Brutus Hamilton of California at Berkeley. But that's a personal reaction with little validity. Another coach would present a quite different list. But all would have in common a primary concern for the boy.

If you do not genuinely enjoy being with young athletes, stay out of coaching. To want to help them is not enough; to be fascinated by the mechanics of track and field is not enough. Genuine friendliness is an essential requirement. Every profession has its special requirements, special conditions, atmosphere, problems. The coach has to feel relaxed and "at home" when travelling with the team, should be one of the team members in laughter and gaiety, while still maintaining their respect and the proper coach-athlete relationship on the field. Without that warmheartedness, without such a sense of mutual enjoyment, there may be victories and record performances, but there is not likely to be the inspiration, zest, and deep satisfaction so essential to great coaching. (Laird, 1956, 191).

Some successful coaches are known as strict disciplinarians. But you'll find that somewhere, someway--on the track or at off-hours--such taskmasters will establish their place in the hearts of their boys. The coaches that fail altogether to be heart-centered are seldom effective and--hopefully--do not remain long in the profession.

Oh, it's not all cream and sugar. There'll be times when you'd like to wipe out the lot of them. There'll be "teams" that just never are able to work or feel together. When the going gets rough, they'll get rough with each other. There'll be men that seem to hate you, and whom you'll--not hate--but at least be glad when they graduate. There'll be times when you feel you're only a policeman, or worse, a spy. But if you like boys, they'll usually buoy you up, infect you with enthusiasm and energy, amaze you with "impossible" performances, and even--now and then and hesitantly--credit you with having been of some small help in some unimportant way. But that'll be compensation enough. I am reminded of Kahlil Gibran's comment that when a true leader dies, the people will say, "We did this thing ourselves."

Quite obviously, an effective coach knows the what and how of his boys' living as they relate directly to track and field. That's his job. But how broadly does he define the word "directly?" Many a boy has withdrawn entirely from track and field because of girl problems, study problems, draft-board problems. How can a coach, with perhaps a hundred boys on his squad, find time and energy for all this, when there's hardly enough time for coaching on the field and for the important demands of coaching clinics, professional improvement, community services, and all the rest? He can't, of course, not really, and yet somehow he does.

Somehow he does maintain personal contact. He realizes the need in all men for recognition and some degree of commendation. He trains himself to look for what is well done--or at least well tried--and finds sincere ways of expressing his appreciation. There is an artless art of such expression, of knowing how an athlete feels, of what is important to him, and what words he will accept--and reject. "Art" because it can be learned; "artless" because it must never seem contrived.

When a disappointed Jerry Siebert returned to California after placing sixth in the Tokyo 800 meters, a letter awaited him from his coach, Brutus Hamilton,

I was never more proud. Knowing something of your condition, [Jerry competed despite illness] I was surprised you ran at all, and I'm not altogether certain that you should have run, but the fact that you did run, and ran well, will always be a source of great pride to your old coach.

Contrived? Insincere? From some coaches it might have seemed so; from Brutus it was as in-character as ham and eggs in a Western breakfast.

Track and field competition and training is a profound experience in which self-doubt and elation, discomfort and joy, numb despair and wild hope, arduous work and surging energy, are all jumbled together. The insensitive "it's-a-job" coach assumes that the outward action is all that is happening to a boy, and reacts only to the hard facts of the situation. But the coach that likes boys, and knows out of his own experiences and his own related emotions what they feel inside the facts, somehow conveys his empathy to the boy, perhaps without saying a word.

Of course, as Ryan[1] pointed out, the father symbol can have a negative influence. To the extent that the boy's father was over-dominant and restrictive, the boy may resent and resist the teachings of the coach, especially when a coach's analysis of a boy's technique becomes, in the boy's mind, a job of surgery on himself personally.

THE COACH AS RELIEVER OF ATHLETE RESPONSIBILITY. The coach plays a very important role in relieving the athlete of the burden of responsibility for planning and making decisions that quite often he is neither ready nor willing to make. This is obviously true for beginning athletes but also for those of long experience at high-performance levels. Dolson tells of George Young's difficulties[2],

The ulcers struck again in 1967, a year before the Mexico City Olympics, and George went through an agonizing summer trying to decide if his track career was over. Maybe he simply couldn't take the strain anymore....He had to do something to reduce the pressure. Anything...

The solution hit him. He had a friend in Silver City...a math instructor and a

---

[1]Frank Ryan, "Some Aspects of Athletic Behavior," NCTCA *Clinic Notes*, 1955, 1.

[2]Frank Dolson, *ALWAYS YOUNG*, Mountain View, Cal.; *World Publications*, 1975, p. 152.

knowledgeable track coach. If George could lean on Jim Fox, maybe the mental strain wouldn't be so great.

"I realized one of my big mental problems...was I would devise workouts for myself, then I wouldn't complete them because I'd think maybe they weren't that good," he said. "Or maybe they were too hard. I felt if I could get him to train me through the mail this would take a lot of the worries off me"....

He followed those workouts religiously--and, more important, unquestioningly--for close on two years. "It did take a lot of pressure off me"...(and he attained) the greatest shape of his life.

Unfortunately, what began as mere helpful relief has gradually become self-righteous power. The coach and sports administrators generally now tend to take such power of decision for granted, quite apart from its uses for the athlete. Eric Fromm, in his *Escape from Freedom*, describes the strong tendency for people to escape from the burdens of responsibility when freedom creates confusion and anxiety, by delegating crucial powers to their leaders, especially to those authoritarian leaders who promise the most at the least cost. Usually, such delegation occurs gradually, in little ways, with little awareness of final implication. But once gained, authority tends to assume an inherent right, and defends itself for its own sake, without regard to the original intent of the people.

This is what has occurred in American sports generally, though to a lesser degree in track and field. As I review this tendency in the light of my own long experience as a coach, I realize with a sense of almost shock the degree to which I assumed this role of the coach. I can't imagine anyone accusing me of being dictatorial in my relations with others; my failings would be on the other side of the scale. And yet, I did make so many decisions--our schedule of meets, our use of college vacation periods, who should make trips, who would room with whom, what would we wear, what would we eat, when would we come and go--with little or no consultation with the individuals involved. It just never occurred to me, nor to all the other coaches doing the same thing, that there was a better way to do it. Nor, with rare exceptions, do I remember that team members ever questioned my right to make such decisions or suggested improvements. That was the way it had always been done. Only in recent years, as one phase of the revolt against the Establishment, have the athletes begun to question such authority and its right of decision. It should be questioned of course, questioned in every way, and its power diminished whenever practicable.

SUMMARY. This discussion of coaching roles is intended, not to advocate this or that role, but to help you understand the varied roles that the track coach in America is expected to play. But if the material is accepted without critical analysis of its applications for your coaching situation and for you specifically as a person, it may delude far more than it helps.

A coach must assess the whole situation--the community, the school, the sports traditions, the athletes, and especially himself--very critically. To a degree he can mould and discipline himself in the roles that are most likely to prove effective. To a degree he can select and train assistants who will strengthen those roles in which he is weak. But in any case and with no exceptions, the roles of the coach and the needs of the situation must somehow mesh, must somehow fit together so as to operate effectively.

GROUP DYNAMICS IN TRACK AND FIELD. Track and field is often described as an individual sport in which competition among individuals predominates, and the team wins if each individual does his isolated best. Usually the organization of the team is low-level. Meetings are irregular, usually for factual rather than morale reasons. Often team members travel to meets separately, and may not even meet together prior to competition. Some coaches succeed by collecting an aggregation of self-centered stars whose contribution to the team is entirely one of scoring points. For such coaches, group dynamics would be of little use.

But when, as in most successful operations, the emphasis is on the team as being, not merely more than, but other than the sum of its individual members, or when the team is felt to comprise the local community and student body, as well as the athletes and coach, then group dynamics becomes a crucial concern.

The word "dynamics," derived from the Greek, means the forces acting in any given field. As related to human groups, it suggests the motivating or driving forces that operate within and upon groups. As a concept for research and related use, it came into acceptance in the 1930s, primarily through the insights and work of Kurt Lewin (1935, 1951). Lewin was impressed by society's need for a more scientific approach to understanding the problems of groups and their relation to individual members: how they are formed, how they function and change, what relationships exist between members, how leaders are chosen, how different leadership methods affect group actions as well as individual actions, and many more.

Once again, lack of space cuts off adequate treatment of the subject, but the following summary may be of value. The words are my own but I have drawn freely from the papers of Dorwin Cartwright (p. 506), Alex Bavelas (p. 474), and Theodore Newcomb (p. 7), to be found in Hollander (1963).

1. The holistic concept of the organism-in-environment is basic to a sound understanding of the problems of track coaching. We easily accept the statement that the human organism adapts the environment to itself; we must learn to accept just as completely that the environment as a truly indivisible whole adapts the human organism to itself. For example, to understand the problems of coaching as they might occur at Manhattan College in New York City would be in a uniquely different context and lead to quite different conclusions from those we might gain from understanding the problems at the University of Oregon at Eugene, or those of Southern University of Baton Rouge, Louisiana. Differences would not be merely those of the physical environment but equally those of the social culture as well.

2. A track team is a dynamic social group. That group may be loosely organized; it may be a mere aggregation of recruited individuals. Such individuals may never see each other except at competitions, and perhaps not even then. But even such a "team" has a dynamic force. A track team always stands for something. That something, whether strong or weak, influences the behavior of its members. How and to what degree that influence occurs is a function of the team family in its widest sense, as well as of its leadership.

3. A track team is a constantly changing and very flexible organization. In any one year, different kinds of meets call for different competitors, different in both number and events. In different years, team members and even the coach may change. At different institutions situated in different environments, attitudes and customs vary greatly. I suppose only personal experience can make one realize the full significance of this statement. I coached for equally long periods at the Universities of Michigan and Pennsylvania. Though the same principles of coaching were used, the applications of those principles were disturbingly different.

But teams vary, not only in the closeness of their internal organization, but also in the scope of those who share team goals and methods. We have advanced the concept of the team family which, as at Harvard or California, might extend to the 50 states of the Union. Or to suggest an extreme example, in the sport of rowing, a Harvard crew can progressively represent its University at Poughkeepsie, northeastern United States at the final Olympic tryouts, and the nation as a whole at the Olympic Games.

4. If a track team is to be a truly effective group, its members (athletes, coaches, trainers, managers, and the loyal family of followers) must have a strong sense of togetherness, of belonging to one group and sharing its common goals. Our team, not my team; our training rules, not his rules; our team success, not my winning record as a coach. This principle does not preclude separate individual goals but when the team is the focal concern, individual goals should lead toward, not away from the common goal.

5. A track team judges the worth of its coaching member in terms of his contribution to team goals and values. That he is an authority in the sport, that he is a valued contributor to state and national coaching circles, that his research or his writings have gained wide recognition, that he has been honored as an athlete or coach, all these may be happily accepted as one may rejoice in the success of a friend, but they will be valued as they serve directly the purposes of the team and its members.

6. The greater the awareness that team goals contribute to the furtherance of individual goals, the greater and more helpful the influence that the team and its coach can exert on its individual members. The team and its members are two aspects of one reality; neither should preclude the other. Just as the individual should further the team, so the team should further

the goals of its individuals. Within this two-way pattern of operation lies the high art of coaching.

7. In attempts to improve the behavior, attitudes, or feelings of team members, the more relevant those improvements are to actual performance on the track and field, the greater the influence that the team and the coach can exert. Consider the relative importance in terms of performance of (1) time and energy on the field, (2) training conduct off the field, (3) length and neatness of hair, (4) clothing on campus and on trips, (5) attitudes toward social problems, (6) problems of sports amateurism. The wise coach focuses on essentials in his efforts to influence the behavior of team members, recognizing that what is essential is often doubtful.

8. Information relating to behavior must be shared openly with all team members that might be affected. It is essential to keep the channels of communication open. One of the first consequences of mistrust and hostility is the loss of free communication about the problem-producing tension. As communication slows, hostility increases.

9. In seeking to maintain mutual respect and discipline, the coach will be less concerned with inflicting punishment for defiance of "my rules" than with creating conditions by which the team and its members will discipline themselves for breaking "our rules."[1]

10. The effectiveness of pressure for change is greatest when it comes from within the group; it thereby creates a shared perception of need, method, and degree of change (Laird, 1956, 153).

11. Different styles of leadership bring forth different styles of aggressive behavior from any given group (team) or from its individual members.[2]

12. Individuals must be valued equally. Equality of opportunity is a critical issue today, both in society as a whole and in the track team. We now recognize this as it applies to race, color, or creed. But it also applies to differences in talent. For example, treatment of star athletes as special persons is likely to disrupt team morale and to ostracize those athletes. Most champions prefer leaders that treat them as regular members (Hollander, 1963, 268). Nelson (1967, 35) gives an excellent example of this in Coach Timmons' treatment of Jim Ryun. Even when Jim returned to the East High School squad after the Tokyo Olympics, he was treated as just "one of the boys" in his conformance with team rules and training schedules. All boys followed the same basic training schedule, but those of higher ability ran each phase faster or longer.

MOTIVATIONAL PATTERNS IN COACHING. One of the more respected theories of human motivation was developed by the late Abraham H. Maslow.[3] He suggested that human needs can be categorized within five levels or hierarchies, as follows:

5--Need for self-actualization (development, growth, creativity, self-realization, achieving the higher levels of one's potential energies and talents)

4--Ego needs (both self-esteem as indicated by feelings of competence, capacity, power, adequacy; and esteem of others as indicated by recognition, respect, prestige, status)

3--Social needs (friendship, love, belongingness, team membership)

2--Safety needs (freedom from possible injury or excessive pain, social security--vocation, finances, student status, religion, an orderly society)

1--Physiological needs (food, water, shelter, activity, sleep, sexual fulfillment, and the like)

---

[1]Dorwin Cartwright, "Achieving Change in People: Some Applications of Group Dynamics Theory," *Human Relations*, 1951, 381.

[2]Kurt Lewin, R. Lippitt and R. K. White, "Patterns of Aggressive Behavior in Experimentally Created 'Social Climates,'" *Journal Social Psychology*, 1939, 10, 271-299.

[3]Abraham H. Maslow, *MOTIVATION AND PERSONALITY*, New York: Harper & Row, Publishers, Inc., 1954, pp. 81-106.

Once a lower-level or more basic need is satisfied, it loses its potency as a motivating force. "Man lives by bread alone only as long as he has no bread." Then the next higher level of need becomes operative. Such theory does not suggest an actual separation of these levels of need. A level does not require 100 percent satisfaction before the next becomes potent. Usually we are partially satisfied-unsatisfied at each level at any given time. For instance, Maslow suggests an average citizen satisfaction of perhaps 85 percent in physiological needs, 70 percent in safety needs, 50 percent in social needs, 40 percent in ego needs, and 10 percent in self-actualization needs.

In studying Maslow's five levels of need, a track and field coach will reach several conclusions: (1) The three top levels (self-actualization, esteem, belongingness) are most related to sports motivation. (2) However, they have lowest priority if the more basic needs are unsatisfied. (3) If finances or student status are in jeopardy, they become dominant as motivators, and the higher levels are diminished or inoperative. (4) Most important, as Likert made clear, satisfaction-unsatisfaction must be measured, not only by actual conditions, but by attitudes and feelings. They determine what is acceptable, even more than do the realities of the situation.

MOTIVATIONS AND COACHING ASSUMPTIONS. On the basis of much related research in industry, we can conclude that the assumptions a coach makes about human nature and its reaction to any difficult task will have a greater effect on his way of coaching and the reactions of his boys than can all his technical skills in planning, directing, coercing and rewarding.

According to Douglas McGregor[1] the authoritarian approach (Theory X) to business management has ignored a great weight of contrary scientific research in its acceptance of basically unsound assumptions:

1. The average human being has an inherent dislike for work and will avoid it if he can.

2. Most people must therefore be coerced, controlled, given extrinsic rewards, directed and threatened with punishment to get them to put forth adequate effort toward the achievement of organization objectives.

3. The average human being prefers to be directed, wishes to avoid responsibility, has little ambition, and wants security above all.

4. Wages are a sufficient motivating force for effective work.

Having made these basic assumptions, management then proceeds to construct situations, procedures and motivations that are consistent with them. It takes away control and responsibility and so finds that workers are irresponsible. The results "prove" the validity of the original assumptions. To round out this circular thinking, such Theory X management uses this "proof" as evidence that its kind of management is best for production and profit and should be supported.

It ignores the possibility that different basic assumptions and related procedures might have brought out quite different responses and greater production and profit. McGregor concludes that management's views of human nature as related to work are of greater significance in the effects on worker response, and so on production and profit than are management's skills, however expert, in the techniques of production, planning, and controlling.

We can assume a similar relationship between coaching assumptions and athlete performance. Perhaps the most obvious example of this was the great success and failure of Mihaly Igloi during the 1960s in this country. Igloi had highest-level expertise in the technology of training for endurance running and a sound background of success in his handling of Iharos, Roszavolgyi and Tabori in Hungary. But his military background induced him to exert complete control and direction of all aspects of training and competition. "It's your job to run; I'll do all the rest." He had success as long as his runners relaxed and followed instructions. His breadth of knowledge of all aspects of running was prodigious. But he failed when

---

[1]Douglas McGregor, THE HUMAN SIDE OF ENTERPRISE, New York: McGraw-Hill Book Company, Inc., 1960, pp. 33-49.

self-esteem caused his men to seek a greater degree of freedom and self-control.

In contrast to the authoritarian approach, McGregor[1] used research in sociology and business management to construct his Theory Y with its more realistic assessment of the motivations of workers. When the proper climate of human relations has been established and basic needs satisfied:

1. Effort in meaningful work is as natural as play and rest.

2. Man will exercise effective self control and direction in work whose objectives have his full commitment.

3. Commitment to objectives enhances the effects of extrinsic rewards for achievement.

4. Under proper conditions, the average worker learns, not only to accept, but to seek responsibility.

5. Success of the business enterprise is most fully assured when workers feel that their personal goals are integrated with those of the enterprise.

Almost all coaches agree in general with such an approach to motivation in track and field. But most still feel that the coach knows best and should exercise some degree of benevolent autocracy. Their problem becomes one of granting certain kinds and degrees of control, giving and seeking cooperation, meeting the more basic levels of need of team members, granting fair treatment and ample rewards in return for successful performance, but always maintaining the reins of control in their own hands.

McGregor favored clear communication of objectives with as much self-direction and self-control as is feasible. However, after serving as president of Antioch College, he wrote:[2]

Before coming to Antioch...I believed that a leader could operate successfully as a kind of advisor to his organization. Unconsciously, I suspect, I hoped to duck the unpleasant necessity of making difficult decisions, of taking responsibility for one course of action among many uncertain alternatives, of making mistakes and taking the consequences. I thought that maybe I could operate so that everybody would like me--that good human relations would eliminate all discord and disappointment. I could not have been more wrong.

He concluded that, even among wise and good men, effective leadership cannot ignore its inherent role as initiator, decision-maker, and executor. Things must get done and effective leadership must lead the action. The questions remain as to how this is accomplished and with what patterns of motivation.

ATTITUDES ARE CRUCIAL. Both McGregor and Likert emphasized that attitudes toward working conditions were at least equally important as the actual conditions of work. McGregor wrote of "the climate of relationships" within the managerial enterprise. "The climate is more significant than the type or personal style of leadership."[3] Similarly Likert wrote,[4]

It is how he sees things that counts, not objective reality. Consequently an individual member of an organization will always interpret an interaction between himself and the organization in terms of his own background, experience and expectations.... In order therefore to have an interaction viewed as supportive, it must be of such a

---

[1]*Ibid.*, pp. 47-48.

[2]Douglas McGregor, *LEADERSHIP AND MOTIVATION*, Cambridge: The M.I.T. Press, 1966, p. 67.

[3]*Ibid.*, p. 134.

[4]Rensis Likert, *NEW PATTERNS OF MANAGEMENT*, New York: McGraw-Hill Book Co., 1961, p. 102.

character that the individual himself...sees it as supportive.

The crucial factor then is the attitudinal climate within which interactions occur. That climate can be a function of local traditions, of the present situation, of the coach himself, or of all taken together. But it is the attitude that counts. High altitude in itself detracts from running performance. But it becomes an asset when attitudes use it as a stimulus to greater performance. Who would have thought that the hot, humid climate and lack of running tradition of the state of Florida could have developed the 1972 Olympic marathon champion, Frank Shorter, as well as a half-dozen or more other excellent distance men? Attitudes must have been influential.

In the 1930s, the University of Chicago withdrew from the Big Ten Athletic Conference and reduced greatly its commitment to the major sports. Conditions for track and field certainly seemed unfavorable. But a few decades later, primarily through the attitudes and energies of Coach Ted Haydon and his fellow-workers, there emerged the University of Chicago track club and program, in my judgment, the most significant development for the improvement of United States track and field of the past fifty years.

I remember with some regret but much satisfaction the limited training conditions of my own track career at Detroit City College (now Wayne State University) in the 1920s; no indoor facility except the college class-room corridors and women's gym when and if they were finished with it; no outdoor facility except the Detroit Recreation Department track on Belle Isle, six miles from school. No hot showers; no training room or trainer; no locker in which to leave one's track clothes overnight; a seldom-brushed or watered cinder track; jumping pits that we often spaded ourselves. But we had no basis for comparison; so far as we knew such conditions were quite normal. And in any case, the boundless enthusiasm and energy of Coach David L. Holmes would have soon quieted any team members inclined to gripe. We just made the most of what we had and thought nothing of it. In fact I could make a strong case in arguing that I won two National Decathlon titles because of those "handicapping" conditions, not despite them. Such conditions meant our squad was small so I competed in every event in which I might score a single point, some times as many as seven events in a dual meet. We developed a toughness and resiliency that were of great help later in the decathlon.

The primary factor is how the coach and the team members perceive and interpret the situation. Such attitudes may be quite unrelated to the actual situation and emerge out of the individual's innate optimism or negativism, or out of a reaction to one seemingly unimportant aspect of the situation to which the individual has a strong bias for or against. Such biases are of all kinds: the provincial attitudes of the student body, of the local townspeople, or of one's roommate; the size and atmosphere of the town; the religious or social conservatism of one's associates; the food and sleeping conditions; or to shift the focus, the extent to which the coach reminds the athlete of his own father or of a former coach. All the ingenuity of an expert leader of men may be unable to establish a mutually supportive relationship if the athlete is personally hostile out of his own preconceptions.

GOALS (ENDS AND MEANS). Success in coaching comes in so many forms and by way of so many methods that a summary is not feasible. But one way to a successful beginning--however "successful" is defined--includes a detailed listing of goals and the means of their attainment, all in order of priority.

Such a plan helps to create a charisma of wholeness and integrity as related to the coach, his relationships and methods. Others know where he stands, what he believes in. He's all-of-one-piece, so to speak. He follows what can be called a hierarchy-of-value system in which lesser values are judged, and decisions made, as they relate to the first-priority value. Having a basis for judgment, decisions--even those of vital importance--can be made quickly, surely and soundly.

Of the coaches described in Chapter 4, Jumbo Elliott of Villanova University has been the most successful in terms of world-level champions in media events--Olympics, invitational indoor meets, ICAAAA championships, Penn Relays. Judged by this goal--though restrained by his "genuine interest in the welfare of his boys," as described by his own Olympic champion, Charlie Jenkins--Elliott has evidenced a one-value system of goals, not only as a coach but as a man. He was a winner in whatever caught his interest and energies. He was a big winner in his earth-moving machinery business, a winner in golf and among its followers, a winner as fund-raiser for his University, a winner in his Church and Community relationships--all within socially accepted rules of the game though interpreted "realistically" by a competitive market-place standard. From his first year as a coach, Elliott knew where he wanted to go, and followed a clear road map of how to get there.

Within a competitive industrial society such as the United States is today, the Elliott-Villanova example is most likely to gain media recognition and social approval. A different example of mutually supportive ends and means can be found, all too rarely, within institutions and communities that focus their primary objectives on what can be called a liberal education: development of well-rounded individuals toward a better society. I think of my present home-town, Swarthmore (Pa.) High School. During the past half century, over 90 percent of its students have gone on to colleges with high-level academic requirements. Its winning record in all sports has been excellent, but winning was only a means to a more important end--a well-rounded education.

Of the college coaches I have known, Brutus Hamilton, University of California at Berkeley (1932-1965), best exemplified such a broader-based and less-controlled system. Note that when winning is the goal, the individual must adjust to the system; when education is the goal, the system in all its phases tends to adjust to the multiple demands of each unique individual--a much more difficult task. Hamilton's goals were clearly centered on his many boys. His biographer, Lawrence J. Baack, makes that clear time after time. Above all else, he was an educator, a teacher, a worker with college students. Winning was important, but as a motivator toward excellence, not at all as an end in itself. Though chosen as United States Head Olympic Coach, he once valued his leadership "as refraining from interference with the normal progress of the boys." Idealistic? Impractical? Read Chapter 4 and make up your own mind. For me, I have never known a man with such well-integrated goals or well-ordered approach to life--within himself, his university family, or with his much-respected boys.

Elliott and Hamilton differed widely in the basic orientation of their goals. But they were alike in that they lived well-ordered lives, followed well-ordered goals, used well-ordered means in seeking those goals. Both were fortunate to coach in universities and communities whose ends and means were supportive of their own. Had they exchanged social environments, both would have been misplaced, less successful, and much less satisfied.

In contrast to these examples of success and well-ordered planning, think of the descriptive phrases one tends to use for the unsuccessful coach: lack of organization, inability to plan, disoriented as to the attitudes and mores of other persons or related institutions, an uncer-tainty of mind and action, a man with problems, lacking in self-confidence. Such a man has goals; in fact he undoubtedly suffers from an excess of goals, centripetal goals that lead away from center at almost any tangent. Or such a man may be well-integrated within him-self as to his ends and means, but finds he's not at all on the same wave length with his institution and community. His goals in the various phases of coaching are not their goals. Their conception of the ways and means of sport just doesn't tune in with his methods. Result--failure and all that goes with it.

At first thought, the problem of integrating one's goals would seem to be much easier for a coach in such planned societies as the USSR or East Germany. There sport is openly regarded as an arm of government and party policy. Sport and those that take part in sport tend to be a means to a one-value system of Communist success. Whatever problems may arise; whatever decisions must be reached, can all be related to that one pre-eminent goal.

THE DYNAMICS OF INDIVIDUALITY. Only in recent years have there been serious scientific efforts to discover the infinite ways in which individuals vary from each other. Though his concern was not for sports, Roger J. Williams (1956, 1967) has contributed greatly to our understanding in this important field. At least three of his conclusions are of practical use to coaches:
1. Both structurally and functionally, individuals are uniquely different in all aspects of their being. Only lack of sufficiently sensitive measuring devices prevents full documen-tation. We accept the statement that no two fingerprints are identical, and use the fact in practical ways. In supporting his assumption that similar variability is present in all struc-tures and functions, Williams gives numerous examples of anatomical variations in heart, stomach, liver, colon, respiratory tract, hand and face nerve patterns, blood composition, and many more; as well as functional variations in nutrition.

2. To speak of normal persons has its uses. Actually, there are no entirely normal persons, or better, no persons that are within the range of normality in all structures and functions. Williams gives many examples of abnormal organs and systems in normal people, and suggests that all of us have such abnormalities. Such deviation helps us to understand the so-called peculiarities of athletes. For example, in studying the characteristics of marathon runners, Ernst Jokl[1] and others have reported that though one might describe the typical marathon runner in various aspects of body size, weight, heart action, age, intelligence, blood chemistry, etc., many men evidence characteristics that must be considered deviates from the normal. In each case, success is achieved through compensating factors, including training, which bring balance and effectiveness to the whole.

3. The common practice of classifying individuals under group names and programs is necessary--necessary to understanding, to communication of ideas, and to overall organization. But the moment such categories are used in actual practice, specific individuality becomes a crucial consideration. Williams (1956, 178) gives the example of the important uses of norms and types as they relate to human eye structure and function. But application of such knowledge requires the services of an expert oculist to prepare glasses precisely ground to the precise needs of the individual eye. The same basic approach must be made to the problems of track and field. Examples will be given from three areas: nutrition, heat-humidity, altitude.

a. NUTRITION. We tend to assume that a well-balanced diet is fully adequate for every "normal" athlete (Johnson, 1960, 285). We assume that there is a natural "wisdom of the body" (Cannon, 1932) that will select what it needs and can do so adequately for all the high-level needs of sport. But Williams (1956, 162) cites experiments that support his thesis that "(1) each human individual has quantitatively a distinctive pattern of nutritional needs, (2) from individual to individual, specific needs may vary several fold, and (3) important deficiencies may exist that have not been discoverable clinically by observing acute outward symptoms."

b. HEAT-HUMIDITY. In 1959, in the USA-USSR dual meet in Philadelphia, the four competitors in the 10,000-meter run were assumed to be of similar ability and condition. But performance varied greatly--one man finished strongly, one dropped out, and two were widely separated at various stages of the race. This great variation in performance was brought about by one factor in the situation: their varying capacities to run under the conditions of 85 degree temperature and 78 percent humidity. The winner, Desyatchikov, held up well, though obviously affected. Bob Soth had some spectators in tears as he fought for several laps in the weird, high-stepping and backward-leaning style of a man undergoing heat exhaustion. He finally dropped and was helped from the track. Pyarnokivi showed similar signs of collapse but stayed on the track to the finish. Truex, more experienced than Soth, slowed down as he felt the effects of heat, then came on with a thrilling sprint at the finish. In summary, their race patterns were specific to their reactions to heat and humidity, not to their over-all conditioning and ability.

c. ALTITUDE. The Mexico City Olympic Games provided numerous examples of specific reactions to high altitudes. Quite obviously, training at altitude improved response to it. But though in some instances the kind and amount of training seemed identical, actual performance in the Games was specific to each individual. Some were able to adapt more readily than others.

SUMMARY. Men are both alike and uniquely different. Our common humanness and our biochemical individuality are two sides of one coin; which side we focus on depends on the purpose and situation. As we focus on alikeness, we construct training systems, well-balanced diets, programs of competition, team goals, or patterns of attitudes ahd behavior. As we focus on uniqueness, we must adapt these systems and goals and attitudes to the special needs of the individual. The art of coaching includes both aspects. But since a coach can adopt the plans and methods of others--for example, those of this textbook--the real art of coaching is one of individual application.

---

[1]Ernst Jokl, M.D., "Response of Body to Distance Running," *The Amateur Athlete,* Feb. 1955, p.24.

Chapter 3
COACHING—PERSONS AND MECHANICS

Strictly speaking, there can be no track and field coaches, only coaches (teachers) of young men and women in the training methods and techniques of track and field, and in mutually supportive relationships with many other persons. To say it differently, effective coaching requires a balance--a vital balance--between expertise in working with persons and expertise in the technology of our sport (Line A-D, Figure 3.1).

In its review of the development of track and field knowledge, Chapter One made clear that during our first 100 years serious study was related perhaps 90 percent to the technology side of this vital balance, only about 10 percent to the human side. Consider the time-energy devoted to physiology, anatomy, kinesiology, biomechanics, and especially engineering as related to facilities and equipment. Now contrast the paucity of serious time-energy directed toward the improvement of mutually supportive human relationships in track and field coaching.

The concept of mutually supportive relationships, so basic to the human side, is complex and needs research just as much as does biomechanics or physiology. From such relationships each member gains and derives satisfactions, not as the prime mover (coach, organizer, management) decides, but as each member feels and determines his own best interests-needs-goals-values. That's the major difference between autocratic and democratic leadership.

Coaches vary from aardvark to zygote in both the "who" and the "how" of such relationships. Chapter 4 will illustrate this. But all successful coaches have been effective--somehow, someway-- in working with people. It is the intent of this Chapter to use the graph of Figure 3.1 as a first effort toward a more analytic study of the human side of coaching. It seeks the meanings of individual squares suggesting individual coaching styles. But the crucial purpose is to emphasize those styles that lie along the line (A-D, Figure 3.1) of vital balance between the human and the technological sides.

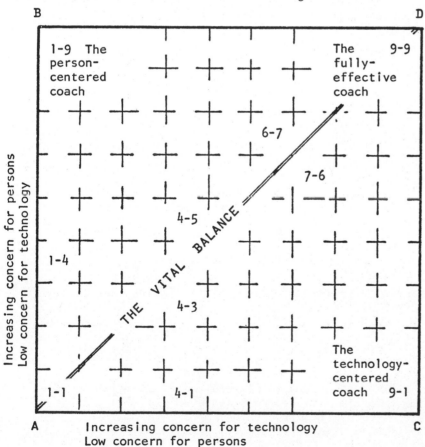

Fig. 3.1 The Vital Balance (line A-D) between expertise in technology and in working with numerous and varied persons. Horizontal lines show increasing concern for technology (training methods, techniques and the related sciences); vertical lines, increasing concern for persons.

Effective coaching seeks a balance between the two, as in the squares 4-3, 4-5, 7-6, 6-7 that lie along the A-D balance line. Only as we approach the fully effective coach (9-9) is there integration of both at highest levels.

VALUES AND LIMITATIONS OF A COACHING GRAPH

The primary purpose and value of this graphic approach is to urge the importance of clarifying goals and the means for achieving them. It is not to describe precisely modelled ways of coaching to be emulated by the coach-in-training. If certain coaching styles, such as a 1-9 or a 9-1 style, are highlighted, they are intended only to suggest basic patterns among an infinity of possible patterns by which coaches can develop what Douglas McGregor called "managerial climates," or what Rensis Likert called "mutually supportive relationships".

To form any useful theory, such as attempted here, the relevant words and viewpoints must be clearly defined so that explanations and understandings can be on an intelligent basis. But such definitions are arbitrarily in support of theory assumptions. The more precise the definitions, the greater the apparent clarity but also the actual delusion. Real situations are not so readily packaged. Real coaches just cannot be squeezed into such neat squares as outlined in a grid. No real-life coach conforms precisely to any description of a 1-9 or 9-3 coaching method. Each coach is uniquely and infinitely himself, just as each athlete-team-school-situation is uniquely and infinitely itself. Each is beyond precise description.

But patterns of coaching can be discerned; climates of relationships can be distinguished. To understand those patterns and relationships enables the coach-in-training to choose better patterns for himself and thereby develop a better product of both coach and athlete. He and his coaching situation will establish the precise "what" and "how" and "how much" in choosing between concern-for-persons and concern-for-sport-methods-and-techniques.

THE 1-9 COACHING STYLE

The coach that follows a 1-9 style is described as having a low-level concern for the sport of track and field in terms of maximum performance and winning, and so of the many ways these are brought about: training methods, techniques, equipment and facilities, competitive program and all the rest. In contrast, his highest-level "9" rating indicates a high concern for his boys. But the nature of this concern is limited by his lack of personal enthusiasm and commitment to his sport, and his low esteem for his job as a coach. This means his concern for athletes-as-persons is more for their goodwill and approval than for their full development through the challenges and hardships of track and field training and competition.

COACHING RELATIONSHIPS IN THIS STYLE. As pointed out by McGregor, leadership in any social situation is always a relationship among the many elements of that situation: the coach-athlete-institution-community-culture, in a variety of ways.

In his relations with his boys, the 1-9 coach thinks of himself as a friend, as an educator, as one who educes performance rather than compelling it, who is primarily interested in the health and character values of sport. For such a coach, losing is no disgrace, in fact, has character-building uses of comparable value to those of winning: "One of the essentials of sport is to be a good sportsman in losing."

Such a coach will have mutually supportive relationships with his school administration and community members only if their objectives for track and field are consistent with such viewpoints. Then they will ask, not how much winning he has achieved, but how much his approach and method of program organization has contributed to the education and character development of his boys. His assumption of a low value for sports participation as compared with the academic phases of school life is in keeping with school-community viewpoints. His demands are few and easily met. His boys are never late for supper or too fagged to eat or do their homework. His training program does not interfere with plans for weekends or vacations.

What schools would seek a close relationship with such a non-winning coach? There are many high schools and colleges where track and field along with other non-spectator sports is simply not a matter of major concern. The coach who keeps his charges reasonably content, who keeps them busy in a recreational sort of way, keeps them out of mischief and in no way disruptive to the community, often retires after long and faithful service following a dinner at which the principal, the team, and even a few team mothers are present to give forth words of praise. To denigrate this coaching style is to question the values of our intramural sports programs so highly praised in our country, or to doubt that "sport for sport's sake" is a worthy motivation.

On the other hand, if a 1-9 coach finds himself in a school or community more typical of what American attitudes are presumed to be--develop character but win; educate but win; have fun but win--his coaching relationships will be much less mutually supportive and his job as coach much less secure. He will never be given a coach-of-the-year award. The news media will totally ignore his program. His community will not point with pride or attend the home competitions. In summary, such a 1-9 coach without supportive relationships will have to go it alone, finding his satisfactions in the pleasant, low-tension associations with those of his boys that have similar low-keyed ambitions in his sport.

CONCERN FOR ATHLETES AS PERSONS IN THE 1-9 STYLE. The concern of the 1-9 coach for his athletes as persons is based on a low estimate of their energy and talent capacities. He assumes limited vital energies and, if training and competition for track and field make copious demands, the energies and enthusiasm for the more primary purposes of education, academic studies, will be lessened and even insufficient. He believes time-energy for studies is vital and that he can serve his role best by a policy of non-interference with such study. He assumes that high pressures for winning and record-breaking work against high performance as students.

He therefore is non authoritarian in his coach-athlete relations. His job is to help them help themselves in the ways and at the stress-levels they seem to prefer. Likert emphasized "a feeling of supportive relationships," as being even more crucial for the achievement of goals than their actual presence. The 1-9 coach is so concerned about how his boys feel toward him and his work assignments that he is inclined to be over-cautious and to expect a lower level of training even if that means a lower level of performance.

The 1-9 coach is invariably likeable. He is interested in his boys' life problems. He coaches by gentle persuasion, by giving reasons for his methods, and by sugar-coating such unpleasant requirements as cannot be avoided. He tries to distinguish between what the athlete does that is unsatisfactory and what he is as a person; the former can be criticized; but loyalty to the latter is never suspect. In return, of course, he expects personal loyalty from his boys and is deeply disturbed when such loyalty is not given.

The 1-9 coach may be emotionally upset about losing; hard not to in our win-centered culture. But he protects his boys. "You made a great effort. That's what really counts--in track and in life. Being a good loser is just as important as winning. Don't let it bother you. We'll do even better next time. Congratulations."

Such a coach assumes that his boys want to do well, do try to make their best effort. He seldom blames them for not trying, and would certainly defend them from any charge of quitting. Such charges would create personal antagonisms, and reduce his effectiveness as a coach and friend.

A 1-9 coach seldom has written or precisely stated rules of training off-the-track. He expects his boys to act as they know they should simply because he believes they are well-intentioned. He prefers that whatever training rules are operative should be set up by the team and policed by the team. If he is forced to discipline a team member, he does so on behalf of the team, not because "my rules are broken" or "my authority is challenged." He avoids checking on his boys and punishing them, and thus avoids resentments and team divisiveness such actions might bring forth.

COACHING METHODS IN THE 1-9 STYLE. The leadership approach of the 1-9 style coach tends to be by consensus, not by personal authority. He says, "This is our team or your team, never my team." High team morale is a focal concern, but "high" should be interpreted at the level of having fun while playing the game more than as the high morale required of high-risk adventure.

The 1-9 coach provides opportunities--movies, books, clinics--by which team members can see and learn sound methods and techniques, but allows them to choose or reject without coercion from him. Encouragement and having fun are major concerns. He's adept in informal conversations, at joking and telling stories, and quick with an understanding smile and pat on the back--an altogether charming fellow. When vaguely defined rules are not followed, he tends to assume the offender will straighten himself out, with only a gentle reminder from the coach that he's always ready to be helpful if asked.

Though anxious to get along with everyone, including school and community critics, the 1-9 oriented coach tends to reject pressures for winning and record-breaking that go beyond the wishes and best interests of his boys. His endurance training program is therefore at energy-pain levels generally considered acceptable and healthful, but avoids—and resents the practice when done by other coaches—any demand for time-energy-pain that might be considered excessive.

For the most part, teaching techniques will not be the forte of the 1-9 coach. More experienced team members will be expected to teach beginners, or, if available, the assistant coach is given this assignment. The head coach would tend to stay in one spot on the track where he could work with numbers of men rather than serving the time-consuming needs of field-event athletes.

GOALS IN THE 1-9 COACHING STYLE. Perhaps the most important function in the coaching enterprise is related to goals. What are we trying to accomplish in this sport? How high can we climb in the time and under the conditions allowed us? What demands on our time-energy-commitment do such goals require? What other interests must be curtailed, even eliminated? All this needs to be done specifically and clearly, and it is vital to know how such general goals are to be sought. Ends are almost meaningless unless we know the specific means. In fact, ends and means are inseparable—two aspects of a single process.

The primary goal of the 1-9 oriented coach is to get along with people—with his administrative superiors, with his community, with his peers in the coaching profession, and above all, with his boys on the track team. He seeks an integration of goals with each of these groups by working within their self-chosen goals. To impose, coerce, or even strongly induce goals of his own preference on others would be personally out of character and worrisome.

Team goals and individual goals would be considered helpful, even essential to everyone's success, but these should be goals reached by consensus: challenging but within rather easy grasp, so as to gain team support with a minimum of argument and discord.

Depending on the situation, a 1-9 coach would probably emphasize dual meets with local schools having a similar viewpoint for sport. Dual meets are non-controversial, are ignored by the news media, are low-tension affairs—for the team members and the coach. Such a coach is unlikely to develop individual star athletes; they require an expertise in methods and techniques he does not have. Further they tend to be disruptive within the team, require special attention, special equipment, special meets in which they can get equal competition. In contrast, dual meets can be won by encouraging large numbers of boys to participate, by keeping them happily interested with no painful demands or competitive tensions. Being local, they cost little, so that large numbers can be handled on a low budget and without disruption of administrative routines. The coach's superiors are likely to be satisfied, even though not enthusiastic or bursting their chest buttons with pride.

Team and individual goals can be high under even a 1-9 coach, depending on the ambition and energy of the team, of the team captain or even of some local enthusiast. Team meetings could be held at which goals could be agreed on well above those the 1-9 coach might choose on his own. Success could follow, success that might carry over into next year and the year after. School and community enthusiasm might be aroused and even an expectation of winning created. Since the 1-9 coach wants, above all else, to get along with people, he can join in wholeheartedly. But not as a genuine forerunner.

MANAGING CONFLICT IN THE 1-9 STYLE. Disagreements and conflicts within the team family disclose the basically weak position of the 1-9 coach. His overriding concern for the good opinions of others makes quick and stern decisions too upsetting to face. His disparagement of winning as an all-or-nothing goal puts him at odds with many strong voices in the community. His lack of knowledge and expertise in track and field, the thing for which his athletes should respect him, diminishes whatever self-esteem he may have. As a result he tends to avoid all direct confrontation in the early stages of opposition, and then appeases or compromises when it can no longer be avoided.

If the 9-1 coach tends to suppress conflict, the 1-9 coach tries to smooth it over, to get along with whoever or whatever is causing it, to talk it over as a reasonable man, and not to fight anyone for any reason. Under such a coach, important issues are seldom settled. An outwardly friendly attitude prevails but important grievances continue on to surface later when conditions worsen.

SUMMARY. In summary, the 1-9 oriented coach is highly concerned with human relations, but in only a partial way. He wants to get along with them as they are, more than pushing them toward what they can become. He has a low estimate of student-athlete energies and willingness to accept discomfort and hardship--in track and field as well as life in general. What is drained away in one area diminishes what can be done in other areas.

The 1-9 coach tries to help the development of his boys, but within the limits of their own estimates and their own sentivity to the pains of fatigue and day-after-day-after-day training. Enjoying the game is more important than peak performance.

Like the 9-1 and 9-9 coach, he also wants to win, but not at high cost; in fact, not at any cost that his boys or his friends might consider excessive. If, by way of illustration, we refer to the Dedication of this OMNIBOOK, page iii, the 1-9 coach would be greatly concerned about the avocational nature of amateur, that is, school-college sports. He would respect the first priority of student work (studies), make time-energy demands within what was left over, and would not wish to interfere in any way with their requirements. Within those limits, the 1-9 coach might urge an athlete's best efforts but lacks the interest or expertise in training methods and techniques that would make such efforts successful in the larger fields of competition.

THE 9-1 COACHING STYLE.
In the symbol, "9-1" the hyphen is important as indicating a relationship--perhaps of balance, perhaps of imbalance--between two complex tendencies. How that relationship is developed, within what climate of attitudes and feelings, is the crux of any given coaching style.

The two competing tendencies in the 9-1 style are (1) a primary concern for winning performance and its rewards, and (2) a low concern for athletes as persons, with all the wide-ranging conflict of interests and energies that the word "persons" implies. The excessive need to win makes of this coach an exacting taskmaster in training for endurance and strength, often an expert in event techniques, facilities, equipment, or in whatever improves performance and the chances of winning, with special emphasis on the recruitment of outstanding talent.

The overall climate of relationship between the 9-1 coach and his athletes tends to be one of opposition and even distrust. He assumes they will work at levels below his needs, and so must be driven or given material rewards of some kind if they are to measure up. He assumes they will break his training rules if given a chance, and so contrives checks and punishments to ensure conformance. He believes their goals as persons with many interests beyond sport are inevitably detrimental to highest performance and winning, and so must be set aside.

The successful 9-1 coach knows the importance of motivation for both competition and training. If he does so begrudgingly at least possible levels, he can be classified as a true 9-1 coach. On the other hand, if he is aware of modern research in industry that concludes a high concern for persons is the best way of increasing production and profit, he may treat his athletes on a first class basis, give them the best of everything, but all for the primary end of winning. Should he relax, discover the satisfactions of helping athletes achieve their own personal goals apart from track and field, he would then be classified as a 9-3 or 9-5 coach. Once again, we remind ourselves that we are interested in describing general patterns of behavior, not in pigeonholing individual coaches.

COACHING RELATIONSHIPS IN THE 9-1 STYLE. The need for a supportive surround is just as important for this as for any style of coaching. But since our culture tends to accept the preeminence of winning as a goal, such supportive relationships are easy to establish. Even where a school or community has no tradition or awareness of such winning viewpoints, a 9-1 coach can usually discover a few enthusiasts to further his winning ways. Once the values of success become apparent by way of the news media and town talk, supporters will multiply amazingly.

In fact, the 9-1 oriented style of coaching may initiate its program by seeking first the support of community and other outside groups and individuals for a greatly expanded program of track and field. This year's team may be neglected so that coaching energies can be more profitably employed. At the college level this takes many forms: improving the local facilities, equipment and home-meet program, raising funds with which more attractive away-meets can be attended, securing scholarships, finding low-energy high-pay jobs, increasing booster-club funds for supplementary financial help, enrolling bird dogs in the broadest possible recruiting fields to help flush out the quarry; all this of course within the written rules of the governing body, though with more concern for getting caught than for observing the spirit of the rules, and all for the purpose of recruiting talent.

At the high achool level, the coaching style would be the same, though limited by the much more restricted supervision and scope of operation. In some areas, recruiting athletes from junior high schools and from nearby school districts is becoming almost as excessive as in college ranks. Highly talented athletes are absolutely essential to the goal of winning of the 9-1 coach. Their development by means of the participation of hundreds of prospective athletes is a far-too-slow and uncertain process. Neither the coach nor his backers can be so patient. He therefore recruits talent, by paying for it in whatever ways are required. Having paid them--within the rules of course--he can and does make demands on the time-energy-devotion they give to his sport.

The crux of the coach-athlete relationship in the 9-1 style is therefore the exercise of authority by the coach and obedience by the athlete. Until his reputation for success is firmly established, until his athletes feel that first-class rewards will be certain to follow first-class performances, such a demand for obedience may be met reluctantly and even with resistance. Failure in the early years, for whatever reason, may nullify the entire project. Bitterness is sure to follow--against failure and against the dictatorial coach that produced it. Today the local newspaper announced the firing of a high school football coach in mid-season who had demanded much from his team, the school and the town. At first he won, beat the perennial league winner and was carried high on shoulders off the field. But the next few years things went awry--injuries occurred to crucial men, some said through overwork; the coach was misquoted; his critics were loud; things got pretty nasty. He could walk onto the field or scratch his ear and the crowd would boo. After all, the local booster club had to maintain its self respect. When he loses, the 9-1 coach has no friends. But once success is assured everyone prospers and is more than willing to go along with the authoritarian mode. However, the 9-1 coach is unlikely to experience personal friendship with rival coaches, because his urge-to-win makes the field of play a battleground and his excessive recruiting and demands for maximum training create resentment as being unfair and illegal. Unwritten codes may lead his rival coaches to hide all open resentment and bitterness but few would interpret their smiles as genuine warmth of feeling.

CONCERN FOR ATHLETES AS PERSONS IN THE 9-1 STYLE. Under 9-1 coaching, athletes are regarded as instruments of winning in meets that gain public attention. Regardless of how well he may treat them or reward them for their work they are but the means to the coach's goal of personal success. He values them as athletes and will help them in every way he can as long as their athletic talents contribute to his goal. Whatever he may seem to do for them as persons should be suspect.

If running more miles or at greater intensities more days per week and more weeks per year will produce faster competitive performance, more wins and records and greater public attention, the 9-1 coach will demand it, with little or no concern for the needs of non-sport interests and activities. Time-energy-commitment to anything other than track and field is resented as interference with the all-out commitment to sport, allowed only if required or necessary.

His concern for beginners and non-talented team members is nil, even negative, as they expect him to give them coaching time that might better be used with more productive members. If the school program requires dual meets in which second and third places are helpful, he may tolerate these incompetents, but since they were not recruited and have no scholarships they are independent and not inclined to accede to his more extreme demands.

THE TEAM CONCEPT WITHIN THE 9-1 STYLE. Under the 9-1 style of coaching, the most valid definition of "the team" is an aggregation of individuals drawn together by the coach for a common purpose. The coach is the producer and promoter of the team, outside and not a member of it. If morale is good, reference is to the coach and the team; if morale breaks down, to the coach versus the team. In both cases the team captain serves primarily an honorary role and a sort of go-between for the coach and the team.

Traditionally this has been the role of the captain in colleges and schools. Coaches who believed in the importance of team morale tried to influence as best they could the selection of each year's captain, so as to ensure a man supportive of team tradition and of the coach's policies. Quite often the captain was the coach's agent for preventing or settling disagreements. He received special privileges including dinners at the coach's home. All quite innocent of course, and in keeping with tradition. Up to about 1960 few had questioned that tradition.

Under such a 9-1 coaching style, the team as a group would have little organization, few meetings, and low team morale. Traditionally, two meetings a year were sufficient: the end-of-the-year team banquet and the get-together for the team picture after voting for next year's captain. In fact, where dual meets are minimal and athletes travel to invitational meets separately, as was the custom in the East when the Madison Square and Boston Gardens dominated the indoor season, track teams have no opportunity to get together before or after competition. On one occasion during the early indoor season, I, as coach, actually introduced one runner to the other three members of a relay team after they had reached the Garden! He had practiced separately and travelled on the train separately.

CONCERN FOR PERFORMANCE AND WINNING IN THE 9-1 STYLE. Success of the 9-1 style, both in college and high school, depends primarily on the recruitment of outstanding talent. But outstanding talent, if it is to be developed to its highest levels, requires highest-level methods of training and event techniques. The 9-1 coach must therefore train himself to become expert in these and all other phases of track and field, if he is to be fully effective.

Not only has the 9-1 style of coaching produced some of our most successful coaches as judged by national individual and team championships, record-breaking, Olympic champions, and the like, it has also produced some of our highest authorities as to methods and techniques from both a scientific and practical standpoint. The urge to win may be the primary motivating force, but it has often led to genuine creativeness that has made important contributions to our sport.

GOALS (ENDS & MEANS) IN THE 9-1 STYLE. The all-consuming goal of the 9-1 coach is clear: victory in meets that draw attention to the accomplishments of my boys, my team, my school and myself. The "my" is not an exaggeration insofar as he rates a lowest possible "1" in his concern for others. If the "my" is less blatant, if it takes the form of "our" even occasionally, then he rates a 9-2 or even higher.

The point has been made that the practical nature of goals, as of leadership, depends on relationships; on the kinds of spectator-oriented meets that are available, on the attitudes of the school administration, the alumni, the community, the news media. Ordinarily, the coach's devotion to winning gives him a wide base of support, for our competitive private-enterprise system, the coach and the athletes requires the athletes to support the system, regardless of their personal goals. Some kind of compensation is therefore essential, and so the prevalence of scholarships as reward and the threat of their withdrawal as punishment. The 9-1 style tends to produce a business-enterprise climate focussed on production and profit for the enterprise.

But during the 1970s, the financial support so essential to the 9-1 college coach has been gradually withdrawn. Greatly increased expenses have caused college administrators to concentrate their resources among the income-producing sports, of which track and field is rarely one. If this trend continues, the path of the 9-1 coach will lead to something less than his goal of personal glory.

MANAGING CONFLICT IN THE 9-1 STYLE. Just as the 9-1 coach tends to be authoritarian in his high concern for performance and winning, so is he authoritarian in his handling of conflicts between himself and team members or among team members. Whatever interferes with the primary goal of winning and attention-getting performance must be dealt with decisively.

In a recruited-team situation in which the coach has the power to withdraw scholarships, serious disagreements are not tolerated. In a non-recruited situation, as in most high schools, the tradition of coaching authority may allow this same dictatorial way of settling disputes. In a more democratically-oriented school or college, the 9-1 style must learn to be flexible, conceding a setback or two in order to maintain its basic position of dominance.

The overall climate of relationships in this style tends to make all differences personal.

The coach must prove himself right and all others wrong; the others tend to react similarly. Any mistake or defeat produces an emotional reaction and the least hint of criticism is taken personally. The 9-1 coach has a low tolerance for human frailty. Arnie Sowell of Pittsburgh was potentially an all-time Great in world half-miling, the probable winner of the 1956 Olympic Championship. Even today, I can hear with a feeling of distaste the "chewing out" that his coach gave him following a bad preliminary race in the Nationals. Arnie was sent home immediately with no chance to even see the finals. I've often wondered what he would have done under a 9-9 coaching style, a style that the Pitt coach would have considered "soft" and "pampering."

THE 9-9 COACHING STYLE

The salient feature of the 9-9 style of coaching leadership lies not so much in the charisma of the man, important as that is, as in the supportive relationships he establishes among all sectors of the team family. Four viewpoints are inherent:

1. The vital energies of men are far more capable of development to higher and broader levels of daily energizing than is commonly realized. When energy development is by gradual increments of stress, daily work at the higher levels of one's potential energies requires no more hours of sleep and rest than does lower-level work, and need not interfere with the time-energy-commitment given to other activities.

2. Integration of the goals, means and attitudes of the various members of the track family is essential; all can achieve their goals best by attitudes and efforts that are mutually supportive.

3. Highest-level performance and winning at both the individual and team levels are important, even indispensable, but important as means to seeking the educational or developmental goals of the athlete and the institution, not as the dominant ends of sport.

4. For a coach to extend full respect and concern for others, he must first have achieved full respect and esteem for himself. Modern psychologists (Erich Fromm, Abraham Maslow, Gardner Murphy and many others) are in agreement on this point. In fact, Maslow[1] makes it an essential element in his description of what he calls self-actualizing people.

THE ENERGIES OF MEN. In 1904 William James wrote the essay, *The Energies of Men*, which, after numerous reprints,[2] has become the classic statement on the subject:

Compared with what we ought to be, we are only half awake. Our fires are damped, our drafts are checked. We are making use of only a small part of our possible physical and mental resources....

But the very same individual, pushing his energies to their extreme, may in a vast number of cases keep the pace up day after day, and find no reaction of a bad sort, so long as decent hygienic conditions are preserved. His more active rate of energizing does not wreck him; for the organism adapts itself, and as the rate of waste augments, augments correspondingly the rate of repair....

Stating the thing broadly, the human individual...energizes well below his maximum as well as below his optimum.

The history of track and field in our world over the past century discloses a gradually developing realization of the truth of James' insights, though undoubtedly to extremes of energizing well beyond those James would have deemed sustainable by normal human beings. In my personal experience over the past 50 years, each generation has used the same words to express a common feeling: "Track coaches can properly demand this level of time-energy-commitment from their boys. But no more than this level! To expect more is to jeopardize studies, social duties and health." But within that same generation some coach-athlete has demonstrated

---

[1]Abraham H. Maslow, *MOTIVATION AND PERSONALITY*, New York: Harper & Row, 1954, pp. 199-260.

[2]John J. McDermott, *THE WRITINGS OF WILLIAM JAMES*, New York: The Modern Library, pp. 671ff.

higher levels were quite attainable without additional sleep and rest, and without unreasonable interference with other activities. In the 1920s I remember Pennsylvania's Lawson Robertson's condemnation of Stanford's Dink Templeton for "burning out" his runners. In the 1930s Charlie Hoyt of Michigan had adopted Templeton's level of energizing but now was criticizing Billy Hayes of Indiana for his work schedules of greater mileage and intensity of training than ever before. Today, Hayes' program would be thought inadequate. Thus each new world record has been the effect-cause of gradual increments of training energies.

My main point is that this rise in acceptable energizing applies, not just to track training, but to life in general. The rate of restoration increases along with the rate of use. If training increases are carefully gradual a college or high school boy of will and enthusiasm can take part successfully in the most rigorous of sports such as running or swimming, have time for studies, and live a normal student life with several hobbies on the side. Just yesterday on TV I watched an All-Conference college football player as he practiced the piano preparing himself for a concerto concert in New York City. He had played the piano and some form of football since he was five years old. To do both, along with studies and other activities was his way of life, certainly nothing to get excited about. "I'd be bored if I wasn't busy all the time. No, I don't feel I have unusual talent or vitality. It's just that I started early and got the habit."

That is the crux, and the excellence, of the 9-9 coaching style. Such a coach conveys to the athlete a high expectation of excellence in all phases of his life, not just in athletics. He knows that the main dangers of stress arise from the negative emotions: self-doubt, fear of failure, worry, inability to "burn away" by physical activity the wastes of stress; and in trying to do too much too soon, before the person is prepared to properly handle such a high level of stress. Such a coach accepts Hans Selye's warning[1] that the vital energies of men are limited and, once depleted, cannot be restored, but is quietly sure that careful and wise use of modern training methods will not encroach on such dangerous levels. The purpose of every training program is to develop powers of recovery greater than the training stress and so increase resistance to competitive stress. A coach would be a fool to provide stresses for which the athlete is unprepared and so result in negative returns. A 9-9 coach carefully and scientifically, insofar as feasible, measures out his dosages of stress to ensure the fulfillment of his high-level expectations.

THE PRINCIPLE OF INTEGRATION. The third principle underlying the 9-9 coaching style is that of integration: the organization of the conditions of competition and training so that the efforts of the coaching enterprise as a whole and those of its individual members are integrated and mutually supportive. The special meaning of this principal in the 9-1 and 1-9 styles of coaching has been described as workable only if the individual members conform to the system; as, in industry, workers conform to the goals of business enterprise for greater production and profit.

In the 9-9 coaching style, integration takes on a new dimension: a dimension of freedom between equals, or better, of freedom within the restraints of inter-dependence of the many parts of one entity. We might call that entity, "the track team family," including the culture-community-school-coach-athletes. Since each of the members of any interdependent relationship must accept a degree of restraint in the full achievement of goals, major conflict is likely to arise unless all members feel that on balance and in the long run this is the best way. Once the restraints are accepted by everyone (especially the coach and his supporters), inter-personal tensions relax and a climate of freedom of action and attitude prevails.

Such an integration between equal partners in a common enterprise implies that the lower level needs (physiological-safety-social) of Maslow's hierarchy are acceptably taken care of and that concentration on the higher levels of esteem (self-esteem and esteem of others) and self-actualization (working toward one's potentials) can become paramount to all members of the team family. To the school, this means that winning is important, but important as a means to the ends of better education and greater service to the educational needs of its members, in and out of school. To the individual athlete, this means that he can achieve his goals best by working with the coach and within the school sport system. Mutual support would

---

[1]Hans Selye, THE STRESS OF LIFE, New York: McGraw-Hill Book Co., Inc., 1956, 324 pages.

be inherent in the situation; suspicion that one was being used by the other for selfish purposes just wouldn't be in the air.

Achieving such integration is not primarily a matter of precise tactics or special methods. These will vary greatly with the overall situation (cultural and institutional), the team, and the coach. The importance of the attitudes of all concerned cannot be over-emphasized: they must all seek diligently to establish a spirit of mutual trust, respect, and confidence.

THE COACH-AS-PERSON IN THE 9-9 COACHING STYLE. Crucial to the 9-9 coaching style is the fourth concept that a coach can extend full concern for others insofar as he has achieved full respect for himself. At first thought, this seems to suggest narcissism and excessive self-concern. But in his fascinating booklet, *THE ART OF LOVING*, Erich Fromm makes clear that,

> *Whoever is capable of giving of himself is rich; the more he is able to give, the richer he becomes....But in giving he cannot help bringing something to life in the other person, and this...reflects back to him....It is clear that respect (for others) is possible only if I have achieved independence: if I can stand and walk without needing crutches, without having to dominate and exploit anyone else.*[1]

Men having such self-respect tend not to worry about themselves or about the basic needs of safety, shelter, esteem from others or belongingness that, according to Maslow, are common to men generally. Their overall orientation is positive and optimistic--toward more and better and greater challenges, with little or no anxiety about all the negatives that might occur. All my life I have idolized Robert Falcon Scott and his companion, Edward Wilson, who starved and froze to death following their desperate attainment of the South Pole in 1912. Despite the deep disappointment of finding that the Norwegian, Roald Amundsen, had beaten them to the Pole, Scott's last diary notes expressed no rancor against his bad luck, or against those who had failed to establish food depots for their return; rather, a calm acceptance of the situation and deep admiration for the "everlasting cheerfulness and courage" of his companions. "We have decided to die naturally in the track....We could have got through had we neglected our sick."

This may seem an extreme example, somewhat far afield from track athletics, but it makes the point clearly. Once full commitment is made to the task and to others, concern for one's own selfish interests is no longer operative. Almost any biography of a track coach or athlete illustrates the point. Self-esteem? Of course, more than most humans. Great achievement would be almost unthinkable without a belief in oneself. But with it, a selflessness or un-concern for self that makes it possible to focus outwardly on the goal and on others.

COACHING AUTHORITY IN THE 9-9 STYLE.
If it is to be effective, the 9-9 style of coaching entails authority; without authority, both leadership and program will founder. But such authority tends to be indirect or as symbol of some higher authority. Among those relevant to track and field we can cite: (1) authority of tradition and institution, (2) authority of team agreements, (3) authority of commitment to excellence, and (4) authority of coaching competence.

In contrast to the 9-1 style, such authority is not authoritarian. The authority of the 9-9 coach seldom requires unquestioning obedience, and even then it is to the situation, not to the coach. It derives its force more from the climate of felt relationships--mutual trust and purpose--than from fear of punishment.

This does not imply approval of the British tradition of centering authority in the team captain, with the coach in a mere advisory capacity, a sort of "help-if-asked" function. This not only rejects authority-as-person but also as representative. Much as though, in our courts of law, we were to reject all authority of the judge, even though it be as symbol of the higher authority of law and order.

Nor does it suggest approval of the 1-9 coaching style in which a "soft" or "laissez-faire" relationship is present. The disciplines of arduous training and high-level competitive

---

[1]Erich Fromm, *THE ART OF LOVING*, New York, Harper & Brothers Publishing, 1956, p. 28.

performance must be maintained; it's inherent in the sport and in the employment of a coach to do a job. Minimal coaching authority is not a workable alternative to authoritarianism. Decisions must be made, often immediately without waiting for group approval. The Chapter 2 story of McGregor's experience as new president at Antioch makes that clear. But always within the climate of mutual trust or of mutually supportive relationships inherent in the 9-9 style.

THE AUTHORITY OF TRADITION AND INSTITUTION. Man's basic urge toward adventure and risk-activity is in conflict with his basic need for safety. Almost inevitably he seeks solutions by way of the leader, especially the leader who impels him to efforts beyond his own self-confidence, and also assumes a major share of the responsibility for defeat.

In the 1930s, the Pennsylvania State High School Athletic Association sought to reduce both coaching authority and pressures for winning by removing the coach entirely from the playing bench. But many complaints--of the weight of over-responsibility on the boys and of incompetence as related to winning--soon forced them to reverse their action.

The point here is rather obvious and needs little further discussion. Under normal conditions (our present tendency to question all authority is quite abnormal) men seek guidance when they enter into new endeavors for which they lack competence. Those who guide them soon acquire a reputation of authority. Their followers must trust that authority, whatever its source, if they are to succeed in their enterprise.

Only when there is betrayal of that trust--as in the Vietnam war, or in the use of University research by those supporting that war, or in the exploitation of college athletes to serve the ambitions of college administrators or coaches--does revolt occur against such authority.

THE AUTHORITY OF TEAM AGREEMENTS. We use the word "team" in the sense of the greater team family. For the establishing of proper conduct is a function of many persons over a long period of time. Such persons include past team members, sports administrators both within and outside the sponsoring institution, parents, members of the local community, and of course the team and coach. This year's team cannot make its own rules exclusive of social tradition. However, once the agreements of such a team family have been established, once they have been discussed, understood, modified perhaps, and accepted by the members of this year's team, they then should take on an authority that is firm and binding. Agreements as to conduct both on and off the field must be adhered to strictly; fairly of course, but without exceptions for special or most-talented members.

Those who punish rule-breakers do so, not to satisfy some unfulfilled need in themselves to rule over others, nor to further their selfish goals; they are merely the agents of the authority of agreements made to achieve the goals of the team, and of its individual members.

THE AUTHORITY OF COMMITMENT TO EXCELLENCE. Every commitment to a program of personal development exacts a loss in personal freedom. Freedom to do one's best in any activity requiring effort assumes, on the one hand, concentration, and on the other, the discipline of all other activities and attitudes that would interfere or distract.

Such discipline is based on an acceptance of authority, though it be only the athlete's freely chosen training schedule. Such a schedule demands that certain work must be done when it needs to be done whether one feels like doing it or not. It has an authority that denies freedom to do as one pleases. Almost every biography of great track or field champions warns that if training is to be successful, it must be adamant in its essentials.

In his biography of Jim Ryun, Nelson (1967, 43) describes a situation that illustrates this problem,

During winter, junior year, State rules did not permit the coach to be with the boy, so Jim came to Timmons in the swimming pool.

All I could do was offer advice and he had to do the approaching....

Once he came to me and I could tell he was down in the dumps. It was the off season and he had been out running in the dark, in the snow and ice and rain, all by himself. There

weren't any other runners out, day after day like that, and it hurt him. And I could see he was beginning to wonder if it was worth it. And I told him, 'Jim, I'm not going to fight you on this. If this goal--the four-minute mile--isn't worth enough to get out and work day after day, then just forget about it. Nobody should browbeat you into achieving anything, as great as the goal may be...But I don't want you to come back at the end and tell me that if I had made you work you could have made it.'

THE AUTHORITY OF COACHING COMPETENCE. Of a thousand evaluations by outstanding athletes of their coaches, the most common adjectives would undoubtedly relate to personal integrity, respect, esteem or trust. But behind the aura of personal worth can be found the persuasive force of competence, what might be called the authority of successful experience.

Faced with such authority, men needing discipline become disciples; the problem disappears. I'm reminded of the comment, "What you've done speaks so clearly, no words are needed." Eamonn Coghlan once said of his coach, Jumbo Elliott, "I feel he coaches and treats his athletes the same way he does his business. He runs a high-class business and he deals with us as high-class athletes...There's no bull. Everything is very honest."

Such authority requires years, including early years in which failure is as frequent as success. Certainly that was true in Elliott's career.

GOALS IN THE 9-9 COACHING STYLE. In his award-winning research on better ways of business management, Rensis Likert studied the nature of highly effective groups in and out of business. Quite clearly their most important characteristic related to goals--clearly stated, long-time and immediate, accepted by common agreement, mutually supportive of the group and its members, challenging but achievable, and requiring the cooperation of all members.

Each member accepts willingly and without resentment the goals and expectations that he and the group establish for themselves. The anxieties, fears, and emotional stresses produced by direct pressure from a boss (authoritarian)...are not present. Such groups seem capable of setting...goals high enough to stimulate each member to do his best but not so high as to create anxieties or fear of failures....Mutual help is an important characteristic.[1]

Clearly, the 9-9 style of coaching must place great emphasis on this goal-centered approach, and give careful consideration to each of the following items.

Setting Goals--Mutually Agreeable and Supportive. Research on the goal-insight approach to coaching track and field is lacking. But related research in social psychology and in business has been extensive. For example, Kurt Lewin (1951) concluded from his classic experiment in group dynamics that methods by which the group (including members and leaders) reached its own decisions for changing group behavior were from two to ten times as effective as was a lecture exhorting change. Again, in industry, Hemphill (1950) found that the setting of clearly defined goals, not for, but WITH individual workers was the most effective of all devices for increasing production. (For other related research see Hollander and Hunt, 1963, 506).

Effective coaching will try in many ways to hold team goals, individual goals, and the coach's goals in common, as inseparable aspects of a single complex of goals. Higher authority and long-established traditions may fix the schedule of meets, the budget, facilities, even attitudes within and toward the sport. To this extent, the framework of team goals is already established. But within this framework, team members should feel that they and the coach, working together, have decided what emphasis shall be placed on what meets, how daily practice will be related to that emphasis, what "off-the-field" training rules shall be established and how they shall be policed, how leadership within the team will be organized, how individual differences between team members or between team members and the coach will be resolved, and many other team-centered problems.

Such goal setting WITH the team need not require many long meetings or discussions. Far

---

[1]Rensis Likert, *op. cit.*, p. 168.

better that it emerge out of a sound institutional tradition in sports, and out of sound coach-athlete relationships over the years. Then the fewer the words, the better. Once a climate of mutual empathy and trust surrounds the team family, only a few details need to be agreed on. On the other hand, never take the team's understanding and acceptance of past traditions for granted. During the past decade the very word "tradition" has been moot.

The Integration of Team Goals with Individual Goals. Effective track teams plan programs that provide opportunities for high-level performances by both the team and its individual members. Dual meets and multi-school championships tend toward the first; invitation meets toward the second. But some coaches such as Bill Bowerman, Oregon, used dual meets to serve both purposes. He began by maintaining a large squad of competitors. He then discouraged doubling whenever it might interfere with best-possible performance in the athlete's specialty. "I don't believe there is any danger of physical damage but psychologically I don't think it's a good thing."[1]

THE COACH HELPS THE INDIVIDUAL SET HIS OWN GOALS. Nelson quoted Bob Timmons, who coached championship teams in both high school and college, that the goal-insight system was the most important aspect of his coaching (1967, 22),

Very few noteworthy achievements come about by happenstance. They're accomplishments of thorough planning, determined sacrifice, genuine effort, and continuing hard work, all of which are given direction and purpose by the use of goals. The backbone of our program is in the establishment of goals. We believe that every boy must have a season and a career goal for his event....

Nothing was permitted to hinder their progress toward their goals. To us early season losing wasn't of great concern if the effort is good; and winning isn't good enough unless the performance is the best possible under the circumstances.

Of course, the athlete's belief in the competence and integrity of the coach is absolutely essential. Nelson writes (1967, 8),

When, six months after starting training, Jim ran a mile in 4:26.4, Timmons approached him, smiling and excited, "Jim, you've got a chance to run the mile under four minutes in high school."

The high school record was 4:08. Jim was 15 years old.

Jim's reaction: "Coach, crazy!" And it might have been such. But Timmons had already coached San Romani, had kept accurate records, and could prove that Jim had done better than Archie at the same age and level of experience.

At times, especially with beginners, the coach must lead strongly (Nelson, 1967, 69),

There were times when Timmons talked very straight to Ryun. If it were to take pressure, Timmons would apply it--and Jim accepted it. Later Jim said, "When we started, I wasn't sold on the idea at all. But as time went on and I began to see what the hard work would do, then I began to understand what Timmie was doing." It was tough work.

But ultimately, the athlete has the final veto; only he can decide whether to run or not to run (Nelson, 1967, 44),

"He has to sacrifice," Timmons says, "just the same Spartan life by his own decision. I don't threaten him or force him. I feel that he ought to become the best miler in the world, but it doesn't matter how we outsiders feel. It's all up to Jim. He does the work; he gets the credit. He should make the decisions about himself. He has to decide if he wants to go to the top of the world himself."

---

[1]Joe Henderson, "A Coach and a Tradition," Los Altos, Calif.: *Track & Field News*, 1 June, 1968, p. 21.

A Planned Time and Place. Reaching agreement as to team and individual goals cannot be left to chance or for the right moment to arrive. For the team, it is a group process that requires a regularly scheduled time and place. This allows informal prior discussions so that agreement in most instances is reached by consensus, not by factional argument and majority rule. Certainly, in the 9-9 style, agreement on goals is not gained merely by acceptance of the coach's statement of goals. But in any case, a climate of mutual trust and respect is essential.

Similarly, the setting of individual goals must have a time and place, even though unscheduled. All too often, the coach's office is not convenient to students. All too often the coach has "important work to do," and students hesitate to interfere. All too often the coach lives far off campus so that evening discussions are at least difficult. Brutus Hamilton had a custom of going early to the field, sitting in the first row of the stand away from technical coaching, and waiting for team members to come to him. He told me he had found this one of the best ways of setting up a relaxed one-on-one situation, away from the action-centered practice field, and open to frank discussion of whatever problems the athlete might have on his mind--personal or otherwise. Hamilton's excellent assistant coach, Al Ragan, was always on the field for coaching techniques.

Is the Goal Worth Its Cost? From time to time doubt arises in the mind of every athlete--great and not so great--as to whether the planned goals are really worth their cost in effort and agony and denial of other worthwhile activities or pleasures. Every biography provides examples. George Young was one of the toughest in maintaining his goals during 20 years of running, including four Olympic Games, despite the demands of full-time teaching, of a wife and family, and of a physical environment somewhat adverse to running. His duties required early-morning workouts, usually at 6 so as to be at school on time.

George Young may have been lonely on those early-morning runs through the desert, but he wasn't alone. There were coyotes and lizards and, above all, there were rattlesnakes....Although he never got bitten, the possibility was always there, and he couldn't help thinking about it at times....

The winter was the worst because it would still be dark when he completed his workout and that, he said, "was kind of demoralizing--knowing everyone else was still asleep...."[1]

Some times George felt, "This hasn't been a sport for me. It's been an obsession. I'm beginning to feel guilty about the time away from my two kids. I've only been fishing once with my little boy. It's been four years since I took Shirley to a movie.[2]

Was it really worth it? Throughout a full score of years, George Young maintained adamantly that it was, and at the end he was deeply regretful that he could no longer continue. But within that adamancy there were many times of self-doubt and even anxiety, as was indicated by his constant battle with bleeding ulcers. "Hereditary," he said, but we can be sure heredity was aggravated by circumstances.

The important point to be made here is that every coach should be aware of this uncertainty, especially in the minds of beginners and the less-talented, so as to provide the encouragement and proper viewpoint. Is what you're doing today satisfying? Then we need not worry about what might happen next month or next year.

Goals Must be Realistic. I remember one fine prospect who was determined to make the American Olympic team. I encouraged such a goal--one never knows--but as something for the future, three years or even seven years from now. But to the boy it was a daily obsession. The value of each practice and of each competition was judged by its furtherance of his Olympic prospects.

---

[1] Frank Dolson, ALWAYS YOUNG, Mountain View, Calif.: World Publications, 1975, p. 138.

[2] Ibid., p. 10.

He was frustrated at his slow progress. His frustration developed into a complex of difficulties. In the end, it was hard to say whether he quit or was requested to leave the team.

Such boys seldom disclose to the coach the hows and whys, or even the goal itself, for fear he may deride them. And therefore the coach will often be at a loss to understand what is going on in the boy's mind. When such a long reach for achievement exceeds the runner's ability to grasp it, his continuing sense of failure may block even those performances that he can do. His goals take on an emotional value far in excess of their real importance; emotion creates tensions which, directly and indirectly, hold him back.

He may blame himself for his failure. He may blame others. He is quite likely to blame the coach, especially if the coach puts forward more reasonable goals, but goals that the boy feels are empty of challenge or will delay his progress toward the goals *he* thinks are really important.

Such cases of over-evaluation of unsound goals are seldom simple. Solutions are likely to be difficult. One or two suggestions based upon my own errors more than my successes might be of interest: (1) be personally concerned about the athlete but not personally involved in his frustrations; (2) try to help the athlete define his problems clearly and matter-of-factly; and (3) help him to keep both the problems and their solutions at the simplest level possible. The tendency of a frustrated athlete and an interested coach is to dig deeper than the situation requires. If attention can be concentrated upon doing well today and tomorrow—and enjoying it—for its own sake, the problem will be well on its way toward solution.

Which reminds us to return to Bob Timmons' statement that "every boy must have a season and a career goal for his event." And we might add, a goal for this week's competition and this day's practice and this work-time-distance. Unless the boy understands and accepts these goals whole-heartedly, his energies in seeking them will be diminished.

High-Level Goals Require Gradual Increments of Effort. The assumption of striving for excellence inherent in the 9-9 coaching style depends on gradual increments of effort. This is as valid at the high school level as at the Olympic, though the potentials are lowered by age and maturity. But so much depends on the way in which "gradual increments" is interpreted by the coach. Does "gradual" apply to the entire career of the athlete, as is so strongly emphasized by Arthur Lydiard and Bill Bowerman, or to the four years of high school as was done by Bob Timmons in training Jim Ryun, or to this present year only, as might be done to a high school senior by a new coach anxious to impress others? Does "gradual" apply to mileage only or to intensities of training? If the latter, and within a six-week time period, doing too much too soon can lead to injury and a loss of faith in the coach.

Goals as Commitment. The Dedication of this OMNIBOOK praises those athletes who, within the limitations of time and energy placed by their higher-priority commitment to the studies, vocation or other services, "strive to their utmost to raise performance ever higher, faster, and farther." But we must balance this with the earlier statement on the potentially abundant energies of men with its assumption that, under supportive conditions and motivations, the everyday student-athlete can do all this and all that too, both at high levels. Average men have reservoirs of energy that far surpass common assessments of their capacity.

Unfortunately, few people agree with this concept that we can strive to our utmost in more than one area of action. The time-energies spent here take away from the time-energies properly spent elsewhere. They fail to realize that the rate of restoration increases along with the rate of use. The 4:00-minute miler needs no more hours of sleep and rest than does the 5:00-minute miler. Nevertheless, many a well-balanced individual with potential in track and field is turned away by this "over-emphasis" on dedication to sport. Brian Mitchell[1] suggests that we distinguish between a dedicated attitude and a dedicated life. To dedicate one's life to track and field would be foolish; life has far greater potentials than that. But we can take

---

[1]Brian Mitchell, "The Right Kind of Dedication," *ATHLETICS WEEKLY*, Vol. 22, No. 19, May 11, 1968.

an attitude of utmost dedication to our sport within its proper merits, without excluding or suppressing the other phases of life.

Following Dave Roberts' world-record pole vault at 18'6½", Jon Hendershott[1] quoted him,

"Actually, my No. 1 priority this year wasn't vaulting--and it still isn't. I've been studying awfully hard in grad school, and I'm applying to medical school. School has been a full time job and I'm trying to vault well, which is also a full-time job. I guess I'm kinda burning the candle at both ends, but it has worked out."

Indeed, for he earned all A's last quarter in school--and his achievements in the other we already know about.

Of course such a multiple commitment must come primarily from within. Most persons acquire it during the first years of life from the climate of action and attitude in their home-community-school. If it's not there, neither the stick nor the carrot can create it. But an effective 9-9 coach can do much to nourish and encourage its development.

ACHIEVED GOALS DESTROY INCENTIVES. When goals are underestimated or when performance exceeds all expectation, it is very difficult to maintain incentives. Perhaps the most amazing example of this was Bob Beamon's superhuman performance (29' 2½") in the 1968 Olympic long jump. No jumper had ever done even 28 feet. His superlative leap brushed aside several decades of normal progress and cleared a distance to be expected in the 1980s or later. It overwhelmed everyone, and Beamon most of all. At this writing (1971) it appears he will never even attempt to reach such a level of performance again.

Somewhat similarly, Dick Fosbury gained his goal of being Olympic champion high jumper during his college junior year, four years sooner than planned. After two years of almost no jumping, he was quoted as saying,[2]

One of my problems was that I went too high in the Olympics. When I jumped 7' 4¼" I exceeded my goal for the year by a couple of inches. That threw me off. I was sort of lost for a while as far as my mind was concerned. I had nowhere to go. Now that I've been completely away from competition for a while I'm starting over again. I can set a goal again, and come close to it, working up gradually.

PERSONAL EXPERIENCE IN THE 9-9 COACHING STYLE. The 9-9 coaching method assumes that young athletes will reach toward the highest levels of performance and so into the highest levels of training energies and the so-called "agonies" inherent in them. (Actually, the idea of "agony" is the invention of the less developed or ill-trained; sound training develops defenses against the feelings of exhaustion as much as against the physical aspects.)

It is therefore very important that the 9-9 coach should have had personal experience in the many aspects of track and field--in both competition and training. Possessing such a knowledge out of muscle spindles and pain endings, a coach can inflict fatigue pains without uncertainty or sense of guilt or fear of harm to his pupil. As Lydiard said to Peter Snell at the Rome Olympics, "Throw up if you feel like it. You'll feel better for it. But then, go ahead and take your workout." No hint of concern or suggestion of easing the work that needed to be done. Insensitive? Yes, from a layman's or inexperienced point of view. But Lydiard had trained for and run the marathon. He knew by personal experience that sometimes insensitivity to discomfort is the only means of impelling a man beyond what he believes possible. As such it can be proof, not of harshness, but of deep personal concern, in contrast to the false concern of allowing the less painful way that leads to lesser performance and a lesser person.

Murray Halberg wrote that when he first worked out under Arthur Lydiard,

---

[1]Jon Hendershott, "Roberts gets his Record and Then Some," *Track & Field News*, September, 1975, p. 4.

[2]"Dick Fosbury Looking for 68 Spark," *Track & Field News*, 1 February 1971, 7.

Lydiard was still developing his system with athletes like Lawrie King, Colin Lousich, and Ernie Haskell....but first and foremost he used himself as a guinea-pig.... But he wouldn't ask us to do anything new until he'd tried it out on himself to find out its effects on the body. He tested theories on us only when he was certain they were worth trying. It was tough training but I thrived on it.[1]

But I also think of Dyatchkov's work with Valery Brumel, of Coach Augie Erfurth's work with his two great vaulters, Fred Hansen and Dave Roberts, or of Coach Bill Dellinger's work with Prefontaine.

Perhaps America's greatest coach of distance runners was Billy Hayes of Indiana. I've never heard that Hayes was a competitive distance runner but he had a muscle-nerve feeling for running that his many greater champions seldom if ever questioned. He was the first of our coaches to spend several summers in Scandinavia where he watched and listened to runners and coaches along the woods paths at Swedish Vålådalen or Finnish Vierumäcki until he knew in his bones the higher levels of what could be done. It was that bone certainty that gave Coach Hayes the authority that impels acceptance.

MOTIVATION IN THE 9-9 COACHING STYLE. The pattern of motivation inherent in this method of coaching is that of McGregor's Theory Y as stated in Chapter 2, "Motivations and Coaching Assumptions." Challenging work is as natural and enjoyable as play or rest. Once committed, men (including boys and girls) will exercise a considerable degree of self-direction in their work. The satisfaction of work well done is more satisfying than the rewards that sometimes attend it. External controls and the threat of punishment are mainly necessary under the assumptions of Theory X.

Examples of this approach are innumerable. Most track Greats tend to be self-dependent and in some real measure, self-coached. I have just finished reading Frank Dolson's biography of George Young,[2] America's first distance runner to compete in four Olympics. During those 16 years, George was almost entirely self-driven. Whatever he received in the way of recognitions and awards was quite secondary to his own need to come up to his own expectations in running. Along similar lines, Brutus Hamilton wrote to the mother of Don Bowden, first American to better four minutes for the mile,[3]

My only disagreement with Don has been in the amount of work that he should do. I usually have to chase him off the track each afternoon because he always wants to do one more straightaway or one more lap. Even this week, after his great effort of Saturday, he still wants to do more than I think he should....

Perhaps no track and field man ever developed himself as close to his maximum potentials as did Bill Toomey. During four years of college track, he was an NCAA non-place-winner in the long jump and 440. In 1969 he was Olympic Champion and world-record holder in the decathlon, a truly amazing development. Frank Dolson, sports columnist of *The Philadelphia Inquirer*, told it this way,

Bill Toomey has done a good many unbelievable things. Over a five-year period he completely rebuilt his body, changing himself from a 165-pounder with pretty good speed into a 195-pounder with blazing speed. His "secret" was dedication. From the day he first set his sights on becoming an Olympic decathlon man to the moment he climbed the victory platform in Mexico City, he let nothing stand in the way of his "impossible dream."....

---

[1]Murray Halberg and Garth Gilmour, *A CLEAN PAIR OF HEELS,* London: Herbert Jenkins Ltd., 1963, p. 27.

[2]Frank Dolson, *ALWAYS YOUNG,* Mountain View, Calif: World Wide Publications, 1976.

[3]Lawrence J. Baack, *THE WORLDS OF BRUTUS HAMILTON,* Los Altos: Tafnews, 1971, p. 19.

[4]Frank Dolson, "Bill Toomey Tells Young People what Winning is All About." *Family Circle,* July 1969, p. 60.

From 1964 through 1968, Bill trained daily. He ran, worked with weights, and did all the things a decathlon man has to do to become No. 1. Except for his family and friends, nobody noticed....It would have been very easy for Bill to give up his Olympic dream.

"The hardest thing is getting out there every day," Bill says, "It's so simple to find something else to do. Your body tells you, 'Forget it; don't work out today.' Your mind says, 'Do it!'"

Bill's mind won.

The 9-9 coaching style can and does accept scholarships and other material rewards within its system, if given and controlled by the regular scholarship faculty of the college. But as Maslow has made clear, the man whose lower-level needs of food-shelter-safety are satisfied is no longer motivated by those needs. In terms of inciting greater efforts on the track or field, scholarships, once granted, are ineffective. Without them, of course, the athlete might not be in college at all. But only in the 9-1 style, where the coach can give and take away, does fear of loss make them a factor in performance.

THE 9-9 COACHING STYLE ENCOURAGES THE ATHLETE'S SELF-DEPENDENCE.

Many related research studies in business and industry (Hollander and Hunt, 1963, 506ff) support actual experience in track and field that development will proceed more rapidly if the individual athlete is critical of his own goals, of his own training methods and techniques, and of his own tactics in competition. On the basis of their work with track athletes and coaches, Ogilvie and Tutko (1966, 28) recommend,

An open reception on the part of your athletes; not an uncritical acceptance, but a measured, thoughtful involvement in your counsel. The athlete retains his integrity as an individual but allows new knowledge or theories to blend with his preconceived notions or past....experiences....Remember that you are always planting seeds.... It will not be until the athlete actually feels in a personal way the significance of your words or instruction that true learning has occurred.

Coaches disagree on the extent of such thinking and self-criticism by their athletes, depending on their concepts of the coach-athlete relationship. A few take the attitude, "I'll do the thinking; you stick to doing what I tell you," and produce record performances and winning teams. But as a group, successful performers in track and field tend to be intelligent, self-dependent men, given to critical analysis of situations, techniques, and methods, especially as these apply to themselves.

One of my greatest joys in coaching was working with Charles Fonville who, considering methods and attitudes of the 1940s, achieved as close to perfect technique in the shot put as has any man. Time after time he came to me saying, "Coach, I've been thinking about that problem we discussed last week. I think this will work." And then he'd execute, with almost no practice, the very point we had not been clear about.

I once asked Parry O'Brien why he wasted so much time working alone and with only one shot. His answer, "Coach, doing it this way gives me time to think about what was wrong with the last effort and what will be right in the next." Some months before the actual event occurred, Gunder Hägg predicted in Sweden that though many men were trying, Roger Bannister would be the first to break the four-minute "barrier" in the mile, not because he possessed the greatest physical powers, but because he approached the problems of training and self-analysis intelligently and with clear concentration upon what such an effort required.

Of course, individuals differ in the benefits they can derive from such self-dependent thinking. Assuming maturity, the greater the intelligence, the more likely good effects will result. Lacking maturity, defined as self-confidence and self-control, to be "thoughtful and critical" of one's own methods can lead to doubt and lack of direction. Some successful athletes seem to adapt themselves best to the rigors of training when they put themselves--body and mind--in the hands of a respected coach. By giving over the mental-emotional stresses of both training and competition, such men tend to relax more, sleep better, enjoy their food more, and perform better.

MANAGING CONFLICT IN THE 9-9 STYLE. During the 1960s and early 70s a spirit of revolt against the Establishment was in the very air we breathed. The authority of anyone who could in any way be representative of the System was open to challenge--and often was challenged. And this carried over from the political and military spheres to that of education and sport. The Princeton University track team voted in midseason to stop the year's competitive schedule in protest of the Vietnam war and the Kent State killings--and had their way.

Many a longtime track coach who had ruled his situation--autocratically perhaps but kindly and without dissent ("It never occurred to me to do otherwise")--found himself beleaguered from all sides. Some 9-1 coaches, firmly established through long success, resisted hard, fired team members for insubordination, and are still coaching. Others were deeply hurt and chose early retirement, long before their years of effective coaching were gone.

On balance, the total result of this conflict against authority was on the plus side. It called into question a full spectrum of problems that had been hidden. And out of it emerged a better understanding of what I have called "the human side of the coaching enterprise." In those colleges and schools where the overall climate of attitude was in keeping with the 9-9 style of coaching, that is, where the goals and attitudes of the institution-coach-athletes were integrated and mutually supportive, there was relatively little difficulty. At Princeton, for example, Ken Fairman, Athletic Director, supported quite readily the vote-to-quit of the team. "They're dropping out because they no longer feel a 100 percent commitment to sports; their hearts are no longer in the game. After all, they always have a veto; they're not hired by us to compete."

The 9-9 style does not prevent conflict. In some ways, its emphasis on freedom and openness stimulates it. But it does so in healthful ways. It does not avoid direct confrontation; it welcomes it as the best means of making the issues clear and open. Since personal authority is not at stake in this style, loss of authority is not feared. Nor is the strong need to get along with people at any cost, that characterizes the 1-9 style, evident here.

Conflict tends to arise from off-the-field conduct. What is the image our track team wishes to convey to others--to other students on campus, to the public when we travel, to the news media if they become interested? Are we fully committed to excellence in our off-the-field efforts just as on the field? What time and energy does this allow for having fun? What kind and degree of fun? How do we travel to meets? Separately? How do we dress on trips and in hotel lobbies? What hotels do we stay in?

In many situations, these are questions for which the athletes feel no concern. They're glad to have such unimportant details settled without any effort on their part. "Give me a quiet place, a good bed, food I like, and a fair chance to compete; that's all I care about." But in other situations, the least hint of neglect, of discrimination, of changing the rules and customs, of restricting individual rights or habits, can become issues leading to revolt and direct confrontation.

The more open the door and the mind of the coach to the suggestions and disagreements of team members, the more open their attitudes to consult with him. The potential conflict is now met at its weakest point--before it congeals or gathers its forces. Discussions now relate to solving problems, not to suppressing persons. Time consuming? In the short run, yes. But in the long run, definitely time and energy saving. One needs to be convinced of that. Otherwise it's so much easier to avoid confrontation now; so much easier to put it off, make do, compromise.

As I look back on my own coaching career, I remember so many instances of person-to-person conflict and one of coach-to-team conflict in which early open discussion would probably have avoided hostility. I can think of various excuses--the long distance from campus to coach's office, the endless demands on a coach's time, the chip-on-the-shoulder attitudes of some youth--but the core of the trouble was failure to establish a sufficient climate of mutual trust and personal concern, the key to the 9-9 style.

Every team operation requires control. In his autobiography, Vince Matthews told of what I consider to be excessive demands by a dozen or so of America's top track and field champions. On the one hand, they wanted the benefits of Olympic and inter-nation team competitions; on the other, they demanded complete individual freedom to arrange their own tours, set their own wage demands, follow their own training and life styles.[1] With such attitudes by team members, not even the most expert coaching leadership could achieve a sound team operation.

A team is not a mere aggregation of individuals. A team has a character of its own that is more than and other than the sum of its individual members. The purpose and goal of the team must be pursued even though this diminishes individual freedom and the pursuit of individual goals. In the long run this will be more than balanced by individual benefits from team efforts--successful or not.

The team must work together to get its job done, and primary responsibility for that work rests with the coach. That's the demand of the school administration and the demand of all that are worthwhile team members. Obviously, the 9-9 coach will seek control first by democratic means as advocated throughout this section. But he must be clear that control, one way or another, must be achieved or the entire enterprise will founder.

COACHING-PERSONS AND MECHANICS--SUMMARY
This graphic approach seeks to improve our understanding of the job of coaching by dividing it into two aspects: one related directly to persons and inter-personal relationships; the other to the methods and techniques of track and field training and performance. In life and on the field, these are inseparable. But distinguishing between them, as in a graph, implements clearer understanding, deeper analysis, and a more sound balance of coaching emphasis between the two.

The major concern of Part I of this OMNIBOOK is with coaching leadership and its mutually supportive relationships with other persons within and outside the track team family; that is, with those aspects of coaching that lie along the vertical axis of the Figure 3.1 graph. The major concern of the remainder (Part II) of the OMNIBOOK is with track and field mechanics and training systems--those evaluated along the horizontal axis of the graph. Both aspects are essential to coaching. However, to simplify and shorten the discussion, these latter concerns were largely ignored throughout this Chapter 3, thus forcing contrasts between the different coaching styles primarily on the basis of differing attitudes as related to persons. Even in this area, we concentrated on only the 1-9. 9-1 and 9-9 styles of coaching. Given more space, much fuller consideration would have been given to other styles such as the 1-1, 5-5 and others, certainly as to their concern for methods and techniques but also as to personal relationships. (There's a field for a much-needed full-sized volume on track and field coaching.)

In the past, both textbooks and lecturers at coaching clinics have dealt almost exclusively with methods and techniques. But coaches have found the problems of persons, both within and outside the team, to be both more common and more complex. Obviously, much more sound research must be done in this area; we've hardly begun to take it seriously. This material is only a beginning, but often making a beginning is the hardest phase of growth.

To make best use of this graphic approach, we must go back to the work of Douglas McGregor and Rensis Likert with their emphasis on climates of mutual trust and mutually supportive relationships, not only within the track team, but among the many other groups that relate to the coaching enterprise--the institution, community, team family and extending to the entire culture. When these are in conflict, the enterprise is diminished.

As a final and crucial point, we must be constantly aware that the graphic use of precise numbers, such as 9-3 or 5-7, is merely a convenience or tool to further analysis and communicate ideas. No coach or coaching style can be circumscribed so precisely. These numbers are value symbols; if valid they may simulate life values but no more than that. Neither humans nor human operations can be squeezed into any mathematical symbol. The word is not the thing. To repeat--there are no 1-9 or 9-1 coaches or even coaching styles.

The full intent of this graphic approach to coaching is to free and expand our sights, not to narrow them; to achieve a better balance in coaching by emphasizing the human side of coaching, not by diminishing its technology.

---

[1]Vince Matthews with Neil Amdur, *MY RACE BE WON*, New York: Charterhouse, 1974, hardcover, 396 pp.

Chapter 4
TRACK AND FIELD COACHES OF INTEREST

These thumb-nail sketches of coaches have a number of uses. First, they serve as examples of the various coaching styles indicated in the Coaching Grid from 1-9 to 9-1 to 9-9. No one of these coaches can be fitted into any one pigeonhole; humans are far too elusive and variable for that. Second, class discussions of the general area of the Grid into which these coaches fall should (1) bring clearer insights into the principles of coaching given in Chapters 2 and 3, and (2) suggest the wide range of coaching styles that have proved successful. Third, these sketches should indicate the many ways you can modify and improve your own coaching style. We change our basic attitudes and behavior in small ways and with great reluctance. But, with time and persistence, they can be modified. So with our coaching styles. It's probably easier to change oneself than to change one's coaching situation.

BRUTUS HAMILTON--UNIVERSITY OF CALIFORNIA, BERKELEY (1932-1965)

It has been my good fortune to be with Brutus Hamilton at many coaching clinics, dual meets, and championship meets. He was inherently impressive--impressive of figure and face and voice and attitude and way of speaking and, most important, of personal and coaching success. What other track coach had been National Decathlon champion, Chief U. S. Olympic coach, Director of Athletics, Dean of Students, and coach of many world and Olympic champions?

But along with all this, he had a clear quality of selflessness, both in his life and in his coaching. No one could question that he got things done, but by his own charisma which impelled others to help themselves, without leaning on him except for inspiration and a direct answer when asked. No one could accuse Brutus of pushing his own weight around. I was with him in 1956 as we were about to enter the Los Angeles stadium for the final Olympic trials. He was chief Olympic coach. At the last moment he discovered he had left his ticket at home. He could have pushed himself into the stadium easily. Everyone knew him. Certainly I could have identified him to the ticket-taker. But he quietly went to the ticket-seller and bought himself a seat!

I was with him in India in 1954 among coaches whose technical knowledge was at least doubtful if not non-existent. During three weeks of coaching, Brutus's strongest admonition was "Look within yourselves for your answers. India has an infinite capacity for good coaching. Believe in it. Work in terms of your own Indian way of life. Adapt Western techniques and details to yourselves. For your sports future lies within you, not in acquiring the secrets of coaches from other countries, no matter how successful those secrets may have been for them."

This was Hamilton's approach when teaching other coaches, but also when coaching his own athletes. He seldom urged a point of view, and never dictated, "Do it my way." Certainly he could never be accused of over-coaching, at least as it applies to teaching techniques. His knowledge of techniques, based on his own experience, was sound. But he evidenced that knowledge in his coaching, not so much by authoritative direction as by suggestion, by asking questions in such a way that the right answers became evident, by encouraging thoughtful analysis and discussion among his athletes, by presenting himself as a resource expert to whom they might come for help in their efforts to help themselves.

At the time of his retirement, Harry O. Bain wrote in the *California Monthly*,

the story of Brutus Hamilton, . . .a man whose life has been stamped with rare idealism, with love of sport, not for the sake of winning alone, but for the will to strive. to compete. Even more it is a tale of loyalty and love for his athletes and their almost mystical devotion to the man they remember as 'The Coach.' Brutus' allegiance to his athletes is a constant in an often unbalanced athletic world where premiums are set on winning. To blame a beaten athlete, or criticise an official's judgment publicly is unthinkable to the Hamilton character . . . .

But Brutus' concern for the athlete goes beyond physical and academic welfare. To him each boy is special, whether he is a world class competitor or a 'little man' whose efforts never pay off in points or records. In Brutus' eyes his athletes are equals. One spring night in 1956, when the great Don Bowden became America's first sub-four-minute miler . . . .Brutus was literally swarmed by well wishers in the stands. On the track where the two mile was about to start was another of Hamilton's athletes, a runner far below Bowden's stature, but a boy gifted with great team spirit and desire to excel . . . . Brutus slipped quietly away from the jubilant crowd, saying simply, "I must be there to tell Val how he looked at the finish." . . .

There is a wide streak of humor in Brutus Hamilton. An inveterate letter writer, his prose fairly glitters with wit, and some of his best shots are aimed at his own head. In 1952, after coaching the U. S. Olympic team to a resounding success at Helsinki, Brutus summarized his contribution "as refraining from interference with the normal progress of the boys."

Shortly after Brutus' death in December, 1970, Dave Maggard wrote the following paragraphs for Track & Field News.[1] Maggard was captain of a Hamilton-coached California track team and was highly recommended by Hamilton to succeed himself as head coach.

Brutus Hamilton was a unique human being. A scholar, philosopher, poet and gentleman, Brutus could have excelled in whatever profession he had chosen. A man of keen intellect, I think he may have been the most articulate man the sport has ever known.

Without a doubt, Brutus was ahead of his time as far as coaching was concerned. Rapport with his athletes was excellent. Respect was mutual. There were times when he drew criticism from his colleagues for not being a tougher taskmaster. Some even felt he did not care about winning. Nothing could have been further from the truth. A great athlete during his competitive days, he was a winner in every respect. None of his athletes were pampered or coddled. Care about them he did but exploiting an athlete never entered his mind. The athlete competed because he had the desire to excel, not because he was being coerced. Brutus could be disturbed by the spoiled athlete--the type who complained that the world owed him a living.

Brutus felt there was one real reason for being part of the team--the athlete had to have the desire to be the best. He could guide an athlete as far as he cared to go toward excellence. Winning was the name of the game--but not at all costs. Not at the cost of sacrificing ideals. He had an excellent understanding of the student-athlete and problems he might encounter along the way. His emphasis was placed on getting an education-- getting through the University and preparing for life. He looked on his athletes as men who could take lessons from athletics for later years. The carry-over values can be great. Many of those he coached continued to improve even after graduation, due mostly to the acquisition of a solid background and the love of competition. His idea of the athlete standing on his own two feet lends to this continued success.

Team morale on Brutus' teams was just great. Not a forced, rah-rah type of enthusiasm but a quiet, sincere dedication. Foolishness and frivolity were not a part of the man's character. Having fun and enjoying what you were doing seemed to exemplify his coaching philosophy. Brutus' long experience and great knowledge gave him a quiet confidence. His enthusiasm for life and sport was almost indescribable--so mellow, yet inspirational. Seldom did he raise his voice either during a meet or practice. A warm handshake or pat on the back with a complimentary remark made it all seem worthwhile. He was a great stabilizing influence. "Keep things in proper perspective" was a common phrase for Brutus. I once heard him say to a young aspiring sophomore, "This is your first race for California, make yourself proud of the association." Or just before an important meet, he might say, "Don't underestimate your competitor, honor him with your best performance." . . .

Shortly after I had taken my first job at the high school level, I received a letter

---

[1] Dave Maggard, "So Mellow, Yet Inspirational," Track & Field News, 1 February 1971, 14.

from Brutus. Many of the things he said then I feel reflected not only his coaching philosophy but also his wonderful sense of humor.

"Coaching track will always be rather a personal coach-athlete relationship....Some coaches know all the techniques except they forget to tell their boys to get there first. They become so form conscious that they invariably forget to win. Form is, of course, important and essential but it should never stick out." ...

Forrest Beaty, now a medical student, relates the manner in which Brutus had recruited him. Forrest was being wined and dined by many colleges all over the country. He was somewhat surprised when his recruiting luncheon was at Fenton's ice cream parlor. Brutus' approach was most refreshing and Forrest ended up at California.

Archie Williams, 1936 Olympic 400-meter gold medalist and world record holder,.... now a teacher in Marin County (near San Francisco), said he often asks himself, "What would the coach want me to do?"

Don Bowden, first American to run the mile below four minutes, talked of Brutus' ability to get the athlete ready at the right time. "Any coach can work an athlete hard but only the great ones know when to ease off."

Lon Spurrier, former world record holder in the 880, tells of the times when Brutus was always there to share the blame for poor performances but never around to accept credit for the athlete's great performances.

The list continues on and on--all influenced by the greatness of Brutus Hamilton.

In my judgment, Brutus was unique among United States track coaches in the great breadth of his activities, his interests, his track and field contributions, and his tolerance of others-- an authentic 9-9 leader. He was a respected Major in the Army Air Corps[1] but I knew him to be a strong advocate of peace among all men of One World, a man cited for "his idealism, sensitivity, light-heartedness, beauty and wisdom." (Strange words to ascribe to a winning coach of a major track college.) He was a second-team end on Walter Camp's 1921 All-American football team, a forward on the National AAU Championship basketball team for the Kansas City Athletic Club in 1923, National decathlon and pentathlon champion and Olympic Games silver medallist in 1920, but along with all that, an excellent student at the University of Missouri specializing in English poetry and prose. Baack wrote[2]

"This did not mean that athletics dominated his life at the University. On the contrary his first love was probably literature and history. As he once wrote, 'one of the dearest and most inspiring friendships of my life' was with John Rutledge Scott, Professor of Elocution at Missouri. 'I made hundreds of trips from the Delt house to his home (a four-mile walk, going and coming) and literally sat at his feet for four years.'"

Brutus was Director of Athletics at the University of California, 1946-1955, with all the problems of big-time sports promotion and alumni relations that job entails, but was also Dean of Men, 1944-1946, Track Coach, 1932-1965, Chairman of the NCAA Track Rules Committee, 1955-1965, and one must add, instructor of English literature and history at Westminster College, Missouri, 1924-1929. This latter interest stayed with him. His wife, Rowena, wrote me that "He always found time to read--very often poetry. He had a wonderful memory and could quote poetry by the hour."

He was an avid fisherman, for love of quiet and the out-of-doors, and also was known through-

---

[1]"He did this because he was very patriotic in a quiet sort of way and because as he said, 'If I'm going to work with boys the rest of my life, I've got to know what they've been through.'" Lawrence J. Baack, *THE WORLDS OF BRUTUS HAMILTON*, Los Altos: *Tafnews*, 1975, p. 14.

[2]*Ibid.*, p. 10.

out Berkeley as "the gentle caretaker of the birds at Edwards Stadium." He once posted a notice that, prior to leaving Berkeley for a long trip, he had weighed each bird very carefully, "Woe to all persons...if one gram is missing from any one bird. Mr. Hamilton is ordinarily a very peaceful man, but he wishes to remind...(you) that he knocked out Benny Herring in the second round of a scheduled four-round bout for the Regimental Light-Heavyweight Championship in World War I. BEWARE!"

Brutus also had a lifetime love affair with the harmonica--always in his travel case or pocket. I remember well the closing festivities of our three-week coaches' clinic at Patiala, India, at which each person was expected to do his thing. Brutus was the hit of the evening with "Turkey in the Straw," the California Bear Fight Song, but most movingly, with "Shenandoah."

To confirm the great variety of friendships that Brutus maintained, he was a close friend of rival coach, Dink Templeton of Stanford, for whose place as an athlete on the 1920 Olympic team he had fought vigorously. To me, Templeton was the opposite of Hamilton--explosive, restless, at least outwardly a tyrant, crudely profane and increasingly alcoholic; somehow they found much in common. But Brutus was also a kind friend of the "Dear Good and Gracious Lady" who owned the flower shop in Berkeley.

No description of Brutus Hamilton would be complete without inclusion of two helpers. The first, Rowena Hamilton, his wife during 44 years. At Brutus' retirement dinner, I had the sharp impression that it was equally in recognition of her many contributions. That seems an exaggeration, but athlete after athlete spoke so warmly, even emotionally, of her personal concern, her ever-present smile, her well-loaded dinner table, or of her help in solving some personal problem for which only such a woman could have empathy and sound suggestions. In one letter Rowena wrote to me, "I have always been grateful that Brutus was in a profession I could share. It was great to know the athletes and their girls--what they thought and what they wanted to be. When an athlete was hurt, both Brutus and I worried and lost sleep." The Hamiltons were clearly a two-person coaching staff.

But there was another important member of that staff, Al Ragan, California's assistant track coach for over 45 years, 1927-1974. Of-one-piece with Brutus, Ragan extended the emphasis on fundamentals and "keeping things simple," so inherent in Hamilton's coaching. He told Ted Brock[1] that "Brutus believed in a very basic approach too. With an athlete he'd take one thing at a time. Keep watching. Keep watching. Sometimes I think the kids didn't realize how much they were being coached. He and I stayed quite close to them, in their work, their academics, their talk of the future."

There you have it all in a nutshell--"He and I (and Rowena) stayed quite close to them." We tend to assume that a coach is restricted to the outline of his own skin. But if the research of McGregor and Likert has any meaning at all, his skin is also an inline of the persons and the devices and the climate of supportive relationships a coach establishes about him, which, working all together, gain their mutual goals.

This sketch neglects entirely Hamilton's attitude toward recruiting--in brief, one that extends a warm welcome to the boy as a worthy member of the California student body, as well as an athlete. His letter[2] to "Woody" Covington of Compton High, the 1958 California State High School mile champion, illustrates this attitude perfectly, but our lack of space allows quotation of only one-half:

I am pleased that you have sent your transcript to the University for evaluation. Your marks thus far completed show that you should have no difficulty meeting the stern entrance requirements here, provided, of course, you continue your excellent work during your last high school semester. This I know you shall do.

You now face three major decisions. First, the university which you wish to attend;

---

[1]Ted Brock, "Al Ragan: The Stuff of Permanence," Los Altos: *Track & Field News*,| June 1972,p.30.

[2]Lawrence J. Baack, *op. cit.*,p. 29.

second, the profession which you wish to follow; and, third and finally, the girl with whom you wish to share your life. I refuse, of course, to have anything to do with this latter decision in any case. However, I might say in passing that there is no dearth of charming, brilliant and high charactered girls on this campus, should you decide to cast your lot with us, and should you evidence an interest in such distracting items.

For the most part, I coach by indirection. I like to coach men without their realizing they are being coached. I want them to enjoy running and not make a grim business of it....

But a coach can only point the way. Inspired performances must come from deep within the boy himself. We work hard on the mental side and try to get a boy to realize and achieve his potential.

But coaching is something more than a craft. We follow a general pattern but no two men are worked exactly alike. Insofar as possible, we follow the rule of a certain voice teacher who was once asked what method she used in teaching her pupils. She replied, "I have twenty-five students. I use twenty-five different methods." So, if you asked me exactly how you would be coached, I couldn't tell you. I can tell you, except for the above generalities, only after I've had a chance to study you and work with you...

JAMES (JUMBO) ELLIOTT -- VILLANOVA UNIVERSITY (1936--)
Skip Myslenski's article, "The 40-year Odyssey of Jumbo Elliott," appeared in the April 13, 1975 issue of *The Philadelphia Inquirer*,

In a time of too many spurious copies, one James Francis Elliott exists as an original,....a kaleidoscopic blend of coach, counsellor, celebrity, dictator, entertainer, hustler, genius, magician and father confessor....

"Yeah, Jumbo is just Jumbo," says miler Eamonn Coghlan, who runs for him now. "He influences a lot of people, but nothing influences him."

"Jumbo is so complex I don't think he understands himself," says Tom Donnelly, who ran for him in the late Sixties. "I don't mean that in a derogatory sense, but it seems like he's always pre-occupied, things are always off-handed, he's off in the distance somewhere. But of course what he says always works out."

"He's an institution, an attraction," says Marty Liquori, who ran at the same time as Buerkle. "He's like the Liberty Bell."

"The Liberty Bell, oh my God," says Jumbo Elliott, laughing heartily. "Old hat'd be more like it."

He began in 1936, barely 22 years old, recently graduated and earning $135 for a year as both trainer and track coach. As a student he himself had run not unimpressively (he still holds the school's 600-yard record), captained the golf team, scheduled meets (golf on Friday, track on Saturday) and often accompanied football coach Harry Stuhldreher to Penn, where they would watch and learn from Billy Morris, the Olympic trainer. He received an appointment to West Point (at the time you could graduate from college then compete four more years for the Academy if you entered before July 1 and were not yet 21), stayed eight months, then returned to begin his career.

For 40 seasons now he has cajoled, tended, directed and ministered to various Villanova track teams. He has coached 22 Olympians, 217 IC4A champions, 61 AAU champions, 52 NCAA champions, 14 world record holders...He has made Penn Relays a personal showcase for his runners, dominated Eastern track since the war, earned the admiration of most all and been denied an Olympic coaching position only because he refuses to play the political game....

It is a mixed bag, Jumbo Elliott's methods, an eclectic blend of showmanship, salesmanship, Irish wit, Irish blarney, parental care, parental discipline, instinct and knowledge. "I think the big thing is he takes a genuine interest in the boys in terms of their welfare," says Charlie Jenkins, who won a gold medal at the 1956 Olympics. "You know, it's hard to fool kids nowadays, and when you find someone like Jumbo who is genuinely interested, you respond. And when you respond to Jumbo, who's an excellent coach, you can't help but come out good."

"He really doesn't create a coach-athlete relationship the same way other coaches do," says Eamonn Coghlin. "I feel he coaches and treats his athletes the same way he does business. He runs a high-class business and he deals with us as high-class athletes. He doesn't worry you about all the bull, busting records, being in the top 10, that crap. It's just run your race, do your job that day then move on to the next race. There's no bull. Everything is very honest."

"If he's anything he's a salesman," says Marty Liquori. "He knows how to handle people, how to sell things and he teaches you how to be quick on your feet, how to think on your feet. He realizes the big thing is psychological and is a master at getting you psyched up, getting you mentally prepared. Then by the time you're a senior you have Jumbo's philosophy, so even if he isn't around for a month, you still have that feeling in the air. You have a feeling that just doesn't let you be anything but a winner."....

Too, he is the successful businessman, wealthy, refined, tasteful, the chief executive of Elliott & Frantz, Inc., dealers in heavy equipment. He lives on the Main Line, drives a Cadillac (he received the first 1975 model shipped to Philadelphia), belongs to the selective Squires Country Club, wears custom-made suits and shoes (the latter from England, where the company has a mold of his feet) and plays golf with Bob Hope, Andy Williams, Mike Douglas, Perry Como and Cardinal Krol. Indeed, he helped found a country club in Florida in partnership with Hope and William Ford III and vacations there for two weeks each March....

When they compete at the NCAA Indoors they stay at the Ponchartrain, Detroit's best hotel; other teams stay at Howard Johnson's. When he was recruiting Billy McLoughlin he took him, Liquori, Dave Patrick and Frank Murphy to Mama Leone's on a Friday night; he ignored the long line, claimed reservations he didn't make, demanded a table immediately and received the best in the restaurant.

"Jumbo is always first class in everything he does and that's important," says Liquori. "He would never, never let us go second class because we were the best. In fact, I think he even sometimes dug into his own pocket to treat us as the best.

"This may be the most important thing about him, his being a first-class guy. Most of us want to be first class sooner or later and there's no better way than to associate with someone who is. And traditionally the winners go first class, the losers go second class. So it's all part of his plan to convince us that we're the best. Oh, we might run some bad races, but that's just a temporary thing, the cream will always come to the top. And we're the cream."

Rain falls on this Tuesday afternoon, so Jumbo Elliott moves his team through its routine quickly before Villanova's old, cinder track turns soft and treacherous. That completed, he ambles up to a second-floor office in the fieldhouse, greets his visitor, then turns his attention to the others in the room. There is a word, a smile, a joke for everyone....

During the talk he will laugh often...when he learns what others have said about him, when he realizes what his visitor has heard of him...."I just don't know, I just don't know," Jumbo Elliott says, slowly shaking his head. "I think you have to communicate with them. I think you have to control them. I think I know what basically is the way to train, that they're all individuals and that they're all different...

"Everybody is handled in an individual way. I couldn't treat Brian McElroy like Dick Buerkle like Marty Liquori, they're each different. I don't like to dominate them, but I do dominate them to the point that I control them. For example, if someone would come out with a workout in his head, it could be anything, well, I've been doing it so much that they'll do what I want them to do but in a way that they think that they're doing what's exactly in their head.

"What I like to have them feel is that at the end of four years they know as much about track as I do and that they can go on a track and run and that they're masters of the situation, that they don't have to wait for a coach to say you ran that first quarter three-tenths of a second too fast and carry on to these extremes like some coaches in the past have done. I feel that's ridiculous...."

In summary, Jumbo Elliott's coaching can be described with reasonable validity as that of a man well-trained in Business Administration at Villanova University, and working wholeheartedly within the values and methods of traditional business management and Dale Carnegie's HOW TO WIN FRIENDS AND INFLUENCE PEOPLE. Forced to supplement the $135 he received from Villanova for his first year of coaching, he became a salesman of heavy earth-moving machinery (somehow that's in keeping with his style), and there learned--the hard way--the best methods of selling his product and himself.

He followed this two-way vocational pattern throughout his career. It was far from easy, with many failures and frustrations in early coaching and sales endeavors. But gradually he acquired a more relaxed and self-confident attitude and a sound formula for success in his rapidly expanding sales business and his coaching: (1) Sell a first-class product. (2) Work within the Business, Church and Social System; believe in its ethic, assume its attitudes and ways of getting along, praise it and don't knock it. (3) Work hard at your selling; concentrate your energies so that all distracting and interfering influences are eliminated. Enjoy your golf and your coaching for their own sakes but conduct them in ways that will further your success in business and social life. (4) All aspects of selling should be done with integrity though without qualms as to the more delicate aspects of integrity; balance conscience with effectiveness, sincerity with making the right impression. (5) Demand high-level effort and performance from your associates and helpers but in return give them first-class compensations; by working hard together, first-class rewards for all--for them and for yourself--will be assured. (6) Show yourself and your product, whether machines or athletes; don't waste time-energy in non-productive showcases. (7) Study carefully the consequences of what you do and what you say; work to make those consequences productive. (8) In summary, analyze and understand what is effective and what is not effective, what secures public recognition and what the public ignores; concentrate on the essentials of success, disregard the non-essentials, shun the hindrances.

One suspects that Jumbo had studied--studied carefully--the various books of Dale Carnegie and Norman Vincent Peale (at least in his emphasis on positive thinking, if not in his Protestant theology). Jumbo may well have simulated the big smile and out-going manner of Charles Schwab, the steel magnate so much admired by Carnegie. He had an easy-going joviality in meeting people, especially those he respected and (I suspect) felt he needed. He took pride in his ability to make many friends and influence them toward acceptance of his programs and himself.

Certainly he attained success--success in business as attested by the 100 or more persons he employed and the six-figured gross income, and success in track coaching as attested by 22 Olympians and 217 IC4A champions--two parts of one Whole.

Was all this coldly deliberate? Was it a carefully planned use of a successful track and field program to advertise and make valuable contacts for a profitable business, Elliott & Frantz Sales? Jumbo would deny it--vehemently, and all but his severest critics would agree with him. Note that his athletes (Coghlin, Liquori, Jenkins) spoke of his integrity. "There's no bull; everything is honest." But Jumbo openly admitted such a business value of his talents in golf--one of the best ways of making effective contacts with potential buyers, friends of Villanova track and, not least, the higher echelons of society. At various times he urged his assistant coach, Jim Tuppeny, to take up golf for similar reasons.

But all would agree that the Elliott track program was a close adjunct to the machinery sales business, and was conducted with similarly effective managerial methods and policies. Certainly he used his track eminence to gain friends and helpers, bulldozing track promoters into giving what he needed. I have a built-in reaction against human bulldozers of all kinds. Frankly, Jumbo and I seldom agreed on anything. When I was director of the *Philadelphia Inquirer Games*, Jumbo insisted that he must have some 35 or more tickets for his friends and the upper hierarchy at Villanova. I, just as adamantly, refused, "I'll treat you fairly-- just as I do every other college coach in the Philadelphia area, and none of them even ask

61

for tickets!" But Jumbo won, I discovered later, by going upstairs to higher *Inquirer* personnel.

Above all, Jumbo was hardworking, never idle. His daily schedule found him at the sales office--early of course. If out of the office, a bleeper system kept him in constant touch with phone calls related to either track or saleswork. He was usually at the Villanova track from three to six P.M. His assistant coach took care of the early or late comers. He was home most evenings but was busy on the telephone--with track and business--until late in the evening.

What were the essentials of the Elliott program of track and field? First, he emphasized competitions that had spectator appeal; minimized those that did not. Second, he and his assistants recruited first-class athletes--mostly runners since these fitted best into the chosen competition. The more mature runners of Ireland, Scotland, England accepted his invitations to become student-athletes gladly, especially after his masterful job in helping Ron Delany rise to the 1956 Olympic 1500-meter championship--perhaps a score of them altogether. But he also had remarkable success with more local talents such as Charley Jenkins and Marty Liquori and such early unknowns as Pat Traynor and Dick Buerkle.

Third, acceptance of his authority and his hard-work training programs. In the early years this took the form of demands, and acceptance was not always easy since there was no proof of his effectiveness. Those were rough years, rough on Jumbo and rough on at least some of his athletes. But with the gradually acquired aura of success and competence, his dominance became less obvious. "I've been doing it so much (successful coaching) that they'll do what I want them to do but in a way that they think they're doing exactly what's in their own heads." Gradually the team attitude became, "Go along with Jumbo; he'll treat you right and your personal success will be certain." Once such general acceptance was attained, everyone prospered. The burden of doubt was removed from the runners' shoulders; they were more relaxed in training and in competition; high spirits, joking even poking fun at the coach became part of the training atmosphere, though never publicly to the detriment of coaching authority.

Fourth, work with each athlete as an individual, treat him fairly, make him no promises you will not fulfill, conduct all aspects of his relationship to your program on a first-class basis, show him off to the public in a first-class way. I first became aware of Jumbo's men through their expensive Villanova sports jackets, their clean overall appearance, their relatively sophisticated manner when meeting the public and especially the news media. Ron Delany, with his delightful Irish brogue and wit, Charlie Jenkins and Marty Liquori were perfect examples of this. Not only did they sell the Elliott public; equally important, they sold other first-class prospects on the advantages of running in the Elliott track program.

And finally, eliminate inner and outer conflicts by co-ordinating the track program with other life activities and interests. For the track-team members, balance the demands of strenuous training with those of academic and some measure of social life. For Elliott, co-ordinate all interests and activities--track and field, business, home, golf, social life--so that they all contribute to the main life goal--success within Elliott's assessment of the System.

ROBERT L. "DINK" TEMPLETON--STANFORD UNIVERSITY (1921-1939), SAN FRANCISCO TRACK CLUB (1944-1962).
Dink Templeton was undoubtedly America's all-time controversial track coach, as well as one of her few authentic track and field geniuses. On the one hand, he was far ahead of his time in field-event techniques, and hard-training methods. And in middle-distance running he openly advocated mileage and year-round training in violation of the widespread concern for over-work that "burned out" runners. But on the other hand, Templeton felt a deep contempt for incompetence and ignorance in high places, especially when dressed in tails and high hat, and an unstoppable urge to express that contempt regardless of the solemnity of the occasion. Add a rasping, far-carrying voice and a penchant for gutter profanity, and it's easy to understand why the number of his many friends was equalled by his enemies.

Templeton was appointed head coach at Stanford at the age of 24, a "boy-wonder." Stanford's track tradition was based mostly on a few champions (Horine, high jump, 1912; Hartranft, discus, 1925), but between 1927 and 1934 Templeton teams won first or second in all the Eastern ICAAAA Championships and three NCAA Championships. Stanford was known for its high academic requirements, but was not averse to well-controlled recruiting. Dink's close friendship with such men as Big Jim Reynolds, number one Stanford proselyte, Douglas Fairbanks, Gene Tunney, Charlie Paddock, and Ty Cobb was no handicap. With Stanford's great reputation and beautiful small-town campus, what track man of talent and good grades would refuse the opportunity?

Most tragically, in 1931 Dink was struck by acute arthritis. Repeated operations left him "a burned-out shell." In 1936 one doctor gave him only one year to live. He survived; in fact lived to the age of 65, but he took to drugs, alcohol and pep pills to ease pain and what could be called a sickness of soul, and from this he never fully recovered. All this, combined with his expressed disrespect for those in authority (at Stanford as anywhere), led to his being fired in 1939, at the age of 42 when he was just coming into his own as a coach--locally, nationally and internationally.

His mind approached almost total breakdown. For months he was at Veterans' Hospital in Palo Alto under the care of Dr. Morris Kirksey, psychiatrist, Olympic sprinter, and Stanford teammate. But Bud Spencer tells it better,[1]

> To face adversity and despair is not enough. To win the struggle, to continue despite the scars, to bring alive again the spark of vanquished youth, to emerge from the snake pit a greater individual--there is the bone, blood and heart of a truly great man.

> From 1942 to 1962, a mellowed Templeton, still possessing a superlative analytical mind, photographic eye, understanding heart, verbal needle and gravel voice...continued to guide thousands....He lived 30 years beyond his first readied obituary, leaving behind a rich tradition that will live as long as men run, jump and throw.

Brutus Hamilton, rival coach at California, wrote the following as part of a foreword to Spencer's biography:[2]

> In a sense Dink Templeton will never be dead for he shall always be remembered--by his vibrant personality, his willingness to defy tradition, his refusal to accept stodgy thinking and his keen perception of the laws of scientific motion as applied to mechanics. . . . There will never be a second Templeton. . . .Never another like him. . . .

> Dink was fiery, explosive, exciting and restless, and he brought a fresh and original approach to coaching. Behind his crusading unique personality was a brilliant, impatient, scientific mind, and he must be considered the pioneer in modern methods and the forerunner of present-day techniques. In his 18 years at Stanford he fought with a vitality and knowingness that were overwhelmingly lacking up to his time. . . .

> His actions were strikingly those of a non-conformist. . . .His continued revolt against the A.A.U., the American Olympic officials, archaic methods and traditions were a natural outlet for this apostasy. He had all the outward appearance of an unbending tyrant but deep inside he was as soft as oatmeal gruel. . . .My boys at California loved him and respected him almost as much as his own boys at Stanford or all those who came to him for patient and kind words of wisdom.

> As a track and field teacher he knew every phase of his subject. He was an articulate, purposeful teacher with a perceptive eye and an analytical mind. He. . .was able to inspire each man to realize unplumbed depths. He took interest in young men beyond their ability to run or jump or throw. . . .

> Dink's longest, toughest crusade was to convert the hardened philistines of the "burned out" school into believing full athletic attainment can only be realized by back-breaking, muscle-aching, brain-wearying work. 'There is no short-cut to supremacy; nothing comes out you don't first put in,' he always preached.

---

[1] Bud Spencer, *HIGH ABOVE THE OLYMPIANS*, Los Altos, Calif.: Tafnews Press, 1966, p. 20.

[2] Bud Spencer, *ibid.*, p. i.

Keep in mind that these words were written by a rival coach, one who experienced both defeat and victory in his meets with Dink's Stanford teams. It is a tribute to Hamilton's ability to judge others without prejudice, but even more, to Templeton's power to influence men. Frankly, though I knew Dink only briefly--on the 1928 Olympic boat, in coaching clinics, and when watching him coach his Stanford men on three or four occasions--I do not share Hamilton's opinion 100 percent. Dink's inside may have been as soft as oatmeal gruel, but his outside--his hard eyes, his cutting voice, his constant swearing, smoking, drinking, his unnecessary belittlement of those lacking his brain power and insight--all this weighed heavily on the negative side of my scale for judging coaches. For example, Templeton was justified in disagreeing with Head Olympic Coach, Lawson Robertson's article on the dangers of men being burned out by over-work, a Saturday Evening Post article that had national influence. But to evidence his scorn a year later at a dinner honoring Robertson was in my judgment inexcusably arrogant and insolent. Bud Spencer, Dink's great quartermiler in the late 20s, who idolized his coach, reported the incident gleefully,[1]

Dink's turn came to pay homage . . . ."Robbie, why in hell did you have to write such crap? . . . I don't begrudge your literary efforts or a natural Scotchman's grasp to pick up an extra buck for something that did not smell exactly like Paris in the spring. Jesus Christ, it set track and field back 50 years. But what really gives me a pain in the fantail is that your pack of jackasses at Penn can't read. But my gang at Stanford can, and you ruined half my track team.

Spencer summarized Templeton's personality as follows[2]

During his active coaching days he was as unpredictable as he was flamboyant; he was as ornery as he was masterful in his coaching. A creature with mischief in his soul, he was warm, considerate and gentle to those who hungered for a crumb of understanding. Although a belligerent who dearly loved to knock over stuffed shirts and raise merry hell, he could, at times, show the restrained wisdom and charm of an old world priest.

Sometimes Templeton could be as cold as a razor, absolutely devoid of emotion, but it was a designed act to shoo away complacency, deadly evil of competitive athletics. He was hard outside--a thoroughbred heart doesn't scream and cry every time it's pinched-- but soft as peach fuzz inside, and he could transform tears of despair into new hope.

BUD WINTER--SAN JOSE STATE UNIVERSITY (1940-1970).
The following paragraphs were all written by Dick Drake[3] for Track & Field News,

Bud Winter has an ego. Not a bloated one, mind you, but should the occasion arise, he can accommodate interested listeners with quite a success story in 25 years at San Jose State. He has aided the careers of 15 Olympic participants, including three gold medal- lists and a half dozen world record holders (with about 25 records). Winter's success with sprinters is world renowned.

"Bud is a remarkably different coach," assesses Dr. Bruce Ogilvie, one of the world's foremost sports psychologists..."We have learned considerable about coaches from their personality profiles. They are very strong in the drive motives: tremendously ambitious, highly organized, high sense of right and wrong, highly aggressive and tough-minded. They have an intact personality. We find them highly conservative--especially in politics, economics and religion. Power and control are important to them....

"Bud's value system is not directed toward these conservative dimensions. He's much more open; he's a laissez-faire sort of guy....On those aspects of track which Bud con- siders important, he is obsessed and totally committed. But through it all, he remains

---

[1]Ibid., p. 10.

[2]Ibid., p. 44.

[3]Dick Drake, "Laissez-Faire Winter," Track & Field News, 11, June 1969, 1.

open, flexible, and willing to explore. He has been a great innovator....

"Bud describes his approach as 'common sense.' While he's not given to over-reaction, he has a strong sense of fairness to guide him in making judgments. 'We get the job done by kidding and cajoling the athletes along. If purple vitamin milk will make them run faster, then we give it to them. But open communication remains the most important element in our coaching. The greatest technician won't be more than a fair coach if he can't impart his knowledge and feelings. There are occasions to be firm but a common sense approach is definitely the answer to all problems.'

Bud is obsessed with track," comments Ogilvie, "In his total commitment, he is living in an insular world. He doesn't let other things intrude very much. Perhaps this is what it takes to be exceptional. His approach is intuitive. He gets a feeling and carries it through. He really doesn't think beyond the strategy of the moment. But Bud can focus down on the unique individual aspects of a performance. It's as though he has some special insight, and he communicates this with high confidence and emotional commitment."

Art Simburg, close observer of the San Jose track scene, elaborated, "Bud is constantly observing and commenting on an athlete's style and method. He zeroes in on special problems, and gets the athlete to think about what he is doing. At the Olympics, Tom Smith hadn't seen Bud until one day he walked up in his hunting cap, fishing shirt and hush puppies. Tom wanted to laugh. But the feeling all turned to inner warmth because he knew that Mr. Knowledge with the special scret would have the answers. He went through the high knee drills and his rhythm came back. And Tom felt confident again."

Bud is at his best in a one-to-one personal relationship. And it's this intense personal interest in individuals and his drive to help and be loved by all his athletes that leads him to spread himself thin. On the surface he appears disorganized. The clutter of papers on his desk and in his car support this conception. Little details don't bother him if they're not directly related to an individual athlete. . . .

Says Ogilvie, "Bud would be an extremely difficult man to work under. As much affection as I have for him, I could never work on a team with him as assistant coaches do. Of all his creative skills, organization is the most difficult for him to come by. He has a chaotic approach. Even if he eventually does get the job done, he spreads himself all over the place. He simply cannot delegate responsibility.

"Loyalty is extremely important to Bud, and the violation of this trust breaks him up. He can't understand it, and yet in his relationships with people he does tricky things, and does not realize why they may not respond to his ideas as innovations. I have seen sophisticated young men like Tommie Smith and John Carlos smiling about being taken in. I would say that there is a humorous, gentle disrespect for Bud."

Bud relies heavily on gimmickry, key phrases, tricks and clever motivating forces to get his job done. And for the most part they seem to be effective. He is interested in the unusual, and perhaps this explains why he will permit more differences than most coaches. His gimmickry is probably most useful with the young, unsophisticated athletes, according to Ogilvie. Imagine the psychic effect as he communicates his 'Rocket Sprint Start' or his 'Jet Sprint Relay Pass.' . . .

And then there's the matter of motivation. Bud challenges his athletes with 'Get something out of the coach.' He posts on the bulletin board the marks athletes must achieve to win milkshakes from the coach. Each time an athlete improves a San Jose State school record he is entitled to a German chocolate cake which Bud's wife bakes at the end of the season.

Bud's involvement in activities and organizations, and his inventiveness are impressive. He was responsible for creating the State Department track tours of goodwill throughout the world; Ogilvie credits Bud with being the first coach in America willing to let Ogilvie 'tamper' with his athletes. "Until then, everybody said, 'Oh God, I wouldn't let a headshrinker near the club.'" He was instrumental in creating, developing and testing the track surface we now know as Tartan. His four books on sprinting and high jumping have been top sellers at Track and Field News. He has a color film on sprinting that has been widely distributed. He was the organizer of the first International Coaches Clinic at Berkeley, California, 1956. He has conducted clinics in India, Burman, Rumania, Ceylon, Finland, Sweden, and Denmark.

TOM BOTTS -- UNIVERSITY OF MISSOURI (1945-1972).

The following article concerning Coach Tom Botts of Missouri appeared in the Kansas City *Star*, February 1, 1972:

It fits the Tom Botts way of doing business that he will retire before a light flashes on a computer, signifying that his working years have run out. The man who has been the head track coach at Missouri for 27 seasons will call it a career this spring because he--not somebody else--thinks it is the right thing to do.

There is no pressure on Tom Botts--not from the university administration, not from Sparky Stalcup (the athletic director), not from Tiger alumni. Tom Botts is a happy man, a man at peace with his world. And he is a healthy man--one issued top-quality equipment by the Good Lord, one who has taken care of what the Lord gave him. He neither looks nor acts nor feels his 67 years.

If he followed the accepted course, he would stay on for another three years. But he says, "For the good of all concerned, I think it's time to change. I felt it was time to drop out last year, but I did want to coach one year in the new field house." He says it apologetically, almost as if it were an admission of selfishness.

Then he adds, "And I'll say it is a disappointment that I didn't coach there. (Construction still is not completed.) But I made up my mind last fall that I would step out before I'm forced out. And I'll enjoy watching athletic events in the new facility."

His Day Starts Early and Ends Late.
Botts says he is just as willing to work as ever, which means he arrives at Brewer Field House (to go through his daily 2-mile run-jog workout) while the rest of the city sleeps and stays until after most have called it a day. He says, "Coaching is no great strain on me. The only thing I notice is that the hurdles are getting a little heavier--and I want to carry my share."

This also fits Tom Botts. Never has he asked more of his athletes than he was willing to give. He coaches by example, not by demand. As Bob Teel, the M.U. assistant since 1961 and the man who will replace Botts, puts it: "He believes in a minimum training program, hoping the athlete will go beyond it. Now his minimum isn't easy--but Coach won't drive anybody. He thinks the athlete must push himself."

And it works. Missouri has fielded good track teams under Tom Botts--winning the league outdoor title four times, the indoor crown four times, the cross-country championship twice. The Tigers even took the national indoor title in 1964. No one appreciates winning more than Botts, so championship squads rank high on his good-memory list.

But when Tom Botts lists the greatest track accomplishment by M.U. during his time at the helm, he goes to a 4-man squad winning the 1964 Texas Relays team trophy. And he didn't see it. Teel took the four to Texas; Botts stayed home for a dual meet.

There have been great track men in these 27 seasons, men who exemplified what Botts values so highly, those who combined attitude and performance. He doesn't like to name names--beyond Robin Lingle, Dick Ault and Teel--because there might be an omission. But he does want this on the record: "Some I remember most fondly have not been great performers." That means attitude ranks first with Botts, just as getting an education ranks above getting a spot on the track team.

He Goes Beyond Coaching.
What it all means is this: Tom Botts is more than a coach. He is an honest man, a genuinely humble man, a genuinely good man. As one of his former standouts put it: "He didn't stop at showing us how to run. He showed us how to live."

Perhaps the best expression of Bott's imprint on his pupils is this: In 1966, when

Botts completed his 25th season at M.U. (and that included three years as an assist-ant), his former athletes came back to M.U. to honor him. There were 120 contacted, and 93 responded--with spoken tribute, with money enough to buy him a new car. That stunned those in the university's business school, those who know a 2 percent response to a solicitation is average and that a 20 percent reply is the ultimate. For Botts, it was better than 75 percent.

And when Botts showed up at a cocktail party before that dinner in his honor, men in their 40s put down cigarettes and drinks. They didn't want to disappoint him. And one who dropped his smoke was a former high jumper who had been dismissed from the squad--for smoking just before a meet in which his sure points could have been the difference between winning and losing.

It is a stern code that Tom Botts follows. Unfortunately, it is one that many con-sider out-of-date. It is one that will not let him knock any fragment of the colle-giate athletic system--not even recruiting that rubs against his grain.

It is a code so strict he will not follow the accepted pattern for retired coaches, writing a book. As he says, "I would not want to impose my ideas on anyone."[1]

The Dedication in the printed program of the 1954 National AAU Championships held in St. Louis, Missouri was to Tom Botts. It read (in part and with my own minor changes--JKD) as follows:

> A Coach of men through excellence in techniques and methods,
> A gentleman proud to be in the coaching profession,
> A Christian who knows no substitute for principle,
> "And when we youngsters reach the evening of our day,
> And gray a little or bald a bit, we still will say,
> 'There was a man!
> A man who coached the right way to run and jump and throw
> While practicing his own right way to live.'"

WILLIAM J. "Bill" BOWERMAN--UNIVERSITY OF OREGON (1947-1973), MEDFORD HIGH SCHOOL (1933-1947)
ROBERT "Bob" NEWLAND--MEDFORD HIGH SCHOOL (1947-1957), NORTH EUGENE HIGH SCHOOL (1957--)

I have placed these two coaches, Bill Bowerman and Bob Newland, under one heading deliberately, not that they were alike in personality, but that together they formed a unified coaching system, a system that involved all the essential subsystems of local community, lower-grade schools, state-wide feeder groups; all with mutually helpful relationships and a complete absence of hard-sell recruiting.

Both men had charisma, though in quite different ways. Bill Bowerman was big and impres-sive: a rough-hewn outdoors face, well over six feet tall, large bones and frame, a low-toned, slow-speaking voice. One tended to listen when he spoke, to believe what he said, and to do without question what he advised doing. Prefontaine, the great long distance runner of the early 70s so tragically killed before reaching his potential, was once quoted as saying, "I'll never forget the first time I met him. I felt like I was talking to God. I still do."

This all suggests authority, and rightly so. But Bill always considered himself a teacher and instructor, not a director of men. In fact he actually discouraged reference to himself as coach, in reaction to his own unfortunate experience as an athlete with an authoritarian coach. In the preface to his textbook, *COACHING TRACK AND FIELD* (title probably chosen by his publisher), he uses the words "teacher" or "teacher-coach" 10 times; "coach" only three times. For example, he writes, "I am proud to be a teacher and to be associated with a group of men and women who, on the whole, love youngsters and do not care a whoop if their critics...cause them to be underpaid, underestimated, and overworked."

Bowerman was a major with the 10th Mountain Division during World War II that fought so successfully in Italy, and somehow that fits. As does his love for the out-of-doors in all

---

[1]Dick Wade, "Talk of the Times," *Kansas City Star*, Feb. 1, 1972.

its aspects. His ranch-style home is on 70 acres of a mountain above the McKenzie River, a great terrain for fishing and hunting, and incidentally for hiking and running.   In summary, the man, his personal and coaching experience, his life style were all of one piece, of one well integrated whole.

His coaching success was great, both in high school and college. Prior to Bill's coming, the University of Oregon track team record was only fair; for example in 1946 they scored no points in the NCAA Championships. Under Bowerman, Oregon won the NCAA team title in 1962, 1964, 1965, and was second in 1961 and 1967. Small wonder he was selected as Head Track and Field Coach for the 1972 Olympic team. Things did not go smoothly at Munich. Not only was the international situation chaotic, a number of our own athletes[1] felt strongly that they could skipper their own boat, and Bill as ship's captain, was not one to hold the steering wheel lightly. In Oregon his benevolent authority during some 40 years of coaching had been accepted without question. But these Olympians challenged everything. Bill spoke out bluntly and openly, and that didn't endear him to these athletes or to the top brass of our Olympic staff. For a while the water was rough but Bowerman maintained control and in the end the respect of most everyone.

But when trying to judge Bill Bowerman's stature as a coach, one tends to think first of his total surround or system, of the Oregon environment--physical and social, much as one does when judging the great running tradition of Finland. The Oregon country is varied in terrain, consistently cool, a perfect set-up for the fartlek type of training that Bowerman emphasizes. The town of Eugene is nuts about running. I once stopped at a gas station there, whose attendant expressed more enthusiasm and personal concern for the track team than those in other states do for football or basketball. And this enthusiasm extends throughout the state of Oregon. Eugene is called "the jogging capital of the world," the initiator of the present American jogging craze.

When the total situation is positive, effective coaching and winning come easily and naturally, with few of the high pressure methods and inducements so often used in more negative situations.   Joe Henderson[2] makes this point very clear:

Bowerman wouldn't admit to having any "secret method" of turning out distance men... He talks openly about his methods and there's little new or startling about them. It's clear that the man and the total distance environment at Oregon are as responsible as the training methods for one of the longest-running success stories in track.

It begins with recruiting--but not the high pressure kind of selling so commonly associated with college athletics. Bowerman neither likes it nor seems to need it. "I'm opposed to all-out recruiting," he says, "I don't like to get into the rat race. If I hear from someone I know, or preferably, if an athlete will write to me, I will do my best to interpret the University of Oregon's educational opportunity and athletic objectives to him....Of the present team, of the 21 who now make the U.S. (best performance) charts, only four ever appeared among the high school listings."

Once in school, the athletes become submerged in an atmosphere of infectious distance running enthusiasm. It's present in their coach who logs several miles of jogging himself each day. They're surrounded by a throng of talented team-mates. They're in a community with thousands of run-for-fun-and-fitness addicts. The newspapers, radio, and TV devote an extraordinary amount of space and time to track. In brief, the Oregon runners feel important and appreciated....

Runner Kvalheim tells about his training. "I think one of the secrets of Oregon's success in distance running is the way we enjoy our training together as a group of buddies. In the fall and winter, we take off every Sunday for a long run up in the mountains or down at the beach, having a lot of fun although training hard. After the run we often drop by Bill's house up on the hills to get served juice by Mrs. Bowerman. Bill is putting

---

[1]Read Vince Matthew with Neil Amdur, *MY RACE BE WON*, New York: Charterhouse, 1974, p.303ff.

[2]Joe Henderson, "A Coach and a Tradition," *Track & Field News*, I June 1968, 20.

a lot of emphasis on the importance of fartlek runs. This way of training makes the whole thing more pleasant than running intervals day after day on the track."

But as first stated, Bill Bowerman's story is only half told if confined to his own person. Beyond any coach I have known, his was one of mutually supportive relationships, of cooperation with and help from so many persons. For example, Bob Newland.

<u>Bob Newland</u>. During the Bowerman era, Medford High won four State High School team titles. During Bob Newland's ten years, Medford won nine team firsts and one second. How? The Bowerman tradition of success had a strong carry-over. Hard work on a year-round basis was accepted by the boys, the school and the community. But most important, Newland practiced organization in all its aspects.

<u>Organization within the school</u>. Every boy in the physical education classes was screened by use of the John Core 5-Star Test. The school paper emphasized track items. A bulletin board included a "Profile of Champions" with pictures and comments on team members--varsity and JV. A trophy case showed track records--school, state, national. During the noon hour, track films (Olympic and national) were shown. The track squad ran between 65 and 80 with everyone encouraged to stay with the sport. Faculty joined townspeople as officials at track meets. Service clubs sponsored meets such as the Kiwanis Relays and the Lions Invitational. In response to related questions, Bob Newland wrote me that,

Our home was open at all times to our athletes, and they frequently dropped in for conversation or a pre-meet meal. We considered them a part of our family and so we were able to discuss problems openly and in general enjoy one another. The athletes get to feel the coach is interested in them personally apart from athletics. As Bill Bowerman said so often, "Remember you are a student first, an athlete second."

<u>Organization among Feeder Schools</u>. This was the primary reason for Medford's success. Newland believed the foundation of the high school track program was based on that within the Medford Public School System. He began by meeting and reaching agreement among all public school teachers interested in track. To encourage as many youngsters as possible to compete, grade school competition was divided into three classes--A, B, C--on an age-height-weight scale. To further uniform methods, a respected track textbook was given free to each grade school and junior high coach, along with a 31-page brochure, TRACK AND FIELD-THE MEDFORD SYSTEM. This was a manual on how to create interest, discover prospects, organize a program, conduct track meets, with a hint as to recommended methods and techniques. Most important, this manual was officially issued by the Medford Public Schools System with an Introduction by the Medford Superintendent of Schools. This added authority to its teaching values. Track clinics began at the 5th-grade level. On call, "star" high school track men would be sent to a grade or junior high school to work with the young athletes; this was found very effective.

Another valuable device was a card-file system whereby the grade school coach started a card for each athlete giving all vital information including performances and personal evaluations by the coach. These cards were passed along as the athlete progressed in school, and gave important background information, especially if a coach wanted to check out why an athlete had failed to report for track.

<u>North Eugene High School</u>. When Newland came to North Eugene High School in 1957 as vice-principal, he was asked to continue being active in track and field. He immediately re-established his close relationship with Bill Bowerman and, working together, they started their age-group all-comers summer track program that became the model for the United States Track Federation's National Age-Group Program.[1] This had the strong support of the University of Oregon and the Oregon Track Club. Newland wrote me,

While the Oregon Track Club did help all high school track programs in the area, that was not its full intent. We wanted to enlist community support for the University track and field program as well as provide a great physical fitness and fun program for the Greater Eugene community.

---

[1] Bob Newland, "Organizing Summer Track Meets," USTCA QUARTERLY, Vol. 64, No. 3, 1964 and Vol. 67, No. 2, 1967.

That first summer, 1957, they had five two-day meets with about 75 athletes at each meet. In 1975, between 500 and 600 competed in the program. Oregon Track Club athletes *and their wives* (most important!) did most of the officiating. But prominent people also help, as when the Mayor of Eugene officiated the high jump and Dick Fosbury put up the cross-bar.

"At first," says Newland, "we had age-group divisions like six-and-under, 7-10 and 11-13, but that was too wide a spread. All the older kids were winning. Since we wanted to encourage as many as possible, we narrowed the grouping to two years. That meant lots more ribbons which pleased everybody. Even Dyrol Burleson, Olympic 1500 place-winner, came up for his ribbon....

Thursday meets are a wonder to behold--swarms of children running, jumping, putting the shot; swarms of parents with stopwatches on the field, grinning maniacally or shouting themselves hoarse from the bleachers....

During the girls' four-and-under race, the shouting from the stands is tremendous. Then the leader stops one foot from the finish, shyly unwilling to break the string.[1]

Add to this summer-long program a series of all-comers long-distance runs called Butte-to-Butte, of which there are many in the area, with 300 or more competitors, and we begin to understand what Newland and Bowerman mean by trying to establish wide and warm relationships.

I have said nothing of Bob Newland's leadership as personal charisma. That's not the word unless we can define charisma in terms of long hours and hard work. Add to his full-time job as vice-principal and track coach, the following activities: Director National Collegiate Track Championships--1962, 1964, 1972. Assistant Manager U.S. Olympic Team, 1976. Director National AAU Track Championships, 1971. Director Portland Indoor Invitational, 1961-1972. Track and Field Chairman Oregon AAU, 8 years. Track and Field Chairman, USTFF, 6 years. Director U.S. Olympic Final Trials, Eugene, 1972. Guest Lecturer, First International Track & Field Coaches Association Clinic, Berkeley, Cal., 1956. President Oregon High School Teachers Association, President University of Oregon Dads' Club, 1970.

Small wonder that Bob wrote me,

Coaching hours are hard to measure. When you aren't writing letters to outstanding coaches and athletes for information, making up workouts for individual athletes, publicizing your program, writing lesson plans for classes, instructing classes, we may be assisting in either football or basketball. Sometimes it seems the day never ends. Many times in the winter months I did not get home until 9 or 10 in the evening.

WAYNE VANDENBURG--UNIVERSITY OF TEXAS EL PASO (1967-1972).

Under the head of "Fastest Super-Mouth in the West," Bert Nelson (*Track & Field News*, I June 1972, 20) wrote the following concerning Wayne Vandenburg,

To use his favorite word, Wayne Vandenburg is a "super" promoter. The young coach at the El Paso campus of the University of Texas may, in fact, have no peers among track and field coaches when it comes to promoting their sport.

It wasn't long after he entered college coaching, as assistant coach at the University of New Mexico in 1965, that Vandy started making a national reputation. A virtually non-stop talker, he soon became known as the fastest mouth in the west. Soon it was realized that a lot of knowledge backed up the flow of words and Wayne was recognized as one of the country's best informed experts on the subject of high school track and field. Track & Field News' far-reaching string of prep correspondents occasionally failed to come up with details of schoolboy athletic feats that Vandenburg could rattle off without pause.

It wasn't long before that knowledge and that gift of gab were put to practical use. Recruiting it was called, and it seemed he was born for the game. He got his chance to

---

[1]Bobbie Conlan Moore, "A Fever Running Through the Streets," *Sports Illustrated*, August 23, 1974, p. 26.

prove it early, being named head track coach of the University of Texas at El Paso.

To some it must have seemed an early end of a promising career. Texas El Paso was nowhere as a track school. Remotely located on the high desert in the western tip of Texas, UTEP wasn't likely to appeal to many hotshots from the rest of the sprawling state, let alone to the sophisticates of either coast. Money was scarce. Team support was close to non-existent. And the physical facilities were less than super.

Was Vandenburg worried? Not to listen to him. No sooner was the job his than he unabashedly admitted "my goal is to win an NCAA title." The laughter could be heard from Los Angeles to Eugene to Philadelphia, but it was doubtful the brash 25-year-old was listening. He was too busy talking--and recruiting.

A short two years later the laughter abruptly ceased. The impossible had happened. UTEP had its NCAA title. Villanova, winner for the past three years, surrendered its cross-country throne to the Texas upstarts. But it wasn't really a Texas team, for of the seven runners three were Australians and a fourth was English. That's capital R Recruiting, and from then on Wayne Vandenburg has been recognized, and feared, as the equal if not the superior of the country's track recruiters.

There are those who say Vandy recruited a little too hard. His early track squads were hastily patched together congregations which included unknown frosh, transfers from other schools and second-chance drop-outs. There were some who probably shouldn't have been in college and some who definitely weren't suited for UTEP. The predictable result was trouble and El Paso had it. There was an official NCAA reprimand and a number of athletes, headed by superstar Bob Beamon, departed.

Pausing only long enough to digest his lesson, a mellowing, maturing Vandenburg began to build on a more solid base. UTEP became firmly established as a track power on the basis of two fifths and a sixth in the NCAA outdoor meet and a second indoors. This year, the Miners, whose coach actually is talking a little less and listening more, have a real shot at the big bauble. They have a fast, deep sprint squad capable of scoring well in five events, a double-threat in Fred DeBernardi, and a lot of others who could get in the money, including, believe it or not, two hammer throwers.

Hammer throwers in El Paso? You bet. And in that unlikely situation is found two of the keys to Vandenburg's success. Peter Farmer hails from far away Sydney, Australia, one more proof of Vandy's unquestioned recruiting ability. But it takes more than recruiting to take a 19-year-old freshman from 195-6 to 220-plus in one season. Or to take the other ball-and-chainer, Pryor Nunn, from the 130-feet he threw last spring as a newly converted discusman to the 195-footer he is today.

But the greatest coach in the world is helpless without material and recruiting long has been known as the name of the US collegiate game. And that is where Vandenburg excels. Of the 48 names in the 1972 press book, only 12 are from Texas, including seven locals from El Paso. Seven foreign countries furnish 14 athletes, including six from Australia alone. New York and California contribute seven and six squad members and the rest are scattered among five other states. That is indeed super promotion.

But super promoter Wayne Vandenburg hasn't earned the title on recruiting alone. To his everlasting credit, he cares, really cares, about track. It's a love with him. And he promotes it.

Item. He's the only track coach I know to have his own TV program "The Wayne Vandenburg Track Show" is aired for a half-hour weekly.

Item. UTEP put up only half the $120,000 cost of the new Tartan track. So Vandy promoted the rest. They got an eight lane Tartan track, complete with field event run-ups.

Item. It takes help to dig up that kind of money, and the additional funds needed for grants and other expenses. So Wayne promoted the El Paso Amateur Track & Field Association and the El Paso Track & Field Officials' Association, which is a division of the former. The latter group has 117 men, each of whom not only bought a handsome uniform at $85 each and worked to become competent officials, but gave their time and energies to promoting track in the El Paso area.

Item. A first-class team deserves first-class competition, and so the 6-2, 200-pound coach put together (an extensive) 1972 home schedule, beginning Feb. 26 and ending May 22...

Item. Such a schedule deserves fan support, requiring promotion. So two large, color posters...were printed by Coors Beer and distributed to 1100 Coors' outlets. El Paso Natural Gas came through with 12,000 folders....Two local gas chains contributed 5000 bumper stickers. Television stations produced 20-, 30-, and 60-second spots over an eight week period and radio did its part. All hammered away at the "Debut '72" theme.

Item. There was no judges stand. So when Wayne spotted some airplane loading ramps no longer needed by El Paso's new terminal, the result was inevitable and the highly suitable stand is in action today....

Item. Not content with a "super facility" he touts as one of the best in the country, Vandy has complete plans for $108,000 worth of electric scoreboard and electronic timing capacity and is on his way to promoting it.

Item. There is more to track than intercollegiate competition and, wanting the best, the hard-working coach created the El Paso Invitational last year. Nearly blown out of the stadium by a dust storm the natives still brag about, Vandy was undeterred. This year the weather was great, the field was super, and the crowd was disappointingly small. The meet took a bath that could cost as much as $10,000. But the true promoter never quits, and within hours Wayne was vowing to come back with another super winner.

Item. Attracting class athletes to an invitational meet, particularly when it's in far-off El Paso, is a promotional art in itself. So Vandenburg laid on the hospitality and provided prizes the likes of which may not have been seen in this country. To the winner went AM-FM cassette recorders, while second placers got AM-FM digital clock radios, and third-placers won AM-FM transistor pocket radios. Each placer received a pair of double-knit slacks. And all took home unique El Paso Invitational plaques. Created by Tiny Barcena, a former track coach and active member of the booster club, the plaques are works of art and would be more than satisfactory prizes themselves. An 11 inch casting featuring the Aztec sun calendar is mounted on a hand carved wooden base 16 inches in diameter. Together, they emphasize the cultural blend that exists in El Paso, the largest American city on the Mexican border. The prizes were promoted, of course. Each event sponsor paid $150 for the privilege, items were purchased at wholesale or less and one sponsor, Chico's Tacos to be exact, came through with a cool $1000.

How and why does this friendly, enthusiastic father of two do it? The question is answered in the UTEP press book: "The secret to Vandenburg's success is work, and here's how he reflects on the subject: 'I like a situation where you never get caught up, no matter how hard you work. So you go at it as hard as you can, as long as you can. You achieve results, but you're never really satisfied, because you know you could have always done more.' He's a high pressure, constant motion man who lives and dies track."

Never stopping, never satisfied, Vandy is even now preparing his talented squad for that NCAA challenge, winding up the finishing touches on a recruiting campaign that already has a flock of goodies headed for Vandytown, planning landscaping for the stadium, and, undoubtedly, working on a super promotion or two.

There is a sequel to this. In November 1972, Vandy[1] was fired by the UTEP athletic director for flagrant violations of university authority and rules. In 1975, UTEP, under its new coach, Ted Banks, won the NCAA team title in indoor and outdoor track as well as cross-country. No school had ever done that before. In 1980, UTEP won the NCAA indoor title with a record 72 points. Sixty four of these were scored by men from seven foreign countries, most of whom

---

[1]"Successful El Paso Coach Vandenburg Fired," *Track & Field News*, Box 296, Los Altos, Cal., 19422, December 1972, p. 27.

were over 21 years of age; two over 27. It seems clear that Vandenburg's excesses in promotion were really quite in keeping with UTEP's belief in winning as the main, if not the only, end.

EDWARD M. "Ted" HAYDON--UNIVERSITY OF CHICAGO TRACK CLUB (1950--).
Ted Haydon's primary qualification as a "coach of unusual interest" is his role as originator, organizer, money-raiser, locker room supervisor, track and pit raker, program editor, father confessor, and--oh yes--coach, humorist and good friend of the University of Chicago Track Club.

That's both a unique and important qualification. In various talks and papers,[1] I have described his program--one that allows non-college athletes of any age or sex or talent to have the advantages of college facilities and coaching for year-round training and competition--as the most significant of the past 50 years in its potential for improvement of our national program of track and field. Why was it so significant? In brief, because this was the first longtime effort to successfully combine our shamefully weak club program with our outstanding school-college program--all at little extra cost to the latter.

Bill Jauss of *The Chicago Tribune* tells the story,[2]

Pick out almost any time in Ted Haydon's 25 years as coach of the University of Chicago Track Club. You're sure to find evidence of the resiliency and the droll sense of humor that make Haydon one of the best liked and most respected persons in sport.

Go back, for example, halfway in the 25-year UCTC history. Haydon's purely amateur runners were being hassled then as pawns in the selfish, senseless power struggle between the two grand poo-bahs of amateur sport.

The Amateur Athletic Union (AAU) and the U. S. Track and Field Federation, an arm of the National Collegiate Athletic Association (NCAA), each told Haydon that his athletes would be barred from competition unless their group--and only their group--sanctioned Haydon's track meets.

Haydon, you must understand, never has been terribly impressed with sanctions or unions or federations or associations. Instead, this white-haired, red-faced, Canadian-born, South Side-reared 62-year-old ex-social worker simply works hard so that the greatest number of people--regardless of sanction, sex, skin color, or speed--can run or jump in his meets....

During the AAU-NCAA "alphabet war" in the 60s, Haydon recalled, during an interview, he had to "get tough" when neither of the factions saw much humor in his unsanctioned "practice meets." "We told both of them," Ted said, "that we, not they, had exclusive sanction to the territory between 56th and 57th and between University and Greenwood. And that our sanction body was 'R.F.F.'" Haydon pronounced "R.F.F." like a dog snarling at a door-to-door peddler: "Rrrrooofff!" The initials stand for "Run for Fun."

Ken Doherty, respected director of the Penn Relays and ex-coach at Michigan, spoke precisely about Haydon last Sunday when, at the UCTC Silver Anniversary dinner, he said that Haydon's "Run for Fun" philosophy and his university's permitting outsiders to run for its club represent "the most significant work of any track coach in the U.S.....and the most significant development in amateur sport in 50 years."

Think of sports as we know them. Imagine how things would change if others dropped their win-at-all-cost, recruit-at-all-cost policies and replaced them with the Haydon-Chicago plan.

Chicago is a school where no candidate is cut from a varsity squad. Haydon conducts a club program where no athlete gets recruited or paid and even a superstar such as the half-mile record holder, Rick Wohlhuter, may be asked to pay part of his expenses to a meet.

---

[1] Ken Doherty, "A Better Future for United States Track and Field," *USTCA Quarterly*, June 1966, 39-47.

[2] Bill Jauss, "The Man Who Keeps the UCTC Running," *The Chicago Tribune*, January 23, 1975.

In 1950, Haydon quit being a volunteer coach and full-time social worker and succeeded Ned Merriam, his old college track coach. He also welcomed postcollege Maroons who still wished to compete....

The UCTC breakthru came in 1954 when miler Lawton Lamb, an Illinois grad training with the club, asked Haydon: "Can I run for this club even tho I didn't go to Chicago?" Haydon relayed the question to his athletic director, T. N. Metcalf, who answered: "Why not."...Drop in at one of the 30 to 40 meets a year at the University of Chicago. You see black and white, Jew and gentile. Male and female. Young and old. Bearded and clean-shaven. Intellectual and barely literate. Champion and plodder.

"We do not discriminate," Haydon said years ago, "against anyone on the basis of race, creed, or talent." Author Hal Higdon, still a competitive distance runner at 40-plus, has told the delightful story of Sam Ash. Sam (like "Murphy the Milkman") walked into the fieldhouse one day and announced to Haydon that he was a miler. When Ted asked how fast Sam ran the mile, he pondered and replied, "oh, 4 or 4½ minutes." Sam Ash, Higdon recalls, probably never broke six minutes. But one time Sam found himself in a race against five class milers including Coleman, Ted Wheeler, and Higdon. Ash finished sixth and dead last, of course. But they awarded medals in this meet to the first six finishers. "Coach," medal winner Ash told Haydon the next day, "that was the proudest moment of my life."

Open to all? You'd better believe it. Higdon once questioned Haydon about the sign painted on the stately Gothic walls of old Bartlett: "Power to the Gay Jocks." First came Haydon's familiar smile. Then, "there's nothing to prevent homosexuals from having a wholesome interest in sports, is there?" Haydon looked up from the notes he'd just taken. "Our group," he said, "is just like a natural gang. It starts somewhere," he said. "It ends somewhere. But you're never sure just where. You can't say 'these are the athletes.' Or, 'these are the officials.' Or 'these are the contributors.' Because we all do each thing."

Haydon withdrew from a file cabinet the current (loose, of course) budget of the track club. It's up $10,000 from last year to $32,000. Home meets took in only $927. In the midst of the "alphabet war," meet receipts were just $300, suggesting why the AAU and NCAA ignored Ted's jiving them. The club, Haydon explained, breaks even because scores of ex-Olympians and Murphy the Milkmen contribute to it. Nearly 80 percent of the expenses ($25,000 last year) went to sending athletes to meets.

Haydon's phone jangled. This time it was a Peoria high school coach expressing some "concerns" about the upcoming weekend meet. "...Just come up Saturday. I'll guarantee you there will be athletes your people can beat. And I'll guarantee, no matter how good they are, your athletes will be beaten by some others..." Haydon listened, then smiled. "...What's that? Oh, 'our neighborhood' here? Well, I've heard some bad things about Peoria, too. No, just park in the street. Nobody will bother you."....

If Haydon sometimes wears a dazed look, his duties as coach of the undergraduate Maroons and the club sometimes take 16 hours a day.

In some unfathomable fashion, in that shipwreck office of his, Haydon handles the budget, travel plans, and correspondence for UCTC. After dark, he has shivered, turned flashlight on stopwatch, and cried out interval times to circling club runners (Olympians and Sam Ashes alike).

"If Ted was paid double time for overtime," says Maroon Athletic Director Wally Hass, "he would be a multimillionaire." Haydon is rich in wealth a bankbook cannot measure. He's helped coach U. S. Olympic teams in Mexico City and in Munich in 1968 and 1972. He holds the respect of hundreds of past and current Maroon and UCTC athletes.

During the past century, our school-college track program has been supreme among the many Olympic nations in providing the essentials of success--facilities, coaching, training and competitive program. But that program covers only the years between about 12 and 22. Beyond those years we have provided almost none of the essentials--no facilities, very inadequate coaching, and a competitive program restricted to only a few hundred of the best athletes.

When we realize that these essentials of the school-college system are largely unused during the hours of the day (evening), weekends, and months of the year (summer) when those with jobs would most like to use them, it seems only common sense that they should be made available as was done by Ted Haydon and the University of Chicago. Add the fact that other successful Olympic nations in Europe and the Soviet Union center their sports programs around the club concept in which people engage in organized sports as long as they feel it's worth doing--any age from 6 to 60. Add finally the keystone of Haydon's approach--Run-for-Fun, and we have a sound formula for a rebirth of track and field in this country. Only long tradition with its fear of what might happen in the way of added costs and misuse of facilities stands in the way.

But the over-25-year UCTC program has effectively demonstrated it can be done--in a large-city college within a less-than-desirable residential area, with an actual enhancement of the college program, and at minimal additional cost to the college administration. How was this done?[1] In all-too-brief summary: (1) An emphasis on numbers--numbers of club members and competitors in club meets. In 1975 the UCTC had 200 members of both sexes and from ages 11 to 53. (2) No formal recruiting of track stars. Welcome those that join of their own free will, provide full opportunities for training, for coaching, and for year-round competition, and the stars will be happy to join. For example, by 1976 the UCTC held the world record for the two-mile relay (7:10.4) and had won six out of seven AAU Indoor Championship two-mile relays (1969-1975), using such Greats as Rick Wohlhuter and Lowell Paul. (3) Organize many meet competitions--indoors and outdoors, winter-spring-summer, as well as some six cross-country runs in the fall--a total of 30 or more with from 150 to 600 competitors in each meet. (4) Emphasize number and needs of athletes, not number or needs of spectators. In 1974 total gate receipts for over 30 meets was under $1000. Pay no expenses to star athletes competing in UCTC-sponsored meets. Welcome but otherwise ignore the news media. (5) Keep the UCTC yearly budget low. Until 1970 it was kept below $10,000, but rose in 1975 to $30,000. Raise money for this budget from (a) contributions by friends of the UCTC--44 percent; guarantees for athletes' expenses from large-meet directors--34 percent; entry fees for UCTC meets--10 percent; gate receipts--3 percent; other--9 percent. Contributions by friends included several hundred small gifts but also a few larger gifts by such organizations as the Mayor Daley Youth Foundation.

True, there has been only one Ted Haydon. True, it requires a near-genius in dedication and energy, in achieving an acceptable organization of meets and schedules within an apparent chaos, in maintaining patience and good humor despite endless frustrations and small irritations, in making-do with less, and in solving all the problems inherent in any attempt to open elitist doors to the many. Perhaps only a very few coaches will be able to equal Haydon's program. But most school-college coaches can exert enough influence one way or another to start such a club program and gradually increase its scope as attitudes and conditions permit. Not only would such a national program upgrade our Olympic performances; even more important it would allow many thousands of young and old to gain the benefits of year-round training and competition in track and field.

Oh, by the way--hardly worth mentioning though when you're speaking about Ted Haydon--Ted was Assistant Olympic Coach at both Mexico City and Munich, was Head Coach for the Russian and Polish meets abroad in 1975, and was inducted into the National Track and Field Hall of Fame, 1975, "for long and outstanding service to United States track and field." When congratulated for such honors, Ted always grins away his embarrassment with some such remark as "Yes, I guess it was a lot of hard work I enjoyed but it took Rick Wohlhuter's world records to bring all this attention, and that was all his doing, not mine."

One further important point. Jauss wrote, "his duties as coach...sometimes take 16 hours a day." Sixteen hours! How much time did that leave Ted to fulfill his other obligations to his home and community? When I wrote Ted's wife, Goldie Haydon, about this, she replied,

Ted is home evenings after 8 o'clock, except for occasional meetings. Sundays he is home except for 4-7 o'clock when he goes to the fieldhouse for team workouts and for high school athletes to have a chance to run on a track instead of in the high-school hall. Holidays and vacation periods he has daily workouts, except that in the summer

---

[1] Ted Haydon, "Starting a Track and Field Club," NCTCA *Quarterly*, 1960, p. 13.

I feel it is good to get away to Michigan for a change, where we have no telephone. But we return to Chicago for meets.

When we have a family date or dinner occasionally, Ted's assistant coach substitutes at practice. He pays his own assistant because the University had to cut down.

Preparations for meets are done by us at home. Ted has no secretary so I help him with stuffing-mailing-sealing-stamping letters. I also pin medals on ribbons and help prepare the judges' record cards, etc. Ted has the use of two rooms for all this. He has a typewriter and copier. We do a great deal of telephoning at home.

Much of our social life is with people involved in the program, and all of it has to be planned around the year's schedule. Occasionally we have athletes staying overnite, as do others from our own club; all join in to help out with meet preparations when needed.

For all-day meets (afternoon and evening), I usually have four buffet suppers a year for the coaches, since there are few suitable places to eat near the University.

All this takes time, lots of work, honesty and real interest. The reward is satisfaction in being able to contribute to others' lives, and the fun of creating something worthwhile.

That says it all. Wait, not quite; I must add that Goldie's letter indicated a typewriter badly in need of repair and a ribbon badly in need of replacement. And that takes care of those who wail that their budgets just won't permit a Chicago Club plan at their school.

CHRIS MURRAY--IOWA STATE UNIVERSITY (1972--), WOMEN'S TRACK.

In the near future, women's track and field will be coached by women at both the college and high school levels, but during these early years, for reasons not necessarily related to competence, schools have tended to employ men. The following story by Cathy Breitenbucher[1] relates the evolution of such a program at Iowa State University:

Before there was a university-sanctioned team, women at this school of nearly 23,000 students competed as members of the Iowa State Track Club. "It was a cooperative effort with the men's track team," recalls Peg Neppel, who joined the team in the fall of 1971, when the club was a year old. "We weren't recognized by the university and there was no funding."

When the team was left without a coach in 1972, the women recruited Chris Murray, an assistant professor in the PE department. Still without a budget, they competed in some cross country meets that fall. "The kids footed the whole bill and I was a volunteer coach," Murray says.

Neppel, who didn't begin running until her junior year of high school, but set a world 10,000 record last year, says there was no improvement in her prep times during her first year of college. "But when Chris Murray got a hold of me, it made a true difference. By the end of our first year with Chris, we had gained some recognition from the university. We got a little money, which we put right back into the program. Things just kept getting better."

Better, indeed. The Cyclone women made their first appearance on the national scene in 1974, winning the AIAW mile relay. The squad has placed nationally in that event every year since.

The Cyclones have also dominated women's cross country ever since hosting the forerunner to the AIAW meet in 1974. Iowa State is undefeated in x-c meets ranging from duals to nationals.

---

[1]Cathy Breitenbucher, "Iowa State's Success Story," *Track & Field News*, June 1978, p. 58.

Since 1972, Cyclone women have set four world and eight American records. Six have represented the U.S. on international teams. At the outset of the intercollegiate program, Murray was hard-pressed to set up a schedule for his team.

But now, Murray sees the central states as a leader in women's track. "The Midwest-- in numbers of schools involved--is one of the top areas in the country," he thinks. "There are some real good programs on the West Coast, but the Big 8 is miles ahead of any other conference in women's track. Our indoor meet showed that. There was great depth in all the events."

Murray's team is young (3 seniors, 10 juniors, 12 sophomores, 6 freshmen), but he feels his squad is representative of a nationwide trend: "Every team is young. Most teams are about 80% sophomores and freshmen. That's a reflection of the newness of the program."

The program is not only new, it is changing. "Women's athletics is progressing very well, but we're feeling the growing pains," the ISU coach comments. "Things are changing so quickly that I'm in a pinch to keep up with it."

Fifteen of the 31 women on the ISU roster are Iowans. "Iowa's been a leader in girl's track for years," Murray says. "The girls come to college after having run for 4 years and they want to continue to compete." The Iowa Girls High School Athletic Union sponsored its first state track meet in 1962, with 100 schools participating. Now, 486 schools field teams.

In the early days of the ISU program, word spread quickly that Ames was the place for a woman to go if she wanted to compete in college. "Somehow Iowa high school girls knew there was someone at Iowa State to coach them," Neppel explains. "The good runners knew where to come." Now that ISU has an established reputation, Murray's approach to recruiting is simple: "If you want to come and work, we'll get you in the good meets. I'll work with you, and you'll get a good education that will benefit you the rest of your life."

While Murray has coached some of the nation's top individuals (Neppel, Carol Cook, Debbie Esser, Debbie Vetter), the 36-year-old former Canadian international runner emphasizes the unity of his team. "We hold the team very importantly," he says. "If someone has an off day, the others pick it up. If every member of the team gives 100% then we're going to have success."

Success for Murray translates into development of each athlete's potential. "We set very high goals," he said, "and our goals are very individualized. Our basic goal is national placing or winning for all our individuals. And to think in terms of international competition if they have the ability." Murray definitely downplays the presence of top-flight athletes on his team, but he knows the other tracksters are aware of their famous teammates. "International-class runners become very real people when you see them every day. Quality is a tradition at Iowa State. Our people see others who have done it before."

While Murray is the guiding force behind the Cyclone women, he is quick to give credit to his unofficial assistant coaches, Bill Nix, Gordy Scoles and John Wagner.

Murray considers himself fortunate to work with athletes who are mature enough to make decisions for themselves. "You can overestimate the importance of the coach," he explains. "We like to get the person going, then have her stand on her own two feet. The good ones are going to do it.

"It's a mistake when a coach has to lead an athlete around by the hand and set up every step of the race. The independence is important. A good athlete has to stand on her own two feet because you never know how a race will go. You have to provide the athlete with the tools so she can meet the situation as it arises."

WHY THESE COACHES? Reviewing the styles of these so-widely-differing coaches has been most interesting. But to what purpose? Why were these particular coaches selected as "of special interest"? In brief, not so much because of their individual merits or demerits as because, taken as a group, they comprise a wide and somewhat valid spectrum of coaching styles and relationships.

These coaches were not chosen as models to be imitated or shunned as you may judge their relative merits, or from whom you may select certain traits or tricks by which to win friends, much as Dale Carnegie plucked out Charles Schwab's "prodigiously winning smile" as being his secret device for getting others to do what he wanted them to do.

Nor were these coaches chosen as examples of coaching personalities and ways of operating to be analyzed and judged as fitting within a 9-3 or 3-9 pigeonhole. In the first place, that can't be done; the infinity of attitudes and actions of any man-in-environment can never be compressed into even a flexible pigeonhole. On the other hand, this process of analyzing and judging, of arguing differences and clarifying agreements should lead to a better understanding of the coaching enterprise and a clearer feeling of the general direction and attitude each student will take in trying to become a more effective coach.

Each student-coach will choose his own path, of course. But on one principle, such prolonged discussions should produce clarity and agreement. The coaching enterprise is not centered within a person, whatever his charisma or knowledge or experienced expertise may be. Rather the coaching enterprise is a relationship among that person and all the other persons within what I have called the team family--team members, administration and faculty of the school or college, the local community, the alumni and bird dogs, the entire track world at home and abroad. A coach always functions within such a complex of relationships. When we evaluate any given coach we need to ask who he was and what he accomplished, but equally crucial, within what team family, what social milieu, what cultural system and subsystems did he operate. Wayne Vandenburg, for a time, was very effective, and, with a few modifications, could have remained effective. But only within a particular climate or complex of relationships, within the kind of system indigenous to himself, to UTEP and to his associates in El Paso. Contrast Vandenburg and Botts or Hamilton as persons, if you will, but also contrast the cultural surrounds in which they worked. What would have happened if Hamilton had gone to UTEP and Vandenburg to Berkeley? Failure? Perhaps, not necessarily. But if either became effective, he would necessarily draw forth--from himself and from the situation--the kind and degree of supportive relationships every leader, whether in sports or business or politics or religion, must have. If this Chapter 4 and Part I make that clear and nothing else, they will be worth the writing, and the studying.

Chapter 5
THE HUMAN SIDE OF COACHING

All agree that the job of coaching is one of personal and public relations at least as much as of training methods and event techniques. But strangely, we tend to assume that only the latter requires special analysis and study. Apparently the former can be mastered by some innate charismatic quality or adequately learned while on the job. Actually, the investigation in this OMNIBOOK of the human side of coaching is but a beginning, a mere hint of what should and can be done in the future. We can be certain that full textbooks and complete college courses will soon be organized as they relate directly to track and field. Generalized courses in educational psychology, sociology or sports administration are essential in understanding fundamentals, but they need to be supplemented by more related and useable materials.

But even though this is a mere beginning or hint, the previous four chapters do attempt to make clear the nature of the problem. Chapter 1 traced the gradual development of track knowledge and related college courses, and led to a study of methods of business management. Of special interest were Douglas McGregor's "management as person-centered," and Rensis Likert's "mutually-supportive relationships" as between persons and groups. Chapter 2 summarized theories on the nature of leadership and the many roles that coaches must play in performing the various facets of their job. Chapter 3 emphasized the importance of striving for a vital balance between expertise in the technology of track and field and expertise in working with persons. A coaching grid was devised by which the problems of balance could be analyzed more precisely--needless to say, with only limited validity. Chapter 4 selected a dozen track and field coaches whose personalities and methods covered a wide range of coaching potentials-- from all-out recruiting of talent for winning to a genuine concern for the development of athletes as persons. The two approaches can occur together but tend to be mutually exclusive.

Throughout all four chapters, special concern was expressed for the importance of compatibility and unity between the coach and his social surround--goals, means, methods, attitudes. The main focus of these can be at any square within the coaching grid, or at any point along a wide range of possible coaching attitudes and actions. But if effective work is to be done, the many parts must dovetail and provide mutually supportive relationships.

For the most part, the term, "social surround" was defined at the local level--all those persons and groups with whom every coach has direct contacts. But there is a greater social sphere within which all United States coaches function and by which they should be judged-- what is often called "the system"--our modern business-centered society with its belief in competitiveness as a primary and unalterable instinct, its worship of winning and of material gains as an almost divine right of winners.

This idea of a social surround out of which we absorb our ideas-attitudes-belief is difficult, even impossible, to realize as related to ourselves. It's not a matter of selection so much as of subconscious diffusion, much as a fish diffuses oxygen from the surrounding sea. Even a genius fish would have no awareness of the sea until he first became aware of the sky. Perhaps the sky of our awareness could be the contrasting social system of communist East Germany.

A 1978 East German textbook for track and field coaches makes a major point of these views,[1]

The coaches of the Athletic Association of the GDR will only be able to accomplish the tasks set them if they are dedicated to their profession, if they have acquired a high standard of political and professional knowledge, educational skill, and if they are distinguished by socialist convictions, habits and qualities so they can set an example to their athletes by their political thoughts and actions. The coach is an official of the workers' state according to his social calling....
(Then on a later page)--*They are to be educated in the love and faith of the working class, its party and our state. When our athletes are convinced that the victory of socialism is the main task of our era, they will fight even more passonately and consistently for the improvement of their athletic performance.*

Extreme? Utter nonsense? Applicable only to a Marxist-Leninist society, but not to our own? Definitely yes, in terms of the details of what is believed and taught. But definitely not so, in terms of the principle of individual-group unity. Although we scorn such mawkish expressions of social duty and loyalty, we tend to be unaware that our system has its own compelling ways of ensuring conformity with what it considers essential.

We use certain names to describe our society--"Capitalism," "Science and Technology," "Materialistic," "Business-oriented." Such names imply certain basic assumptions--private enterprise, work for material gain more than for satisfactions inherent in the work, analysis into separate things more than synthesis toward wholeness, individualism that views society as an aggregate of separate individuals--all confirming competitiveness as a primary instinct in human nature, and winning for material gain as a main goal in sports, as in life generally.

Can we be certain that these assumptions are any less extreme or nonsensical than those of the East German textbook? These assumptions are among those that such leading social analysts as Erich Fromm, Karen Horney, Renee Dubos or Lewis Mumford describe as "dehumanizing," "Neurotic," "alienating," and "destructive of self and society."

Over many years we have gradually accepted the custom of calling ourselves track and field coaches. That seems an innocent habit, one that distinguishes us from football or swimming coaches. And it is, unless--and here's the catch--unless such a focus on the medium obscures our real goal, the human goal. It's not innocent at all; it's downright dangerous if we begin to think and act as though techniques-methods-performance-winning are our REAL goals; the youngsters we work with, only the tools for reaching those goals.

Bill Bowerman, longtime coach at Oregon and 1972 United States Head Olympic Coach, hated the very word, "Coach," and refused to answer when called by such a title. His early exper- ience as an athlete led him to relate "Coach" to dirty tactics in recruiting, to promotion more than education, to using sports and athletes to satisfy the lust for winning. In the preface to his textbook, *COACHING TRACK AND FIELD*,[2] he wrote,

I am proud to be a teacher and to be associated with a group of men and women who, on the whole, love youngsters and do not care a whoop if their critics...cause them to be underpaid, under-estimated, and overworked.

Bill was a tough competitor--as an athlete and a coach. He battled hard to win; in fact, won three NCAA team titles while at Oregon. But his main emphasis, and his great contribution to United States track and field related to the many thousands that he encouraged to take part.

All this leads up to the point that, if such assumptions are really inherent in our business- oriented society, those coaches who follow the ways of winning-as-the-main-goal are its natur- al offspring, entirely worthy of the high praise and material rewards that such a culture grants to loyal disciples that embrace its teachings and follow its ways. In contrast, those

---

[1]Gerhardt Schmolinsky, *TRACK AND FIELD*, Berlin: *Sportverlag*, 1978, pp. 30ff.

[2]Bill Bowerman, *COACHING TRACK AND FIELD*, Los Altos, Cal.: *Tafnews Press*, 1974, 400 pages.

that deny such teachings and seek other and better ways are likely to be rewarded only with discouragement, general alienation, and even loss of their jobs.

The important point to be gained relates to understanding the scope of the problem, to awareness of the vital importance of knowing just where you-as-coach stand in relation to your own social surround--in America, but more precisely in Philadelphia, or Ames, Iowa; in El Paso, Texas or Eugene, Oregon. If such relationships among you-team-school-community are mutually supportive, you're likely to achieve success, along with such rewards as that kind of success warrants, from cold cash to deep personal satisfaction. When such compatibility of ends and means is lacking, the end result is likely to be a sense of personal isolation, anxiety, and little accomplishment--for you, your school, and your athletes.

Our great society is not monolithic, all of one kind. Its varied communities and institutions do provide opportunities for work motivations other than those of business. An intelligent young coach will face the issue squarely--to find a school-community whose ends and means for sport are compatible with his own, or to mold his own attitudes and methods to conform with those that surround him. Otherwise success will come hard, however success be defined. Both Villanova's Jumbo Elliott and Berkeley's Brutus Hamilton enjoyed great success, though quite differently oriented. There is a choice.

CERTIFICATION OF TRACK AND FIELD COACHES. One of the most important aspects of improving United States track and field at all levels, as related to both the human and the technical side, is that of the certification of coaches. Certainly no aspect has been so widely neglected. Primarily this has occurred through lack of a national consensus--and certainly of program--as to the place of sports in our Educational and social system.

At the college and club levels, no qualifications are needed, other than convincing local employers that their concept of what the job requires will be fulfilled. During its 50-year history, the College Track Coaches Association has prepared no formal Statement as to the level of competency needed to coach our sport. During its 100-year history, our national governing body, the National AAU, has taken no position on the matter. Anyone with the will, energy and means could organize and coach a club team.

As a result of such a lack of nation-wide policy, many entirely unqualified persons have coached our sport--unqualified on both the technical and the human side. We've had great coaches--the best in the world--great coaches of techniques and methods, beloved educators of young men and women. But such great coaches have emerged almost by chance, out of trial-and-error guided only by the assumption that whoever can do it well, can coach it; and whoever can coach well enough to win is a fit person to teach in institutions of higher learning. For instance, the 1980 Charter of the newly-formed TFA/USA contained 17 detailed statements of purposes and objectives. Number 15 was "to train and certify competent track and field officials." But no such specific statement related to track and field coaches. Apparently their competency was of lesser concern.

At the high school level a similar lack of national consensus is present. But at this level, studies of the problems of certification have been made for many years, and a few States have actually adopted requirements, however minimal. Among the better published statements for high schools is that by Samuel Adams, Washington State University,[1]

Requiring certification of all interscholastic athletic coaches would be a major step forward for the coaching profession and interscholastic school sports. If sports are educational, it is logical that specific criteria be established for high school coaches just as there are special requirements for other special areas of education--driver's education, vocational education, counseling, speech therapy, and special education....

The need for more qualified coaches that had been accentuated by more participation by both boys and girls in sports in secondary schools since the late 1960s became acute with Title IX.

---

[1]Samuel Adams, Ph.D., "Coaching Certification: The Time is Now," Mobile, Ala.: *United States Sports Academy News*, Vol. 3, No. 4, Sept. 1979, p. 1. (The excerpt given here is not complete.)

Administrators of secondary schools had historically relied upon physical educators to handle the coaching responsibilities. The problem inherent in the increase in participation in sports is the lack of teaching positions related to coaching positions. For example, in a typical high school of 1,000 students there are approximately 20-25 coaching jobs for 10 boys' sports. In this same school there are usually two to three fulltime men physical education and health education teachers. Even with each man coaching three sports, only nine of the 20 positions are filled. Personnel from other teaching and district positions have had to be utilized, many of them without any form of professional training. This same staffing problem is now facing girls' sports. Therefore, there is a dire need for professional training for coaching personnel from the other areas of education. Following the 1972 Olympic Games the United States Sports Academy sent out a series of surveys in an attempt to evaluate the credentials of people in coaching. Results indicated that over 70% of the coaches in schools don't have a physical education major; over 65% don't even have a P.E. minor; and over 50% have never competed in sports themselves. ......

What are the implications for coaching? It seems that there is a definite need for certification of coaching. Coaching is a specialized area of education. It is an area that must be regarded as an entity in itself. It is different although similar with some basic qualities and characteristics of physical education. Being a good physical educator doesn't assure one of being a good coach. There are specialized knowledges needed for coaching expertise; in sports medicine, sports psychology, sports technique, sports administration, sports physiology, public relations, sports facilities and equipment, and sports problems that include law and liability and assessment of personnel and programs. ......

However, the task is not the formulation of a certification program but realization that it is needed now. Only a few states have moved into certification. In 1976 45 states, Puerto Rico, and the District of Columbia had no specific certification requirements for coaching; however, most of them require that a coach be a certified teacher. Only six states have minimum certification requirements for coaching in addition to teachers certification. These states are Minnesota, Nebraska, Iowa, Wyoming, Pennsylvania, and South Dakota. Only three of these states, Iowa, Nebraska, and Minnesota have additional coaching certification requirements for physical education majors. All of these coaching certification programs are sub-minimum with the exception perhaps, of the requirement for women coaches in Minnesota, which could be considered minimum.

Most proposals for certification of coaches have come from persons not in the coaching profession--from members of the AAHPER or of college teacher-training departments. A review of such proposals makes clear two phases of certification: (1) standards related to safety and health, to educational and ethical purposes, to backgrounds in related social sciences; and (2) standards related to coaching competency in a particular sport or sports event.

Quite properly, the concern of State Boards of Education and of State Associations for HPER are primarily with the first of these. Their concern is that sports should be planned and conducted in accordance with sound educational practices by persons trained in related education and science courses. To achieve this, they tend to propose legislative measures leading to State-wide and even Nation-wide requirements.

Such widespread requirements reduce local autonomy and so are slow to be approved by school boards overwhelmed by the need for lowering school costs, and quite happy merely to maintain the status quo in the conduct of sports. Athletic directors and coaches tend to resent interference, and may even fear loss of their jobs through their own failure to qualify under proposed standards. Traditionally, sports in American colleges and schools have been community-oriented. Unfortunately our communities have not been strongly on the side of the higher aspects of education. After more than 100 years, no educational requirements have been established for coaching in colleges, and only some five States have even minimal requirements for the secondary-school level.

But the second phase of certification, that related to coaching competency in methods and techniques of sport, need not be organized in terms of requirement. Any formal recognition of work done or knowledge acquired could gradually gain respect within coaching ranks and, more importantly, among school employers as a valid indication of competency in an applicant's file. That is the intent of college courses using this TRACK AND FIELD OMNIBOOK. But there is no official recognition of such courses, no official standards by which their effectiveness can be judged. Of two student-coaches at different teacher-training colleges, one may have needed to study the entire 550 pages of this book; the other may have needed only to glance at the sequence drawings. But both might receive grades of "A" and be recommended as fully qualified to coach track and field.

Such a careless lack of organization is disgraceful in terms of our modern level of knowledge, training and performance in sports. It's a natural outcome of our early development as outlined in Chapter 1. But it can no longer be tolerated, even if only our own self-respect as professional coaches is at stake. Certainly, under such a slovenly disarrangement, we cannot hope to compete with the systems of coach qualification and training now being used in European and Eastern-bloc countries. There, certification as a Master Coach requires years of study in related physical and social sciences, and receives widespread respect and even official honors. I remember so well a clinic in Moscow at which all arose as Vladimir Dyatchkov, "Honored Master and National Coach of High Jumping for the USSR," came down the aisle of the lecture room. We tend to scorn such respect for authority, but it has its values for effectiveness of both persons and programs.

In 1975, the Canadian Track & Field Association started a CTFA Coaching Certification Program, with Fred Wilt as Provincial Coordinator.[1] This program sought to standardize coaching levels across the country through a common framework of both theory and practical knowledge. Its approach served the two-pronged needs of health, safety and education, on the one hand, and those of "learning-by-doing" as related to techniques and methods, on the other. The program for each event or group of events is planned on five levels of competence. On completion of any given level, a certificate is given that is recognized in every Province of Canada. The CTFA used its best coaches, as well as experts in related sciences, in preparing materials, and in the actual training of student-coaches. By upgrading the overall level of coaching competence, the CTFA hopes to improve performance at all levels from grade school to international.[2]

In summary, certification can be at several levels of competence and relate (1) to overall qualifications as coach of track and field; (2) to a group of events, such as distance running; or (3) to a single event, such as the pole vault. A person might well be an overall coach at a lower level, but a Master Coach for sprint events. At first, such certification should relate only to competence in coaching techniques and methods. Qualifications in such areas as health, safety and sound educational practices, though essential, could be dealt with later, or in cooperation with other groups.

Such a program should not be retroactive; coaches now employed need not be involved. It should be planned in terms of the next 20 years or more before becoming fully effective. But just plain commonsense--that rare quality--would rule that it needs to be started, and the sooner the better.

---

[1]Fred Wilt, An editorial on certification of coaches, *Track Technique*, Vol.71, March 1978, p. 2248.

[2]"Coaching Certification Program," *Track and Field Journal*, #2, April 1980, p. 31, published by CTFA, 355 River Road, Vanier City, Ontario, K1L 8C1.

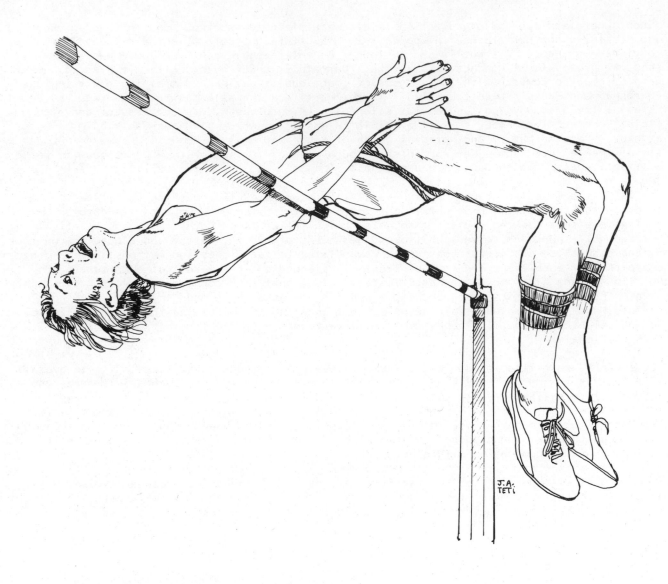

PART 2A
Coaching Field Events

Chapter 6
TRAINING FOR FIELD EVENT POWER AND FLEXIBILITY

Up to about 1950, improvement in performance in field events was gained through a 100 percent emphasis on technique. For example, in 1948, Charles Fonville set a startling world record for the shot at 58¼", with no concern for resistances greater than 16 pounds. Perfection of skill at maximal velocities was both his goal and the means to that goal.

But during the following decade or so, this approach was reversed to one in which a 90 percent emphasis was placed on maximal strength, with only a 10 percent concern for skill, or even for the velocity factor in the formula for power. This change occurred through actual experience by such shotputters as Otis Chandler (Stanford), Stan Lampert (NYU) and Parry O'Brien (USC). But it was based on research that used static (isometric) strength as being more reliable in its measurement. Conclusions drawn by such careful scientists as Thomas De Lorme and E. A. Muller were precisely stated and entirely valid. But the assumptions made by others, both coaches and textbook writers, were often not valid for actual use on the training field, and led to confusion that, even today, is far from cleared.

Gradually, awareness has developed that the goal of power training for field events is not maximal strength, but maximal velocity through strength--more specifically, velocity of movement in a particular field-event technique that is biomechanically sound. Such velocity is the true goal; strength, the means to that goal.

From such statements, the question arises--what is the relationship between "strength," "power," or "velocity."

THE MEANING OF HUMAN POWER.
Such words as "strength," "power," "velocity," or "skill" are just that--words, symbols, ways of thinking and speaking by which we identify aspects of sports action that, in the real world, are never separate. These words are tools, not entities, tools that we use AS IF the structures and functions they symbolize actually exist separately. Unfortunately, we forget, all too quickly the "as if"; we forget that these are merely ways of analyzing wholes that have no actual parts.

It makes a significant difference if a training system assumes that strength and power and velocity and skill are separate entities rather than strength-power-velocity-skill abstracted out of a continuous spectrum of movement. As an analogy, we might consider the relationships among the colors that emerge when sunlight is passed through a prism. We name them and use them--red, yellow, blue, violet--AS IF they are separate entities, but such use should be within the context of the continuum out of which we abstracted them. Colors are ways of analyzing and understanding sunlight. Or, as a second analogy, we can take "still-life"--note the self-contradition--sequence photos of human movement. To do so is entirely valid and very useful, as long as we maintain awareness of the continuous life-movement from which they were "stilled."

To think of strength as one thing; then of power or velocity as another separate thing leads to confusion and misuse not unlike that inherent in trying to separate muscle fibers from the neurons that excite them. A knife that attempts to do so not only destroys both but makes a certain non-sense of of their separate names.

Strength, as related to sports, always involves movement, though at a relatively slow speed. On the other hand, even weight-lifters insist, "It is of the utmost importance that the athlete *think speed*...if he is to activate fast-twitch (FT) fibers."[1] In weight-lifting, the amount of resistance moved is the goal; speed of movement is essential as a means to that goal. *But in training for field events, the opposite is true--speed of movement is the goal; contractions against maximal resistances, a means to that goal.*

Power Begins in Trunk Muscles. The power phase of every field event begins with contractions of the large, strong muscles of the trunk; then, almost simultaneously, extends to the smaller-faster muscles of the extremities.

One might compare this sequence of power to that in the propulsion of space rockets by stages. Rocket movement begins through the more powerful--though slow--thrusts of Stage 1. Such thrusts continue to a point of diminishing returns, when the inertia of Stage 1 is greater than its thrusting power. At this point, Stage 1 drops off; Stage 2 fires, with lesser power but also with lesser weight to move. At the start, lacking Stage 1, the lesser power of Stage 2 would have been totally ineffective. But for both stages, the goal was final velocity; maximal power was a means to that end.

It is the same with throwing events. As Robert Vigars states in his "Analysis of Critical Factors in the Throws,"[2] "Large body parts (hips and trunk) having greater inertia must precede the movement of the smaller body parts (throwing arm), so that all related joint forces can be used in a coordinated effort to propel the implement being thrown." In such statements lies the solution to the argument between the advocates of heavy-weight lifting and those of optimal power at maximal velocity.

THE PROGRESSIVE-OVERLOAD PRINCIPLE
The principle of progressive-overload is one of the most basic and universally accepted of all methods of training, not only as related to strength and power but to endurance and persistence and will-to-succeed. Challenge leads to related response, but only within the limits of stress inherent in the challenge. For example, our chapter on training for endurance states that "more running leads to better running but only within the degree of stress produced by such running."

The actions of any field event, during practice or competition, develops strength commensurate with the resistances inherent in that event. An emphasis on greater speed of action increases resistance and leads to greater strength, but only within the limits of stress produced in the related motor units.

Recently, on TV, an Olympic long jumper was shown running up the steps of a stadium--one at a time. He said that during early season he did this regularly--up and down, two and even three times a week--all to develop power for the long jump. Such exercise is great for that special kind of endurance, but its values for power are limited to the strength required in thrusting the body-weight to the height of one stadium step.

Greatest credit for the statement of this principle as related to strength is generally given to Thomas DeLorme[3] who made use of the overload principle in rehabilitating the wounded from World War II. He concluded (1) that strength can be developed only by workloads that are above those regularly experienced, (2) development in strength can occur only within the limits of the intensity of a given workload, and (3) overloads must be measured in terms of the intensity of a few contractions, rather than of the number of repetitions.

----

[1]Carl Miller, *OLYMPIC LIFTING TRAINING MANUAL*, self-published, 302 Chula Vista, Santa Fe, NM, 1977, p. 47.

[2]Robert Vigars, "Analysis of Critical Factors in the Throws," *Track Technique*, #77, Fall 1979, p. 2447.

[3]Thomas L. DeLorme, "Restoration of Muscle Power by Heavy Resistance," in *CLASSICAL STUDIES ON PHYSICAL ACTIVITY*, ed. Roscoe C. Brown and Gerald S. Kenyon, Englewood Cliffs, N.J.: Prentice-Hall, Inc., 1968, 236-261.

This means, first, that if lifting 25 pounds is the regular workload of a certain muscle, its strength will be limited to the developmental values of 25 pounds. This holds true, even though that 25 pounds is lifted at maximum velocity. This was the situation in the shot put prior to 1950 in which we had only 16-pound strength, so to speak. To gain ever-greater strength, resistances must be progressively increased.

DeLorme's conclusions also mean that many repetitions of a workload that is less than an overload will improve only the endurance of a muscle, not its strength. Weight trainers vary in the exact number of repetitions they advocate, but between eight and 12 is usually considered most effective for strength. For example, Ryan (1969, 57) recommends as a rule of thumb that a weight is most effective for strength if it can be lifted only eight times for each of three sets. The number of "reps" (repetitions) is gradually increased to 12, at which point the weight can again be increased so that three sets of eight reps is again a maximum.

A second important source of research knowledge of the progressive overload principle was the work of Hellebrandt[1] and Houtz. Among their conclusions were (1) the amount of work done per unit of time is the critical variable on which continuous development depends; (2) determination not to reduce the rate of working when the stress imposed seems insuperable is a crucial element in overload training; (3) strength and endurance increase together when repetitive exercise is performed against heavy resistance; (4) the rapidity with which work overloads increase the power capacity suggests that changes in the central nervous system are important aspects of training development.

THE UNIQUE VALUES OF MODERN STRENGTH TRAINING

Prior to our present use of heavy-weights for strength training, the resistances to be overcome were limited to those of the implements--16# for shot and hammer; 1.7# for the javelin--and of the weight of the body. Chin-ups, sit-ups, push-ups were done but body weight was constant and that both fixed and limited the strength that could be gained.

In contrast to such limited tools, modern strength training provides for maximal resistances, for movement patterns that simulate those of the intended skill, for extensive variety, for precise measurement of weight increments even if not of strength gains, and for considerable control of many significant factors. Resistances of weights or of weight-training machines can now be fixed to require maximal exertion, or changed by whatever increments seem best--100#-50#-10#-5#. All aspects of such increases can be controlled--weight, repetitions, rest periods, pattern of movement, velocity sequence of exercises--and all in ways that simulate the movements of the event for which training is done.

Furthermore, the organization of weight-lifting allows for a variety of periods for recovery and muscle-fiber development--those between repetitions, between sets, and between workouts. Repetitions provide alternating periods of a few seconds of work and rest. Sets ensure similar periods of longer duration. Workouts are usually every other day, so that work bouts are alternated with some 46 hours of potential recovery and development. Such recovery periods are as important to strength development as are the work periods, for it is then that the processes of muscle-fiber development occur.

MAXIMAL STRENGTH IS ESSENTIAL

The goal in all strength training for field events is maximal velocity--velocity of the implement thrown or of the body moved. But maximal velocity is possible only through maximal strength during each phase of action.

As previously stated, movement in all field events begins in the largest and strongest muscle groups in the trunk area[2], then extends quickly downward to the feet on the ground and, in the throwing events, upward through the shoulder-arm-fingers. During Stage 1, to use the

---

[1]F. A. Hellebrandt and S. J. Houtz, "Mechanisms of Muscle Training in Man: Experimental Demonstration of the Overload Principle," in CLASSICAL STUDIES ON PHYSICAL ACTIVITY, ibid., 288-304.

[2]Geoffrey Dyson, THE MECHANICS OF ATHLETICS, 7th edition, London: University of London Press, Ltd., 1978, p. 36.

space-rocket analogy, movement despite the inertia of the trunk requires the great strength of the trunk muscles. (This is as essential for the 1.7# javelin as for the 16# shot or even the 56# weight throw.)

With rockets, Stage 1 completes its work, drops away, then Stage 2 takes over. In the human body, Stage 1 begins only an instant before Stage 2--just enough to ensure an explosive start-- then maintains force until the implement is released. That instant of delay is all-important; resistances (body + implement) are now moving at a critical speed that enables the faster-weaker muscles (shoulder-arm-wrist-fingers) to exert their maximal force and so have a significant effect on release velocity of the implement.

But the point being made here is that maximal force (strength) is required throughout--in the slower, stronger muscles of the trunk, but equally, in the faster, weaker muscles of the more distal segments. Maximal force from both muscle groups depends on all-out firing of the fast twitch fibers; the greater the number of such fast-twitch fibers that have been activated by relevant strength training, the greater the force-velocity they can exert. It is this point that makes clear the need to maintain heavy-weight lifting for the trunk muscles up to the weeks of important competition, and at the same time to develop maximal strength of the smaller, faster muscle groups--all relevant to the competitive event.

SPEED-STRENGTH IN TRAINING FOR POWER

The view held here is that, when training for power for field events, velocity of muscle contraction is the goal; strength gained through maximal resistances, one of several possible means. What is the argument in favor of lesser resistances moved at greater velocities? Is it only maximal resistances that can create a maximal stimulus for power development? Or is intensity of stress within the muscle the essential stimulating condition, stress that can be created by high-velocity contractions against lighter resistances? And, most important, are there various answers to such questions, depending on (1) whether we are developing slower-heavier muscles of the trunk in which slow-twitch fibers predominate, or the lighter-faster muscles of the more distal parts in which fast-twitch fibers predominate; (2) whether it is early pre-season or late competitive season; or (3) whether heavy or light implements are to be thrown--56# weight or 1.7# javelin?

Experience and research agree that highest-velocity contractions are best, whatever the amount of resistance, the pattern of movement, or the event for which training is done--Olympic weight-lifting or javelin throwing. On the other hand, potential increases in velocity of movement--whether in speed of any given muscle group, in greater efficiency of neuromuscular coordination, or in more effective inhibition of negative factors--are much less capable of development than are those for strength.

Fast-Twitch and Slow-Twitch Muscle Fibers. For many decades, physiologists have distinguished between two kinds of fibers present in all muscles of the body--identifiable by color (red and white), but also by function. Muscles in which red fibers predominate tend toward long-term, slow, powerful contractions and are not easily fatigued. Such muscles relate mainly to posture, the diaphragm and extensor muscles. Muscles in which white fibers predominate are specialized toward speed of contraction and are more easily fatigued. They are most numerous in such high-velocity muscles as the flexors.

Both types of fibers are present in all muscles of the body, but it is generally agreed that which type is developed in any given muscle is largely the effect of the kind of work it performs. That is, fast contractions tend to develop white fibers; slow, prolonged contractions, red fibers.

During more recent years, physiologists have re-examined these facts, with significant results for strength training. Red fibers are now called slow-twitch (ST) fibers; white, fast-twitch (FT) fibers. Such re-naming suggests no changes in our views of structure but does ennable us to relate muscle development more precisely to training for strength, velocity and endurance. For example, Gideon Ariel[1] reports research by Swedish workers who conclude

---

[1]Gideon B. Ariel, "Resistance Exercises and Muscle-Fiber Typing," *Track Technique*, #70, December 1977, p. 2239.

that fast-twitch fibers are developed most effectively through exercises of high intensity in which high velocity and maximal effort are present. Since the intensity of muscle performance varies throughout the range of motion of joints, power-training machines are used that require high-intensity effort throughout the full range of movement. From these findings, Ariel concludes: (1) it is important to identify the dominant muscle groups involved in the event for which training is done, and (2) to develop fast-twitch fibers, resistance to muscle contraction should be applied throughout the full range of motion at a velocity that most closely simulates the goal-activity.

In an attempt to clarify and simplify methods for developing fast-twitch fibers, Garhammer[1], a specialist in biomechanics and exercise physiology, explains (1) three most popular training methods: variable resistance machines, isokinetic machines, and free weights such as barbells and dumbbells; and (2) the importance of the specificity concept: exercises should simulate their target events in body position, muscles groups, pattern of movement, speed, duration and range of joint action. Of these methods, Garhammer concludes that "low cost free weights, benches and racks usually prove far superior in producing desired results than do expensive machines." By proper techniques, variations in loading, careful simulation of event movements, and always an emphasis on explosive effort, excellent gains can be obtained.

Methods for developing fast-twitch fibers are of great interest to Olympic weightlifters. Carl Miller,[2] former National Coaching Coordinator for the sport, studied Eastern European methods--especially Bulgarian--and concluded that dormant fast-twitch fibers are most effectively activated by "thinking speed" when lifting. "Thinking normally will activate more slow-twitch fibers; thinking speed, more fast-twitch fibers....This way fibers would be activated in the proportion used in the actual snatch or clean-and-jerk, or when rising from the clean."

A DEVELOPMENTAL STIMULUS FOR FIELD-EVENT POWER

Weightlifting experts are in general agreement that optimal gains in strength occur only from repeated contractions against highest-level resistances; that is, resistances that can be rhythmically lifted a limited number of times, say from one to 12. DeVries states that such a program "seems to rest on sound experimental bases."[3] Asmussen concurs, "As a general principle for an effective training of muscular strength, it must be emphasized that only maximal or near-maximal contractions will produce measureable results."[4]

Such statements seem clear when the goal, as in Olympic weightlifting, is for maximal poundage. Weightlifting entails very limited patterns of movement, movements in which the slow-heavy muscles of the trunk and upper legs are predominant. True, weightlifters insist on maximal speed in all their work, but for reasons of heavier weights to be lifted.

But every field event also requires maximal strength in the weaker-faster distal muscles; in the throws, the muscles of the shoulder-arm-hand-fingers. For these, the heavy weights of Olympic lifts prepare the way--not unlike the rocket's Stage 1--but do not directly increase distal strength. These muscles require their own maximal resistances that conform to their special strength potentials and fast movements. Now we use the word, "power," for velocity is vital to their work.

An optimal stimulus for full use of potential power will vary in resistance from those that this muscle group fails to move (isometric contractions), to those that are lighter than that of the target load (16# to 1.7#). The latter is still a "maximal contraction," as required by Asmussen, but now the more effective factor is velocity, not resistance.

---

[1] John Garhammer, "Muscle Fiber Types and Weight Training," *Track Technique*, #72, June 1978, p. 2297.

[2] Carl Miller, *ibid.*, p. 47.

[3] Herbert A. deVries, *PHYSIOLOGY OF EXERCISE*, Dubuque, Iowa: Wm. C. Brown Co., 1974, p. 317.

[4] Erling Asmussen, "The Neuromuscular System and Exercise," in Harold B. Falls, *EXERCISE PHYSIOLOGY*, New York: Academic Press, 1968, p. 35.

As to the relative emphasis within a year-round training program to be put on heavy versus light resistances, de Vries[1] points out that "speed of movement improves rapidly in the training program to a plateau, above which it can be increased only with great difficulty. On the other hand, very few athletes have even begun to approach their maximum strength levels, and thus huge gains in power are possible by improving strength--while simply maintaining speed." That is, we should use such low-weight-maximum-velocity loads as a late-season "peaking" procedure.

A second essential point as related to a developmental stimulus for power in field events relates to the particular movement pattern of each event. *Even a slight change in pattern will increase the load on certain muscle groups and decrease the load on others.* It is this essential that has led to the use of 20# shots, over-weight discuses, and 4-5# balls for the javelin. Such light-weight loads develop power within the flow of muscle contractions that most closely simulate those of the actual event, a flow or pattern that is not feasible with heavier loads. Warning: When practicing for more perfect skill, no additional weights or resistances of any kind should be used. To do so is to change the pattern of skill in coordination, strength required and velocities of contractions; that is, to learn a significantly different skill.

RATE OF STRENGTH GAIN

Low reliability in measurement has prevented research on the rate of gains in dynamic-strength training. Research in isometric training tends to conclude that gains occur at about five percent a week; about 50 percent in seven weeks; near-maximal gains, in about three months. In general, gains are rapid when present strength is low in terms of potential strength, and increasingly slow as strength approaches maximal levels.

Such conclusions are roughly similar to those of experience. During preliminary stages, the processes of recovery from "wear and tear" are slow and inadequate; those of development and growth are rapid. As development proceeds, the processes of both recovery and growth are rapid and effective. In later stages, the processes of recovery are most effective but those of development and growth are increasingly difficult. When an athlete reaches a critical age, further development tends to stop altogether, though sometimes a changed approach in both kind and extent of training will induce even greater performance.

In planning a year-round program of training for throwers, Tschiene[2] outlines a six-month period of basic preparation, in which strength training increases in extent and intensity during the first three months or so. Similarly, Miller[3] states that a six-month program is best, but that a three-month program can be adequate. For both authorities, strength training is continuous throughout the year, but varies in both loading and intensity from one phase to the next.

RETENTION OF STRENGTH

Crucial questions arise: (a) when and to what degree can this basic strength phase of training be diminished, and (b) is there a period in the late competitive season when it can be stopped entirely. Answers can be gotten from both research and experience; neither is final. As a generalization, Steinhaus (1963, 136) states that rapid training induces a loosely "anchored" strength in the muscle which is lost at about the same rate as gained. However, strength maintained for many weeks becomes firmly anchored and tends to be lost very slowly. Muller reports that strength maintained for 12 weeks undergoes little loss during the following 12 weeks, and in the next 28 weeks "was still far from having returned to the level it started from at the beginning of the experiment" (see Steinhaus, 1963, 136).

We must keep in mind that a "little loss," as judged by a scientist, might be a crucial loss to an athlete's competitive performance. For example, Vladimir Dyatchkov (1969, 1123) reported that the cessation of all weight training during the competitive season resulted in a measureable decrease in strength and, even more important, in competitive performance.

---

[1]DeVries, *ibid*, p. 302.

[2]Tschiene, *ibid.*, p. 1642.

[3]Miller, *ibid.*, p. 9.

Whether or not to stop or even diminish heavy-weight lifting depends on whether one's goals are related to maximal performance near the end of a sport season, or to a lesser performance over many weeks of the full season. Heavy-weight lifting produces an overall lethargy or fatigue. This is greatly diminished after 48 hours or so of rest. But highest-level performance requires a longer period--one to two weeks; for some men, even more--of both recovery and growth.

As a matter of interest, Olympic weightlifters continue some lifting right up to the day of competition. But they gradually reduce both the number of exercises and the intensity percentages some two and even three weeks before major competition.[1]

STRENGTH EXERCISES AS AN ENERGIZING FACTOR

Dyatchkov, coach of Brumel and other USSR jumpers, emphasizes not only the strength values of weight exercises but their restorative and energizing values also.

During many years, experimental investigations and observations have been carried out by us, first independently, then in combination with physiologists and physicians. It was established after intensive high jumps (competitions--J.K.D.) a considerable decline of the functional state of the central nervous system occurs under the influence of exhaustion, while after exercises with a barbell, even with a greater total load. . . a positive action is observed during the following 24 hours. The rehabilitation processes occur more rapidly if the exercises with the barbell are combined with exercises of a low intensity--slow running, relaxation exercises, etc. . . . . Strength exercises as a stimulating factor should be used at all stages of training, including the competitive season.[2]

Such use of strength exercises in recovery from the nervous exhaustion of competition is most interesting, and, coming from such a serious student of the sport as Dyatchkov, should be tried by other coaches. In a follow-up statement, Dyatchkov suggests barbell exercises using snatches and presses with 85% maximum weights.

THE STRETCH REFLEX AS RELATED TO POWER

Experience in various sports such as weight-lifting, gymnastics and field events has made clear that maximal efforts are often preceded by a stretching and reflex contraction of the muscles that initiate action, what is commonly called a stretch reflex. Perhaps the simplest example occurs when a doctor taps the patellar tendon and produces a knee-jerk response. The tap causes related muscles to stretch and contract in quick reflex action.

The potential advantages of the stretch reflex for power is confirmed by research. For example, Astrand states, "An unattached unstimulated muscle is at its equilibrium length, and the tension is zero....Normally, when attached by its tendons to the skeleton, the muscle is under slight tension, since it is moderately stretched (resting length). Measurements of the tension developed by the stimulated muscle show that tension is maximal when the initial length of the muscle at the time of stimulation is about 20 percent above the equilibrium length (1.2 to 1)....and decreases at lower and higher lengths."[3]

A 20 percent increase in strength would be of great significance. But in sports action, this potential force is reduced, since the line of pull under stretch tends to coincide with that of the related levers as their arms become straightline. For example, in the chinning exercise, the drop to full extension places the biceps at their strongest in contractile pull. But this potential strength is partially lost through the mechanical disadvantage of the fully extended elbow.

The value of the stretch reflex is shown clearly in the discus throw. During the turn, the throwing arm is held back--"on stretch." As the left foot is fixed at front-circle, an explosive counterclockwise rotation of the left hip produces a counter-rotation of the right

---

[1]Carl Miller, *ibid.*, p. 78

[2]Vladimir Dyatchkov, *Track Technique*, 1969, p. 1151

[3]Per-Olof Astrand, *ibid.*, p. 71

shoulder that places all related muscles on stretch at what is potentially their most powerful length. One feels and others can see this reflex as a reactive "bounce" that can be significant performance wise.

VARIETY IN TRAINING ROUTINES

We have emphasized the importance of careful organization of year-round programs of strength training, programs that include a few basic exercises such as the Olympic Lifts--simple in their movements, precisely measured, clearly progressive within a given year and also from year to year. But equally essential to good planning is an emphasis on variety in all phases of the program. Such variety maintains enthusiasm and motivation, but also ensures development of all related muscle groups, as well as full recovery and neuromuscular growth.

For example, we have suggested three sets as a rule of thumb. But Miller[1] recommends a three month program: first two weeks--three sets of 10 reps; next six weeks--eight sets of five reps with emphasis on strength; next four weeks--eight sets of five reps with lesser weights but emphasis on power.

Peter Tschiene's excellent review[2] of power training among top throwers in West Germany and the USSR is primarily a statement of the necessity for continuous variety: variety in work-rest periods; variety in loads per exercise, per day and in total lifted in a given number of days; variety in muscle structures and patterns of movement; variety in simulation of exercise to the movement of the projected event. As one example, he cites these monthly changes in the weight training of Dieter Moser, West German shotputter: Preparation period 1: November--3 sessions per week, submaximal (85%); December--5 times weekly, extensive (60%); January--3 times weekly, submaximal (85%); February--5 times weekly, extensive (60%); Preparation period 2: March-April--3 times weekly, intensive (75-80%); May--4 times weekly, maximal (90-95%); Competition period 1: June--twice weekly, intensive (75-80%); July--once weekly, maximum in 'pendulum' training (West German Championships); Competition period 2: August--once weekly, submaximal (80%); September--'pendulum' training for Olympic Games.

INDIVIDUAL DIFFERENCES IN POWER TRAINING

Individuals differ in all aspects of developmental training. Study after study reports that "individuals react to exercise in a manner unique to themselves." or that "great individual variations occur under the same experimental conditions." True, men are more alike than they are different, and the same basic principles of training apply to all individuals. But the specific blend of training factors that is optimum for any one individual is always unique.

1. Individuals differ in their responsiveness to heavy resistances in strength training. Some are innately heavy muscled; others, light muscled. Some, generally slow; others, generally fast. Even with outwardly equal physiques, two individuals may differ greatly in both natural strength and velocity of muscle contractions.

2. Individuals differ in the pattern of strength-velocity-coordination in different parts of the body. One individual may be superior in the movements of his arms but inferior in those of the legs, or vice versa. For example, de Vries (1968, 353) states that "this specificity extends even to the type of task and the direction of movement...It has been shown...that speed is 87 or 88 percent specific to the limb. Even within the limb, speed is 88 to 90 percent specific to the direction of movement." (Keep in mind that "speed" is not a separate entity but a way of looking at "power," and that what is said of one relates to what can be said of the other.)

3. As a generality, we tend to assume a 1:1 ratio between muscle cross section and its

---

[1]Carl Miller, *HOW TO USE WEIGHT TRAINING FOR YOUR SPECIFIC SPORT*, self-published, 1977, p. 7.

[2]Peter Tschiene, *ibid.*, pp. 1642-1654. (Though written in 1972, this article by a National Coach of West Germany is of present-day value for all throwing events. Examples are drawn from diaries of great performers, including Walter Schmidt, former world-record holder in the hammer.)

absolute strength (Hettinger, 1961, 12). Individuals differ, of course, in such cross sections. But Morehouse (1960, 195) points out, "there are repeated observations that exercised muscles can increase in size, but not in strength," as witness the "body beautiful" of the muscle pumper.

4. Very important: Individuals vary widely in the relative lengths of the bony levers of the body, as also in the effectiveness with which these levers function at various angles.

5. Individuals also vary greatly in what can be called "willed control" of strength. For example, Ikai[1] and Steinhaus concluded, "Our findings appear to support the thesis that in every voluntarily executed, all-out maximal effort, psychologic rather than physiologic factors determine the limits of performance." Such psychologic inhibitions, or lack of them, vary infinitely with each individual's unique environmental influences.

Bruce Jenner had his weight-training eyes opened when, in 1975, he shifted from his kingpin role at Graceland college to San Jose where the Big Boys--Feuerbach, Wilkins--were training,

I'd always thought I was strong, but very soon I found out different. The first time I went to the weight room at the YMCA...I did a few squats and thought I was real hot stuff. Then along comes Maren Seidler, a woman shot-putter, and she outsquats me like it was nothing at all. A girl!....It made me realize how underdeveloped I was, how much further I had to go, seeing all these guys so much better than I was.[2]

This list of five areas of individual differences is merely suggestive. Roger J. Williams' life-time studies[3] led him to conclude that just as our fingerprints are individually unique, so are all aspects of our structures and functions.

EVENT DIFFERENCES IN POWER TRAINING

The initial force of the power phase of all field events has a common origin--the strong-slow contractions of the large muscles closest to the center of weight, the trunk muscles. But the precise pattern of movement and innervation of motor units even in this central part is unique for each event.

This suggests that basic strength training as in the Olympic lifts has values for all events. But also, *even in basic strength training*, there should be a variation of loads and exercise movements that correspond to those of the event being trained.

Following a year-round plan for strength training by USSR Master Coach V. Kuznyetsov, Peter Tschiene[4] divided the program into three interwoven parts: basic strength work (BSW), diversified conditioning (DC) and specialized strength work (SSW). For the hammer and javelin he indicated the following changes from the 1960 period to that of the 1970s:

	BSW	DC	SSW
1960s	60-70%	20-30%	5-10%
1970s	10-20%	20-30%	50-60%

These figures should be interpreted loosely of course, but they do suggest distinct changes in attitudes and programs.

The pattern of movements and the particular motor units among the distal muscles vary even more markedly among field events. Contrast, for example, the shot and javelin, or the high jump and pole vault. What now is the specific need for strength? Here the answer is less

---

[1]Michio Ikai and Arthur Steinhaus, "Some Factors Modifying the Expression of Human Strength," in Steinhaus, *ibid.*, p. 137.

[2]Bruce Jenner and Phillip Finch, *DECATHLON CHALLENGE*, Englewood Cliffs, N.J.:Prentice-Hall Inc., 1977, p. 72.

[3]Roger J. Williams, *BIOCHEMICAL INDIVIDUALITY*, New York: John Wiley & Sons, 1956, 215 pp.

[4]Peter Tschiene, *ibid.*, p. 1650.

clear and requires an understanding of the previous discussion, "The Meaning of Human Power." As with the proximal muscles, highest-level strength is needed if resistances, however light, are to be moved at greatest velocity. But since these muscles are light-fast in both their structure and use, the strength concept now takes the form of power (strength x velocity) in which the velocity factor becomes more and more relevant as between the 16# shot within its 7-foot circle and the 1.7# javelin with its unlimited run that builds high velocity prior to the power-thrust at the foul arc. That is to say, optimal resistances must conform with muscle limitations as well as their special energy outputs.

SAFETY IN TRAINING FOR POWER

Even with trained supervision and careful organization of strength training, there is always danger of injury from overloading skeletal-muscle systems when doing power exercises. On beginning a weight-lifting program, strength develops rapidly; young boys and girls become enthusiastic; they attempt weights beyond their readiness, or use techniques that place over-strain on points of skeletal weakness.

Injuries, as in all aspects of strenuous sports, will occur. The all-important responsibility of both the coach and the weight-room supervisor is to make certain that the risk of injury is minimal. When it occurs--and it will occur--they each should feel they took all precautions to avoid it. I know all too well! Even now after more than 30 years, I get a tight feeling in my throat whenever I think of Charlie Fonville, world-record holder in the shot put, 1948. "The American most likely to win a gold at the London Olympics," he failed to make the U.S. Olympic team because of a lower-back injury while practicing the shot. No weight-lifting, of course, in the 1940s, but 10,000 repetitions of putting a 16# weight is a power exercise that can put all related structures on strain. Note that the shotputting action is identical to that of the lower figure in Figure 7.1. We weren't aware of that in 1948, but the bone-and-joint medics were, and we should have been.

Gunter Fritzsche[1], of West Germany, summarized the pros and cons of safety in weightlifting, the gist of which is as follows:

1. "The coach should continuously inform young athletes of the danger of premature tests of strength."

2. "Particularly important is the all-around development of the youngster in his early years." "Barbell work should not be performed until after the 13th year."

3. "There is basically no difference in teaching weight training to boys and to girls. However, because of less power, initial poundages for females should be 10-15% less."

Youngsters of widely different ages and abilities should work out separately. Supervision and teaching can then be more precisely fitted to both knowledge and capacity.

4. An all-round conditioning program, one that ensures good muscular development of the torso (medicine balls, sandbags, bars, etc.), should precede weight lifting.

5. "Correct lifting technique is particularly important...Correct motions should first be learned with unweighted bars."

Fig. 6.1--Movements that tend to cause injury.

[1]Gunter Fritzsche, "Safety Factors in Weightlifting," *Track Technique*, #64, June 1976, p. 2025. Translated by G. A. Carr from *Leichtathletik*, #7, 1975.

6. "The objective for each training session must be carefully thought out and well under-stood by all."

7. Adequate warmup, both general and specific, must precede each exercise. As to possible dangers of heavy-weight training programs in general, Fritzsche cites the work of Falameyev and Lukanov, USSR, "Exercises with weights cause no particular changes to the spine but actual-ly favorably influence its structure in that weight training develops a supportive 'corset of muscles.'"

8. Until both the supervisor and the youngster are sure of what can be handled without strain, weights should be lifted easily; repetitions, low so that the last lift on the last set involves sub-maximal effort; and progressions from week to week, gradual.

ORGANIZATION OF TRAINING SESSIONS

It is not within the scope of this book to detail the many phases of training for basic strength and basic power. Such training requires personal supervision at all times, instruc-tion from an expert experienced in weightlifting, and more complete explanations of a full textbook on this particular subject. But a few background comments should be helpful:

STARTING WEIGHTS. Assuming the all-round conditioning program has been of sufficient length and gradually developed, starting weights should be those that can be lifted about 20 times without strain. After several sessions with satisfactory recovery, increase weights to those that can be lifted 12 times.

REPETITIONS. Authorities differ as to a specific number of repetitions that is optimal, once serious weightlifting is started. As a basic rule, Ryan[1] suggests three sets that can be done with eight reps, then increased, one rep at a time, to 12. Now increase the weight so that eight reps is a maximum, again gradually increasing the reps to 12. Ryan makes no claims of "this being the one and only way. It just seems to work well and is a good way to get started." With certain exercises, such as squats or heel raises, Ryan suggests more reps--"probably 12 to 15."

Lukk,[2] of Estonia, reviewed related research and recommended a three-stage program: when medium weights will gain the intended purpose, eight to 10 reps are best; for heavy resis-tances, four to seven; for maximal or near-maximal resistances, one to three.

Taking a different approach, Miller[3] gives an example of progressions in repetitions in four exercises--split squats, front squats, knee-ups, and bench presses. After two weeks of gradual build-up with moderate weights, one of his athletes followed this program:

The following four weeks he did eight sets of five repetitions. This first set was done with moderate weight and 7-12# were added with each set, hitting his maximum on the fourth or fifth set, and then trying to stay with as much weight as possible until eight sets were completed....On every repetition, every effort was made to explode... Admittedly the last repetition did not go very fast, but the nerves were being told to explode. Since we were striving for strength, we took a long rest (three to five minutes) between sets.

SETS. The number of sets in any given session varies in keeping with the time of year as related to competition, with the purpose of that particular session, and with the nature of each exercise. For example, when the purpose is focussed on basic strength, as distinguished from velocity and special movement patterns, the number of sets--as of repetitions--is usually kept low with ample rest periods between sets: three sets of 6-8 RM (Repetitions Maximum-- the maximal weight that can be lifted six to eight times.) But diaries of champions often disclose sessions in which six sets are used for cleans, snatches, and squats but only two

[1]Frank Ryan, WEIGHT TRAINING, New York: The Viking Press, Inc., 1969, p. 57.

[2]T. Lukk, "Science and Throwing," Track Technique, #72, June 1978, p. 2307.

[3]Carl Miller, HOW TO USE WEIGHT TRAINING FOR YOUR SPECIFIC SPORT, self-published, p. 8.

sets for dead lifts and trunk twisting.

Hooks[1] seeks to develop both strength and velocity by sessions of three sets of ten, eight, and six reps each. In the first set of an over-head press, for example, the lifter presses ten times with a weight about 50% of maximum with concentration upon all-out speed of movement. On the second set, weight is added so that speed is reduced, even though maximum explosiveness is attempted; repetitions are reduced to eight. On the third set, the weight is further increased; the reps reduced to six. When ten reps can be done in the third set without straining, all three sets are increased by 20 pounds (larger muscles) or 10 pounds (smaller muscles).

Pickering[2] recommends the pyramid system as "the most favored of all systems." He suggests five sets with a decreasing number of repetitions from five down to two, and with increasing weights for each set (ten pounds for weaker muscles; 20 pounds for stronger ones). When two repetitions with a maximum weight can be done, the beginning weight with five reps is increased, and the series repeated until again two reps can be made with a heavier maximum weight.

RECORD KEEPING. It is essential to knowledge of progress, to planning of each year's program, and to maintaining motivation that a record be kept by both the coach and the athlete of the essentials of each day's workout: exercise, sets, repetitions, rest periods, training intensities, and most important, purpose of the workout.

A competent coach must be able to refer back to workouts of previous years by this athlete and all others that have come under his care.

ISOMETRIC (STATIC) STRENGTH TRAINING

The isometric craze of the 60s has now receded to its proper level, as reported by its original research workers--Theodor Hettinger, E. A. Muller, F. M. Henry and others. Actually, these men were not concerned with sport or work so much as with greater knowledge--the nature of muscle development, of a minimal developmental load, and the like. They chose isometric contraction because it met the needs of science for validity and reliability. Today, after years of field experience, we realize that isometric training is useful primarily in research; only secondarily in the cautiously derived insights such research can provide for dynamic training. Among such insights are the following:

1. "There is no doubt that isometric muscle training, performed daily, and with greatest possible intensity and frequency, will result in an increase in isometric muscle strength.... But if the muscle strength is intended. . . for performing certain tasks in labor or sport, isometric training probably is rather worthless. This is because the obtained isometric strength apparently cannot be transferred directly to other forms of activity. . . ."[3]

2. DeVries (1966, 310) states that well-controlled studies show no significant correlations between the strength gains from isometric and dynamic training programs. In part this results from the unreliability of dynamic strength measurements. It also suggests that conclusions from one such program should be used very cautiously as related to the other.

3. Isometric training increases isometric strength without affecting significantly the endurance of related muscles (Astrand, 1970, 401). Training by repeated isometric contractions develops endurance only for this particular kind of action. Dynamic endurance results only from repeated dynamic contractions.

4. Static strength gains occur very quickly when a muscle's present strength is a small percentage of its potential strength, but occur very slowly as muscle strength approaches its maximum. Gains usually range from one to ten percent per week, but some investigators have reported gains in beginners of as much as 73 percent per week for static training, and 168 percent for dynamic training.

---

[1]Gene Hooks, *APPLICATION OF WEIGHT TRAINING TO ATHLETICS*, Englewood Cliffs, N.J.: Prentice-Hall, Inc., 1962, pp. 24, 47.

[2]Ron Pickering, *STRENGTH TRAINING FOR ATHLETICS*, London: AAA, 1970, p. 51.

[3]Erling Asmussen, "The Neuromuscular System and Exercise," see Harold B. Falls, 1968, 36.

THE OLYMPIC LIFTS.

The Olympic lifts shown in Figures 6.2 to 6.5 are the foundation of every program for developing basic strength, that is, maximal strength of the large muscles of the torso moving against heavy resistances. Of course "torso" is itself an extensional word. We use it AS IF it were between the shoulders and hips; actually it extends in all Olympic lifts upward through the shoulders-arms-wrists-hands-fingers, and downward through the hips-legs-feet. But development goals should be centered on the largest, strongest, slowest muscles surrounding the body's center of gravity, those that initiate all power movements of field events.

Fig. 6.2 -- Two-arm clean and press.

Fig. 6.3 -- Two-arm snatch.

Fig. 6.4 -- Two-arm clean and jerk (split).

Fig. 6.5 -- Two-arm clean and jerk (squat).

---

[1]These drawings excerpted from Nikolai G. Osolin, *Modern System of Sports Training*, Moscow: USSR Gov't Printing Office.

POWER EXERCISES

POWER EXERCISES

FLEXIBILITY FOR TRACK AND FIELD

A well-designed program of flexibility based on stretching exercises can be an important factor in preventing injuries, as well as in improving performance. In simplest terms, flexibility relates to the range of movement within a joint or series of joints. For some joints, such as the elbow or knee, the bony structure fixes the limits of this range. But for most, as in the ankle, wrist or hip, the range of motion depends on more stretchable tissues: (1) muscles and their fascial sheaths; (2) connective tissue including tendons, ligaments, and joint capsules; and (3) the skin. Related research has established that, of these factors, resistance to extension arises almost entirely from the fascial sheaths that closely bind muscles and muscle-fiber units. It is these fascial sheaths that are the primary concern of a program of flexibility exercises.

Herbert deVries,[1] after a careful survey of related research, identified two types of flexibility: static--a measure of range of motion; and dynamic--a measure of a joint's resistance to motion. In his study of static flexibility, deVries distinguished between two methods: (1) ballistic--the usual calisthenic exercises such as trunk rotators, benders and lifters, or leg and arm lifters. Antagonists are stretched by contraction of the agonists, and vice versa, in bobbing or bouncing movements. (2) Static stretching methods, not unlike the static positions (*asanas*) of Hatha yoga. Joints are locked for a period of time so as to extend muscles and connective tissues maximally.

DeVries found that both methods made significant and similar gains in flexibility, but concluded that the static stretching method has three distinct advantages: (1) less danger of injury by over-extension; (2) lower energy requirements; and (3) in contrast to ballistic stretching, it seems to relieve muscle soreness, not cause it.

Cyril Carter[2] prefers the word, "suppling"--bending easily without strain or breaking--as used in ballet and gymnastics. He suggests ballistic movements during the warm-up phase, with emphasis on complete relaxation; then moves toward the extremes of a joint's range of motion, again with a first concern for relaxation. In many instances this relaxed stretch can be held for as long as 30 seconds.

The main principle governing this type of suppling is that...the athlete should never use his own muscular strength to force a joint beyond its "natural" range... The natural reaction of a training muscle, when encountering a sudden forceful movement, is to tighten up...to prevent injury to the joint. This counters the intent to stretch and lengthen (supple) the muscle and ligaments, and often causes small tears...in the muscle.

In all exercises for suppling the emphasis is on relaxation of the limb to be worked on. Therefore, whatever position is being practiced, the athlete must attempt to go to the extremes of his range and stay, relaxed, for a period of time. It is the number of times,...together with the length of time spent in such positions, that determines just how supple (and how quickly) one is likely to get. The only effort is (that) required for relaxing.

Suppling is an all-round (two-way) process....It is of little use suppling in one direction without spending an equal amount of time suppling in the opposite direction. Example: if one requires suppling of the hamstrings for the lead-leg action in hurdling, one must also supple the opposing muscle (the quadriceps) on the same leg.

(Carter's exercises are similar to those described here, though with a greater emphasis on

---

[1]The views stated in this section have been drawn primarily from Herbert A. deVries, *PHYSIOLOGY OF EXERCISE FOR PHYSICAL EDUCATION AND ATHLETICS*, Dubuque, Iowa: Wm. C. Brown Co., Publishers, 1974, Chapter 22--Flexibility.

[2]Cyril A. Carter, "Suppling: the Myth of Mobility Exercising," *Track Technique*, #73, Fall 1978, p. 2329.

complete relaxation and on the length of time positions are held. He ends his article as follows:)

Remember that (suppling) is a long and slow process (often painful but not injurious), in which the emphasis is on relaxation, not on activity. If you feel any sharp or sudden pain, stop immediately. Take your time and persevere for, just as the results are slow, so too are they certain and safe.

Consistent with these findings, Croce[1] and DiPaolo selected 32 static exercises (positions) that stretch the various joints and muscles that incur greatest stress in sports. Joints are gradually extended toward their maximal range of motion. Positions are held for from five to ten seconds, then repeated three to five times, with complete relaxation between.

To avoid muscle soreness and possible injury from over-stretching, the authors emphasize (1) such warm-up exercises as easy calisthenics, jogging-in-place and rope skipping, and (2) gradual increments of stretching during first movements. Among their recommended exercises, the following seem of special value for track and field:

Head to Floor--Sit with legs straddled wide; keeping legs straight with hands grasping lower legs loosely, bring forehead slowly forward toward and eventually to the floor. Repeat with increase of leg spread. Muscles stretched--trunk extensors, groin, hamstrings.

Knees to Floor--Sit with soles of feet together; use hands to pull heels maximally toward crotch; lean forward, using elbows to push knees down to floor. Muscles stretched--groin.

Heels to Buttocks--Lie prone; keeping chin on floor, grasp both ankles; slowly pull heels to buttocks. Muscles stretched--quadriceps. (As an extension of this exercise, lift chin and pull knees from floor; then rock forward and back.)

Palms to Floor--Stand with feet together; keeping knees straight, bend slowly forward until the palms touch the floor. Muscles stretched--hamstrings, trunk extensors.

Head to Floor--Stand with feet spread about 3-4 times shoulder-width; keep knees straight; hands should grasp lower legs to aid forward bend bringing head to the floor. Muscles stretched--hamstrings, trunk extensors, groin.

Calf Stretch--Stand with feet about four feet from wall, extended palms on wall; keeping entire body straight and heels on floor, slowly lean forward using arms for support. Muscles stretched--calf, ankle plantarflexors.

Prayer Stretch--Place palms of hands together in front of chin at shoulder level; raise elbows maximally. Muscles stretched--wrist flexors. (To stretch wrist extensors, reverse this exercise with backs of hands together; pull elbows down.)

----

[1]Pat Croce and Matt DiPaolo, *STRETCH YOUR LIFE*, C & D Publications, Box 447, Springfield, Pa., 19064, 1980, paperback, 48 pps. A completely illustrated guide to static stretching exercises.

BASIC FLEXIBILITY EXERCISES

Basic Flexibility Exercises. Most of these exercises can be done by both the ballistic and static stretching methods as described by deVries. However, the work of all three investigators reviewed here confirms that major emphasis should be placed on the static (suppling) method. In most instances, the ballistic method is better used when warming up.

Chapter 7
THE HIGH JUMP

In contrast to the single-line approach of the other jumping events, the 180-degree area in front of the running-high-jump crossbar is unrestricted. During the past 100 years of trying to jump higher and higher, men have run down or curved across each of those 180 degrees, and each variation has produced its own unique technique--in the run, in the gather and spring, and in the method of clearing the bar. In this last phase alone, we can distinguish at least eight different styles, as will be described in a later section.

Actually, the method of clearing the bar is not at all the crucial phase of jumping high. Geoffrey Dyson, the English expert in biomechanics, estimated (1967, 135) that this phase contributed only about ten percent to the height obtained, as compared with 90 percent from what he called spring. This analysis was confirmed roughly by Hay's study[1] of a 7-foot jump by Matzdorf from which he concluded that the takeoff (vertical impulse) contributed 8.9 times as much to height cleared as did the method of clearance.

In their use of the words "spring" and "takeoff," these researchers included the forces gained from all phases of the run to the instant of leaving the ground. For our purposes, spring is better understood as having two phases: (1) the horizontal force of the run, and (2) the vertical impulse as achieved in a standing high jump. Using Harold Osborn's standing high jump record (5'6", 1936, at age 35!) as compared with his running high jump record (6'8¼", 1924), and making allowance for the height of his standing center of gravity, we secure a difference of roughly 70 percent. If we then subtract Dyson's estimate of 10 percent for clearance style, we obtain 60 percent for spring and 30 percent for the value of the run. I hardly need add that these figures are merely suggestive. Actually, Osborn's run was with "long easy bounding strides, a little faster than a dog trot," so we can assume an even higher percentage might be derived from a more forceful run.

It follows that a valid attempt to summarize the development of technique in the running high jump must consider, not just the styles of bar-clearance, but also the various phases of the run (direction, length, velocity, pattern), and what can be called the conversion phase from horizontal to vertical force. Jumpers have unique styles in these phases just as they do in the bar-clearance phase. But first, to make such a history clearer, a review of certain basic concepts is in order.

BASIC CONCEPTS RELATED TO JUMPING HIGH.
(1) Dyson's estimate of 10 percent for clearance, 90 percent for spring including the run, suggests that *in terms of high-jumping techniques a jumper's major concern should be to develop better methods for increasing his upward velocity at takeoff, much more than for his style of clearing the bar.* Such velocity (plus the flight angle) determines entirely the height to which the jumper's center of mass rises. Clearance styles affect this only indirectly, by the way they may change the run and conversion phases.

The first corollary of this principle is that high-jumping styles should be valued on a

---

[1]James G. Hay, "A Kinematic Analysis of the High Jump," *Track Technique*, Sept. 1973, 1698.

TABLE 7.1
OUTSTANDING PERFORMANCES -- HIGH JUMP

OLYMPIC CHAMPIONS -- MEN

Date	Record		Name	Affiliation	Age	Hgt.	Wgt.	Style
1948	6' 6"	1.98	John Winter	Australia		6' 4"		Eastern
1952	6' 8¼"	2.04	Walt Davis	Texas A&M	21	6' 8½"	190	Western
1956	6' 11½"	2.16	Charles Dumas	Compton	19	6' 1½"	179	Straddle
1960	7' 1"	2.17	R. Shavlakadze	USSR	27	6' 1¼"	183	Straddle
1964	7' 1 7/8"	2.19	Valeriy Brumel	USSR	22	6' 1½"	175	Straddle
1968	7' 4¼"	2.25	Richard Fosbury	Oregon St.	21	6' 4"	183	Flop
1972	7' 3 3/4"	2.24	Juri Tarmak	USSR	26	6' 4"	161	Straddle
1976	7' 4½"	2.26	Jacek Wszola	Poland	19	6' 3"	168	Flop
1980	7' 8 7/8"	2.36	Gerd Wessig	E. Germany				

PERFORMANCES OF SPECIAL INTEREST -- MEN

Date	Record		Name	Affiliation	Age	Hgt.	Wgt.	Style
1887	6' 4"	1.93	W. Byrd Page	U. of Penn.		5' 6 3/4"		Mod. scissors
1895	6' 5 5/8"	1.97	Mike Sweeney	Xavier A.C.		5' 8¼"		Eastern
1912	6' 7"	2.01	George Horine	Stanford		5' 11"		Western
1917	6' 9½"x	2.07	Clint Larson	Brig. Young	25	5' 9½"		On back
1924	6' 8¼"	2.04	Harold Osborn	Illinois	25	5' 11½"	178	Western
1932	6' 6"	1.98	Jim Stewart	So. Calif.	23	6' 3"		Straddle
1933	6' 8¼"	2.04	George Spitz	N.Y.U.	24	6'		Eastern
1936	6' 8 3/8"	2.04	Kalevi Kotkas	Finland		6' 6"		Eastern
1936	6' 9 3/4"	2.08	Dave Albritton	Ohio State	23	6' 3"	176	½D-Straddle
1938	6' 8 3/8"	2.04	Gil Cruter	Colorado	23	6' 4"	174	Dive-Straddle
1941	6' 11"	2.11	Les Steers	Oregon	24	6' 1"	190	Straddle
1956	7' 5/8"	2.15	Charles Dumas	Compton	19	6' 1½"	179	Straddle
1960	7' 3 3/4"	2.24	John Thomas	Boston U.	19	6' 4 3/4"	187	Straddle
1963	7' 5 3/4"	2.29	Valeriy Brumel	USSR	21	6' 1½"	175	Straddle
1971	7' 6¼"	2.30	Pat Matzdorf	Wisconsin	21	6' 3"	172	Dive-Straddle
1976	7' 7¼"	2.32	Dwight Stones	L. Beach St.	20	6' 5"	175	Flop
1978	7' 8"x	2.34	V. Yashchenko	USSR	20	6' 5¼"	180	Dive-Straddle
1980	7' 8½"		Jacek Wszola	Poland	23	6' 3"	172	Flop

x Exhibition

HIGH SCHOOL BOYS

Date	Record		Name	Affiliation
1971	7' 1½"	2.17	Dwight Stones	Glendale, CA
1974	7' 1 3/4"	2.17	Dean Herzog	Russelville, Kansas
1978	7' 4¼"	2.24	Gail Olson	Sycamore, Ill.

OLYMPIC CHAMPIONS-- WOMEN

Date	Record		Name	Affiliation	Age	Hgt.	Wgt.
1972	6' 3¼"	1.91	Ulrike Meyfarth	W. Germany	16	6' ¼"	154
1976	6' 4"	1.93	Rosie Ackermann	E. Germany	24	5' 9"	130
1980	6' 5½"		Sara Simeoni	Italy	27	5' 9¼"	151

OUTSTANDING PERFORMANCES -- WOMEN

Date	Record		Name	Affiliation
1976	6' 1½"[1]	1.87	Paula Girven	Garfield, Woodb. Va.
1978	6' 7"[2]	2.01	Sara Simeoni	Italy
1979	6' 4"[3,4]	1.93	Louise Ritter	Texas Western U.
1980	6' 4 3/4"		Louise Ritter	Texas Western U.

[1] High School Record
[2] World Record
[3] College record
[4] American record

basis of their effectiveness in the run-and-spring phase of the jump (90 percent), rather than on the traditional basis of economy of clearance (10 percent). On such a scale, how does the Flop compare with the Straddle or Dive Straddle? How does the Brumel Straddle compare with that of Dumas with its four slow and three fast steps to the takeoff?

A second corollary is that practice time should be focussed on first things first--on the run, conversion and spring phases of high jumping, and on specifically related power training. The specific movements of bar-clearance will tend to emerge, without special emphasis, from such practice and early-career competition.

(2) *An emphasis on related power training is absolutely essential--to highest jumping and for prevention of injury.* The vertical velocities involved in jumping seven feet or more require great power exerted during a very brief time--power in the takeoff leg (torso, thigh, lower leg, knee and ankle, foot), and power in the lead leg to aid its rapidly accelerating drive upward. In addition, the faster run and sudden braking actions of high-level jumping place great strain on the related muscles and tendons. Ecker states that "top-level high jumpers exert a force against the ground that is as much as four times their body weight."[1] Prevention, always best, requires power training prior to actual jumping.

(3) *The greater the velocity of the run, the greater its potential as an aid to jumping high.* To explain this principle, I think of an indoor game my grandson has. By pulling a rod, a steel spring is compressed. Its release shoots steel balls horizontally into an upward-curved slope, hopefully into holes at various heights--low and high. The more the spring is compressed, *the greater the velocity of the ball, and the higher it is projected into the air.* Dyatchkov[2] states that an increase of 0.1 m/sec linear speed increases the pressure against the ground by the takeoff foot by 26-35 pounds which, if used effectively, can increase vertical height by about 3.5 cms.

In the indoor game with the steel balls, a curved slope provides the means for converting horizontal force upward. In human jumping the body is self-propelled and there is no curved slope, but the principle is still effective. In fact, in the late 1950s it led to experimentation with an "inclined-plane shoe" having a thick sole, and this in turn to the present rule fixing the thickness of the sole at 13 mm. Saying it differently, a major focus of high jumping technique is to acquire a built-in substitute for the curved-slope or inclined-plane concepts.

(4) *The greater the velocity of the run, the greater its tendency to shorten the time during which force can be exerted against the ground during the takeoff phase,* and so to decrease the impulse (force x time) upward. Note that this is the negative aspect of concept #3. There is no benefit in a faster run if a man lacks the power or technique for using it. Dyson (1978, 7th edition, 142) suggests that each jumper and each jumping style has a "critical speed beyond which takeoff efficiency can be impaired." That is, if the height of present jumping is important, a jumper should use a running velocity that is relative to his present related-muscle power and conversion technique. In the past, this has meant that, lacking power training and effective conversion technique, men have tended to slow their run.

Today we understand that the negative effects of faster running is only a tendency that allows a range of possible use, not a fixed value. It follows that in early season or with beginning jumpers the run should not be slowed to ensure critical speed. Instead, primary concern should be to gain greater power in the related muscles, and better techniques to increase the duration of force against the ground so as to make full use of a fast-as-possible run.

(5) *Impulse = Force x Time. Other things being equal, the greater the time that force is applied upward, the higher the center of mass is propelled.* This concept has many implications, and we are still discovering better ways of making it more effective. During the last few strides the center of gravity must be lowered, thus compressing the muscle springs, and

---

[1]Tom Ecker, "High Jump Take-Off," *The Athletic Journal*, March 1975, p. 18.

[2]Vladimir M. Dyatchkov, *HIGH JUMPING*, Moscow: State Publishing House, 1966.

providing more time for the application of force. Pre-Brumel Straddlers did not get as low and started the center of gravity upward sooner. Brumel carried it low during the final strides and started it slightly upward only during the last step.

Fig. 7.1. Valeriy Brumel--The Conversion Phase. The down-through-up action of the arms (a-b-c) keeps the center of gravity low. The forceful upward thrust of the arms (c-d) and of the lead leg (b-c) increases force against the ground. Great strength in the takeoff leg creates the reactive impulse upward (d-e). These same forces are present in the Fosbury style.

Some recent research has shown that on higher jumps, the takeoff foot is on the ground for a shorter length of time. This is only an apparent contradiction to this concept #5. Highest-level jumpers have greater muscular power which gives them greater quickness in all the related aspects of the jump; their time factor is therefore shorter. Given equal power (quickness), the technique that lengthens the time in which force is applied will exert a greater vertical impulse.

(6) *Rotational movements seeking an efficient clearance style are of two kinds--direct and indirect.* Direct rotation occurs while the jumper is still in contact with the ground, when a force in any given direction produces an effect in that same direction--leaning forward produces a forward rotation; to the inside, an inward rotation, and so forth. Since its direction of force is always to one side or the other of the line of flight of the center of gravity, direct rotation diminishes vertical force, and so the height reached by the center of gravity.

Indirect rotation occurs after contact with the ground has been lost, and so has no detrimental effect on vertical force or the height reached by the center of gravity. Now movement of the extremities has an action-reaction effect. A left-ward thrust of the right arm turns the torso to the right; a downward thrust moves it upward. An upward lift of the head lowers the torso; a lowering of the torso tends to lift the extremities.

In general, effective jumpers seek maximal vertical impulse with minimal direct rotation, and achieve efficient clearance by way of indirect rotation. Attempts to coach direct rotation in the Flop by emphasizing an inward eccentric drive of the lead knee tends to increase rotation directly and diminish the vertical thrust of the takeoff leg.

(7) *Improved technique and higher jumping are acquired together; each aids the other.* A higher height of the bar forces a more vertical effort and also allows more time for the movements of indirect rotation and clearance.

(8) *To provide maximal upward force, the lead leg must accelerate maximally during the first 90 degrees of its upward swing while the takeoff foot is still on the ground.* Once takeoff is completed, such acceleration cannot add to the jumper's velocity. Since a flexed lead leg can drive upward more quickly, and so contributes more force in the brief time the foot is against the ground, it is so used in the Flop and Dive-Straddle styles. (See Figure 7.44). In the Straddle, the great concern for vertical force allows more time in which a

straighter (longer) lead leg can contribute greater angular momentum and upward pull to the body. But in every style, early maximum acceleration of the lead leg's forceful upthrust is crucial.

A SUMMARY HISTORY OF THE RUN.

Over the past century of high jumping we have gradually learned to run faster and make more effective use of the potential values of such speed. But this is an over-simplification of what actually happened. It was no straight-line development; each generation of jumpers had advocates of a somewhat longer-faster run, and other advocates of a forceful spring with emphasis on only the last three or four strides of the run.

THE RUN IN THE EASTERN STYLE. Prior to about 1940, most of those favoring a faster run followed some variation of the Eastern style. Such a run was inherent in the style with its outside-foot takeoff and forceful swing-up of the inside leg.

Mike Sweeney (N.Y.A.C., 1895, 6'5 5'8") was the first major jumper to achieve a full layout from an outside-foot takeoff. In fact, his achievement was so startling that for many years men spoke of the Sweeney style (Figure 7.4a) much as we now do of the Fosbury Flop. Not until some years after the Horine style came to be called the Western Roll was Sweeney's style called the Eastern.

Sweeney started his run in the middle of the runway (about 75 feet back), and swung slowly towards the right edge of the cinder track, turning sharply to the left at an exactly fixed point. He then took three strides as rapidly and with as much force as he could compel. This brings his left foot on the take-off, and gives his body a sort of twist that aids greatly in getting over the bar.[1]

There's no evidence that Dick Fosbury ever read that 1896 quotation, but it's a striking instance of history repeating itself, for his run, though from the opposite side, was remarkably similar to that of Sweeney.

One variation of the Eastern style, that used by Clint Larson (1917, 6'7"; 1924, 6'9½" exhibition), made an even greater use of speed in the run. Larson described his clearance (Figure 7.5) as "a face-upward, back-to-the-bar position", and wrote that,

I feel certain that I ran farther and faster than any other high jumper of my time. I gave particular attention to the practice of sprinting and under favorable conditions could cover the 100 yards in 10.2 seconds. I believe that my jumping ability is due to speed and direct co-ordination of action from the time I start the run until I land on the other side of the bar....I ordinarily cover a distance of from 12 to 14 feet....from takeoff to point of landing.[2]

As with Murphy, Larson's words might have been taken from a talk by Dwight Stones ("I consider speed in the run as of primary importance") but we must deduct heavily for 1920 conditions (soft surfaces for run-up and takeoff, heavy shoes with two-spiked heels, no power training) when we interpret the meaning of "speed" in action. In any case, this emphasis on a forceful run gradually faded as the Eastern style lost favor.

THE RUN IN THE WESTERN ROLL. The Western Roll and its variations had a built-in tendency to slow the run so as to ensure a maximum spring and efficient clearance style. Its inventor, George Horine (1912, 6'7"), described his run,

I used a short preliminary run--actually a walk--except for the last three or four steps....I never measured my run and never marked my takeoff.[3]

---

[1] *TRACK ATHLETICS IN DETAIL*, compiled by Editor of *Harper's Round Table*, New York: Harper & Brothers Publishers, 1896, p. 56.

[2] Clinton Larson, "Larson on High Jumping," in R. L. Templeton, *THE HIGH JUMP*, American Sports Publishing Co., 1926, p. 125.

[3] George Horine, "My Development of the Western Roll," in R. L. Templeton, *THE HIGH JUMP*, ibid., p. 109.

Harold Osborne (1924, 6'8¼"), with his own back-to-the-bar version of the Western Roll (Figure 7.7b) was very exact in his way of running but gained little momentum,

I measure my approach with a great deal of care, allowing 24 feet between my takeoff and first check-mark, and 12 feet to the second mark. I take three steps to the middle mark and four more to the takeoff--about three feet from the crossbar. I approach from an angle of about 45 degrees and use a long easy bounding step, a little faster than a dog trot. On the last step I "settle" for the spring, then swing the outward leg up and over the bar with considerable force.[1]

THE RUN IN THE STRADDLE STYLE. In its early stages, the Straddle style was developed as an improvement in economy of clearance, without reference to the run or to differences in training methods. That is, Straddlers followed the minimal speeds in the approach and in amount of practice as established by Horine and Osborn.

But Les Steers (1941, 6'11") changed this. Of course power training was unknown at that time. But Steers partially offset this by gradually increasing, during a 12-year career, his ability to jump many times at high heights day-after-day-after-day, probably more than has ever been done in jumping history. Bowerman[2] states that Steers often "jumped twice a day, sometimes taking 20 to 30 jumps on the morning of a meet as a warm-up." Steers said that he ran without any special emphasis on speed, but actually he ran much faster than his contemporaries.

As a spectator-coach, I was greatly impressed by Steers--by his insistence on practice to gain both power and skill, and by the potential value of his running velocity. In 1953, in the first edition of *MODERN TRACK AND FIELD*, I wrote:

It is my considered opinion that a man can learn to use greater speed at the takeoff than has heretofore been used, and that some means of suddenly "bracing" against horizontal momentum can be acquired....The jumper will have Les Steers' ability to take work, developed through years of effort, and will have Clint Larson's speed and gather up to the bar. Only by combining the two will the best-ever performance be forthcoming.[3]

Unfortunately, most coaches and jumpers did not agree and Steers' methods met strong resistance. They found that repeated jumping tended to "deaden" the jumping muscles, as of course it does if too much is attempted too soon. They therefore concluded that Steers was one-of-a-kind and, lacking his gradual 12-year build-up and having no knowledge of the values of power training, they tended to accept a slower approach as being the more practical way.

In 1956, the Olympic Champion, Charles Dumas, first man ever to clear seven feet, reduced the run to its minimal values. From an angle of 43 degrees, he took eight strides to the takeoff, almost walking the first few and accelerating rapidly only on the last three, much as Harold Osborn had done in 1924.

In my judgment, the longer-faster runs of today were originated by the great Swedish jumpers of the 1950s. In 1954, at the Swedish National Championships, I watched Bengt Nilsson's efforts to become the first to clear seven feet. He used a 13-stride run in which the last seven or eight accelerated to give great force at takeoff. Though jumping Dive-Straddle style, Nilsson used a two-arm upward thrust as an aid to converting that force vertically, a method that was first copied by the Russians and later, by the jumping world.

Valeriy Brumel. The most perfect development of all aspects of the Straddle style came through the work of Valeriy Brumel, USSR, 1963, 7'5 3/4". (I have a strong inclination to

---

[1]Harold M. Osborne, "Championship Competition," in R.L.Templeton, *THE HIGH JUMP*, p. 162.

[2]William J. Bowerman, *COACHING TRACK AND FIELD*, Boston: Houghton Mifflin Co., 1975, p. 171.

[3]J. Kenneth Doherty, *MODERN TRACK AND FIELD*, Englewood Cliffs, N.J.; Prentice-Hall, Inc., 1953, p. 376.

write the name as Brumel-Dyatchkov, since the influence of this great National Coach of High Jumping was so vital to Brumel's success.) Perhaps their greatest contribution was that they contrived the means for making a fast run of practical use in increasing upward force. Their method had at least four aspects: (1) a related power training program, (2) a forward-upward thrust of both arms that delayed the rise of the center of weight during the spring, (3) a "settling" of the body during the last three strides, and (4) as an effect of these, an actual increase in the speed of the run.

How fast did Brumel run? Certainly faster than any world-rank jumper prior to 1960, with the possible exception of Larson, whom I never saw. He took seven strides plus three or four preliminary steps, with full acceleration on the first stride beyond his checkmark, a total run of 50 feet. During one of the great dual competitions (1962) in Madison Square Garden between Brumel and John Thomas (1960, 7'3 3/4"), several coaches[1] found he averaged 2.15 seconds from his deep checkmark to takeoff. Dyatchkov reported that Brumel's speed at the next-to-last stride was 15.65 mph.

THE RUN IN THE FLOP STYLE. The Flop style of high jumping is best understood in all its phases if it is related to the Eastern style--more specifically, the Sweeney-Larson version of the Eastern style. Fosbury began jumping scissors-style in grade school. His high school coach tried to teach him the Straddle, but in one meet, age 16, he reverted to the Scissors with a back layout. At first his body angle was about 45 degrees to the crossbar but by his senior year he had rotated to the full 90 degrees during clearance. Without coaching, Fosbury found that he could run faster and faster up to his takeoff, with little tendency to decelerate during the last few strides.

Since Fosbury, the majority of great jumpers have adopted his style, and all have run at speeds greater than those generally used in the Western or Straddle. Dwight Stones (1973, 7' 7¼") said repeatedly that the key to his jumping lay in speed, speed and more speed-- "the faster I run, the higher I can jump." It seems clear that, not only is this an innate feature of the style, but the use of a curved approach during the last few strides also has special values. The natural lean into the curve and back from the takeoff foot balances centrifugal force and prolongs the compression of the body springs that Brumel contrived only with special techniques and long practice. This, added to the outside-foot takeoff and inside knee thrust upward, somehow makes the style more tolerant of limited leg strength, limited leg spring, and even limited skill.

Fig. 7.2. The run by Dwight Stones. Contrast this higher-speed style (forward lean, high on toes) with the more flat-footed and "settled" style of Sapka (Figure 7.45).

Did Stones attain maximal speed for the Flop as Brumel did for the Straddle? Probably not. Stones took ten strides in his run from a checkmark about 64 feet from the crossbar. This length certainly gave him the potential for great speed. His one-year coach (1974), John

---

[1]W. Harold O'Connor, Carl Seaman, Edward Boyle and Roger Howard, "Brumel vs Thomas," *Scholastic Coach*, March 1962, p. 7.

Tansley of Glendale College, wrote that "he accelerates on the last three steps, coordinating the right amount of speed with the maximum available strength." How much strength was available? Stones did make use of related power training, but not at all to the extent available to Brumel who had the great advantages of experts in biomechanics and sports medicine as well as of a National High Jump Coach, Dyatchkov, whose concern was solely for that event and its champions. In contrast, Stones moved from college to college and never had consistent single-minded coaching.

Furthermore, like Fosbury, Stones seldom jumped in practice. Even if the Flop style is relatively simple, and requires less time to gain acceptable proficiency, we are not entitled to assume that perfection can be attained with little practice. *It never can in any sphere of human activity.* For example, some musicians say that, of all composers, Mozart demands the greatest amount of practice for the very reason that his music is so simple. That is, Mozart requires a higher level of excellence, not a lower level of application.

In the Straddle style, we thought in the 1940s that Les Steers ran as fast as any man could. In fact, many such as Dumas (he merely ambled up to the bar) thought Steers ran too fast. But by use of power training and speed-oriented techniques, Brumel and Yashchenko proved that even greater speed could be used effectively.

So with the Flop. Present-day floppers, by proof of their failure to work hard and long at both related power training and perfection of technique, are well below maximums in speed of the run and in conversion of that speed into vertical thrust.

A SUMMARY HISTORY OF STYLES OF BAR-CLEARANCE.

Each champion tends to have his own unique way of clearing the bar. For example, though they both jumped "Western," Osborne (1924, 6'8¼", Figure 7.7b) lay parallel with the bar and on his back, whereas Horine (1912, 6'7", Figure 7.7a) was across the bar and on his side. (Osborne claimed his style was original and that he knew nothing of the Horine style.) Similarly, Brumel differed from Thomas, and Stones differed from Fosbury. On this basis, there have been as many styles as there have been champions. But among these individually unique thousands, we can validly distinguish nine bar-clearance techniques: the Scissors, the Modified Scissors (Page, 1887), the Eastern Cut-Off (Sweeney, 1895), the Eastern Trail-Leg Lift (Oler, 1914), the Eastern Back-to-the-Bar (Larson, 1917), the Western Roll (Horine, 1912), the Straddle (Stewart, 1930), the Dive-Straddle (Cruter, 1938), and the Flop (Fosbury, 1968).

Fig. 7.3a. The Scissors style as jumped prior to 1880 or by any beginning schoolboy jumper of today.

Fig. 7.3b. A Modified Scissors style as jumped by Egon Erickson, National Champion, 1910. Compare with Larson (Figure 7.5).

THE SCISSORS AND MODIFIED SCISSORS. Every schoolboy knows the natural style of springing with the torso erect and the legs "scissoring"--first the inside leg upward, then the outside-- over the bar. Fosbury says he started jumping that way, and all that followed was a modification. Using only a slightly backward layout, W. Byrd Page, 5'6 3/4" tall, was the first (1887, 6'4") to achieve widespread recognition for this style. Almost a century of improvement of all kinds (techniques, practice methods, power training, equipment, facilities, motivation and mind-set) have added only about 14 inches to Byrd's achievement, the smallest relative gain in any field event.

THE EASTERN STYLE. Mike Sweeney (1895, 6'5 5/8") changed the Page method of lowering the heavy shoulders by reducing the high throw of the second leg, pulling it under the lead leg (the cut-off) and landing on it.

Sweeney's record lasted 17 years but his technique was gradually improved by such men as H. F. Porter and Wesley Oler who whipped the almost straight takeoff leg as high and forcefully as possible while twisting the shoulders down and in the opposite direction, then brought it down quickly for the landing, facing the bar (See Figure 7.4b).

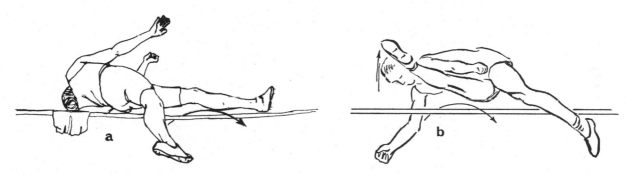

Fig. 7.4a. Eastern Cut-off Style. Drawn from actual jump by Mike Sweeney in setting 1895 world record of 6'5 5/8" that lasted 17 years.
Fig. 7.4b. Eastern Style with straight-leg vertical lift, as jumped by George Spitz (NYU, 1933, 6'8¼").

Oler, who held the schoolboy record in 1912, 6'3 5/8", considered the lift derived from the two-leg upward drive as most significant,[1]

The lead leg should be kicked up with all possible force and high above the head.... As the function of this leg is about over, the rear leg provides the upward action called the lift, accomplished by driving the leg up with every bit of force at one's command. The knee of this leg is slightly bent and the toe of the foot is turned out almost to 90 degrees....The paramount importance of the lift cannot be overemphasized...the maximum height the jumper attains will be governed by the amount of lift he is able to develop.

This Eastern trail-leg lift style persisted for many years, despite its tendency to a higher center of gravity during clearance. Throughout the 1930s, almost all the jumpers in the Eastern states and in other countries of the world used the Eastern style. In 1933, George Spitz of NYU cleared 6'8¼"; in 1936, Kalevi Kotkas of Finland, 6'8 3/8". In 1948, John Winter of Australia used the Eastern in winning the London Olympic title.

THE EASTERN BACK-TO-THE-BAR STYLE. Though very different in his method of spring and clearance, Larson's face-up, back-to-the-bar style (1917, 6'9½" exhibition) is best understood as a variation of the Eastern style. Larson (Fig. 7.5) described his method this way,[2]

[1]Wesley M. Oler, Jr., "Four Essentials of High Jumping," in R.L.Templeton, *op.cit.*, p. 143.

[2]Clinton Larson, "Larson on High Jumping," in R.L.Templeton, ibid., p. 127.

The last step before the spring upward is an extra long one. I drop into a low crouching position, so that I can get force to kick the right leg upward as high as possible. I...then spring upward with the left leg. In this way I get a double force....

As I approach the top of the crossbar, after the takeoff, I am in a sort of sitting position and when I reach my highest elevation, I shoot my legs straight out, "bob" my hips and throw my shoulders backward for a complete layout. At this time my body is parallel with the ground and forms practically a straight line....As the upper body clears the bar, I whip my right arm downward as sharply as possible, so that I land on my right leg and right arm.

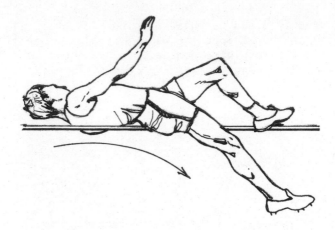

Fig. 7.5. Eastern Style by Clint Larson (1917, 6'9½'' in exhibition).

THE FOSBURY FLOP. Though out of chronological order, the Flop belongs here from a technique standpoint, following Sweeney and Larson, and not following Brumel or Matzdorf. Roy Blount tells the story,

Then, in the course of a momentous meet when Fosbury was 16, he reverted to the scissors. As a straddler he had never jumped higher than 5'4". Scissoring he went higher and higher--and a strange thing began to happen. "As the bar got higher, I started laying out more," he recalls, "and pretty soon I was flat on my back."...

Fig. 7.6. The Flop Style by Dick Fosbury (1968 Olympic Champion, 7'4¼''). Note that the run-gather-takeoff of Fosbury and Sweeney are very similar.

By his junior year, Fosbury's back was intersecting the bar at a 45 degree angle and he was clearing a little more than six feet. By the end of his senior year he had just about attained the pure 90-degree-angle Flop.[1]

Fosbury's ultimate clearance style will be described in detail later, but can be quickly understood by studying Figure 7.6.

THE WESTERN ROLL. In 1912, George Horine of Stanford startled the high-jump world, and the Sweeney advocates in particular, by taking off from the inside foot, clearing the bar at 6'7" in a side-to-the-bar position, and landing on the takeoff foot (Figure 7.7a). Horine wrote how it happened,[2]

I was forced into the "Western" form through an accident....As the available grounds were only 12 feet wide...we had to place the standards (to one side-J.K.D.) and leave them there.

I had always jumped scissors fashion off my left foot...The other boys...were using the same style except that they took off from the right foot, running from the left side....

So I had to run from the left side, though taking off from the left foot as before. This was the beginning of my new form....(At first I) used a straight (almost 90-degree) run and then in 1912 I changed back to my left-side run....

Within a week...I cleared 5 feet 9 inches and a few days later made 6 feet 1 inch.

The Western Roll gained both nation-wide and world-wide acceptance with begrudging slowness. On the West Coast, Eddie Beeson of California (1914, 6'7 5/8") demonstrated it was no trick style. But Eastern advocates claimed the Roll was a dive and not a true jump. A new rule required the head to precede both feet over the bar and not be below the hips at the moment of clearance. Even after Harold Osborne (1924, 6'8¼") of Illinois proved the Roll was not a West-Coast monopoly, critics were unconvinced. In 1924 the cross bar rested on 3" pegs projecting from the side of each standard. They said Osborne actually depressed the bar, pushed it against the standard, then rolled around it, gaining an unfair advantage by never achieving the true bar height. First, one new rule placed the crossbar as it is today. Then, after much quarreling and elimination of great jumpers for fouling (for example the famed Babe Didrickson at the 1932 Olympics), the rules on clearance were simplified--"a jumper must take off from one foot."

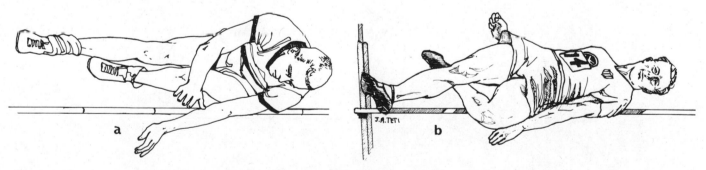

Fig. 7.7a. Western Roll as jumped by George Horine (1912, 6'7", World Record).
Fig. 7.7b. Western Roll by Harold Osborne (1924, 6'8¼", World Record).

---

[1] Roy Blount, Jr., "Being Backward Gets Results," *Sports Illustrated*, Feb. 12, 1969.

[2] George Horine, "My Development of the Western Form," in R. L. Templeton, *op. cit.*, p. 109.

THE STRADDLE STYLE. According to Dean Cromwell, Jim Stewart (USC, 1930, 6'6") "was the first outstanding athlete to use the belly roll successfully in major competition." Cromwell gave a tongue-in-cheek explanation of its origin,[1]

Jim picked up the belly roll so quickly that I asked him if he had ever tried it as a youngster. He said that he had been raised on a ranch and had needed considerable agility at the fences whenever the cattle went rampaging. At first he took the barbed wire fences with the scissors high jump form, but he found this dorsal clearance both destructive for the seat of his trousers and unpleasant anatomically. Finally, he said, since the cattle didn't get any more peaceful and the fences didn't get any lower, he was forced to use the technique of the belly roll, for with this form he could hold down the barbed wire as he rolled over it. I never believed Jim's yarn either.

The changeover from the Roll to the Straddle also occurred gradually. Most Rollers, such as Les Steers (1941, 6'11"), felt that the Straddle created a tendency to dive and so lose vertical force during the takeoff. They continued to practice the Roll and in competition shifted to the Straddle only at highest heights. The first Straddler to achieve a world record was Dave Albritton (1936, 6'9 3/4") who, surprisingly, combined a very fast, though short approach with a modified dive position over the bar.

During the 1940s and later, many coaches and jumpers were greatly concerned about vertical lift and the negative effects of diving. In part this was caused by the controversy between Eastern stylists and Western Rollers. But we should also be aware that some of these jumpers were well over six feet tall and attempting heights only a little above eye level. Diving "down" to the bar was a natural tendency and easily exaggerated. In contrast, our present-day heights of over seven feet provide time-distance to concentrate on vertical force and then, later, on bar clearance. Effective technique is easier when the bar is higher.

As a result, runs were shortened and slowed and great emphasis was placed on a forceful upward thrust of a straight lead leg as shown by Charles Dumas in Figure 7.8.

Fig. 7.8. The Straddle Style by Charles Dumas (1956 Olympic Champion, 7' 5/8"); though just out of high school, he was the first man to clear seven feet.

By the year 1960, perhaps 99 percent of jumpers were using some variation of the Straddle. To my knowledge, Gene Johnson (1962, 7' ½") was the first and possibly the last Roller to clear seven feet.

---

[1]Dean B. Cromwell, *CHAMPIONSHIP TECHNIQUE IN TRACK AND FIELD,* New York: McGraw-Hill Book Co., Inc., 1941, 207.

THE DIVE STRADDLE. As might be expected, the Dive Straddle evolved with and emerged out of the Straddle, for actually they are variations of a single technique. In 1936, Dave Albritton took off perhaps five feet from the line of the bar and "dove" forward-up in setting his world record. A Dive-Straddle? Perhaps, though he held his head and right shoulder well up during clearance. I'm inclined to credit Gil Cruter (Colorado, 1938, 6'8½") with being the first to use a valid Dive-Straddle. In 1938 his style was criticized as emphasizing diving more than jumping high; actually his clearance was very similar to that of Yashchenko (Fig. 7.28), 40 years later.

Fig. 7.9a--
Bengt Nilsson, Sweden, 1954--6'11"

But as a deliberately coached method, the Dive-Straddle emerged primarily out of Sweden. Between 1952 and 1961, at least four Swedish jumpers (Svensson, Dahl, Nilsson and Petterson) all used a pronounced dive while attempting world-ranked heights. Between them they contributed two important innovations. First, a longer, faster and more forceful run. Pettersson, for example, took 15 strides with increasing speed throughout. Second, they acquired a means for converting that running force upward by using first, what we now call a two-arm thrust, along with a flexed lead leg whose shortened lever drove more quickly and forcefully upward.

The next great Dive-Straddler (Yuri Stepanov, USSR, 1957, 7'1¼") was more famous for his "inclined-plane" takeoff shoe than for his world-record. At that time, the rules ignored sole thickness. A sole 3/4" thick enabled Stepanov to make more effective use of a faster run. A year later his record was approved, but sole thickness was set at one-half inch.

In the 1971 USA-USSR dual meet, Pat Matzdorf upset everyone, including himself (his previous best was 7'2"), by setting a new world record at 7'6¼" while using a Dive-Straddle similar to that of Cruter, Avant and Nilsson. Matzdorf acquired his style in high school without knowledge of any previous jumper. But his coach at Wisconsin, Bill Perrin, had been persuaded by the research of John Cooper[1] who found the Dive-Straddle of Bob Avant (1961, 7 feet) had definite mechanical advantages in both takeoff and clearance

Though neither he nor his coach use the term, the next Dive-Straddler was Vladimir Yashchenko (19, 6'4", 180#) who cleared 7' 7 3/4" (2.33m) in a USA-USSR dual meet at Richmond, Va., 1977. His coach since age 12, Vasiliy Telegin, started him with a dive-straddle style, but combined it with Brumel's techniques in the run and conversion phase that permitted a much faster run than Brumel's. He led the takeoff with the outside arm, as did Brumel, but thrust the inside hand-arm quickly up-across-and-down beyond the bar as shown in Figure 7.40, in what has been called "a dive-through-a-window" style.

Fig. 7.9b--Dive-Straddle style by Pat Matzdorf (1971, 7'6¼", world record).

[1]John M. Cooper, "Kinesiology of High Jumping," *Biomechanics*, I, 1st International Seminar, Zurich, 1967, New York: Karger Publishers, 1968, 291-302.

ESSENTIALS OF TECHNIQUE IN THE STRADDLE STYLE.

To say that an athlete has high technical skill is to describe him as able to perform in ways that are biomechanically sound and that produce a maximum level of performance. A man can't run slowly in the long jump or javelin throw and still exhibit a high level of technical skill; velocity in the run is essential to maximum performance and is therefore inherent in high-level skill. In this important sense, whatever physical actions may enhance performance should be included within technical skill and given regular practice.

THE WHOLE ACTION. In Chapter 16 we described a system of coaching field events in which the whole action of jumping or throwing was given first priority. Applying this system to high jumping, our first drawing and related captions describe the entire movements from the first step in the run through clearance of the crossbar (Figure 7.21). We all tend to classify high-jumping styles, as Western or Straddle or Fosbury Flop, in terms of the action over the bar. This leads to serious misjudgments of what is essential in training.

Thirty years ago, Dean Cromwell, America's most successful college coach, wrote, "Most high jumpers run too far and too fast and their energies are dissipated in moving forward instead of upward." In contrast, today's most eminent high jump coach, Vladimir Dyatchkov, (1969, 1124), U.S.S.R., writes, "The principle problem in all jumping is the effective utilization of great horizontal speed so as to aid greater power in the spring and a greater takeoff speed at the optimum angle."

Today we emphasize that bar-clearance methods are related to inches and fractions of inches in heights cleared, whereas the run-gather-takeoff relate to feet. Dyson has estimated a ten percent contribution by the first; 90 percent, by the second. In summary, take a whole-phase-whole approach to high jumping as in coaching other field events.

THE RUN IN THE STRADDLE STYLE

It must be emphasized again and again that the run is at least as crucial a phase of high jumping as is clearance technique. The run comes first, and so develops the potential force, the degree of relaxation, and the means of converting horizontal power upward. If the run is too short or too long, too slow or too fast, from an unuseable angle, or with mechanically unsound

Fig. 7.20 -- The potential force of a full and fast run requires related power training for effective use. The skill of the run-and-gather is equally important as that of clearing the bar and needs just as much practice.

positions of the body and its parts, the height of the jump will be diminished. A sound run which moves effectively into the conversion phase of the takeoff is the foundation of a sound jump.

DIRECTION OF THE RUN

In the straddle style, the angle of the run as related to the crossbar has varied among world jumpers from 43 to 28 degrees. Dumas, with a short, slow approach, ran at 43 degrees; Thomas, medium speed, at 37; Brumel, at faster speed, 28. Yashchenko, with his dive-straddle style, ran fastest of them all at 35 degrees.

Usually, the greater the angle at which one runs, the greater the awareness of the bar. This awareness tends toward a more vertical takeoff, but also toward a slower run and/or a distant takeoff. In contrast, the lesser the angle, the easier it is to get a close takeoff

Fig. 7.21. Valeriy Brumel, USSR; 1964 Olympic high jump champion, 7'1 7/8"; 1963 world-record holder 7'5 3/4". Modified Straddle style.

THE WHOLE ACTION

The running high jump is just that--one action; one run-gather-takeoff-clearance-landing. From the standpoints of technique and training, all phases of that action are crucial. For 50 years or more we thought of high-jumping technique as related only to bar-clearance, but since Les Steers (1941, 6'11") and especially since the Dyatchkov-Brumel duo, the run-and-gather have been emphasized, precisely analyzed, and given special power-and-skill training.

The problem is to put it all together in one all-out flowing movement--in competition! There's the crux. It's a whole man that jumps, not just a body. If a man is to do his best, his energies cannot be drained away by thought of the details of technique, or by doubt as to what he can do. To do his best, he can have only one focus of mind and technique--running-and-jumping HIGH! When Yashchenko tried 7'8½" (2.35) after his world-record 7'7 3/4", he said afterwards "It was not really a test as such. For me, the height did not exist as a barrier or limit."

but the greater the tendency to lean in to the bar and dive along it.

Beginning jumpers are usually instructed to run at 40-45 degrees, as this induces a more vertical jump and a free swing of the lead leg straight ahead along the line of the run. This is enhanced if the bar is imagined as being well above the head. But a coach or jumper would be justified to begin at a theoretically sound angle--say 30 degrees--and then work in terms of the strengths and weaknesses of that angle. (Soviet high jumpers, having learned how to combine a fast run with the technique of a more vertical jump, use angles of 28-35 degrees.) Whatever the chosen angle, be certain to maintain one direction of force: one direction of run-foot placement-body lean-swing of the arms and of the lead leg. This is crucial. Dyatchkov (1969, 1126) puts it this way,

> *In order to use the force of the takeoff fully . . . the entire run-up should lie in a straight line without any deviation to the side; the feet should be placed strictly along this line, and, if possible, without turning the toes out. This is especially important during the last steps of the run-up. Misplacement of the takeoff foot to the right of the line of run is a very bad technical error, leading to a sharp decrease in the effectiveness of the spring.*

LENGTH OF THE RUN

The run should be long enough to enable the jumper to build up optimum velocity *before*--we emphasize--before the transition stage of converting horizontal momentum upward, that is, before the last three steps. Dyatchkov advocates seven to nine steps. Brumel used seven measured steps but added three or four more preliminary steps from about 50 feet out (Figure 7.22). Thomas took seven strides from a fixed point. The Swedish jumpers (Pettersson, Nilsson) who influenced the modern methods of run and conversion so much, ran a total of 15 strides but accelerated very slowly.

Actually, length and speed of the run are inseparable. If the speed, for whatever reason, is slow, there is no point in a run of more than seven strides. But if the speed of the run is fast, as it must be for highest heights, seven strides from a fixed point is hardly enough to acquire speed smoothly before the transition to the conversion phase of the run and takeoff.

SPEED OF THE RUN

In principle, the optimum speed of a maximum high jump must be very fast, limited only by the developed power and skill by which a jumper converts such speed upward. As world-champions acquire greater power and related skill, the speed of their run-ups will be increased, will be maintained until the last two strides before takeoff, and then converted explosively upward. Proponents of the Fosbury style claim this is one of its great assets, that the actions of the gather and takeoff make more effective use of a fast run than can any other style. Almost all Fosbury jumpers do run fast into the takeoff.

How fast did Brumel run? Dyatchkov states, "Our jumpers develop a speed which reaches 15.65 mph or 7 to 7.5 meters per second before the takeoff." When Brumel met Thomas in Madison Square Garden in 1962, Harold O'Connor and other coaches put a stopwatch on them. "The Russian on his best jumps took from 2.1 to 2.2 seconds from his deep check mark to his takeoff."

Dyatchkov favors "a rapid increase in speed from the starting point, with a gradual decrease of acceleration in speed at the end of the run-up. . . ." Note that he says a "decrease in acceleration," not an actual decrease in speed. There is no slow-down, only a shift of attention from greater speed to a smooth use of speed. Velocity "reaches its maximum at the next-to-last step."

On the other hand, a strong case can be made by those who favor a slower and less forceful run. They say that velocity in the run is of value only to the degree that the jumper makes use of it. Dyson (1967, 137), the English authority in track and field mechanics, states

> *The value of approach speed to spring lies in contributing to range, force and speed beyond what is attainable in a standing high jump. Jumpers should experiment to see if they can benefit from a faster run up; yet each will possess a "critical speed" beyond which takeoff efficiency will be impaired, varying greatly from jumper to jumper, largely because of variations in strength and intrinsic muscular speed. Some, to gain time to evoke their maximum force at takeoff, will use a slow approach; while others can benefit*

from a faster run up (and therefore, a more exaggerated backward lean at the end of it) and still have time to evoke maximum takeoff force, the technique now more generally used. For most good high jumpers a run of only a few strides is necessary. The majority of champions use from seven to nine.

In American college competitive schedules, and especially in those high schools where time for training is restricted, there is seldom enough time for a sound foundation of training in power and skill. From a practical standpoint, then, how fast should such men run to ensure a good performance in a competition only a few weeks away? Obviously, something has to give-- either run velocity or meet performance. The easy solution is to slow down to an immediately useable speed. At once the jumper performs better, and feels better. A slower approach is satisfying, and as in all learning, whatever satisfies, tends to be learned, and tends to be- come a habit that is not easily changed. The coach may intend that run velocity will be in- creased in later months when strength and related skill make it useable, but by that time there is a strong resistance to change and increases tend to be minimal.

In summary, no matter how you achieve it, never abandon velocity in the run any more than you would abandon skill in the jump as a whole; in fact, velocity is inherent in skill and cannot really be separated from it.

THE USE OF CHECK MARKS

The use of check marks should be learned as soon as a man starts to jump, even before he learns the techniques of layout. By acquiring a fixed pattern of run up--fixed in angle, length, speed, rhythm, and emphasis--a sound foundation for the jump is established, and check marks become a natural, even unconscious part of the whole pattern.

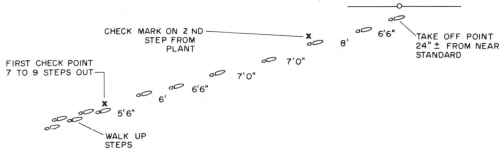

Fig. 7.22 -- Diagram of run and checkmarks as used by Valeriy Brumel. Acceleration of the run began at the first checkmark.

Brumel used two check marks throughout his career, plus one other unmeasured mark. The crucial mark was seven measured strides from takeoff. But he also used a second mark for his next-to-last left foot placement. Some jumpers place this mark three strides from the takeoff, as being the point of transition from horizontal velocity into the upward drive. But Dyatchkov, after many years of coaching great jumpers, has concluded that this transition should occur at the last possible moment; if too early, the power built up in the run is dissipated. There is an inevitable anticipation of this mark wherever it is used. If used for the next-to-last stride, anticipation produces transitional effects on the previous stride, as Dyatchkov prefers.

Check marks do not merely fix the point of takeoff, crucial as that is. Equally important, they fix the pattern of the entire run-jump: its rhythm, emphasis, coordination, potential power. In this way, the mechanics of the run-jump are always the same; the jumper feels "right," and his attention can be concentrated on the skill of exploding upward.

THE TRANSITION PHASE

Dyatchkov and his Soviet jumpers have proved beyond all doubt that relatively great velocity in the run up can be used effectively to increase the height of the jump. As in all jumping-- and throwing--such velocity must not be dissipated gradually; it must be maintained until the last moment, then converted forcefully, quickly, and smoothly.

1

This figure with kind permission from Fred Wilt and Tom Ecker, *International Track and Field Coaching Encyclopedia*, West Nyack, N.Y.: Parker Publishing Company, Inc. 1970, 135.

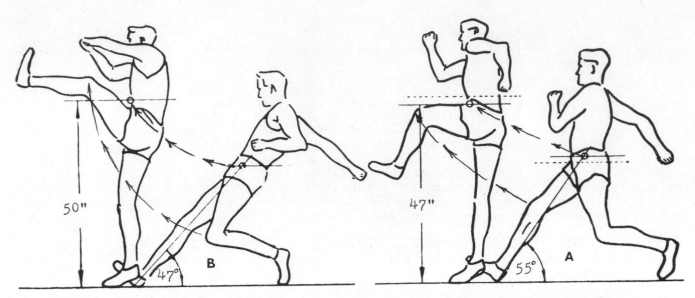

Fig. 7.23 -- Two takeoff methods having at least four points of difference: (1) The 8-degree difference in body angle of B gives greater potential conversion force; (2) Through greater knee-hip flexion, the pelvis in B moves more flatly forward-and-up, thus compressing the springs of force; (3) Vertical power can be applied in B through a greater time-distance; (4) In the bent-leg style (A), the distance through which its force is effective is 3 inches less than with a straight leg.

How does this transition occur? Dyatchkov explains (1969, 1127),

This transition is made in the third step from the takeoff. . . . The usual rise of the center of gravity is decreased, and the jumper . . . must run on his heels. . . . On setting the foot on the ground, the leg is somewhat bent at the knee, causing the jumper, in spite of his being carried forward, to pass through the resistance of the leg with his momentum. (However) the knee should not be bent excessively (this pertains to the last steps also), but only enough to permit the jumper to pass through the resisting leg freely and flatly forward. . . . His eyes remain focused on the takeoff spot, not on the bar. . . . The jumper keeps his shoulders forward . . . At the last moment . . . the pelvis, drawn forward by the forward action of the free (right) leg, moves ahead of the shoulders. . . .

Fig. 7.24 -- The last three strides. The body settles, with knee-hip flexion throughout; the foot plant is on the heel; the body angle inclines beyond the vertical; the two arms move down-forward-up. This figure deserves careful study.

As the jumper passes through the free leg, the body should gradually incline backward. . . . This is attained, not by bringing the shoulders back but by moving the pelvis forward. . . . At this time the right knee traces an arch, moving forward and down. There is a sharp decrease in running activity . . . the jumper pushes forward with the right foot very easily, so as to have great speed in the forward movement of the pelvis as related to the shoulders. . . . The right knee remains bent throughout the action.

At this point Dyatchkov is concerned with pelvis momentum more than with the action of the shoulders. He emphasizes several times that, to implement this pelvis momentum, the takeoff foot should be brought through low to the ground and placed firmly (Figure 7.24), not stamped on the ground. To bring it high and stamp it forcefully is a most common error. The tremendous force of the run up is braked strongly by the takeoff leg which, however, quickly gives way, bending under the force of the body moving forward, and thus compressing the powerful springs of action. Only powerful muscles can keep this "giving way" in control and forcefully reactive upward.

All actions during this transition phase are directed toward reducing resistance and shock, and increasing the speed of change in the direction of force upward. It should be an organic flow or curve of change.

Fig. 7.25--The last stride, transition phase: Note how both arms and hips are thrust through-and-up to increase takeoff time-force. Brumel's takeoff time was about .21 second.

USE OF ARMS DURING TRANSITION AND TAKEOFF
We've had a tendency to value the two-arm thrust of the Swedish-Russian style only in terms of increased upward force. But Dyatchkov also uses them to aid his forward or through-and-up approach Figure 7.25

The movements of the arms during this transition phase are very important. . . . During the phase of passing through the free (right) leg, [Several strides later than one might expect--JKD] the arm movements change. The right arm is held up slightly in front and to the side for better balance. At the same time, the left arm moves backward until level with the right. Then both, sharply bent, drive vigorously downward, forward and upward as the spring begins.

THE TAKEOFF
The takeoff should be understood, not as the instant at which the foot leaves the ground, but as a flow of movement of the pelvis through the takeoff leg, the reaction to compression, and the forceful drive upward. The change in action of the takeoff leg from resistance and absorption of shock to that of exploding upward must occur instantly and with great force. Both power and great skill are needed.

Fig. 7.25a--This sequence is similar to the technique of Yashchenko. The first four figures illustrate Dyatchkov's through-and-up technique in which the pelvis moves horizontally from figures 2 to 4 ahead of the shoulders. But in figure 5, the lead leg, as with Yashchenko, is more flexed; the lean toward the bar slightly greater. The left arm now thrusts across and down as shown in Fig. 7.28.

Each increase in the linear speed of the run by 0.1 m/sec. increases pressure on the takeoff foot by 26-35 pounds. Similarly a decrease of radius (curve B versus curve A) by 10 cm. also increases pressure by 44-88 pounds.

Such increased pressures have commonly induced a slower run, a lesser knee bend, and lower heights cleared. Dyatchkov prefers the more difficult way of developing power to resist and use such pressures, and thereby jumping higher. He has found that "every increase of the initial speed of the takeoff by 0.1 m/sec. (assuming no change in takeoff angle) increases height by 3.5 cm." (1.37 inches).

<u>INCREASING THE TIME-DISTANCE OF APPLICATION OF FORCE</u>. Such an increase in upward velocity can be gained by greater related power as derived from the many exercises described here (Read caption for Figure 7.60), but also by a correct technique which increases the time-distance through which such power is applied. By a momentary non-resistance which allows the center of weight to move through and then up-and-over the takeoff leg, that is, by greater compression of the springs of jumping--the jumper in Figure 7.23 curve B, achieves a greater time-distance of force and a greater vertical velocity.

In this action, Dyatchkov (1969, 1130) emphasizes the role of the pelvis,
The jumper, leaving the free leg in a pose of readiness for the takeoff [This is a way of speaking--JKD], *moves his pelvis in, somewhat leading the shoulders. Thus the pelvis achieves momentum onto the takeoff foot which is placed far forward. To use this momentum effectively requires . . . moving the takeoff leg (and foot) low along the ground. . . with the knee almost completely straightened as the heel hits. The last step of our jumpers varies somewhat with the height of the bar and the speed of the run, but averages between 6' 4 3/4" and 6' 6 3/4". Most importantly, the center of weight moves flatly forward as the knee bends, moving onto the whole sole of the foot and toes.*

Saying this differently, the most effective force provided by the lead leg and the arms occurs while the takeoff foot is still in contact with the ground and so can still exert force against it. The longer the time through which a reactive acceleration of upward velocity can be exerted, the more effective the upward drive by the lead leg and arms.

Fig. 7.25b--Vladimir Yashchenko (1978--7'8"), Dive-Straddle style. Compare all aspects of this figure with those in Figures 7.25 to 7.28, with special attention to follow-up Figure 7.40. Note rotation of takeoff foot as contrasted to straight-line drive of Figure 7.26 (Dumas) and 7.21-21 (Brumel). The lead right leg is flexed; foot is turning. Right hand is well above bar, but left trails so as to be thrust across-and-down as shown in Figure 7.40. Since the crossbar is 16" above Yashchenko's head, his C.G. remains directly above the takeoff foot until the latter leaves the ground. A lower relative bar height, as with most jumpers, would tend toward an ineffective dive.

THE LEAD LEG

The most powerful lead leg is one that swings through in a definitely flexed position (to increase acceleration of the swing), then straightens quickly as it swings up to the 11 o'clock position as shown in Figure 7.26

Such an explosive thrust requires great power, and much related power training of those specific muscles, usually neglected, that drive the lead leg toward the vertical.

Note in Figure 7.26 that though the lead thigh is well above the horizontal, the takeoff foot has just left the ground. This is both unusual and helpful from an increased force standpoint. The higher the leg can swing while the takeoff foot can still apply a reactive force against the ground, the greater its effectiveness. (This applies to the upthrust of the arms also.)

A lead leg that remains flexed, as shown in Figs. 7.26a and b, lacks the inertia of Dumas' straight leg, but more than compensates: (1) by greater velocity in the preceding run, (2) by its shorter lever that speeds the upward thrust of the leg, and (3) by its effective use in gaining the "through-a-window" clearance of Yashchenko, Fig. 7.40.

Fig. 7.26--A straight lead-leg by Charles Dumas. First high school boy to clear 7 ft., 1956.

Fig. 7.26a -- Dive-straddle style with flexed lead leg by Nilsson.

Fig. 7.26b -- Modified flexion of lead leg by Ernie Shelton (1955 - 6'11¼"). No right shoe prevented dragging of spikes as lead leg passed takeoff foot.

Note similarity of these two Figures with that of Yashchenko (Fig. 7.25b).

Fig. 7.26c -- Fiberglass heelcup, individually fitted, prevents crippling heel bruises.

CLEARANCE OF THE BAR. Various effective methods of clearing the crossbar are shown in Figures 7.27 to 7.30 in a clearer way than words can describe. Only a few summary points need emphasis.

Once contact with the ground is broken the angle of flight is fixed and the total rotary momentum of the body cannot be slowed or speeded up. However, the actual speed of rotation can be increased by shortening the arms and legs around the body's frontal axis, just as do ice skaters in their spins. This principle is of great value when the jumper wishes to speed up the actions of clearing the bar, as occurs in the early flexion of the trail leg.

Second, any movement--up, down, or around--on one side of the center of gravity produces an equivalent "opposite" movement on the other side. An upward counterclockwise lift of the trail leg both produces and is increased by a downward clockwise thrust of the "opposite" head-shoulders-arms (Figs. 7.28--7.30). Geoffrey Dyson once demonstrated this principle very dramatically by standing on a turnstool that moved freely on ballbearings. When he thrust his arms-shoulders clockwise, his legs-feet rotated counterclockwise. This is of crucial importance in attempts to clear the bar with the trail leg. Most photographs show a high trail leg being counterbalanced by a low right shoulder-arm (Figs. 7.29, 7.30).

Actually the counterclockwise lift of the trail leg is aided by a quick upward lift clockwise of the right arm (Fig. 7.27). That is, the right arm is first lowered, then raised quickly, and lowered again for the landing. To insist that the right arm be kept low beyong the bar can result only in resistance to the lift of the trail leg.[1]

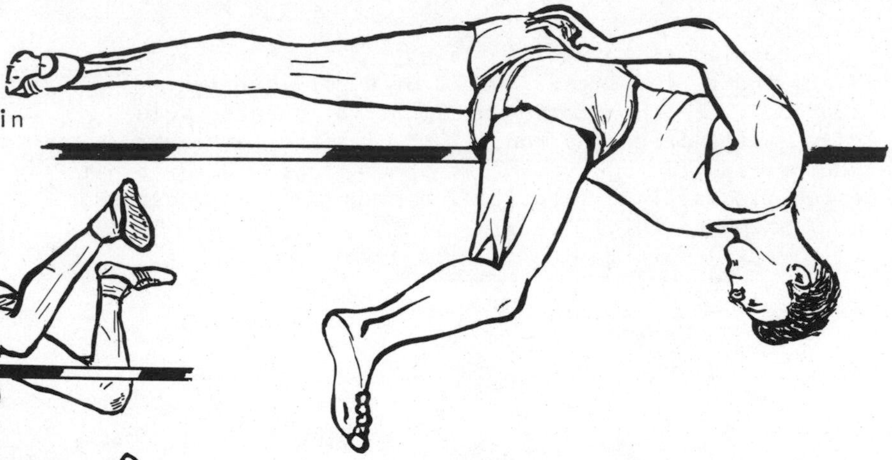

Fig. 7.27-- Trail-leg clearance by lifting it straight up with little torso rotation.

Fig. 7.28--Trail-leg clearance by emphasis on rotation of head-shoulder and down-thrust of left arm.

[1]Tom Ecker, TRACK AND FIELD DYNAMICS, Los Altos, CA: Tafnews Press, 1971, pp. 72-79.

As a third principle in all such efforts to clear the bar by the various body parts, place first emphasis on the desired action directly, rather than on its opposing action (Figures 7.28, 7.30a,b,c). That is, evert up and away from the bar the left hip, the left knee, or the left toe. Automatically, with or without awareness, the body parts that are on the opposite side of the rotational axis will move in the opposite direction around the axis.

Some men, as in a modified dive straddle, are able to clear the crossbar effectively by simply lifting the trail leg straight up without rolling around the longitudinal axis or even everting the foot (Figure 7.30a). Others gain the same end by quickly rotating the pelvis; the various related actions of the legs and arms follow in keeping with the inexorable laws of motion, regardless of the jumper's awareness.

Each jumper finds his own individual method that is mechanically sound but individually unique in its specific execution. Be sure there are no fixed positions or wrong actions that inhibit or prevent the natural movements. A rigidly-held head or lead arm may be the cause of clearance failure by the trail leg.

Lift power of the trail leg is aided by extreme knee flexion. It then straightens as in Figure 7.30B.

Right arm lifts quickly as counter to upward thrust of trail leg, then drops down again as in Figure 7.30B.

Fig. 7.29 -- Straddle style - Valeriy Brumel, USSR, 1963 world-record holder -- 7' 5 3/4".

Fig. 7.30 A-B-C -- Three variations of trail-leg clearance. Fig.A is similar to that of Yashchenko, Fig. 7.28; Fig. B is drawn from Brumel (Fig. 7.29) but taken from other side of bar. Fig. C emphasizes rotation.

SPECIAL EXERCISES FOR THE STRADDLE STYLE.
Dyatchkov (1969, 1141) is adamant on the necessity of special exercises for greater skill, taken regularly throughout the career of every high jumper.

However perfectly the technique of jumping may be learned, special related exercises do not lose their crucial value. Their specific applications vary with individual peculiarities of style and work. But failure to use such exercises leads to a decrease in technical mastery, as well as of mental control of the jumping situation as a whole. Maximum jumping requires a maximum mobilization of all mental-physical forces. As technical mastery develops, training jumps at near-maximum and maximum heights play an increasing role, but such jumps must always be supplemented by special related exercises.

Dyatchkov provides a number of progressive exercises which he considers effective, especially for beginners, in learning the unique coordinations of transition-takeoff-clearance. He warns, however, that such exercises can be harmful if emphasized separately from jumping for any length of time. As soon as a jumper gains the kinesthetic feel of a movement, it should be integrated with the actual movement of jumping. This is in keeping with the whole-phase-whole approach of this textbook.

1. EXERCISE TO COORDINATE THE MOTIONS OF THE PELVIS AND THE FREE LEG SWING. The jumper stands on the takeoff leg and grasps the wall with his left hand. The free leg, along with the pelvis, is brought well back (Figure 7.31). The pelvis is then thrust quickly forward, bringing the free leg with it. The leg straightens quickly at the knee and swings forcefully forward and up. Be sure the pelvis precedes and initiates the pull of the leg forward.

Extension 1. As flexibility improves, thrust the hip forward more forcefully, causing the leg to swing higher and higher to as much as a one o'clock position.

Extension 2. The forward thrust of the pelvis and swing-up of the lead leg should now be so forceful as to lift the jumper from the floor; the more forceful and high, the better (Figure 7.32). As a stunt, Brumel was able to kick the iron ring holding a basketball net.   Gradually the thrust, swing-up and spring-up will become coordinated as one smooth movement. To gain a vertical jump, the spot of landing should be the same as that of takeoff.

Fig. 7.31

Extension 3. Similar to extension 1 but with emphasis on the forward thrust of the pelvis ahead of the shoulders. The body weight is moved forward on to the sole of the takeoff foot (knee well bent) by the force of the actions of the pelvis and leg. A slightly backward inclination is maintained throughout, so that, upon landing, the weight swings back to the original position on the swing-up (right) foot. As a further extension, increase the force of the movements as in extension 2 so as to lift the jumper high off the floor.

Fig. 7.32

Extension 4. Lying supine on the edge of a firm table, swing the lead leg high in the air (Figure 7.34). Lead the action by an upthrust of the pelvis. Exercise without and also with ankle weights, using great caution against strain in all instances.

Fig. 7.33   Fig. 7.34

2. EXERCISE TO LEARN THE SHIFT OF MOVEMENT THROUGH-AND-UP INTO THE SPRING. In Figure 7.35 the body weight (a) moves forward onto the heel of the right leg; the body angle is slightly forward of vertical. The backward lean of Figure 7.35cd results from the forward thrust of the pelvis under the shoulders which--very important--move forward with no lean to the left. To do this, the left knee, which in (c) is almost straight, must bend and so gain the compressed spring action essential to the spring-up. Note (cd) that the right leg remains bent as it passes the left, then straightens quickly and forcefully in coordination with the spring-up from the left foot.

a b c d e

Fig. 7.35

Variation. 1. Perform this exercise with the shoulders under parallel bars, without spring-up. This forces a horizontal movement of the shoulders. By gradually lowering the bars, deeper bending of the knees is required, eventually to as much as a right angle. One should feel the center of weight move forward-and-up in a convex curve, rather than up-and-over the takeoff foot.

Now, without the parallel bars, follow the same pattern with a gradual increase in the depth of the knee bend. Jump higher and higher, with a gradual increase in the force of all movements. The forward thrust of the pelvis must predominate.

Variation. 2. Shift to the jumping area and exercise the same flat through-and-up action (Figure 7.36 abcd).

Fig. 7.36

3. EXERCISE TO LEARN THE TECHNIQUE OF ARM MOVEMENTS. The arms are brought back by a circular motion of the elbows, somewhat away from the sides. This occurs within the single stride (Figure 7.24), not before. For better control, the hands should remain inside the elbows. The force of the forward arm swing is up vertically; the hands rise only to about head level. This requires increasing flexion at the elbows and a drive of the hands toward the centerline of the body. Such action ensures that the tendency to incline the head-body to the left and toward the bar will be checked. The head should not pass outside the line of the left hip, nor ahead of the pelvis. All such actions--and the landing--should be along the line of the run.

4. EXERCISE TO LEARN THE TECHNIQUE OF THE TRAIL LEG. The pattern of action of the trail leg in the straddle style is unique, and so requires special exercise. Individual jumpers differ in the exact pattern of action but all require special training for full force and flexibility. Dyatchkov emphasizes the predominant action of the pelvis and left shoulder "up-and-away from the bar," with the everted knee and foot following. For rotational quickness, the knee angle as the movement begins is less than 90 degrees.

But there are other methods as shown in Figures 7.27 to 7.30, 7.37 and 7.38.

Fig. 7.37

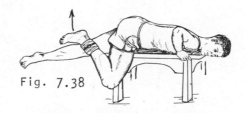

Fig. 7.38

ESSENTIALS OF TECHNIQUE IN THE DIVE STRADDLE

There's no sharp line by which the Dive-Straddle can be distinguished from the Straddle. In brief it is a variation that tends to emphasize what one observer called "a dive-through-a-window" method of clearing the bar (Fig. 7.40), as contrasted with Brumel's body-leg extension along the bar. It therefore does not justify a separate and full explanation as has been done with the Straddle.

Both styles seek maximal useable--what Dyson called "critical"--speed from a straight-line run. Both seek maximal vertical impulse and minimal rotation during takeoff. Both seek a lowest-possible center of gravity during bar-clearance. These basic concerns are alike; but there are differences in the degree of emphasis on each phase.

Following Matzdorf's world-record (1971, 7'6¼"), his coach at Wisconsin, Bill Perrin wrote in a letter to me:

In training we tried to compensate for the things supposedly missing from not using a straight leg. We worked on three things: improving his speed to the crossbar, lowering the center of gravity as much as possible in the approach without losing speed, and developing a powerful arm thrust before and during takeoff....

We feel the transition of horizontal forces to vertical forces is much faster and more efficient with the bent-leg style. Any time a shorter lever is used to compensate and get more force, it has to be faster.. Pat's lead leg comes through much faster than with a straight leg...

Fig. 7.40--Vladimir Yashchenko (1978--7'8"), a "dive-through-a-window" clearance style. Note how similar this position is to that in Fig. 7.30A; how it differs in the use of the left arm with that of Fig. 7.9 (Matzdorf); and how it contrasts with that in Figs. 7.29 (Brumel) and 7.27, in which the body-leg is parallel with the bar. In keeping with Dyson's principle, the continuing lift of the left leg will be aided by a down-thrust of the right arm and lift of the left. The hands will touch the pit almost simultaneously.

By using the special techniques developed by Coach Dyatchkov, Valeriy Brumel (USSR, 1963, 7' 5 3/4") was able to run faster than any previous Straddler. Yashchenko's coach, Vasiliy Telegin, taught similar techniques in the run. But Yashchenko, possessed of lesser leg-power but greater height (6'4"), ran even faster. Being a Dive-Straddler, he differed from Brumel in his use of slightly greater rotation at take-off by an eccentric thrust from the take-off leg (Fig. 7.25b) combined with greater flexion of the lead leg across the bar--not along it as with Brumel--and thrust of the left inside arm across the bar.

The downward thrust of the head and arms--contrast Yashchenko's left arm (Fig. 7.28) with that of Brumel (Fig. 7.29)--raises the hips and trail leg. As Yashchenko's trail leg clears the bar, his center of gravity is some inches below that of any regular Straddler--a definite advantage of the style.

ESSENTIALS OF TECHNIQUE IN THE FOSBURY FLOP.

The most conspicuous feature of the Fosbury style is its method of clearance with the back to the bar, hence its name. But its most valuable asset lies in its style of run and method of converting the high speed of that run into vertical force. Though men such as Larson, Steers, and Brumel have demonstrated for some 50 years or more the greater potential values of run velocity as compared with those of clearance economy, it was not until the Flop proved the point beyond all question that everyone--researchers, coaches, jumpers--came to realize its full significance. This was brought out clearly in the early sections of this Chapter.

In keeping with this "new" emphasis, most of this discussion of Flop techniques will be related to the run-conversion phase. To re-state what Dwight Stones has said repeatedly-- clearance is merely the follow-through phase of a proper run and takeoff; it's no problem--a natural outcome of the style.

RELATED POWER. Acquiring related power is a first priority over that of technique, if not in ultimate value, at least in order of training. Without prior power training, the critical speed of the run is diminished and the dangers of injury from attempting too much too soon are increased. Most of the exercises suggested for the Straddle style are germane to the Flop, but the Flop does have its own unique stresses and related-power requirements. Not only are the horizontal yield-reactive forces greater, the short-radius curve at the end of the Flop run puts unique strains on the related muscles and tendons. Special exercises are required. Examples:

1. Repeated windsprints around the curve of a flat 220-or-shorter indoor track. Emphasize the inward lean and cross-body drive of the outside arm.
2. Sprinting over hurdles on the curve of such a track.
3. Short sprints with sudden turns and sudden braking as occurs in the Flop run.
4. Hopping in place, with or without a weighted vest or other device, on the inclined curve of a wooden indoor track, with the takeoff foot on the lower side.

SAFETY IN THE FLOP STYLE. The landing in the Flop Style should be made on the middle-back (Figure 7.41). The focus of the eyes on the bar during clearance of the feet brings the chin forward to the chest and so prevents the head-first landing so feared during the first years of the Flop. At various clinics, Coach Wagner questioned some 1700 coaches as to injuries while Flopping. They reported only two (a broken collarbone and a concussion), both in- curred when the jumpers missed the landing mound entirely.

Fig. 7.41. Landing by Dwight Stones on lower back.

The Committee on the Medical Aspects of Sports of the AMA made a thorough investigation of the Flop....Its con- clusion: "It is recognized that all forms of athletic endeavor carry with them the risk of injury....When per- formance is according to recommended coaching techniques, the Fosbury method of high jumping does not bear greater risks than other methods of high jumping, pole vaulting or gymnastics. It is strongly urged that the rules committee create rules requiring foam rubber or equi- valent landing pits for the high jump."[1]

Up to 1973, Coach Berny Wagner had had more experience with seven-foot Floppers than any

---

[1]Berny Wagner, "The Fosbury Flop High Jump Style," Report of the 1973 Congress of the ITFCA, Madrid: Real Federacion Espanola de Atletismo, p. 262.

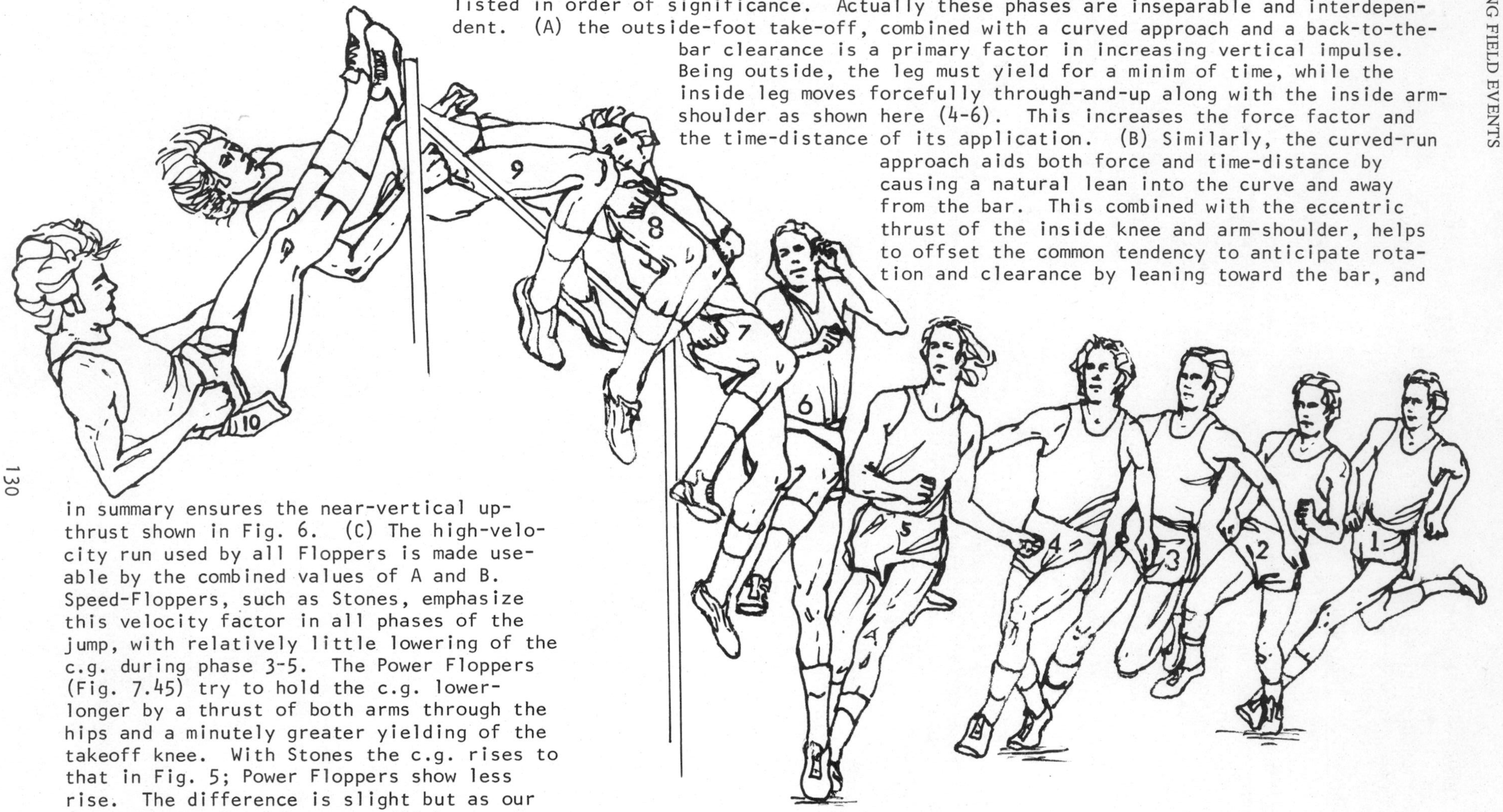

Fig. 7.42. The Speed-Flop as jumped by Dwight Stones (1976 world-record, 7'7"). Superiority of the Flop style can be attributed to four phases: (A) an outside-foot takeoff, (B) a curved-run approach, (C) a high-velocity run, and (D) method of bar-clearance, listed in order of significance. Actually these phases are inseparable and interdependent. (A) the outside-foot take-off, combined with a curved approach and a back-to-the-bar clearance is a primary factor in increasing vertical impulse. Being outside, the leg must yield for a minim of time, while the inside leg moves forcefully through-and-up along with the inside arm-shoulder as shown here (4-6). This increases the force factor and the time-distance of its application. (B) Similarly, the curved-run approach aids both force and time-distance by causing a natural lean into the curve and away from the bar. This combined with the eccentric thrust of the inside knee and arm-shoulder, helps to offset the common tendency to anticipate rotation and clearance by leaning toward the bar, and

in summary ensures the near-vertical up-thrust shown in Fig. 6. (C) The high-velocity run used by all Floppers is made useable by the combined values of A and B. Speed-Floppers, such as Stones, emphasize this velocity factor in all phases of the jump, with relatively little lowering of the c.g. during phase 3-5. The Power Floppers (Fig. 7.45) try to hold the c.g. lower-longer by a thrust of both arms through the hips and a minutely greater yielding of the takeoff knee. With Stones the c.g. rises to that in Fig. 5; Power Floppers show less rise. The difference is slight but as our grasp of technique improves will become increasingly significant. In general it seems one of $(velocity^8 + time\text{-}distance^7 = height^{15})$ as compared with $(velocity^7 + time\text{-}distance^8 = height^{15})$. But Stones' 1976 $height^{18}$ (7'7") suggests that his velocity factor might be valued as high as 11. It will take a decade however before the final tally is recorded. (D) The method of bar-clearance is listed last as a matter of relative significance in height cleared. In one way it is merely a follow-through of the preceding actions. Stones says "It just happens. No problem at all." On the other hand, Stones extends his bar-clearance all the way up-and-over--no quitting at the top, no tension of muscles that reduce quick-ness, as occurs to often with lesser jumpers.

other coach. He reported,

> *We have found only two injury problems with the Flop. One is strained or irritated*
> *ligaments in the takeoff foot from the vigorous heel plant that converts the fast*
> *run into upward force....The other is a jarring of the back from the shock of the*
> *vigorous plant.*

Both types of strain call for prevention by a program of specifically related power training
prior to jumping, and a gradual approach once it is begun.

SPEED FLOP AND POWER FLOP. In a recent conversation with Frank Costello, University of
Maryland head track coach, and himself a technically-expert, seven-foot Straddler, he made a
very valuable distinction between two variations of the Flop Style--the Speed Flop and the
Power Flop. Keeping in mind the formula (power=strength x velocity), the Power Floppers tend
to emphasize the strength aspects of jumping in both technique and training; the Speed Floppers,
the velocity aspects. Such a definition clarifies two extremes of a multiple-point scale, of
course, with actual jumpers falling at any point along that scale.

Fig. 7.44. The Speed-Flop by Dwight Stones (1973, 7'6 5/8"), taken from angle different from
   that of Figure 7.42. Contrast style with that of Sapka's Power-Flop (Figure. 7.45).

The Speed Flop. Those that emphasize the velocity aspects of Flop jumping are typified by
Stones, Fosbury, and most American Floppers. They believe in and practice great speed--speed
in the run, in the conversion curve, in the use of the arms and the bent-knee lead leg, and
speed in the kind of power training and the amount of time devoted to it. They do power training of course but with a lesser emphasis on basic strength. They use a two-arm thrust during
the conversion-takeoff, but tend to bend the arms, shorten the radius of the thrust, and so
raise slightly the angle at which the pelvis (c.g.) lifts during the last strides. Though
this tends to diminish the duration of thrust against the ground, they seek to balance this
loss through faster arm and lead-leg actions.

For example, Donald Chu, coach of jumping events at California State Hayward, stated in a
letter to me,

> *A true double-arm action is difficult to achieve without deceleration in the approach.*
> *Therefore Stones, by film analysis, has poor arm technique by comparison with Brumel.*
> *But what he does so effectively, and through such a short range it is almost never*
> *seen, is to "punch" the arms through-and-up. This, well timed with a quick lead-leg*
> *knee drive (bent for a shorter and faster thrust), must provide great impulse against*
> *the ground. Not unlike what the Karate expert achieves with his sharp jab-like kicks*
> *and punches.*

The Power Flop. Costello, who trained for a time under Dyatchkov in Moscow, told me that Russian coaches and jumpers recognize the advantages of the Flop style but are seeking to maintain those of the Brumel version of the Straddle. Brumel's run was the fastest of all Straddlers, and Power Floppers would not lessen such velocity. But they argue that greater useable velocities of the run will be achieved indirectly, by way of power training and power techniques, more than by a direct emphasis on velocity with an inadequate power background. The greater the strength of the related muscles, the more effectively speed can be used. Also, by power techniques in the use of the arms and a slight prolongation of the "settle," they seek to increase the force of thrust against the ground and the duration of the vertical impulse. (Compare the more horizontal through-and-up action of the pelvis of Sapka in Figure 7.45 and that of Stones, Figure 7.44.)

Fig. 7.45. The Power Flop by Kestutis Sapka (USSR, 1974, 7'4½''), showing an approach style similar to that of Brumel (Straddle style). Sapka tended to lean toward the bar during takeoff. Contrast high throw of arms with Stones in Figure 7.44.

True, their use of a low double-arm action and tendency to run flat-footed during the last few strides has a definite slowing effect on the run. But this is at least partially countered by their more effective conversion effectiveness from horizontal to vertical force.

In summary, this distinction between a Speed Flop and Power Flop is of value in clarifying different approaches to the same problem, not unlike the non-essential differences that Kerssenbrock found between Brumel's Straddle and Matzdorf's Dive-Straddle when he cleared 2.29m. The Speed-Floppers, such as Stones, will achieve vertical thrust by way of power training and a direct emphasis on running velocity. The Power-Floppers, such as Sapka or Woods, will achieve vertical thrust by way of power training and a direct emphasis on using that power by prolonging the duration of power application. As with Brumel and Matzdorf, when each is performed maximally, differences will disappear.

THE RUN. An effective high-velocity run is inherent in the Fosbury style. Three phases of the run require special attention: its velocity, its length, and its pattern.

Run Velocity. The run should be as fast as possible, even a little faster than a jumper feels he can now use effectively. Prior to the introduction of the Flop, Dyson wrote, "too fast an approach gives insufficient time for the application of the various forces against the ground; vertical velocity is then reduced, as is the takeoff angle."[1]   But the Flop style inherently increases the time factor. What Brumel, using the Straddle, acquired by power training and endless practice during years under a meticulous coach, Fosbury acquired while working alone, almost haphazardly, as a natural outcome of his style. Coach Wagner said, "Fosbury approaches the bar faster than any previous jumper." Dwight Stones has said repeatedly, "The key to my jumping more effectively lies in using more speed-speed-speed." I have yet to see a Flopper who runs slowly.

Each man does have his own critical speed determined in part by heredity but even more by present muscle power, by skill in the techniques of the run, and by the pattern of his run. But each man's goal is to increase that critical speed to his highest levels of use. About 30 percent of clearance height is gained from effective use of horizontal velocity.

Run Length.   The run should be long enough to ensure optimal velocity prior to the first strides of the conversion curve. "Optimal velocity" is not fastest-possible velocity, but is that speed that enables the jumper to gain fastest-useable velocity during the next-to-last stride before takeoff. Fosbury ran a spiral curve from his first step 42'6" from the crossbar extended, using eight strides; Stones took ten strides from 65 feet out; Woods, 8 strides from 56 feet (1973); and other seven-foot jumpers, eight to 11 strides from 55 to about 70 feet out. (See Figure 7.46.) During the indoor season, jumpers must be prepared to shorten both the length of run and the lateral location of their starting point so as to adjust to the limited space of indoor facilities.

Run Pattern.   Two distinguishable patterns have gained wide acceptance in the Flop--the arc and the J. The arc was used by Fosbury, primarily because of the narrowness of his own back yard where he first tried the style. But later jumpers prefer it as providing a gradual adjustment to the increasing centrifugal forces of curve running.

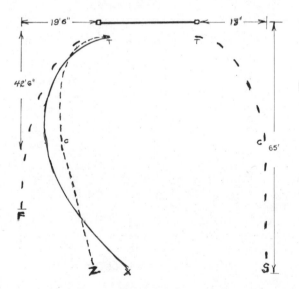

Fig. 7.46. Run Patterns for the Fosbury Flop. Curve FT--Fosbury's pattern; curve ST--Stones; curve ZT--five strides straight-line, five curved with decreasing radius; curve XT--spiral curve with long radius during early strides, short radius during last strides. In curve ST, note precisely measured turn-mark at point "c". Stones curved during fifth stride without a measured turn-mark.

Individual patterns vary. Some have tried a single-radius circular run. But running in a tight circle not only tends to limit running speed, it also makes consistency in strides and arm action more difficult. Therefore most arc-style runners use a spiral pattern with a long-radius curve during first strides and a short-radius curve during the final three to five strides (Figure 7.46-FT).

Those using the J pattern argue that acceleration occurs more easily if the early strides are straight-line; the change into curve running can still be made smoothly and effectively. Variations also occur in the J pattern: some, such as Stones, start their straight-line run at 90 degrees to the crossbar (Figure 7.46ST); others angle their straight-line run at 80 or even 70 degrees to the crossbar, claiming that this eases the transition to curve running (Figure 7.46-ZT).

[1]Geoffrey H. G. Dyson, *op. cit.*, p. 146.

Stones explained his pattern this way:[1]

For the 15-foot measurement (crossbar extended) I put one foot in front of the other 15 times (shoe length=12 inches). For the 65-foot measurement, I walk 19 strides and that's it. This mark varies with run-up conditions, psych, bar height, etc. My plant foot is 3 feet away and parallel with the line of the bar. As the bar goes up, my plant position moves out gradually. I then adjust my starting point by moving it back three times that change in distance.

Some J-style Floppers, such as Mel Embree (Harvard, 1975, 7'2¼"), are more concerned with the exact location of the point at which they start their curved run. Embree's turn mark was 15'1" laterally and 26'1" at right angles to the crossbar. He started six running strides from the turn mark. "This allows me to set my starting point so that I will be relaxed to the turn mark and able to drive my last four strides consistently on every jump."[2]

The Conversion Curve. In both the arc and J patterns, the radius of the conversion curve is of great importance. A longer radius with its more gradual curve can either lessen centrifugal force and so decrease its potential values for vertical force, or it can utilize greater velocity in the run without decreasing vertical force. A shorter radius has the opposite potential effects. Given a fixed velocity, a "sharper" curve creates greater centrifugal force, tends toward a greater lean into the curve and back of the takeoff foot, and so a longer time in which force can be applied against the ground during takeoff. As jumpers improve their technique and clearance height, they tend to increase running velocity and decrease the radius of the conversion curve, but this is only a tendency that varies from man to man. Frank Ryun[3] reports Stones as saying,

During the first five strides I work on establishing rhythm and, at the same time, develop velocity. From the sixth step on, I go toward the curve. While running in the curve I try to maintain or even increase my speed. At this stage I can feel the pull of centrifugal force and I lean into what would be the center of the circle.

Length of the Final Strides. Normally, the length of the final strides will be a natural consequence of the pattern and technique of the approach. Analysis by the use of movies usually finds the next-to-last stride is longer; the last stride, shorter but this varies with the style of jump and the individual jumper.

For example, using the Straddle, Brumel's next-to-last stride had these measurements:[4] length--230cm, duration--0.275sec, cadence--3.63 strides per sec, and horizontal speed--7.5m/sec. Measurements for these same measurements of his final stride were 200cm, 0.250sec, 4 steps per sec, and 7.24m/sec. That is, he shortened his last stride and slowed his horizontal speed. In contrast, Kerssenbrock found these values for Matzdorf's last two strides. Next-to-last-stride--0.243sec, 156cm, 4.11 strides per sec, about 6.5m/sec; last stride--0.272sec, about 193cm, 3.6 steps per sec, and about 6.95m/sec. That is, Matzdorf lengthened his last stride and increased his horizontal speed. Similar differences will undoubtedly be found among individual Floppers and between those using a Power Style as contrasted with a Speed style of the Flop.

But our main point here is that such differences are inherent in style variation and so need no special coaching emphasis. In fact, attention directed to such differences is more likely to disrupt coordination than to help it.

---

[1]Dwight Stones, "Competitors' Corner," *TRACK TECHNIQUE*, No. 55, March 1974, p. 1974.

[2]Mel Embree, ibid., 1974.

[3]Frank J. Ryan, Ph.D., "The Fosbury Flop with Dwight Stones," *SCHOLASTIC COACH*, March 1976, p. 24.

[4]K. Kerssenbrock, *op. cit.*, p. 46.

Placement of the Takeoff Foot.   After years of experimentation, jumpers and coaches now seem generally agreed that the takeoff should be from a point about three feet directly out from the near standard. This ensures clearance of the bar at its lowest point, relates the takeoff point to a fixed and easily seen object, and most important, produces a landing on a safe foam-rubber mound. Otherwise, men tend to slide along the bar and end up on the concrete apron, more than slightly bruised.

To be most effective, the line of placement of the takeoff foot should balance two con-cerns--alighment with the curve of the final strides, and facilitation of rotation during takeoff. The latter is essential, even though minimal. Coach Wagner states[1] that Fosbury's foot was placed at 15 degrees to the crossbar. Stones tried to plant his foot parallel with the crossbar. The difference lies primarily in the shortness of the radius of the approach curve, more than in attempts to ensure rotation. A short-radius curve tends to lessen the angle of foot placement; a wide radius, to increase it. In both cases, a straight-ahead place-ment and vertical thrust take precedence over rotation. Wagner says Fosbury "does not twist his spikes in the takeoff surface," though how that is determined from synthetic surfaces is hard to imagine. Actually a curved approach would produce a slight rotation of the foot from outside heel to inside big-toe, during which the line of foot-placement would swing as much as five degrees.

Little or no coaching of these points is needed if the principle is understood. But in-expert jumpers do tend to anticipate rotation in all takeoff movements, including rotation of the takeoff foot. In contrast, men with excellent technique as well as those attempting heights well above their standing height have a longer time in which to achieve rotation, and so can concentrate on jumping high with a minimum of rotation--takeoff foot, lead knee, right shoulder and all.

SPRING.   Strange as it may seem, high jumpers are not necessarily able to jump high, certainly not if we use the Sargent jump-and-reach test as our criterion. For years coaches have used performances in the latter event to discover prospects for high jumping, but the

correlation between high jumping and the Sargent jump is apparent-ly not high. Both Fosbury and Stones denied exceptional ability in the latter. In one interview[2] Stones said that "Al Feuerbach (260-pound shot putter) can easily out-jump me in the standing-jump test." This seems incredible. Donald Chu[3] found supportive evidence at the 1975 Olympic Development Camp at Indiana University,

At the Camp one of the tests for high jumpers and shot putters was the jump-and-reach test. The shot putters had a higher mean jump-and-reach than the high jumpers. Matzdorf had the best mark for the high jumpers--32 inches, but the best shot putter went three inches higher--35 inches. Everyone went "zonkers" thinking how high the high jumpers would go when they acquired the leg strength of the weightmen. But they were ignoring task specificity. High jumping is specific to the special skills of the run-conver-sion-spring-clearance.

Franklin Jacobs (Flop style, 1978, 20--5'8"--150#). The all-time master of "spring" was undoubtedly Franklin Jacobs, Fairleigh Dickinson University, who at age 20, set an indoor world record of 7'7¼". Jacobs was 5'8" tall, a difference of 23½" as between head and clearance heights. This was an amazing achievement, com-parable in its superhuman quality to Beamon's 29' 2¼" in the long jump. A rather careful examination of the record discloses no other

Fig. 7.47 Vertical Thrust by Stones.

[1]Berny Wagner, "The Fosbury High-Jump Style," *Track & Field Quarterly Review,* Vol. 75, No. 2, Summer, 1975, p. 111.

[2]John Tansley, "How They Train--Dwight Stones," *Track Technique,* No. 55, March 1974, p. 1757.

[3]Donald A. Chu, personal letter to me dated January 13, 1976.

jumper with more than a 17-inch difference: Brumel--16¼"; Stones--14¼". Yashchenko--15¼"; Mogenburg--12". Jacobs ignored his shortness and emphasized the positives of greater relative explosiveness in lifting his lighter weight (150#) as compared with the 170 pounds or more of other jumpers. (Yashchenko weighed 183#).

It follows that spring is specific to each method of jumping high. In contrast to the jump-and-reach, the high jumper runs prior to jumping, takes off from only one foot, and uses special techniques to exert a force against the ground greater than that supporting his weight. In the Flop style, spring is initiated by a faster-than-usual run that ends with a short-radius curve and a sudden change of direction from horizontal to vertical. The faster run tends to shorten durations of force during the spring but the Flop style compensates by increasing force-time through (a) an outside-foot takeoff, (b) a lean into the curve and lowering of the c.g. during the last few strides (called by some the "settle"), (c) a momentary bracing of the takeoff leg against horizontal force, and follow-up "yielding" as occurs in the exercise called depth jumping, (d) a quick acceleration of the arms and lead knee during takeoff that, by action-reaction, increases force against the ground, and (e) a vertical thrust by the takeoff leg with minimum loss of force to rotation and clearance.

Dyson emphasizes the value of early forceful acceleration of the arms and lead leg in increasing thrust against the ground. The greater that acceleration the greater the vertical-force reaction. "Ideally, the free leg and arms should be moving at their maximum velocity at the instant of takeoff, for their acceleration afterward cannot add to the athlete's vertical velocity.[1]

In the Straddle style, a straight lead leg aided vertical thrust and clearance. In the Flop style, both the direction and the force of upward thrust are aided by emphasizing a flexed leg that does not allow the foot to swing forward of the knee. If the foot does swing forward it tends to carry the c.g. along the bar and slows the accelerated drive of the knee Dyson considers essential. The line of the thigh rises very little above the horizontal, then drops down to gain clearance simultaneously with the takeoff leg.

Fig. 7.48. Takeoff by Sapka. Compare with Stones (Fig. 7.47).

In contrast, the arms are free to punch vertically and early while the takeoff foot is still flat on the ground, and with maximum force. They are effective in increasing ground thrust only as long as there is ground contact, but their ballistic follow-through over the head does aid the later clearance of the hips and legs.

All this assumes, and it's a critical assumption, that the related takeoff leg muscles have sufficient power (strength x velocity) to react to such great force. Only progressive and related strength training can provide the power required by the bracing-yielding and explosive reaction of these movements.

In summary, spring in the Flop style is the resultant of skill during the conversion strides, accumulated force against the ground, and vertical impulse (force x duration). Power Floppers tend to emphasize all three phases; Speed Floppers accumulate less force but utilize greater velocities throughout.

Acquiring Rotation. If there is a potential "problem" as related to rotation in the Flop style, it comes from over-emphasis--by the athlete and by the coach. As a rule of thumb, it needs minimal direct coaching. If the jumper has watched other Floppers and gained a muscle-nerve feel of the technique, and if he has made a sound approach to the takeoff, the specific

[1]Geoffrey H. G. Dyson, *op. cit.*, p. 145.

movements of rotation tend to be learned naturally, without special emphasis. If we analyze a slow-motion movie of the Flop, we abstract certain counter-clockwise movements (left-footed Flopper)--a slight rotation of the takeoff foot, an away-from-the-bar thrust of the lead knee, a slight swing of the inside shoulder and head. But such details of rotation will usually evolve naturally if the jumper observes other Floppers and gets a feel of the whole movement.

The primary value of the lead knee lies in its explosive and early thrust vertically, increasing the force against the ground. The athlete should have a sense of keeping such actions (including the arms) in close to the c.g., so as to increase their velocity and minimize rotation. Beyond that, the less coaching of details the better. Provide good examples by way of competitions and movies, then let the jumper work out his own details. Fosbury developed his style in his own back yard without benefit of coaching.

CLEARANCE. To the spectator, the method of clearance in the Flop style is its most spectacular feature--hence its name. Cameramen commonly catch the moment of buttocks-clearance when it appears certain the legs can never be lifted above the crossbar. But, strange as it may seem, clearance like rotation, occurs quite naturally *if the Flopper is aware of the crossbar as each part approaches it.* As Stones says, "it just happens." As the head-shoulders clear the bar they lift, both to see the bar and to prevent landing on the head. As the hips clear the bar and the head lifts, the hips drop. As the hips drop, the legs lift. It's as natural and simple as that. Similarly, the forceful thrust of the lead knee produces a wide spread of the knees (Figure 7.51), slows rotation, and aids both the arch and clearance of the legs.

Fig. 7.49. Stones' last stride.
The inward lean is rising toward vertical; the takeoff foot will be placed in line with the bar.

Fig. 7.50. Clearance by Dwight Stones. Eyes are focussed on the bar; arms are in close; knees spread; as buttocks clear, head is lifted, buttocks drop, legs and feet lift. Stones -- "It's as simple as that."

In describing Fosbury's clearance, Coach Wagner stated[1] that as his head passed the bar, the chin swung to his left collarbone as he looked over his left shoulder at the crossbar. He found that knowing the precise location of the bar was essential to clearing each part of the body--back, hips, thighs, lower legs. The arms were held close to the body--for better control.

The Arch During Clearance. Floppers vary greatly in the amount of arch of the back during clearance. Fosbury and Stones had relatively flat arches (Figures 7.6, 7.44, 7.50); Woods, a medium arch; various female Floppers, high arches. The arch raises the back and hips by dropping the head-shoulders (Figure 7.51). As these clear the bar, the head lifts, the hips drop, and the legs are lifted. The higher the arch, the higher the legs can be lifted.

All this occurs within a brief instant, as one rapidly-flowing movement, requiring perfect timing. Anticipation of the arch sometimes shortens the vertical thrust of the lead leg, or causes the head to drop too soon or too far, so as to lose sight of the crossbar. However its potential for adding to clearance height is significant.

Anticipation as a Potential Fault. Premature anticipation is probably the most common fault among Flop-style jumpers--anticipation of rotation to the detriment of a straight-line placement and thrust of the takeoff foot, anticipation of an arched clearance that tends to lean the torso toward the bar and decreases the vertical drive, anticipation of the landing that lifts the head too soon and drops the hips into the bar. In introducing the high jump, I estimated that about 60 percent of height cleared could be attributed to spring, 30 percent to the run, and only 10 percent to clearance. That estimate, accurate or not, clearly establishes the priorities of technique--each in its own good time and not before.

Fig. 7.51. Clearance by Chris Dunn (Colgate, 1975, 7'2¼").

THE ORGANIZATION OF PRACTICE

The overall organization of practice and training for field events is discussed at length in Chapter 6 and Chapter 16. But even with such exhaustive analysis, this book can provide only guidelines to organization. The local climate, conditions for training indoors and out, the schedule of competitive jumping, and of course, individual differences--all combine to require each coach to organize his own practice schedule for field events, as well as a particular schedule for this particular athlete. How else can a coach help a Fosbury who says, "I only jumped five or six times in practice all last year," the year he won the Olympic title.

TRAINING FOR POWER AND PRACTICING SKILL

This book assumes year-round related training for all events. The principle is sound for the high jump as for the shot put or six-mile run. But just how time-energies are portioned as between power and skill and body-mind relaxation is specific to each event. Dyatchkov (1969, 1141), after years of coaching great jumpers, concluded that basic power and flexibility training should comprise about 50 percent of total training time, both for the beginner and the expert. About half of this time would be taken with associated activities: gymnastics, acrobatics, ballet, and performing other track and field events. The other half would be given over to activities for enjoyment and relaxation. Variety is important. Competition should be low key. Whatever is fun and without tension: recreational basketball, soccer, swimming, tennis.

The remaining 50 percent of total year-round training time is divided between power training and skill practice. Practice to improve skill tends to be continuous, though with varying emphasis. But strength (basic-related-imitative) is also necessary to

---

[1]Berny Wagner, op. cit., p. 9.

allow the athlete to fulfill his potential in skill. Dyatchkov[1] reports that in 1960, the 18-year-old Brumel spent only 16 percent of his time in early season in jumping over the bar; the remainder, to basic and related conditioning. His meticulous records show that a total of 1260 practice jumps were taken. But in 1961, Brumel's year of greatest progress, "he went over the bar only 268 times, devoting the greater part of his efforts to building up his physical strength as related to high jumping." Keep in mind that Brumel was under a carefully controlled regime of both training and competition. No competition was important except as it pointed toward the Rome Olympics. They trained in terms of ONE BIG MEET only.

HOW TO BEGIN.
Appendix A examines in detail the basic methods for improving motor skills. Here we need only suggest examples of how these apply to jumping high. How, for example, does the principle of whole-part-whole learning function in practice? Obviously one cannot begin by making a well-executed run-spring-straddle or run-spring-flop. As indicated in Appendix A, the whole jump of the beginner is of a low order, as whole$_1$, which then progresses by gradually more complex wholes (whole$_2$--whole$_3$--etc.) to levels of complete mastery. The all-important concern is that each whole should be basically sound in terms of the next and, of course, the ultimate technique. Saying it differently, a high-jump coach must establish learning priorities; the actions and forces that contribute most to jumping high should be learned first, not as separate parts or progressions which, added together later will form a whole, but always on a whole-part-whole-part-whole basis.

Consistent with this principle, beginners in the high jump should use the scissors style. In that way they learn the highest-priority essentials first--jumping high from a preliminary run. We began by emphasizing that spring contributed about 70 percent to height cleared; the run, about 20 percent; clearance, about 10 percent. Learning procedures should follow this same emphasis.

In jumping scissors style (Figure 7.4a), efficiency of clearance is not a concern; attention can be concentrated wholly on jumping high. Soon, the beginner will crouch a little prior to takeoff. He may speed up his last three or four strides or emphasize their force against the ground. As this occurs, a checkmark at the point where these strides begin will be helpful in improving consistency of strides and fixing an effective point of takeoff. At first the beginner will feel his way to that checkmark, but the need for consistency and smoothness will soon produce a starting mark about five strides beyond. He now has the primary essentials of a sound high jump--a consistent approach and a vertical jump. Up to this point, the coach has said nothing about clearance style or rotation during takeoff. The torso remains upright; the landing is on the lead leg.

Speed of the run should at first be natural and uninstructed, though a casual suggestion to take it easier or move a little faster may not confuse the jumper. Similarly, little attention should be called to the run pattern. The beginner may have seen a Flop-style curved run, or a Straddle straight-line run. At this stage either is sound. But gradually, the jumper should become aware of the potential value of the run-up for applying force against the ground and jumping high. Once he realizes that 90 percent of jumping high lies in this phase, and not in the more obvious and more talked-about phase of clearance efficiency, he is well on the road to sound learning.

As soon as the beginner shows interest in continuing with the high jump, his attention should be shifted to related power training, especially in the form of sprinting, hurdling, long jumping, high bounding from the takeoff leg--from short strides or from a stand. Exercises such as those shown in Figures 7.60 to 7.79 will be of value, if the jumper is interested and they fit his time schedule. Approach this phase of training gradually and carefully; plenty of time later to follow a scheduled progressive program of weight training. But it is important that the high-jump prospect should understand that jumping high is an outcome of developed power as much as of practiced technique.

If the coach and the jumper favor the Fosbury Flop style, the curved approach should be learned before mention is made of rotation or method of clearance. Most now use the straight-

---

[1]Vladimir Dyatchkov, "How the Russian High Jumpers Succeeded at Rome," *Track Technique*, June 1961, 100. Translated from *Light Athletics*, Moscow, 12, December 1960.

line J approach during the first five or six strides. But the last three or four strides are the crucial ones--in terms of consistency, of velocity, of inward lean, of use of the arms in keeping the c.g. low, of stride length. Until the jumper can master all such details so that they are done confidently in the same way every time, he is not ready for the details of clearance. Just last week I watched 18 high-school high jumpers at the Pennsylvania Relays. Nine cleared 6'9''; three, 6'11''. Not one of the 18 had what could be called a sound approach. Somehow, the first priorities of jumping high had been neglected.

Even when the jumper is ready for coaching rotation and clearance, details should be kept to a minimum. Usually he will learn the idea of these movements by watching others, and will need little direct instruction. To suggest a thrust of the lead knee away from the bar, or a turn of the inside shoulder, or of the head will tend to lead to exaggeration or to the common fault of anticipation. It's intriguing that Fosbury learned his style without benefit of any coaching.

All of this assumes a safe landing mound--high enough to reduce the distance of descent, and soft enough to minimize impact shock. If the eyes concentrate on leg clearance, the landing will be made on the upper back, with no danger to the head or neck. No mention should be made of the arch-clearance during early learning as this tends to lower the head.

WHICH STYLE--STRADDLE OR FLOP?

Which Style is Best? Each individual will determine his own style out of his first attempts to high jump, his own unique physical characteristics, his own personal preference. A coach must work within the limits of such individual uniqueness; to coerce a high jump prospect to conform to some theoretically "best" style is always difficult and often ends in failure. Fosbury's coach, Berny Wagner, Oregon State, tried for over a year to change the outlandish Flop to a more respectable Straddle, then threw in the towel. After setting his world record with a Dive-Straddle, Matzdorf tried hard *and* long to shift to the Flop style--without success. But one thing is clear--the Straddle and Flop are mutually supportive in their contributions to our knowledge of each style and of the essentials of jumping high. After a century of experimentation, we are still conscious of how much more there is to understand and use.

Which style is best? No need to give an either/or answer. For it seems that an eclectic approach--not to modern styles as wholes, but as related to each phase of high jumping--would have the greatest potential for the future. What style and velocity of run has greatest potential? What techniques are best during the transition phase--use of arms, stride-lengths, lowering of c.g., body lean, etc.? What techniques in the upward drive? In clearance? Within such specific questions lies the answer to potentially best style.

Yashchenko combined great velocity in his straight-line approach with an excellent transition and vertical thrust, but it took him some five years or more to perfect what Floppers learn in a year or two. Most experts agree that the curved approach of the Flop J-style has greatest potential in ease of learning, but also in velocity and conversion of force upward. Such a curved approach has been used only when the takeoff foot is on the outside, as in the Flop. But I mentioned in the history of the run that, in 1895, Mike Sweeney (Eastern cutoff style--6'5 5/8'') used a curved approach, an outside-foot takeoff and feet-first clearance. Using all our modern improvement, could it be that some variation of the old Eastern cutoff style has potential in the future of high jumping?

To go even further, it would seem quite feasible to use such a high-velocity, curved run with an inside-foot takeoff. True, the weight would tend to be to the inside of the curve and behind the takeoff foot. The lead leg would need to be flexed to avoid dragging the ground. Techniques of conversion during the last stride-takeoff would be extremely fast--explosive punch of the arms upward, very short last stride, forceful drive upward of the takeoff knee, and the like. Admittedly this is an armchair speculation but it might be done.

As a second example, experts in biomechanics generally agree that, all other considerations aside, some variation of the Dive-Straddle is most economical in terms of bar-clearance. Use Yashchenko's method as a starting point but let actual techniques emerge out of forces created by the run and vertical jump. You can't afford to waste a talented youngster in making such an experiment? Then encourage a retired Dive-Straddler to try. It would be fun.

As between the Flop and the various versions of the Straddle, one thing is clear and certain. The Flop is much easier and quicker to learn. Neither Fosbury nor Stones--its strongest advocates--practiced technique very much. Beginners are learning acceptable technique in a year or so. All over the world the percentage of Floppers seems to be increasing. In 1979 of West Germany's four jumpers to clear 7'6½'', all were Floppers. At the 1979 NCAA Championships, all 28 competitors were Floppers. In 1980, all 14 U.S. women high jumpers over six feet were Floppers. In 1977, Louise Ritter (1979--6'4'') improved over two inches within weeks of changing from the Straddle to the Flop. "It's just so much easier. The Straddle is so technical." French National High Jump Coach, Andre Daniel,[1] confirmed this view, "It only takes a coach 2 to 4 months to teach the Fosbury technique, whereas it takes 3 to 4 years to discover the subtleties of the straddle jump." (Despite this, he preferred the Dive Straddle as having greater potential.)

Quite naturally, champions tend to defend their own style. Yashchenko: "For me personally the Straddle is best....I tried it (the Flop) but not very successfully." Rolf Beilschmidt (E.G., 1979--undefeated, 7'6½'' Straddler) "had toyed with the flop in training, and his best of 6'10 3/4'' is only four inches behind his practice best with the Straddle. 'But the Straddle,' he says, 'seems to be more economical. I feel more at ease there....But the technique is much more difficult to master....In the straddle one is always able to improve.'"[2] Hardly a weighty argument for each master understands and feels at ease with what he does best.

HOW MUCH JUMPING IN PRACTICE?
The way to better technique is through more and better practice; there's no other way. That's true for every complex human skill--for gymnastics, for hitting a baseball, for playing tiddley-winks, and certainly for high jumping, whatever the style. It's also true that jumping over a high crossbar is a unified skill not easily divided into separate parts such as the run, the takeoff, or the clearance. To practice properly such a whole skill requires all of its phases. Certainly clearance requires a takeoff; takeoff, a run. But also, a run without takeoff and clearance is a different skill; one should at least be doubtful of its usefulness for the real event, a running high jump. Attention can be focussed on whatever detail is of interest in a particular jump--on eye focus or the thrust of an arm--but always within the whole action.

For the Flop style, there is a tradition of minimal jumping in practice, as though the Flop has some unique and bizarre quality that sets it apart from other human skills. Two years after his Olympic victory, Fosbury was quoted as follows,[3]

But I never jump in practice anyway. That's one of my eccentricities, I guess. If I do jump in practice, I don't get psyched up for meets. I pick up bad habits. Most high jump coaches will tell you that the way to learn to high jump is to high jump. As far as I'm concerned, the way to learn how to high jump well is to high jump in competition only. I know that I'm lucky. I know my style. I've already got it down. Any bad habits I have is just a slacking off of mental concentration. It's always been within me. Nobody ever taught me the style. I just did it.

Dwight Stones did far more jumping at higher heights than Fosbury ever did, and has followed a power-training program far beyond that of Fosbury's reluctant sessions. He trained almost year-round at repeated speed-endurance work, triple-jump bounding, and weightlifting. But, like Fosbury, he almost never jumped for technique in practice. As he explained to Robert Pariente,[4]

"The Flop is simple. It rests on the principle of speed. It is my speed that lifts me to that height. Of course, that is dependent on the amount of strength I have in my legs; the two go together...Technique is secondary, so I don't Flop in training. I don't feel the need. I just do intervals and limbering exercises, and in the winter, lots of weightlifting--that's enough."

---

[1] Andre Daniel, "Yashchenko and the Straddle," *Track Technique*, June 1978, Vol. 72, p. 2304.

[2] *Track & Field News*, September 1979, p. 19.

[3] "Dick Fosbury Looking for 68 Spark," *Track & Field News*, 1 February 1971, 7.

[4] Robert Pariente, "A Glorious Return to Munich," *Track & Field News*, 11 July 1973, p. 16.

But even specifically related strength training does not use muscles as they are used in actual high jumping. Depth jumping comes closer but Stones shunned it, as being too stressful and even dangerous; that is, he failed to make the gradual approach that Veroshanskiy warned was necessary. Stones attributed 80 percent of his success to his "hard training" in the Fall-- quite possibly a valid assumption. He also placed great reliance in triple-jump bounding and interval training (speed-endurance training) as a means of peaking for highest performance.

In my judgment, the minimal jumping-in-practice of Fosbury and Stones is more an indication that we're still not near human ultimates than that practice jumping isn't needed for the Flop style. True, a degree of skill sufficient for competition can be acquired in a remarkably short time, but this is far from full mastery. A precise number of jumps in practice is almost meaningless, for the answer depends so much on individual differences and maturity as related to jumping, time of year, purpose of the workout, and so forth. Yashchenko[1] mentioned 25 or 30 jumps as a maximum, and to make effective use of such a number requires a gradual build-up of the jumping muscles. Muscle "deadness" is the result of jumping too much-too high-too soon.

PERFECTING TECHNIQUE IN HIGH JUMPING.

Sometimes cliches, however trite, are justified: only perfect practice makes perfect. Chapter 16 reviewed the basic means to improving motor skills. But how do such means apply specifi- cally to the skill of jumping high?

First place emphasis on whole-part-whole jumping; that is, upon jumping at highest poss- ible heights with concentration of attention on how you jump, rather than on how high. After warming up well, in terms of flexibility and springiness, move the bar up rapidly to a height near your personal maximum. Now take each jump just as you would in competition, though with your attention on some detail of technique that needs improvement. Always use check-marks, even though you so perfect your run that you're hardly aware of them. Always run at meet velo- city so that, like your check-marks, such velocity will be automatized; it will be your way of jumping and will need little, if any, attention in a meet. The speed of its execution is an inherent part of every high jump style, just as much so as the mechanics of arm or leg move- ments; all such aspects of style should be practiced together, as one whole and inseparable movement, until they become "out of mind," so to speak. Now, the jumper can concentrate on simply jumping, with no inhibitions, no seepage of power or attention.

Before each jump, think through, or rather, feel through in a mind-muscle sense, the jump as a whole, including the run and all. Now feel through the special aspect of the jump you are concerned with. Jump in terms of this part-in-whole awareness. Immediately, as you walk back from the pit, think-and-feel through both the right and wrong of what you just jumped. The thinking and feeling aid learning, along with the actual jumping. Attentive right practice makes perfect.

MAINTAIN A DETAILED DIARY.

Can you imagine the complete dedication of Dyatchkov's coaching when he could state exactly how many practice jumps Brumel took in 1961 as compared with 1960? Actually, in his writings he tells us how many jumps at each height of the crossbar, and exactly how many vertical jumps with each weight on the shoulders. Of course, Dyatchkov was the National High Jump Coach, with no other responsibilities.

But only by keeping a complete record of his daily work can a man really plan his program. Just what and how much was done last year? What were its effects on performance? How can this year's training program improve on it--both in general and in particular? How does this man's development in power and performance compare with that of a former great jumper at a similar level of development. Such questions are the very backbone of competent coaching in any field event. At least, to have a written record of the related answers sure helps to straighten the backbone; coaching humans is always an uncertain business.

---

[1]Garry Hill, "Yashchenko," *Track & Field News*, May 1978, p. 7.

POWER TRAINING FOR SOUND TECHNIQUE

Until the late 1950s, the way to better jumping was exclusively by more jumping. At least 90 percent of the time-energy of daily practice was given to jumping and directly related activities. Today, more jumping is not nearly enough. Jumping skill is probably practiced as many hours now as then, but an eleven-month year of related work allows time for much more than skill. Essential as skill is, it is now allotted only about 50 percent--and even as low as 15 percent--of practice time-energy. Today, one must develop a foundation of related power, flexibility and relaxation from which to project skill upward. Without that foundation, skill can be developed only within the limits of relative weakness, stiffness and mental inhibitions. It is power--at least as much as skill--that determines how fast-far we can run, what body flexion can be used during the last two strides, or the speed with which the springs of jumping can react after being compressed. Keep in mind that power-velocity-skill, in reality, is a unity; only as words and ideas are they separable.

Chapter 6, "The Dynamics of Power," emphasizes the importance of building basic strength, but also related power that simulates specific patterns of movement of each phase of the target event. For example, the upthrust of the lead leg needs power training of that specific pattern of action, a pattern that is somewhat different in the Straddle from that of the Flop. Optimal power training would reflect that difference.

The discussion in Chapter 6 of the extent to which strength is retained concluded that a significant degree of strength is lost in a matter of weeks. As evidence, Dyatchkov, (1969, 1123) found that when heavy-weight lifting exercises are stopped altogether, strength decreases, muscle tension increases, and competitive results suffer. It seems clear that, along with the imitative power exercises, some basic strength exercises should be continued throughout the year.

The trend during early season is to increase weights, that is, to emphasize the strength factor; that during the later season is to decrease weights and emphasize the speed-force factor. During the latter period, exercises with weights should be combined with exercises involving explosive jumping without weights. These usually are done at the end of a training session. In general, weight exercises should be stopped well before exhaustion occurs; power, not endurance, is the goal.

POWER EXERCISES FOR THE LEGS AND FEET[1]

These power exercises have been selected because they overload muscles and joints in ways that relate directly to the movements of high jumping, whatever the style may be. Each tends to concentrate on one phase of such actions, but all taken together cover the full range of all high jumping actions. These exercises are not all inclusive; the resourceful coach and jumper will invent his own exercises for those actions we have neglected.

Poundages given are intended to suggest relative resistances, not actual weights for all jumpers. A maximum weight is the heaviest an athlete can lift when rising from the squat position.

Figure 7.60. Squats, barbells on shoulders (220-270 lbs.).

Figure 7.61 Half-squats with explosive rise on toes (350-530 lb.).

---

[1] I wish to acknowledge my great indebtedness for the many excellent line drawings in the remaining pages of this chapter, in particular those figures with black shirts, taken from Vladimir Dyatchkov, *THE HIGH JUMP*, Moscow: *FIZKULTURA I SPORT*, 2nd edition, 1970.

    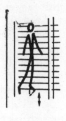

Figure 7.62. Jumping from partial squat, not more than half-maximum weight (barbells or sandbags); do sets of 6-7 jumps each.

Figure 7.63. Vertical jumping for maximum height from 140-degree angle of knees, less than half-maximum weight.

Figure 7.64. Vertical jumping, alternating feet forward and back, half-maximum weight; do sets of 6-10 strides each.

Figure 7.65. Rise high on toes, weights 400-480 lbs.

Figure 7.66. On stall bar, lower heel as far as possible, then rise high on the toes; first both feet, then each foot separately.

   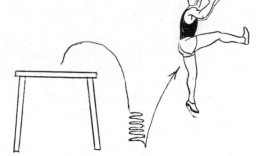

Figure 7.67. Skip on the toes with knees slightly bent (170-220 lbs.).

Figure 7.68. Takeoff-leg press. By fixing pins in vertical posts, can be made isometric.

Figure 7.69. Stepping up on stool 12-18 inches high. Alternate legs. Increase weights gradually; knees are susceptible to strain.

Figure 7.70 Depth Jumping.[1] Jump high in the air in explosive reaction to jumping down from a platform 30" (75cm) to 43" (110cm) high. Do not use weights, since reactive speed, not strength, is the desired outcome. By research, Verhoshanskiy determined that these precise heights give optimal value (1) in developing maximum speed in switching from yielding to overcoming work so crucial in the last strides of the high-jump run, and (2) in developing maximal dynamic strength. Do in sets--2 x (10 @ 75cm) plus 2 x (10 @ 110cm). Jog between sets. Maximum use is twice a week; once a week for the less prepared. Depth jumping, approached gradually and carefully, can be of great value; too much too soon can strain or injure muscles and ligaments. In general, beginners and young jumpers should avoid it until after months of jumping with weights.

Stop all depth jumping 10 to 14 days before important competition.

---

[1] Yuriy Verhoshanskiy, "Depth Jumping in the Training of Jumpers," *Track Technique*, # 51, March 1973, p. 1618. The serious coach should study this report carefully. (Reprinted in *Track & Field Quarterly Review*, Vol.79, #1, Spring 1979, p. 60.)

POWER EXERCISES FOR THE EXTENSORS OF THE FEET-LOWER LEGS

Figure 7.71   Jump or skip, with or without skipping rope, with or without weighted vest or belt.   Keep knees locked to emphasize foot-ankle power.

Figure 7.72   Jump high emphasizing explosive push of the takeoff foot; thrust lead leg upward as in high jumping; with or without weighted vest or belt.

Figure 7.73   Rise on the toes with a narrow board attached to a ski shoe.   Walk or skip; at first use hip and knee muscles; later, emphasize ankle-foot muscles.

Figure 7.74   Place one foot on gym horse or table; bounce high on toes of other foot; with or without weights.   Emphasize ankle-foot power.

POWER EXERCISES FOR DEVELOPMENT OF THE PELVIC MUSCLES

Figure 7.75   Jump high from a partial squat; begin with little flexion, then gradually drop lower.

Figure 7.76   Jump high from solid platform with weight in hole.   Keep back erect; eyes up.   Do not use gym stools--unsafe.

Figure 7.77   Jump up using takeoff leg from platform whose height produces a 140-degree angle at the knee; with or without weighted vest or belt.

Figure 7.78   Jumps from alternating legs; drop down low, jump high; with or without weighted vest or belt.

Figure 7.79   Jump successive hurdles, emphasizing hip action in dropping low and rising high.

MEASURING PROGRESS IN THE VERTICAL JUMP

A valid and reliable measure of progress in vertical jumping power is important as a motivating device and as a means not subject to variations in skill or attitude.   The Sargent jump is often used but Zivkovic[1] seems to have found an even better method.   Note in Figure 7.81 that a cloth tape, pulled through a metal staple, measures the height to which a man can jump vertically.   The tape spool can be fastened or held in the hand; a slight pressure against the spool will prevent it from running too freely through the staple.

Figure 7.81

[1]Miodrag Zivkovic, "How I Train Yugoslavian High Jumpers," *Track Technique*, 14, December 1964, 420.

HOW THEY TRAIN
The previous discussions have given in some detail the training programs of Les Steers and Valeriy Brumel as being basically sound for all jumping styles and, within the limits of individual differences, for all jumpers. But the training of these more modern jumpers may also be helpful.

The Training of Pat Matzdorf
Pat Matzdorf did relatively little power training until his sophomore year in college under Coach Bill Perrin. For years, Perrin had been a power-training expert who organized power exercises for the specific movements of all events, though especially his "Bill Perrin Pole Vault Trainer," using rubber tubing whose resistance varies with its length.

Perrin was familiar with the research of Dyatchkov that strength and competitive performance diminish together when weight training is stopped entirely, so that along with simulated-power exercises, Matzdorf lifted heavy weights within one month of his record performance. However, the primary exercises for power development were high-hopping, especially up the stadium steps, and depth jumping as advocated by Verhoshanskiy (Figure 7.70). The stadium-step jumping was without weights but involved great force in bounding 2 and 3 steps at a time. In depth jumping Matzdorf rebounded so as to touch with his forehead a cloth 3 to 4 feet above his head.

These two training exercises combined with three practices per week of 10-15 jumps each at bar heights within about 3 inches of his maximum comprised the bulk of his work.

In the interview previously cited[1] Perrin was quoted as follows,

"This involves some weight training but more important, exercises like hopping stadium seats on one and both legs. Notice I said seats, not just the stairs. Pat will bound over one and maybe miss one, but it's a constant pop all the way up. He tries to put in such an intensity of effort that if he goes much past 10 seconds or so he is virtually exhausted. So it's always a concentrated, explosive effort; all the exercises we do are power-related and there is such an overload that the athlete can only do one for a short period because of the intensity of the drill. This power training is the basic training in the fall and into the indoor season when he does it three times a week. During the competitive season, he follows this program twice a week.

"We concentrate on the play of the arms in all exercises. If they are used correctly, the arms alone can give tremendous lift," Perrin remarks. "We also use what I call 'depth jumping' where the athlete stands on a table or bench three or four feet high and then drops down and immediately explodes back up as high as possible. As the body drops, the weight doubles or triples and the athlete gets all the advantages of squats or leg presses and similar weight routines without the restrictions of weights. Of course, Pat has a fundamental weight training routine, but again everything is done with explosive quickness. All the exercises are done with the total body in mind plus tying in all the various phases of the jump."

The Training of Tom Woods.[2]
Born: April 7, 1953. Ht/Wt: 6'5"/175#, 1.95/79.
Background: A 6'11½" high jumper as a prep, Woods went on to Oregon State and placings in four consecutive NCAA competitions (including 1st in 1972) and 3 AAU meets. In 1975, after a dismal day in the rain at the NCAA, Woods went on to win the AAU with a PR 7'5½" and the Pan-Am Games HJ with a meet record 7'4½" to complete his best season ever.
Best Marks: HJ, 7'5½", 100y, 10.5.

Basic Approach: Twice per week, Woods does intervals, either 100 or 165s, starting slowly and

---

[1]Jon Hendershott, "Another Jump Style: Bent Knee," *Track & Field News*, 1 August 1971, 2.

[2]Gene Willis, "Tom Woods," *Track Technique*, #63, March 1976, p. 2009. (Note that Tom Woods' training program was at Oregon State, and influenced by Coach Berny Wagner's experience with Dick Fosbury.)

working up to 3/4 speed, then back down. 10 x 100s or 5-8 x 165s. Tom feels that the basketball stuffing and triple jump bounding he does are especially effective for him. Tom never jumps for high heights in practice, though he does have a 7-3 practice mark. Woods competes every week for 3 months during the indoor season and for 5 months during the outdoor season.

Non-Competitive Season.

<u>Mon.</u> Weightlifting; half-squats, 5 x 135, 5 x 225, 5 x 305, 3 x 355, 3 x 405, 2 x 455, 1 x 485, 5 x 375; toe-risers, 10 x 450, 10 x 500, 10 x 550, 10 x 600; bench presses, 5 x 110, 5 x 120, 5 x 130, 3 x 140, 2 x 150. 20 incline situps. Basketball stuffing.

<u>Tues.</u> Jumping for technique; 10 x 100; 5 x 220.

<u>Wed.</u> Weightlifting: jump squats, 10 x 80, 10 x 90, 10 x 100, 10 x 135; toe-risers, 10 x 450, 10 x 500, 10 x 550, 10 x 600; bench presses, 5 x 110, 5 x 120, 5 x 130, 5 x 140, 3 x 150. Basketball stuffing.

<u>Thurs.</u> Hopping steps, 5 x 20 on left leg, 10 x 20 right leg; 10 x 165.

<u>Fri.</u> Same as Monday.

<u>Sat.</u>,<u>Sun.</u> Rest.

Competitive Season.

<u>Mon.</u> Weightlifting; halfsquats, 5 x 135, 5 x 225, 5 x 315, 3 x 365, 2 x 405, 2 x 455, toe-risers, 10 x 450, 10 x 500, 10 x 550, 10 x 600; bench presses, whatever he feels like. Basketball stuffing.

<u>Tues.</u> Technique work; 10 x 100.

<u>Wed.</u> Same as Monday, but add TJ bounding drill.

<u>Thurs.</u> Technique jumping; 5 x 165.

<u>Fri.</u> Jog, break a sweat, run through approach.

<u>Sat.</u> Compete.

<u>Sun.</u> Rest.

Training for the High Jump by Don Chu[1]

A training program for high jumpers, devised by Don Chu, Ph.D. of Cal-State U. at Hayward, distinguishes two main phases: (1) basic and related strength training, and (2) high jumping for technique, endurance and maximal height. On a year-round basis, the first is given about 50 percent emphasis; jumping for technique, about 25 percent: the remainder on related activities including jumping for endurance and height.

Strength Training.

A. Maximal Loading Base Period (Quantitive work--July-September).

This is an early pre-season period. During this time the jumper does a great volume of lifting, usually measured in total pounds (or kg). A larger number of sets and repetitions at moderate weight are utilized--i.e., 4-6 sets of 10-15 repetitions at 60-70% of maximum.

B. Power Development Period (October-January)

During this phase, emphasis is placed upon the maximal amount of weight which can be moved during a specific time, usually one second. This is the Russian "optimal load" concept, used to enhance faster movement response. Lifting is interspread with jumping drills-bounding and box drills-twice a week, usually Monday and Friday.

Example:

Half-squats	8 box jumps
1 set x 6 reps @ 80%	1 set x 8 @ 70%
optimal load (O.L.)	1 set x 10 @ 60%
1 set x 8 reps @ 90%	8 in-depth jumps
8 single-leg hops (each leg)	1 set x 5 @ 100%
1 set x 5 @ 100%	
1 set x 4 @ 110%	

Exercises Used:

Half-squat		Snatch
Inverted Leg Press	Power-clean	Squat-Jump

[1]Don Chu, "Training Methods for Jumpers," *Track & Field Quarterly Review*, Vol. 79 #1, Spring 1979, p. 50. Reprinted from *Olympic Development Technical Bulletin*, Utah State U., Logan, Utah.

Train three times per week--M-W-F. (No jump training on Wed.)

C. Power Transfer Period (February-April)
These exercises are more specifically related to the jumping movements. They should be carried out at maximal speed.

Do 4 sets x 5 repetitions at maximal intensity (85-95% of single RM):
Double-legged jumps with barbell   Inverted leg press
Single-legged jumps   Shoulder and biceps curl
Bounding split squats

D. Transition Phase-Preparation for Major Competitions.
This consists of two weeks of circuit training. Set-up 6-7 stations. Do 40-50% of single RM-30 seconds work, 15 seconds rest. 3 circuits.

E. Power Retention Phase.
This helps to maintain gains made earlier, and is used during late season championship meets. One day per week. 4 sets x 6 repetitions for major muscle groups.

High Jump Work-Outs
Three types of high jump work-outs are used to emphasize different aspects of the training program.

A. Technique.
This is the commonest type of session, usually done twice a week. The bar is set 6 inches below the jumper's maximum jump. 15-18 jumps are taken. Adequate rest is taken between jumps so that the jumper can be fresh and go all-out with each jump. The bar is raised 1-2 inches after the first few jumps, if all is going well. The jumper must concentrate on the specific points to be stressed in the technique during this type of session.

B. Endurance.
This is aimed toward taking many jumps during a session--up to 30 when the athlete is well-trained. Start the bar 8 inches below best jump attained. Clear 3 times at this height, and raise the bar by 2 inches. Repeat this process until the jumper has missed twice--then lower the bar by one inch and clear.

C. Maximal Height.
Take 12-15 jumps at the jumper's lifetime best. Continue to jump regardless of whether the bar is cleared. Stress concentration on each jump. Try to relax and allow technique to remain and carry the athlete over.

Some kind of high jumping occurs during all five phases of the year's training. High jumping for technique occurs about as follows: Phase A--once in 2 weeks; B--2 per week; C--2 per week; D--1 or 2 per week; E--1 per week. When power training and high jumping occur on the same day, jump first. High jumping for technique and for either endurance or maximal height are done on separate days. During the A-B, Power Development Periods (July to January), high jumping for technique occurs uncertainly, perhaps once in two weeks.

Chapter 8
THE POLE VAULT

<u>A BRIEF HISTORY OF EQUIPMENT</u>
The development of techniques and performances in the pole vault is so intimately related to equipment and facilities that a preliminary summary of the latter seems desirable.

   <u>THE VAULTING POLE</u>. In the earliest competitions, the pole was of either ash, hickory or spruce, and had an iron device at its tip--a three-inch tripod with three spikes weighing, one author said, 25# but more likely much less, or an iron cup with a single iron spike. Between 1900 and 1915, tape-wrapped bamboo gained general acceptance--at first with a spiked end, then, as a stopboard and takeoff box were introduced, with a wood plug in the hollow end-section.

   At the back of Michael C. Murphy's *COLLEGE ATHLETICS*, probably printed in 1909, A. G. Spalding advertised various track and field impedimenta, including pictures of three single-spiked vaulting poles: (1) a "thoroughly seasoned" spruce pole, 8 to 16 feet long, at $3 to $7 each; (2) a hollow spruce pole "considerably lighter than the solid poles, and the interior is filled with a special preparation which greatly increases the strength and stiffness," of similar lengths at a cost of $8 to $10 each; and (3) a bamboo pole "thoroughly seasoned, tape wound at short intervals, and fitted with special spike," 16 feet long, $7 each.

   With a plug, a medium-sized bamboo pole weighed about $5\frac{1}{2}$ pounds. In the 1930s, an aluminum pole was tried that weighed about the same, but lacked the flexibility of bamboo. Somewhat heavier but more flexible steel poles came from Sweden to the United States in the late 1940s but broke easily after several abrasions from falling. Fiberglass poles became available just after the war. For each pole, it took about ten years to gain acceptance.

   <u>THE TAKEOFF BOX</u>. Prior to 1900, there was no one place for planting the iron spike of the pole; any spot the vaulter preferred was acceptable. But by the 1912 Olympic Games at Stockholm, a small depression and stopboard were allowed. In his 1914 book for coaches, Mike Murphy stated "the plank in the ground should be at least six feet in length. It is sunk 12 inches in the ground leaving an edge of about two inches above ground. In front of the plank is dug a small hole (4 to 6 inches in depth) so that the force of the pole as it strikes the ground will be against this plank."[1] This "hole" was gradually widened at its front end to become a slideway. Schulte's *POLE VAULTING*[2], 1927, contains a picture of Frank Foss (1920 Olympic Champion, 13'5") with just such a stopboard and dirt slideway, but also an article by Harry Hillman describing a "take-off box" of wood, very similar in size to that used today. In contrast, even as late as 1926, our National AAU Rules Book stated as a first choice, "Any competitor shall be allowed to dig a hole not more than one foot in diameter at the takeoff, in which he shall plant his pole. A wooden box or stopboard sunk in the ground may be allowed." (Specifications followed.) I should add that use of the stopboard and box made an iron-spiked pole a liability, and so produced round ends on the bamboo poles as well as on the diminishing ash and spruce. As a later and probably final improvement, the wooden takeoff

---

[1]Michael C. Murphy, *ATHLETIC TRAINING*, New York: Charles Scribner's Sons, 1914, p. 109.

[2]Henry F. Schulte, *POLE VAULTING*, New York, American Sports Publishing Co., 1927, p. 166.

TABLE 8.1

OUTSTANDING PERFORMANCES -- POLE VAULT

OLYMPIC CHAMPIONS

Date	Record	Name	Affiliation	Hgt.	Wgt.	Grip **	Time 100y	Run	Comments
1896	10'10"	Wm. W. Hoyt	NYAC			* Grip height is here			Ash Pole
1900	10'10"	Irving Baxter	NYAC			measured from top of			Bamboo
1904	11'6"	C.E.Dvorak	Michigan			the upper hand to the			
1908	12'2"	E.T.Cooke	USA			Tip of pole.			
		A.C.Gilbert	Yale						
1912	12'11½"	H.S.Babcock	USA						
1920	13'5"	F.K.Foss	Chicago						
1924	12'11½"	Lee Barnes	USC	5'8"	150	12'4"		115'	
1928	13'9½"	Sabin Carr	Yale	6'1"	168				
1932	14'2"	William Miller	USC						
1936	14'3¼"	Earle Meadows	USC	6'1"	160	13'2"	10.4	115'	
1948	14'1¼"	Guinn Smith	Calif.	6'2"	170	12'11"	9.8	125'	Bamboo Pole
1952	14'11¼"	Bob Richards	Illinois	5'10"	160	13'7"	10.0	115'	Steel Pole
1956	14'11½"	Bob Richards	Illinois						
1960	15'5"	Don Bragg	Villanova	6'3"	192	13'10"	10.2	125'	Steel Pole
1964	16'8 3/4"	Fred Hansen	Rice	6'	167	15'0"	10.2		Fiberglass
1968	17'8½"	Bob Seagren	USC	6'	175	15'2"	9.8	130'	Fiberglass
1972	18' ½"	W.Nordwig	E.Germany	6'½"	160	15'4"	10.8m	126'	Fiberglass
1976	18' ½"	T. Slusarski	Poland	5'10"	168	15'7"			
1980	18'11½"	W.Kozakiewicz	Poland	6'1-3/4"	185	16'0"	11.0		

WORLD-RECORD PERFORMANCES OF SPECIAL INTEREST

Date	Record	Name	Affiliation	Hgt.	Wgt.	Grip **	Time 100y	Run	Comments
1887	11'5"	Hugh H.Baxter	NYAC	6'1"		(Ash Pole)			First over 11'
1904	12'1½"	Norman Dole	Stanford			(Bamboo)			First over 12'
1912	13'2¼"	M.S.Wright	Dartmouth			"			First over 13'
1927	14'0"	Sabin Carr	Yale	6'1"	168	"			First over 14'
1942	15'7 3/4"	C. Warmerdam	Fresno St.	6'1"	165	"	10.2	140'	First over 15'
1960	15'9¼"	Donald Bragg	Villanova	6'3"	192	13'10"	10.2	125'	Best ever steel
1962	16' 3/4"	John Uelses	U.S.Marines	6'0"	168	14'0"			First over 16' indoors
1962	16'2"	Dave Tork	U.S.Marines	5'8"	150				First over 16' outdoors
1963	17' 3/4"	John Pennel	N.E.La.	5'10"	170	14'10"	9.8	145'	First over 17'
1970	18' ¼"	C.Papanicolaou	Greece	5'11½"	168	15'10"	10.0	134'	First over 18'
1972	18'4¼"	Kjell Isaksson	Sweden						
1972	18'5 3/4"	Bob Seagren	USC						
1976	18'7¼"	Earl Bell	Kansas St.	6'3"	170	15'9"			Banana pole
1976	18'8¼"	Dave Roberts	Fla. T.C.	6'2½"	185	16'0"	9.7	138'	Banana pole
1980	18'8 3/4"	Mike Tully	U.S.	6'2"	181	15'10"			
1980	18'11¼"	P.Houvion	France	6'1¼"	176	15'10"	10.9		

BEST PERFORMANCES -- HIGH SCHOOL

Date	Record	Name	Affiliation	Hgt.	Wgt.
1969	17'4 3/4"**	Casey Carrington	Orting, Wash.		
1972	16'4"	Craig Brigham	So. Eugene, Ore.		
1974	16'8¼"	Mike Tully	Long Beach, Ca.		
1978	17'4¼"	Anthony Curran	Encino, Ca.		
1979	16'6"	Greg Duplantis	Lafayette, La.		
1980	17'5¼"**	Joe Dial	Marlow, Okla.	5'8½"	131#

** National High School record

box, which tended to rot and break with use, was changed to one of metal or other all-weather materials as done today.

THE LANDING PIT. First landings from the vault were undoubtedly made on unaltered grass. Turned-over sod is little softer and less level, and so was improved by uneven stages in this country and abroad by using, first sandy loam, then sawdust with sandy loam, and later shavings. Pits tended to be ground-level, though men were allowed to pile up the material in the center of the pit. But gradually they were raised. Hillman's 1926 article, just mentioned, advocated "For indoor vaulting a pit, two feet high, can be constructed on the floor and filled with sawdust, with mattresses arranged against sides of pit and on bottom underneath the sawdust." Very quickly, such construction was moved outdoors. Writing in 1940, Dean Cromwell complains[1] of European vaulting pits "as soft to land on as a cement sidewalk" and strongly recommends "a generous pile of wood shavings" both deep and wide. Shavings were supplanted in the late 1950s by huge mounds of loose foam rubber, and they, in the 60s, by the wonderfully soft though most expensive foam or air bags now in use.

THE RUNWAY. If not over-used and properly cut, rolled and watered, a grass runway gives excellent footing, and did so throughout the early years. With heavy poles and short runs, no one cared for more than level footing. Even when cinder-loam and clay-loam runways were constructed, runs of more than 50 feet were unusual. Mike Murphy's 1914 book[2] for coaches suggests "Two checkmarks--six and twelve ordinary paces from the plank," less than 60 feet in all. But lighter poles and realization of the value of greater run velocities rapidly increased runway lengths to 100 and even more feet. Present-day synthetic runway surfaces were not introduced until the 1950s.

A BRIEF HISTORY OF TECHNIQUE

The early development of vaulting with a pole had a multiple ethnic origin, with each nation contributing to the event out of its own unique customs and viewpoints. The Germans and those they influenced used pole jumping as a gymnastic and physical-culture exercise; the English, Scottish and Irish used it as a competitive event in their athletic games that "have been one of the chief characteristics of both town and country life in 'Merrie England' as far back as chronicles will reach."[3]

First printed mention of pole jumping seems to have been made in Germany--in Johann Basedow, *A BOOK OF METHODS*, 1774, a complete system of primary education, in which he proposed leaping with a pole as an exercise in his "naturalistic" approach to German physical culture. But in Johann Guts Muth's *GYMNASTICS FOR THE YOUNG*, 1793, a full section was given to vaulting, with drawings and a detailed explanation of vaulting mechanics. Heavy wooden poles were used, forcing a slow and probably short run. Crossbars two or three feet higher than the vaulter's head were cleared.

In contrast to this formalized approach in Germany, jumping with a pole in England evolved out of the natural terrain, the long-held customs of beagling and crosscountry running, and the centuries-old tradition of competitive sports and pastimes. As one might expect, no one kind of pole nor one style of jumping was used, and just who did what with which is not at all clear. In my 1954 search for the facts, I received a letter from Harry Askew, track coach at The Royal Liberty School, England, who spoke with the son of Edwin Woodburn who held the record of 11'7" in 1874. "The son attributes the growth of pole vaulting in Ulverston to the fact that men following the beagles took a pole with them to jump over the many stone walls (about five feet high), and so keep up with the hunt. Since there were many such limestone walls enclosing tiny fields, this explanation seems most plausible." Askew added that beagling (hunting with hounds) on foot is still done in some parts of England. For such a purpose, one can assume that any stout pole, with or without a metal point, and any technique would be used that brought the pole on the far side of the wall, or watery ditch for that matter, so as to be carried to the next obstacle.

---

[1]Dean B. Cromwell, *CHAMPIONSHIP TECHNIQUE IN TRACK AND FIELD*, New York: Mc-Graw-Hill Book Co., Inc., 1941, p. 181.

[2]Michael C. Murphy, *op. cit.*, p. 113.

[3]Montague Shearman, *ATHLETICS AND FOOTBALL*, London: Longmans, Green and Co., 1889, p. 4.

Without giving his sources, the English coach and writer, F. A. M. Webster, tells a different version of the Ulverston story,[1]

The method employed by the Ulverston men was unique, and for years the world's record holders came from that small town. Their poles were of ash or hickory, long and heavy, and shod at the lower end with a tripod of iron, forming a three-inch triangle. The weight of the pole necessitated a wide separation of the hands and a slow run-up. At the end of the approach run the tripod was planted some three feet in front of the cross-bar. The athlete then allowed his body to swing up and began to climb. The upper hand was shifted a foot up the pole and the lower hand brought up to it. The climbing continued until the pole had passed the vertical position. As it began to fall forward, the athlete drew up his knees and went over the bar in a sitting position, a last backward push preventing the pole from following through to remove the bar.

The Ulverston method obtained until 1889. The American athletes contended that the performances of Ray and Stones were nothing but acrobatic balancing feats, requiring neither strength nor endurance, and a new rule was passed prohibiting the athlete from shifting the grip of the upper hand and from placing the lower hand above the upper hand after the feet have left the ground. About this time too, several men suffered death by impalement, through their wooden poles snapping transversely, and the pole vault began to disappear from the programmes of British school sports.

The most authentic source for the early development of United States vaulting is from the article by Hugh H. Baxter,[2]

Up to 1879, American pole vaulters used various styles, all of them crude and unscientific. The upper grip on the pole was in all cases at least 3 feet higher than would be used by a modern pole vaulter for the same height. Some carried the thumb of the right hand up, and that of the left hand down, and all pulled with the upper hand alone, using the lower hand simply as a prop.

In 1879, W. J. Van Houten of the Scottish-American Athletic Club, New York, won the American championships with 10'4 3/4", using the same style as the record holders of today except that he did not have some of the fine points which have developed in recent years. He knew nothing about the shift, but being a very light man and using a very light pole he was able to carry it with both hands close together, thus obtaining the two hand pull which is the essential difference between the new and old styles and mainly accounts for the difference in records....

It is impossible to say just when or where the Van Houten style of pole vaulting returned and came into general use, but it is certain that R. G. Clapp of Yale used it when he made a record of 11' 10!" in 1898, and all subsequent records were made in practically the same style.

A BRIEF HISTORY OF PERFORMANCE

With increased use of lighter weight, more flexible and less dangerous bamboo poles, longer and faster runs, combined with a shift of the lower hand during takeoff, achieved greater upward velocity and higher heights. From 1904 to 1912, five world's records were made, beginning with Norman Dole's first-over-12 feet vault of 12' 1½" when winning the 1904 Olympics, and ending with Marcus Wright's 13' 2¼" at the 1912 Games, the first vault over 13 feet.

---

[1]F. A. M. Webster, *ATHLETES OF TODAY*, London: Frederick Warne & Co., 1929, p. 228.

[2]Hugh H. Baxter, "An Historical Contribution from an Early Champion," in Henry F. Schulte, *POLE VAULTING*, New York: American Sports Publishing Co., 1927, p. 172.

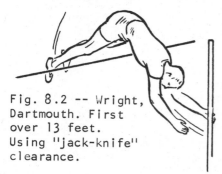

Fig. 8.2 -- Wright, Dartmouth. First over 13 feet. Using "jack-knife" clearance.

The "man's ultimate height" of 14 feet was not cleared officially until 15 years later (1927) by Sabin Carr (Yale). But the real innovator and influence of this period was Charles Hoff of Norway who cleared 13' 11 3/8" as an amateur, then 14 feet on various occasions as a professional. Hoff was a champion decathlon performer, 6'3" tall, and had run the 100 under ten seconds. The ease and speed of his run, high handgrip (12' 10"), free swing-up and quick flyaway and up from the pole, in contrast to the usual delayed release, opened up new potentials for the event.

What had been, up till then, a trick event for gymnasts, became a single-action jump and swing with a pole for tall sprinters and high jumpers with strong shoulders. In the next few decades, it was realized that the primary problems of vaulting were related to velocity rather than to strength and bar-clearance techniques.

Fig. 8.3 -- Hoff, Norway; first over 14 feet (professional). Using fly-away clearance.

Quite properly, Cornelius Warmerdam (Fresno State) was the first to clear 15 feet (1940), as well as the greatest height with a bamboo pole--15' 7 3/4", 1942. On over 50 occasions, indoors and out, when no others could do so, he cleared 15 feet or higher. As with Hoff, his success lay in the speed of his run-takeoff-swingup, rather than in his gymnastic ability over the bar. I remember well that, as I studied his style in competition, I felt he had contributed nothing new in technique other than the more perfect execution of all that was then considered good form. Though two inches shorter than Hoff, he was able to raise his handgrip to 13' 11", thus gaining a smaller braking angle at the takeoff and a higher point of pushup at the top of his vault.

In general, pole flexibility was not a major concern in these years, though Nikolai Osolin (USSR, 1939, 14' 1¼"), and Sueo Ohe (Japan, 1937, 14' 3¼"), with their 135-pound body weights and slender 4 3/4-pound bamboo poles, did demonstrate the uses of pole flexibility.

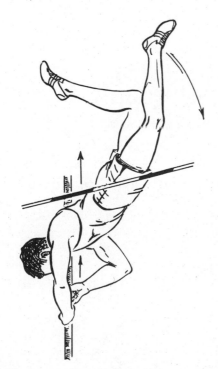

Fig. 8.4 -- Warmerdam, Fresno State; first over 15 feet. Using bamboo pole.

Then came the metal poles (aluminum-magnesium alloys and steel) with their false claims of "Lifetime durability" and "no need to transport your own poles to meets!" Their weights varied, of course, but averaged slightly heavier than the bamboo poles--about six pounds. The aluminum poles were lighter but very rigid; the best Swedish steel poles were relatively flexible but heavy. Ganslen (1970, 20) states that the steel poles of heavier men, such as Donald Bragg (192#) did bend 2-2½ feet out of line, but reacted very quickly in straightening. With such a pole, Bragg held a handgrip of 13'10" and cleared 15'9¼" for a world record and all-time high with a metal pole.

Introduction of the fiberglass pole brought about the most controversial and exciting change in both technique and performance since vaulting began. First used in the early 1950s, it was not fully effective until the 1960s. Its opponents said performance was now the effect of a machine's catapult action, but gradually all agreed that its main value was in its flexion at takeoff that (1) eased the jarring shock at the moment of pole plant, with reduced slipping of the hands; (2) it allowed a

smoother and more gradual change of direction from horizontal to vertical, with less loss of momentum; (3) it permitted higher handgrips, and so a higher body position at the top of the vault; and (4) its extension aided greater upward momentum during the push-up.

Fig. 8.5. Bragg, Villa-
nova. Best ever with
steel pole - 15'9¼"

The first world record made with a fiberglass pole was in 1961-- George Davies, 15'10¼". In 1962, the first-ever vaults over 16 feet were achieved: indoors, John Uelses, 16'3/4"; outdoors, Dave Tork, 16'2". Within the next five years (1962-1967), fiberglass vaulters dominated the event with 15 new world-record performances-- nine of them by John Pennel with a final best jump in 1967 of 17'6 3/4". For the first time in this century, the record left the U.S.A. with Finland's Pentti Nikula at 16'2½", June 1962. But in 1963, Pennel (16'4") and Brian Sternberg (16'8") brought it back. Sternberg had all the qualities of true greatness as a vaulter but a trampoline neck injury cut his career tragically short. Pennel then climaxed four world-record jumps in 1963 to become the first over 17 feet. In 1964, Fred Hansen raised the record to 17'4", then won the Tokyo Olympics at 16'8 3/4". Bob Seagren (17'5½"), Pennel (17'6 3/4"), Paul Wilson (17'7 3/4"), Seagren (17'9") and Pennel (17'10¼") each held it briefly, but again the record moved abroad, this time to Greece with Chris Papanicolaou in a first-over-18 feet (18'¼" 1970). In 1972, Seagren and Kjell Isaksson of Sweden cleared 18'4½" on the same day in April but Seagren upped this in June to 18'5 3/4". In 1980, the record was held by Dave Roberts (18'8¼") of the Florida Track Club, but there was no longer the assurance that the pole vault was an American monopoly. In 1965, United States vaulters made 13 of the best 25 vaults in the world, placing 1-4-5-6-7-10; in 1975 they made 10 of the best 25, placing 3-5-6-9-10; in 1979 it was 9 of the first 25, placing 3-8-10-17-20.

Have human ultimates been attained? Few believe so, including Dutch Warmerdam, who, after

Fig. 8.6. Comparison of takeoffs with steel pole (A) and with fiberglass pole (B). In A note earlier pole shift--forward-up--and takeoff at plumb line below upper hand. In B shift is upward-forward; takeoff is midway between hands; the spring-swing is forward-up forcing a bend of the flexible pole.

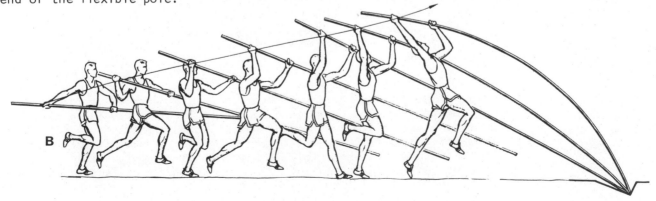

Papanicolaou's 18-foot vault, predicted that an additional 12 inches was entirely possible. "though it may take longer than we now think." In his first 1980 competition, Wladyslaw Kozakiewicz set a new world record at 18'9¼" (5.72m), then failed narrowly at 18'11¼" (5.77). His reaction--"that goal is only postponed, perhaps until the Moscow Olympics."

HOW TO BEGIN

The problem of "how to begin" should assume a year-round program of related practice. A different approach would need to be made if less time is available. Such a year-round program must include at least four areas of development: basic and related power, skills related to vaulting, related speed-endurance, and actual vaulting in practice. Competitive vaulting should be delayed until skill is well established, and even then kept at a low level.

In keeping with the training system outlined in Chapter 16 we first need to motivate power and related skills training. Watching expert vaulters in important competitions is the best way of all. Studying slow-motion films of technical experts gives a feeling of the whole action. Or look over the various phases of the whole action in Figure 8.7.

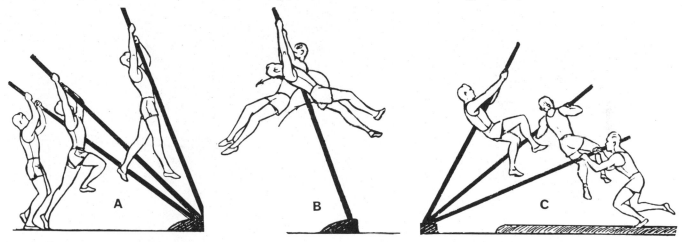

Fig. 8.8 -- How to begin. A - With a low handhold, and a short run, swing and pull up without turning. B - Do the same but turn round the pole and back to the runway. C - Do the same but swing through and turn.

But this visual insight of the vaulting movements as a whole needs to be translated into muscle-nerve language. Get a stiff metal pole in your hand, take a few jogging steps, and get the feel of swinging, not on some fanciful star, but on a sturdy and dependable pole as shown in Figure 8.8--just enough to convince you that this event is exciting and worth working for.

Now how you divide your time as between the various phases of training: (1) basic strength training (Chapter 6, all figures), (2) related power training (pp.158-9), and (3) skills as related to vaulting, and (4) actual pole vaulting, depends on your own unique schedule and judgment. Almost all vaulters have used such related activities as gymnastics, tumbling, diving, and trampoline to aid their basic coordination and confidence for vaulting. Keep vaulting in mind as you do this and emphasize the actions of vaulting. For example, when Fred Hansen (1964 Olympic Champion) did trampoline work he held his hands steadily about 18 inches apart as though holding a vaulting pole. The many drawings of related exercises should provide ample suggestions for what to do.

But sooner or later, one must vault. How should a properly conditioned vaulter proceed? First, proceed on the basic principle that the first actions of the running pole vault should be learned first. Learn how to run and shift the pole (Figure 8.9); then how to run, plant the pole, and spring off (Figure 8.10). These actions create the kinetic energy for the vault;

cont'd page 160

Fig. 8.8b -- The whole action with a
fiberglass pole. This drawing excerpted
from V.M. Yagodin, *The Pole Vault*,
Moscow: USSR Gov't Printing Office,
1970.

POLE VAULT

Pole vaulting is one action; one unified and undividable action which begins with the first step of the run and ends with the landing. Within that single movement, there are no separate actions, such as the run, take-off, swing-up, or pull-up. These are merely words, devices of understanding and communication. This seems obvious, a waste of space and time, but too often, simply by naming and writing or speaking of these phases of action, we make a vaulter aware of them as distinct and separate parts.

We all remember the frustrated centipede who was asked which leg came after which; we often forget that men are susceptible to similar frustrations. For example, both as coaches and as vaulters, we tend to ignore the principle that actions which precede tend to be more crucial in their effects on total performance. Certainly the potential height to which the body mass can go is first limited by the kinetic energy of the speed of the vaulter prior to takeoff. All our coaching and practice of the swing-up and tuck and pullup-pushup will go for nothing if these have not been preceded by a smooth transition, during the pole plant and takeoff, of horizontal momentum toward the vertical.

Pole vaulting is one undividable action. I once knew a coach--at least he used the title--who, either through laziness or obtuseness of mind, refused to coach details. He said the all-important element in a vaulter was competitive spirit. "Have fun! Clear the bar! Go higher than the other guy!" was the sum of his coaching. In one way he was right. In competition, it must be a single action--single minded and single bodied. But without analysis of the detailed phases of technique and specific emphasis in practice on those phases, coaching would be meaningless.

At the other equally invalid extreme is the coach who makes a man so aware of this or that part of the vault that he loses his integrity, so to speak. His flow of action, timing and balance are lost.

Above all else, a sound coach will try to maintain the wholeness and flow of action throughout the run and vault. In practice the complexity of the action requires dissection, but be sure it is merely the action that is being dissected and not, as with the centipede, the man himself.

RELATED POWER EXERCISES

The black-shirted figures are excerpted from Nikolai G. Ozolin, *Modern System of Sports Training*, Moscow: USSR Gov't Sports Publishing Office, 1969.

POLE VAULT

Use this
approach in
this exercise

159

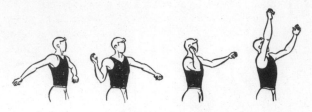

Fig. 8 .9 -- Simulation of pole plant. Note that hands shift very little if at all.

until they are learned, even the greatest gymnastic ability will be wasted.

As soon as a low-level skill in holding the pole, running, and shifting the pole to its spring-off position has been gained, include some degree of swinging in the air in your practice. That is, run and vault as soon as you can; don't just learn to run separate from vaulting. But concentrate your attention on the techniques of how to run and plant and spring-off.

Fig. 8.10. Shift and takeoff, fiberglass pole. Shift is upward-forward. Takeoff by this vaulter is below upper hand, producing a more forceful spring from the takeoff foot and quicker drive of the lead knee upward.

With what kind of pole? We now assume that the flexible pole is here to stay and will be used in high schools as in all other vaulting. But it's both wasteful and foolhardy to risk both the vaulter and a fragile pole when first learning. The vaulter's confidence is all important; let him gain it first with a controllable and unbreakable pole.

POWER TRAINING FOR SOUND TECHNIQUE

The basic program of power training for the specific movements of each of the eight field events is outlined in Chapter 16 and needs no repetition here. Of course, the movements of pole vaulting are unique and specially related exercises must be selected. But the need for basic strength in vaulting is just as crucial as for shot putting or hammer throwing, even though the proportion of strength in the power formula (power = strength x velocity) is less. It follows that, just as emphasized in the high jump, basic strength exercises (Chapter 1) should be given at least two days a week during the early season and at least one day every two weeks during even the late competitive season. Dyatchkov's (1969, 1123) experiments in the high jump led him to conclude that, otherwise, both strength and performance would decrease.

But because of the unusual movements of the pole vault which involve muscles not ordinarily developed, both related and imitative power exercises are a major and continuous part of year-round training. There is no real distinction between the two words "related" and "imitative." But as indicated in Table 1, Chapter 11, their use helps to make clear the different emphases on the crucial factors of strength, velocity of movement, and the specific skills of pole vaulting that are made (1) in basic strength training, (2) in related power training, (3) in imitative power training, and (4) in practice of the specific skill of vaulting.

That idea is so crucial as to bear re-statement. Along with other qualities, competitive performance requires power and skill. Power involves both strength and velocity in varying ratios from 10:1, when doing a bench press, to 1:10, when doing a pull-up and flyaway on a swinging rope. Since strength recedes with disuse, exercises with 10:1 ratios occur in a significant degree throughout the year. But as the year progresses, exercises with 1:10 ratios become more and more vital, *especially when they imitate the specific movements of the running vault*. Related power exercises are those that tend to use the resistances of artificial weights or of another person in movements that involve vaulting muscles but not necessarily in vaulting movements. The ratio of strength to velocity tends to be about 5:5, though this is flexible. Imitative power exercises are very similar to the movements of vaulting and at the velocities of vaulting, or even faster. The amount of resistance is a lesser concern, though it tends to be greater than that in actual vaulting.

You will note that the various related exercises on pp. 158-9   tend to use weights that can be increased progressively, while the imitative exercises do not. No verbal description of each of these exercises seems necessary. However, the serious student will review carefully the discussions in Chapters 15 and 16.

Figure 8.11

The swinging rope - a "must" for pole vaulters. Fred Hansen and other great vaulters also found the trampoline of great value.

ESSENTIALS OF SOUND TECHNIQUE (Fiberglass Pole)[1]

It is sometimes argued that vaulters differ so much in the details of technique, it is useless to speak of the essentials of form. Give a man a pole, a place to work, a few fundamentals, and leave him alone. This attitude is very much in error. Men are much more alike in every way than they are different. The biomechanics of vaulting are the same for all individuals. True, biomechanics allow for a range of tolerable variation, but with all the changes that have occurred in vaulting since 1900, once the run and fixed hand grip were established, the essentials of technique have remained the same.

Simply stated, the running pole vault is an attempt to conserve as much as possible of the

Fig. 8.12--The double-pendulum action in the pole vault. Pendulum #1 is shown as X-Y (the pole whose fulcrum is at Y, whose bob or weight is the body's center of gravity, and whose length of pendulum is measured from the pole-point in the box to the constantly changing c.g. of the body. Pendulum #2 is the body itself (X-Z). This drawing from Nikolai Ozolin, previously cited.

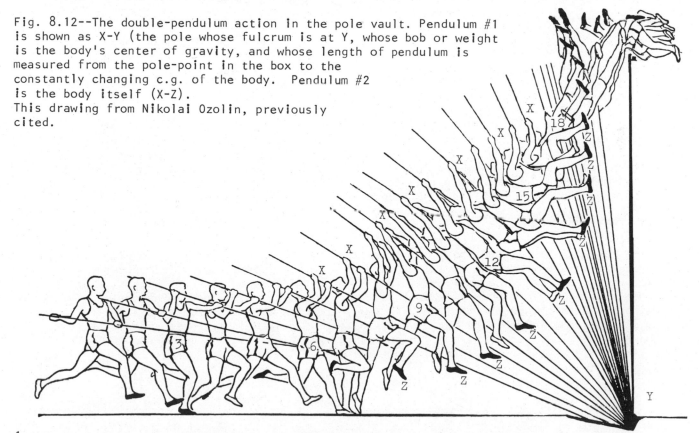

[1]Acknowledgement: This discussion of "Sound Technique" relies primarily on the various editions of *MECHANICS OF THE POLE VAULT* by Richard V. Ganslen, Ph.D. The 1980 edition, paperback, 176 pps. with many line drawings and detailed comments by world performers can be obtained from Dr. Ganslen, 1204 Windsor Dr., Denton, Texas, 76201. Ganslen is undoubtedly the world's foremost authority on vaulting, with book translations into German, Russian, and Japanese.   [Any errors of fact or judgment in this OMNIBOOK are of course my own.]

horizontal momentum of the body, derived from a fast run, and to gain maximum height of the body through the use of a lightweight, flexible pole. Forward progress of the point of the pole is stopped by placing it in the box. But forward progress of the upper part of the pole is lost gradually as its pendulum swings to the vertical. Similarly, forward progress of the hands is slowed suddenly (less so with the flexible pole) as they tightly grip the pole, but the forward-upward progress of the body slows gradually as its pendulum swings upward.

HOLDING THE POLE

A close look at Figure 8.13 reveals a pole carry that aids both the speed and relaxation of the run and the planting of the pole in the box. The point of the pole is at head height and slightly to the left of the centerline of the runway. This relaxes the shoulders and arms so they can swing freely with the rhythm of running while still holding the pole quite steady. Certainly the pole should not swing forward and back during the run.

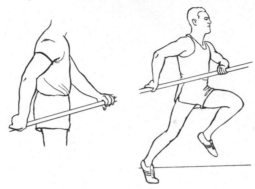

Fig. 8.13 -- The handhold and carry of the pole. The pole tip is at eye height.

Separation of the hands varies greatly from 15 to as much as 36 inches (Ganslen, 1980, 18.) A very wide separation does ease the pole carry during the run but makes a smooth plant of the pole more difficult. Most major vaulters hands are between 18 and 24 inches apart. The grip of the upper hand must be firmly fixed, for the pull at takeoff is tremendous. Most vaulters use firm-grip paste or spray to ensure against slipping.

Of 23 outstanding pole vaulters that answered Ganslen's questionnaire (1970, 84), five carried the pole straight down the runway, 16 swung it slightly to the left, two did not answer this question. As to the height of the pole tip while running, 11 held it at about eye level; three raised it above eye level; eight did not answer this question. As to the hand spread while running, two said they had a "medium" spread; two were spread 24"; one, 27"; one, 28"; three, 30"; one, 34"; one, 40"; one, 42"; nine did not answer this question.

HEIGHT OF THE UPPER-HAND GRIP ON THE POLE

Grip height   is commonly measured from the top of the upper hand to the tip of the pole. Some writers speak of "effective height" which subtracts the eight inches below ground level taken by the vaulting box. Each vaulter, by simple trial-and-error, must work out his own effective handgrip--all depending on skill-speed-personal height. When first introduced, the fiberglass pole allowed an increase of roughly two feet in handgrip. But later champions raised this another foot. A USSR study[1] concluded that 15 world-best vaulters averaged 15'8" (4m 80cm) in their handgrip when clearing highest heights, an average difference of 3'7" (1m 10cm). [This seems extremely high--JKD.] When clearing his world-record 18'8¼", Dave Roberts held at 15'7", a difference of 3'1¼".

---

[1]V. Mansvetov, "Contemporary Technique in the Pole Vault," *Track & Field Quarterly Review,* Vol. 79 #1, Spring 1979, p. 14.

THE RUN. A vaulter should run as fast as possible within his limits of strength, skill, and relaxation. He is first limited by grip and arm-shoulder strength, for it requires great strength to resist the body momentum as it hurtles forward and up at the takeoff. He is equally limited by skill, for the efficient re-direction upward of a 170-pound body moving at less than 10 second-per-100 speed is probably the most difficult action in all of track and field. But he must also run within the limits of relaxation, for forced speed and uncertain control bring muscular tensions that work against an effective vault.

Though done over 35 years ago, Warmerdam's study[1] of many aspects of vaulting is still mostly valid. He found, for example, that greater heights were almost invariably related to greater speed in the run: while vaulting, 22 men (12'6") attained 11.3 sec/100y; 18 men (13'), 11.4 sec/100y; 9 men (13'6"), 11.1 sec/100y; 8 men (14'), 10.7 sec/100y. Warmerdam concluded that faster men tend to clear greater heights and also that great vaulters tend to increase their speed as the height of the bar is raised.

Fig. 8.14 -- Organization of the run -- length and checkmarks.

LENGTH OF THE RUN

A vaulter should run as far as is necessary to attain near-maximum speed about two strides before the action of planting the pole is started; that is, about four strides before the takeoff. Figure 8.14 indicates run lengths from 114 to 135 feet. Since even with maximum acceleration, sprinters require about six seconds (180 feet) to attain highest velocity, we must conclude that, running with a pole, a distance of even 140 feet is still short of highest speed potentials. Since expert vaulters tend to state that they accelerate gradually at the start of their run, not all-out, they probably achieve only 90 percent of maximum velocity or even less. Dave Roberts' (18'6½", 1975) run was 139 feet long.

Typical answers by outstanding vaulters to Ganslen's questions about this problem were: Bob Seagren--"I build speed all the way down the runway." Les Smith--"I try to gain my speed as soon as possible, then drive into the box." John Pennel--"Gradual build-up, maintaining speed in the middle of run, then driving strides at the end." Jeffrey Chase--"Slowly pick up speed, then blast." Dave Roberts--"slow start, gradual acceleration, really accelerate 4-5 strides from plant."

THE USE OF CHECKMARKS

Almost all vaulters use two checkmarks: the first at the start of the run; the second, after about seven strides from the start and about 16 strides from takeoff. We recommend standing on the first checkmark but some excellent vaulters prefer to begin two or three short strides back of it, and hit it as they start. The second checkmark usually indicates no change in acceleration or body action; it simply gives assurance that the beginning strides have been made precisely right.

Various methods of securing check marks are used. We suggest getting away from the pole-vault runway to a surface where stride marks can be seen. An observer can note the seventh, and later the 23rd stride. After measuring, these marks can be transferred to the vault run-way. Since such trial runs are free of all tension, they are likely to prove accurate. Stick to them for a while until certain they are incorrect. Eventually, of course, adjustments will probably be made.

Important--the value of checkmarks is as much mental as physical. A positive attitude is as vital as accurate measurements. Once doubt enters the mind, rhythm leaves the legs. Louisiana Tech coach, Aubrey Dooley,[2] a fine vaulter in his day, suggests five checkmarks-- start, second stride, about 2/3rds down runway, four strides from takeoff, actual takeoff. This seems physically valid but mentally distracting. In contrast, Dave Roberts used only one mark.

[1]Cornelius Warmerdam, "Factors Associated with the Approach and Takeoff in Pole Vaulting," an unpublished Master's Thesis, Fresno State College, Calif., 1944.
[2]Aubrey C. Dooley, "Pole Vaulting Technique," *Track & Field Quarterly Review*, Vol. 79 #1, Spring 1979, p. 15.

THE TRANSITION PHASE

From the standpoints of degree of difficulty and effective vaulting, this transition phase is the most crucial in the entire vault. If it is effective, body momentum is maintained, even increased, and the later phases of the vault are relatively simple. The transition phase of the run begins about four strides from takeoff. Full velocity has been gained; the mind shifts from running speed to the smooth transfer of momentum (mass x velocity) to a pendulum pole whose point is fixed in the vault box. First, the pole must be shifted forward and up (Figure 8.12). Second, the body's center of gravity lowers a little during the transition strides, much as does a long jumper before takeoff. Ganslen (1980,20.) writes, "But the vaulter must relax the last few strides and run in flat-footed as he prepares himself for the spring from the ground." Third, the flexible pole must be bent by the combined actions of the arms and the forward force of the body. All of this in ways that merge and flow into one another with a minimum loss of kinetic energy and, at the end, a maximum height of the center of gravity.

PLANTING THE POLE

The vaulter has three crucial concerns during the planting of the pole: (1) to maintain and even increase momentum, (2) to cushion the shock of stopping horizontal momentum so as to convert as much kinetic energy as possible upwards, and (3) to establish good balance for the remainder of the vault.

(1) During the plant, the vaulter should try to drive forward into a strong spring-off that will aid the momentum of the pendulum swing of the pole. The body drops down just a little; the foot-plant is lower, though not on the heel until the final stride.

Of 21 outstanding vaulters who answered Ganslen's (1970, 91) inquiry as to their method of shifting the pole, 12 indicated an early and straight-up shift to a point above the forehead; five described an "underhand" shift; four, an "overhand" shift. These words require some interpretation but they do suggest methods. Nordwig started his pole and hand shift three strides out.

(2) It requires great skill to cushion the shock of suddenly stopping all forward movement of the tip of the pole so as to maintain high velocity in the pendulum swing upward of the body and pole. First, the pole must be planted in the box before the takeoff foot touches the ground. The right hand pull-pushes the pole forward-and-up in a straight line past and in front of the face. Figures 8.12 and 8.18 show this angle of shift very well. In contrast, Figure 8.16 shows an upward and delayed shift of the pole which some great vaulters have used successfully but which tends to increase shock, not cushion it. The arm muscles must have just the right balance of relaxation and tension. The right hand grip must be fixed with no slipping. But the flexion of the elbows and shoulders must be such as to cushion the transfer of the torso to the pole, and also force the bend of the flexible pole out in front of the torso.

Using a stiff metal pole, vaulters achieve these goals by shifting the lower hand up the pole to within a few inches of the upper hand. Using a flexible pole most vaulters do shift their hands but to a wider spread than is used by stiff-pole users. Of 22 outstanding vaulters that answered Ganslen's (1970, 87) question on this point, nine stated they did not shift the hands; 13 that they did shift. Dan Ripley (18'5 3/4")--"Yes, I do shift my left hand. Too wide a grip can inhibit the rock-back; too narrow, decreases control."

(3) Achieving good balance in the vault is equally crucial. Success lies first in shifting the pole forward exactly along the line of the run so that the hands are on a plumb line to the takeoff foot (Figures 8.17,8.18). To bring the pole around and up, out of line and away from the body is certain to produce imbalance. Such a roundhouse pole plant is often caused by running on or to the right of the centerline of the box and runway. The run should always place the right foot just to the left of this centerline and thereby line up the pole with the vault box. Failing this, some men veer to the left during the last few strides which also tends to produce imbalance.

THE POINT OF TAKEOFF

Vaulters using stiff poles tended to take off with the toe of their shoe on a point reached by a plumb line from the top of their upper hand. Flexible-pole vaulters tend to place their foot closer to the vault box. In Manzvetow's study previously cited, all 15 champion vaulters-- (best heights from 5.20 m (17'1½") to 5.70m (18'8½"))--had a takeoff point under the top hand, varying from 10cm (4") to 80cm (31"). Most were at about 13 inches. World-record holder Roberts was at 16 inches.

THE TAKEOFF

Understanding the mechanics of the takeoff warrants repetition that the pole vault is a continuous unified action having many phases, each of which, to be effective, depends on those that
precede it. When George Moore--a student of vaulting and manufacturer of an excellent fiberglass pole--analyzed the takeoff,[1] he first explained such earlier phases as pole carry, hand
spread, pole plant, and proper position of the takeoff foot. Only as these actions are well
done can an effective takeoff be made.

The action of the takeoff foot should be a forceful spring off the ground--more forward-
through than upward; a follow-through of the run; not a jump as implied by "foot-stamp." Dan
Ripley (5.63m., 18'5 3/4")--"The timing of the takeoff (and plant) is the most crucial and
difficult to master....the most explosive action of the vault." (Ganslen, 1979, 117). Earl
Bell[2] said that Mike Tully's (18'3") ability to hold his trunk vertical an extra instant while
driving through as the pole is bending was one of his greatest assets.

Fig. 8.15--Dave Roberts (1979 world record--5.70m, 18'8¼"). Best 100y--09.7. Top-hand grip--
16'; "One should hold as high as he can...to reach maximum height." Handspread--18"; "As
close as possible to facilitate storing (circular) momentum into the pole....a wide spread
kills the swing." Pole plant--"Begin plant 3-4 steps from box. Push both hands forward at
45 degree angle forward and upward one step from box." Takeoff--"I drive the lead leg forward
and down toward the box to aid swing with both legs straight and nearly together." Rock back--
"Delay the rock back as long as possible to maintain forward motion, especially with high grip."
Delay of pull-up--"Keep arms straight, don't pull on pole....Most of delay should be in swing."
(All quotes from Ganslen, 1980, pp. 106-117.)

---

[1]George Moore, "An Analysis of the Pole Vault Takeoff," *Track Technique,*Vol. 74, Winter 1978,
p. 2352.

[2]Tom Jordan, "An Interview with Earl Bell," *Track & Field News,*July 1977, 11.

THE SWING-UP (First Phase)

The swing-up is a continuing phase of the spring-off, having validity only in words, not in action. It continues the forward action but begins to shorten the lever of the body pendulum and thus speed its swing-up. The rate at which this lever is shortened is a crucial point, and great vaulters do differ in this respect. Some do it relatively early. They tend to drive the lead leg up with quick knee flexion (Figure 8.19a), to lift the head back early, focus the eyes upward, and arch the back. This action lengthens the lever of the pole pendulum, tends to slow its momentum, but does gain an early increase in the height of the center of gravity, relative to the grip on the pole.

But it must be timed exactly right or, as happens so often with beginning vaulters, the hips will swing forward ahead of the pole, will slow pole velocity, and probably stall the vault. Expert vaulters do emphasize the upward drive of the lead knee but they counteract this by holding the head in line with the torso and the eyes focussed straight ahead.

Fig. 8.16. In this Figure the shift is somewhat more forward than in Figure 8.10: the takeoff is closer to the lower hand, with a lesser tendency to spring as balanced with swing.

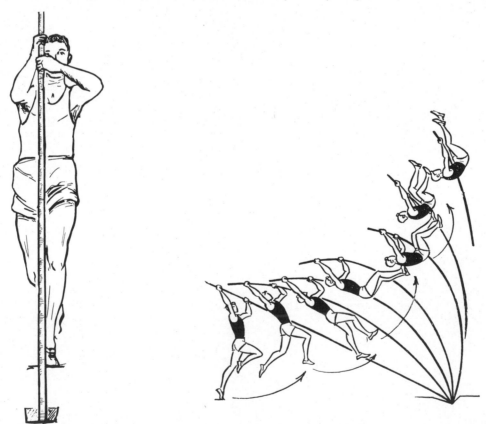

Fig. 8.17 -- A plumb-line takeoff   Fig. 8.18 -- Takeoff and full swingup.

The best single means of control of this curve of body flexion lies in the focus of the eyes and thereby the inclination of the head. To ensure the desired flat curve, the eyes at takeoff should focus at a very low upward angle. Ganslen (1970, 41) suggests that "the focus of attention is all directed at the box and back of the pit. Do not look at the crossbar."

Of the 21 answers by outstanding vaulters to Ganslen's (1970, 94) question as to their way of taking off, seven said they simply ran forward with no special emphasis on jumping; 13 said they sprang forward and up, somewhat as is done in long jumping; only one said he jumped up.

The degree to which the lead leg is bent at the knee and driven upward greatly influences the angle of spring-off and the first phase of the swing-up. Of the 18 answers by outstanding vaulters to Ganslen's (1970, 94) question on this point, 11 indicated a definite and early drive upward with the flexed knee; 12 indicated a more forward-and-up direction of the lead knee. This latter figure is consistent with the answers to the previous question.

POLE BEND DURING THE SWING-UP. During the swing-up and rock-back, the flexible pole has at least four advantages over the stiffer metal and bamboo poles. (1) It allows a higher handgrip on the pole which gives greater leverage in bending the pole. We can assume that the maximum straight-line grip is the same as that reached by the metal-pole users--about 14 feet. But the bend of the flexible pole extends this grip to 15'6" or even higher when measured along the vaulting pole. (2) Pole flexion provides a cushioning of the change from horizontal to vertical momentum. Study of Figure 8.8 will show that the center of gravity of the body travels forward in a flat upward curve after takeoff. A steel-pole vaulter who has changed to fiberglass speaks of a sinking sensation at this point, comparable to that felt when using a rubber cable on the end of a hanging rope. (3) Pole flexion creates a greater time-distance for execution of the second phase of the swing-up, or rock-back as some prefer to call it. At the start of the swing-up, the distance of the center of gravity from the crossbar is significantly greater than when using a stiff pole. There's more room for movement. On the other hand, the pole straightens with great quickness, so that the time factor is very limited. (4) The bend of the pole stores kinetic energy to be released at the last instant, in the so-called catapult effect, and thus increases the effectiveness of the pull-up along the straightening pole.

THE SWING-UP (Second Phase)
The second phase of the swing-up, often called the rock-back, acts primarily to shorten the body pendulum *but involves no upward pulling by the arms*. The bend of the pole is still increasing; in fact, greater body flexion during the rock-back increases pole flexion. Any pull-up during this phase could use only the inertia of a moving five-pound pole and so would greatly reduce momentum.

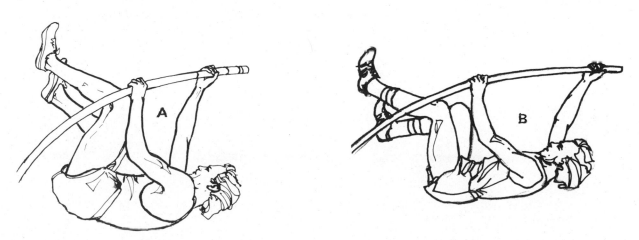

Fig. 8.19ab. Showing different effects of lower grip-shorter handspread (Figure A) with higher grip-wider handspread (Figure B). Lohre[1] attributes in part the recent improvement of Polish vaulters to the "Eastern style" with its higher upper hand (Figure B). The left arm is stiff and almost straight during the rock-back to keep the body's c.g. well behind the pole.

---

[1]Gunther Lohre, "Wide Pole Grip," *Track Technique*, #62, December 1975, p. 1988.

The takeoff (left) leg catches up with the right. The fixed, though relaxed, arms provide the fulcrum of the body lever. By rapid flexion of the hips and knees, the long axis of the body is shortened and the swing of the body pendulum is speeded up. The effect of this action on the pole pendulum is to move its center of weight (its bob if we think of a clock pendulum) away from the pole point and so to slow down its upward swing. It is therefore crucial to an effective vault that the rock-back be delayed till just the right instant (Figures 8.20, 8.21, and 8.19ab).

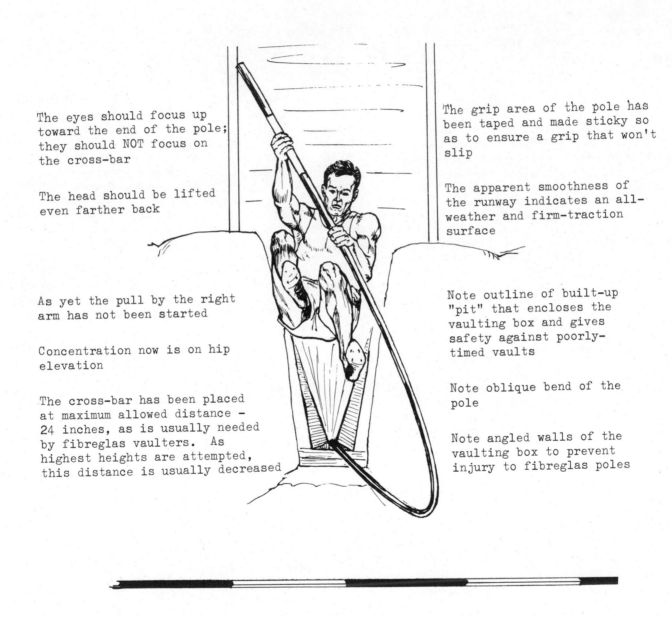

The eyes should focus up toward the end of the pole; they should NOT focus on the cross-bar

The head should be lifted even farther back

As yet the pull by the right arm has not been started

Concentration now is on hip elevation

The cross-bar has been placed at maximum allowed distance — 24 inches, as is usually needed by fibreglas vaulters. As highest heights are attempted, this distance is usually decreased

The grip area of the pole has been taped and made sticky so as to ensure a grip that won't slip

The apparent smoothness of the runway indicates an all-weather and firm-traction surface

Note outline of built-up "pit" that encloses the vaulting box and gives safety against poorly-timed vaults

Note oblique bend of the pole

Note angled walls of the vaulting box to prevent injury to fibreglas poles

Fig. 8.20 -- The swingup - second phase, commonly called the rollback. Drawn from a photo of Bob Seagren, 1968 Olympic champion and 1966 world-record holder - 17' 5 3/4".

The overall orientation of the vaulter during this rock-back phase is upward "toward the sky" (Abada), or "toward the tip of the pole" (Nordwig), or "I just swing and try to get my feet as high as possible" (Isaksson). Many vaulters speak of the "feel" of pole bend and adjust their actions to it. Beginners that extend the feet toward the crossbar tend to swing under it, but experts acquire an orientation to the crossbar and adjust in terms of it. For all vaulters, pole extension carries the body toward the crossbar; no effort toward it is needed.

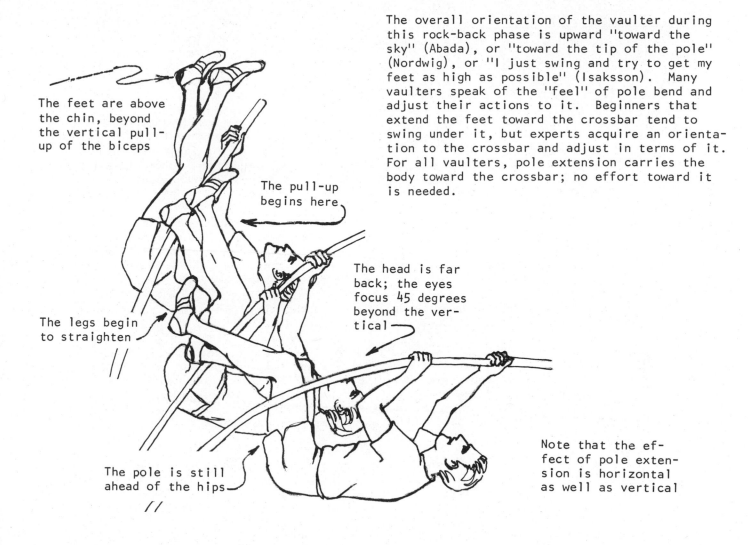

The feet are above the chin, beyond the vertical pull-up of the biceps

The pull-up begins here

The head is far back; the eyes focus 45 degrees beyond the vertical

The legs begin to straighten

The pole is still ahead of the hips

Note that the effect of pole extension is horizontal as well as vertical

Fig. 8.21. The rock-back.

Any so-called waiting or "hang" in the vault should be related to the swing, certainly not to the rock-back. This is crucial. All the developed momentum of the run and takeoff, all the conserved momentum of the swing and shortening of the body pendulum centers within the aggressive actions of the rock-back and pullup-pushup. During the rock-back, the action is not to delay but to increase velocity of the c.g. upward. The kinetic energy of the straightening pole is now greatest so that shortening the body pendulum has the least negative effects. Once the trail knee rises above the level of the hands, the forceful pull lifts the body in perfect timing with the "catapult" extension of the pole. Some vaulters offset a tendency to turn too soon by emphasizing the pull of the lower hand and upward extension of the trail leg.

During the pull-turn-pushup, the feet should be kept together, with the turn being made through the c.g. or longitudinal axis of the body, that is, with a minimal transverse axis, thus improving body control as related to clearing the crossbar.

THE PULL-UP -- TURN -- PUSH-UP

As is implied by the hyphens, this is one continuous action, with no hint of hesitation between (Figures 8.22, 8.23). This is the crucial instant when, if all the previous actions have been in good balance and full force, the vaulter explodes upward. Its effect might be compared to that of the finger-wrist action in the shot or javelin, a gathering culmination of force behind the projectile which, in this case, is the vaulter himself.

The pull-up does not begin as the pole starts to straighten; this would be too soon and would work against upward velocity. Rather, it begins an instant later when the pole is nearly straight and the pull-up can be along the pole with its base firm in the vault box (Figure 8.21). By this time the center of body weight is close along the pole and to the source of power. The body pendulum is at its shortest and so gains its greatest rotational energy about the hands as well as being in a most efficient position for the final pull-push.

Ganslen (1970, 47) reminds us that the much-publicized catapult action of the pole during this phase has been greatly exaggerated. First, the direction of this pole force is more horizontal than vertical; second, this force is actually rather weak as related to the inertia of a 170-pound body. It is muscle power, more than pole power, that lifts the vaulter. But every little bit helps and the vaulter should make the most of it.

As with the pull-up, the turn should be delayed until the hips have lifted to or above the level of the hands. But then it occurs very quickly in coordination with the pull-up.

The explosively forceful push-up should do just that--push the center of weight vertically up higher. This requires great power in the arm triceps and related muscles, and related power exercises should be done to develop the quick force with which this can be done. Certainly the push-up is not a weak pushaway of the pole that develops merely enough rotational force to ensure a proper landing. It should drive the heavy hips and legs, especially the right leg, UP; for that's what it is, a push UP as high and as explosively as possible.

CLEARING THE BAR

This description of the push-up establishes the method of clearing the bar. To be effective, any push-up must have a weight (in this instance, the hips and possibly right leg) to drive upward. Of course, some degree of arch over the bar is necessary to make a landing. Much as he might wish to do so, a vaulter cannot really push himself up into the sky.

But it should be clear that the hips should be close to the pole and above the hands until the hands have completed their push up from the pole (Figures 8.22, 8.23). If such a style needs a name, it might be described as a lancet-arch style, one that reaches fully upward before starting its descent.

The perfect maximum vaulter will be much concerned about economy of clearance and will try to maintain his center of gravity at or even below the crossbar. But even then the push-up phase of the vault would have priority over economy of clearance. An emphasis on clearance style will tend to drop the legs too soon, before the hips have reached their potential height.

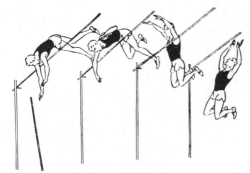

Fig. 8.22 -- Clearing the bar.

THE LANDING

Modern vaulting at high heights demands, not a pit, but a full three-foot high, foam-rubber landing area. On such a buoyant surface, a vaulter can land any which-way without danger of injury. But most vaulters pull their legs quickly upward in an inverted pike position and land on their upper back.

Fig. 8.23 -- Clearing the bar.

COMMON FAULTS IN POLE VAULTING

1. To use a pole that is too flexible and therefore breakable, dangerous, and expensive.

2. To misuse a pole by allowing it to drop when vaulting, or to use it when the pole is cold and the fiberglass brittle.

3. To fail to achieve 95 percent momentum three strides from takeoff, and to drive forward on the last 3-4 strides.

4. To fail to start the pole plant early, so that the pole is in the box just before the takeoff heel lands. (The flexible pole tends to hide this fault but it is nevertheless a crucial error.)

5. To swing the pole forward during the pole plant out of line with the run and a vertical vault; the entire vault is then off-balance.

6. To shift the hands too close so that they have little power in bending the pole and controlling the swing-up.

7. To merely run-off at takeoff rather than to spring-off as does a long jumper. This is not a foot stamp but a compression-expansion of the springs of jumping.

8. At takeoff, to lift the eyes and head too soon, and so to cut the forward swing.

9. At takeoff, to fail to bring the lead knee up fast and forcefully.

10. To relax the lower arm so that the legs and hips swing ahead of the pole during the early phase of the swing-up and so reduce pole velocity.

11. To fail to rock-back with maximum force and velocity.

12. During the rock-back, to look at the crossbar, rather than looking toward the upper tip of the pole or even back at the runway.

13. To pull up too soon, before the pole is almost straight, and before the weight of the hips is above the hands.

14. To be more concerned for the method of clearing the bar than for making a maximum push upward off the pole.

THE ORGANIZATION OF PRACTICE

The overall organization of training and practice for the pole vault should follow the pattern established for all events in Chapter 16, in the development of basic strength, Chapter 6, and in the dynamics of skill, Appendix A.

Development in the pole vault should assume a year-round program, for no event in track and field is so complex in its skill or so demanding in its need for related power, for running speed and speed-endurance, and for patience in continuing on despite the frustrations of slow progress and injuries of many kinds.

TRAINING FOR RELATED POWER. Even more than in the other events, power, speed, and skill develop together. Certainly to say that a vaulter can be skilled though lacking in related muscle power or in speed in the run and swing-up is self-contradictory. All agree that training in skill should be based on a solid foundation of related power training. As examples of this need, the more powerful (strength x velocity) and the pull-up-push-up as the pole straightens, the higher the body can be thrust above the grip on the pole. Again, the rock-back requires a tremendous flexion of the abdominal and leg muscles; the more powerful they are, the faster the action; the faster this action, the longer the swing can be sustained, the shorter the pole pendulum, and the faster the pole velocity. That is to say, increased power brings increased mechanical efficiency in vaulting.

TRAINING FOR IMITATIVE SKILL AND POWER. Assuming that the suggestions for power training given in Chapters 6   have been followed, the main emphasis in pole vault training will be on vaulting and on those power activities that most nearly imitate the movements of vaulting. For example, Fred Hansen, 1964 Olympic champion did a great deal of trampoline work in which he fixed his hands in the same position they would have on the pole when vaulting. That is, his body flexions and extensions were learned within vaulting restrictions. The Perrin[1] vault trainer (Figure 8.25) which uses a rubber cable on a climbing rope is another such attempt. As the vaulter's weight drops on the rubber cable, he experiences a sinking sensation comparable to that of the bending fiberglass pole; later he practices pull-ups as the rubber contracts, similar to the lifting action of the straightening pole. As preferred exercises on the rings, Sternberg[2] listed both uprises, shoot handstands, and such holds as levers and crosses. He further noted that not only were such exercises helpful for the vault

Fig. 8 .25 -- Perrin pole-vault trainer, using rubber tubing.

but challenging in themselves. Sternberg competed on his college gymnastic team on the still rings and trampoline.

Almost all successful vaulters have made great use of gymnastics. They require almost all the related ingredients: power, in the sense of both strength and quickness; coordination while being supported by the hands; similar actions as in the single action pull-up-push-up; and, of special importance, endurance through repetition of movements. Men vault only some 15 to 25 times in one practice and so perform each movement only this same number of times. But in gymnastic and related work, a given movement can be done to exhaustion or as many times as contributes to learning.

In general, pole vaulting suffers from too few repetitions. Forty to sixty repetitions per week of such a complex movement are far too few for mastery within a desired time. That's why men turn to gymnastics. Many have tried to invent a vaulting device which would make more repetitions possible.

TRAINING FOR RELATED SPEED-ENDURANCE. Short-distance interval training can be of real help in building the stamina by which more vaults can be made in practice. The distance run should be similar to that of vaulting--50 to 60 yards. The pace, about 9/10th maximum. The recovery interval, 20 seconds or less. The number of repetitions, gradually increasing over months of training to about 20. The total time for such a workout at the end of a training session would be only ten minutes. But the purpose should be clear--more speed-endurance by which to take more vaults for greater skill.

PRACTICING SKILL IN POLE VAULTING. During the early competitive season, most men vault three times a week. Men vary greatly in the number of vaults per practice. But certainly as compared with the throwing events or with the skills of other sports, the total number per week is very meager. All the more reason for making full use of each vault in terms of faster and more effective learning. Again, we suggest a review of the sections on holistic learning in Appendix A on "The Dynamics of Skill." Also read the section "Learning Better Technique" in the high jump chapter. As applied to the pole vault, these methods suggest that, just before starting down the runway, think-feel through in a mind-muscle sense both the whole of the vault and the one phase you wish to emphasize on this vault. Feel both the whole and the part in your muscles. Research has shown that nerve impulses go to the muscles when you do this, though below the threshold of action. Now vault, while maintaining this same part-in-whole concentration of attention. The moment you're out of the pit, again think-feel through what you just did, both the right and the less right of it. It is attentive right practice that makes perfect.

---

[1]For information, write Bill Perrin, University of Wisconsin Athletic Dept., Madison, Wisconsin, 53703.

[2]"Brian Sternberg--Vaulting profile," *Track Technique*, 16, June 1964, 509.

HOW THEY TRAIN. In his outstanding book, MECHANICS OF THE POLE VAULT, Dick Ganslen provides answers by 27 world-ranked vaulters to his request, "in a short paragraph, describe your basic physical training program." Answers by seven of these were as follows:

Dave Roberts, Florida Track Club, born 7/23/51, 6'2½", 185#. Best height, 18'6½", 1975, world record. Running cross country, mostly in the fall 3-8 miles. Interval training (220s, 330s, 440s) as needed, about 2-3 days a week, in fall, but about once a week in season. Sprinting (50-100) with a flying start is very good. I do relaxed, rhythmic-type running on grass with some type of track work every day. Gymnastics: do everything--rings, parallel bars, hi-bar, trampoline, ropes, etc., 2-4 days a week. Weights: emphasis is on overall body strength movements--cleans, jerks, squats, and some presses. I do a lot of stomach work. Vaulting: I vault as little as possible to develop and maintain technique. Technique work is done in the spring and fall. Jumping 1-2 days a week. At all other times I jump only enough to maintain things.

Jan Johnson, Alabama, born 11/11/50, 5'11", 158#. Best height, 18'½", placed third 1972 Olympics. Fall: Weights three times a week: cleans, squats, snatch, curls, ropes, high bar, and rings, and three times a week of cross-country running. Winter: one optional day and a rest day. The optional day may be gymnastics. Spring: three vault days, one sprint day and a competition day.

Reinhard Kuretsky, West Germany, born 12/1/47, 6'½" 168#. Best height, 17'4 3/4", 1972. Before the Olympics in 1972 I worked out with an exercising machine 1-2 times per week. Much emphasis on abdominal and shoulder muscles and on strengthening the legs. For strengthening of the legs, I often use the ladder. For speed: 2-3x(6x50m)@100%. From an upright standing start, 2x30m, 2x50m, 2x80m (100%), 5x100m (70%). During the summer I cut down this training considerably and pole vault often. Since the winter of 1973 I am not using the exercise machine, but exercise on gymnastic apparatus...this gives the feeling of movement at the same time.

Mike Bull, Great Britain, born 9/11/46, 6' 3/4", 168#. Best height, 17' 3/4", 1972. Weights. I am coached by Buster McShane, a famous strength coach. This program is 3 times a week and includes: sit-ups, leg raises with weights, vertical jumping with weights (belt) 1/2 squats, cleans and bench presses up to 350 lbs. plus some special exercise routines. Vaulting is 3 times weekly, 2 days with a full approach, and 1 day with a short approach. Running is 3 times weekly--60s, 150s, and 300s.

Scott Wallick, Miami, Ohio, Best height, 17'0", 1972. Fall: Heavy weights and long road runs. On alternate (weight days) I use gymnastics. Winter: I shorten up and do 440s, and 300s along with vaulting 2-3 times a week at most. Spring: due to our bad weather in Ohio, I go back to a bit longer work on the roads for 3-4 weeks. After that I go to 220s, and 100s; lifting weights all the time, and jumping 2-3 times a week. I lift even the week of a large meet. I need to feel a bit tight to jump well. Summer: I lift only and do not do any running or vaulting. In the future I plan on trying other types of all-year training, including extensive jumping.

Greg Smithey, Idaho State. Best height, 16'1", 1972. Pre-season months: I run lots of distance 4-8 miles every other day. I run steep hills and try to run up stairs at least twice a week. Weight lifting for fun, gymnastics and general physical fitness activities is a part of my off-season training. In season, (which for me is about 8 months): I vault two or three times a week. I lift weights throughout the entire season at least twice a week. I also work on gymnastics (tumbling, rings, parallel bars). My running workout consists of 220s, 150s, 110s, and 75s. I also mark the distance I run (while vaulting) on the track and go through the distance as if I were vaulting.

Kjell Isaksson, Sweden, born 2/28/48, 5'8¼" 150#. Best height, 18'4¼", 1972, world record. Weight lifting 3-4 times a week, 30-45 minutes. Running 4-5 times a week for 60-90 minutes, 90-100% of maximum speed @ 50-100 - 150 yards. Jumping once a week; however, in 1964-68 I was jumping 5 days a week. I always try to jump as high as possible in practice. You get used to the heights!

Mike Tully, UCLA, born 10/21/56, 6'2", 185#. Best height, 18'8 3/4", 1978 (world record not accepted); high school record, 16'4¼". Weight training is done twice per week year round. Exercises include clean and jerks, bench presses with a free-bar, and a few pull-downs. He does no full-squats, only partial squats to build the quad muscles. While Mike was an accomplished gymnast as a prep, he does no gymnastics work per se for the vault. He does do a little diving to work on body position. Tully divides his training about 50-50 between vaulting and running technique. He feels the most useful component of his program is the short-run vaulting to work on specific techniques.[1]

Non-Competitive Season.
Mon: Short-run vaults, 16 stride runup. Weights: clean & jerk; 3 x 10 at 120 lbs. bench presses 3 x 10 at 200.
Tues: Pole runs; 6 x 165; gymnastics or diving; hill running.
Wed: 16 stride short-run vaults, pole runs.
Thurs: 4 x 75; diving.
Fri: Weights, same as Monday; hill running.
Sat: Short-run vaults.
Sun: Rest.

Competitive Season.
Mon: Long warmup; stadium steps. Weights: clean & jerk, 3 x 5 at 120 lbs. bench presses, 3 x 5 at 200; leg squats, as he feels.
Tues: Short-run vaults.
Wed: Repeat 50s or 75s, numbers vary.
Thurs: 5 pole runs from 20 strides distance.
Fri: Stretch, easy jogging.
Sat: Meet; lift weights after meet, same as Monday.
Sun: Rest or surf.

Earl Bell,[2] Arkansas State, born 8/25/55, 6'3", 170#. Best height, 18' 7¼"--1975, age 20; best high school mark, 15'8". Earl trains year-round, although he does no weight training during the summer. During the regular season, he weight trains 3 times per week, then cuts down to 2-1-0 as the championship meets approach. Reps and poundages remain the same, however. Bell estimates that 25% of his training is taken up by weight training, 50% by running, and 25% by gymnastics-technique work. Running training consists of 330s, 220s, and 110s done at a fast pace (e.g., 24.0 for the 220s). In addition to vaulting a great deal in practice, Bell works out on the trampoline and rings to improve body control. Earl does vault at 100% in practice, "because there isn't any other way to pole vault." Length of Bell's approach run is 127 ft., taking 18 strides. He holds at 15-3 on a 16-5/190 lb. pole. Bell competes at least once per week during both indoor and outdoor season.

Non-Competitive Season.
Mon: Weight training: 3x(6x200 lbs. in the bench, 6x180 lbs. in cleans, 20x situps with 10 lb. weight, 10x200-450 lbs. in squats).
Tues: Easy running; technique work; gymnastic work on tramp, rings.
Wed: Weights, same as Monday.
Thurs: Same as Tuesday.
Fri: Weights, same as Monday.
Sat-Sun: Rest.

Competitive Season.
Mon: Vault.
Tues: 3-4 x 330 in 40.0.
Wed: Vault.
Thurs: Easy running.
Fri: Rest.
Sat: Compete.
Sun: Rest.

---

[1]Dan Sherrod, "Mike Tully," *Track Technique*, #60, June 1975, p. 1912.

[2]Mark Nadarsky, "Earl Bell," *Track Technique*, #63, March 1976, p. 2013.

Chapter 9
THE LONG JUMP

From a technique standpoint, the long jump is by far the simplest of the field events. Its approach is from a single direction, in contrast to a potential 180 degrees in the high jump. True, the transition from running speed to an optimum height in the jump, and the most effective way of landing in the pit do present certain problems in body mechanics, but, as compared with the other three jumps, these are not complicated. It is not surprising that, until about 1950, long jumpers were usually sprinters-on-holiday, doing a second event for fun and team points, with almost no emphasis on special training for the event.

A SUMMARY HISTORY OF PERFORMANCE AND TECHNIQUE

Long jumping has always been a natural part of man's everyday living as he cleared streams or fallen trees "at a bound," whenever the need was urgent. Certainly the mythology of every people tells stories of great feats of jumping from the Nibelungen tale of Siegfried's leap of 72 feet and more, carrying King Gunther with him beneath his Cloak of Darkness, to that of the Hindu monkey-god, Hanuman, who could clear oceans without use of the intervening islands. It was quite natural therefore that the long jump should be included in the Ancient Greek Olympics, though neither the high jump nor pole vault were contested. Gardiner's[1] carefully re-searched description of their methods is both interesting and instructive as it relates to modern jumping:

> For the long jump a firm hard take-off was provided called the Threshhold. We do not know whether it was of wood or stone. In vase paintings the take-off is marked by spears stuck in the ground or by stone pillars similar to those used to mark the start of a race. . . . The ground in front of the take-off was dug up and leveled to a certain dist-ance. This was called the Skamma. "To jump beyond the skamma or the dug-up" was the pro-verbial expression for an extraordinary feat. Phayllus, the hero of a fabulous jump of 55 feet, is said to have jumped 5 feet beyond the skamma, and we are not surprised to hear from one commentator that he broke his leg in the performance. . . .

> The Greeks always used jumping weights, halteres, in the long jump. These jumping weights, which somewhat resemble and were probably the origin of our dumbbells, were made of metal or stone and varied in weight from 2 1/4 to more than 10 pounds. . . . The jumper with weights depends for his impetus partly on the swing of the weights, partly on the run. The run is short and not fast. . . . As the jumper takes off he swings the weights for-ward, so that in mid-air arms and legs are almost parallel. Before landing he swings them backwards, a movement which shoots the legs to the front and so lengthens the jump.

Little is known of the true distances made by the Greeks, for they paid more attention to style than to records. But a few professional sprinters and jumpers in England during the 19th century used 5-pound dumbbells as a part of certain trick jumping acts. Gardiner appears

---

[1] E. Norman Gardiner, ATHLETICS OF THE ANCIENT WORLD, London: Oxford University Press, 1930, 144.

TABLE 9.1
OUTSTANDING PERFORMANCES -- LONG JUMP

OLYMPIC CHAMPIONS

Date	Record			Name	Affiliation	Best 100y/m	Best High Jump
1936	26'5¼''	8.06m		Jesse Owens	Ohio State	9.4y	6'
1948	25'8''	7.82m		Willie Steele	San Diego St.	9.6y	
1952	24'10''	7.57m		Jerome Biffle	Colorado	10.4m	
1956	25'8¼''	7.83m		Gregory Bell	Indiana	9.7y	6'2''
1960	26'7½''	8.12m		Ralph Boston	Tenn A & I	9.7y	6'9''
1964	26'5½''	8.07m		Lynn Davies	Grt. Britain	9.5y	6'2''
1968	29'2½''	8.90m		Robert Beamon	USA	9.5y	6'2''
1972	27' ½''	8.24m		Randy Williams	USA	Triple jump	6'5''
1976	27'4.7''	8.35m		Arnie Robinson	USA	9.4y	
1980	28' ¼''			L. Dombrowski	E. Germany		

WORLD-RECORD PERFORMANCES OF SPECIAL INTEREST

1921	25'3''	7.70m		Ed Gourdin	Harvard	(First over 25 feet)	
1928	26' 1/8''	7.93m		Silvo Cator	Haiti	(First over 26 feet)	
1935	26'8¼''	8.14m		Jesse Owens	Ohio State		
1965	27'43/4''	8.35m		Ralph Boston	Tenn A & I	(First over 27 feet)	
1967	27'43/4''	8.35m		I. Ter-Ovanesyan	USSR	10.4m	6'6 3/4''
1968	29'2½''	8.90m		Robert Beamon	USA	(First over 28 & 29 ft.)	

OUTSTANDING PERFORMANCES -- WOMEN

1976	21'10.2''[4]	6.78		K. McMillan	Raeford H.S.,N.C.	2nd O.G	
1976	22'2.5''[1]	6.72		Angela Voigt	E. Germany	25	5'7¼''	139
1978	23'3¼''[3]	7.09		V. Bardauskiene	SU	25	5'9''	143
1978	22'7½''[2]	6.90		Jodi Anderson	Los Angeles	20	5'5''	119
1980	23'2'' OR			T. Kolpakova	USSR		

[1] Olympic champion   [2] American record   [3] World record   [4] High School record

to accept the statement of one of them that "J. Howard jumped 29 feet 7 inches at Chester in 1854" and that use of the weights "added at least 8 feet to his jump." Incidentally, in 1928 I trained for the decathlon under Steve Farrell, head coach, University of Michigan. Steve held the professional record for the standing long jump with weights, not forward but backwards. Distance--over 11 feet!

In more modern times, the long jump has been competed since the early Victorian period. The McWhirters,[1] experts in great human feats, inform us that

The prospectus of the inaugural "Grand Annual Games" of 1860 at Oxford University invited entries for a "wide jump," though, when the programme came to be printed, the event was designated a "running long jump." The winner was Powell of Oriel with a "length of 17 feet 4 inches," which, incidentally was the same distance at which the first American championship was won 16 years later.

Of course, the conditions for jumping were then very poor. The pits were of turned over dirt and the first takeoff board was not used until 1886 when M. W. Ford reached 23' 2''. During the next 15 years, the unofficial world's record was broken 10 times by three Irish and four American jumpers. The best of the Irish was Pat O'Connor who cleared the remarkable distance of 24' 11 3/4'' in 1901, a record that held up for 20 years.

Webster[2] states that O'Connor "did not use the hitch-kick but simply drew the knees up

---

[1] Ross and Norris McWhirter, *GET TO YOUR MARKS!*, London: Nicholas Kaye, 1951, 175.

[2] F. A. M. Webster, *ATHLETICS OF TODAY*, London: Frederick Warne & Co., Ltd., 1929, 215.

toward the chin and trusted to his initial velocity to carry him sailing through the air. . . . Had he known the modern hitch-kick method, I think he might well have exceeded 26 feet instead of just failing to reach 25 feet." (We are entitled to our own opinion in this regard.)

The first jump over 25 feet was made in 1921 by Ed Gourdin of Harvard, who, after first beating the next Olympic champion, Harold Abrahams, in the 100-yard dash, leaped 25' 3" in the long jump. Pictures of Gourdin indicate that he also used a "float" style, with little leg action in the air.

DeHart Hubbard, Michigan, cleared only 24' 6" in winning the 1924 Olympic title, but the following year achieved 25' 10 7/8". Hubbard's style included a very short run of less than 100 feet, great acceleration, good height in the air (he was a six-foot high jumper), a single fast kick of the lead leg, and excellent forward placement of the feet in landing.

Ed Hamm, Georgia, (25' 11 1/8" -- 1928) and Luz Long, Germany, (25' 11" -- 1936) demonstrated most effectively the "hang" style with its delayed hip and leg swing (Figure 4.9). At takeoff, they leaped high in the air with the head and chest up but with the legs trailing. Then, just before landing, the legs came up and the head forward.

The style of Silvio Cator, Haiti, first to clear 26 feet officially (1928), is shown in Figure 4.1. Three years later, 1931, Chuhei Nambu, Japan, set a new record at 26' 2 1/8". Stocky of build, yet a good high jumper, a 10.5 100-meter sprinter, and world-record holder at 51' 7" in the triple jump, he combined speed, height, and balance.

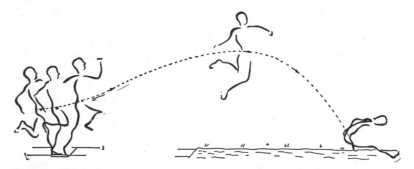

Fig. 9.1 -- The long jump ,from movies of Silvio Cator, Haiti, first to clear 26 feet.

Then came the great Jesse Owens, Ohio State, with his 26' 8¼" in 1935 that was to last for 25 years, the most long-lived of all track and field records. I was meet director of the Big Ten Conference meet in which Jesse not only made this record but also new world records in the 220 and 220 low hurdles, and a tie for the record in the 100, the greatest day any modern track man has ever had. To bring the long jump in front of the spectators, we dug into the sod and installed a board and pit just one week before the event. The runway was on the old grass, cut short, watered and rolled.

Owens stood on his one checkmark, only 108 feet from the board. At the takeoff, he seemed to simply run off the board with no special try for height. He used a simple one-leg swing, a natural movement for balance only. Owens seldom practiced the long jump. He was a great sprinter, trained on a minimum schedule of work as was the custom in 1935. To risk injury in long jumping would be foolhardy. Had Owens the use of today's perfect runways, had he had benefit of related power training, had he been able to practice the exact techniques of the gather and takeoff, who can say how far he might have jumped? His record might have lasted even beyond 1968 and Beamon's 29' 2½"!

This is more a history of technique than of performance. Lorenzo Wright, Wayne State (25' 11" -- 1950), stiffened his almost straight knees at the landing so as to produce a bounce up and forward out of the pit. Willie Steele, San Diego State (26' 6" -- 1948), along with others, slid off to the side after landing, rather than straight forward. But there was danger in this of touching the ground to the side or even out of the pit. Gregory Bell, Indiana (1956 Olympic champion -- 26' 7"), was a long jump specialist with a style so excellent that we shall discuss it in detail under "Essentials of Technique."

During the next decade, world long jumping was dominated by two men, Ralph Boston, Tennessee A & I (27' 4 3/4" -- 1965), and Igor Ter-Ovanesyan, U.S.S.R., (27' 4 3/4" -- 1967). In both cases, great performance was the result of great natural ability plus mastery of individually different but quite orthodox styles. Both were fine decathlon prospects.

In a very detailed report on Boston's career, Dick Drake[1] made no mention of jumping techniques. Instead he concentrated on Boston's great competitive spirit and all-round athletic ability. In 127 meets indoors and out during six years (1960-1966) his best marks per meet averaged 26' 2 3/5". In these meets he won 115 times; lost only 12 times. He never lost outdoors to Ter-Ovanesyan, and only once to Lynn Davies (Great Britain), 1964 Olympic Champion. On various important occasions, though behind throughout the competition, he managed to so concentrate his energies as to win on his last jump.

Drake states also that "a tally of Boston's best marks for each of the 10 decathlon events reveals he would score 8045 points, fifth best in history." Among his best events were the high jump-6'9", high hurdles--:13.7, triple jump--52' 1½", 100 meters--:10.5, pole vault--13'9", javelin--210'.

For eight straight years (1960-1967) *Track & Field News* ranked Boston first among world long jumpers. In six of those years, his best jump was over 27 feet. No other modern field event man can claim such a long span of dominance while competing regularly both outdoors and in. His only rival in this respect, Al Oerter, discus, was primarily an Olympic Games competitor.

But in 1968, even Ralph Boston had to accept second ranking to the most shocking and perfect single performance in all field event history, that of Bob Beamon at Mexico City. Boston had dreamed of 28 feet, though it was over seven inches beyond his best. But Beamon ignored that mountain peak entirely and leaped all the way to a Mount Everest distance of 29 feet 2½ inches. As verest is the world's ultimate in the height of man's climbing, so I believe Beamon's record is the ultimate in man's, not merely long jumping, but his ultimate for all field events. It's a relatively simple event; no inventions of gadgets as in the pole vault or javelin are likely to change the base of performance. It was a perfect jump. *Track & Field News* (Oct/Nov 1968, 30) put it this way,

It was a rare jump indeed. But then, Beamon is a rare talent, and a combination of circumstances led him from a previous best of 27' 4" to 29' 2½". He was obviously fired up, his step was exactly right, his form bordered perfection, his speed (09.5 - 100y) came as a great asset, the runway was consistent and fast, the assisting wind read a maximum of 4.473 mph, the high altitude (7350 feet) provided reduced air resistance, and he put together perhaps the ultimate technical effort that all field event performers dream about but rarely realize.

On the other hand, both Arnie Robinson (1976 Olympic champion--27'4 3/4") and Larry Myricks (1979 World Cup -- 27'11½") jumped with conditions that were far from ideal. Robinson--slow runway, slight headwind, overstride to hit board--felt that, with Beamon's "perfect" conditions, he could have done 29 feet. Myricks' jump--second best ever--was made at sea level (Montreal) and with "absolutely no aiding wind."[2] Experts estimate this handicapped him as much as a foot as compared with the conditions of Beamon's 29'2½".

HOW TO BEGIN

Long jumping begins with sprinting, for greater sprinting speed not only provides the potential kinetic energy that makes greater distances possible, it also develops much of the speed-stamina and toughness of muscle-tendon that is so essential to great jumping. Interval training with short sprints of from 50 to 100 yards at 9/10s speed should be started as soon as muscle condition permits.

---

[1]Dick Drake, "Ralph Boston: Super Giant, *Track & Field News*, November 1966, 11.

[2]Jon Hendershott, "Larry Myricks," *Track & Field News*, Oct. 1979, p. 11.

By way of preliminary practice, short runs with pop-ups into the jumping pit should gain the feel of long jumping. But very early, the full run with checkmarks should be introduced and practiced regularly. As demonstrated so perfectly by Beamon, an all-out runup uninhibited by any doubts as to checkmarks or to hitting the board is the way to best performance.

Related power training is important and should be started early. Greater power is an aid to greater sprinting speed but even more so, to more powerful jumping off the board. True, Ralph Boston never trained with weights until the end of his career (Fall, 1966).[1] But even at that 11th-hour period, he felt they were helpful.

Incidentally, many a fine long jumper started his career as a high jumper or hurdler.

ESSENTIALS OF SOUND TECHNIQUE

The distance a man can long jump is strongly influenced by four "physical"[2] factors: (1) the speed with which he can run about 40 yards, (2) the forward-up force he can apply against the takeoff board, (3) the time-distance and angle through which he can apply that force, and (4) the efficiency with which he can make a landing. Height in the air, so essential to distance, is an effect of the first three factors. Other influencing factors can be analyzed. Though they tend to be developed through the usual training methods, they may need specific attention. For example, the dropping of all acquired inhibitions against all-out speed in the run and all-out force against the takeoff board.

THE RUN

The run in the long jump includes four aspects: length, speed, method (including the use of checkmarks), and what we call the gather.

THE LENGTH OF THE RUN. The run in the long jump should be the shortest distance in which a man can gain near-maximum velocity some four strides from the toeboard. Henry's[3] research on acceleration in sprinting is helpful,

The place at which a sprinter running a 100-yard dash reaches peak velocity . . . turns out to be a function of his speed, but is reached in almost exactly 6 seconds regardless of the speed if he is running at full effort. The runner will be within 1 percent of his greatest speed at 50 yards if he runs a 10.5 hundred, at 53.7 yards for 10 flat, 57.0 yards in case of a 9.5, and 60.6 yards in a hypothetical 9 flat. (Naturally these figures will vary slightly depending upon the characteristics of the individual.)

These conclusions are drawn from sprinters who concentrate solely on all-out acceleration from their first movement. Long jumpers tend to be inhibited subconsciously (1) by the fact that they are jumpers, not sprinters, and (2) that speed must be tempered by the necessity of hitting the toeboard exactly right, as well as hitting the checkmarks on the way. Either of two conclusions is open: (1) the length of the run must be more than 200 feet (180 feet four strides from toeboard), or (2) long jumpers must be content with only about 95 percent maximum speed. Henry found that sprinters achieved 95 percent speed at about 66 feet, but for the reasons given, long jumpers would need a greater distance.

Actually, great long jumpers have varied in the length of their run from 108 feet to about 145 feet, using from 19 to 23 strides. The shortest of these was the 108-foot run of Jesse Owens (26' 8¼" - 1935), but Jesse began from a low crouch and attempted all-out acceleration from his first step. At the other extreme, such champions as Ralph Boston, Igor Ter-Ovanesyan, Willie Steele (26' 6" - 1948), and Greg Bell (1956 Olympic champion - 25' 8¼") used runs of over 140 feet. On his record 29'2½" jump (1968), Bob Beamon ran 130 feet.

---

[1] Dick Drake, *op. cit.*

[2] The quotation marks are an easily forgotten reminder that these so-called physical factors have their mental-emotional aspects that are just as crucial and just as much in need of specifically related training.

[3] Franklin M. Henry, "Research on Sprint Running," *The Athletic Journal*, February 1962, 32.

RELATED POWER EXERCISES

LONG JUMP - - TRIPLE JUMP

Assuming a certain degree of endurance and sprinting ability, even beginners should use a run of some such length; 21 or so strides are all too few in which to gain all-out relaxed velocity in time for the gather for the jump.

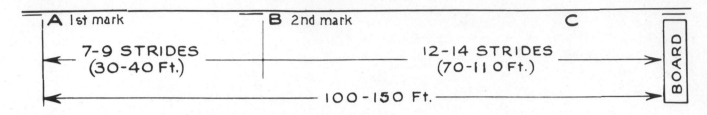

Fig. 9.3 -- Checkmarks and distances in the long-jump run.

THE SPEED OF THE RUN. In summary, a long jumper should accelerate and sprint as fast as he can within the limits of relaxation and readiness for the gather and precise takeoff. Dyson[1] has estimated that a jumper with great speed has only 5/36 second during which his take-off foot would be in contact with the board, only about one-half the time a high jumper uses. But this fact should not be used to argue for reducing speed, so much as for developing the speed-power and skill with which compression of the body springs and their reaction can be used effectively, in that brief instant. Such an approach is positive and in contrast to the negative assumption that the time factor is so limited that the speed of the approach must be equally so.

As long as a man is running relaxed, no concern for hitting the checkmarks and toeboard, or for providing more time in which to apply force against the board, should be allowed to decrease his speed. Assuming power and skill, the faster a man can run the farther he can jump.

On the other hand, despite this strong plea for greater speed, the distance actually jumped is a function of power and skill in jumping forward off the board, as well as of running speed. Boston broke Owens' 25-year old record though he could sprint only a "slow" :09.6 as compared with Owens' :09.4. But he could high jump 6' 9" as compared with Owens' 6 feet even. Another even more striking case is that of Rainer Stenius (Finland and Cal State at L.A.), who had a best time in the 100 of 10 flat and a best high jump of 5' 8", but long jumped 26' 9½" (1966). I heard Stenius talk before the USTCA coaches, and was greatly impressed that he used a full 40 minutes emphasizing the many aspects of skill in the gather and takeoff as well as the need for power in the particular muscles involved in these movements.

THE METHOD OF RUNNING. Three factors are crucial: velocity, relaxation, and exactness. We have already emphasized the first two, but exactness is of equal importance. A man must KNOW, must FEEL: in his muscles, in his mind, and in his heart, that he will hit just short of the front edge of the takeoff board *on every jump*. Actually, even with a master jumper, this won't always happen, but an occational failure will not disturb his calm assumption of a perfect run every time. Such a sense of certainty is the result of three requirements: (1) a positive mental attitude toward the run and its check-marks on the part of the coach and the jumper throughout all his practice and competition, (2) persistent and thoughtful practice using a whole-part-whole method, and (3) repeated and varied competitive experience.

Drake[2] reports that Ralph Boston fouled only seven times in 62 jumps taken in his most important competitions. He concluded that this was the result, not so much of endless practice, as of a positive mental attitude toward the situation. (I almost wrote the word "problem" but that's just the point--to think of fouling as a problem is to multiply its probabilities.)

---

[1] Geoffrey Dyson, *The Mechanics of Athletics*, London: University of London Press, 3rd edition, 1970, 152.

[2] Dick Drake, *op. cit.*

THE USE OF CHECKMARKS. The purpose of checkmarks is to ensure the three factors just discussed: velocity, relaxation and especially, exactness of the run. Of the three checkmarks shown in Figure 9.3, A is most important; B is necessary for beginning jumpers and helpful for most jumpers throughout their career; C is more to indicate an area than a specific point--an area within which attention shifts to the final approach steps and takeoff.

Actually, marks B and C might better be called go-marks, for their import is positive, a green light clearing the way in contrast to the checkmark's yellow light of caution and hesitation. For the well-training long jumper, there are not three parts to the run; it is one unit which, as training progresses, is invariably the same on every jump. The position of the feet at mark A is always the same; the forward lean, first step, and all succeeding steps are always the same; the degree of acceleration and the transitional final strides are always the same. Always the same in competition, and, as much as a sound approach to training can make it, always the same in practice.

THE APPROACH STRIDES. The approach strides are the most crucial phase of the long jump--the difference between the inexpert, however talented, and the true long-jump technician. In fact, as I think back over 50 years of great jumpers--DeHart Hubbard, Jesse Owens, Greg Bell, Ralph Boston, Bob Beamon--the only important change in emphasis and training for this event is primarily related to improving technique and power in the muscles related to the approach strides and, I must add of course, the takeoff. We used to think in terms of coasting, relaxation, "settle" or lowering the body's center of weight, foot-stamp or thrust--even if these required a loss of velocity in the approach. Today, all of these aspects are still relevant and valid but all within the limits of maximum velocity off the takeoff board.

Fig. 9.4. Jesse Owens who, from a run of only 108 feet, with minimal practice on technique and no power training, set a 1935 world record of 26'8¼", unbroken for 25 years.

That's an important change in emphasis, one that affects our entire year-round approach to training--as indicated in that section of this chapter--as well as the distances made in modern competition. In Chapter 7 we allocated 90 percent of height cleared in the high jump to the run and takeoff; only ten percent to the technique of bar clearance. This emphasis is even more marked in the long jump--probably 95 percent of the distance cleared is the resultant of velocity and technique in the run and takeoff.

Slow-motion film of the approach strides of expert jumpers discloses individual variations of these adjustments:

(1) The center of gravity lowers--the eyes focus down at the toeboard, then on the last strides, to the area above; the hands thrust forcefully but lower to aid the "settling" of the torso; the placement of the feet is lower--not so high on the toes.

(2) The next-to-last stride is longer--a natural effect found with all beginners and champions; only the degree of difference may need coaching. One study[1] reports a difference between a fast-approach jumper (Boston) and a slow jumper (Auga, East Germany) of over eight inches. Boston's last three strides were 2.10m, 2.30m., 2.10m, a difference of 8½ inches; Auga's last three strides were 1.95m, 2.43m, 2.01m, differences of 18" and 16". The effect of these two strides with their lowered pelvis and more erect torso is to place the takeoff foot

_____

[1]"The Long Jump," author unnamed, in Fred Wilt, ed., THE JUMPS, Los Altos: Track & Field News, 1972, p. 99.

somewhat more ahead of the c.g. than when sprinting (in preparation for the upthrust off the board), though less than in high jumping. Figure 9.5 portrays this clearly.

(3) The two adjustments just described must occur with a minimum loss of forward velocity. For beginners or those inadequately trained, this is difficult if not impossible. Verhoshanski reports[1] that two 22-foot jumpers on pre-training efforts were able to jump significantly farther using 3/4 speed during the approach than when using maximum speed. One might conclude that "coasting," or running at relaxed, controlled or optimal speed is better. But Verhoshanski concluded that these men lacked proper year-round training in both technique and related power to make a maximum-speed approach effective. Following such training, "the jumpers were able to jump confidently using maximum speed without any loss before the takeoff. Their performances improved significantly."

Fig. 9.5. The gather and takeoff as done by Ter-Ovanesyan, USSR, 1967 world-record co-holder, 27' 4 3/4". This drawing excerpted from *Light Athletics*, USSR publication, 1966, #2.

These findings are supported by the experience of Lynn Davies, Great Britain's 1964 Olympic Champion--26' 5½". With a total run of 132 feet, Davies' checkmark "B" was only seven strides (54' 6") from the board. During his early years of jumping, he tried to coast or gather for the takeoff. But in his later years when jumping his best, he tried to "change gears and sprint at the board." His coach, Ron Pickering[2], stated that "No longer does Lynn think of settling and sinking before reaching the board, but of really accelerating..." This change did not come easily or quickly but required months of related training.

(4) Placement of the takeoff foot on the toeboard is shifted laterally inward a few inches to ensure a position directly under the c.g. where the takeoff leg can best apply its power upward, and body balance in the air can be best achieved. As with the longer next-to-last stride, this tends to be a natural action for which coaching is only a distraction.

In summary of this all-important approach phase of the running long jump, several points need re-statement. (1) Perfect execution of the techniques of the approach strides (often called the gather) and takeoff makes the long jump a specialized skill-event, one that requires repeated practice as in any complex motor skill. (2) Since practice, to make perfect, must simulate the velocity as well as the skill of competitive performance, the danger of injury is always present. (3) Such danger is best avoided, not by a policy of minimum practice, but by one of gradual progression in training so that the muscles and tendons can be developed to withstand such high-level strains.

THE TAKEOFF
By giving the takeoff a name, we tend to imply an entity that can be separated from other phases of the long jump. On the contrary, whether by word or action, the takeoff extends back to include the approach strides and forward to include the flight into the air. "Takeoff" is only

---

[1]Yuri Verhoshanski, "The Long Jump and Triple Jump Approach," in Fred Wilt, ed., ibid.,pp.120-122.

[2]Ron Pickering, "Coaching an Olympic Champion," *Royal Canadian Coaching Review*, Dec.1967, p.1.

a convenience of communication and understanding; if thought of in any separate sense, both are lost.

Keeping in mind, therefore, that the technique of the approach strides will determine the forces and movements of the takeoff, the latter can be discussed in three aspects: (1) yield-reaction to the takeoff board, (2) uses of the arms and lead leg during takeoff, (3) active extension off the board.

The same forces of yield-reaction discussed in the high-jump chapter are present in the long jump, but here the goal is distance rather than height, so that the yielding phase is minimal. Keep in mind that expert long jumping allows only about 0.12sec. for the complex movements during contact with the board. Dyson (1970, 152) estimated a contact time of 5/36ths as compared with 7+/36ths for the high jump. The yielding phase includes a follow-through of the lowered c.g. during the approach strides: the foot placement is lower on the ball-heel; the ankle, knee and hip joints bend (yield) slightly; the lead arm thrusts forcefully forward-up, not simply "up" as formerly taught. If the yielding is too "soft," the joints will give way and the jumper will collapse into the near-end of the pit. If too "hard", and if the bracing of the takeoff leg has a significant braking effect, both velocity and distance jumped will be diminished.

As in high jumping, the uses of the arms and lead leg during the takeoff are primarily to increase the force of downward thrust of the takeoff leg against the board. During the first phase of takeoff, the forward-slightly downward thrust of the arms has the opposite effect; they help to cushion the momentary yielding phase and reduce pressure on the takeoff leg. But as the direction of arm and lead-leg force swings upward, their force of inertia is directed downward, increasing the load on the takeoff leg. Assuming the reactive power of this leg is adequate, the greater this downward force, the higher the jump.

Verhoshanski emphasizes the importance of precise timing of these related actions. With expert jumpers, maximum force from the lead arm and leg occurs at the end of the yielding or shock-absorbing phase and before the straightening action of the takeoff leg; beginners tend to start these actions earlier, before they can be effective. "In this detail lies the essential differences in the technique of a qualified jumper and a beginner."[1]

At the end of the takeoff actions, the upward thrust of the lead arm and leg slows. The hand stays below the shoulder and the line of the lead leg below the horizontal (Figs. 9.5, 9.6, 9.7), thus reducing pressure and aiding the final explosive extension of the takeoff foot.

TAKEOFF ANGLE. The ultimate effect in terms of distance of such forces against the board is determined primarily by the takeoff angle. Various studies have shown that this angle, in contrast to 45-degrees for projectiles, varies in the long jump between 15 and 25 degrees. In theory the latter figure has greater potential for distance, but it is fully effective only if all the other factors in creating force have been mastered: those in the run, approach strides, and takeoff actions as perfected by year-round practice on technique and training for related power.

THE LANDING
The most effective method of landing is one that ensures the greatest horizontal distance between the center of weight (for all effective purposes, the pelvis) and the heels at the moment they touch the pit, and still allow the buttocks to clear the ground as they fall forward. For every inch the heels are kept up, a jumper will gain about an inch and a half.

Fig.9.6. Ralph Boston, 1960 & 1964 Olympic Champion. World-record co-holder, 1965, 27' 4 3/4".

[1]Yuri Verhoshanski, op. cit., p. 117.

ACTION IN THE AIR

First movements off the board are concerned with getting maximum height. The head and chest are up, the back is arched, the lead-leg is flexed, the arms drive forcefully (Figures 9.1, 9.5). Some such movements are natural, even unavoidable. Any schoolboy will demonstrate them on his first attempt. But their exact timing, their maximum force, and their optimum direction are far from natural, must be carefully evaluated, and persistently practiced.

Subsequent movements in the air depend upon the manner of takeoff. In this, jumpers vary greatly. At one extreme of little action, there is the "sail" style by which a man jumps high, sits down in the air, and waits for the ground to come up. Next in simplicity is the "hang," a style which emphasizes the arch of the back and backward throw of the head (Figure 9.7a, with a forward jack-knife action just before landing. With most such jumpers, the feet drag behind prior to the "jack;" with others, they aid balance by quick, tiny steps in the air. Then there are two "running-in-the-air" styles: one and one-half strides is often called the hitch-kick (Figure 9.7b, by far the most common style used today. But some do use two and one-half strides.

Some years ago, there was much argument as to the relative value of these styles for increasing momentum in the air. But there is no scientific basis for such opinions. For every forward action there is an equal and opposite backward action. Momentum is a resultant of the run and takeoff and cannot be changed while in the air.

Head is back

Back is arched

Right arm drives high

Left knee drives high

A heel-ball-toe foot placement

Fig. 9.7b-- A hitch-kick style -- one and one-half strides in the air. This sequence drawn from movies of Greg Bell, Indiana, 1956 Olympic champion - 25'8¼", best distance - 26' 7", 1957.

But these styles do have different values in terms of efficient landing. There must be relaxation and balance in the air so that at exactly the right moment, not too soon and certainly not too late, the heels can be extended forward as far as possible and the buttocks can be brought through without touching the pit. In general, no movement at all, as in the "sail" style, tends toward tension and imbalance. The "hang" is an active style but must be precisely timed. Most champion jumpers today find the "hitch-kick" very satisfactory for balance, relaxation, and action. But Geoffrey Dyson, generally accepted as the expert on track and field mechanics, prefers two and one-half strides as best combining action, and proper timing for an efficient landing.

Arms high for balance

Fig. 9.7a -- The "hang" style. After a delaying "hang" in the air, the head and feet jack-knife forward.

Both legs extended

Feet are together

Head-shoulders are thrown forward and down

Both legs are pulled forward, flexed for greater quickness

Buttocks just clear the sand

Various factors tend to lower the heels. The jumper is overconcerned about sitting back in the pit. He holds his torso erect too long. (This will drop his feet even though he tries to extend them.) For the beginning jumper, forward rotation off the toeboard may lower the legs. But most important of all is the action of the arms. Dyson (1970, 157) states,

Landing efficiency is increased in long jumping when, immediately before contacting the pit, the arms are behind the jumper, for he then adds to the horizontal distance between his Centre of Gravity and heels, and when he lands he can then throw the arms vigorously forward to assist the forward pivoting of his body, transferring momentum.

Fig. 9.8. An exaggerated but clear indication of the distance to be gained from an economical landing as contrasted with one in which the torso inclines forward causing the feet to drop.

In actual practice there is much variation in just how this is done. Boston thrust his arms, especially the left, high, but then brought them forward outside his legs. Ter-Ovanesyan brought them forward and down past the hips, then forcefully up just before the buttocks reached their lowest point. The jumper in Figure 9.8 probably brought his head down between the knees by pushing the hands upward-backward.

Fig. 9.9. Bob Beamon, 1968 Olympic Champion, 29'2½", the greatest single performance in all track and field history—the equivalent of 7'10½" in the high jump or 61'5 3/4" in the triple jump! This drawing is taken from a photo of the actual jump. The left leg seems to trail but is moving forward to a position similar to that of the right (Note middle figure in Figure 9.8). The out-of-balance impression one derives is the outcome of camera angle.

PREVENTION OF INJURY IN THE LONG JUMP

In past decades, the long jump was considered the most dangerous of all jumping events in terms of strain of the leg muscles and tendons. Primarily this was due to lack of proper training. The event was dominated by sprinters who were too valuable to risk in practicing the jump but did take just enough jumps in meets to score the needed points. This led to a "kid-glove" attitude--a minimum of training work, and extremely little jumping. Despite his great record in competition, Jesse Owens was a typical example of such an attitude and practice.

Today, long jumping tends to be an event for specialists who train 12 months of the year in ways related to their specialty. The suggestions in Chapter 15, as well as those in Chapters 6 and 16, are just as valid for the long jump as for the high jump or shot put, especially as they relate to a toughening of tissues to prevent injury.

Fig. 9.10 -- A fiberglass heelcup for prevention of heel bruises in all jumping events. Produced commercially but can be form-fitted.

In summary, prevention of injuries is primarily a result of foresight in toughening the particular muscles and tendons on which long jumping places greatest strain. Some of the most important of these are the groin, the hamstrings, and the lower back muscles. Gradual overloading of these tissues in movements which imitate those of jumping and sprinting can be very helpful in prevention. Most common of all injuries is that to the heel during the takeoff, especially when the area just behind the board is depressed. Modern synthetic runways make this injury less likely, but every long jumper should wear a heelcup as shown in Figure 9.10, not merely after, but before injury occurs.

THE ORGANIZATION OF PRACTICE

By reason of the apparent simplicity of the long jump, the development of its technique and the training of related power and toughness has been neglected more than for any other field event. Actually, technical simplicity calls for greater perfection, not for carelessness. Artists in music agree that the most simple melodies are often the most difficult of all to play perfectly.

In summary, practice organization should consider at least six factors: (1) greater speed by which to gain greater kinetic energy during the run, (2) greater power in the muscles used in the transition from horizontal to more vertical momentum, (3) greater skill in all phases of the event but especially in the gather and takeoff, (4) greater toughness of tendons and tissues in the prevention of injury, (5) greater speed-endurance by which to ensure greatest velocity at the end of a 140-foot run, and maximum energies at the end of a long competition, and (6) the elimination of all inhibitions against an all-out effort at the takeoff (Steinhaus, 1963, 137).

Chapter 16 indicates the pattern by which these factors are organized during a 12-month training year. But only the unique needs and conditions of each individual and his situation can determine the exact what and when and how this pattern shall become actualized.

Now that the triple jump has been added to our program, we have become aware of the numerous exercises and devices that can aid performance when taking three long jumps. A similar approach should be made for taking a single long jump. In selecting power exercises, think through the various movements of the long jump in which power (strength x velocity) is an important factor. Sprinting can be improved by related power training. But of greatest concern are the movements that occur during the 5/36th second the jumper is in contact with the board, and the upward drive of the flexed lead leg and the opposite arm. How does one acquire the power for such explosive actions? By following the same pattern of (1) strength, (2) related power (3) imitative power, and (4) the skill itself that have been proved helpful in all other jumping and throwing events.

These movements involve takeoff-leg extension, including the foot, ankle, knee, and hip. For the foot-ankle, do heel raises and vertical hops with heavy weights on the shoulders. Also, lighten the weight (a dumbbell in each hand), and leap high and explosively reversing the feet or keeping them together. If emphasizing the foot-ankle, keep the knees and hips relatively straight; if not, then drop down lower and extend the entire body. When stair-climbing with weights, rise high on the toes on each stair. When running against the resistance of a stone drag, emphasize the full extension of the feet.

But gradually include more imitative power exercises. After a short run, leap high off the long jump board trying to touch with your forehead a 10-foot high cloth hung from a pole vault crossbar. After about ten years of great jumping, Boston still found this exercise helpful. Try using a weighted vest to increase the strength factor. Or, as another device, take a short run and jump from an inclined plane such as is used in gymnastics. This will increase the resistive shock of changing horizontal to vertical momentum, emphasize the flat forward movement of the pelvis, increase knee bend, and thereby the time-distance in which the power of leg extension can drive upward. (Warning--This artificial aid to height will need to be counteracted in subsequent practice.)

All such methods require a little imagination. Think of the specific movement to which you wish to bring greater power. Now imitate it, both closely and roughly. Keep in mind that strength, to be retained, must be overloaded at least once every two weeks. (Steinhaus, 1963, 136).

And certainly, do not neglect skill. True, to take a full run and jump cannot be repeated many times without endangering muscles and tendons. But the full run with a minimum effort off the board can be done once or twice a week with a dozen or so runs each time. These runs should be done exactly as in competition, with the same mental concentration. Secondly, the skills of the jump phase can be practiced with shorter runs of from 7 to 9 strides, or with longer runs of from 11 to 13 strides. Again, though the full-speed run is missing, concentrate on the jump as though in competition. Practice does not make perfect nearly so much as does consciously right practice.

The fact is that, for all our great performances in competition, we in the United States have not taken the long jump seriously from a training standpoint. The serious research and thinking has been done abroad in Great Britain, Germany, Yugoslavia, and the USSR. Ter-Ovanesyan of the USSR once wrote,

I am not afraid to tell you Americans that I have learned a lot from you and I wasn't ashamed to learn. Thousands of times I studied the movies of Jesse Owens' jumps. I tried to acquire the harmony of running form and speed which were peculiar to him and very much his own. From Bell I tried to learn the art of keeping balanced while in flight. From Bennett I wanted to learn his softness, from Shelby his impeccable landing. Boston forced me to see the take-off in a new light. I commit no error when I say that I know the mistakes and strong points of these broad jumpers better than they know them themselves.

Verhoshanski's Approach to Training.[1] Verhoshanski made the obvious but unusual assumption that a jumper's inability to make effective use of a maximum-velocity approach was caused, not so much by some defect in technique or lack of related power, as by an irrational program of training. In particular, he assumed that learning is specific to the skill that is practiced, that if 75 percent of technique practice consists of short-approach jumps with emphasis on the takeoff, that specific skill is learned, with only a partial carry-over to jumping with a full-distance and maximum-velocity run. *Velocity of movement is as essential to the skill concept as is the pattern of movement.* The specific techniques of a 50-foot-approach jump are therefore quite different from those of a 130-foot-approach jump. *Somehow long jumpers must find a training program by which they can practice the precise actions and velocities and powers they use in competition.* Startling? Yes, for long jumpers of the past 50 years, but only common sense in all areas of motor learning.

By-passing other needs of training including related power and flexibility, Verhoshanski recommended the following year-round program for practicing technique, based on a competitive season from May to September:

November-December. Goals: to improve sprinting technique; to improve the long-jump approach rhythm emphasizing acceleration from the first stride. Means: many repetitions (at least 8-10 times per session) of the full approach @ 3/4 effort without jumping. In these

---

[1]Yuri Verhoshanksi, *op. cit.*, p. 120.

runs, emphasize the approach phase by taking slightly faster and shorter strides. As physical condition improves, add an easy takeoff-run through the pit to more closely simulate actual jumping.

January-February. Goal: to master the techniques of increased speed throughout the approach phase and takeoff. Means: many repetitions of the full approach as in the preceding period. In these runs, 3/4 effort is still used during the early strides, but with maximum speed during the approach strides. However, though these strides do increase in tempo, there should now be no significant decrease in stride length. By concentrating on the specific skills of power sprinting--explosive push-off by each foot, high knees, full leg extension, forceful arm drive--the jumper gradually learns to drive through these approach strides and up into the takeoff with increasing power. Practice should include a normal takeoff and action in the air. The landing may be on one foot with a run-through beyond the pit, or with the usual two-foot style into the pit. In summary of this period, all the specific techniques of the approach phase of maximum long jumping are practiced, limited only by the 3/4 effort during the early strides.

March-April. Goals: mastery of the techniques of maximum velocity throughout the run-approach-takeoff. Means: repetitions of such maximum-velocity jumps in practice sessions. The gradual six-month progression in velocity of jumping, augmented of course by related power training and flexibility exercises, has now toughened the muscles and tendons to withstand the strains of all-out jumping. Strains are always a danger, and all precautions should be taken to avoid them, but basically the body is prepared and the danger is minimal.

May-September. Competitive period. Goal: perfection of the artless art of maximum long jumping in which the details gradually fall away, as has happened at least once when Beamon cleared 29 feet 2½ inches at Mexico City. Means: practicing the jump as a unified whole with attention to its parts only as seems necessary.

In my judgment, Verhoshanski's approach to training for technique is a sound one; sound in terms of basic motor learning and sound for the special problems of long jumping. Our problem is to adjust this Russian time schedule to our own school-college schedule with its indoor competitive season and tendency to lay off during the summer months. To hurry the gradual increments of effort and strain so carefully planned by Verhoshanski would decrease improvements of techniques and increase the dangers of injury. Where attitudes or competitive schedules permit, competitive performance during the indoor season should be secondary to proper training for the more important outdoor season.

Fig. 9.11. The Hang Style. A method that tends to produce a powerful takeoff with maximal height. But also one that prolongs the "hand" phase (Figures 3-4), delaying the forward pull of the legs and arms, so that the feet trail into the pit and reduce the distance of the jump.

191

All this taken together makes clear that there is hardly enough time in a 12-month year for a man who specializes in the long jump to get his work done--that is, done right!

THE TRAINING OF LYNN DAVIES

The following material has been excerpted and re-stated from a report by Ron Pickering[1], coach of Lynn Davies, Great Britain, 1964 Olympic champion--26' 5 3/4". Davies' example is of great value because (1) he was a long jump specialist, (2) he was trained by one coach throughout his career, a weight-training and long-jump expert, (3) he was not a great natural talent and had to work hard for his achievements. As Coach Pickering says, "Athletes who do not inherit a great natural gift of spring possessed by such men as Boston (or Beamon--J.K.D.) have to earn it the hard way. Improving their basic leg power/bodyweight ratio, though not the whole answer, can at least close the gap."

Davies was first subjected to a comprehensive range of tests to measure his basic physical capacities and thereby plan a priority of training activities. Throughout his career, a strong emphasis on strength training as related to long jumping was maintained, with emphasis on six exercises: (1) Modified squats (thighs at horizontal), up to 580#; (2) Jump squats (thighs at horizontal), up to 250#; (3) Clean and jerk, up to 265#, using the pyramid method with a maximum of 5 reps with lesser weights to a single lift with maximum weight; (4) stepping up and down from a 16" bench, up to 400# (3 reps of 8 reps each); (5) bouncing split squats, up to 225#; (6) skipping with weight on shoulders, 250#. The bench press, up to 250#, was also included as an aid to the more effective use of the other exercises.

This basic strength program was followed four times a week in winter and at least twice a week in summer. It is of great importance that, in a training session in the Olympic Village, Tokyo, just six days before the long jump final, Davies made personal best lifts in three of his weight-lifting exercises. This supports the experience of Dyatchkov in the high jump that strength training must be continued to some degree even during the late competitive season.

Every lifting session was combined with sprint training, jumping when possible, gymnastics, and special calesthenics to improve mobility.

Long jumping occurred whenever weather, takeoff surfaces, and physical condition permitted. Much of this was with a short approach of 7-9 strides, to develop height in the jump. Later, Davies concentrated on what Pickering considers the first pre-requisite of good long jumping-- maximum terminal velocity at the board. The best way to learn this is to practice jumping for height with a short approach, then gradually increase the length and speed of the run. The full approach run (21 strides for Davies) must be practiced for a month or so before major competition.

Throughout 1964, in addition to the usual sprinting, jumping, and weight training, resistance running and related jumping activities were added, the latter with fun competition: (1) running up steep sand slopes up to 300 feet high; (2) resistance running in a belt, pulling a partner or some weighted object; (3) repetition hopping, skipping, bouncing, and jumping on grass or through soft sand; (4) hopping and jumping for speed and distance; (5) abdominal work on an inclined bench.

Davies' best vertical jump--32½ inches; best standing broad jump--10' 7"; best triple jump-- 50' 7"; best time for his long jump run of 132 feet--4.4 seconds.

Despite his emphasis on weight training throughout his career, Davies' lowest bodyweight during the three prior years was at Tokyo--165 pounds. Pickering claims to have kept the muscle power/bodyweight ratio high by insisting on few repetitions in weight training and thereby reducing muscle bulk.

---

[1] Ron Pickering, "Training an Olympic Champion," *Royal Canadian Legion Coaching Review,* December, 1967, 1.

THE TRAINING OF LARRY MYRICKS[1] (1979--8.52m (27'11½'')--2nd best all-time long jump.
Born: March 10, 1956, Clinton, Miss. Ht/Wt; 6'1½''/165.
Best Marks: 100y--9.4; 220y--20 6w, 21.01; 440--47.5 relay.
Length of run: approximately 120 feet.
Training: In summary, concentrate on speed work, accuracy of steps, proper takeoff, hitch-kick movement in air, extension and forward lean with arms behind body at the end of jump. Speed work is major; weightlifting is not emphasized. He never jumps for distance in practice. On run-throughs, a short jump off the board is more effective than simply running through.

September--Sprint Capsule
Mon--(speed)--Warmup; 2 x 75 buildups; 3 x 30 meters working on technique; 2 x 30 meters out of blocks, 1 x 60 meters out of blocks; 2 x 30m fly; easy 440 warmdown.
Tues--(drill)--5 x one-legged hops (knee to chest) for approx. 30-40 yards; 5 x jumps in place with knee to chest; 10 x high knee action for 50 yards; weights on own.
Wed--Rest.
Thurs--(sprint holding power)--Warmup; 2 x 150 buildups; 2 x 30m starts, working on technique; 3 x 30m at 7/8ths effort; 2 x 60m out of blocks; 1 x 60m fly.
Fri--Same as Monday.
Sat-Sun--Rest.

Oct.-Nov.--General Foundation Period
Mon--(endurance & mental)--1-2 x a fartlek circuit.
Tues--(strength & speed endurance)--Weights and flexibility exercises: 2 x high knee sprints up freeway exit ramp; 2 x 110 (brisk) on grass; 25 x bounces on toes with weighted vest.
Wed--(endurance & mental)--steady 3-4 miles.
Thurs--5-10 x starts into a curve like a 220; weights and flexibility exercises.
Fri--Warmup; 4-6 x 440 with 440 jog between on grass.
Sat-Sun--Rest.

Jan.-Feb.--Indoor and Pre-Outdoor
Mon--(strength)--Warmup; 3 x popups for height; 5 x box popups; untimed 550, 440, 330, 220, 110 at medium speed; weights.
Tues--(speed endurance)--Warmup; 10 x 30m starts; 4-6 x 110 fast and relaxed, timed, but not all out; 1 x 300 untimed; 5 x high-knee action 50s.
Wed--(specialty)--Warmup; 5 x form starts; 6-10 x full long-jump runup; 5 x box popups.
Thurs--(specialty)--Warmup; 6 x full LJ runups as in meet; box popups for form.
Fri--Regular pre-meet day routine (individual).
Sat--Travel.

March-April-Outdoor Competitive Season
    Emphasize sprints and team effort. Larry usually runs 100,220, 440 relay and long jump for conditioning and motivation.
Mon--Warmup; 550, 440, 330, 220, 110 untimed at medium effort, walk the distance run. These get faster, but effort remains the same as condition improves.
Tues--Warmup; 5 x 30m timed out of the blocks, with gun; 4 x 150 fast and relaxed, hitting 16, with 3/4-lap walk interval; 5 x high-knee action 50s.
Wed--Warmup; 3 x 300 in 34 fast and relaxed, with a full rest; 5 x high knee action 50s.
Thurs--Relay handoff; LJ runups; starts.
Fri--Individual preparation.
Sat--Competition.
Sun--Rest.

May-July--Rest and Specializing Period
    Running workouts are gradually tapered away. Myricks no longer runs 100s and 220s but still competes on the 440 relay during May.
Mon--Warmup; 6-12 x full runups as in a meet; 2-3 high-knee action 50s.
Tues--Warmup; perhaps 1-3 popups for height; 10-20 box popups working on form.
Wed--Same as Mon. Thurs--Same as Tues. Fri--Same as Mon. Sat-Sun--Active rest; e.g.,swimming.

---

[1]Staff of *Track Technique*, Vol. 67, March 1977, p. 2133.

Chapter 10
THE TRIPLE JUMP

The triple jump is a most challenging event, comparable to the pole vault and high jump, and certainly when compared with the long jump. Its challenge arises from (1) its demand for great speed in the run combined with great agility and spring, (2) its demand for strong, resilient muscles that can be pliant under resistance and rebound vigorously against it, and (3) its demand for great skill in the multiple actions of the gather and three jumps. These demands call for studious planning, year-round training, and persistent practice of related skills.

SUMMARY HISTORY OF TECHNIQUE AND PERFORMANCE
The evolution of technique in the triple jump can be summarized as having three phases: (1) that of changing emphases on the three jumps, (2) that of the use of related power training in developing the reactive or bounce power for each of the jumps, and (3) that of greater velocity in the approach run as well as within the jumps.

Pat Tan Eng Yoon[1] credits the Irish with having used an early prototype style of hopping twice, then jumping--an L-L-L-jump style, with the English adopting the present accepted method around the turn of this century. Quite naturally, the early jumpers thought in terms of each phase somewhat separately, and tended to emphasize first, the hop or first jump; then the final third jump; and more recently, the step or second jump. Today, the event is thought of as a single, undividable action, having various phases which must be emphasized within the total action so as to produce the greatest total distance.

One of the mysteries of our sport is why the triple jump was ever dropped from the American program, and why we waited until about 1962 before the event was restored on a full college schedule. Or why even today many State High School Associations do not sponsor it. Certainly it had a strong beginning here, for American athletes dominated the event in the first three Olympic Games. J. B. Connolly, Boston, won in 1896 with 45 feet; Meyer Prinstein, Syracuse, in 1900 and 1904, with 47' 4¼" and 47' even, despite the dropping of the event from the National AAU championship meet from 1893-1906.

Since then no American has ever won this event in the Olympic Games, though in 1911 Dan Ahearne of Ireland and later, the Irish-American AC, did jump 50' 11" which remained the world record until 1924. According to Richard Ganslen, the breakdown on Dan's jump was 20' -- 11'3" -- 19' 8", a ratio characteristic of early jumpers who took a relatively short step and emphasized the hop and jump.

Dan Ahearne's durability in a tough event was just as amazing as his record. He won the American championships on eight different occasions from 1910 to 1918, and in 1924, at something over 40 years of age, was still expert enough to represent America in the Paris Olympic games. Incidentally, his younger brother, Tim, won the 1908 hop, step, and jump event in the London

---

[1]Pat Tan Eng Yoon, "Research into the Hop, Step and Jump," *Clinic Notes*, NCAA Track Coaches Association, 1959, 16.

TABLE 10.1

OUTSTANDING PERFORMANCES--TRIPLE JUMP

OLYMPIC CHAMPIONS

Date	Record	Name	Affiliation	Hgt.	Wgt.	Hop	Record Jump Analysis Step	Jump	Best 100m.	Best L.J.
1896	44' 11 3/4''	J.V.Connolly	Boston							
1900	47' 4 1/4''	Meyer Prinstein	Syracuse							24' 7 1/4''
1908	48' 11 1/4''	Tim Ahearne	Ireland	5' 7''	130					24' 1''
1912	48' 5 1/8''	G. Lindblom	Sweden							
1920	50' 9 1/2''	V. Tuulos	Finland							
1924	50' 11 3/4''	A.W.Winter	Australia							
1928	49' 10 3/4''	Mikio Oda	Japan	5' 6''	130				:10.7	24' 8''
1932	51' 7''	Chuhel Nambu	Japan	5' 8''	140	21' 0''	14' 6''	16' 2''	:10.5	26' 2''
1936	52' 5 7/8''	N. Tajima	Japan	5' 10''	140	20' 4''	13' 1''	19' 1''		25' 5''
1948	50' 7''	Arne Ahman	Sweden	5' 8''						
1952	53' 2 1/2''	A.F.da Silva	Brazil	5' 10''	148	20' 4''	15' 1''	17' 9 1/2''	:10.7	24' 1''
1956	53' 7 1/2''	A.F.da Silva	Brazil	5' 10''	152					
1960	55' 1 3/4''	Josef Schmidt	Poland	6' 1/2''	170					
1964	55' 3 1/2''	Josef Schmidt	Poland							
1968	57' 3/4''	Viktor Saneyev	USSR	6' 1 1/2''	180	22' 4''*	16' 7''	19' 10'' (Altitude, 7350')		
1972	56' 11''	Viktor Saneyev	USSR	6' 2''	176		(*includes 8'' takeoff before board)			
1976	56' 8.7''	Viktor Saneyev	USSR	6' 2''	176					
1980	56' 11 1/8''	Jaak Uudmae	USSR							

WORLD RECORDS OF SPECIAL INTEREST

Date	Record	Name	Affiliation	Hgt.	Wgt.	Hop	Step	Jump	Best 100m.	Best L.J.
1911	50' 11''	Dan Ahearne	Eire	5' 8''	140	20' 0''	11' 3''	19' 8''		
1931	51' 1 3/8''	Mikio Oda	Japan	5' 6''	130	21' 4''	11' 6''	18' 3''	:10.7	24' 8''
1935	51' 9 3/8''	Jack Metcalfe	Australia			18' 6''	13' 6''	20' 4''		
1937	52' 3/8''	K. Togami	Japan	5' 8''	148	19' 0''	14' 0''	19' 2''		25' 1''
1950	52' 5 7/8''	A.F.da Silva	Brazil	5' 10''	143	18' 1''	15' 10''	18' 6''	:11.0	23' 7''
1951	52' 6 1/4''	A.F.da Silva	Brazil							
1953	53' 2 3/4''	I. Shcherbakov	USSR			19' 8 1/2''	16' 3 1/2''	17' 2 1/2''		
1955	54' 4''	A.F.da Silva	Brazil			20' 7''	16' 4''	17' 5''		
1958	54' 5 1/4''	O. Ryakhovskiy	USSR			21' 2 1/2''	16' 3 1/2''	16' 11''		
1959	54' 9 1/2''	O. Fyedoseyev	USSR			21' 4''	15' 9 3/4)	17' 7 3/4''	:10.7	23' 2 1/2''
1960	55' 10 1/4''	Josef Schmidt	Poland	6' 1/2''	170	19' 8 1/4''	16' 5 1/4''	19' 8 3/4''	:10.5	
1968	57' 3/4''	Viktor Saneyev	USSR	6' 1 1/2''	180	(altitude--7350')				
1969	56' 3 1/4''	Viktor Saneyev	USSR			(sea level)			:10.5	
1968	56' 2''	Art Walker	USA			(altitude--7350')				
1971	57' 3/4''	Pedro Perez	Cuba			(sea level at Pan-Am Games)				
1972	57' 2 3/4''	Viktor Saneyev	USSR							
1975	58' 8 1/4''	Joao Oliveira	Brazil	6' 2 1/2''	165	20'	17' 7''	21' 1 1/2''	10.4m	26' 10 1/2''
1978	56' 6 3/4''*	James Butts	USA							

*USA Record

OUTSTANDING PERFORMANCES--HIGH SCHOOL

Date	Record	Name	Affiliation	Hgt.	Wgt.
1965	50' 3 3/4''	Bob Beamon	Jamaica, N.Y.		
1970	52' 6 1/4''	Dave Tucker	San Joaquin Mem., Fresno, Cal.		
1973	51' 7 3/4''	Ron Livers	Eisenhower, Norristown, Pa.		
1974	51' 3''	Willie Banks	Oceanside, Cal.		
1975	51' 7 1/2''	Nate Cooper	Clarke Central, Athens, Ga.		
1976	51' 8 1/2''	Greg Caldwell	Fremont, L.A.		
1977	51' 5 1/2''	Greg Artis	Fike, Wilson, N.C.		
1978	53' 4 1/4''	Sanya Owolabi	No. Tarrytown, N.Y.	6' 1''	165#
1979	52' 6''	Henry Ellard	Hoover, Fresno, Cal.		

Olympics while Dan was trying to get settled after his emigration to America.

Following the world monopoly of the Ahearne brothers, men from Sweden and Finland won the event in the 1912 and 1920 Olympics, with jumps of 48' 5" and 47' 7" respectively.

JAPANESE DOMINANCE. But in 1928, Mikio Oda, (5' 6" tall, weight--130#, best 100 yard time-- about :09.9) began a 12-year world-dominance in the event for Japan. This was specially signi- ficant because many of the Japanese jumpers were slow as sprinters. Tan Eng Yoon reports that neither Oda, Tajima, nor Harada could break 11 seconds for 100 meters, though they all bettered 51 feet. But they did have great leg power and resiliency, acquired, some said, from the Japanese custom of sitting on the floor and using the power of crossed legs in rising. In any case, we know that they studied the event very carefully, emphasized a deeper knee-hip flexion and rebound on each jump, and a better balance of distance between the three phases of the jump. By 1932, their greatest natural athlete, Chuhei Nambu, combined excellent speed (100 meters-- :10.5) with great jumping ability (world-record long jump--26' 2") to gain the Olympic title and the world record at 51' 7". In 1936, Japanese athletes won 1st, 2nd, and 6th at the Berlin Olympics, including Tajima's world record of 52' 5 7/8". But the War destroyed all Japanese development in sports, and when they recovered, others had passed them by.

ADHEMAR da SILVA. Surprisingly, the next world champion, the fun-loving Adhemar da Silva, came from Brazil. Da Silva failed in 1948 at London because, he said, "I was so awestruck by the multitude of people that I forgot to warm up or anything else!" But in the years that fol- lowed, he forgot spectators in the sheer delight of jumping at any time and in almost any place in the world. First (1950, 52' 5 7/8"), he tied Tajima's record with the greatest series of jumps up to that time:

	HOP	STEP	JUMP	TOTAL
1.	18' 8 3/4"	14' 5 1/4"	16' 4 7/8"	49' 6 7/8"
2.	17'10 5/8"	15' 2 5/8"	18' 7/8"	51' 2 1/8"
3.	17' 8 1/4"	15' 3"	18' 2 1/2"	51' 1 3/4"
4.	18' 2 1/2"	15' 6 1/4"	18' 6"	52' 2 3/4"
5.	18' 2 1/2"	15' 8 5/8"	18' 7 5/8"	52' 6 3/4" (foul)
6.	18' 1 3/8"	15'10 1/2"	18' 6"	52' 5 7/8"

The relative lengths of the hop, the step, and the jump warrant careful study for they are very similar to those of modern jumping. On a percentage basis, the three phases of his final record comprised 34.5 -- 30.1 -- 35.4 percent of the total effort, a very well-balanced performance, even by modern standards.

Then, at the 1952 Olympic Games at Helsinki, he set new world-records on three consecutive jumps with a final best of 53' 2 1/2". He planned to retire, but when Shcherbakov of the U.S.S.R. beat his mark by one-quarter inch, he went into training again, with a new record of 54' 4".

Once again he announced his retirement. But this time, according to his own telling, his wife agreed to present him with a third child if he would present her with another Olympic gold medal. Which, at Melbourne, he did; and which, in good time, she did. It was a boy!

SOVIET DOMINANCE. But individual efforts, even those as brilliant as da Silva's were being outshone by the mass athletics program of the Communist countries. The U.S.S.R. took this event very seriously, as being one that was relatively undeveloped in world competition. Coaches who specialized in this one event were appointed. Scientific studies were made. In 1961, these studies were summarized in a 214-page book on this event alone. All aspects were reviewed, past history, prevalent techniques, but especially, the outlook for the future. One table, for example, projected the probable performances of a 27-foot broad jumper, such as Ter-Ovanesyan or Ralph Boston. The result? Just over 59 feet! The world's record when the prediction was made was 55'10¼" by Jozef Schmidt of Poland!

The Russian technique seemed to place great emphasis on the hop. Both Ryakhovskiy and Fyedoseyev cleared more than 21 feet, comparable to the efforts of Oda and Nambu of Japan back in 1928-1932. This great effort was maintained in their step (between 15'9" and 16'3"), with least emphasis on the jump (16' 11" to 17' 7"). Perhaps their projection of an ultimate 59 feet influenced their methods; at least they used their momentum to a maximum degree on each phase, in the hope that some one at some time would have enough balance and relaxation to permit the momentum to continue into the last phase, the jump. Considering that none of their champions were even good sprinters or broad jumpers, their performances were truly remarkable.

THE POLISH METHOD. However, the next great break-through in performance and perhaps in method came from Poland, not the U.S.S.R. Just before the 1960 Olympic Games, Jozef Schmidt surpassed Fyedoseyev's world's record by more than a foot with 55' 10¼", in which the three phases were 35.2--29.4--35.4 percent of the total jump, a very well-balanced performance. Schmidt placed his emphasis where he was most capable--on velocity (best time 100 meters--:10.5). By keeping his trajectory low on his first\two jumps, he maintained momentum for a long third jump. His splits on his record jump were 19' 8 1/4" (relatively short), 16' 5 1/4" (relatively long), and 19' 8 3/4" (long). This came to be known as the Polish "flat" technique, and still has its advocates today.

MEXICO CITY. Schmidt's record lasted eight years, a long time in today's world. But in the eighth year, at the Mexico City Olympics (altitude - 7349 feet), it was broken not by one man, but by five. All related factors were on the plus side--altitude, wind, sunny weather, and the presence of the ten top triple jumpers on the all-time listings. Most competitors made personal-best records, topped by Saneyev's 57' 3/4".

LATER RECORDS. Great as 57 feet was in terms of past performances, it was some three feet short of our projected human ultimate of over 60 feet. As was soon demonstrated. In 1971, at sea-level, Pedro Perez of Cuba equalled Saneyev's distance, only to be outdone in 1972 when the Master, following his second gold at Munich, regained the world record at 57'2 3/4". Then, at the Pan-Am Games at Mexico City, Joao Oliveira's great runway speed (10.4 100-meters) combined with low-density air to achieve a milestone 58'8¼" (17.89m), with a three-jump break-down of 20' - 17'7" - 21'1½". As a matter of interest, if not great significance, this ratio is closest to that projected by Mikio Oda of Japan (35-30-35), with excellent balance as between the first and last jumps and a full second jump in between. Other than repeated sprints with weighted vest, Oliveira used a minimum of weight training. Even better jumps are undoubtedly forthcoming.

BASIC QUALITIES NEEDED FOR THE TRIPLE JUMP

Even a moment's thought about the triple jump makes it clear that ultimate human performance calls for at least four basic qualities: great sprinting speed, great rebounding or jumping ability, great power in the related muscles, and most important, great skill in mastering the most effective technique. But to date, and this includes Saneyev with his 57' 3/4" world record, no triple jumper has been able to claim all four qualities. When such a man comes along, the world record will approach or even better 60 feet.

As with the long jump, velocity at the takeoff provides over 90 percent of the distance covered. On the other hand, even world-record triple jumpers have not possessed world-level sprinting ability. Valid sprint times for triple jumpers are seldom available but these have been reported: Josef Schmidt (55'10¼") 10.5; Victor Saneyev (57' 2 3/4")--10.6; Joao Oliveira (58'8¼")--10.4. It follows that, as better sprinters master this event, even greater distances will be achieved.

Second, aptitude for triple jumping is related to long jumping and high jumping. Table 10.1 shows that most champion triple jumpers had excellent marks in the long jump. One (Nambu, Japan, 1932) held the world record in both. Victor Saneyev long jumped 25' 11"; James Butts, 1979 American record holder (56'6 3/4"), 25 feet; Joao Oliveira (58'8¼"), 26'10½". High jump marks are less available. Saneyev cleared 6'2½". Long jumper Ralph Boston (27'4 3/4") triple jumped 52' 3/4" and high jumped 6'9" straddle style. Arnie Robinson (27'4 3/4") triple jumped 50'11 3/8" and high jumped 6'9".

Cont'd. on p. 200

THE WHOLE ACTION

THE WHOLE ACTION

The triple jump demands a whole-action approach as much as does any field event, comparable to that of the pole vault and high jump. It is in fact a single triple-jump, not three separate jumps as was implied by the former American name of the hop, step and jump. In a true sense it is one action, a run-and-three-jumps as one indivisible movement.

In that action it typifies the three essentials that are often held up as the symbol of the Olympic Games: faster--higher--farther. Other things being equal, the faster a man can run the greater his explosive power in absorbing each of three landings and rebounding high into the air, and the smaller his loss of velocity on each of the first two jumps, the greater his potential distance as a triple jumper. In addition, there is a speed-endurance factor here, for it takes a special kind of endurance to sustain six all-out sprints of about 125 feet each with three jumps at the end, and still be able to do one's best on the last effort, if need be.

Second, it is a whole-action event in its demand for high-level skill beginning with the first step of the run and the difficult coordination of three successive jumps. The leg and torso muscles must relax for an instant as they yield during the gather of each jump but must then react quickly and powerfully during each rebound. This is not done easily, and we see the best-trained and most-skilled champions occasionally flub a jump by settling a trifle low, and then be unable to rebound.

The triple jump is one of the most fascinating of all track and field events, especially for boys of even 10 to 12 years of age. It can be done from a stand, with any given length of run, and any combination of hops on one foot, or jumps. Even the first few trials will bring forth performances that are far more satisfying than are those of high jumping, and certainly of pole vaulting. In jumping from a stand,

Figs. 10.1 & 10.2 -- These two remarkable drawings are excerpted from the USSR publication, *Light Athletics*, 1965, #9. The distance of Fig. 10.1 was given as 16.81 meters (55' 7/8"); Fig. 10.2 16.43 meters (53' 10 3/4").

The techniques shown deserve careful study and comparison beyond my comments. They are uniquely different in almost all details. Fig. 10.1 seems lower on his first jump but farther, perhaps by greater speed. Note how Fig. 10.2 uses a two-

TRIPLE JUMP

beginning jumpers may tend to take a long hop. They will jump farther and also learn the technique of triple jumping if the emphasis is on velocity as well as distance of jumping. This will cut the first hop somewhat and produce a ratio between jumps of perhaps 6-8-10 or 7-9-11, as in clearing 24 or 27 feet.

Actually, the triple jump is a much more interesting event than the long jump, and it is surprising that American high schools and colleges did not adopt the event some 75 years ago. It cannot be dominated by sprinters as has happened in the long jump, unless they undergo a rather long period of special related training in both power and skill. Therefore men specialize as triple jumpers just as they tend to do for the high jump and pole vault. Even today many State High School Associations do not recognize the event officially, but it will soon be universally accepted. Why rule out such an exciting action?

But though relatively simple at the beginner's level, the triple jump is sufficiently complex in its skills and demanding in its requirements for related power, as to challenge the most talented athletes over a period of ten or more years of year-round training and competition. Though speed is a very important factor in triple jumping, rebounding power and mastery of technique are even more essential. This is indicated by the fact that perhaps 90 percent of past world-level performers have not been great sprinters. In fact, of all the Japanese who once dominated world triple jumping, only a very few such as Nambu, 1932 Olympic champion and over-26-foot long jumper, had great sprinting ability. Josef Schmidt, Poland, was a fine sprinter but very few of the Russian champions had great speed. In all such instances, what they may have lacked in velocity at the point of takeoff, they balanced by great resilient power and excellent technique during the jumps.

arm thrust, especially on the two later jumps. Both men settle during the last two strides before takeoff, rolling on the heel, with pelvis low. This is also clearly indicated in the later jumps. The arms of Fig. 10.1 are better controlled throughout, though they do go high and then down before the landing. In contrast, the arms of Fig. 10.2 tend to be high, then go low and forward at the landing. Measurement of the drawings indicates 10.1s advantage lies in his first two jumps.

Toni Nett once theorized that one's best potential triple jump could be estimated by the formula--(LJ distance x 3 x .75). Example: 20' x 3 x .75 = 45'. This seems to be an acceptable rule-of-thumb, though Beamon's long jump of 29'2½" would project a possible triple jump of 65'7". Even Larry Myrick's best at sea level (27'11½") would project 63'. Either the formula is too high or our best triple jumps are far short of what lies ahead.

Third, best performance in the triple jump requires great power specifically related to the movements of this event. Such power is similar to that needed in the long jump but, of course, for both legs, and with a greater need for reactive or bounce power on the last two phases. The emphasis on related power exercises is therefore much greater.

Finally, the triple jump is a complex movement that requires great skill for mastery. Consider: the skill inherent in achieving maximal useable speed at the board; that of gaining optimal height on each of three jumps; that needed to ensure a minimal loss of velocity throughout; that of the yielding-rebounding phase of each jump; and that of an effective landing. It seems clear that no field event, such as the pole vault or discus, is so dependent on mastery of technique.

From these four essentials of great triple jumping, two conclusions are obvious. First, the event needs to be included in the high school program nation-wide; and second, even after years of careful, related training, there will be too few days in which to attain full competence.

HOW TO BEGIN

The decision as to "How to Begin" depends so much upon the individual jumper--his age, ability, jumping experience, and related power training. The overall approach for all field events has been outlined in Chapter 16; that for the long jump, especially as related to power training, in Chapter 9. Those sections should be reviewed.

However, the following procedures for the triple jump should be considered for beginning jumpers:

1. <u>The Standing Triple Jump</u>. Practice three quick jumps from a standing start (either two feet on the line or the takeoff foot forward) R-R-L-jump and also L-L-R-jump. Encourage resilient ball-heel-toe landings and takeoffs. Emphasize forward velocity rather than height, and so develop a feeling for one unified effort with its three phases.

As boys develop proficiency, coach increasing height in the three phases--low on the first; higher on the second; highest on the third. A low first-phase jump is achieved by spending less time in the air, by not lowering the center of weight, by focussing the eyes and face forward and not up, and by continuing the natural swing of the arms. A highest third-phase jump is achieved by lowering the body weight through greater flexion of the takeoff leg (hip, knee, ankle) and rebounding explosively by lifting the eyes-head-chest upward, by dropping both arms down-back then driving them forward-up in rhythm with the lead leg. (Note--this two-arm drive is disruptive and, though mentioned, should not be emphasized.)

2. <u>Getting Checkmarks and Practicing the Run</u>. With our emphasis on the whole action and the crucial importance of the run, we feel it should be practiced early in the learning process. Follow the same methods as for the long jump, using a minimum hop-step-jump off the board. Take a positive approach; coach simple learnings before they become problems.

3. <u>Develop Related Power</u>. (a) From a stand, triple hop on same leg for distance or for height; shift to other leg; gradually, during training, increase number of hops to 10 or 12. (More than that increases endurance, not power.) Later in development, use weighted vest or belt. (b) Repeated hops with sand bag or weights on shoulders, either in place or advancing, emphasizing each leg in turn, or using both legs. For explosive power, use lighter weights-- higher jumps; for strength, use heavier weights. Other combinations of hops and jumps are easily devised.

---

[1]Toni Nett, "Economy in Triple Jumps," *Die Lehre der Leichtathletik*, Berlin, June 6, 1961 and reprinted in *Track Technique*, December 1961, 191.

4. Short Run and Triple Jump. Quick-striding runs of from three to seven strides will provide the exciting sense of speed, rhythm and power that makes the triple jump so challenging. Only the athlete with a rather high-level natural ability is likely to do well in the triple jump; such men learn to combine velocity with jumping techniques without difficulty. Emphasize low forward quickness on the first phase; increasing height on the second and third.

5. Competition for Fun. Triple jump exercises are inherently competitive and fun. Any combination of hops, with or without steps or jumps, can be measured for distance. Heinz Rieger[1] reports a scoring system, commonly used in East Germany, which trains for greater speed-power in jumping. By scoring on a combined basis of distance covered and time required (Example--46-49 feet in 3.8 seconds), the jumper learns the crucial importance of forward velocity while still covering long distances. An approach run of seven rapidly accelerated strides is used. Note that each improvement in distance is achieved in a lesser time, which illustrates the importance of the velocity factor in gaining greater distance.

TABLE 10.3

CLASSIFICATION OF SPEED-POWER IN JUMPING

Action	Class III	Class II	Class I	Master
Steps (RLRLR)	46'-49' (3.8s)	49'-55' (3.5s)	55'-62' (3.0s)	65'-75' (2.8s)
Hop-step-hop-jump	46'-49' (3.8s)	49'-55' (3.5s)	55'-62' (3.0s)	65'-75' (2.8s)
Hop (RRRRR or LLLLL)	43'-46' (4.0s)	46'-52' (3.8s)	52'-59' (3.3s)	65'-69' (2.8s)

ESSENTIALS OF CORRECT TECHNIQUE

As with all field events, the triple jump is actually a single-action event which begins with the first step at the start of the run and ends in the pit. This single action has whatever number of phases one's powers of analysis can discern. Usually we speak of four phases--the run and the three jumps--but each of these can be analyzed further into the gather, takeoff, action in the air, landing, rebound (from the first two jumps), etc. Our emphasis in this first essential is on unifying the whole movement, and on considering the effect of emphasizing one phase upon the total performance. (See Figure 10.1 and the related discussion of the whole action.)

BASIC SIMILARITIES BETWEEN LONG AND TRIPLE JUMPING. The entire discussion in the preceding chapter has direct application to the triple jump. This is especially true as to the run, the use of checkmarks, and the action in the air and landing in the third jump. In summary, every triple jumper should understand, and use with modifications, the various means to development in long jumping. This applies in large measure to basic training, as is implied by placing all training exercises in the long-jump chapter.

TRIPLE JUMP TAKEOFFS. The most effective takeoff for each of the three jumps is one that balances horizontal with vertical velocity; that is, one in which the resistance against forward velocity is the least possible, while a maximum impulse upward is thrust through the body's center of weight. The first jump tends to give greater weight to the first of these two forces; the third jump, to the second; with the middle jump, somewhere in between, depending on the method emphasis.

DEGREE OF LANDING SHOCK. Experts in triple jumping are able to minimize the shock of bracing the leg as its foot first touches the ground, and then to extend the leg more quickly and powerfully in the takeoff. The USSR coach, Verhoshanski[2] speaks of this shock phase as "yielding work," and concludes that the master jumper actually allows less flexion in the knee joint. Perhaps we can compare this phase of movement with a rubber ball. If a very hard ball, the shock of striking the ground would be great and the reactive power, low. If a very soft ball,

--Continued on page 208

---

[1] Heinz Rieger, "Training for Triple Jumpers," (translated by Gerry Weichert), *Track Technique*, September 1964, 538.

[2] Yuri Verhoshanski, "Jumping Downward as a Means of Training Jumpers," Moscow, USSR, *Legkaha Athletika*, September 1967. Translated by Dr. Michael Yessis, California State College.

The first jump (hop) as shown here comes after a full and fast run, gather and take-off which is basically the same as described in the preceding section for the long jump. All the discussion there as to length and velocity of run, check-marks, method of running, relaxation, and use of momentum also applies here for the triple jump. Some argue that velocity for the triple jump must be curtailed. Perhaps so, but only temporarily; a sounder approach is to assume full relaxed velocity, then develop the power and skill to make full use of it.

The head is erect but not back; the eyes are straight-ahead, not up toward the vertical

The attitude at take-off is for-ward-upward, rather than upward-forward as occurs in long jumping

The first jump (hop).
Fig.-10.3

As compared with the long jump, the lead knee is not as high, and the take-off leg comes up sooner

Most jumpers begin by using the stronger leg for the first and last jumps, but by power training try to develop equal power in both legs

This is a simple hop on the right foot; there is no hitch-kick as in the broad jump

202

JUMP (THE HOP)

The first jump does not strive for maximum distance as might a long jumper. Rather it strives for a less-than-maximum distance while maintaining as much velocity as possible for the next two jumps.

The head and eyes are straight ahead, not up

Note the shock-absorbing relaxation of the right knee, both here and in figure 10.4G This is all-important. By gradual flexion the knee cushions the landing and is ready for the re-bound into the next jump. <u>This</u> <u>takes</u> <u>power</u>!

With some jumpers, the thigh would be horizontal or even higher

The right knee is thrust high and remains high

The right foot is extended well ahead of the center of gravity. To drop it sooner would throw the weight forward and shorten the step

This jumper lands on the right foot: heel-ball-toe; other jumpers land: ball-heel-ball-toe to ensure forward velocity

Extension of the right leg and preparation for a long step causes the left leg to trail far behind

The crucial problem in the triple jump is to integrate a relatively long step with a minimum loss of velocity and a maximum gather and re-bound into the final jump. "To integrate" implies a fine but precarious balance between these aspects. To go all-out for an extremely long step would decrease both velocity and height - and over-all distance. To over-emphasize velocity and height would lose more in the step than would be gained in the jump.

A recognition of the flow or continuity of triple jump action is essential, not merely for performance, - it is inevitable there - but for the sound coaching of per-

The direction of movement is <u>forward</u>-upward, that is, distance by way of height

The line of the thigh is close to the horizontal

Fig. 10.4
The second jump

Compare the action in G-H with that in the long-jump (Figure 9.8   Note similarities, but also that emphasis here is forward, with a lesser effort for height

Both arms tend to be forward (G-J), then back (L-M), in keeping with leg action.

Lowering of the c.g. in action G compresses the springs for their re-bound action in H

JUMP (THE STEP)

formance. Actually, there is no more valid reason for separating figure 10.3F from figure 10.4G, other than the attempt to explain action, than there would be for separating 10.4G from 10.4H. Actually the gather for the explosive spring into the air shown in action H began with figure 10.3F, and even 10.3E. To gain a feeling of continuity, follow the action of the left leg through D-E-F-G-H-J-K. A coach who understands continuity of action will never speak of a deliberate "foot stamp" on each take-off; rather, the entire hip-knee-ankle-foot, along with the arms, flexes smoothly under the lowering weight of the body, then extends explosively upward.

The eyes-head are forward, not up ──>

Both arms are back, ready for the forceful forward thrust of the action N-O

The trail leg swings forward and flexes (J-K), then backward in reaction to extension of the lead leg (L-M). To remain back, extended, would be awkward,and shorten the step

A heel-ball-toe foot placement ──────>

Note how closely action M follows action F

In this third and final jump, an all-out effort is made to integrate height and distance. Velocity has declined so that a compensatory height is crucial. There is a deeper settling of the center of gravity, and an even more resilient re-bound. Follow the action of both arms from figure 10.4L to figure 10.50 as they thrust together upward. Similarly, follow the action of the right leg in these same figures as it drives with full flexion for a greater thrust upward and forward.

The left knee and hip are deeply flexed as is indicated by the extreme bend in the right knee

Fig. 10.50
The third jump

A most forceful effort for height is shown here. The center of gravity is thrust upward at a 20 degree grade

Between figures N to R, arm action changes three times; they lift (O), lower (P), lift (Q), and finally move forward (R-S); all as a significant balancing agent for the actions of the legs: up-back-forward

JUMP

This triple jumper is using a modified "hang" style, advocated by many but especially by Japanese jumpers and coaches. The typical action of this style is that shown in P-Q with the arms up and back and with both legs back. A more extreme "hang" would throw the head back, as in figure 9.9 but this would tend to over-emphasize height when velocity is at min-imum levels. Other jumpers use a simple "sail" style in which the feet are pulled forward for the landing a little earlier than shown here. Lack of velocity on this third jump gives little energy for a hitch-kick or for one or more strides-in-the-air as is often done in the long jump.

With the above modifications, the methods of landing used in the long jump apply here

The aim is to place the feet as far as possible in front of the line of flight of the center of gravity

To prevent the buttochs from touching the pit, the knees and ankles must relax and flex, allowing the c.g. to move forward

The landing action is commonly described as a jackknife style in which (1) both arms and legs are behind the center of gravity (Q), then (2) jackknife together at the landing (S)

207

the shock would be negligible and the reactive power, low. If a medium-soft ball, the shock would be low but the reactive power high. The last would be descriptive of an expert triple jumper.

Dyson (1978, 161) explains the problem in mechanical terms,

The acute angle at which he lands tends severely to check his forward movement. To reduce this resistance, the expert triple jumper moves his leading foot back quickly immediately before landing to reduce its forward speed in relation to the ground, lands with the greatest practicable angle between his leading foreleg and the ground, and then "gives" at the hip, knee and ankle joints. Yet he must stress none of these movements at a cost, subsequently, of essential vertical speed.

This important aspect of triple jumping will be discussed again as related to special exercises that may develop the necessary yielding-reactive power.

HIGH KNEE LIFT. Study of the related Figures will disclose a high knee thrust and carry in each phase. In the first jump this is most pronounced in the takeoff leg as the leg thrusts forward for a long placement ahead of the body's center of weight. Without such a reach there could be no upward jump; the man would simply fall forward. On the second jump, the knee of the lead leg is thrust high and stays there, waiting for the ground to come up. Again, the reach must place the foot ahead of the pelvis if height is to be gained. This is repeated in the third jump, though coordinated with the demands of an economical landing.

EFFECTIVE POWER = TIME-DISTANCE THROUGH WHICH IT IS APPLIED. The significance of the three essentials just discussed can be summarized in terms of the time-distance through which power can be summarized in terms of the time-distance through which power can be applied during the landing and takeoff for each jump. Assuming that power, and therefore greater velocity, is being developed in the related muscles by progressive overloads of special exercises, we must also acquire the skill by which that power can be applied through a greater time-distance. Although Veroshanski stated that he found less flexion in the knee joint among expert long and triple jumpers, he also says later that "the angle of flexion in the knee joint should be optimal so as to . . . achieve a maximal takeoff."

The problem of achieving an optimal flexion in the knee joint, as well as in the ankle, foot, and hips, is what "landing shock," and "high knee lift" and "two-arm thrust" and "a flat forward movement of the pelvis" are all about. As we discuss the details of technique, this essential will take on increasing significance.

FORWARD LEAN. The degree of forward lean during each of the three jumps is crucial to just the right balance of velocity and height. To be well forward tends to aid velocity but decreases height and distance. The high knee lift helps to compensate for this loss. To carry the body erect tends to produce the opposite effect. A small difference in body angle can make a great difference in performance.

SKILL PRACTICE SHOULD NOT BE OVERLOADED. When practicing the skill of the full run and triple jump, there should be no overloading of the action. To wear a weighted vest or other device is to change the coordination and thus disrupt the precise balance and skill that is being learned. (See the related discussion in Appendix A)

THE RUN AND FIRST GATHER. For the details of these phases of the triple jump, we refer you to the related discussions for the long jump. Since the triple jump is a more complex skill than the long jump, mastery of that skill will enable a man to achieve very creditable distances even though he lacks great speed in the run. We were aware of this as related to the world-record Japanese and early Russian triple jumpers. For the first few years of triple jumping, first priority should be given to skill and to the power by which high-level skill is made possible.

However, this in no way implies that speed in the run is not essential for best performance. The faster a man can run, the farther he can jump—assuming he can make full use of the kinetic energy of that run. That's a sneaky sentence but it needs to be stated and its implications need to be used. The length and acceleration of the run, the use of checkmarks, the importance of the gather, are all the same as for the long jump.

TRIPLE JUMP METHODS

Discussion of different methods of triple jumping has been deliberately held back in favor of the essentials of good technique. Method differences cannot be equated, for example, with high jumping styles which are clearly distinct from each other. In the triple jump, such differences are in terms of degree of emphasis on the three phases of the jump, or on the trajectory of each of the jumps, or on the amount of flexion in the lead-leg knee, or in the use of the arms during each of the three jumps. These can be described, not so much as different styles of jumping, as different emphases on the details of jumping.

RELATIVE DISTANCES FOR THE THREE JUMPS. Table 10.1 gives us the actual distances for each of the three phases of the triple jump made during world-record performances. These are acceptably correct, though world statisticians do differ slightly on details. Needless to say, such measurements would be secondary to those of the official triple jump distance.

Our interest however, is for relative distances. These, and the resulting measurements for each phase of triple jumps of different lengths, are given in Table 10.2. Various coaches and researchers have advanced the merits of different ratios, such as the 6:5:6 or 10:8:9 ratios, which we have converted to distance percentages, since these provide a single basis for comparison.

1. 35-30-35 ratio. This was advanced in 1949 by Mikio Oda , the Japanese Olympic champion and coach. In seeking to improve the weak "step" phase of Japanese jumpers, Oda increased the step percentage as compared with the 37.5-25-37.5% they had used previously.

This revision consisted of injecting more speed into the three parts of the jump. In the past we ran about the same distance as in the running broad jump without attaching importance to speed and considering the balance and rhythm after the initial takeoff to be very important.

Thus in the new method we tried to increase the distance of the hop by relying on the speed of the run before the hop, one of the aims being not to overdo the hop (about 20 feet), and to land on the takeoff foot with a very deliberate stamp of the foot, and then to stretch the step over 15 feet. The objective is to extend the overall distance of the jump through speed, rather than by the rhythm of the jump. To do this one must hop lower than formerly and, moreover, one must move his legs quicker.

2. 37-30-33 ratio. In 1957 Pat Tan Eng Yoon[1] made a very exhaustive study of this problem at the world-renowned Loughborough Athletics Training School, England. He concluded his research by recommending Mikio Oda's percentages but also suggested a 37-30-33 ratio which places first relative emphasis on the step, second emphasis on the hop. This method intends that, when all the early phases of the triple jump have been mastered, sufficient momentum will have been maintained to achieve a long final jump. Yoon also suggested that beginners would do better with a ratio of 37-26-37. He agreed that this method de-emphasized the second phase, the step, and was unbalanced for the best performers.

Yoon's ratios were supported by Dietrich Gerner, Brazil, who is reported to have coached Adhemar da Silva for several years. He suggested that the combined distance for the first two jumps should double that for the third, but these figures were gained by averaging the results of past champions, not by reason of research in biomechanics--if such is possible. Such a formula produces a ratio between the hop and step of 5:4, almost identical to that obtained by Yoon.

3. 38-30-32 ratio. Vitold Kreyer[2] USSR National Triple Jump Coach and Olympic bronze medallist at both Melbourne and Rome, recommended this ratio, though with some flexibility as to the precise numbers. He found that beginners do well using a 38-27-35 ratio, and reported: Josef Schmidt: 35-30-35; Viktor Saneyev: 37-30-33; Joao Oliveira: 34-30-36--all of which are consistent with the figures given in Table 10.1.

[1] Pat Tan Eng Yoon, "Research into the Hop Step and Jump," *Clinic Notes, National Collegiate Track Coaches Association,* 1959, 16-41.

[2] Gabor Simonyi, "Vitold Kreyer's Training for Soviet Triple Jumpers," *Track Technique,* #79, Spring 1980, pp. 2505-2508.

TABLE 10.4

RELATIVE DISTANCES OF THREE JUMPS UNDER DIFFERENT RATIO SYSTEMS

Distance	35-30-35 Ratio			37-30-33 Ratio			37.8-28.9-33.3 Ratio		
40	14' 1''	11' 10''	14' 1''	14' 9½''	11' 10½''	13' 4''	15' 1''	11' 6''	13' 5''
42	14' 10''	12' 4''	14' 10''	15' 6½''	12' 5½''	14' 0''	15' 10''	12' 2''	14' 0''
44	15' 6½''	12' 11''	15' 6½''	16' 3½''	13' ½''	14' 8''	16' 7''	12' 9''	14' 8''
46	16' 3''	13' 6''	16' 3''	17' ½''	13' 7½''	15' 4''	17' 4''	13' 3''	15' 5''
48	16' 11''	14' 2''	16' 11''	17' 9½''	14' 2½''	16' 0''	18' 1''	13' 10''	16' 1''
50	17' 7 3/4''	14' 8½''	17' 7 3/4''	18' 6½''	14' 9½''	16' 8''	18' 10''	14' 4''	16' 10''
52	18' 3 3/4''	15' 3½''	18' 3 3/4''	19' 3½''	15' 4½''	17' 4''	19' 7''	14' 11''	17' 6''
54	19' ¼''	15' 11½''	19' ¼''	20' ½''	15' 11½''	18' 0''	20' 4''	15' 5''	18' 3''
56	19' 8 3/4''	16' 6½''	19' 8 3/4''	20' 9½''	16' 6½''	18' 8''	21' 1''	16' 0''	18' 11''
58	20' 5¼''	17' 1½''	20' 5¼''	21' 6½''	17' 1½''	19' 4''	21' 10''	16' 6''	19' 8''

For example, the hop phase for 50 feet under the three ratios would be 17' 7 3/4'' -- 18' 6½'' -- 18' 10''.

The Significance of Ratio Theory. Such ratio systems are of significant value in help-ing us understand the various emphases on the three phases of the triple jump that are most likely to produce maximum performance. They do make clear the crucial importance of balancing the maintenance of momentum with an optimum distance on each jump so as to produce greatest distance. On the other hand, the individual jumper or his coach should not become so concerned about discovering the exactly right ratio that they lose the unity of performance as a whole. Each change in jumping power and skill, or in running speed, will be likely to change the effective ratio.

THE POLISH "FLAT" METHOD. Josef Schmidt, Poland, (1960--55' 10¼''), emphasized speed in the approach run and the maintenance of momentum through both the first and second phases of the jump. To do this, he de-emphasized the gather and upward leap on the first jump, achieving 19' 8¼'', as compared with about 21 feet by long hoppers. He continued this same low trajectory on the second jump, then put all his energies upward in his final effort. As another way of looking at the problem, we can assume that he required fewer seconds for the first two jumps than would the longer and higher jumpers. This "flat" method has general acceptance today. We should add, however, that giving priority to momentum did not lead to neglect of the step, in which Schmidt achieved a very respectable 16' 5¼''.

THE DOUBLE-ARM ACTION. In the early 1950s, the Swedish high jumpers introduced a two-arm upward drive during the gather and takeoff of the high jump. This was adopted and improved by the Russian high jumpers and their coach Dyatchkov, not so much because of the upward impulse given by the arms, as of the lowering of the center of gravity (the pelvis) aided by the swing of the extended arms as they came forward-downward. It was only natural that the Russians should have attempted the use of this same action in the triple jump (Figure 10.6). In the long jump, a two-arm action tends to disrupt the high-velocity gather and takeoff, though un-doubtedly some jumpers are trying to master its difficulties. Similarly, the two-arm action in the triple jump is of doubtful use in gathering for the first jump; most men are following the method shown in Figures 10.1 and 10.7.

Simonyi[1] is convinced by personal experience that this double-arm action is of signifi-cant force value, not only in its own forward-upward drive but also in its effects on body flexion in increasing the time-distance in which leg force can be applied. As the rather ex-tended arms come forward and downward (Figure 10.6), they tend to keep the center of gravity low just an instant longer. The hips now ride flatly forward, thus delaying for an instant the upward extension of the legs and torso. We speak of the springs of action being compressed

---

[1] Gabor Simonyi, op. cit., 1377.

until they can be fully effective. Then they expand quickly with the forceful upward drive of the two arms.

Fig. 10.6. The technique of the two-arm thrust in the triple jump. Its values relate to keeping the pelvis low during the "settle", and to the upthrust at takeoff. It can be used on one, two, or all three of the jumps.

Simonyi is sure that this double-arm action can be helpful for both of the last two jumps, and perhaps for the first jump also.

However, use of the two-arm drive is not an all-or-none problem. It can be modified to meet the specific and different needs of the three jumps. On all three jumps there is a great need to move the pelvis flatly through-and-over whichever leg is involved in the takeoff. This

Figs. 10.7 & 10.8 These two drawings, excerpted from the USSR publication, *Light Athletics*, 1964 #6, show two similarly-styled jumpers. Fig. 10.7 cleared 52'10¼"; Fig.10.8, 53'. Fig. 10.8 seems to get a longer second jump and does use a two-arm thrust on the last two jumps. Also his balance and effectiveness of landing are better on the third jump.

maintains knee-ankle flexion an instant longer and so increases the potential for jumping power. It can therefore be argued that the downward-forward thrust of the two arms is helpful for this reason alone.

On the other hand, each successive jump tends to place greater emphasis on height as it tries to compensate for loss of horizontal momentum. Since height is least in the first jump, the thrust of the two arms should be 90 percent downward-forward. Since height is greatest on the final jump, the thrust of the two arms should be downward-forward plus an explosive upward thrust to add their impulse to that of the body as a whole. Since height is of medium concern in the second jump (or even less if following the Polish "flat" technique), the use of the two-arm thrust should be tempered accordingly. Careful examination of Figs. 10.1, 10.2, 10.7 and 10.8 seems to justify this difference in the precise use of the arms.

POWER EXERCISES FOR THE TRIPLE JUMP

To emphasize the crucial importance of training for the long jump, we deliberately placed Pages 180-1 which include some 25 exercises for the long and triple jumps in that chapter, rather than in this. In addition to these more basic power exercises, the following should be of use in overloading the specific movements of the triple jump or in teaching its various skills:

1. Exercises to Teach Double-Arm Action.

Note: The above figures excerpted from the USSR publication, *Light Athletics*, 1965 #9.

Note in the above figures that the arms are flexed as they swing back-and-up. The time in which they do this when triple jumping is very limited, so that speed of movement is essential. Second, as they drive forcefully forward, they extend downward, thus aiding a flat forward movement of the pelvis, maintaining torso and leg flexion an instant longer, and so increasing the time-distance through which power is applied in the upward jump. This is especially crucial on the third, and to a lesser degree, the second jump.

Fig.10.9a & b. Two examples of depth jumping to develop the "yielding-reactive" power as described by Verhoshanski. Note in item 3 his distinction between different-height tables in developing either power or strength. This difference is significant.

2. <u>Exercises to Overload Jumping Power.</u>

Fig. 10.10. 2 x RRL, and 2 x LLR, then increase distances between boxes by 12"; repeat.

Fig. 10.11. 2 x RRL and 2 x LLR, then increase distances between boxes by 12"; repeat.

Fig. 10.12. 2 x RRL and 2 X LLR. From take-off to box 15'; then increase distance by 12".

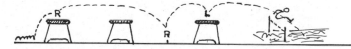

Fig. 10.13. 2 x RRL, and 2xLLR. Absorb landing shock with knee and rebound to top of next box, then over a string for distance.

These illustrations show boxes or stands of very sturdy construction. They should be specially built with wide bases to prevent overturning and possible injury. Height--18 to 24 inches since this produces the proper knee flexion on the rise, as well as an overload on the descent.

Only four exercises are shown. However, a little imagination will produce any number of jump combinations. Rule of thumb--think of a specific movement in triple jumping and overload it. Use a weighted vest or belt when needed for overloading.

3. <u>Exercises to Develop Yielding-Reactive Power.</u> Verhoshanski[1] emphasizes the need for special exercises to develop the power of flexion-extension. It's more than resiliency, the ability to rebound, that is required. The ability to "give" just enough at the right instant, to yield to compression is equally important. To develop this two-phase power, Verhoshanski concluded after research that what he calls depth jumps are most effective. For example, he suggests jumping from a height of either .75 or 1.10 meters (30 or 43 inches), landing on both legs and bounding upward quickly and powerfully. Use of a cloth on a string above the head will motivate higher and higher jumps. To prevent injury and further relaxation, the landing should be made on "a thick elastic or felt cover (a gymnastics mat is not sufficient) resiliently on the forward portion of the foot. The angle of flexion in the knee joint should be optimal so as to soften the landing in the 'yield' phase and achieve a maximum reaction upward."

Verhoshanski warns that such depth jumping needs no overloading such as weighted vests. This would increase strength but slow down the speed of reaction and rebound. He also confirms the exact heights of the depth jumps. At 30 inches, maximum velocity in the yielding-reactive power formula (power = strength x velocity) is achieved; at 43 inches, maximum strength. Increasing table height changes the mechanics of the action so that the exercises tend to lose their meaning for jumping. (We must add that individual differences require a certain flexibility in Verhoshanski's figures.)

---

[1]Yuri Verhoshanski, *op. cit.*

The jumps are done in sets (2 x 10 reps at 30") plus (2 x 10 reps at 43"). Between sets do light running and relaxation exercises. Fatigue effects of these jumps are usually long-lasting. He suggests they be discontinued 10-14 days before important competition.

To prevent knee injury, gradual build-up exercises should precede depth jumping. Beginning jumpers should avoid depth jumps altogether until power training has developed the necessary toughness of tissues. In general, depth jumps are effective only when combined with other power exercises of a reactive-explosive nature.

THE ORGANIZATION OF PRACTICE

The triple jump is a most challenging contest in skill, in resilience in bounding high, not once but three times, in related power in the sense of both strength and velocity of movement, in endurance, and certainly in sprinting speed.

That's an impressive list of necessary qualities. It follows that the organization of a year-round and well-planned training program must be similarly impressive. Perhaps two of the 12 months can be allowed for recreation and renewal, but these should include vigorous activity along with the fun and rest. Of the ten that remain, organization will, as always, depend on the individual, his opportunities for practice, and his competitive schedule.

The overall plan for organization should follow that suggested in Chapter 16, and supplemented in Chapter 6 which review the problems of training for power. More specifically, however, we urge an early emphasis on learning the skill of triple jumping. It's fun to triple jump, even on the first attempt; there's none of the embarrassment or doubt that is inherent in the shot put, when weakness is exposed, or in the pole vault, when skill is lacking. Such early exposure build motivation for the long weeks of power training that lie ahead.

Table 10.5

YEAR-ROUND BASIC TRAINING PROGRAM[1]
(Victor Saneyev, USSR, 3-time Olympic Champion)

Month	10 11 12 1	2 3	4 5	6 7 8	9
Period-ization	PREPARATION PERIOD (I)	COMPETITION PERIOD (I)	PREPARATION PERIOD (II)	COMPETITION PERIOD (II)	TRANSITION PERIOD
Mon.	-Sprinting -Strength	-Rest	Technique -Sprinting	-Rest	-Ball game
Tue.	-Jump power	-Technique -Sprinting	-Jump power -Strength	-Technique -Sprinting	-Rest
Wed.	-Ball game (Active rest)	-Rest	-Rest	-Jump power -Strength	-Ball game
Thu	-Rest	-Sprinting -Strength	-Rest	-Rest	-Rest
Fri.	-Sprinting -Strength	-Rest	-Technique -Sprinting	-Rest	-Ball game
Sat.	-Jump power -Ball game	-Warm ups	-Jump power -Strength	-Warm-ups	-Ball game
Sun.	-Rest	-Competition	-Rest	-Competition	-Rest

[1] Yukito Muraki, "A Study of Selected Prominent Jumpers," *Track & Field Quarterly Review*, Vol. 78 #2, Summer 1978, p. 38.

January 9. Morning. General exercises; jumping up and down on both feet 100 times, from foot to foot 100 times, on one foot 20 times.

Afternoon. In stadium. (1) Five exercises with the shot, repeated four times, (2) 500 m. running and general exercises, (3) 2 × 60 m. with short but fast strides, (4) 2 × 60 m. relaxed running with fast long strides, (5) 2 × 100 m. acceleration runs, (6) 4 × 75 m. of "hops," (7) 3 × 100 m. of "steps," (8) 260 m. with many successive jumps, (9) 50 m. "frog" jumping, (10) 260 m. of "steps," including 97 "steps," and finally (11) 500 m. running. (We can assume that these 500 m. are jogging runs—J. K. D.)

January 10. Rest in morning; General exercises in afternoon.

January 11. Morning. General exercises; jumping on two feet 100 times; jumping from foot to foot 100 times; jumping on one foot 20 times.

Afternoon. (1) 500 m. running; general exercises, (2) 6 × 50 m. acceleration runs, (3) standing hop, step, and jumping eight times (about 8.50 m.), (4) hop, step, and jumping on two feet four times, (5) hop, step, and jumping on one foot three times, (6) 400 m. covered with many successive jumps, (7) 2 × 10 sit ups, (8) strength exercises with a 32 kg. dumbbell, 2 × 10 repetitions, (9) hop, step, and jumping two times, (10) throwing 32 kg. dumbbells 3 × 4 series, (11) swinging dumbbell on the right side (like hammer throwing) eight times, (12) 400 m. covered with many successive jumps, (13) 250 m. running, (14) hop, step, and jumping with dumbbells in hands, two series.

January 12. Morning. General exercises; jumping on two feet 100 times; jumping on one foot 20 times; jumping from foot to foot 100 times.

Afternoon: (1) 1000 m. run, general exercises, (2) weight lifting with barbell. Two arm snatch, 60 kg., 2 × 3 repetitions. 65 kg. twice; 60 kg. once; 70 kg. two times; clean and jerk, 75 kg., three times, (3) jumps with 32 kg. dumbbell, 50 and then 40 times, (4) ten sit ups, (5) standing shot put, eight times, (6) throwing the shot overhead, backwards, six times.

January 13. Rest.

January 14. Morning: General exercises; jumping on two feet 100 times; jumping from foot to foot 100 times.

Afternoon. In stadium. (1) 1000 m. run. General exercises; 50 m. running with short but fast strides, (2) 3 × 100 m. acceleration runs, (3) six starts, (4) 5 × 80 m. performing "hops," (5) 5 × 100 m. performing "steps," (6) 200 m. covered with many successive jumps, (7) 800 m. run.

January 15. Morning: (1) General exercises, (2) weight lifting with barbells, two hand press using 60 kg. once; snatch, 60 kg. four times; snatch 65 kg. twice, 70 kg. once; clean and jerk, 70 kg. once, 75 kg. once, (3) jumps with 32 kg. dumbbell, 43 times and then 41 times, (4) throwing the dumbbell like the hammer 12 times, (5) shot putting nine times, (6) "sit ups," ten times and then eight times, (7) exercises for back muscles with dumbbells, ten times.

Though we might argue the relatedness of some of this training, we cannot question the zeal with which Kreyer prepared for competition.

To achieve such a high level of related condition requires a well-planned year-round program. A rough idea of what is needed can be gained from Table 10.5, an outline of the year-round training of Victor Saneyev, three-time Olympic champion with a PR of 57'2 3/4". At first glance, it does not seem a hardship. Note that during the second competitive period (June-July) he works hard only two days per week, and that during his toughest training period, he takes three days of rest. However, Saneyev was 31 when this was written, had years of training behind him, and so may not have needed the usual tough Russian work schedule.

In terms of workload, that of Vitold Kreyer (USSR, 54'1¼", 1956 & 1960 Olympic bronze medalist) was much heavier, certainly more than the average college jumper could sustain.[1] Note that this is a seven-day schedule during the month of January. The Russian competitive indoor season begins in February.

---

[1]Ruddi Toomsalu, "Training and Technique of Soviet Triple Jumpers," *Track Technique*, Sept. 1960, 26.

PEAKING FOR THE TRIPLE JUMP

In his article, "Triple Jump Peaking," John Gillespie,[1] coach at South Eugene High School, Oregon, gives a down-to-earth summary of year-round training:

This article will discuss methods of peaking triple jumpers for the big meets at the end of the season. It is possible to peak a triple jumper in five separate areas: speed, strength, spring, technique and mental attitude.

Speed is essential to a good triple jump. Basically, the faster the approach, the longer the jump. But speed kills. The beginner, or the veteran at the start of the season, should either run at less than full speed or else use a shorter approach. The jumper is not able to handle too much speed early in the year or his form will deteriorate. Besides, less speed means less force so it is easier to concentrate on jumping and correct technique. In this way the athlete has to improve by jumping farther in each phase rather than allowing improvement because of an increase in momentum. At the end of the season the athlete will be able to handle more speed and will naturally jump farther because of the longer, faster approach.

Sprinting speed itself can also be peaked by gradually shortening the length of interval runs and increasing the tempo. In this way the jumper should actually be faster at the end of the season.

Strength training is vital to triple jumping. The basic weight training principle for peaking is in three parts, plus. In the beginning we lift three days a week for endurance, or lots of repetitions with a medium weight in all exercises. During the preseason and early season we lift three days a week for strength by using only 1-4 repetitions with maximum poundage. Finally, during the middle of the season we change to lifting two days a week and then one day in the late season for quickness. A submaximum weight is used, increasing the repetitions slightly, but trying for quickness or speed. The plus in weight lifting peaking is achieved through rest or no lifting at all during the week of the final meet of the year.

Spring is really a combination of speed and strength. In jumping, however, we shall refer to bounce. One of the easiest ways of peaking a jumper is to control the amount of bounce in his legs. Some of the principles of "bounce control" are: (1) no days off before dual meets but give the athlete a day off prior to a big meet; (2) jumping takes a great deal of bounce out of the legs, so gradually give the jumper more rest between the last jumping practice day and the meet. You can usually jump the day prior to a meet in early season; run only on the day before a meet in the middle of the season, allow two days jumping rest near the end and have no jumping at all the week of the last meet of the season. Also, (3) depth jumping is great for the triple jumper, but it requires a lot of rest. Therefore, gradually give more rest so that there is no depth jumping during the last two weeks of the season.

The principle of technique peaking is to gradually teach the event concentrating on the fundamentals early and saving some ideas that can be picked up easily until later in the season. Stress an upright body position (no forward lean) and heel-ball-toe foot placement during the early season. This will not increase the length of a jump, only put the athlete in position to jump farther. Since most jumpers do not have a long enough step, work on that phase at the start of the season. Then work on the jump at the end. Finally, during the late season emphasize hopping as far as possible while staying low. (A good way of learning this is to practice hopping into the long jump pit with a towel at a specific distance, and gradually increase that distance.) Not only will the athlete hop farther, but he will create more momentum for the rest of the jump. Another late season clue is to have the jumper think about pushing off with the toes during each phase. This helps to create more forward speed.

The positive mental attitude, however, is the most important point in peaking. The athlete needs to pick a goal and believe that he can attain it. We use a system of goal and date pace with our jumpers (similar to distance running) to keep track of how well they are proceeding toward their goal. Auxiliary goals (in related events) give the athlete motivation for training and show progress toward the big goal. The quarter-mile and the long jump are good indicators for the triple jump. Note that it is quarter-mile speed plus the stamina which a triple jumper needs to survive the pounding of six jumps in a meet. Keep reminding the athlete that you are peaking him for the big meet and explain how bounce control and strength peaking work. The more he believes in the system the better it will work.

[1]John Gillespie, "Triple Jump Peaking," *Track Technique*, #73, Fall, 1978, p. 2313.

Chapter 11
THE SHOT PUT

The men that contrived the shot put must have sprung from a long line of Puritan gaolers who believed the stocks which secured both ankles and wrists were the best punishment for the sins of mankind. Of course, the event itself is no promoter of free movement. The shot has no wires by which to create far-flying centrifugal force, no flat surface to aid aerodynamics, no cord grip or long axis to assist being airborne. The shot is inherently a stodgy iron sphere which prefers above all else staying where it's at.

Any man with half a heart would have given such an event all possible freedom. But one of the first rules these masochists set up was that all its action must be restricted to a meager 7-foot circle. Not even a genius could be creative in devising better techniques within such a penned-in area. Oh, a few men have tried; some men just have to try. They tried throwing the ball. But a new rule decreed it must be put or pushed, not thrown. They tried holding the ball at arm's length at the back of the circle, then pulled it forward to its proper position on the neck as they glided toward the toeboard. But another restraining order stated that at no time could the shot drop behind or below the shoulder. As if the impounding circle were not enough, someone conceived a puny 40-degree enclosure within which the shot must land if the effort was to be legal. And then, to curb any remaining shreds of revolt, a new rule shackled the putter even after the shot had landed, and required him to leave the circle from its back half. In sheer unreasoning desperation, the human animal tried to free himself by rotating along a 580-degree arc (the discus style). One claimed a distance several feet beyond that ever achieved by the straight-line method. But problems of falling and fouling led more to failure and frustration than to fame and fortune.

No wonder shot competitors like the great Parry O'Brien seem to be bursting with frustration. No wonder *Time Magazine* once described Parry's performance as "a vaudeville act of O'Brien and O'Brien, with Parry snarling around, sinking into what he calls his 'competitive trance,' beneath which lies the quick temper of a scalded hog." No wonder Joel Sayre, writing in *Sports Illustrated*, had a similar impression of suppressed energy,

He has blue eyes, curly brown hair, a fair skin, high cheekbones and an almost permanent dead-pan expression which he maintains during competition even though he is boiling inside. It is fascinating at a track meet to watch O'Brien even between heaves. He speaks to nobody. He trots up and down the field, sometimes bending nearly double and revolving his clenched fists swiftly as he gives off a series of ferocious woofs. Sometimes he sits in a sort of trance: "working up to the big one" as he calls it. From time to time he will take a snort of liquid honey from a plastic bottle to accelerate his energy. . . .

Interested in the Athletes' Lib movement? Better stay away from the shot put.

TABLE 11.1
OUTSTANDING PERFORMANCES IN THE SHOT PUT

OLYMPIC CHAMPIONS

Date	Record		Name	Affiliation	Age	Hgt.	Wgt.
1952	57' 1½"	17.41	Parry O'Brien	USA	20	6'3"	223
1956	60' 11"	18.57	Parry O'Brien	USA	24	6'3½"	230
1960	64' 6½"	19.68	Bill Nieder	USA	26	6'3"	240
1964	66' 8½"	20.33	Dallas Long	USA	24	6'4"	260
1968	67' 4½"	20.54	Randy Matson	USA	23	6'6½"	265
1972	69' 6"	21.18	Wladyslaw Komar	Poland	32	6'5¼"	276
1976	69' 3/4"	21.05	Udo Beyer	E. Germany	20	6'5"	249
1980	70' ½"		V. Kiselyov	USSR	23	6'2½"	265

OUTSTANDING WORLD RECORD PERFORMANCES -- MEN

Date	Record		Name	Affiliation	Age	Hgt.	Wgt.
1948	58' ¼"	17.75	Charles Fonville	USA	20	6'2"	195
1950	58' 10½"	17.96	James Fuchs	USA	22	6'1½"	224
1956	63' 2"	19.26	Parry O'Brien	USA	24	6'3½"	230
1960	64' 6½"	19.69	Dallas Long	USA	19	6'4"	265
1960	65' 10"	20.07	William Nieder	USA	26	6'3"	240
1964	67' 10"	20.68	Dallas Long	USA	23	6'4"	260
1967	71' 5½"	21.80	Randy Matson	USA	22	6'6½"	265
1973	71' 7"	21.84	Al Feuerbach	USA	25	6'4½"	262
1976	71' 8½"	21.88	Terry Albritton	Hawaii	21	6'4½"	260
1976	72' 2¼"	22.00	A. Barishnikov	USSR	28	6'6¼"	280
1978	72' 8"	22.15	Udo Beyer	E. Germany	22	6'5"	265

OUTSTANDING PERFORMANCES -- WOMEN

Date	Record		Name	Affiliation	Age	Hgt.	Wgt.
1972	69' 0"[1,3]	21.04	N. Chizhoua	USSR			
1976	69' 5"[1]	21.17	Ivanka Christova	Bulgaria	35	5'8"	183
1980	73'8"[3]	22.45	Ilona Slupianek	E. Germany	22	5'11"	198
1979	62' 7 3/4"[2]	19.09	Maren Seidler	Santa Clara,CA	30	6'2"	220
1980	73' 6 1/2"[1]	22.41	Ilona Slopianek	E. Germany	23	5'11"	198

BEST HIGH SCHOOL PERFORMERS

BOYS -- 12# Shot

Date	Record		Name	Affiliation	16# Shot
1968	72' 3¼"[4]	22.03	Sam Walker	Dallas Texas	
1970	71'9 3/4"	21.91	Jesse Stuart	Glasgow, Kentucky	60' 10"
1972	70'1 3/4"	21.79	Ron Semkiw	Pittsburgh, Pa.	
1974	69' 8½"	21.26	Paul White	Russellville, Ark.	
1977	69' 11"	21.32	Vince Goldsmith	Tacoma, Wash.	
1979	81' 3½"[4]	24.80	Mike Carter	Jefferson, Dallas	67' 9"

GIRLS -- (8# Shot)

Date	Record		Name	Affiliation
1975	52' 6½"[4]	16.01	Ann Turbyne	Winslow, Maine
1978	51' 5"	15.69	Carrie Albano	Meadowdale, Wash.
1979	50' 10½"	15.52	Jackie Henry	Lynnwood, Wash.

---

[1]Olympic champion   [2]American record   [3]World record   [4]High school record

A SUMMARY HISTORY OF TECHNIQUE AND PERFORMANCE

This introduction was obviously with tongue-in-cheek, but it does point up the difficulty of setting up a system for explaining progress in the event. The shot has had no 180-degree approach area, as for the high jump, in which various styles could be attempted. It includes no helpful implement, such as a vaulting pole, which has undergone stages of development. As we wrote--it's just a stodgy, apparently uncomplicated sphere, or at least it is until you sell your soul for it, as did such putters as Parry O'Brien or such coaches as Dink Templeton of Stanford, or, if I may, myself, before and after I coached Charlie Fonville.

At the risk of confusing as much as clarifying, the development of the shot can be classified within five periods: (1) that of the hop and wide-open experimentation, (2) that of a 90 percent emphasis on skill, (3) that of Parry O'Brien, (4) that of strength training, and (5) that of a unity of power and skill. Needless to say, actual history never followed any such over-simplified pattern.

SIZE PLUS TRIAL-AND-ERROR. (1875-1934). Few coaches and athletes were interested in the event. Naturally, those few tended to dominate it. For example, G. R. Gray, of Toronto and the NYAC, set his first world record in 1887 at 43' 11", raised it in 1893 to 47", and won his last U. S. title in 1902 at 46' 5". Similarly, Denis Horgan of Ireland continued to compete to the age of 43, winning his first English title in 1893, his last in 1912, and setting his world record at 48' 2" in 1900.

The greatest putter of this period was Ralph Rose, of California and the University of Michigan, whose 51 feet in 1909 stood for 19 years as the world record; some said it would never be broken. His size, though common now, was rare then (6'4"--286#). His style--up and down and around and out. Templeton, Stanford's great weight coach, watched Rose perform many

Fig.11.1 -- Ralph Rose, Michigan, 1909 - 51 feet. (6'4" - 286#).

Fig.11.2 -- Jack Torrance, Louisiana, 1934, 57' 1" (6'4" - 260#). No glide or shift here; rather a hop up and gather in the center.

times. He said Rose began by facing about 45 degrees clockwise to the front of the circle (Figure 11.1). Action started with a high forward kick of the left leg and a high hop across the circle in which his right foot was perhaps six inches off the ground. Upon landing in the center of the circle, a clockwise hitch or rotation of the shoulders tried to ensure greater power. Momentum of the shot across the circle was actually negative as he stopped for the hitchback. But Rose held the world record and most putters followed his style with little variation.

I was learning to put the shot in the middle 1920s and I can recall, somewhat wryly, the ineffective methods we tried. For one year we tried facing the toeboard when at the back of the circle, then rotated clockwise as we hopped high across it. Another year we tried hopping from both feet with no preliminary movements. Needless to say, we and our coach abhorred actions that even hinted of heavy resistance work, though for some reason chopping wood and making home ice deliveries was permitted. Of course, the best shot-putters were making some progress in technique, though Rose's record was not broken until 1928 by Emil Herschfeld, Germany, 51' 9½".

The greatest putter of this so-called "hop" period was Jack Torrance (6'4" tall, 260#) who achieved 57' 1", a distance so amazing that the astute Brutus Hamilton used it as a starting base on which to build a table of human-ultimate performances in all events in track and field. Torrance moved across the circle much faster than Rose, but he too depended mainly on size and natural strength. Figure 6.2 shows him hopping upward, so that he had to hesitate and gather in the center of the circle.

TECHNIQUE 90% -- OTHER FACTORS 10% -- STRENGTH TRAINING 0% (1920-1948). During these decades, the more basic and sound techniques of shot putting were worked out. We have chosen 1920, quite arbitrarily, as beginning with Bud Houser, USC, who won the Olympic shot in 1924 (50'1") and the Olympic discus in 1924 and 1928. Bud was only 6 feet tall and 180#, so that he had to make up in the sound application of force what he lacked in size. (I use the word "size" rather than "strength" deliberately, for strength was not an "in" word in the 1920-1950 period.)

There were many fine technicians during these years--John Lyman, Stan Anderson, Wilbur Thompson--all of Stanford and Templeton-coached, and Hans Woellke of Germany, the 1936 Olympic winner. All these men devoted at least 90 percent of their energies to the virtues of sound technique.

But the all-time Master in terms of body velocity and straight-line explosion across the circle was Charles Fonville, Michigan, who in 1948, though only 195#, 6'2", and 20 years of age, surpassed Torrance's 14-year old record with 58' 3/8". What were Fonville's special assets?

Fig.11.3a. Fonville's shot lowered during the glide, and so aided velocity across the circle.

Fig.11.3 -- Charles Fonville, Michigan, 1948 - 58' 3/8" (6'2" - 195#). No weight training. Year-round practice on technique only. Perfection of skill.

First, an amazing degree of explosive power and quickness of muscle action. Second, a perfection of all the aspects of form which were then approved by the experts, not merely concerning proper position but also in the momentum he achieved across the circle and in the high efficiency with which he coordinated this momentum so that it led to great body force. And third, an ability to concentrate his energies in competitive performance that, to me, his coach, is still beyond the level of understanding. Fig. 11.3 conveys something of his shift of the weight of the hips ahead of the powerful extension of the right leg which drove him across the circle. Notice the way the left foot drives directly and flatly toward the toeboard so there was no hesitation at all in the bracing action of the left leg.

One other man of this period earns mention because of his style of putting--Jim Fuchs, Yale, 58'10 3/4". Jim was not as fast across the circle as Fonville but at the toeboard he did achieve a backward lean so extreme that the line of his back was almost horizontal. This also is crucial in increasing the time-distance in which power is applied, and points a way to future improvement.

STRENGTH 60%--TECHNIQUE 30%--MENTAL PREPARATION 10% (1952-1967.) Both the heading and the dates describe the career of Parry O'Brien, THE Mr. Shot Put of all time. He won two Olympic

Parry O'Brien's shoulders are at right angles to the centerline of the circle. His eyes are focussed along, or even to the right of this centerline.
During the glide, the shoulders and eyes try to maintain these positions.

O'Brien's shot and his body in general rises during the glide. His head at pt.6 is higher than at pt.4. This meant a loss of power.

The heel leaves last, not the toes.

Fig.11.5 -- Parry O'Brien, USC, 1952, 1956 Olympic champion. 1956 world-record holder - 63' 2".

titles (1952, 1956) plus a silver medal in 1960, numerous world records outdoors and in, and a personal-best put of 64'7¼" in 1966 at the age of 35! We have mentioned and will mention again, his tremendous emphasis on emotional training and preparation for competition, which we feel was as useful in shot development as was his invention of better mechanics. Also his use of a program of weight training in the same year (1951) that he adopted his new technique, so that we are inclined to conclude that greater strength was the secret of his tremendous success even more than was his unique style. In fact, he was once quoted as saying "the shot is 60 percent pure strength; 30 percent technique; 10 percent mental."

The crux of O'Brien's style lies in the 10-12 inch rotation clockwise of his right shoulder and torso at the back and in the center of the circle. (Compare the 6th figure in Fig. 11.5 with the 4th figure in Fig. 11.3). Though this may seem a small difference it is actually very significant, for it comes at the beginning of the forward-up impulse, when the shot is moving most slowly and the body's forces are most effective in accelerating the shot's velocity (Dyson, 1967, 35).

Dallas Long, USC, (height--6'4"; weight--246-270) also belongs within this "O'Brien" period. Dallas was weight-trained in high school and college, but his O'Brien technique was superior even to that of the Master. He held his shoulder position steady and his center of weight low as he came across the circle; all with excellent momentum. His first world record (1960, 64' 6½") came at age 20; his final record (1964, 67' 10") at age 24. Though weight training was primary, he did not neglect practice of sound technique.

THE WEIGHT-LIFTERS (1946-present day). Though the dates of this period dovetail with those of the preceding period, the 95 percent concentration on strength training of its champions warrants a separate listing. Most agree that it began with Otis Chandler, now publisher of the *Los Angeles Times*, who in 1946 started lifting weights and putting the shot along with Norman Nourse at Andover Academy. His improvement in distance was immediate but, as happens so often, it required some four or five years before others could accept his radical and "mad" approach. Not even the perceptive coach Templeton gave approval until Chandler's senior year at Stanford.[1]

But then, again as happens so often, some men swallowed strength whole. They argued that muscle-fiber speed is innate; therefore greater speed of movement can come only through greater strength; that is, through greater basic strength regardless of its direct relatedness. Dave Davis achieved 63' 10½" when Dallas Long's world record was 64' 6½", almost exclusively, he said, on a program of heavy-weight lifting. Gary Gubner (6'2", 270#) did 64' 11", and was an active member of the U. S. international weight-lifting team. One of the better articles on the subject is by Joe Henderson[2],

Today's bigger, more powerful shot putters owe their amazing progress to weight training more than anything else. The world record is 13 feet beyond the 1950 figure, and last year (1968) 50 men topped 60 feet....The means--weightlifting for shotputting success- almost seems to be an end in itself, lifting for its own sake. They love it..... (The following) statistics apply to the time the athlete was doing his best putting:

	Long	Gubner	Matson	Steinhauer	Woods
Best Put	67'10½"	64'11½"	71'5½"	68'11¼"	72'2 3/4"
Body Weight	270	280	265	270	295
Bench Press	550	500	425	440	480
Squat	500	630	505	600	635
Incline Press	475	440	325	---	445
Dead Lift	---	700	---	715	600

---

[1] As confirmed by a personal letter to me dated 4/14/70.

[2] Joe Henderson, "Weight Training Yields Power," *Track & Field News*, 11 March 1969, 20.

<u>Randy Matson</u> (Texas A & M, 6'7", 265#).
Randy Matson's best put (1967, 71'5½") was at
least three feet 7½" beyond that of any previous shotputter--a "human ultimate" some
thought. But even today, the sources of his
great achievement are somewhat of an enigma.
He wasn't strong, as compared with the weight-
lifters of shotputting. He wasn't fast across
the circle, as compared with O'Brien or certainly with Fonville. But he did evidence
tremendous power at the front half of the
circle--power in the sense of velocity x
distance x force. His coach, Charlie Thomas,
wrote me in October 1965,

*On the push off or glide Randy keeps his
shoulders well back and shifts only the
weight of his left leg and hips; consequently the toes of the right foot leave
the ground at the back of the circle
last, not the heel as does O'Brien.
With Matson's size and power (fast, explosive power) he does not have to rely
on speed to the center of the circle from
the push off. We think the position in
the center of the circle is more import-*

Fig. 11.6. Basic strength training: the
means to speed-power and greater distance
in the shot put, even at a loss in skill.

*ant than speed up to it....If you study films on the good boys I think you will find that
Matson is much faster than Long and O'Brien from the upward motion in the center of the
circle through to the release--here is where he applies speed and power. He is slower
than others from the push off to the center.*

Actually, neither Matson nor his coach had much concern for perfecting technique, as compared with Parry O'Brien, Dallas Long and a 50-year tradition in shotputting. Coach Thomas
wrote that in his senior year, twice-a-week practices on skill, "if he can immediately throw
64-65-66 feet, he will only throw 5-6-7 times. I think that most coaches will agree that
technique reaches a leveling-off period kind of early." Compare this minimum view with the
90 percent emphasis on skill of 26 years before, as evidenced in my own writings,[1]

*Practice on the skills of shot-putting should occur five times per week during eight or
nine months of the year. During a 90-minute workout, a man should make as many puts as
he can. Three or more shots should always be available and rolled back by the coach or
manager so that there is no delay between puts. A hundred puts is not too many.*

True, we were over-balanced then, but surely not completely so. While agreeing with Matson's assumption that explosive power at the front of the circle should have high priority
over velocity across it, it is hard to believe that mastery of that specific skill can be
gained or even maintained by two or three practices a week, only about six months of the year,
and only a dozen or so puts per session. Certainly I can think of no other event in or out of
sports in which highest-level skill can be so maintained, let alone improved.

How then can one explain Matson's tremendous performances, considering his lack of practice
on technique and lack of strength as compared with other great putters? True, he worked hard
on skill in high school, and skill does tend to be retained. But the better answer has two
aspects. First, Randy's muscles had an inborn explosiveness, a high-velocity factor. He may
not have been strong but he was powerful, as is suggested in the formula (power = velocity^6
x strength^4). Second, Matson was tall (6'7") and kept his weight well back over the right
foot at the front of the circle. Therefore the distance through which his high-velocity power
was applied probably exceeded that of any previous putter.

---

[1]J. Kenneth Doherty, *MODERN TRACK AND FIELD*, Englewood Cliffs, N.J.: Prentice-Hall, Inc.,
1953. 332.

This advantage apparently impressed the East German coaches[1] to the point of deliberately shortening the glide so as to increase the spread of the feet at the front of the circle and so the distance of power application. By-passing the possible values of this method, it is of interest that they found Matson's glide to be 0.83 meters (2'8 3/4") as compared with Briesenick's (E.G.--70'8") 0.68 meters (2'3"). Briesenick's wide putting-stance gave him a power-application distance of 1.70 meters (5'7"). Another East German, Gies, applied force even longer--1.82 meters (6'10"). No comparable figures are given for Matson. For the record, the height of Briesenick's shot at the start of delivery was 1.16 meters (3'9 3/4"); at the end, 2.27 meters (7'5½"), a difference of 1.11 meters (3'7 3/4").

A BALANCE OF STRENGTH-VELOCITY-SKILL-MENTAL PREPARATION.

Though this fifth period in the evolution of shotputting began a quarter-century ago with Fonville, O'Brien, Long and Matson--each contributing his portion on either side of the balance scale--Al Feuerbach (Emporia State College, 6'1", 250#) was the first to put it all together with his world-record put of 71'7" in 1973. Bob Daugherty wrote,[2]

> *Feuerbach trains almost the same--year-round, doing both weight and technique training. However, perhaps more than any other world-class performer, Feuerbach stresses technique and actual throwing in practice. (He says,) "In this country, there's too much emphasis on strength development and not enough on technique development. You have to train your nervous system to throw with more speed and explosiveness. Throw, throw, throw."*

To which I of course add my loudest-possible "Amen" and even "Bravo"! Maximum performance in any human skill--shotputting, high jumping, flag-pole sitting or thumb-twiddling--requires balanced, year-round practice over many years; the greater the number of years, the more the emphasis on the perfection of skill, on what only the real Masters comprehend--the artless art of highest-level performance. Feuerbach says,[3] "The key is the mind. It takes ingenuity and a type of creativity to utilize all the things that are already known about the nervous system, muscular system, and so forth. You need an intelligent plan of attack."

But even "perfect" skill must give way to greater power-with-skill. In 1974, George Woods (Southern Illinois University, 6'2", 290#) put the iron shot indoors 72'2 3/4", and gave indications of putting it even further. His technique was excellent but to this was added some forty pounds of muscle power and an extension of at least one inch in power application. Just before the 1972 Olympic Games Woods achieved a personal-best standing put of 65'7" followed by a personal-best practice put across the circle of 72'10" the same day.[4] Sixty five feet seven inches! That suggests 90 percent of putting distance is derived from raw power; only 10 percent from the velocity-skill across the circle. Clearly human ultimates are still in the future.

In 1978, Udo Beyer, E. Germany (22, 6'5", 265#), the 1976 Olympic champion, achieved 72'8" (22.15m) by means of a sound balance of the essentials, but it was clear such balance at higher levels was, not merely possible, but certain.

For some 30 years or more, various putters had played with a new discus or rotational style. The small 7-foot circle was a great handicap, but finally, 1976, Barishnikov (USSR, 6'6¼", 280#) confirmed the value of the method through a world-record 72'2¼". Full explanation of the method in this OMNIBOOK follows that of the Feuerbach (O'Brien) style.

---

[1]"Shot Put the East German Way," by the Staff of *Modern Athlete and Coach*, in *Track Technique*, #57, Sept. 1974, p. 1814.

[2]Bob Daugherty, "Al Feuerbach," *Track Technique*, #58, Dec. 1974, p. 1852.

[3]Bob Daugherty, Ibid.

[4]Fred Wilt, "George Woods," *Track Technique*, #56, June 1974, p. 1786.

RELATED EXPLOSIVE POWER

Development of explosive power for the shot put must first establish a foundation of basic strength. Such strength for shot-putting, as for all field events, is centered about the mid-section of the body, in the muscles of the lower back, sides, and abdominal area. Exercises for such muscle groups have been described in Chapter 6.

But power training for the shot-putter must enable him to put the shot farther; he is not concerned about his reputation as the strongest weight-lifter in the shot-put competition. Exercises for the development of shot-put power, therefore, must also be closely related to and even imitate all the power movements of putting the shot. It really requires little knowledge of human anatomy or of biomechanics to identify these movements and to devise power exercises directly related to them.

First, the horizontal glide across the circle requires great power in the leg extensors-- especially of the right leg--to initiate the action. Then the hamstrings of the right must flex the knee explosively so as to pull the lower leg across and under the body's center of weight at center circle. Inadequate power in those muscles produces an inadequate shift--not fast enough and probably not far enough. Practice the shift within a discus circle or on any concrete surface, using a heavily weighted vest or belt. Exaggerate both the velocity and the distance of the glide. In fact, this can become a backward standing hop for distance--right foot only, with or without weights. Using a weighted vest aids in keeping a horizontal line of the torso during the shift.

Second, as the right foot lands at center circle, an explosive rotation of the hips counter-clockwise produces a reactive clockwise rotation of the right shoulder. This puts the related torso muscles on stretch and increases the time/distance through which power is applied. This rotation upward is tremendously fast, and requires repetition of these movements, using weights heavier than that of the shot--a heavily-weighted vest or belt, for example. With the shot in its usual position, do this exercise with a glide. Plant the right foot at right angles to the circle diameter. Concentrate on an explosive rotation of the hips but also try to accelerate the forward movement of the shot, with no hesitation or slow-down between the glide and rota-tion. It will be found that correct placement of the left foot--hard against the toeboard-- is of critical importance.

Third, one must devise power exercises related to extensions of the extremities--of the legs-ankles-feet, and of the right arm-wrist-fingers. Examples of these are shown in the double-page of drawings, and need no further explanation.

In all of this, perhaps the most important point relates to the degree of commitment and effort. Power training cannot be realized from a short-time, half-effort approach. Early progress should be gradual, unhurried. Late-season efforts should be at maximal levels of power. That means continuous, year-round increments of effort and resistances, not unlike the gradual increments of endurance training done by modern distance runners. Greater related power tends to be the result of greater related effort over a longer period of time.

RELATED POWER EXERCISES

Imitative putting with Perrin rubber cable. Isometric and isotonic. Increase resistance by shortening cable.

Hamstrings flexion.

Bicycle with weights.

SHOT

Isometric leg extension

One-arm press.

Wrist extension.

Push-up, finger-tips.
Weights (sand-bags) can be added.

THE WHOLE ACTION

Fig. 11.7--Al Feuerbach (Emporia State College, 6'1", 250#, 1973 world record--71'7"). After studying Feuerbach's technique very carefully, and reviewing the details of technique by the many great champion shot putters of the past 75 years, it is my judgment that he put it all together more perfectly than any other--and I'm weighing the special merits of such men as Charles Fonville, Parry O'Brien, Dallas Long and Randy Matson. Matson was 6'6½" tall--5½" more than Feuerbach--and that gave him a significantly greater time-distance through which to apply his power at the front of the circle. Feuerbach lacked that asset but in his mastery of shot-

putting technique as a whole, he was supreme--the first modern Great to believe and practice-- "Technique is what counts in skill events like the shot: I spend at least 60% of my training time on technique, 40% on strength work."

Figures 1-10 show the preliminary movements that, though of minor significance in themselves, are so important in setting the pattern of the entire put. The left arm is relaxed, even limp. The eyes are focussed at 90 degrees downward. The left foot rises (Figure 8) to balance the body weight dropping down, but no higher than necessary. Note that the foot in 9

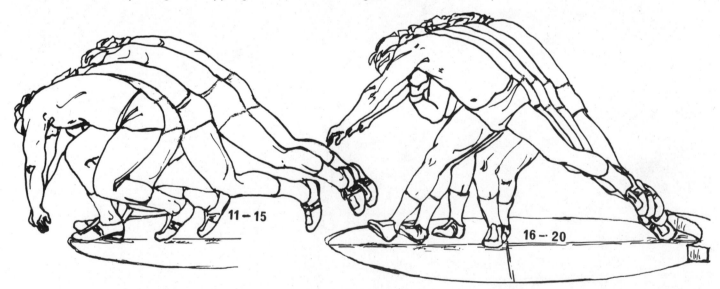

and 10 is dropping down to the just-off-the-ground position of Figure 11. The right foot points straight back to 180 degrees to the toeboard.

The glide begins by shifting the weight of the buttocks across the circle and extending the left leg--keeping the foot as low as possible (Figs. 15-16)--toward its crucial spot (Fig. 21)

228

with the toe in line with the heel of the right foot. The important
action of pulling the right foot from the back to the center of the
circle (Figs. 11-19) is very difficult to do with great quickness
and precise timing; in fact, only specifically related power training can make it possible. Note that the heel leaves last (14-16).

The line of the back, horizontal at the start (Fig. 11), does
rise gradually--and this may be Feuerbach's one flaw in technique--
to that in Fig. 21. A lower line would help to increase the
time-distance of power application in which he is deficient as a
consequence of his short height. In Figs. 11-21, Feuerbach's
eyes--though he says he is unaware of this--are still focussed on
the rear of the iron circle, one method of trying to stay low
during the glide.

Feuerbach considers the placement of the right foot in Fig. 21
of great importance. Centered on the line that bisects the toeboard, it is just behind and parallel with the circle centerline.
To plant the foot at a 30 to 60-degree angle (O'Brien, Fig.11.5)
is to slow hip rotation and decrease stretch-reflex of the upper torso muscles. In contrast, Feuerbach's parallel position
aids rotation and increases stretch-reflex that not only ensures
greater power in the related muscles but also the time-distance through which that power can be applied.

The double function of the left leg (21-27) as a brace or
fulcrum for the right-leg power unit, while also "yielding" so
as to conserve its own power is shown clearly in Figs. 21-30.

Fig. 11.7a--Full explosive
extension.

Its subsequent explosive extension (27-30) adds significantly to the power (force x velocity x
distance) behind the shot.

The rotation of the left shoulder-arm (21-30) is as "straight-line" as possible; that is,
there is a minimal swing of the left arm away from the line of the put. Study Fig. 11.7a; note
that the fingers of the left hand are shown close to the chest; the left elbow is down and close.

HOW TO BEGIN
How to begin is more a problem in arousing and maintaining enthusiastic motivation than one of body mechanics, though actually the two are inseparable.   A wise coach will first decide just how he can get this big and, at least potentially, powerful young man to complete his first put and his first day's practice with a sense of excitement. "This is something I want to do and feel I can do well."

Such a sense of future success must always begin with some feeling of success today, no matter how small or how deliberately contrived. One way open is to build strength first before touching the shot. How to begin, then, will be found by reference to the sections on power training (Chapter 6).   Basic strength is the initial goal but this will later need to be supplemented by power training more related to the muscles and pattern of movements of shotputting. A gradual approach requires weeks, even months of regular training. Be patient! If the prospect seems to forget he's a shotputter in his enthusiasm for greater power, so much the better. That will simply raise the base from which he starts his putting.

Sometimes, however, these weeks of power training are not possible, or the coach or athlete is unwilling to sacrifice the early-season meets in order to build a foundation of power. One worthwhile suggestion is to use a lighter weight shot in the first practices: a 12# for the 16; or an 8# for the 12. The putter now has a feeling of explosiveness and his distance compares well with that of the better conditioned men. He can see the validity of the coach's statement, "All you need is time, practice, and some weight-lifting. Right now, you're just not strong enough." So he comes back tomorrow, and the next week. He begins to believe he's a shot-putter.

Another good suggestion is to keep him away from the other shot prospects during his first practices. If he's going to feel awkward or weak, let him do so alone, or with only the coach. While he's alone, try to concentrate his interest in *how* rather than in *how far*. In doing this, emphasize the most basic fundamentals only; make it sound simple; not easy, but simple. For example, keep hitting hard on the idea of a straight-line put, of the shot travelling along a single plane from the first movement until it lands. Or, concentrate on the up-over-and-out action which involves the upward drive of the right leg and the lift of the head. Those two ideas alone will keep him involved for some days. Sure he wants to compete, but for a while let his competition be with himself and that iron ball.

Teach him how to put from a stand first, preferably away from the toe-board since that makes just one more distraction. Then have him try shifting on concrete but away from the circle; first without, then with the light-weight shot. This shift requires real strength in the legs and a complex coordination of the entire body. It looks easy when the champion does it; it's tough when you try it yourself. That right leg has to be tremendously strong and fast to catch up with the body's imbalance and get under the center of weight. Try to get him to over-shift, to shift four or five feet so he'll get a sense of movement along the ground.

Take it easy on those fingers and that wrist. Too much putting too soon may strain the tendons and hold a man back for some weeks.

In most cases, however, time for power training is available. The prospect now reports to the shot circle strong and ready for full action. After a few preliminaries to get the feel of things, such a man should be able to try the entire putting action across the circle on his first day of practice. To restrict such a man to a series of so-called progressions (a step-by-step approach) is to waste valuable time and dilute enthusiasm. He's put in his period of disciplined training; now let him enjoy the fruits of his work. Even for him, however, keep your coaching simple: fundamentals first; details, only as they are related to fundamentals.

ESSENTIALS OF TECHNIQUE

HOW TO HOLD THE SHOT

The shot should rest on the base of the fingers and high on the thumb.

Some, for greater strength, hold the fingers closer together, and the little finger behind the shot; ⟶

Others widen the fingers with the little finger on the side for better control.

Fig.11.9 - Parry O'Brien. Right forearm is well below shoulder level with about 90 degree flexion at the elbow.

Fig.11.10 - Dallas Long, 67' 10", 1964 Olympic champion.

PUTTING FROM A STAND

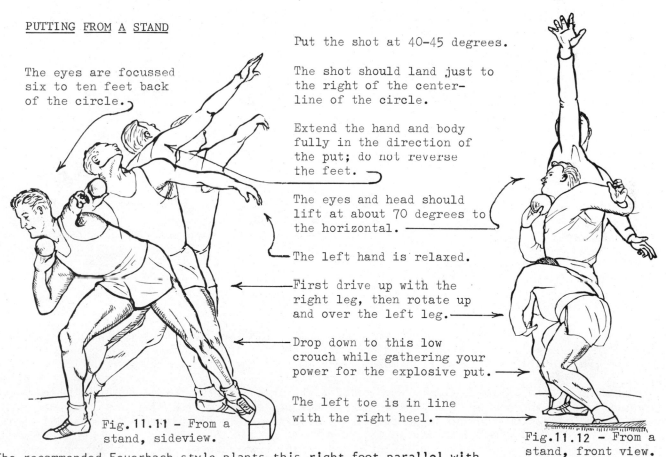

The eyes are focussed six to ten feet back of the circle.

Put the shot at 40-45 degrees.

The shot should land just to the right of the center-line of the circle.

Extend the hand and body fully in the direction of the put; do not reverse the feet.

The eyes and head should lift at about 70 degrees to the horizontal.

The left hand is relaxed.

First drive up with the right leg, then rotate up and over the left leg.

Drop down to this low crouch while gathering your power for the explosive put.

The left toe is in line with the right heel.

Fig.11.11 - From a stand, sideview.

Fig.11.12 - From a stand, front view.

The recommended Feuerbach style plants this right foot parallel with the circle center-line.

PRELIMINARY MOVEMENTS

When using the full circle, shotputters usually make certain preliminary movements that establish the rhythm of action across the circle. Feuerbach's movements are best understood by studying carefully Figure 11.7 (1-3). But however they are made--with what speed or pattern--they must be repeated until they are always the same, until balance and relaxation and rhythm become automatic.

THE SHIFT
The shift of the weight of the body and the shot across the circle, while holding the head and shoulders back in a powerful putting position, requires great power (strength and speed) in the related leg muscles. Although the right foot is last to leave the back of the circle, it must be pulled very rapidly under the body's center of weight before the upward drive can be started. If this action is slow, the foot will not shift far enough, and both momentum and power will be lost. A pre-season program of related strength exercises, especially of the push-off and pull-under, will aid greatly. During early season, try shifting as far as possible, with a 40-50# sandbag on the left shoulder, or with a heavily-weighted vest.

During the shift, the upper body (shoulders, head, eyes) must be held steady. There is a strong tendency (1) to let the shoulders fall forward across the circle with the hips, (2) to anticipate the forward rotation by swinging the eyes around, and (3) to straighten the body so as to lose the low powerful putting position. Such actions do aid momentum across the circle. But they lose much more in force for the up-over-and-out drive of the shot than they gain in momentum.

Various methods have been used to maintain both body torque and a low shot position. O'Brien fixed his eyes about ten feet directly back of the circle; others held this line of vision but rotated it to the left 15 degrees or so. This helped, but eye focus did not fix body position; torque was decreased; the shoulders did lift.

Fig. 11.14. The glide or shift across the circle, as done by Al Feuerbach.

Feuerbach took this method a step further by focussing his eyes down vertically at the back of the circle (Figure 11.14-6). By fixing a point on the rim about 10 degrees clockwise to the right of the centerline, he was much more likely to hold torso torque and angle.

A second method is to concentrate on holding unchanged (1) the position of the shoulders during the shift, or (2) of the right forearm and shot, or (3) of the left arm. Any one of these may be effective and should be tried. It is extremely difficult to flex-extend-flex the right leg in minimal time with no rise in torso angle or lift of the c.g. It is extremely difficult to avoid the gross error of anticipating the upward thrust against the shot during the shift. But it must be done. The power drive at the front of the circle provides some 90 percent of shot distance. Any loss of time-distance through which such power is exerted will more than negate what might be gained from full-circle momentum.

Note in Figure 11.14 that the line of Feuerbach's right foot in the center of the circle is about parallel with the circle diameter. Since his left foot is placed properly and quickly, this right-foot position speeds the explosive drive up-and-out.

MOMENTUM ACROSS THE CIRCLE

The final velocity of the shot at the last whip-cracking flick of the fingers starts with the first movement of the body at the back of the circle. Other factors such as balance and position being equal, the greater the acceleration of movement throughout the shift, the greater will be the shot's final velocity. Momentum is started by shifting the weight of the body off its base (the right foot) in the direction of the put. The heavy hips "fall" toward the toe-board (Figure 11.14), aided by the throw or backward kick of the left leg, and later, the powerful extension of the right leg.

Momentum across the circle is gained primarily by shifting the great weight of the hips across the circle. How far should they be shifted? Most shot putters have followed O'Brien's example, have shifted the hips so far and so fast as to cause the right heel to be the last to leave the back of the circle (Figs. 11.15 and 11.16). Explosive extension of the right leg increases momentum.

In general, a coach should avoid a direct emphasis on momentum across the circle. In general, a man will shift naturally at the natural speed of his muscles or in terms of the acquired strength and skill he now possesses. On the other hand, technique affects momentum. No putter could move fast with the methods taught 30 years ago. The method that is taught by which the putter moves across the circle will establish the limits within which the natural speed of the putter can be effective. The less time in the air during the shift, the greater the momentum across the circle.

HIP ROTATION AND STRETCH-REFLEX

Placement of the right foot parallel with the circle center-line (Fig. 11.14) puts the right hip in a relatively open position from which it rotates explosively to the left, producing a counter-rotation of the right shoulder to the right. The torso muscles are now "on stretch"-- at greatest contractile and time-distance power. This is a great advantage of the Feuerbach over the O'Brien style.

Fig. 11.15 The glide by Al Feuerbach is more straight-line than is that of O'Brien. The c.g. remains lower; the angle of the torso to the ground is less; the left foot, low to ground, will land sooner.

Fig. 11.16 -- The shift or glide across the circle. From a photo of O'Brien. In contrast to Matson, O'Brien's try for quickness across the circle caused him to shift his weight so that the heel was last to leave the back of the circle. Note the eye-focus on the spot six feet directly back of the center of the circle.

THE LEFT FOOT AND LEG

Correct placement and action of the left foot is a major factor in the powerful action of up-over-around-and-out. Figure 11.18 indicates the range of probable placement at the toe-board. Position "1" provides a closed stance and a solid brace or fulcrum which would force an upward drive, but rotation would be hindered. The shot would tend to land too far to the right. Action would be slowed and less powerful.

Position "4" would be "in the bucket." Rotation would be free but there could be little bracing action or upward drive of the left leg. The body would rotate and tend to fall off to the left. Usually, the shot would land to the left and at a lesser distance. There could be little follow-through up-and-out behind the shot.

This "in the bucket" position occurs (1) when the left leg is thrown too high or too far to the left across the circle and makes a late landing at the toe-board *after* body rotation has started; (2) when the eyes lose their focus upon the spot at the back of the circle and swing around too soon, rather than up-and-around; and (3) when, in summary, the "J" rotating action occurs too soon.

Position "2" is best of all. The toes of the left foot are about in line with the heel of the right. The left foot can now serve momentarily as a fulcrum, then as an aid to the upward drive. At the same time, it gives the hips full freedom to rotate upward (Figures 11.17, 11.18).

It must be added that shot putters who attain great momentum across the circle make crucial use of the toe-board. The left foot slams hard against it at exactly the right moment and the right placement. A really great shot-putter should feel without measuring that a circle is one inch too wide.

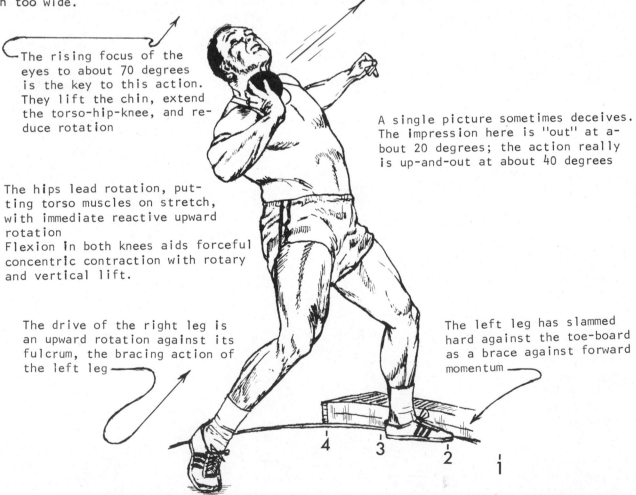

The rising focus of the eyes to about 70 degrees is the key to this action. They lift the chin, extend the torso-hip-knee, and reduce rotation

A single picture sometimes deceives. The impression here is "out" at about 20 degrees; the action really is up-and-out at about 40 degrees

The hips lead rotation, putting torso muscles on stretch, with immediate reactive upward rotation
Flexion in both knees aids forceful concentric contraction with rotary and vertical lift.

The drive of the right leg is an upward rotation against its fulcrum, the bracing action of the left leg

The left leg has slammed hard against the toe-board as a brace against forward momentum

Fig. 11.18 -- Taken from photo of Parry O'Brien, emphasizing proper placement of the left foot. This drawing by Oren Lyons of Roselle, N.J.

234

UP-OVER-AROUND-OUT-EXPLOSIVELY

By far the most powerful (strength x velocity) action of putting the shot lies in the explosive upward extension of the massive back and leg muscles, the same muscles that are strengthened by the squat, dead lift and pull-up and press. O'Brien described his style as a "J" action, one that drives up first, over the braced left leg, then around and out in the direction of the put.

Note that to be able to drive up, one must first be down; to be able to apply force counter-clockwise in rotation, one must first be rotated clockwise. *That is, it is no advantage at all to assume an "O'Brien" position at the back of the circle, if the shoulders are allowed to come up and rotate forward during the shift across the circle.*

THE FOLLOW-THROUGH

The follow-through is of crucial importance to skilled shot-putting: (1) in extending the time-distance through which power can be applied behind the shot, and (2) as an active effect of earlier correct actions. When all preceding movements have been along the plane of the put, or, to take account of O'Brien's "J" style, have been directly related to that plane: (1) when balance and control have been maintained throughout; (2) when the eyes and head have not been too low or too high, too far to the left or held back too far to the right; (3) when the toes of the left foot have landed at the toe-board in line with the right heel, then follow-through in direct line with the put will occur naturally and even inevitably.

However, it does help the putter to know that, after the final push of the fingers, they and the body in general should extend out in the direction of the put. (See especially Figures 11.3, 11.5 and 11.19). A proper follow-through has several phases: a lift of the eyes and chest, an arching of the back, a rotation of the upper body but not beyond the line of the put, a propulsive upward extension of the left leg in which the left foot leaves the ground an instant before the shot leaves the fingers.

FOULING

Some may ask whether such a follow-through will cause fouling? On the contrary, a proper follow-through will prevent fouling. Since the forces of the body are directly in line with the flight of the shot, an opposite and equal reaction will tend to drive the body back into the circle. Fouling is much more the effect of imbalance and non-alignment than of over-extension of the body.

However, none are perfect, and a tendency to foul haunts many. Preventive steps include: (1) establish non-fouling habits in practice just as in meets, never foul through carelessness; (2) at the moment the shot leaves the fingers, drop the eyes down to the toe-board; (3) lower the center of gravity by flexing and relaxing the right knee and hip; (4) keep the left leg in line with the direction of the put.

CONTROLLED RECKLESSNESS

In shot-putting, as in all great competitive efforts, there must be a degree of recklessness, of setting aside all caution, of ignoring all the rules of proper technique, of blanking-out all doubts and distractions. The great shot-putter, in practice as in competition, so masters the details of technique that he can concentrate completely on the wholeness of the putting action. All his physical-mental-emotional powers are channeled in terms of putting the shot, much as a hypnotized subject centers all his energies on some directed goal, or as a madman performs feats of strength far beyond his normal powers.

Such reckless competitiveness is inborn; some have it more than others; but all have it within a wide range of possible action. An athlete reaches the upper level of his own range by the usual methods of learning, not by some mysterious inner magic, by related practice, every day and in competition.

This book has emphasized the techniques of putting the shot. In general, proper technique aids performance. But no over-serious concern for technique should be allowed to distract from concentration on all-out performance. The distance the shot travels is your real goal, not merely perfection of the mechanics of technique.

THE DISCUS-STYLE SHOT PUT

The discus-style shot put has now been used in competition for a score or more of years, time enough in which to establish its potential and useable value. The first is certain. Using this style, at least two men (Barishnikov and Oldfield) surpassed the then-existing world record. The second--its widespread use, its time required for mastery, its consistency in competitive performance, its actual gain as compared with the O'Brien style--all these are still to be established.

Barishnikov and Oldfield both did better with the discus style than they had ever done with the O'Brien style. But it took some seven years of inconsistent performance before Barishnikov attained his best distance of 72'2¼". No one can know how far he might have put if the same time-effort had been used in mastering the O'Brien style. Oldfield had a similar history.

The point of view taken here is admittedly conservative. The main questions are: To what extent is the discus style easier or more difficult to master? What are the best methods for ensuring balance-control and gradual acceleration during the back half of the circle, without diminishing power during the front half?

HISTORY OF STYLE DEVELOPMENT. Claims for discovery of the discus style come from many sources, including at least four nations. I remember, for example, that in the 1940s, Fred Tootell, world-record hammer thrower and coach at Rhode Island, told me of his own experiments with a hammer-style put of the shot--for fun. He thought it had potential. In the early 1960s, without knowledge of any other similar efforts, Bob Ward, coach at Fullerton College, encouraged various shot putters to try the rotation method. One, John McGrath, after graduation from Occidental, won the 1963 AAU title at 63 feet, using the discus style.

Tom Ecker[1] credits Toni Nett, West German author-coach with articles on the discus style in *Die Lehre Der Leichtathletik*, written in the early 1950s. Similarly, Fred Wilt[2] cites a 1957 article by Kerssenbrock, West Germany, in which he used a photo-sequence of a Czechoslovakian hammer champion, Josef Malek, to illustrate a rotation style. The *Yessis Review of Soviet Sports*[3] credits Coach Viktor Alexeyev with teaching "two young shot putters the circular swing in the 1950s. Certainly he coached Alexander Barishnikov who brought world-wide attention to the style with his 1976 Olympic bronze medal and later world record of 72'2¼".

But the most shocking of all shot-put performances, regardless of style, was that by Brian Oldfield of 75 feet even, in a professional meet on May 10, 1975. Oldfield (30, 6'5", 275#) had put the shot, O'Brien style, for some ten years or more,

> *I started using the rotation style about three years ago (1972), just playing with it, although I had seen John McGrath use it in the 1968 AAU. I tried it then but just fell down. But I soon discovered that I was getting better throws this way--and I didn't even know what I was doing...Having made a study, I now know what shot putting truly is...This is THE style, although it's taken me three years to learn how to do it.[4]*

Having occurred in professional meets, Oldfield's performances have received no official recognition. But a put of 72'6½" was measured and his shot weighed as being 3½ ounces heavy by none other than Bert Nelson of *Track & Field News*. We have no such authentication of the 75-foot effort.

Sequence photos of Oldfield's style indicate a more upright body throughout the turn. In contrast to Barishnikov, his eyes focus horizontally and the line of his back is upright at

---

[1]Tom Ecker, "The Whirl Just Might be Better," *Track & Field News*, June 1975, p. 49.

[2]Fred Wilt, "Oldfield Revolutionizes the Shot," *Scholastic Coach*, Sept., 1975.

[3]Viktor Alexeev, "Alexander Barishnikov in the Shot Put," *Yessis Review of Soviet Sports*, Vol. 8 #2, June 1973.

[4]Brian Oldfield, "As The Whirl Turns," *Track & Field News*, May 1975, p. 49. Note: This was written after his put of 72'6½" but before his 75-foot put on May 10.

Fig. 11.19--Alexander Barishnikov (USSR, 28, 6'6¼", 280#). Study of a 33-frame sequence-photo (taken 1975) of Barishnikov suggests torso-legs whirling around a head held steady along the circle diameter. At the back of the circle, his eyes focus straight down at his feet. He crouches low until the line of his back is horizontal, knees bent at about 120 degrees. Keeping his eyes down vertically so that his head stays close to the circle diameter that bisects the toeboard, he leads the "whirl" with his right knee. The shift of weight from left foot to right foot at center circle is very rapid; actually the left toe leaves the ground at the instant that the ball of the right foot touches ground. During this action, the right knee angle increases to about 140 degrees and the line of the back lifts to about 60 degrees to the horizontal.

In this photo series, his left leg swings high and wide to an in-the-bucket position to the left of the toeboard. This fault, inherent in the rotation style, must have been corrected in his world-record put of 72'2¼". To help maintain body torque to the right, Barishnikov held his left arm both down and to the right, but such torque was lost through the delayed plant of the left foot.

In summary, though Barishnikov used a discus style, he followed to an amazing degree the basic tenets of O'Brien's straight-line drive within the back half of the circle.

237

about 80 degrees. At the back of the circle, his right leg swings well outside the circle, but his center of weight does move close along the diameter that bisects the toeboard. At the front of the circle, the overall action is the same as that in the O'Brien style. But overall rotation greatly aids the crucial left transverse rotation of the hips that, in reaction, puts the torso muscles on stretch. (This may be the primary advantage of the discus style.) This sequence shows at the toeboard that Oldfield's center of weight is higher than would be that of Feuerbach. On his best puts, he must have started his power drive from a lower position.

Commenting on his 75-foot series, Oldfield[1] said,

On my fourth put I had a foul at about 74 feet, and I just knew I could do better, so on the next put I just tried a nice smooth one with good technique and went 73'1/4". Then I knew if I just tightened my turn and stayed a little lower I could really get a big one--and I did.

In my judgment, to "tighten my turn" means to start the turn slowly, to maintain body torque, to hold the right knee in close, and, in summary, to follow a relatively "straight-line" curve along the circle diameter. "To stay a little lower" puts emphasis on increasing the distance-time through which power can be applied.

GUIDELINES TO THE DISCUS STYLE

1. The discus style requires years of exacting effort before mastery is attained. But it can be argued that to master the O'Brien style as did Feuerbach--to keep low in the glide, to plant the left foot immediately after the right, to minimize the slowing of linear momentum at center-circle--also requires years of exacting effort. Which style is more effective or more easily learned is open to argument--probably more a matter of individual differences and preferences than of biomechanical advantage either way.

2. Parry O'Brien's repeated improvements over prior world records came primarily as an effect of weight training, not of his unique style. However, his style did increase the distance/time and so the power that could be applied behind the shot. Feuerbach's improvements increased such distance/time. The primary objectives of the discus-style shot put are (1) to maintain all the values of the Feuerbach style, and (2) to increase angular momentum just prior to the Feuerbach power drive by utilizing the stretch-reflex contractions of torso muscles that are inherent in the discus-like turn.

3. In both the Feuerbach and the discus style, the great proportion of force--90 percent or more--is derived from the power drive at the toeboard. Dyson[2] estimates that, in the O'Brien style, about seven percent of a 60-foot put is derived from horizontal speed at the end of the glide. It is unlikely that even a most effective discus style could derive more than about ten percent from the turn; that is, a potential gain over the O'Brien style of about three percent.

4. The term, "discus style," is misleading in several ways. It was chosen here over such names as "rotation style" or "whirl style" because the movements of the discus are well known, and so provides a basis for understanding. However, learning the discus style will occur most effectively if we think of it as a modified O'Brien or straight-line style with minimal circular motion of the body's center of weight and the shot. The movements in the back half of the circle should form a flat oval, not a wide leg-hip-shoulder swing, as done by some discus throwers. The latter produces a three-foot sweep of the discus at the start of the turn, away from the vertical axis of the body. In contrast, the length of the "sweep" of the shot in the discus-style is only one foot or so, since the rules require that the shot shall be put from on or near the neck and not behind the line of the shoulders.

It may help the beginner if he makes the shift of weight, first to the left foot, then the right, as two pivoting steps during which the time when both feet are off the ground is

---

[1]"The Unreal Becomes Fact: Oldfield 75 Feet Even," *Track & Field News,* June 1975, p. 23.

[2]Geoffrey Dyson, *THE MECHANICS OF ATHLETICS,* London: University of London Press, Ltd., 7th edition, 1978, p. 212.

minimal. Such champion discus throwers as Bud Houser and Hugh Cannon proved years ago that such steps can be made just as rapidly as in a whirl. In fact, modern discus-thrower, John Powell (1974-227'11") stated,[1] "Basically, I try to develop linear, instead of circular, motion across the circle. I want to develop slow-to-fast across the ring." That's the key to the discus-style shot put.

5. The critical phase of the discus-style lies within the first 60 degrees or so of the pivot at the start--in technique, in relaxation, in balance-control, in gradual acceleration. A sound start tends to ensure a powerful drive at the toeboard. For most men, a fast start disrupts control and slows later action just when it should be accelerating.

6. In both styles, the shot must be put from a position close to the chin and in front of the line of the shoulders. In the discus style, force must be exerted to counter the centrifugal force of the shot during the turn. In the flat-curve style recommended here, centrifugal force is minor so that control and consistency are increased. The greater the radius and velocity of the whirl, the greater the forces that tend to fly away from center, and so, the tendency to lose balance and power.

7. In both the discus and O'Brien styles, effective use of body momentum at center circle can occur only through the hard bracing or fulcrum action of the left leg as it slams against the toeboard. This fulcrum stops the linear momentum of the left leg-hip so that the power-levers can accelerate the upper-body and shot velocity. Shift thinking for a moment to the high jump. Consider how much the modern emphasis on run velocity and the sudden bracing action of the take-off leg has contributed to increased vertical velocity and heights cleared. In a similar way, both shotput styles achieve greater distances as compared with the zero momentum of putting from a stand. But in the discus style, body movements are rotational so that the left foot tends to swing high and to the left of the toeboard, beyond the right heel ("in the bucket"). Such a position nullifies all the potential benefits of the discus style.

8. Experts in biomechanics, such as Fred Wilt[1], believe that the special value of this style, the value that makes it superior to even Feuerbach's style, lies in an increase in potential power an instant before the power drive at the toeboard. As the right foot pivots at center circle to 90 degrees to the circle diameter, the left foot is braced against forward motion but implements a counterclockwise rotation of the left hip. In reaction, a clockwise rotation of the upper torso-head-shot produces a stretching of the powerful torso muscles that greatly increases their reactive power. The angular momentum resulting from these stretch-reflex contractions is potentially greater than can be produced using the Feuerbach style.[3]

9. Men with prior experience with the discus may adjust to this discus-style shot put more quickly. But such men will also be handicapped by the need to unlearn certain phases of discus technique. The discus, weighing only 4.4 pounds, is carried "like a sling" well out from the center of body weight. In contrast, in the discus-style shot put, the rules require the shot to be held firmly against the neck, close to the axis line of the body. In the discus throw, the c.g. may sweep with a wide radius; with some throwers, such as Fitch and Silvester, this was quite wide. In the shot, such wide-radius rotation is likely to diminish power more than it gains in momentum.

10. In both the linear and discus styles, the line on which the shot moves, as related to the horizontal, rises from the back to the center of the circle. At what angle? How low should the shot be at center-circle? Individuals vary of course, both in potential and actual performance. Barishnikov sometimes started his turn from a very low position--the line of his torso was horizontal--but then he straightened as he moved across, more than did Feuerbach, for example. When a man puts the shot from a stand for maximal distance, he always squats very low, lower than is ever attained in a full drive across the circle. This suggests that, regardless

---

[1] Jon Hendershott, "Interview with John Powell," *Track & Field News*, Nov. 1974, p. 16..

[2] Fred Wilt, "Oldfield Revolution-izes the Shot," *Scholastic Coach*, September 1975.

[3] Tom Tellez, "Shot Put--Emphasis on Rotation," *Track & Field Quarterly Review*, Vol. 79, #4, Winter 1979, p. 22.

of the style used in getting across, the closer one can get to such a squat from-a-stand, the greater the potential power at the toeboard. This is a very important guideline--for this discus style, as for all others.

11. Consensus seems to be that the discus style is most easily and effectively learned when physiques are shorter--though powerful--with great quickness and agility. A circle only seven feet wide greatly handicaps the tall and heavily muscled, especially in the upper torso. For these reasons, J. B. Durant[1] argues that "the rotation technique actually favors the female:" (1) a lower center of gravity "should make spinning easier and generate much less centrifugal force requiring resistance," and (2) angular velocity helps to overcome a woman's natural deficiency in power.

DETAILS OF TECHNIQUE--DISCUS STYLE

At the Back of the Circle. Stand with the feet shoulder-width apart, the left foot just to the left of the circle centerline (Fig. 11.20). If the shot were dropped, it would land 6-8 inches to the right of the centerline. The eyes focus down at about 30 degrees to the horizontal--now and throughout the turn. The line of the head-torso is only slightly forward, to aid relaxation and control.

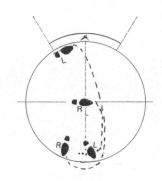

Fig. 11.20--Foot positions and flat-curve movements, discus style.

After a few preliminary short-range swings of the shot-shoulders, squat as low as leg power and the mechanics of the turn make feasible--a slight forward lean, head up. Lead the turn by pivoting on the ball of the left foot. This tends to produce an open left hip and a counteracting torque to the right of the right shoulder-arm-shot. The eye focus should aid torque by following the turn, not by preceding it. (Note: At first, this "unnatural" turn of the eyes-head to the right disorients. But many repetitions will overcome this and ensure a proper tail of the right shoulder.) Consistent with this, the left arm--elbow at about 70 degrees--should be held to the right during the turn.

As weight shifts to the left foot at the back of the circle, the right knee swings close within a short-radius curve (Fig. 11.20). To do this most effectively, individuals should try different positions of the left foot in the preliminary stance. Try moving it a few inches toward the toeboard, or closer to the right foot. This eases the pivot on the left foot. Some argue that it cuts the circle-size when it's already much too small. But since we're starting slowly, not seeking momentum at this phase, whatever works for smoothness and balance is worth trying.

At Center-Circle. As the right foot swings around the left, it stays close to the ground to ensure a very quick "placement" at center-circle at right angles to the circle diameter (Fig. 11.20). Important: Actually there is no fixed placement of the right foot. The foot "placement" drawn in Fig. 11.20 is that from which the linear power drive begins. To have drawn that foot at a 45 degree angle to the centerline would tend to impede the explosive angular rotation of the hips to the left and countering torque of the shoulders to the right-- an essential aspect of the discus style.

As with the right foot, the left swings close--to the ground and to the left leg--along a flat curve to its position hard against the toeboard, toe in line with the right heel, *as quickly as possible after placement of the right foot at center circle.* This is essential if the linear momentum of the shot is to be maintained, then accelerated during the power drive.

Important: None of this description is intended to establish precisely fixed actions or positions. It all assumes a non-existent average person. All statements are subject to

---

[1] J. B. Durant, "Women and the Spin Shot Technique," *Track Technique*, #70, Dec. 1977, p. 2229.

individual variations in body size, levers, power, mastery of technique--all the factors that make each putter's style unique.

But four basic tenets are sound for everyone: (1) As with the discus throw, the effectiveness of the discus-style shot put relates first to the degree of relaxation-balance-control during the start. Start slowly; accelerate gradually; emphasize a pivot on the left foot, not a sweep of the right; feel weight on that left foot. To suggest two pivoting steps--on the left, then the right--may be extreme but it's close to what is intended. (2) All turning occurs within a short radius; the shot should move quite straight-line (flat curve) along the circle diameter. (3) During the turn, assume a partial squat with the line of the torso-head only slightly forward to aid relaxation-balance-control; this will keep the feet close to the ground throughout. The degree of squat at the start is related to balance-control; that at center circle is of first importance as contributing directly to both velocity and strength in the power drive. (4) The power drive in the discus style is identical to that in the Feuerbach style.

ULTIMATES IN SHOTPUTTING

The previous section on the discus style raises the question as to which style--Feuerbach or rotation--will ultimately produce greatest results. No answer can now be given; the discus style has been attempted by only a very few over the ten-or-more-year period needed for perfection of technique. Each style has certain advantages and certain drawbacks; a decade will be needed before making valid conclusions.

But we can be certain that the best is yet to be. Oldfield's unofficial 75 feet, plus his repeated puts over 71 feet in 1980 after two years of active rest, suggest what lies ahead. A related study by *Track & Field News*, November 1977, compares best performances with the 16# shot by the all-time U.S. top ten putters with their best high school distance using the 12#:

	16#	12#		16#	12#
Brian Oldfield	75-0	58-10	Fred DeBernardi	70-3½	60-7
George Woods	72-2 3/4	60-11	Ron Semkiw	70-½	70-1 3/4
Terry Albritton	71-8½	67-9	Pete Shmock	69-3	64-11
Al Feuerbach	71-7	60-9½	Neal Steinhauer	68-11¼	55-1
Randy Matson	71-5½	66-10½	Karl Salb	68-9 3/4	69-6

The average improvement of these men in distance using the 16 over that with the 12 was an amazing 7 feet 5½ inches. Only one, Ron Semkiw, made no improvement. Greatest improvement (16-2) was by Brian Oldfield, counting his 75-foot put. His second-best put of 72-6½ produced a 13-8½ improvement, as compared with Neil Steinhauer's 13-10¼.

Many factors could affect these figures--relative physique, age of first-putting, high school mastery of technique--but the most important seemed to be number of years with the 16. Only three of the 10 did their best while in college--Matson, Semkiw, and Steinhauer. Two-- Oldfield and Woods--got their PRs more than 10 years after their best with the 12.

In the light of this study, Mike Carter's potential seems unbelievable. At age 18 (6-2, 250#), he put the 12# 81-3½; the 16# 67-9. If we have the unmitigated gall to add the average improvement of the top ten putters just cited, we arrive at a distance of--I hesitate-- 88 feet 9 inches. Nothing more needs to be said.

However, one related note. The 1980 official world-record holder, Udo Beyer (6-5, 265#) was only 22 when he put the 16# 72-8. He had run the 100m in 11.2s, and had high jumped 6-4½, indicating high all-round ability. By comparison, Carter's height of 6-2 would work against him. But--.

THE ORGANIZATION OF PRACTICE

Five essentials should guide the organization of practice:

1. The first, the last, and all the in-betweens must be concerned with the many aspects of the problem of motivation. Motivation can never be taken for granted. Without proper motivation, even the most perfect presentation of the mechanics of technique will go down the drain. Whatever goals, whatever rewards or incentives, whatever encouragements or kicks in the gluteus maximus, whatever competitions in practice or in meets, whatever coaching methods will lead to increased personal commitment to shot-putting as a challenging and exciting activity in itself or as a means to achievement or superiority should all be thoughtfully considered and used.

2. An adequate period of strength and power training should precede all shot-putting. To put the shot before one is strong is as unwise from a motivational standpoint as to enter competition with no practice in the skills of putting. Assuming at least ten months of work related to shot putting, the first two or even more should be devoted to strength exercises that are basic for all sports events. Most putters today continue these throughout the year and their entire career, though, to maintain strength, the number of days per week need not exceed one, (Steinhaus, 1963, 323). As the season moves along, power exercises that are more related both in movement and in velocity are introduced. The organization of training sessions in strength and related power is given in Chapters 6 and 16.

3. Maximum performance demands both strength and skill at maximum levels. Once mastered at a high level, skill diminishes rather slowly as compared with strength. But as I look back over some 50 years of great shot putters, only a dozen or so have really mastered the skill of putting. After about 20 years of practicing for greater skill, Parry O'Brien was still trying to improve. Even if skill is but 30 percent of performance, as O'Brien once said (but the validity of which I question seriously), that 30 percent is still crucial. Skill requires regular practice.

4. Sports on an avocational basis provide all too little time in which to perfect the many aspects of training for shot-putting. Careful planning must seek to make the most of this time. Should one work alone or with others? With competition in practice or with concentration on the details of one's own technique? What percentage of time should the coach be present: analyzing, encouraging, criticizing? The answers to these and other such questions will be found in Chapter 16, "A Field-Event Training System," and Appendix A, "The Dynamics of Skill."

5. The organization of any given day's practice of technique will depend on the personal, the seasonal, and the weekly goal for that particular day. The following pattern suggests what might be done during the competitive season:

a. The warm-up (At least 15 minutes). Warm up the legs first by jogging, striding, sprinting. Do calisthenic exercises consistent with shot put action (jumping jack, squat thrust, push-up) as warm-up movements, not as stretching exercises. Such "stretching" will occur more naturally and less dangerously through the full-extensions of strength training and putting the shot.

b. Put the shot from a stand without a reverse (Figure 11.11). From a standing position, the putter simply drops down into a low crouch such as he should attain in the middle of the circle when using the full action. He then drives up-over-and-out into the put, following through in the direction of the put as far as possible but delaying the rotation of the right hip and not reversing the feet. Such an action emphasizes the upward drive of the right leg-hip, the 70-degree upward movement of the eyes which aids the single-plane action of the put, and the crucial value of the left leg, first, as a fulcrum against which the levers of the right leg-hip can brace, and then, when the right foot has left the ground, as a power unit behind the shot. When done properly, the putter will end up high on the toes of the left foot with the right hand-arm, and the eyes-head extending as far as possible, without fouling in the direction of the put (Figure 11.20).

c. Achieving competitive skill. (Whatever time can be used; two hours is not excessive.) Emphasize "competitive-skill" as a two-phased unity. A man may learn competitive attitudes but lack the mechanical skill to make them effective. Another may have mastered the mechanical skills of shot-putting but lack the know-how of mobilizing and controlling the tremendous power that is potentially his. Such a man should experience repeated competition in practice, even when working on technique. The degree of competitive climate will be low, of course, as compared with that in a meet, but much can be learned.

During this period, with or without competition, all efforts should be at near-maximum levels. Skill is specific, not only to the mechanics of the action but to its velocity and its degree of effort. To learn mechanics at 3/4th velocity and effort is to learn exactly that. For a 50-foot shotputter, any put under about 48 feet tends to be of lesser value in learning competitive performance.

Gradually increase the number of "good-form" puts that can be taken in one day's practice. Working with at least two shots that are being returned to the circle, a man in condition can profitably take 30 or more puts per hour. Such a man has no time for general conversation or "horsing around." He's working at a challenge that demands his best; he's trying to accomplish more in less time.

Obviously, a practice situation where three or four putters are working at one circle, or with one or two shots will frustrate such a dedicated athlete. To achieve his goals, Parry O'Brien sought out his own practice area where he could concentrate on his work. As he walked out after each shot, he analyzed the last put and practiced mentally the next.

This phase of the practice session should be ended when fatigue disrupts skill.

d. <u>Use varied-weight shots</u>. The practice of using varied-weight implements has spread rapidly and world-wide in recent years. Its source lay in Finnish success in using 5# iron balls while simulating javelin technique. But the values of lighter-weight implements for increased velocity have also been recognized. East German shotputters have used 14-16-18# shots twice a week during the pre-season,[1] and Terry Albritton reported[2] that "I've also been throwing 75 feet with the 14-pound shot just about every time I go out." The important point is that while simulating regular shot-put technique, a man can emphasize either greater power or greater velocity as seems to meet his special needs.

A word of caution--heavier shots should be put from a stand as they disrupt the feel and pattern of putting; shots lighter than 14# tend to produce hyper-extension and strain. Use a gradual approach.

e. <u>Achieving endurance-strength-speed-skill</u>. The emphasis now is upon endurance, upon developing the ability to make more puts each day. Work in spurts of about ten puts, with short rest periods between. Make as many puts in as short a time as good form will permit. Explode on every put. Shots must be rolled back immediately to the putter. PUT! PUT! PUT! PUT! Many worthwhile learnings result: how to concentrate when tired; how to relax when tired; how to move with quickness when tired; how to do one's best when tired. On many occasions, a putter will be amazed that his best puts of the entire practice session will come during this "gut" workout. It gives him a competitive toughness and confidence not achievable by other more comfortable methods.

I recognize clearly the contrast between this recommended practice and that of Coach Thomas for the world champion, Randy Matson. In brief, this plan does not suggest a lesser emphasis on strength and related power training; it does call for a greater emphasis on skill in both its physical and emotional aspects. The strength-trainers have thrown out the baby with the bathwater.

f. <u>Shift to the discus or other events</u>. One might argue that by this time the athlete has no energy left for the discus or for sprinting or high jumping. Actually, the change of attention and action will bring about recovery. The real limits are produced by the athlete's attitudes or by the total time he has available for practice, not by his physical fatigue.

---

[1]"Shot Put the East German Way," *op. cit.*, p. 1813.

[2]Tom Jordan, "A Sound Mind in a Sound Body," *op. cit.*, p. 16.

HOW THEY TRAIN

Al Feuerbach[1] (In my judgment the following year-round program of training for related power and practicing for skill at the highest levels of velocity, competitive motivation and performance is well balanced and sound--JKD.)

Born: January 14, 1948 in Preston, Iowa. Ht/Wt: 6-1/240, 1.86/110.
Best Marks: Shot, 71-7 (World Record). Discus, 181-0.
Background: Emporia St. College. Two-time NAIA shot champion. AAU shot champion '73, '74.

Training (Non-Competitive Season, Oct.-Jan.)

Mon: 30 hard throws; then to the weight room. Seated dumbbell inclines; warmup with lighter weights, then 5 x 5 at maximum (Max at the beginning of season 85; by competition around 140). Seated press from behind neck; warmup with lighter loads, then 5 x 3 with max load (Starts at 185, by season's end up to 240. Poundage increase is rapid in this and all other lifts). Triceps press lying on bench; warmup to 4 x 8 with 100 (130 by season's end).

Tues: 30 throws; Snatch; 2 x 220, 2 x 250, 2 x 280, 300 max. Full squats; warmup to 5 x 5 400 (max). Best is 480.

Wed: Rest.

Thurs: 30 hard throws; continue rest from weights.

Fri: throw for maximum distance (record for the week); approximately the same weight workout as Mon. Perhaps do bench presses: 2-3 x 400.

Sat: 20 hard throws, going for good distance like Fri. Weights same as Tuesday, except go for maxes on snatch and clean & jerk (400). "Saturday is a big psych day. Max throw on Friday, max lift on Sat (320), and hard training in between. Everything is pointed towards breaking barriers on those weekend days. The record throw attempts are important in developing the nervous system. They are the source of my consistency."

Sun: Rest.

Training (Competitive Season, Jan.-Sept.)

Feuerbach does essentially the same workouts, but rearranges lifting days to ensure plenty of rest before meets. The structure changes only to the extent that he goes with more max single lifts and less reps. He is no longer trying to get fatigued, but to be sharp every day. Mondays and Tuesdays remain the same; Thursday would become the big lifting day and Saturday would be competition. Then, either after meet or on Sunday, Al works on the lower body (e.g. full squats).

At the end of the indoor season, Al does an intensive month of training preparing for the outdoor season: Hard throwing every day, even twice a day; up to 50-75 throws. Lifting stays essentially the same, working with max weights and returning to the number of reps in the Oct-Jan. period.

After the start of major outdoor competition (April), Feuerbach is forced to train on a catch-as-catch-can basis. When he does have time to train, he works on any specific weakness he has discovered.

Feuerbach tries to gain satisfaction from each throw and spends a great deal of time analyzing his technique. "The key is the mind. It takes ingenuity and a type of creativity to utilize all the things that are already known about the nervous system, muscular system, etc. You need an intelligent plan of attack."

---

[1] Bob Daugherty, "Al Feuerbach," op. cit., p. 1852.

Chapter 12
THE DISCUS THROW

To throw any disk-like object is inherently fascinating. Its aerodynamic qualities make it sail far beyond what its size and weight would seem to allow. Remember the fun of skipping stones far out over the lake? Who doesn't enjoy seeing and throwing the modern Frisbee? Or reading in science fiction of the Flying Saucers that now threaten the earth?

Apparently this same fascination was felt by the Ancient Greeks, for despite the warnings of their leaders that the inaccuracy of the discus made it useless for war, it continued to be one of the regular competitive events even in Games that occurred during their wars. This was true in their Olympic Games as in such games as marked the death of Patroclus at Troy.

Both the size and weight of the Ancient Greek discus varied greatly. Some weighed nearly 50 pounds; a metal ingot now in the museum at Cagliari weighs almost exactly the same as our modern discus.[1] But we can be quite sure that the method of throw was not basically different from our own. The Greek vases and sculptures tell us very little; a pose, such as that of Myron's "discobolus," that can be held for long intervals was more important to the artist than one more athletically valid. But Homer, among other poets, stated that Epeius "whirled and threw it." The Greeks threw the discus, not for a mere 75 years as have we moderns, but for centuries, and we can be sure their inventive minds would have created much sounder techniques than the stilted throw from a raised platform, without a turn, that was required in the Modern Olympic Games until 1908, and was known as the "Greek style." The style of the Ancients probably varied with the diameter and weight of the implement but one can assume a rather vertically-held discus with an up-and-down hop in the "whirl"; not even an Al Oerter could maintain a high-held flat turn with a 25-pound metal ingot whose diameter was as much as 15 inches.

A SUMMARY HISTORY OF THE DEVELOPMENT OF TECHNIQUE AND PERFORMANCE

Modern discus throwing in America began with Robert Garrett's (Princeton) victory at Athens, 1896, despite his never having seen the event prior to his arrival. But the real champion of this earliest period was Martin J. Sheridan, a powerful Irish-American of the New York City Police Department. (Along with such other "whales" as Pat McDonald, Matt McGrath and Pat Ryan, who dominated world weight-throwing for decades.) Sheridan broke the unofficial world record seven times, was national champion four times, Olympic champion three times (1904, 1906, 1908), and made his best distance in his last year, 1911, -- 141' 4½" from a tiny 7-foot circle.

The constant difficulty in avoiding fouls when working in this small circle finally produced an increase to 8'2½" (2½ meters) and a new world's record by James H. Duncan in 1912 of 156' 1 3/8". Duncan's style began with the discus high above and behind the head. From there it followed a down, up, down, up, and out motion. A single turn of 360 degrees was used, a so-called spin in which at least one foot was on the ground at all times.

---

[1] For a fuller discussion of all these points, see H. A. Harris, GREEK ATHLETES AND ATHLETICS, London: Hutchinson & Co., Ltd., 1964, 85-92.

TABLE 12.1

OUTSTANDING PERFORMANCES -- DISCUS THROW

OLYMPIC CHAMPIONS

Date	Record		Name	Affiliation	Hgt.	Wgt.	Age
1924	151-5	46.14	Bud Houser	S. Calif.	6' 1"	187	22
1928	155-3	47.32	Bud Houser	USA			26
1932	162-5	49.48	John Anderson	Cornell	6' 3"	215	25
1936	165-7½	50.48	Ken Carpenter	S. Calif.	6' 3"	225	22
1948	173-2	52.78	A. Consolini	Italy	6' 5"	120	24
1952	180-6½	55.02	Sim Iness	S. Calif.	6' 6"	240	26
1956	184-10½	56.36	Al Oerter	Kansas	6' 3"	230	20
1960	194-1½	59.18	Al Oerter	USA	6' 3"	240	24
1964	200-1½	61.00	Al Oerter	USA	6' 3½"	255	28
1968	212-6½	64.78	Al Oerter	USA	6' 4"	270	32
1972	211-3½	64.40	Ludvik Danek	Czech.	6' 4"	260	35
1976	221-5.4	67.50	Mac Wilkins	USA	6' 4"	255	26
1980	218-7	66.62	V. Rasschupkin	USSR			

WORLD RECORDS OF SPECIAL INTEREST

Date	Record		Name	Affiliation	Hgt.	Wgt.	Age
1939	172-4½	52.57	Phil Fox	Stanford			
1943	174-10 1/8	53.33	Hugh Cannon	Utah			
1946	180-2 3/4	54.97	Robert Fitch	Minnesota	6' 2"	220	24
1953	194-6	59.32	Fortune Gordien	Minnesota	6' 2"	224	27
1961	198-4½	60.50	E. Piatkowski	Poland	5'11½"	195	25
1963	205-5½	62.66	Al Oerter	USA	6' 3½"	245	26
1965	213-11½	65.25	Ludvig Danek	CSR	6' 4"	231	28
1968	224-5	68.36	Jay Silvester	USA	6' 3"	230	32
1972	224-5	68.45	Ricky Bruch	Sweden	6' 6¼"	298	26
1975	226-8	69.13	John Powell	USA	6' 2"	235	28
1976	232-6	70.86	Mac Wilkins	USA	6' 4"	245	26
1978	233-5	71.16	Wolfgang Schmidt	E. Ger.	6' 5½"	243	24

OUTSTANDING PERFORMANCES -- HIGH SCHOOL BOYS

4.6# discus

Date	Record		Name	Affiliation	
1971	201-7	61.49	Jim Howard	Scottsdale, Ariz.	
1976	202-9	61.84	Greg Martin	Pascagoula, Miss.	
1977	205-8	62.72	Dock Luckie	Ft. Pierce, Fla.	
1978	209-6	63.86	Dave Porath	Atwater, Cal.	
1979	207-4	63.23	Clint Johnson	Overland Park, Ks.	177-7

OUTSTANDING PERFORMANCES -- WOMEN

Date	Record		Name	Affiliation	Hgt.	Wgt.	Age
1972	218-7[1]	66.62	Faina Myelnik	USSR			
1976	226-4[1]	69.00	Evelin Schlaak	E. Germany			
1978	232-0[2]	70.72	Evelin Jahl	E. Germany	6' 0"	198	22
1980	177-7[3]	54.16	Leslie Deniz	Gridley, Ca.			
1980	207-5[4]	63.22	Lorna Griffin	Modesto, Ca.			
1980	229-6[1]	69.96	Evelin Jahl	E. Germany	6' 0"	198	24

---

[1]Olympic champion   [2]World record   [3]High School record   [4]American record

Duncan's 1912 record was not broken until 1925--by Glenn Hartranft, Stanford, and a year later, by Bud Houser, USC, and 1924 Olympic Champion. Cromwell states that Houser made two separate steps (left then right) in completing 1½ turns. Houser was 6'1", 197#, and extremely quick. He could step around as fast and as smoothly as later throwers could whirl. To the best of my own knowledge, the last and best "stepper" was Hugh Cannon, Utah, whose no-hop style achieved 174' 10" in winning the national title, 1943.

THE HOP STYLE. The modern hop style began as an upward hop in which both feet were as much as 10 inches off the ground. In 1929, Eric Krenz, Stanford, dropped very low at the back of the circle, hopped high, then down and up for the final pull. But beginning with Phil Fox, Stanford, 1939, an attempt to gain greater momentum in the whirl, kept the feet close to the ground so that it became a horizontal hop around, not up and down. From a technique standpoint, very little improvement has been made over the methods advanced by Fox in his talk, 1941, before the National College Track Coaches Association,

From this initial position, you lead with your back and gain momentum with an off-balance drive. . . . The more centrifugal force you build up, the more you travel in an arc, rather than the old straight-line drive across the diameter of the circle. Instead of eight feet, you have about 10 feet to travel, measuring the line that the feet follow across the circle.

Instead of moving from the right foot straight across, you move almost backwards, letting your back lead the action. In this manner you shift the drive off your right leg onto the left, and around to the right so that you land in the throwing position in the proper place, with the left foot about one foot behind the diameter line, and the right toe on the straight diameter line. To do this you have to cut down somewhat on the drive--if you want to do it right. . . . I don't care how fast you whirl. You have to be in good throwing position before you can make a good throw. That is the important thing, landing in a good throwing position, and at the same time utilizing . . . the centrifugal force principle.

My follow-through action, rather than being a straight line action like Harris (Indiana) and Carpenter (U.S.C.) use, is a whirl, and the natural follow-through is a reverse. . . . When I get a good whirl, the momentum is so fast that, if I don't change my feet, they will wind up on me like a couple of pieces of rope. I have to change my feet into the reverse position. If I get a good whirl, I may turn several times after the reverse. My weight against the discus, in the proper way, will tend to throw me back into the circle, rather than throwing me out.

BODY MOMENTUM IN THE WHIRL. Both the speed of the whirl and the clockwise torque of the torso during the whirl have been improved since Phil Fox. But only one significant modification of his style has been used by an outstanding discus thrower–Bob Fitch (Minnesota, 1946, 180' 2 3/4"), whose style was carried to a somewhat extreme but remarkably successful degree by Fortun Gordien (Minnesota, 1953, 194' 6"). Fitch's style (Figure 12.1) emphasized momentum and centrifugal drive through an extreme leading of the turn with the left shoulder and entire upper body. He permitted the great weight of the upper body to "fall" around the circle, with the feet trying desperately to catch up and only succeeding after the reverse and after the

Fig. 12 .1 -- Robert Fitch, Minnesota, 1946 world-record holder - 180' 2 3/4".

right foot had landed at the front of the circle.

All other successful throwers have used the left leg as a firm brace against which they could stop the momentum of the lower body, accelerate momentum in the upper body and especially in the right arm and hand, and still remain in the circle without fouling. Fitch did brace against the left leg, yet he carried his upper body momentum right on over the left foot with no hesitation for bracing, and drove his right shoulder into a very quick reverse which was an actual part of the throw rather than a consequence of it.

Al Oerter. Our interest here is in the evolution of technique more than in the history of performance, but Al Oerter, the only man ever to win four consecutive Olympic titles in a single field event, deserves special mention. Beginning as a 19-year old sophomore at Kansas U., Al not only won but set new Olympic records four times in succession--in 1956 (184' 10½''), in 1960 (194' 1½''), in 1964 (200' 1½'') and in 1968, at the age of 31, threw a personal best (212' 6½'').

The key to this unparalleled performance lay primarily in meticulous preparation--preparation ahead of time for all the difficulties (rain, wind velocity and direction, circle surface, early fouls or mis-throws, long delays between throws) that might arise. For example, major power in the discus is derived from the time-distance in which power is applied at the front of the circle. Body torque is essential. But in high-tension competition, men have a tendency to whirl too fast, to uncoil the hips and put the left foot in the bucket. The bracing function of the left leg is lost and force dissipated. Oerter is reported[1] to have planned ahead to offset this tendency at both Tokyo and Mexico City by deliberately slowing down his whirl and accentuating his body torque. It worked!

One other important contribution of Oerter deserves mention, though it has to do with preparation rather than technique. For 16 years he maintained his world ranking in the discus with a minimum of competition, of practice of technique, and of strength training. That is, each of these factors had been developed during the course of years near to Oerter's potential. His problem became one of organizing his training time and energies within the requirements of his full-time vocation and family (three daughters) responsibilities. There were periods of heavy training, of course, both as to strength and technique, but by and large, he found that "technique and strength can be maintained over prolonged periods of time with minimum effort."[2] Just what "minimum effort" means for most experts has still to be determined.

THE POWER TRAINERS
But modern improvement in distance thrown is primarily the effect of strength and related power training. For example, Jay Silvester threw the discus 181'8'' and the shot, 57'½'' in 1958, without a weight-training program. In 1961, after three years of heavy-weight training, but no noticeable change in technique, he achieved 198'8'' in the discus and 61'5¼'' in the shot, for the greatest double in history. In 1968, he upped this to a world-record 224'5'' and 64'4½''. His weight during this same period increased from 220 to 245. We shall write of his weight-training program under "Practice Organization."

Silvester's technique was marked by several inter-related features. First, his beginning stance was to the left of the centerline of the circle, so that his left foot was on the centerline. This tended to increase the number of degrees in his 1 3/4 turns. Second, as he started, he swung his right foot in a wide arc outside the circumference of the circle. This builds up the angular momentum of his leg so that when it is pulled in closer, body momentum is increased along with torque as between the hips and shoulders (Dyson, 1967, 207). However, this wide swing had a tendency to place the right foot in the front half of the circle, to give him a short throwing stance, a less effective bracing of the left leg (not unlike the technique of Al Fitch), and all too many "lost" throws and even fouls. When all went well, the result was tremendous--a world-record 224'5''. In 1976, at the age of 40, Silvester was still competing and hoping for that Olympic gold, following the example of Ludvig Danek.

Danek was first world-ranked in 1963 at age 26. He set world records in 1964 and 1965 (213' 11½''), took the Olympic silver in 1964, and bronze in 1968, then finally won that much-

[1] Jeff Johnson, "Al Oerter: Olympic Spirit," *Track & Field News*, December 1968, 10.

[2] Cordner Nelson, "Three Discus Stalwarts," *Track & Field News*, October 1966, 16.

desired Olympic title in 1972 at age 35. Danek (6'3", 230#) was a fine stylist, with a sound balance between time-distance power during the throw and velocity in the whirl, as well as between power training and technique practice.

In 1972, the irrepressible egoist, Ricky Bruch (Sweden, 6'6½", 298#) finally achieved his first goal by tieing Silvester's 224' 5". Bruch was--well, Ricky Bruch, an individualist of the first order who at 23 was predicting a personal record for 1970 of 73 meters (239'6"), and an ultimate of 80 meters (262').[1] By weight training, and tremendous food intake, he raised his weight from 199# to 298#.

His typical training day includes two periods of about two hours each. In the morning he generally concentrates on running a 1.5 mile course. In the evening he works with weights. His target under both accounts is the same--a steady increase of tempo and weight. "On the way to greatness in throwing," he says, "there are no short cuts. only hard work will pay."

The next world-record holder, John Powell (1975, 226'8") felt that his "small" size (6'2", 235#) forced him to emphasize technique even more than power.[2] Silvester oriented his style toward that of Al Fitch (Figure 12.1) and Fortun Gordien, by leading with the torso at the back of the circle and swinging the right leg wide (Figure 12.15). Powell patterned his style along the lines of Oerter and Danek. He agreed with Silvester's tenet of keeping the first circle big and controlled; the second circle small and explosive. But he felt this could be achieved by actively turning the left foot at the back of the circle while swinging the right leg at short radius, holding the upper body and discus arm in full torque, and the left arm fully extended. Whereas Silvester's c.g. shifted toward the circle circumference, Powell's tended to follow the more linear diameter of the circle. By this means, less time would be wasted in the hop-around with both feet off the ground; more time used in driving with the foot on the ground (left foot in the first 360-degree turn; right foot in the second). At the front of the circle, Silvester's left leg, swinging minutely wider and higher, required an instant longer in getting to the ground, and often landed "in the bucket." Powell wanted the right-left feet to land almost simultaneously--snap-snap--so the left leg could be used immediately as the fulcrum for the powerful drive of the right and uncurling of the torso. The difference is not easily seen, one of degree, of 60-40 so to speak, but it is nevertheless significant in its effects. Which style is superior depends on the individual thrower's mastery of his own technique.

Powell's record was short-lived, as we can be sure will be those that follow it. In his first meet of the 1976 season, Mac Wilkins (6'4", 238#) reached 226' 11"; in his second, three consecutive world-record throws of 229' 0", 230' 5" and 232' 6". He was competing with Powell and the wind was perfect--"nice, steady 5-10mph wind drifting in across the right quarter, occasionally gusting to 15-20....Wilkins still wasn't happy with his technique. 'It just isn't there yet,' he ventured, 'I made some terrible mistakes out there today. Not one of my throws was really technically excellent. I've still got that big one inside me.'"[3]

But three years later, 1978, it was Wilkins' friend, Wolfgang Schmidt (E.G., 24, 6-5½, 243#) that held the record. Using excellent technique, great velocity in the turn, and a favorable quartering breeze, he added almost a foot--233-5 (71.16m)--to Wilkins' best mark. In addition to his silver medal at Montreal, Schmidt was selected by *Track & Field News* as number 1 in the world for 1975, 1977 and 1979, and also achieved a best-ever shot-discus double on a single day of 67-2 3/4 and 226-1; all-in-all, one of the greatest throwing talents ever.

---

[1]R. L. Quercetani, "Bruch Swedish Discus Talk," *Track & Field News*, November 1969, 6.

[2]"John Powell on the Discus," TRACK TECHNIQUE, #59, March 1975, p. 1875.

[3]Garry Hill, "Not Once, Not Twice, But Thrice," *Track & Field News*, May 1976, 18.

THE WHOLE ACTION

Fig. 12.2---The Whole Action. In this sequence-action drawing, the discus is being thrown toward the viewer, perhaps 30 degrees to his left. The actions shown in Figs. 1-3 comprise the critical phase of the throw as related to technique--balance, control, turn velocity, body torque; those in Figs. 4-5 relate primarily to power. At the back of the circle (Fig.1) the back is erect, slight flexion in the knees, left foot 2-3 inches in from the circle, discus arm relaxed near the hip. Movement begins (Figs. 1-2) by shifting the heavy weight of the hips to the left and, gradually, toward center circle. As technique improves, this action speeds up, but for all, a controlled beginning helps ensure a good throw. The right leg swings wide but the foot remains relatively close to the ground. In Fig. 3, the left foot swings close to the ground to avoid an in-the-bucket position in Figs. 4-5. As turn velocity increases, inertia of the 4.6# discus causes it to move naturally into a high power position an instant after Fig. 3.

DISCUS

Fig.5--the discus has left the hand but the right foot is still on the ground. The reverse is merely a follow-through action.

Figs. 4-5 comprise the power phase of the throw. Hip rotation, so crucial in achieving maximal power, is greatly accelerated as between Figs. 3-4. Such acceleration--what John Powell calls a "hip pop"--actually begins the instant the left foot touches down. Hip pop increases body torque, extends the muscles of the torso to a stretch-reflex phase that ensures greatest muscle power, and, by moving ahead of the discus, increases the time distance through which discus velocity is increased. Mac Wilkins emphasized the importance of speed-power in the actions of the large torso-hip-leg muscles and spoke of his constant amazement at how little effort came from his arm. He said the arm is used only to transfer force from the body to the discus. Note the fulcrum effect of the left leg in Fig.4--left toe in line with right heel. The knee is slightly flexed, thus allowing full extension and added power (Fig.5) at the instant of discus release. In summary, perfect technique + maximal power = discus velocity and distance.

HOW TO BEGIN

How to begin is primarily a problem in arousing and maintaining enthusiasm for discus throwing.
The first day's practice should be considered a success only if the prospect leaves with a
sense of excitement and anticipation: "That discus sure does sail and I think I can throw that
thing!" In the case of the shot, we emphasized the crucial importance of developing strength
BEFORE trying to put. The difference between 40 to 50 feet for the experienced and strong
putter and the 30 to 35 feet of the weak beginner is so noticeable as to embarrass and discourage the latter.

Related strength is important for the discus also, but not to the same degree. Its weight
is only 4.6 pounds; even a weak prospect can handle that. Further, the difference between 150
feet and 100 feet is not quite so noticeable. The crucial factor with the discus is skill in
throwing and lack of skill is not nearly so embarrassing as an exposure of muscular weakness.
The straight-armed, lateral pull of the discus out away from the body is not duplicated by any
other sports event. This, added to the unique platter-like shape of the discus, means that a
new prospect has had no background of related skill such as is the case with the javelin or,
to a lesser extent, the shot.

If then the beginner is to feel encouraged after his first day's practice, it will be because he has gotten the feel of it, more than because of brute strength. Since self-conscious-
ness is so disrupting to skill, a wise coach would do well to emphasize encouragement rather
than coaching. Give the man time and freedom to throw it thoughtlessly, or almost so. Let
his eyes pick up hints, rather than his ears. If he wishes to turn, let him do so naturally
with just a hint of the rhythm involved and the footwork. Let him feel the rhythm of a prolonged "tur-r-n-n-n-n and throw" with almost no concern for the direction the discus goes.
You'd better mention that the discus rolls clockwise around the first finger (Figure 12.9), and
that it will sail flatter if held out away from the hips (Figure 12.8). But beyond that, let
him have fun doing it his way. Out of some 25 to 30 throws he's sure to get one that sails
out--and out--and out, and that's all he needs to ensure he'll be back tomorrow.

But now that you've given him a chance to get his bearings, and before he establishes any
bad habits, you'll wish to emphasize a few fundamentals. Most coaches try to teach a throw
from a stand first, (Figure 12.7), or a simple one step forward and pivot on the right foot
into a throwing position. Emphasize at the beginning that power in the discus is derived primarily in terms of centrifugal or "twisting" force, what in mechanics is called body "torque."
But neither a throw from a stand or full turn is merely rotational. To the forces of rotation
are added a powerful upward extension of the right leg-hip combined with a bracing and extensional force of the left leg. That is, the power of the whirl is enhanced by a very powerful
upward-forward drive as the body weight moves from the right foot to the left. Usually, the
left foot remains in contact with the ground until the discus leaves the hand, though in expert and high-velocity throwers, this may not be true.

Emphasize that the arm and discus during the forward pull should travel along the same plane
as does the discus in its flight; there should be no down-and-up dip. This means the discus
will be about six inches below shoulder height when the arm is at right angles to the direction
of the throw. Similarly, the eyes should move along this same plane.

As he gets the feel of things, encourage him to twist clockwise as far as he can go: with
his hips, his shoulders, his arm and hand, and importantly, with his eyes and head as well. If
he can catch a sense of power from such a long time-distance pull on the discus, it'll be of
great help to him later. When throwing from a stand, do not reverse the feet. The reverse
should be merely a follow-through as a result of the momentum of a full turn. To reverse from
a standing throw is to leave the base of force, the ground, too soon.

Keep a close check on his use of the left leg and foot when turning. The habit of bending
the left knee too much, then dropping the foot too far to the left
"in the bucket," is a tough one to break. Get him to keep the knee in close and the left foot
low to the ground.

In summary, how to begin will depend upon each man and his year's time-table for practice.
If he's likely to be a discus specialist and has a place and good conditions for throwing
throughout the year, he had better concentrate first on developing related power. But keep in
mind that, with the discus, the skill to make full use of that power comes slowly. Maximum
performance requires both perfected skill and full power.

LEARNING TO THROW

Fig. 12.5 -- Grip for greater control of the discus. The discus rotates clockwise around the first finger -- not the second!

Fig.12 .6 -- Grip for greater finger strength. Position of finger does not change from that in Fig. 12.5; the second finger moves to it.

Fig.12.7 -- Throw from a stand. Beginners make low throws with a flatly angled discus. Start the throw by pulling on the discus, not by rotating the eyes-face, nor the left arm-shoulder. The left foot should be in line with the right heel.

Fig.12.8 -- Make a flat swing; Keep discus away from the hip.

Fig.12.9 -- Chin up, back arched, discus almost shoulder height.

LEARNING TO TURN

For beginners, the turn should begin by simultaneously twisting the left heel counter-clock-wise and by shifting the heavy weight of the buttocks to the left foot and toward the center of the circle (Figure 12.10). For beginners, it should not start through the shift of the left arm-shoulder-head as is shown here by the various drawings of champion throwers. That will come later as the need for momentum in the turn increases. By maintaining a clockwise rotation of the left arm and shoulders, body weight will be held an instant longer over the left foot, balance will be aided, and the right will not swing so far across and to the left of the circle centerline. For better control, hold the bent right leg in close to the left. Later, for greater momentum, you may wish to swing it wide (Figure 12.2-2) as did Silvester.

There should be no feeling of the discus pulling the body around. On the contrary the right shoulder, arm, and discus drag well back behind the body. They hang back, relaxed and waiting, waiting as might a sling for throwing stones, or as might the head of a golf club, waiting for the final explosive centrifugal pull around-up-and-out.

Fig. 12.10--Mac Wilkins (6-4, 245#; 1976 Olympic Champion-- 68.28 OR, made in trials). Wilkins sprinted with great velocity into the first turn, right foot wide, discus arm back, loose and away from the hip. This produces torque within the hip-torso that is maintained until the left foot touches down at the front of the circle.

Fig. 12.11 - Turning with strapped discus. Eyes focus on discus. By twisting face to right, arm-shoulder are held well back.

Some 25 years ago we used to step around into a series of positions, so that the term, "throwing stance," as shown in Figure 12.14, had a certain validity. Not today. Today, we work for a rhythmic flow of action from the first "bounce" counter-clockwise at the end of the wind-up until the discus explodes around the tip of the first finger.

Therefore, just as soon as some measure of control of the discus when throwing from a stand has been achieved, start turning: turn, turn, turn, perhaps without throwing. Try a strapped discus as shown in figure 12.11; try making three or four continuous turns away from the circle, without stopping. Soon you'll get the feel of the discus hanging back behind the arm, waiting for the throw. Yes, you'll get dizzy, but stick to it. (Note: This use of the strapped discus with many continuous turns could be helpful throughout a man's career; each year he would learn to turn faster and with greater control, with no loss of power in the final sling of the discus.) Turn at the speed that seems natural; don't slow down to find balance or better foot position; keep the speed natural, then gradually acquire balance. An expert discus thrower must make thousands of turns. Be patient; have faith; it'll take time, but speed in the turn with balance will come.

Figure 12.12. The right foot is ———→ held in close; body torque is the left foot for an instant; the center of the circle. The body legs and feet. The right To increase speed of rota- to the hips. Beginners will balance. Note focus of eyes is horizontal.

kept close to the ground; the knee is maintained which delays the weight on then the right foot is placed quickly in weight (hips) is pushed around by the arm-shoulder hangs back, limp as a rope. tion, the expert lowers the discus close do better to hold it out for easier

This drawing is from a movie of Al Oerter, 4-time Olympic champion.

When actually throwing the discus with a full turn, move right into a long turn-n-n-n-n (on the left foot)-and-throw, no matter how off-balance you may be at first or in what direction the discus may go. Hold the head up; body only slightly forward; eyes focussed just below the horizontal and trailing--not leading--the rotation. This eye-focus aids upper-body torque to the right. This torque is maintained during the turn so that, at the front of the circle, the explosive rotation of the hips to the left produces a reactive contraction of the upper-torso muscles (stretch-reflex). With eyes-head-shoulder-arm trailing, there's no loss of discus momentum; only a muscle stretch-rebound.

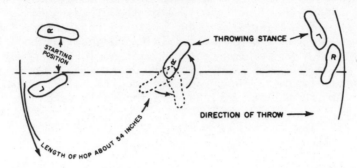

Fig.12.13 - Correct foot placement in the discus turn.

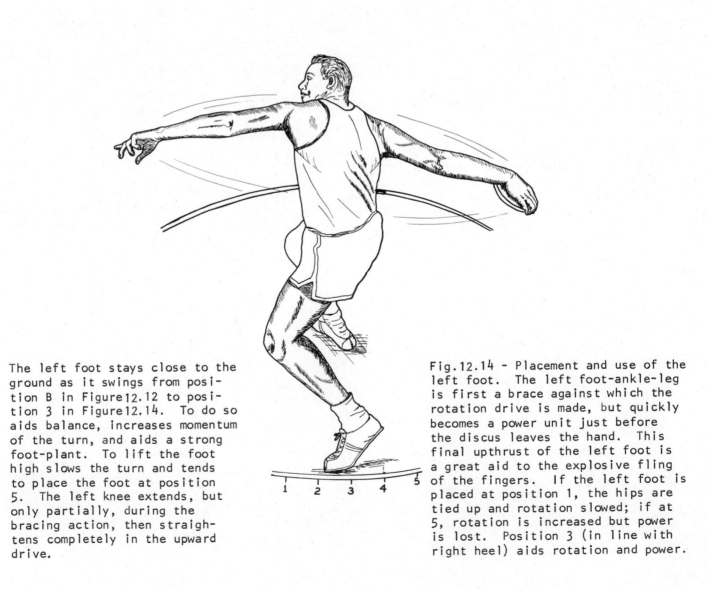

The left foot stays close to the ground as it swings from position B in Figure 12.12 to position 3 in Figure 12.14. To do so aids balance, increases momentum of the turn, and aids a strong foot-plant. To lift the foot high slows the turn and tends to place the foot at position 5. The left knee extends, but only partially, during the bracing action, then straightens completely in the upward drive.

Fig.12.14 - Placement and use of the left foot. The left foot-ankle-leg is first a brace against which the rotation drive is made, but quickly becomes a power unit just before the discus leaves the hand. This final upthrust of the left foot is a great aid to the explosive fling of the fingers. If the left foot is placed at position 1, the hips are tied up and rotation slowed; if at 5, rotation is increased but power is lost. Position 3 (in line with right heel) aids rotation and power.

EXPLOSIVE POWER

The development of explosive power for the discus must first establish a foundation of basic strength as outlined in Chapter 6, and explained in Chapter 16. Such power is centered about the legs and torso, with emphasis on the actions of rotation. Dale O. Nelson, former assistant coach at Utah State, has reported that Jay Silvester made special use of five basic exercises: (1) Clean and jerk -- 3-4 reps @ 177#; 3-4 reps @ 225#; 2-3 reps @ 250#; 1-2 reps @ 275#; 1 rep @ 300#. (2) Dead lift -- 8 reps @ 225#; 6 reps @ 275#; 5 reps @ 325#; 3 reps @ 375#; 1 rep @ 400#. (3) Bench press -- 8-10 reps @ 225#; 8 reps @ 275#; 6 reps @ 305#; 4 reps @ 330#; 2-3 reps @ 260#; 2-3 reps @ 375#; 1 rep @ 400#. (4) Jumping squats -- 8 reps @ 225#; 8 reps @ 250#. (5) Lateral raises on bench (arms fully extended)--starts with easily controllable weight; progresses up to 60# in each hand. Silvester emphasized basic strength throughout his long career, with a much lesser concern for related power.

But basic strength in the large, slower muscles of the torso must be supplemented by related power in the smaller, fast-twitch muscles of the extremities--all within the unique rotational pattern of discus technique. Most of the exercises illustrated on pp. 258-9 are related to such rotational movements.

Note that all these exercises are against resistances greater than that of the discus; that is, though emphasis is on velocity of contraction, greater strength is still a major concern, as it will continue to be throughout the year. However, as the season advances, and velocity becomes primary, resistances on one or two days each week will decrease--at some point, even below the 2 kg-weight of the regular discus. As emphasized in Chapter 6, when practicing technique, use only the regular discus.

One of the more vital actions is the forward pull of the right shoulder produced by the horizontal flexors of the shoulder: the pectoral is major and anterior deltoid. The lateral raise exercise, especially of the right shoulder (p. 258D) should receive great emphasis, along with the imitative movements of pp. 258-9 A and N-Q. Notice that the action of page 259Q, with its heavily weighted discus, exactly imitates throwing from a stand, and develops the horizontal flexors, all the muscles that rotate the trunk, and also the crucial muscles of the fingers and wrist. Just before the discus is released, the force against the fingers is terrific. They must be strengthened, for example, with a grip device as in page 259M, or by squeezing a small rubber ball that can be carried in the pocket.

The twisting of the body counter-clockwise is produced primarily by the rotators of the trunk: the obliques and quadratus lumborum, and by the leg extensors: the gluteus maximus, the quadriceps, the gastrocnemius, and soleus. Keep in mind that the discus action is one in which upward extension is equated with rotation. The final snap of the wrist is a unique action in which the wrist is flexed laterally through the contraction of the flexor and extensor carpi muscles on the thumb side of the hand. The exercise shown on page 258F will prove of help since it imitates this unique movement.

As outlined in Chapters 6 and 16, selection and use of related power exercises on a year-round basis requires careful planning. On pp. 258-9, 22 exercises involving a large number of implements--pulley weights, throwing weights, a rubber cable, barbells, dumbbells, over-weight discus--are shown. Such a wide variety has several values, physical and motivational. But variety does not imply lack of organization. Each exercise has its special uses and weaknesses. Contrast, for example, Exercise G with P or Q. Not only the amount of resistance but the patterns of movement are quite different.

RELATED POWER EXERCISES

Closeup of wall-pulley with welded attachment for heavy weights.

Leg press with weights. For isometric press, place pins through pipes above couplings.

DISCUS

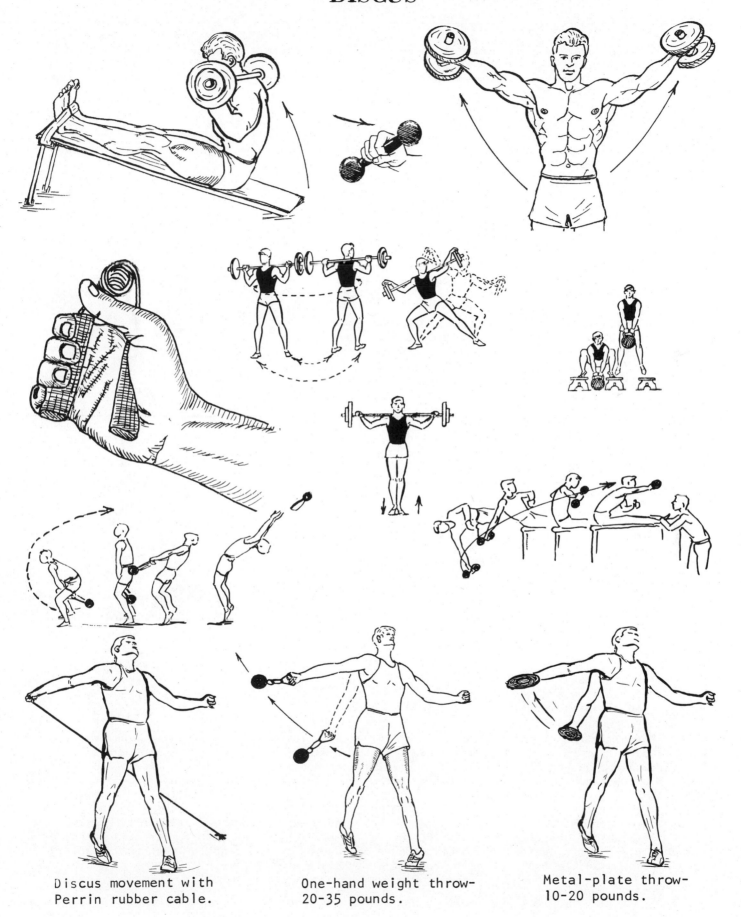

Discus movement with Perrin rubber cable.

One-hand weight throw—20-35 pounds.

Metal-plate throw—10-20 pounds.

259

COMMON FAULTS IN THE DISCUS

1. To allow awareness of momentum to become a problem before a degree of skill and a good sense of balance have been established. Ignore momentum in the turn during the early learning. Coach a style in which high momentum is inherent, but let action be as slow, or fast, as seems natural to the athlete.

2. To allow the eyes to focus above or below the line of the plane in which the discus is moving. Eye focus determines balance; if upward, the weight will tend to be on the heels; if down, too far forward on the toes. Horizontal focus keeps the body erect, the head up, and the shoulders horizontal.

3. To allow the eyes to lead the turning action. To focus them at right angles to the shoulders will aid good balance. Let the hips lead.

4. To lead with the discus in starting the turn. The discus should be held well back during the turn, until the final explosive pull. Start the turn by leading with the buttocks and by twisting on the left foot.

5. To throw the shoulders around and forward at the start of the turn. This creates too long a hop, makes balance precarious, application of power difficult, and fouling likely. Those champions that have used this method have found its potential excellent but have experienced years of inconsistent throwing.

6. To hop up rather than to hop around. A hop in which both feet are off the ground is an accepted part of discus form today. However, such a hop should lift the body upward as little as possible. The drive off each foot which creates the hop should push the falling body even faster in its whirl.

7. If left foot is in-the-bucket, or if head-shoulders lead the turn, hip rotation to place upper torso muscles on stretch will be ineffective. To be effective, torque must be maintained and left foot placed properly and quickly. It then serves as a brace to aid hip rotation; later, as a power unit in left-leg extension.

8. Explosive acceleration of discus momentum occurs at the instant the left foot touches down. Momentum begins slowly at the back of the circle, accelerates slowly during the turn, then explosively and powerfully. This explosive hip rotation to the left does not cause a counter-rotation that slows discus momentum; only a stretch-reaction that increases power in the upper torso muscles.

Fig.12.16 - The follow-through in the direction of discus flight; chin up, eyes on discus first, then to left.

9. To permit the discus to wobble in flight or to slide off to the right. Usually this fault results from failure to maintain the pressure of the first finger so that the discus rolls around the second finger instead. Sometimes the cause can be found in the tendency to pull the discus around in a low arc close to the hip. This brings the discus up on a concave curve with its front edge too high.

10. To over-emphasize the rotation of the head and eyes during the final action of the throw. If they pull hard to the left, force will be applied to the left rather than up-and-into the throw. In practice try holding the chin and eyes to the right of the circle center-line, or emphasize the pull on the discus rather than the head rotation.

11.   To allow the upper torso to control the turning and lead the throwing. Throughout the 1 3/4 turns, Powell emphasized the pivot of the foot on the ground to lead the turning. This pulled the other foot-leg within a shorter radius circle, placed it on the ground sooner, increased upper-body torque throughout, and ensured a firm base at the front of the circle from which to apply maximal power up-and-out at the earliest possible moment.

POSSIBLE IMPROVEMENTS IN DISCUS TECHNIQUE

Considering the rotational technique of the discus, as contrasted with the more restrictive straight-line action of the shot within a 7-foot circle, it is somewhat surprising that no major changes in discus style have occurred in the past 30-40 years, since Phil Fox and Al Fitch.

Improvements related to two aspects of technique seem mechanically sound and feasible: (1) that related to a greater time-distance in which power is applied as the final pull is made, and (2) that related to greater rotational momentum in the early movements.

GREATER POWER + TIME-DISTANCE. Consensus is that the turn adds only about 10 to 20 percent to the distance made with a throw from a stand. The inexpert thrower derives only 10 percent or less, mainly because he uncoils (loses torso torque) as he starts his turn or during it; so that, as the left foot touches down at the front of the circle, the discus--along with the hips--has already moved to position 4 in Fig. 12.17. The hips are now "open;" little additional rotation is possible; whatever stretch-reflex occurs is too late and too little. Loss in both power and time-distance of power application is major.

In contrast, the expert discus thrower maintains torque during the turn. As the left foot lands, the hips rotate explosively to the left. A reaction of the upper torso occurs that places related muscles on stretch, increasing their power. But since torque has been maintained, little or no reactive rotation of the upper torso to the right occurs; the counter-clockwise momentum of the arm-discus is not slowed. Now stretch-reflex increases power; pull on the discus can begin from positions 1 or 2, Fig. 12.17; time-distance of power application is maximal.

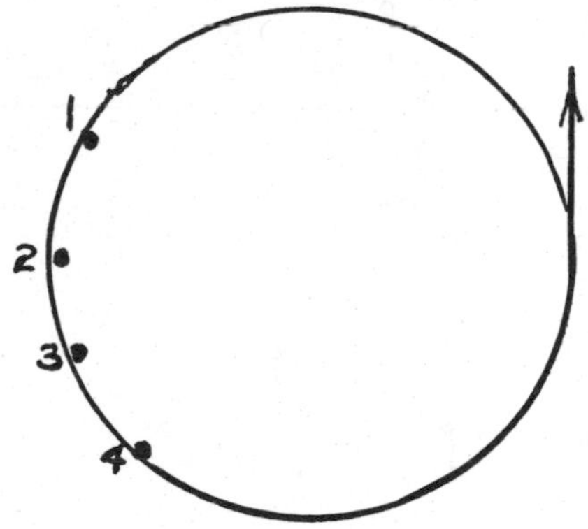

Fig. 12.17--Time-distance of pull on the discus.

To maintain body torque is extremely difficult. Most throwers, inexpert and expert, lead the turn with eyes-head. That's the "natural" way. But this tends to uncoil the upper body; that is, to anticipate counter-clockwise rotation. To prevent this, some throwers hold the left arm in an awkward position clockwise; others hold the torso rigid.

Based on my own long-time experience, the focus of the eyes during the turn is a far more effective way of staying relaxed while maintaining torque. Think of an eye focus at right angles to the line of the shoulders as being at 12 o'clock. During the turn, the eyes should never focus beyond this line; for example to 11 or 10 o'clock. The more they focus behind this line--to one, two, even three o'clock--the greater torque is maintained, and the greater the time-distance through which power can be applied at the front of the circle. Since torque is already maximal, the effect of the explosive hip rotation to the left is to put upper-torso muscles on stretch immediately, with no loss of discus momentum through a counter-rotation of the shoulders to the right.

This eye focus causes one to lose orientation while turning, and balance is precarious. But this is only temporary--hundreds of whirls, in and out of the circle, with multiple rotations, will restore orientation and balance. The time-distance of power application is greatly increased; one feels the weight of the discus and can really work on it to increase momentum. Admitted that body power implemented by clockwise torque affords more than 80 percent of distance; body rotation, less than 20 percent. It still remains that, if torque can be maintained (perhaps by some method as suggested above), any increase in speed of rotation means an increase in distance.

Apparently the most serious modern attempt at two turns was made by Bob Humphreys (USC, 1958-65, 202' 4½"). Lockwood[1] reports that:

The starting position at the back of the circle is identical with that used in the orthodox back-to-the-direction-of-throw technique. Having swung back the discus, the thrower "sets" the left foot in the same way as if he were starting a normal turn, but instead of driving forward off that foot, he continues to pivot on the ball, taking care to keep the body-weight over the feet. He then snatches up the right foot, which has been kept in contact with the ground as long as possible, and lifting the knee close in to the left leg, snaps the right foot down again in the place where it came from, having now reached the backward-facing position again. For a split second the body-weight is taken mainly on the right foot as the left continues to pivot into the "set" position once again. The thrower then drives across the circle from the left foot and completes the throw in the orthodox fashion.

Lockwood goes on to emphasize the importance of a powerful throwing position at the front of the circle, and the greatly decreased time that a faster whirl provides in which that power can be applied. The feet must move with great speed and the upward drive of the right leg against the fulcrum of the left leg must be instantaneous. But this is the same kind of problem faced by those who, over the years, have attempted greater momentum in any of the other field events--javelin, shot, hammer, high jump.

Humphrey's precise method may not be the way, but some such way will be developed, and new records gained. Of course, all such speculation is primarily for the more expert. The beginner should learn to walk before he tries to run.

A DISCUS WIND. The importance of just the right combination of discus angle of projection, angle of inclination (attack), wind velocity, and wind direction has been recognized for 40 years and more. I remember that when Bud Houser made his winning toss at the 1928 Olympics, he shifted his starting position some 90 degrees so as to throw into the wind.

Such knowledge was supported by research. For example, as early as 1932, Taylor[2] presented the results of wind tunnel experiments as to the effects of various wind velocities both with and against the discus. He concluded (1) that any following wind was progressively detrimental, (2) that "up to between 7 and 8 miles an hour, the elevating effects of a head wind is an increasing help, but that when greater than 7 to 8 m/hr. such help decreases steadily up to 14.5 miles per hour, when the head wind becomes a detriment, and (3) that an angle of 35 degrees is optimum for both the initial path of projection and the inclination of the discus.

But some 27 years later, Ganslen[3] found that there are too many variables in discus throwing to state the precise values of any given wind. The velocity with which the discus is thrown, and its angles of projection and inclination will affect wind values. He also made clear that the latter two angles should not be the same. That of projection should be at about 35 degrees; that of discus inclination at 10 to 15 degrees less. The discus is not a flat platter as were those of the Ancient Greeks. Its surface inclines upward toward its center, and this makes a difference in aerodynamic effects. Ganslen also emphasized that a greater angle of projection should not be the result of a flat arc in the forward swing of the discus. Rather it comes from an explosive extension of the right leg and a lift of the right shoulder which has the effect of flattening the discus inclination.[4]

---

[1] Bert Lockwood, "The Double-Turn Throw," *Track Technique*, 35, March 1969, 1110.

[2] James A. Taylor, "Behavior of the Discus in Flight," *ICAAAA Bulletin*, February 27, 1932.

[3] Richard V. Ganslen, "Aerodynamic Forces in Discus Flight," *Scholastic Coach*,

[4] For a much more complete discussion of aerodynamic factors in the discus throw, see Geoffrey Dyson, *The Mechanics of Athletics*, London: University of London Press Ltd., 7th edition, 1978.

THE ORGANIZATION OF PRACTICE

The time, energy, interest, and opportunity for practice of different discus throwers vary so much as to make any one program of work of doubtful value. Many discus throwers are primarily shot putters in interest; some are primarily football players or basketball players with only a few weeks for discus practice. Some have year-round outdoor-indoor facilities; others, no indoor facilities and a late spring.

1. Whatever the length of time available, careful planning of the many aspects of training and competition is essential to good performance. This has always been true. But we never realized the real significance of such planning until the all-out concern for sports as an instrument of government policy was evidenced by the USSR and East Germany. Their term for year-round planning of both training and competition is "periodization";[1] in brief, identification of various periods of time in which gradual changes in emphasis are made in both training and competition. The key to periodization lies in analysis--identifying essentials--and re-synthesis of those essentials into a more complete and better way.

2. A first step in such planning relates to the balance in emphasis on strength-related power, on the one hand, and on technique, on the other. Both are essential to excellent performance. Usually basic-strength training comes first. But in our American school program, the first months of school provide such excellent outdoor weather that first priority should be given to technique. Weather, not theoretical planning, will determine when, and how, and how much the emphasis should be shifted toward strength and power.

3. If working for basic strength and related power, follow the approach provided in Chapters 6 and 16, but also your own preference. Some champions have chosen to do strength training three times a week; discus throwing for technique five or six times. When the two coincide, either may be done first but must be modified in both length and intensity. All champions set aside some days for lifting only; others for throwing only.

4. When throwing the discus, awareness of the specific purpose of each throw is essential. When skill in the full turn-and-throw is no longer a problem, practice throws can be at 80-100 percent effort. That is, throw habitually at maximum distances, but keep awareness on some phase of technique. After each throw, review mentally what was done, how it felt, how it could have been done better. Throw for distance but rarely measure distance in practice. Keep awareness on "how," not on "how far."

To make more throws in less time, someone should return the discus; if working alone, use three or four discuses. More than two throwers working from a single circle upsets concentration, and tends toward frustration more than improvement.

5. Establish your own practice routine; one that meets your needs and with which you feel comfortable. Some men have found this routine of value:

a. After a little running, and related warm-up exercises, start the session by throwing the discus from a stand. A dozen or so throws are enough.

b. Use your major time and energies throwing with a full turn from the circle. Emphasize the over-all balance and rhythm of the whole action. Put off attention to parts of action until a later period. Within the restraints of good form, throw again and again as though you were in competition. Your primary purpose is to develop a set pattern of movement such as you will use in competition. As you step into the circle, do everything the same way every time. Such unvarying routine will develop balance, skill, and especially, confidence, better than any other way.

c. As long as you are throwing well, continue the above method. As you begin to lose your coordination, or whenever judgment suggests, shift to throwing with a full turn from the circle, but with greater attention for the details of good form. Even here, maintain the routine of throwing, but become aware of whatever phase seems to be causing difficulty. Try the various suggestions for overcoming faults in the discus. Throw both with and against the wind. Shift your starting position in the circle so that you can throw into any sector of the landing area.

---

[1]Frank Dick, "Periodization: An Approach to the Training Year," *Track Technique*, #62, Dec. 1975.

a later period. Within the restraints of good form, throw again and again as though you were in competition. Your primary purpose is to develop a set pattern of movement such as you will use in competition. As you step into the circle, do everything the same way every time. Such unvarying routine will develop balance, skill, and especially, confidence, better than any other way.

c. As long as you are throwing well, continue the above method. As you begin to lose your coordination, or whenever judgment suggests, shift to throwing with a full turn from the circle, but with greater attention for the details of good form. Even here, maintain the routine of throwing, but become aware of whatever phase seems to be causing difficulty. Try the various suggestions for overcoming faults in the discus. Throw both with and against the wind. Shift your starting position in the circle so that you can throw into any sector of the landing area.

d. If much difficulty is had in maintaining balance during the turn, practice with the strapped discus (see Figure 12.11) in the circle, or take multiple turns on concrete away from the circle. Initiate the turn with the hips; hold the head, shoulders, and discus back during the turn. Relax! The main reason men do not turn with good balance is that they do not practice the turn often enough. A hundred turns in one workout is not enough!

e. Finish the workout by throwing from a stand. Have three or four discuses and a manager to return them. Experiment with wind velocities and directions. Try for high throws by emphasizing the upward drive of the right leg and hip. Try for low throws into a strong wind. Keep the discus off the hip as it is pulled through. Be sure the discus rotates around the first finger, not the second finger, of the discus hand. This ensures greater power and better control.

f. Patience! Persistence! It takes years, even as much as ten years, to make a skilled discus thrower.

HOW THEY TRAIN -- Ken Stadel (1977: age 25, 6'6", 270#; best mark---222-9)[1]
Ken estimates that 40% of his training time is taken up with weights, 15% with unning, and 45% with technique work in the ring. He practices all-out occasionally, "because when you reach meet conditions, you must throw hard, you must know how your technique will work when going all out."

Stadel weight trains 3-4 times per week in the fall and winter, increases to 5 times per week in the spring, and decreases to 3 in the summer competitive months. He trains year-round. Ken follows no specific warmup or warmdown procedure, as they "vary according to workouts, time of year, and how I feel." During the off-season, he runs half-miles to stay in condition; during the season, this running is changed to sprint work, mainly 100s and 40s mixed with some distance work.

Non-Competitive Season
Mon--Half-mile run. Weights: 7 sets of bench presses, increasing resistance until max on final set; 7 sets of power cleans, increasing resistance while decreasing reps; 5 sets of 10 squats; 2 x 15 situps; 3 x 10 flys.

------

[1] N. A. Firth, "Ken Stadel," *Track Technique*, #70, Dec. 1977, p. 2236.

Tues--Run 880. Throw, 30 spins with discus; 50 without. Working on technique only; no hard throws.
Wed--Run 880. Lifting per Monday, but with dead lifts, push-presses, snatch, clean & jerk substituted during the week for benches, power cleans etc., to keep variety.
Thurs--Run 880. Technique throwing.
Fri--Same as Wednesday.
Sat--Run 880. Go to ring and think, throw a bit, reflect.
Sun--Run 880. Throw hard: 20 easy first, then 10 hard, without discus; review films. PM, half-mile of fartlek.

Competitive Season
Mon--Lifting: one heavy exercise, e.g. power cleans, clean & jerk, snatch, etc. and one light one, e.g. flys, sit-ups, trunk torque, tricep extension.
Tues--Lifting: one heavy exercise, one light. Throw.
Wed--Lifting: 2 light exercises, plus squats. Throw.
Thurs--Lifting: one heavy, one light. Lots of stretching, flexibility exercises. Throw.
Fri--Very light lifting for about 30 minutes. Dry spins only.
Sat--Compete.
Sun--Lifting: 2 heavy sets, one light. Some light throwing; all technique, non-hard.

HOW THEY TRAIN -- Mac Wilkins (1976: age 26, 6'4", 255#; 1976 Olympic Champion; best mark--232-6, world record.) [1]
Wilkins estimates that 40-50% of his training time is taken up with weight training, 3% with running, and the rest with technique. Mac weight trains 2-3 times per week during the fall, 6 during the winter, 5 in spring and 4 in summer.

Before workouts, Wilkins runs 1-2 miles of fartlek and does stretching exercises. Before competitions, he does 200 meters in 30-35 seconds and stretches. He considers his long pull to be the best part of his technique, while balance is the segment most needing work. He competes 1-5 times indoors in the shot, and 30-40 times outdoors in the disc. His only unique feature, believes Wilkins, is "an unusual mind--it is very strong."

Technically speaking, Wilkins starts with his left foot resting on the midline. In the turn, his leg "swings wide and away from the body and then snaps in close, as with Silvester."

Non-Competitive Season
Mon--Run one mile or more daily for warmup and warmdown. Hard training day. Weights:
Hi-pull cleans 4 x 3 from 300 to 375 lbs., depending on the time of season; incline press 5 x 5 at 225-325; straight arm flys 5 x 5 with 25-60. Abdominal exercises. Throw hard 30-50 times.
Tues--Snatch 4 x 2 with 225-275 (max); squats 5 x 5 with 455-550, or 3 x 10 with 350-455; benches 5 x 5 with 355-425 (max), or 8 x 3 with 250-290. Abdominals. Throw medium hard 30 times.
Wed--Narrow-grip snatch technique with 200-235; seated neck bench press 5 x 4 same as Monday; flys same as Monday. Abdominals. Throw 30-50 times.
Thurs--Same weight workout as Monday. No throws.
Fri--Throw 20 easy throws for technique and feeling.
Sat--Same as Tuesday with added set of snatches; or lift for PR and throw for PR.
Sun--Same weight workout as Wednesday. Throw 25-30 times medium.

Competitive Season
Mon--Same weights as non-competitive season. Hard throwing.
Tues--Medium throwing.
Wed--Same weights as off-season. Hard throwing.
Thurs--Medium weights and medium throwing.
Fri--Squat 3 x 8 at 330; bench to 2 x 90% of max; snatch 3 x 60% of max. Or, rest. Or, 10-15 easy throws.
Sat--Compete.
Sun--Light throwing and lifting.
On his throwing, Mac notes that he throws at 100% on about 80% of his practice throws. His best practice mark is 215-feet.

---

[1] C. L. Drown, "Mac Wilkins," *Track Technique*, #65, Sept. 1976, p. 2075.

Chapter 13
THE JAVELIN THROW

Because of its uses for both hunting and war, the javelin has been included in the athletic competitions and legends of most peoples. We are all familiar with its use among the Ancient Greeks as a part of the pentathlon in the Olympic Games as well as a single event in other competitions. Also in the German legend of Siegfried, we read that as a precondition for King Gunther's suit for her hand, Queen Brunnhilde included the javelin throw as a trial of strength and skill. King Henry VIII of England is reported to have been adept in its use, and in the 16th century, Rabelais cited its values for the education of the young Gargantua.

A SUMMARY HISTORY OF THE DEVELOPMENT OF TECHNIQUE AND DISTANCE

Vase paintings and various brief hints from writers indicate that the Greeks used a thong in throwing the javelin. According to Harris[1] this thong was probably not fixed to the javelin but fell away from it in flight. His personal experiments indicated that when the thong was wrapped around the javelin to produce spin and steadiness in flight, distances tended to diminish. Many vases show the thrower using his left hand to press the javelin back to keep the thong taut just prior to the throw. However,

> Apart from these details consequent upon the use of the thong, Greek javelin throwing appears to have been identical with our own. The thrower ran up to the mark carrying the javelin on a level with his ear, took it back for the throw, at the same time extending his left arm to help his balance, and threw without overstepping the line. . . .
>
> Of Greek standards of performance with the javelin we know even less than of their achievements in the jump and discus throwing.

Evidence indicates that their javelins were about eight feet long of lightweight elder wood, and since the use of the thong increased distances considerably, Harris concludes that they probably could achieve some 300 feet or more in distance. The Greeks had no devices for accurate measurement.

EARLY AMERICAN TECHNIQUES. Acceptance of the javelin throw as a regular part of the United States track and field program was both late and uncertain. The first National AAU winner was the world-record shot putter, Ralph Rose, at 141 feet--"through brute force and beastly ignorance," as one writer commented. The ICAAAA, started in 1876, did not include the javelin until 1922. The NCAA threw the javelin in its first championships, 1921, but only a relatively few schools included it in their dual-meet program. For alleged reasons of "danger to others" and "lack of throwing areas," the Big Ten Conference discarded the event in 1943 and, until 1979, has not restored it. The NFSHSAA accepted national records for the javelin as early as 1914 but only a few states--notably California--promoted it.

Quite naturally, such uncertain acceptance was reflected in American javelin techniques-- more related to throwing baseballs than to the unique skill of throwing an 8½-foot spear.

---

[1]H. A. Harris, GREEK ATHLETES AND ATHLETICS, London: Hutchinson & Co., Ltd., 1964, 92-97.

TABLE 13.1

OUTSTANDING PERFORMANCES -- JAVELIN THROW

OLYMPIC CHAMPIONS -- MEN

Date	Record		Name	Affiliation	Age	Hgt.	Wgt.
1952	242' ½"	73.78	Cy Young	USA	24		
1956	281' 2"	85.70	Egil Danielsen	Norway	23	5'11½"	185
1960	277' 8"	84.64	Viktor Tsibulenko	USSR	30	6'2"	222
1964	271' 2½"	82.66	Pauli Nevala	Finland	23	5'10"	179
1968	295' 7"	90.10	Janis Lusis	USSR	29	6' ½"	196
1972	296' 10"	90.48	Klaus Wolfermann	W. Germany	26	5'10"	187
1976	310' 4"	94.58	Miklos Nemeth	Hungary	30	6'0"	194
1980	299'2-3/8"	91.29	Dainis Kula	USSR			

OLYMPIC CHAMPIONS--WOMEN

Date	Record		Name	Affiliation	Age	Hgt.	Wgt.
1964	198' 7"	60.54	Mihaela Penes	Rumania			
1968	198' 0"	60.36	Angela Nemeth	Hungary			
1972	209' 7"	63.88	Ruth Fuchs	E. Germany	26	5'6½"	138
1976	216' 4"	65.94	Ruth Fuchs	E. Germany	30	5'6½"	141
1980	224' 5"	68.45	Maria Colon	Cuba	22	5'9"	154

SELECTED RECORD HOLDERS -- MEN

Date	Record		Name	Affiliation	Age	Hgt.	Wgt.
1955	268' 2½"	81.80	Bud Held	USA	27	6'	170
1959	282' 3½"	86.10	Al Cantello	USA	28	5'7½"	163
1964	300' 11"	91.78	Terje Pedersen	Norway	22	6'3¼"	181
1969	304' 1½"	92.76	Jorma Kinnunen	Finland	28	5'9"	165
1970	300' 0"[2]	91.44	Mark Murro	Arizona St.	20	6'	230
1972	307' 9"	93.86	Janis Lusis	USSR	33	6' ½"	196
1973	308' 8"	94.14	Klaus Wolfermann	W. Germany	27	5'10"	187
1976	310' 4"	94.58	Miklos Nemeth	Hungary	30	6'0"	194
1980	317' 4"	96.78	Ferenc Paragi	Hungary	26	5'10½"	215

SELECTED RECORD HOLDERS -- WOMEN

Date	Record		Name	Affiliation	Age	Hgt.	Wgt.
1976	226' 9"	69.12	Ruth Fuchs	E. Germany			
1977	227' 5"[2]	69.32	Kate Schmidt	USA	24	6'1"	175
1980	229' 6"[1]	69.96	Ruth Fuchs	E. Germany	34	5'6½"	158

SELECTED HIGH SCHOOL PERFORMERS -- BOYS

Date	Record		Name	Affiliation
1971	259' 9"[3]	79.22	Russ Francis	Pleasant Hill, Oregon
1972	247' 11"	75.61	Bruce Dow	Hillsboro, Oregon
1975	239' 1"	72.92	Tom Sinclair	Gig Harbor, Wash.
1977	224' 7"	68.50	Terry Daffin	Baton Rouge, La.
1978	231' 1"	70.49	Gray Barrow	Baton Rouge, La.
1979	229' 2"	69.89	Norm Roth	Rockaway, N.J.

SELECTED HIGH SCHOOL PERFORMERS -- GIRLS

Date	Record		Name	Affiliation
1967	198' 8"[3]	60.56	Barbara Friedrich	Manasquan, N.J.
1978	166' 8"	50.83	Debbie Williams	Euclid, Ohio
1979	175' 6"	53.52	Mary Osborne	Billings, Mon.

---

[1]World record   [2]American record   [3]High school record

Until about 1940, most Americans used a "back cross-step," not unlike the natural skip with which every schoolboy tosses a stone or ball. At the 1952 Olympic Games, Helsinki, the United States gained its greatest javelin success, with Cy Young (242' -- Olympic record) and Bill Miller (237'9") taking 1-2, using a variation of the back cross.

The Hop Style. Even as late as 1961, Bill Miller[1] argued that a "hop-shift" method provided a most powerful throwing position without loss of momentum, if practiced perseveringly. No world-level throwers use such a style today, but it is easily learned. When motivations are low, or time for practice limited, acceptable distances can be achieved.

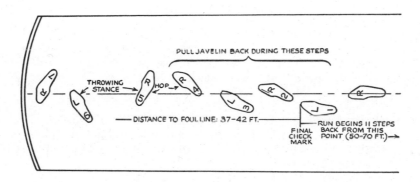

PULL JAVELIN BACK DURING THESE STEPS

THROWING STANCE

HOP

DISTANCE TO FOUL LINE: 37-42 FT.

FINAL CHECK MARK

RUN BEGINS II STEPS BACK FROM THIS POINT (50-70 FT.)→

Fig. 13.1 -- Foot pattern in the now little-used American hop style.

In brief, the run-up and checkmarks are similar to those in the Finnish style. During the six-count transition phase, as shown in Fig. 13.1, the 2nd, 3rd, and 4th footsteps turn gradually more clockwise so that the 4th-count right foot is at about 60 degrees to the line of the run. Then, during the hop, that same foot makes a long, fast, and low rotation to a position that is at or beyond 90 degrees to the direction of the run. On this hop, Bill Miller travelled 8'6" and recommended as much as 11 feet during which the foot would be only a few inches off the ground. Note that the right foot (R5), as advocated by Miller, will produce a closed-hip position that delays the explosive hip rotation and stretch reflex so essential to modern throwing. But the foot angle (R5) can be modified to meet modern requirements.

United States Performance. Other than the 1952 Olympic 1-2 placement, United States achievement in the javelin world has been sparse. In 1953 (263'10") and 1955 (268'2½"), Bud Held (California, Berkeley) set two world records by emphasizing rotation of the right hip-shoulder and javelin to the right, while trying to increase time-distance in the pull. In 1959, Al Cantello (5'7½", 163#) of LaSalle College, Phila., threw 282'3½", also a world record. Cantello's forte lay primarily in a gradually accelerated and fast approach, maintained until the last possible moment, suddenly checked by a perfect left leg, then exploded into a full follow-through into the javelin that ended in a full-length sprawl at the toe-board. Cantello had been praised for several years as having a style that made maximum use of his power but had not thrown over 250 feet in 1958. He attributed the improvement to a more perfect use of the new Held javelin but even more to regular strength training which had boosted his weight of 153 by ten important pounds, as well as the power of his throwing muscles. In 1970, Mark Murro of Arizona State set the American standard, up to 1980, at 300 feet even.

But America's greatest contribution to the event was through the genius of Bud Held and his brother Dick in developing the modern aerodynamic "Held" javelin. This javelin had a surface area that was 27 percent greater than the then-accepted Swedish Olympic model, which improved its "sailing" qualities. During the next five years, world distances increased by an average of about ten feet, as witness, Al Cantello. There were no IAAF rules as to javelin diameters, and controversy, world-wide, was heated. Later, Held made hollow and wider javelins that floated

[1]Bill Miller, "The Transitory Hop Shift Method of Javelin Throwing," *Track Technique*, December 1961, 174.

farther and farther, until precise specifications by the IAAF (1959) settled the issue.

Finnish Javelin Throwing. Finland has dominated Olympic javelin throwing since its inception in 1908. This, despite a population of only about four million (1980--4.7 million), and a climate more conducive to winter sports such as endurance skiing than to thinly-clad javelin throwing. The Finns make much of the word "sisu," that relates to hardiness, toughness and indomitable will. Add to their climate the long-time threat of the Russian Bear and it's small wonder that "sisu" is so deep an aspect of the Finnish character.

At the 1920 Antwerp Olympics, Finland won the first four places; in 1932, the first three. Of a possible 45 medals (1908-1976), she won 17; of a possible 90 places, 31--leaving less than two-thirds for all the other Olympic nations. A most amazing record.

Perhaps the most important reason for such success lay in Finland's early adoption of a throwing technique that held a potential for maximal distances. At the 1920 Games at Antwerp, American Olympic Coach, Dean Cromwell observed Jonni Myyra use what he called a "front-cross style." But not until 1939 did any American champion (Bob Peoples, 234'2") adopt such a style. In describing the fundamentals of the Finnish front-cross, Cromwell stated, "Speed for the toss comes from the run, with the legs transferring momentum to the upper body, but one of the principle effects...comes from the mighty pull on the left side of the body."[1] Even modern biomechanics would accept such a description.

Perhaps the most famous of all Finnish champions, other than Paavo Nurmi of course, was Mr. Javelin, Matti Jarvinen. He set his first world record (234' 9 3/4") in 1930, age 21; won the 1932 Olympic title (238' 6", OR); set his 8th world record (253'4½") at age 27, and was still throwing over 220' in 1950, age 41.

In 1976, *Track & Field News* rated Finnish throwers 1st, 2nd, and 4th among the top ten in the world, but at Montreal, Siitonen (288'5") could gain only second place of Miklos Nemeth's (Hungary) world-record 310'4". In 1978, 12 Finns threw beyond 262'6" (80m); 54, over 229'8" (70m); 220, over 196'10" (60m).[2]

East European and Russian Throwing. In the three years (1977-1979), *Track & Field News*[3] selected the top 50 javelin throwers for each year by nations: Finland--25, USSR-22, E. Germany--19, Hungary--13, U.S.--12, Sweden--10, W. Germany--10, all others 39. In 1979, the top ten (rated by all throws, not best throws) included: 1. Wolfgang Hanisch (EG)--296'5"; 2. Arto Harkonen (Fin)--295'10"; 3. Detlef Michel (EG)--294'5"; 4. Ferenc Paragi (Hun)-- 302'3"; 5. Pentti Sinersaari (Fin)--307'10"; 6. Helmut Schreider (WG)--304'2". Clearly, the all-out use of sports as an instrument of national policy was paying dividends. More specifically, the means for this great upsurge in performance among Communist nations related to (1) scientific planning of the specifics of year-round training; (2) scientific use of basic weight training, related power training, and imitative power-velocity training; (3) biomechanical analysis of javelin-throwing techniques to produce maximal effectiveness.

Finland has demonstrated clearly that concentration on one event can gain international success, even though the population be but four million or so, and the climatic conditions negative. We can assume that the East European superiority will continue. But since we are now approaching human ultimates and using scientific methods common to all, both throwing style and training methods will no longer be distinguishable by nations.

Russia learned from Finland and added improvements; Finland learned from and improved on Russia; East Germany and Hungary gained from both--all learning from each and gradually establishing a base common to all. In 1978, the United States set up its own Olympic Sports Development Center at Colorado Springs, with research teams in biomechanics and related sciences. If we fall short in future javelin performances, it will not be for lack of knowledge but of national commitment.

---

[1] Dean B. Cromwell, *CHAMPIONSHIP TECHNIQUE IN TRACK AND FIELD*, New York: Whittlesey House, 1941, p. 299.

[2] *Track & Field News*, Sept. 1979, p. 36.

[3] *Track & Field News*, January issues, 1978-1980.

PHYSIQUE IN JAVELIN THROWING

Size and strength are essential to greatest distances in javelin throwing, but at a level peculiar to the javelin and definitely lower than required for the other three throwing events. As might be expected, size increases as distances lengthen. Below 250 feet, physiques of 5'8", 165# are not uncommon. But between 1976 and 1980, of the five men surpassing 300 feet, physiques ran: Miklos Nemeth (310'4")--6', 194#; Michael Wessing (309'1")--6', 194#; Pentti Sinersaari (307'10")--6'3½", 176#; Seppo Hovinen (306'11")--6'½", 220#. Perhaps the largest of all excellent throwers was Sam Colson, U.S. (284'3")--6'5¼", 270#.

But an unlimited length of run combined with a lightweight (800g) implement makes it possible for relatively small men to attain world levels. In 1969, Jorma Kinnunen, Finland, threw 304'1½" though 5'8", 165#; in 1959, Al Cantello, U.S., set a world record at 282'3½" though 5'7½", 163#.

It should be added, however, that body mass should not be equated with body power. Some relatively small men have a quality of explosiveness against resistance that is far beyond normal. Cantello was such a man, but his 30-foot improvement in 1959 came only after power training had added 10# in weight and many ergs in power.

THE EXPLOSION OF SPEED-POWER

Figure 13.2---All the gradually accumulated force of the run and transition phase is concentrated at the point captured by this figure. The left foot is in line and firmly planted. The hips have rotated explosively, placing the torso muscles on stretch, with all power converging toward the final whip-cracking thrust of the right wrist-hand-fingers.

This explosion of power, if a throw from a stand is an indication, gains about 60 percent of total throwing distance. For example, Mazzalitis states that Janis Lusis could throw in practice 271' (86.7m) using a full run; 258' (79m) using three steps; and 165' (50m) from a stand--a five percent loss as between the first two; a 40 percent loss between the first and third. *Track & Field News* (May 1980, p. 24) reports that Ferenc Paragi warmed up, using three steps, with 262' (80m) prior to his world record throw of 317'4" (96.72m); difference--18 percent.

RELATED POWER EXERCISES

Note - The black-shirted figures are excerpted from V. Mazzalitis, *Throwing the Javelin*, USSR Sports Publishing Office, 1970.

Imitative javelin power exercise using Perrin rubber cable.

JAVELIN

Imitative power javelin throw with rubber grenade.

Grip-wrist power exercise: roll rope on bar - weights.

rubber buffer

Imitative power exercise with heavy leaded pipe on nylon rope against rubber buffer.

HOW TO BEGIN

In my own coaching experience, how to begin has been more a problem of selecting the real throwers and rejecting those who merely enjoy throwing, than one of increasing motivation. Everyone wants to pick up that spear and try to sock it out of the stadium. Begin then with safety measures so that no skulls are pierced or javelins broken. A special section on this problem has been included in this chapter.

One worthwhile rule for both safety and performance is that NO ONE throws the javelin without the permission of the coach; another, that all javelin prospects must first put in a period of power training before throwing. This alone will discourage the play-boys.

Begin training early in the Fall, the best time for basic training. Follow a gradual conditioning program such as that described by Ed Tucker at the end of this Chapter. First emphasis is made on developing the lower two-thirds of the body--the legs and torso. Run for fun and power away from the track--repeated slow-fast running, up and down hills, without or with a weighted jacket--but emphasize the enjoyment aspect. Sprint on the grass with driving elongated strides. Run up the stadium steps, perhaps two at a stride, then hop down on one leg--both left and right.

Other basic activities include handball, swimming, volleyball, gymnastics that include javelin-related movements, and that useful tool, the medicine ball which can be thrown in movements that closely simulate those of throwing the javelin. Along similar lines, the practice of log-splitting with a sledge and wedges has great value.

While good weather prevails, do repeated front-cross strides as in javelin throwing, running the full length of the field, while holding a Stubby javelin or training ball at full arm extension. Do this primarily for muscle-tendon development but also for a foundation of technique. After some weeks, add a weighted vest or belt.

If actual throwing during the Fall seems best, keep the regulation javelins under a padlock to ensure against muscle-tendon strain, broken javelins, broken heads of other athletes, and broken sleep, from anxiety, of the coach. Best to use steel balls weighing about 1500 grams (3½#), preferably rubber covered. Again, power development outweighs precise technique. A few preliminary steps consistent with later teaching; use the "power reach," as described here with full body torque; throw along a straight line with a high elbow, the hand above the right ear, and a full follow-through up-and-out with javelin flight.

Fig. 13.3- Acceptable method of holding the javelin.

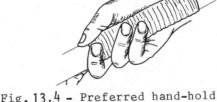

Fig. 13.4 - Preferred hand-hold. The first finger aids javelin rotation and also gives a lift to the tail which helps keep the javelin in line of flight.

ONE AND TWO AND THROW

Fig.13.5 - Beginning to throw. Point the javelin at an object on the ground only about 10 yards away Throw while keeping the point down; Throw at more distant object with javelin at 15 above horizontal.

ESSENTIALS OF SOUND TECHNIQUE

THE GRIP. Two acceptable ways of holding the javelin are shown in Figures 13.3 and 13.4 (1) The grip must be firm to prevent any slipping in the throw. (2) However, the hand-arm-shoulder must be relaxed during the run and especially during the power reach. (3) the javelin should lie within the hollow of the "heel" of the palm so that it is in line with the direction of run and throw. (4) The grip in Figure 13.4 is preferred, as it tends to impart a more rotary javelin action during the throw, and so ensure a more steady flight.

THE CARRY. Before the start of the run, the javelin thrower faces straight ahead, with no rotation of the shoulder girdle. The javelin is carried approximately horizontal and over the shoulder, so that the hand is even with the ear. (Note in Figure 13.8 that Cantello's javelin slants downward.)

LENGTH OF THE RUN. Most champions take 10, 11, or 12 steps from their first mark to their second, depending upon whether they start with the same or the opposite foot as that which hits the second check-mark. This distance will range between 50 and 60 feet. The second check mark should be hit with the left foot, as marking the point at which the javelin is pulled straight back in preparation for the throw. The distance of this mark from the foul line will range from 30 to 60 feet depending on whether the thrower uses a five or seven-step count. Seven steps aids proper javelin position but tends to slow the run at its most crucial point. Most champions use a five-step count. Hannu Siitonen (1973--308'1") took ten short bounding strides during the power reach.[1]

SPEED OF THE RUN. This is an all-important point. The run should be gradually accelerated up to the second stride <u>beyond</u> the final check mark. *It should not slow as the final check mark is approached.* The key to maximum use of the run lies in maintaining useable momentum until the last instant, then braking the speed of the lower body by the shocking resistance of the final right- and left-leg positions, and maintaining the speed of the upper body during the throw. A beginner may run "too fast," faster than he can handle during the throw. If he slows down, he'll throw better today and tommorrow. If he slows down, he will also limit

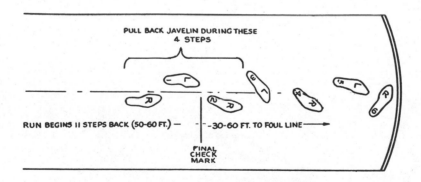

Fig. 13.6 - Steps in the Javelin Run.

his potential use of the run when his technique is improved later. Unless today and tomorrow are extremely important, better to let him maintain "natural" momentum in his run, then gradually acquire the leg power and skill that will fully utilize that momentum. Since momentum tends to carry the upper body ahead of the braking action of the final right-left feet, the latter must be placed well ahead of the body (Figure 13.7)..

Only about one-fourth of the velocity with which a javelin leaves the hand of a champion thrower has been gained from the momentum of the run; the remainder, from sheer throwing power. Prior to Ferenc Paragi's (Hun.) world-record throw of 317'4"[2], he warmed up with throws over 80m (262'5") using three steps--a difference of only 18 percent. But this difference is the <u>one that makes the</u> difference between mediocrity and greatness.

[1] Fred Wilt, "The Javelin: Hannu Siitonen," *Track Technique*, 71, March 1978, p. 2270.

[2] *Track & Field News*, May 1980, p. 24.

THE POWER REACH (Fig. 13.6)

The expression, "power reach" emphasizes perhaps the most critical phase of the entire run-and-throw. The right hand-arm-shoulder do reach back to a position of maximal power; in this thrower, straight back in line with the run; in others (Nemeth, Paragi) farther around (10-15 degrees) beyond the line of run.

The power reach occurs during three strides: L-R-L-R, as shown here. Momentum of the run is maintained--smooth-flowing, rhythmical, completely relaxed.

Full backward reach and rotation occurs during the four steps 1 to 4.

During steps 1 to 4, mainta the full speed and rhythm o the run. Do not slow down.

Javelin point drop down; tail is rela tively high.

Second check-mark on 11th stride. Javelin starts back at this point.

Shoulder-hip rotation causes right foot to turn about 15 degrees.

Throughout the three strides of the power reach, momentum is maintained by moving the feet quickly, low to the ground, and so keeping the center of gravity (hips) low; no upward bounce from one stride to the next. The legs drive forcefully forward (3L to 5R) to place the right foot (5R) quickly and as far forward as possible, well ahead of the right shoulder. Body alignment (figs. 5-6) is now at 20 to even 30 degrees from vertical.

Withdrawal of the javelin (figs. 1-4) achieves a single alignment of the right arm and shoulders (figs. 5-6) to ensure maximal mechanical advantage.

Face turns naturally with the shoulders; eyes maintain focus on direction of throw.

Here, the hand is in front of shoulder alignment; other throwers (Nemeth) swing it slightly behind the shoulder.

The next right-leg stride must be longer, to ensure the backward lean of the torso (30 degrees) and allow time for the left foot to land as quickly as possible during a full stride and extension.

3

3

Figure 13.7. For 13 strides the emphasis has been on building and maintaining momentum. Now within the space of two strides, the brakes are applied hard so as to block the forward movement of the lower body and concentrate power up into the right arm and hand. The greater the speed of the run and the more sudden the stop, the greater the accumulation of power from the run.

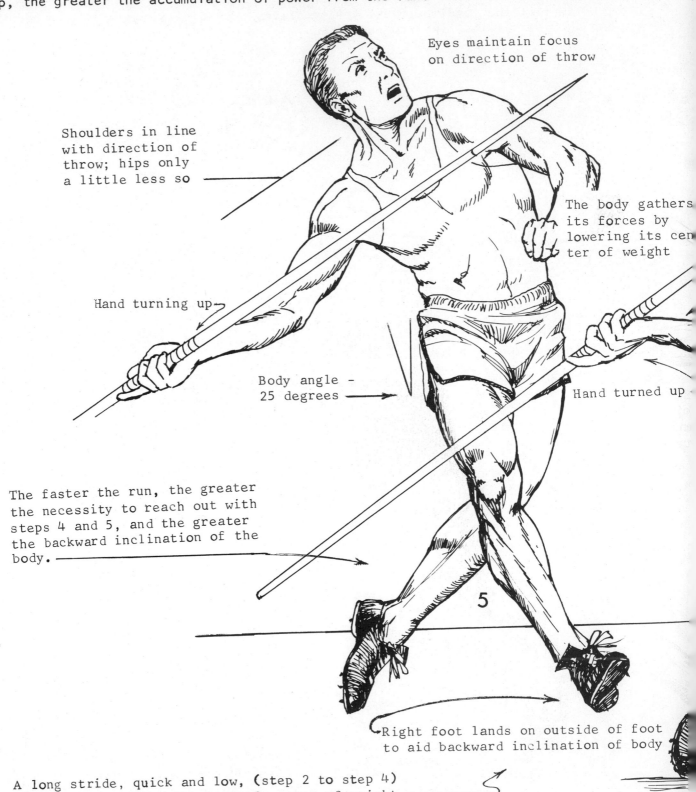

Eyes maintain focus on direction of throw

Shoulders in line with direction of throw; hips only a little less so

The body gathers its forces by lowering its center of weight

Hand turning up

Body angle - 25 degrees

Hand turned up

The faster the run, the greater the necessity to reach out with steps 4 and 5, and the greater the backward inclination of the body.

5

Right foot lands on outside of foot to aid backward inclination of body

A long stride, quick and low, (step 2 to step 4) places right foot well ahead of center of weight

The degree of rotation in the power reach affects directly the important alignment of the hips (figs. 5-6). Greater rotation increases time/force but slows hip
rotation and related actions--counter-torque, stretch-reflex, power-pull. Fig. 6
indicates hip rotation at about 45 degrees. In turn, this relates to degree of
rotation of the right foot (fig. 5). Actual placement will be at about 30 degrees.

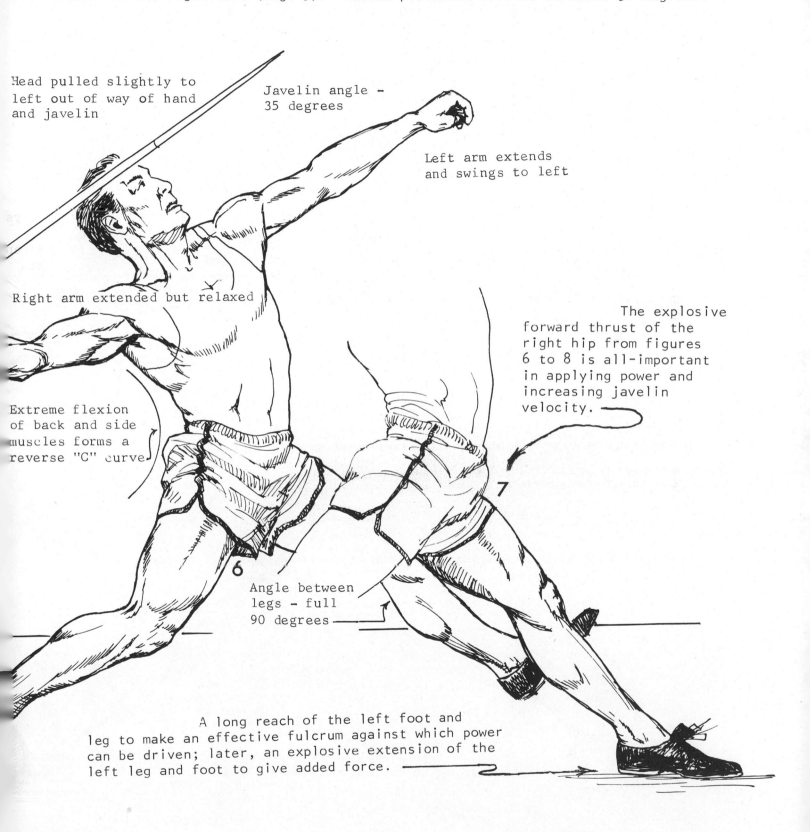

Head pulled slightly to
left out of way of hand
and javelin

Javelin angle -
35 degrees

Left arm extends
and swings to left

Right arm extended but relaxed

The explosive
forward thrust of the
right hip from figures
6 to 8 is all-important
in applying power and
increasing javelin
velocity.

Extreme flexion
of back and side
muscles forms a
reverse "C" curve

Angle between
legs - full
90 degrees

A long reach of the left foot and
leg to make an effective fulcrum against which power
can be driven; later, an explosive extension of the
left leg and foot to give added force.

THE THROW

Figure 13.8. Though actually one unified flowing movement from the first step of the run to the final actions of the follow-through, we can still speak of "the throw" as being the final forward pull-thrust of all the related muscles on the javelin. We have written of the power potentials of the left leg in the shot put and discus. The much higher momentum of a 150-foot run makes those potentials much more crucial in the javelin. There are three aspects: (1) The left leg braces to establish the "hinged moment effect" (Dyson, 1967, 215) by which power is made effective. (2) The throwing action must be forward-up; the left knee therefore bends to allow the pelvis to move forward on a rather flat rising curve. Throwers differ greatly in the degree of this knee bend. In this drawing, Cantello main-tains a

rather straight knee, and so moves over the left leg rather than through it. (3) Just prior to the crucial instant when the whip is cracked and final finger power is applied against the cord grip of the javelin, the left leg extends explosively high on the toes and adds its force to the throw.

To give greater freedom and force to hip rota-tion, the left foot is placed about ten inches laterally to the left of the right foot.

The angle of javelin flight varies among throwers, and also with direction and velocity of the wind--on an average, between 20 and 30 degrees--so as to make most effective use of the aerodynamic qualities of the javelin. Explosive extension of the left leg aids a higher point of javelin release and increased throwing distance. Throughout all such powerful muscle contractions, complete dynamic relaxation is essential, climaxed by the whip-cracking pull of the wrist-fingers.

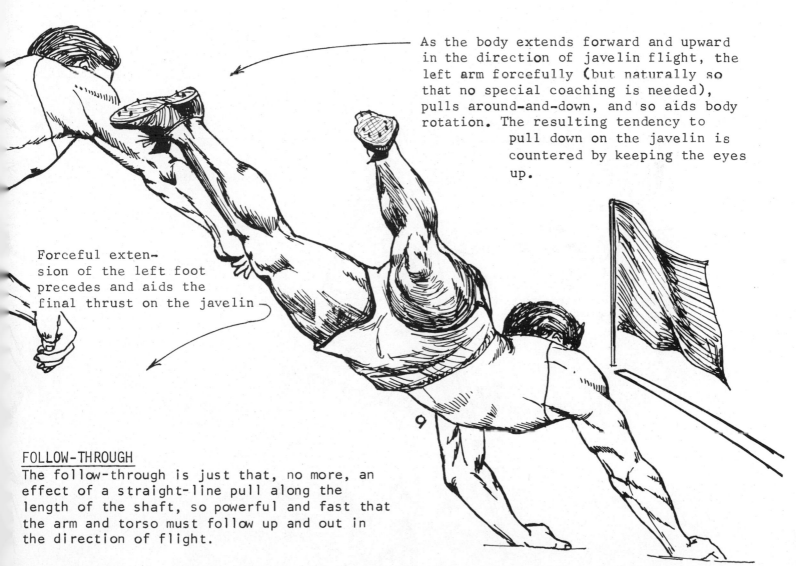

As the body extends forward and upward in the direction of javelin flight, the left arm forcefully (but naturally so that no special coaching is needed), pulls around-and-down, and so aids body rotation. The resulting tendency to pull down on the javelin is countered by keeping the eyes up.

Forceful extension of the left foot precedes and aids the final thrust on the javelin

FOLLOW-THROUGH
The follow-through is just that, no more, an effect of a straight-line pull along the length of the shaft, so powerful and fast that the arm and torso must follow up and out in the direction of flight.

The method of follow-through shown here by Cantello was unique. By trial-and-error Cantello found that when he made an all-out throw with reckless abandon, his torso carried up and out too far and too fast to be restrained by the right leg, without wasting precious feet in a series of hops. He therefore concentrated completely on the throwing action, and caught the full weight of his body on his two arms a few feet from the foul line. Cantello's momentum was great, but he seldom fouled. For him, the method was sound; almost all others prefer to follow the traditional method as shown in Figures 8.3 and 8.16.

LENGTH OF STRIDES. Most champions today take a "natural" length of stride up to the second check-mark, that is, a length which seems most effortless and rhythmical to them individually. However, the modern tendency is to shorten these strides a little, rather than to lengthen them, in the belief that better control and preparation for the throw are gained.

TRANSITION PHASE. Run velocity is greatest at the second check mark just prior to the transition. Acceleration ceases but momentum of the center of gravity is maintained until the last instant. The time interval of the last transitional stride (Fig. 13.8, 4-5) must be minimal. Feet must be close to the ground; the center of gravity (hips) moves forward fast and low, knees flexed. Actual length of this stride depends on various factors--body velocity, body inclination, leg reach for stride length--but about five feet is an effective distance.

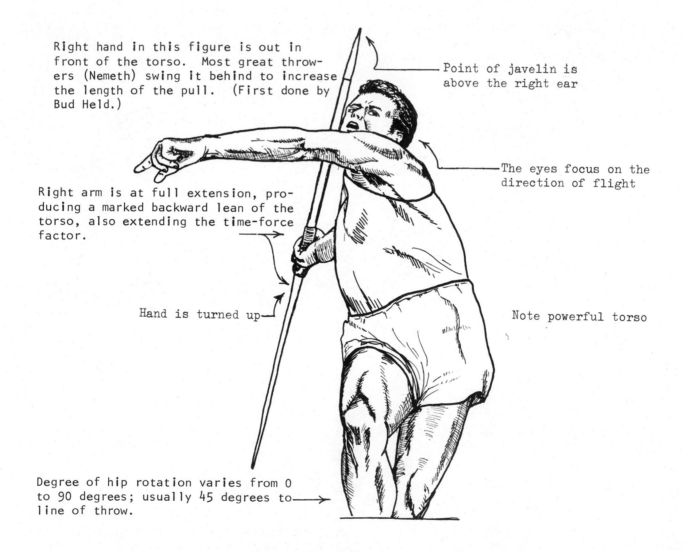

Right hand in this figure is out in front of the torso. Most great throwers (Nemeth) swing it behind to increase the length of the pull. (First done by Bud Held.)

Point of javelin is above the right ear

The eyes focus on the direction of flight

Right arm is at full extension, producing a marked backward lean of the torso, also extending the time-force factor.

Hand is turned up

Note powerful torso

Degree of hip rotation varies from 0 to 90 degrees; usually 45 degrees to line of throw.

Fig. 13.9. A straight-forward action pulling through the javelin. Degree of rotation relates directly to extent and direction of the withdrawal of the javelin. Here, rotation is minimal. Greater stretch-reflex power and time-distance for power application is gained by reaching 10-15 degrees clockwise.

COMMON FAULTS IN THE JAVELIN

1. <u>Failure to align the javelin along the line of throw</u>, and therefore to pull straight along the javelin shaft. This applies both horizontally and laterally. If the javelin point drifts out or up as it is drawn back into throwing position, force will be applied <u>across</u> the shaft. Possible causes are too numerous to fully list here. The grip may be too loose. The right arm may be coming around to the rear; the left foot may be "in the bucket"; the eyes-face may be too high.

2. <u>Too great a concern for the actions of the feet in the so-called cross-over</u>. This cross-over might be compared with the reverse of the feet; it is the result of an action, not an action of which the athlete must be aware when throwing. Emphasize the proper pull-back of the javelin, rotation of the hips to the right rear, the backward lean of the body, and the bracing action of the left, and to a lesser degree, the right leg. This action is very difficult to do when taking a run with full momentum. We have quoted Coach Wetzler's conviction that Cantello's perfection of style could be attributed to perfection of this phase of the throw: "It became part of him. He never had to think of the cross-over as such."

3. <u>Throwing primarily with the arm</u> rather than through the momentum and force of the body in motion. The thrower can be compared with a whip whose explosive "crack!" of the tip would depend on flexibility, of course, but also on the forward velocity and the suddenness of the braking action of the handle. That is, force begins within the handle for the whip; within the legs-body, for the javelin. In the javelin the full momentum of the legs is suddenly stopped by the bracing, or braking action of the right-left legs; force then travels upward through the torso toward the tip (the wrist, hand, and javelin). Keep in mind that this fault must be balanced with that of #6, "failure to explode during the throw."

4. <u>Improper placement of the left leg</u>. This leg placement is crucial. If too far to the left: (a) the body will follow, and the line of force will be down and <u>across</u> the line of intended flight; (b) its bracing action will be lost; and (c) the final powerful extension of the left foot will not coincide with the final whip of the hand as it explodes the javelin on its way. This last point is very important.

If the left leg is extended too far in front, it may brake too much against the forward pull of the javelin; if not extended far enough, it will fail to provide the bracing action by which force is accumulated upward. For beginners the tendency is to cut the leg down too soon and too short, so that the body is above or ahead of it.

5. <u>Too much momentum in the early run; too little during the last three steps before the throw</u>. Only good judgment on the part of the coach can say which portion of this fault should be corrected. To cut down the momentum of the run may aid performance today and this week, but to do so permanently will limit ultimate distance. If time permits, a sounder policy is to maintain momentum of the run by ignoring it, then concentrating attention on the means of utilizing that momentum to the full: on perfection of the cross-over, on a full swing-back or pull-back of the javelin, etc.

6. <u>Failure to explode during the throw</u>. The term we have used in "controlled recklessness." An over-concern for the technical details of javelin throwing may cause the thrower to unlearn his natural tendency to "sock it out there," to forget everything except an uninhibited, all-out explosion of energy. After all, skill is merely a method of accumulating, controlling, and <u>releasing</u> energy. Any sense of caution or concern for style which limits this release of energy is a drawback. A sound style should aid good throwing, but they don't give medals for style; only for distance. EXPLODE!

7. Failure to realize that javelin excellence requires years of practice on technique and training for related power. Coach Joe Haines[1] of David Lipscomb College divided javelin throwers into three groups according to best distance thrown. Group averages were 273', 251' and 233'. He found they differed as follows: number of years between first throwing and peak performance--7.5, 6.0, 5.6; average age--26.3, 23.9, 21.8; threw in high school--13, 9, 9; height--6'1", 6'½", 6'0"; weight--201, 197, 189; maximum bench press--280#, 258#, 255#; best 100 dash time--10.4, 10.8, 10.7.

[1]Bert Nelson, "Of People and Things," *Track & Field News*, 1 March 1973, p. 26.

SAFETY IN THE JAVELIN

1. _Injury to the thrower_. "Muscles that have been properly tuned up and made 100% supple never tear. . . no matter how strenuous the exercise may be." Though this may be an extreme statement, the modern approach to injury prevention is based upon it essential correctness. Traditionally in America, the almost universal prevalence of injury to javelin throwers caused coaches to shy away from the event, to cut fast running and hard throwing to a minimum, and, in general, to avoid injury by doing as little as possible. Today, the reverse is true.

Every link in the javelin thrower's chain of toughness must be gradually forged to withstand every test. Such links are numerous. "Javelin elbow" was so common as to become a by-word in sports. The back muscles are under tremendous strain as the javelin is pulled explosively forward. Tendons in the groin have often weakened as the fast run is suddenly stopped during the last two strides. In fact there are few muscle groups in the body that have not been injured at some time by javelin throwers.

The solution to this aspect of the problem lies in the year-round gradual toughening program outlined in this book. If a muscle or tendon is injured, the fault lies in improper or insufficient preparation, not in the event.

2. _Injury to others_. On the first rule, the coach must be a tough dictator who enforces without favor: No one throws a javelin unless he has the specific permission of the coach. Second, no one gets such permission until he has undergone a period of power training. Enforcement of just those two rules will avoid the greatest danger, that from casual passersby who want to give it a fling, then fling it into somebody's flesh.

Javelin throwers, that is, men who know something of how to throw, can control the direction of flight to a reasonable degree. The problem then is one of preventing others from approaching the landing area. A separate field for the javelin is one obvious solution. Though even then, the throwers must be taught to be constantly aware of danger, to follow a warning system of calls and arm signals. Lacking such a field, ropes should set off the landing area.

Most importantly, the coach must accept full responsibility for this danger; he cannot ignore it; he cannot leave it to the throwers, then blame them for what may happen. If he is constantly aware of danger; his men will be likewise. Certainly the answer does not lie in eliminating the event from our school program as has been done by some States at the high school level, and by the Big Ten College Conference. The javelin is an essential part of the track and field program. When they eliminate football or ice-hockey because of their numerous injuries, then let us consider eliminating the javelin; not before.

The use of safety javelins with rubber tips, such as the Stubby or Winship types thrown into safety nets, is fully justified both for safety and performance, especially when we compare their costs with those of jumping runways and landing mounds.

Fig. 13.10-- For both greater power and safety in the javelin, use 3-4# steel balls, rubber-coated. This drawing from V. Mazzalitis, _Throwing the Javelin_, USSR Sports Publishing Office, 1970.

ORGANIZATION OF TRAINING

The great success of Hungary's javelin throwers, as evidenced by Nemeth (1976-310'4") and Paragi (1980--317'4") makes a summary[1] of their training program by Hungary coach, Jiri Simon, of special interest. The following is my own more concise restatement:

Four aspects of developmental training are emphasized: (1) Work on technique occurs year-round, even indoors when outdoor conditions are unfavorable. Primary emphasis on technique occurs in the spring. (2) Basic strength training follows the pyramid system. For example, during five of six series of squats, resistances are increased, repetitions are decreased, length of recovery periods are increased; during the 6th series, resistances decrease, reps increase, recovery periods increase. (3) Related power training parallels strength training and consists of (a) heavy-resistance movements that simulate javelin patterns of action, and (b) throwing overweight implements--iron rods, weightlifting discs, shots--weighing 1-4kg (2-9#). Gradually progressive overloading, as to both weights and number of throws, is carefully monitored to ensure against injury and for development. (4) Lightweight implements, including underweight javelins, are used for velocity training that closely simulates javelin movements.

Related power training for arm-shoulder development: (1) From throwing stance (left leg forward), lift upward 6 x 25 kg, 6 x 30 kg, 6 x 35 kg, 4 x 40 kg, 6 x 20 kg. (2) Inclined board with dumbbell behind the head, elbows in front. Repeated arm-extension lifts--10 x 5 kg, 3 x 10 kg, 10 x 5 kg. Use a barbell for two-arm extensions.

Related power development of legs: Repeated hops on one leg (R & L) with barbell or sandbags on shoulders--6 x 45 kg, 6 x 50 kg, 6 x 45 kg. For each leg, simulate javelin movements that place greatest stress or require greatest power.

The training year is divided into four phases: (1) September-January, transition periods I & II, (2) January-March, winter periods I & II, (3) March-July, pre-season I & II, (4) July-September, competitive season. Each phase merges smoothly into the next, with careful planning and testing of development throughout. Winter training is extremely intensive and time consuming. All phases include work on technique, on basic strength, and on related power, but the emphasis is constantly changing. For example, the relative emphasis on basic strength and related power (throwing heavy implements) varies for each phase: transition I--1/1, transition II--2/1, winter --3/4, pre-season I--2/3, pre-season II--1/2, competitive period--1/0.

The Tucker Training Program. This method of organization of training is consistent with that devised by Ed Tucker[2], based on his studies of Finnish javelin throwing during several summers in Finland. Finnish summers are warm and pleasant, great for javelin throwing. But Finnish winters are cold-d-d and long-g-g. What we'd consider throwing weather comes in late May and leaves in late August. But for 75 years the Finns have dominated Olympic javelin throwing--a marvel of training organization and of performance.

Tucker found that, as in Hungary, the Finns put major emphasis on basic conditioning in strength, in related power and velocity training. They devised many implements that allowed patterns of movements similar to that of the javelin--implements that were both over and under the 800-gram weight of the javelin, including iron balls.

[1] Jiri Simon, "Hungary's World-Record Javelin Program," *Track Technique*, #69, Sept. 1977, p. 2194.
[2] Ed Tucker, "Javelin Training Program," *Track Technique*, #60, June 1975, p. 1904.

But Tucker points out that the technique of ball throwing is slightly different from that of straight-stick throwing. As the season moves along and technique becomes of greater concern, the Finns use Stubby javelins with weights at both ends to total 3#-2½#-2#. This provides greater safety, develops power, and imitates all aspects of actual javelin technique.

By this time, the javelin prospect will probably move indoors to the weight-training room and basic power development. But indoors or out, such power training should be combined with throwing Stubby javelins into large nets. Tucker found that such nets eliminate javelin hazards and the wasted time spent walking several hundred feet required in throwing a regulation javelin. Many more throws can be taken; coaching time is saved; coaching supervision is closer; the throwers attention is focussed on the how of throwing, not on how far. Where weather permits, the nets are equally effective outdoors.

Flexibility. Tucker[1] reports that the Finns place great emphasis on flexibility and extensibility of the related muscles and tendons--the torso but especially the arms and legs, that is, in the areas where injury is most likely to occur. Few javelin throwers go through a career without straining such parts; prevention can be achieved by proper exercises prior to explosive throwing. Note that the power-training exercises illustrated here can be given a flexibility emphasis as well as one on power. This is important!

A Gradual Year-round Approach. A review of the above discussion will reveal quickly that a gradual development over six months or more is mandatory--for safety, for an unhurried, low-tension approach, for maximum development. Neither power nor technique come easily or quickly. A high, positive correlation could be drawn between javelin distance on the one hand, and years of training-competition as well as months of training within those years on the other.

Fig. 13.11. A Winhill Slo-flite Safety and Training Javelin, as developed by the Winhill Corp.   Has soft-rubber tip. Projecting distance, about 1/3rd javelin distance.

Fig. 13.12. A Stubby javelin as developed by Ed Tucker.

---

[1]Stubby javelins and throwing nets (size, 18' x 24') of Dupont Dacron fiber can be bought from the T-N-T Corp., Attn: Ed Tucker, 2039 Valley Lake Drive, El Cajon, Cal. 92020.

THE ORGANIZATION OF PRACTICE (as devised by Ed Tucker[1])

The intent of this project is to list numerically the key workouts and then show how they fit into a 6½ month training program. They are listed on a daily basis and in suggested order. These, however, are only suggestions and can be altered according to the needs and desires of the coach and/or athlete.

The equipment needed other than the weight lifting room, some form of stadium steps, and common benches are: (1) Medicine balls (weight can vary from 7 to 15 lbs.); (2) Set of "Stubby" Training Javelins (3, 2½, 2 lbs.); (3) T-N-T training net or some other form of catching net.

Note - September is set up as if the man is a beginning thrower. If he or she is a veteran thrower, follow the October program for both September and October.

SEPTEMBER

1st Week
Mon.—1, 2, 3, 5, 28, 31, 8, 9, & 21.
Tues.—1, 2, 3, 5, 11, 12, 13, 14, 15, 16, 18, 19, 20, & 25.
Wed.—1, 2, 3, 5, 28, 31, 22, 23, & 24.
Thurs.—1, 2, 3, 5, 15, 17, 19, & 20.
Fri.—1, 2, 3, 5, 28, 31, 8, 9, & 21.
Sat.—1, 2, 3, 5, 11, 12, 13, 14, 15, 16, 18, 19, 20, & 25.
Sun.—Rest or recreation type workout

2nd Week
Mon.—1, 2, 3, 4, 5, 6, 7, 28, 31, 8, 9, & 21.
Tues.—1, 2, 3, 5, 7, 11, 12, 13, 14, 15, 16, 18, 19, 20, 25, 26, & 27.
Wed.—1, 2, 3, 4, 5, 6, 7, 28, 31, 22, 23, & 24.
Thurs.—1, 2, 3, 5, 15, 17, 18, 19, & 20.
Fri.—1, 2, 3, 4, 5, 6, 7, 28, 31, 32, 8, 10, & 21.
Sat.—1, 2, 3, 5, 7, 11, 12, 13, 14, 15, 16, 18, 19, 20, 25, 26, & 27.
Sun.—Rest or recreational type workout.

3rd Week
Mon.—1, 2, 3, 4, 5, 6, 7, 28, 31, 32, 8, 10, & 21.
Tues.—1, 2, 3, 5, 7, 28, 31, 11, 12, 13, 14, 15, 16, 18, 19, 20, 25, 26, & 27.
Wed.—1, 2, 3, 4, 5, 6, 7, 28, 31, 32, 22, 23, & 24.
Thurs.—1, 2, 3, 5, 7, 28, 31, 15, 17, 18, 19, & 20.
Fri.—1, 2, 3, 4, 5, 6, 7, 28, 31, 32, 8, 10, & 21.
Sat.—Same as Tuesday.
Sun.—Rest or recreational type workout.

4th Week
Same as above (3rd week)

OCTOBER

1st Week
Mon.—1, 2, 3, 4, 5, 6, 7, 28, 32, 35, 8, 10, & 21.
Tues.—1, 2, 3, 5, 7, 28, 31, 11, 12, 13, 14, 15, 16, 18, 19, 20, 25, 26, & 27.
Wed.—1, 2, 3, 4, 5, 6, 7, 28, 32, 35, 22, 23, & 24.
Thurs.—1, 2, 3, 5, 7, 28, 31, 15, 17, 18, 19, & 20.
Fri.—1, 2, 3, 4, 5, 6, 7, 28, 32, 35, 8, 10, & 21.
Sat.—Same as Tuesday.
Sun.—Rest or recreational type workout.

2nd Week
Same as above (1st week).

3rd Week
Mon.—1, 2, 3, 4, 5, 6, 7, 28, 32, 35, 38, 8, 10, & 21.
Tues.—1, 2, 3, 5, 7, 28, 32, 11, 12, 13, 14, 15, 16, 18, 19, 20, 25, 26, & 27.
Wed.—1, 2, 3, 4, 5, 6, 7, 28, 32, 35, 38, 22, 23, & 24.
Thurs.—1, 2, 3, 5, 7, 28, 32, 15, 17, 18, 19, & 20.
Fri.—Same as Monday.
Sat.—Same as Tuesday.
Sun.—Rest or recreational type workout.

4th Week
Same as above (3rd week).

NOVEMBER

1st Week
Mon.—1, 2, 3, 4, 5, 6, 7, 29, 33, 36, 39, 8, 10, & 21.
Tues.—1, 2, 3, 5, 7, 29, 33, 11, 12, 13, 14, 15, 16, 18, 19, 20, 25, 26, & 27.
Wed.—1, 2, 3, 4, 5, 6, 7, 29, 33, 36, 39, 22, 23, & 24.
Thurs.—1, 2, 3, 5, 7, 29, 33, 15, 17, 18, 19, & 20.
Fri.—Same as Monday.
Sat.—Same as Tuesday.
Sun.—Rest or relaxation type workout.

2nd, 3rd, & 4th Weeks
Same as above (1st week).

DECEMBER

1st Week
Mon.—1, 2, 3, 4, 5, 6, 7, 29, 33, 36, 40, 8, 10, & 21.
Tues.—1, 2, 3, 4, 6, 29, 33, 11, 12, 13, 14, 15, 16, 18, 19, 20, 25, 26, & 27.
Wed.—1, 2, 3, 4, 5, 6, 7, 29, 33, 36, 39, 22, 23, & 24.
Thurs.—1, 2, 3, 4, 6, 29, 33, 15, 17, 18, 19, & 20.
Fri.—Same as Monday.
Sat.—Same as Tues.
Sun.—Rest.

2nd, 3rd, & 4th Weeks
Same as above (1st week).

JANUARY

1st Week
Mon.—1, 2, 3, 4, 5, 6, 6, 30, 34, 37, 41, 8, 10, & 21.
Tues.—1, 2, 3, 4, 6, 30, 34, 11, 12, 13, 14, 15, 16, 18, 19, 20, 25, 26, & 27.
Wed.—1, 2, 3, 4, 5, 6, 7, 30, 34, 37, 41, 22, 23, & 24.
Thurs.—1, 2, 3, 4, 6, 30, 34, 15, 17, 18, 19, & 20.
Fri.—Same as Monday.
Sat.—Same as Tuesday.
Sun.—Rest.

2nd, 3rd, & 4th Weeks
Same as above (1st week).

FEBRUARY

1st Week
Mon.—1, 2, 3, 4, 5, 6, 7, 30, 37, 42, 8, 10, & 21.
Tues.—1, 2, 3, 4, 6, 30, 34, 11, 12, 13, 14, 15, 16, 18, 19, 20, 25, 26, & 27.
Wed.—1, 2, 3, 4, 5, 6, 7, 30, 41, 22, 23, & 24.
Thurs.—1, 2, 3, 4, 6, 30, 34, 15, 17, 18, 19, & 20.
Fri.—Same as Monday.
Sat.—Same as Tuesday.
Sun.—Rest.

2nd, 3rd, & 4th Weeks
Same as above (1st week).

---

[1]During the competitive season, workouts each week should include one day of hard throwing—thinking technique and medium distance—and one day of 75% throwing—thinking only technique and competitive effectiveness. On other days, continue with related power training with submaximal weights, with flexibility and stretching, and with running.

WORKOUT KEY

Warmup

1. 15 to 20 min. General—300 to 880 yd. jog, general stretching, 50 fast sit-ups, 4 to 6 wind sprints.
2. 20 to 30 min. Specific—

 A. Medicine Ball (2 hands overhead). Do 10 standing and then 10 kneeling against wall or net.

 B. Stretching for throwing arm. On vertical pole or javelin—hold high with right hand (7') and then push head and chest forward and down causing stretching in the throwing shoulder. Do 10 times and hold.

 C. Arm in throwing position with javelin in hand (palm up)—Force arm back (towards spin but keep javelin tip and arm in throwing position), hold it there, relax, then push back even further. Repeat 5 to 10 times.

 D. Take 10 to 20 EASY throws (standing in front of Training Net with "stubby" javelin) to loosen up arm and shoulder.

Medicine Ball

3. 20 to 30 hard. Standing with ball held with both hands over head. Lean back with arms bent about 90° then deliver with abdominals pulling first and deliver ball (triceps) following.
4. 10 to 15 hard. Same as No. 3 except you twist about 30° by "opening the hip" when going back. Start by punching the hip, then abdominals.
5. 20 to 30 hard. Same as No. 3 except you're on your knees. This tends to put more emphasis on the abdominals.
6. 10 to 15 hard. Same as No. 4 except you're on your knees.
7. 20 to 30 hard. Sitting on bench with feet hooked under another bench, lean back (stretch) with ball in both hands. As ball just touches floor, pull quickly to vertical position with abdominals and release ball with both hands.

Stadium Steps

8. 4 to 5. *Run* stadium steps taking two at a time.
9. 4 to 5. Hopping down steps but landing only on lead leg. (One step at a time).
10. 4 to 5. Hopping down steps—two at a time. (lead leg).

Box Work

11. 8 to 10. Standing on special "boxes" on bench, drop to floor with both feet and immediately jump back to next box which is about 4' to 5' from the first.
12. 6 to 8. Standing on "box", drop to floor landing on the left leg and spring to the next box landing on the left leg.
13. 6 to 8. Same as No. 12, only using right leg.
14. 8 to 10. Drop from box or bench to floor but this time travel forward so your body is dropping at an angle of about 45°. Extend your left leg (as you would in stopping the body in a real throw) and quickly stop the body. Then, drive the body up and back in the direction from which it came.

Weight Lifting

15. 3 sets of Snatch Exercise—weight according to man. 7 to 10 reps.
16. 3 sets of Squats (quarter to half). 7 to 10 reps.
17. 3 sets of Leg presses (use very heavy weight). 7 to 10 reps.

18. 3 sets of Rise on toes (quick bouncing action). 7 to 10 reps.
19. 8 sets of Trunk twisting (forward & sideways) with 5 twists, barbell behind neck.
20. 10—left. Stand in front of chair or bench. Place left foot on bench—step up, then press 10—right, off of toes, back to floor. Repeat.

Running

21. 20 to 40. Short 50 yard wind sprints.
22. 10 to 15. Running up 10 to 30 degree hill for 40 to 60 yards with weight jacket.
23. 8 to 10. Uphill sprints (no jacket) fast for 50 yards.
24. 4 to 5. Bounding strides. 30 to 40 yds.

Triple Jump Type

25. 7 to 10. Alternate leg jumping for 30 to 40 yds.
26. 4 to 5. Left leg hopping for 20 to 30 yds.
27. 4 to 5. Left leg hopping for 20 to 30 yds.

Hip Drills

28. 20 to 30. Hip, then arm drill. Standing in front of training net with 3 lb "Stubby" training javelin, punch hip forward and rotate slightly down (heel or right foot rotates outward). Arm delays then comes through very fast once the hip & shoulder are parallel to the scratch line. Think "high hand release."
29. 20 to 30. Same as No. 28 but use the lighter 2½ lb Stubby.
30. 20 to 30. Same as No. 28 but use the 2 lb Stubby.

Footwork

31. 20 to 30. Take final 4 steps (start with right as No. 1) with 3 lb Stubby in hand. Release javelin into net at ½ effort. Think footwork!
32. 20 to 30. Take a 2 to 4 approach before the final 4 steps. Think footwork and form. Release 3 lb Stubby into net at 2/3 effort.
33. 20 to 30. Same as 32 but use the 2½ lb Stubby.
34. 20 to 30. Same as 32 but use the 2 lb Stubby.

Approach & Coordination

35. 20 to 30. Using a full run, think rhytym, footwork and smoothness prior to releasing the 3 lb Stubby at ¾ effort.
36. 20 to 30. Same as No. 35 but use the 2½ lb Stubby.
37. 20 to 30. Same as No. 35 but use the 2 lb Stubby.

Technique Drill

38. 30 to 50. Full run & throw 3 lb Stubby into net. Emphasis on FORM. In this drill, with the help of the coach and visual aids, the thrower can fortify his strong points and eliminate the poor parts of his throw.
39. 30 to 50. Same as No. 38 but use the 2½ lb Stubby.
40. 40 to 60. Same as No. 38 and No. 39 only do more repetitions.
41. 40 to 60. Same as No. 38 only use the 2 lb Stubby.
42. 15 to 20. These should be the super, all-out throws. The form should be near perfect and you are tuning up for the coming competitive season. You take fewer throws but make each one as close to perfect as possible.
43. 30 to 50. Full run & throw competitive javelin into a training net or outdoors if weather permits. Emphasis here is on proper technique and good angle of release or "down the shaft".
44. 15 to 20. These are all out throws with the competitive javelin. Concentrate on each throw trying to make it your best in all aspects. ‡‡

Chapter 14
THE HAMMER THROW

Throwing the hammer is a very ancient event, having been traced as far back as about 2000 B.C., when the Tailteann Games were held at Tara, Ireland. Folklore still tells of the amazing exploits of Cuchulain, the Irish Hercules, who in one instance performed what was called the "Roth Cleas" (wheel feat) in which, as one teller has it, he threw a single spoke of a chariot wheel to which the hub was still attached. While spinning with it at incredible speed, Cuchulain and the weight parted company and, much to the delight of the onlookers the weight (or was it Cuchulain?) would fly through the air far beyond the marks of ordinary men.

According to the English historian, Joseph Strutt,[1]

Casting of the barre is frequently mentioned by the romance writers as one part of a hero's education, and a poet of the 16th century thinks it highly commendable for kings and princes, by way of exercise, to throw "the stone, the barre, or the plummet" . . . The sledge hammer was also used for the same purpose . . . and, among the rustics, if Barclay is correct, an axletree.

An axletree! Perhaps the tale of Cuchulain had some truth in it, though that would be odd for a brawny Irish hero!

A SUMMARY HISTORY OF TECHNIQUE

Moving ahead a few centuries, Shearman[2] informs us that at a championship meeting, 1886, at the London Athletic Club grounds at Stamford Bridge,

a gigantic Irishman, J. S. Mitchell . . . has won the hammer throwing (a 16# hammer, four feet long, thrown from a 7-foot circle) with a throw of 110'4". . . . The original rules allowed the hammer-thrower to use a hammer [wooden handle--J.K.D.] of any length, to take as much run as he liked, and throw from any place he liked, the judge marking the place where the thrower had his front foot at the moment the hammer left his hands. . . . In 1887 the circle was enlarged from 7 to 9 feet, and in 1896 a handle of flexible metal was legalised.

When the size of the circle was finally standardized in 1907 at a diameter of seven feet, most of the throwers were using one or two turns (not until the 1920s did three turns become accepted.) In part, this was because of the method of turning on the ball of the left foot (often called a "toe turn"), which required a jump around with both feet momentarily in the

---

[1] Joseph Strutt, *SPORTS AND PASTIMES OF THE PEOPLE OF ENGLAND*, London: William Tegg and Co., 1855, 75.

[2] Montague Shearman, *ATHLETICS*, London: Longmans, Green & Co., 1904, 61.

TABLE 14.1

OUTSTANDING PERFORMANCES --HAMMER THROW

OLYMPIC CHAMPIONS

Date	Record	Name	Affiliation	Age	Hgt.	Wgt.
1900	163' 1½''	J. J. Flanagan	USA			
1904	168' 1''	J. J. Flanagan	USA			
1908	170' 4¼''	J. J. Flanagan	USA			
1912	179' 7''	Matt McGrath	USA			
1920	173' 5½''	Pat Ryan	USA			
1924	174'10''	Fred Tootell	USA	24	6'2''	215
1928	168' 7¼''	Pat O'Callaghan	Eire			
1932	176'11''	Pat O'Callaghan	Eire			
1936	185' 4¼''	Karl Hein	Germany			
1948	183'11½''	Imre Nemeth	Hungary			
1952	198' WR	Joszef Csermak	Hungary	20		
1956	207' 3½''	Harold Connolly	USA	25	6'	235
1960	220' 1½''	Vasiliy Rudenkov	USSR	29	6'1½''	211
1964	228' 9½''	Romuald Klim	USSR	31	6'1''	240
1968	240' 8''	Gyula Zsivotsky	Hungary	31	6'3''	205
1972	247' 8½''	Anatoliy Bondarchuk	USSR	32	6'	245
1976	254'3.9''	Yuriy Syedikh	USSR	21	6'3/4''	220
1980	268' 4''WR	Yuriy Syedikh	USSR	25	6'1''	225

RECORDS OF SPECIAL INTEREST

Date	Record	Name	Affiliation	Age	Hgt.	Wgt.
1904	172' 11''	John Flanagan	USA			
1911	187' 4''	Matt McGrath	USA			
1913	189' 6½''	Pat Ryan	USA			
1956	220' 10½''	Mikhail Krivonosov	USSR			
1967	235' 11''2	Ed Burke	USA			
1968	242'	Gyula Zsivotsky	Hungary	31	6'1''	240
1969	247' 7½''	Anatoliy Bondarchuk	USSR	29	6'	240
1971	250' 8''	Walter Schmidt	W. Germany	23	6' 3½''	253
1974	251' 6''	Aleksey Spiridonov	USSR	23	6' 3½''	260
1975	260' 2''	Walter Schmidt	W. Germany	27	6' 3½''	253
1978	263' 6''	Karl-Hans Riehm	W. Germany	27	6'1 3/4''	234
1980	267' 11''	Sergei Litvinov	USSR			

BEST PERFORMANCES -- HIGH SCHOOLS

12#

Date	Record	Name	Affiliation		
1972	227' 8''	Alvin Jackson	Classical, Providence, R.I.		
1976	231' 11''3	Manny Silverio	North Bergen, N.J.	16# -- 202' 9''	
1977	190' 8''	Robert Menard	Woonsocket, R.I.		
1978	200' 4''	Robert Colantonio	Classical, Providence, R.I.		
1979	222' 3''	Keith Bateson	E. Greenwich, R.I.		

2American record   3High School record

290

air. This loss of contact with the ground made balance and straight-line progress across the circle very uncertain. Even with but two turns, fouling was very common and throws flew off in almost any direction.

In consequence, the danger to nearby athletes and spectators was very great, and the event was barred from all high school and most college programs. Only in recent years has the prod of Olympic needs produced an increase in college participation. A few Eastern preparatory schools have maintained hammer competition through the years, primarily through the enthusiastic dedication of a few coaches and ex-throwers like Sam Felton and Harold Connolly.

THE IRISH WERE FIRST. In the early years, the Irish were clearly the chief movers in the event. At least in America, from about 1890 into the 1920s, it was dominated by such good Irish-Americans as John J. Flanagan, Matt McGrath, and Pat Ryan, known as the "whales" of the New York City police force. Between the three of them, they won every Olympic Games from 1900 through 1920. Flanagan won the first three and moved the world record to a very respectable 184'4" in 1909. McGrath won in 1912 and extended the record to 187' 6½". Pat Ryan won in 1920 after having achieved 189'6½", a record that stood for 25 years. Each of these men turned on the ball of the foot in a low-hop style, but were able to maintain balance and control through their great body-weight which averaged about 270 pounds. By the way, in defense of the Irish--as if they ever needed it!--they also won the 1928 and 1932 Games through the throwing of Pat O'Callaghan.

Another great hammer thrower, Fred Tootell, appeared during the twenties. Fast and extremely powerful, Tootell perfected the "toe turns" method and added the concept of letting the hammer "hand" during a portion of each turn. He would permit the hammer to lead him for an instant at its highest point, then, with a burst of speed, turn his body so it was ahead of the hammer as it approached its low point. In this manner, Tootell was able to pick up a tremendous amount of speed and still secure a strong finish position. The record books credit him with a best throw of 185', but after leaving amateur ranks, he officially whipped the hammer some 212', truly remarkable when compared to Ryan's world record of 189'6½". By the way, Tootell was a native of Rhode Island, the only State in the Union to sponsor hammer throwing in its high school program.

In the early 1930s, the upsurge of interest in sports in Germany led to the work of Sepp Christmann who carefully analyzed the hammer throw in terms of its mechanical principles and their application to human powers and movements. He concluded: (1) For good balance and control the left foot must maintain firm contact with the ground throughout all turns. This was done by starting the turn on the outside of the heel of the left foot, rolling on the outside of the foot to the ball-toe, and around to the heel again. The pattern of the foot now moved in a straight line toward the front of the circle. This method is still valid today. (2) The hammer must hang from passive arms directly in front of the thrower's chest so that it neither leads the turns nor retards their movement. The net effect was a smooth, seemingly effortless progression across the circle, with constant acceleration of the ball of the hammer.

Using these two methods, Karl Hein and Erwin Blask of Germany placed one-two in the 1936 Olympics, and moved the world record to 193'7" where it remained for 12 years.

MODERN TECHNIQUES. In the 1950s, three new approaches radically changed hammer methods and performance. Between 1911 and 1951 (40 years) hammer world records improved approximately 20 feet; in the next decade they improved about 30 feet (201-231'). Primary among these new approaches was basic strength training. Second, the extension of training greatly increased--in hours per week and number of weeks until the latter became year-round. Third, hammer-throwing techniques were improved to provide greater velocities in the turn and greater power in the final pull on the hammer. These three concepts are interdependent; certainly the last could not have been achieved without the first two as a foundation.

In the Olympic Games, the Hungarians first led the assault with Imre Nemeth winning in 1948, and Jozsef Csermak in 1952 with a world-record 197'11". In 1956 Hal Connolly (US) set an Olympic record at 207'3".

But from then until the present, world hammer throwing has been dominated by the Soviet Union, West Germany, East Germany and, in the Olympics, Hungary. In the Olympic Games, 1960-1976, the Soviet Union won 11 places including four golds; Hungary, seven places; W. Germany four; East Germany, two; leaving six lower places for all others. Of the top ten world hammer throwers selected by *Track & Field News*, 1975-1979, the Soviet Union claimed 25 including eight in the first three; West Germany, 11; East Germany, 9 leaving only five places for all other nations. Strangely, despite its Olympic success, Hungary took no places among the top ten during any of these five years.

In the decade 1951-1961, the world-record improved about 30 feet (201' to 231'); between 1961-1971 about 20 feet (231' to 251'); between 1971-1980 about 17 feet (251' to 268'). Such a low rate of decrease in record performances suggests continued improvement for many years into the future.

During the most recent period, it would be difficult to select the most outstanding throwers. Bondarchuk (SU), won the 1972 Olympics was third in 1976, and held a world-record at 247'7½". Riehm (WG), was selected as best-in-the world for two years--1975, 1978--and set a world standard in 1978--263'6". Litvinov (SU), was selected 9th in 1978, 1st in 1979, and threw 267'11" for a new world record in 1980. But there were other great performers not far behind. In 1979, according to *Track & Field News*, 10 men in the world bettered 250'7" (5-SU, 3-EG, 2-WG). Fifty bettered 236'3" (SU-25, EG-4, WG-4). The top American (Emmitt Berry) threw 228'9".

Russian Techniques. At the Montreal Olympics, 1976, Yuriy Syedikh (SU) established an Olympic record--254'4" (77.52m). His coach, A. Bondarchuk, had these comments,[1]

Yuri Syedikh, the winner of the Montreal hammer throw, has obviously made good use of the changes in the technique that have taken place in the last few years. What is noticeable in Syedikh's technique is the duration of each turn's double support phase, the placement of his right foot in the single support phase, ideally straight arms throughout the turns, and excellent balance in all support phases. Observations of Syedikh's turns show that he spends relatively long periods in the double support phases after the shoulder and hip axis correspond. On each turn Syedikh turns 90° to the left, something no other hammer thrower in Montreal did.

Another notable aspect in Syedikh's technique is his ability to use the hammer's inertia, created in the single support phases. It must be kept in mind that the hammer head, not the body of the athlete, is the leading link in the thrower-hammer system.

The athlete does not perform active movements with the lower part of the body (hips, legs) until the rotation has passed the highest point. After that, the active rotation around the support point (the ball of the left foot) begins with the right leg, aiming to activate the hammer as fast as possible. Syedikh, at this stage, does not move ahead of the hammer through the active turning of the hips and legs compared with the shoulder axis. He does it with the whole body, except the arms, contrary to the previously recommended action.

In addition, the axis of the shoulders, hips and legs of Syedikh's have not turned in the frontal plane, which is one of the single support phase and therefore makes it possible to lengthen the double support phase. The most active part at this stage is the right leg, not the hip as was previously thought to be correct. This can be explained by the fact that the hammer head can be accelerated towards the end of a single support phase efficiently only when the thrower's body rotates somewhat faster than the hammer. To use the rotational speed of the hip makes such action virtually impossible. Consequently, the early acceleration of the hammer is achieved through the work of an active right leg. The faster the right leg lands on the surface of the circle, the larger the acceleration of the hammer at the start of the double support phase.

The lengthening of the double support phase, in turn, allows for an ideal rotation of the whole system of thrower-hammer around the vertical axis and balances this system during the single support phases.[2]

---

[1] A. Bondarchuk, "Yuri Syedikh's Hammer Technique," *Track Technique* #71, March 1978, p. 2273.

[2] A more detailed discussion of modern techniques is given by Robert P. Narcessian, former U. S. hammer champion, "The Evolution of Modern Hammer Throwing Techniques," *Track & Field Quarterly Review*, Vol.80, #1, Spring 1980, p. 59. Eleven other articles on hammer throwing by coaches and researchers appear in this same issue.

THE WHOLE ACTION

Fig. 14.1 -- These drawings adapted from Harold Connolly, *The Hammer Throw,* published by The Southern Pacific Association of the U.S.A.A.U., Los Angeles, Calif.

HOW TO BEGIN

Begin with the wholeness of action. Allow your new prospect to begin by throwing the hammer: first, with only preliminary swings, but soon, perhaps within 15 minutes, with one and even two turns. It won't actually be *throwing* the hammer; more like stumbling around and letting it go. But the thrill of swinging and releasing that ball on a wire sling can be experienced on the very first day, even on the first effort, regardless of strength and skill. True, one might begin as in shot-putting, by weeks of strenuous power training. This would help the hammer throwing of course, but on the other hand, the thrill of hammer throwing on the first day would help greatly to motivate strength training later on.

THE PRELIMINARY SWINGS. Now that he's caught a feeling of the fun of it, a new and more logical start can be made. First, teach the preliminary swings. (Some use a sandbag without handles; some a sledgehammer--the rigid handle is more controllable than a flexible steel wire; others, the official hammer). Begin with the hammer head far to the right (250 in Figure 14.1). Now as the thrower moves slowly through two flat swings (swings with a low high-point) the coach can hold the hammer head and explain what should be done and felt at each stage. In general, while holding the head position quite steady on its original center-line, the hammer head should be swung at all times in the widest possible arc. To do this, the throw-er should be in a "sitting-down" position: Knees bent, buttocks low; upper body bent forward a little, but head erect and eyes fixed straight ahead throughout the swings; arms straight and shoulders reaching forward whenever possible (Figure 14.2). As the hammer head swings to the left, the head should not sway to the left; to do so would have a similar effect on the shoulders-arms-hammer and cause the low-point to move ten or more degrees to the left, a serious fault.

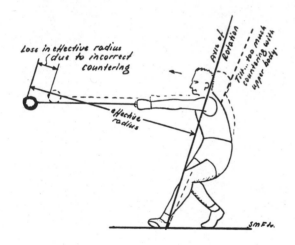

Fig. 14.2 -- Increasing the radius of the hammer by countering (sitting back with the hips while extending the arms and shoulders forward. This drawing by Sam Felton, Jr.

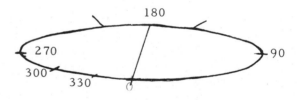

Fig. 14.3 -- Degrees of arc in the hammer circle.

During the turns, there is a strong tendency for this low-point to shift progressively to the left (In Figure 14.3, from 300 to 330 to 350 degrees). The farther the initial low point is to the right during the preliminary swings, the greater the tendency to remain there during the turns. This not only gives the thrower better over-all balance but crucial time in which to sit back hard against the hammer's pull and thus accelerate its momentum--with no loss in radius of the hammer arc.

As the hammer head swings behind the head, a slight forward lean of the torso counter-balances the pull of the hammer and shortens the backward reach of the arms, but the arms, and especially the right arm, are straightened as soon and as quickly as possible so as to ensure a low-point closer to 280-290 degrees.

LEARNING TO TURN. At first, a man may progress faster if he merely holds his arms out at the horizontal, with no hammer, or perhaps with a 16-pound sand bag. But the hammer must be used very soon to ensure sound learning. As the hammer approaches 270 to 280 degrees, the thrower must sit down a trifle lower and harder against the left heel. The knees are bent. The arms are stretched out fully, relaxed and passive--a mere extension of the wire.

At this point the hips lead the shoulders and the shoulders turn left faster than the hammer. As the hammer reaches its low-point, and certainly before the hammer reaches the line of the right knee, the left toe and right heel are lifted and the turn started with a twisting on the left heel and right toe. The weight shifts over to the left heel.

As the hammer reaches about 60 degrees, the body twist pulls the right foot off the ground; the right knee turns in close to the left. These actions aid the right foot to return as quickly as possible to the ground. The hammer can be accelerated only when both feet are on the ground; the longer this time, the greater the acceleration. Centrifugal force and imbalance will tend to swing the right foot and knee wide, but they must be kept in--close!!

As hammer velocity increases, its centrifugal force must be countered by lowering the buttocks and bending the knees, by "sitting-down" *lower* on each turn, not by pulling with the arms or straightening the upper body. This point is crucial and must receive constant attention. The left arm-shoulder remains stretched to its fullest extent throughout the turns.

As soon as the right toe lands at the end of each turn, the thrower must sit back hard against the outward pull of the hammer; the harder and faster this is done, the greater the acceleration of the hammer.

Foot-work. Throughout all phases of the turns, the left foot must maintain contact with the ground. As the hammer head passes about 290 degrees, the weight shifts toward the left heel, the left toe lifts and rotates to the left, the foot rolls on its outside surface around to the toes and ball of the foot, then on around at the end of the turn to the heel again. The axis of this left foot, when on the ground, is a straight line toward the front of the circle.

The right foot remains on the ground as long as possible. It is not deliberately lifted; rather it is pulled off the ground by body rotation. When off the ground it must swing low and in close, so as to return to the ground as soon as possible.

Countering. To maintain control and momentum, there must be a counter-balancing of forces as between the centrifugal force of the hammer and the centripetal force exerted by the body. Traditional techniques countered with the entire body. The body was held relatively straight and leaned away from the hammer. In contrast, modern throwers use only the hips and legs for this countering action; by bending the knees and lowering the buttocks into a "sitting-down" position, these angle strongly away and against the pull of the hammer. The greater the velocity of the hammer head, the greater its centrifugal force, and the lower the thrower must sit-down in order to counter its effects. The increasing momentum of each successive turn tends to straighten and lift the thrower; on the last turn, there will seem to be almost no weight on the turning left foot. This effect must be countered by trying to sit-down lower on each turn.

Such countering is made even more difficult by the modern technique of extending the upper body and arms forward so as to lengthen the radius of the hammer and thus increasing its peripheral velocity. This full forward reach can add as much as four inches to the hammer radius, and Felton[1] claims as much as five to six feet in distance for each inch of radius increase. Assuming a given throwing angle, the primary factor in throwing distance is hammer head velocity at the point of release. Though the turns of modern throwers are not appreciably faster (exception: those now using four turns), this technique of countering with the hips while extending the hammer radius with the upper-body reach may have produced an increase in throwing distance of twenty feet.

The Hammer Plane. During the preliminary swings and the turns, the plane on which the hammer head moves should be kept flat; that is, with a low high-point and a low-point that just clears the ground. During the turns, never allow the hands to rise higher than the shoulders. Two common errors which tend to produce a high-angled plane are (1) to allow the

[1] Sam Felton, Jr. and Gabor Simonyi, *MODERN HAMMER TECHNIQUE.* (See note under "Essentials of Sound Technique.")

the hands to rise higher than the shoulders during the turns, and (2) to try to lift and accelerate the hammer head as it begins to rise from its low-point.

Hammer Acceleration. The very fast placement of the right foot at the end of each turn carries the hips with it and creates a body torsion in which the hips are well ahead of the passive shoulders (Figure 14.4). This torsion is increased as both legs now twist powerfully into the next turn. This acceleration of the feet-legs-hips is conveyed upward through the shoulders and arms to the descending hammer head, when it is most susceptible to acceleration. It ends as the hammer reaches its low-point. If this action if to be effective, the eyes-head must be on the hammer; if they are allowed to lead the turning action, the shoulders will be turned to the left with them, the hammer radius will be shortened, the torsion between hips and shoulders will be lost, and the potential for hammer acceleration dissipated. Similarly the arms do not aid acceleration either directly or actively; they hang passively throughout, and merely transmit the power produced by hip-shoulder torsion.

The Throwing Action. As the last turn is completed, the low-point of the hammer is reached at about 315 degrees (Figure 14.3). At this point both feet are firmly on the ground, knees bent, and at least some of the forward flexion of the upper body-shoulders is still present. Now, by a powerful twisting extension of the left leg, sharp lifting of the eyes-head, and backward extension of the torso (Figure 14.1-21 to 25), tremendous force is exerted to accelerate hammer-head velocity. As its great momentum rips the hammer grip from the hands, the left foot must still be in contact with the ground, though extending powerfully upward.

Head Radius. In an analysis of the techniques of hammer place-winners in the 1972 Olympics, Jabs[1] concluded that the shortness of the radius of the circles outlined by the thrower's head had a high correlation with the distance thrown, that is, best results were reached when the head radius was small, indicating a smooth "linear" progression across the circle.

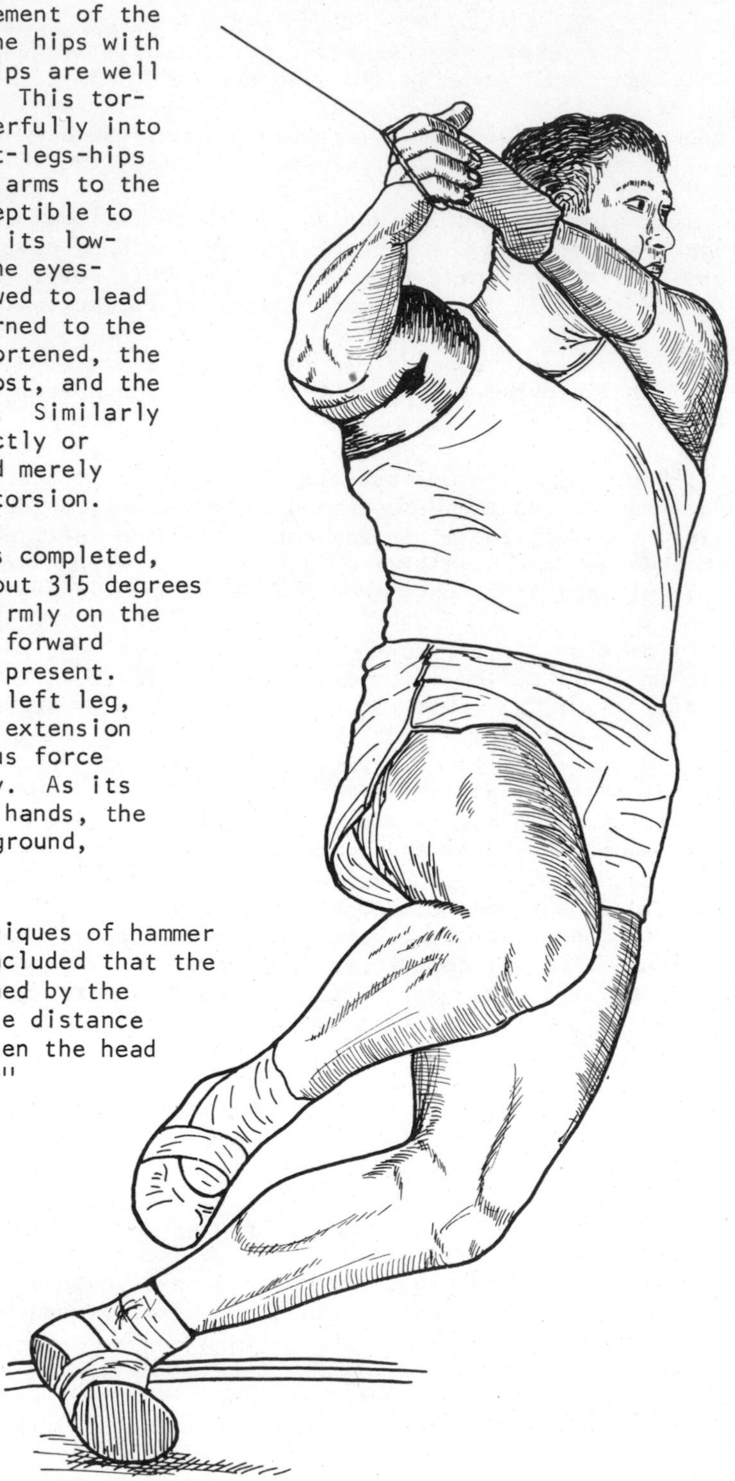

Fig. 14.4 -- Body torque and momentum. Note the balance of forces--the weight and angle of the body counters the centrifugal force of the hammer.

[1]Rolf-Gunter Jabs, "Analyzing the 1972 Olympic Hammer," *Track Technique*, #52, June 1973, p. 1656.

DEVELOPING POWER FOR THE HAMMER

It takes great strength to throw the hammer--great basic strength as is developed by basic weight-lifting exercises, but also great related power as is developed by heavy-resistance exercises involving high velocities of movements similar to those of hammer throwing. Throwing the 56# or 35# weight is probably the best of these.

The organization of a program of building both strength and related power should follow the plans presented in Chapters 6 and 16. In general, hammer throwers, here and abroad, spend a greater percentage of training time on heavy-weight training than do other throwing-event men. This fact, added to their multi-year careers, creates a special problem in monotony and physical plateaus or sticking points. A constant variation in training loads is mandatory to maintain continuous progress--variation in the number of days per week, the degree of intensity of loading from about 60 percent to maximal (95%), variation in extensity or total tonnage per day, per week and per month, and other ways. For example, Tschiene[1] reported that during December 1971 Walter Schmidt worked at this program four times a week: First week--power cleans, 6 x (5 x 265#/120kg); snatch, 6 x (5 x 220#/110kg); squats, 6 x (5 x 364#/165kg); deadlift, 2 x (5 x 375#/170kg); trunk twisting sitting, 2 x (20 x 243#/110kg). Each following week 11#/5kg in weight was added.

When working for power extensionally, Tschiene's throwers lifted weights five times a week with only 60 percent loads--this to develop endurance as well as power. During the early-mid competitive season, once a week of intensive lifting was used with loads of 80 percent to maximum. But whatever the purpose, variation was emphasized throughout.

As the season progressed, greater attention was given to what I have called related-power training, that is, to resistance work (moderate to heavy) for the various muscle groups in movements similar to those of hammer throwing. Such work is alternated rhythmically ("pendulum training") with basic-strength workouts, and later, with specific or imitative power training. In the American schedule, 56# and 35# weight throwing should be considered very effective related-power training but the other exercises illustrated here should also be used for purposes of variation and all-round development.

But relatedness is carried one step further to what I have called imitative-power training-- performing actual hammer throwing from within the 7-foot circle, using hammer weights varying, according to Tschiene, from 27.5#/12.5kg down to 11#/5kg, including other weights of 22#, 20#, 18# and 13½#. Heavier weights develop the strength factor in the formula (power = strength x velocity); lighter-than-competitive-weights, the velocity factor. Each weight has its own rhythm-technique-speed which tends to disrupt 16#-hammer coordinations in competitions. As the competitive season moves forward, increasing emphasis therefore is placed (1) on 16# throwing, and (2) on 20# and 18# throwing.

As final remarks, Tschiene concludes that "strength training occupies the main role in conditioning the thrower....In every instance an increase in performance can take place only through an increase in the extent of the loading" and this in turn can occur only through a wise experience-based variation of loading and its methods.[2]

For the record, Tschiene presents these figures as maximums for these world-class hammer throwers:
   Walter Schmidt (WG),250'8"/71--power clean, 397lb/180kg; squat, 617lb/280kg; snatch, 303lb/137½kg; dead lift, 726lb/330kg; bench press 408lb/195kg.
   Karl Hans Riehm (WG), 242'6", 1972--clean (split), 364lb/165kg; squat, 485lb/220kg; snatch, 298lb/130kg; dead lift, 573lb/260kg; bench press, 276lb/125kg.
   Anatoliy Bondarchuk (SU), 248'11½", 75.88m, 1972 (weightlifting performances from 1969)-- clean, 397lb/180kg; snatch 287lb/130kg; dead lift, 770lb/350kg; squat, 551lb/250kg.

---

[1]Peter Tschiene, "Power Training Principles for Top-Class Throwers," *Track Technique*, #52 June 1973, pp. 1642-1655.

[2]These conclusions are supported by the later research of A. Bondarchuk and others, "Power Development Problems," *Track Technique*, #64, June 1976, p. 2052.

RELATED POWER EXERCISES

HAMMER THROW

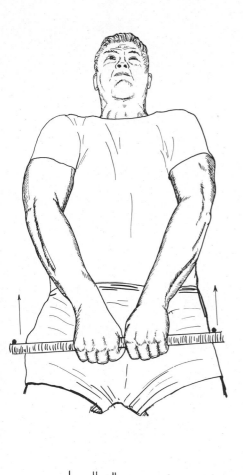

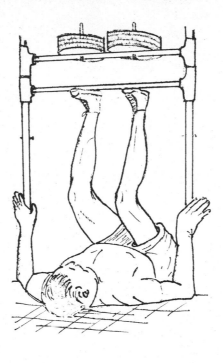

Fig. 9.6 - <u>The Hammer Throw</u>. In figures 1 - 8, note (a) the head is held steady with little sway to the left or right, (b) the knees are bent, (c) the hips are low in a sitting-down position so as to counteract the pull of the hammer, (d) the arms-shoulders in 1-2 and 6-7 are reaching forward so as to increase the hammer radius, (e) the left arm straightens as soon as possible from positions 5 to 6, and 8 to 9.

The second swing is faster than the first. The low-point of the first swing is on the thrower's right at about 300 degrees; that of the second swing, at about 315. The low-point of the first turn (Figure 14), is at 330 degrees; of the second turn (Figure 18), 340; and of the third turn (Figure 22), 350 degrees.

At the beginning of the first turn (Figure 9) and throughout the remaining phases

of the three turns, the weight is over the left foot. The axis of the left foot forms a straight line across the circle (Figures 12, 15+, and 20). Note the countering action of the hips and the full arms-shoulders extension in figures 9 to 12. The right knee-foot in figures 12, 15, 19, and 20 stays low and close to the left so as to gain an early landing just prior to figures 13, 17, and 21. The right foot is not so much

HAMMER

picked up as it is dragged from its place on the ground by body torque. The most important phases in the entire throwing sequence occurs just prior to and during figures 13-14, 17-18, and 21-24. The right foot has just landed; the torsion between the hips, and the shoulders-arms-hammer is at its maximum; both feet are on the ground and now exert maximum power in increasing hammer acceleration. Figures 12 and 20, and to a

lesser degree, figure 16 indicate a flat plane of the hammer sweep - important for proper countering, increased acceleration of the hammer, and overall balance and control throughout the action.

During the final <u>throw</u> of the hammer (Figures 21 - 24), the entire body extends

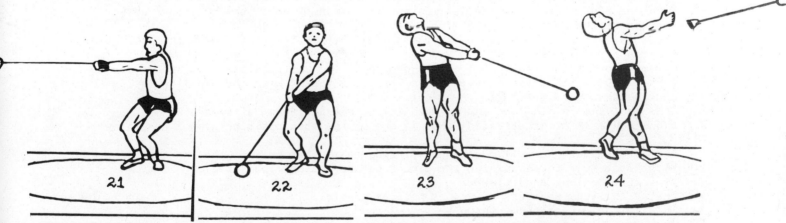

powerfully so as to exert maximum lift on the hammer: the eyes-head drop far back and up, the back-muscles left, the left foot-knees-hip extend with maximum force. The hammer flight should be between 40 and 45 degrees.

*These drawings are adapted from Harold Connolly, <u>The Hammer Throw</u>, Southern Pacific Association AAU, Los Angeles, Calif., 1961, 54 pages. Connolly's contributions in Education and Amateurism exceed even his great performances in throwing the hammer.

ESSENTIALS OF SOUND TECHNIQUE
One of the better outlines of hammer-throwing requisites and techniques is provided by Tom Pagani, field event coach, Indiana University:[1]

A. Physical Characteristics of the Thrower
    1. Should be tall--this allows for a better release angle at the finish.
    2. Long arms--everything else being equal, the further the ball is from the thrower, the faster it will be moving.
    3. Good rotational speed--sprinting or running speed is not the same as turning speed-- a good hammer thrower must be able to turn quickly.
    4. Well coordinated--the hammer is a complex event and a well coordinated athlete will be able to learn it much more quickly.
B. Winds Over the Head (usually two)
    1. This is the single most important part of the throw as it sets up the turning position.
    2. Thrower assumes a position at the front of the circle with the shoulders turned about 45° to the right.
    3. Legs bent to aporximately a quarter squat position--feet pigeon toed, about shoulder width apart.
    4. Ball is either positioned at the back of the circle or swung to that point.
    5. *Wind the ball with as little arm involvement as possible*--use a weight shift from right foot to left foot and back again--these are the forces which accelerate the ball.
    6. Dividing the circle into quarters, assume that 270° is parallel to the throwers right side. During the wind the thrower attempts to have the "low point," which the ball passes through, go over 270° or slightly back from that point.
    7. Accelerate each wind.
    8. Shoulder rotation is constant to keep the proper relationship to the ball.
    9. The "high point" that the ball passes through (at approximately 90°) should not be higher than the head.
C. Entrance into the Turns
    1. If the winds are done properly and the entrance into the turn is smooth, the turns will be simple mechanics.
    2. *Allow time for the ball to move from the right side to the left after the final wind.* When the ball is on the right side, body weight is also on the right. Since *all of the turns are made with the body weight on the left side,* the thrower must allow the ball to move from right to left.
    3. Hip and shoulder lines almost come into alignment.
    4. A triangle is formed between the chest and both arms.
    5. Shoulder line *never* moves ahead of the hip line.
D. Turns (usually three, however some world class take four)
    1. Assume that body weight is now over the left side.
    2. Turn on the heel of the left foot and the ball of the right foot for 180°.
    3. Turn the right knee into the left at this point and keep thighs pressed together throughout the turns.
    4. After the first 180° the turn is made on the ball of the left foot with the right foot off the ground.
    5. Attempt to get the right foot on the ground as soon as possible--ie: before the ball passes 270°. (This is referred to as "crossing the X" with the hip line facing toward and the shoulders turned to the right.)
    6. *Arms must remain straight and relaxed throughout the throw* after the winds.
    7. *Each turn must be accelerated*--this is one of the most basic points of the throw.
E. Finish.
    1. Body weight must be well over the left side to counter pull of the hammer.
    2. Right foot must touch down on the circle before the ball passes 270°.
    3. Arms must be long and relaxed.
    4. Extend the legs and back upward as hard as possible.
    5. Turn in the direction of throw.
    6. *"Low Point" which the ball passes through must never be to the left of 0°.*

---

[1]Tom Pagani, "Hammer Throw Technique," *Track & Field Quarterly Review,* Vol. 80, #1, Spring 1980, p. 30.

ESSENTIALS OF SOUND TECHNIQUE

SUMMARY.[1] Hammer throwing can be made overly complicated. Don't let it be. Keep it simple. Work for a powerful, explosive, rhythmical build-up of great hammer head speed. Combine this surging speed with the widest hammer radius you can control, with particular emphasis on letting the hammer sweep way to your left as you fly into each turn.

Strive for quick, tight turns. During the turns, continually feel your feet and hips gain on the hammer. With each turn, be sure to increase your lead-angle on the hammer. Drive your head and hips around together, and leave the hammer farther behind with each turn. As you do this, counter the hammer's pull with your hips, by letting your arms and shoulders relax and stretch with the hammer from when the hammer is about knee-high, until the ball of your right foot alights at the completion of each turn. If you counter properly as you do this, and if the hammer sweeps far enough to your left, you will have to hang correctly from the hammer's pull or be pulled out of the circle. If you hang correctly, you will complete each turn well ahead of the hammer, with legs well "under the hammer."

Fig. 14.7 -- Hang! This drawing by Sam Felton, Jr.

During the turns, use your legs as the primary source of turning power. They can add power only when both feet are on the ground. During the turns, don't let your left foot be pulled from the ground, even for an instant, and do all you can to insure that your right foot is airborne for the briefest possible instant between the turns.

Between each turn, you must hit a strong lifting position, with legs deeply flexed, before the hammer passes its lowest point, and you must then stretch them ahead of the hammer . . . but, of course, not all the way. The critical "hip-angle" must be maintained throughout the turns. In the second and third turns, the ball of your right foot must alight before the hammer falls below shoulder-height.

During the turns, keep your eyes up. Don't look down.

Hit a powerful finish-position, with both feet in position way ahead of the hammer, with flexed legs "under the hammer" before the hammer passes its lowest point, which must be to the right of 330°, and explode with every ounce of strength to whip the hammer on its way. Use your legs and back as the main lifting force. Keep your left foot firmly on the ground until after the hammer is released.

WHAT TO WATCH FOR--A CHECKLIST
The following are the main points coaches watch for.

1. Note throw's overall tempo. It must be one smooth, rapidly accelerating, continuous action, from start through release. Each turn must be faster than the preceding one. There must be a pronounced, continuous build-up in hammer-head speed. There must be no pauses.

2. In evaluating speed, pay more attention to hammerhead speed than thrower's turning speed.

3. Make sure the thrower stays ahead of hammer during turns. Sense that he gains on the hammer with each turn (Figure 14.1).

---

[1] This summary and the checklist that follows are excerpted with permission from *MODERN HAMMER TECHNIQUE* by Sam Felton, Jr., and Gabor Simonyi.

4. Watch the hammer wire. Sense that it picks up great speed from turn to turn, and gets tighter and tighter. It must not become slack at any time, particularly during back portion of any wind or turn.

5. Watch for a smooth, but dramatic and pronounced pick-up in hammer-head speed as ball of right foot alights at completion of each turn.

6. Stand off at 270° point and watch where the hammer is at the instant ball of right foot alights at completion of each turn. It must alight ahead of hammer, before it passes 270° (Figure 14.1-12), and it should alight farther ahead with each succeeding turn. In addition, it should alight before hammer drops below shoulder height at completion of 2nd and 3rd turns (Figure 14.6-13).

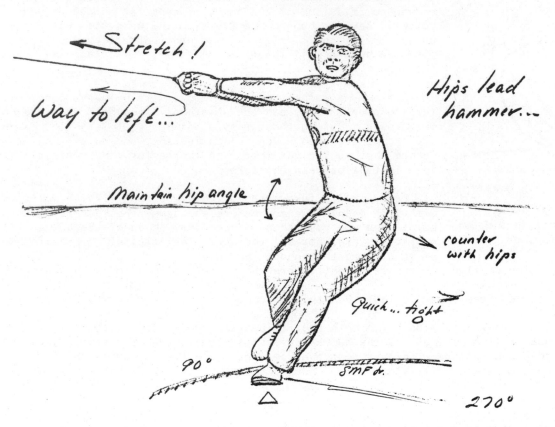

Fig. 14.7 -- Stretch to the left! This drawing and hand-written comments by Sam Felton, Jr.

7. Watch the right foot. It should not be lifted too early at the start of each turn, and it must not be lifted way up, or fly too far out. It should travel the shortest route possible and alight quickly so thrower can bring both legs to bear on hammer to make it go faster.

8. Watch the distance between the knees while the right foot is off the ground. They should be very close to each other (Figures 14.1-11, 14.6-12).

9. Watch the right foot as it completes each turn. Only the ball of right foot should contact ground between turns (Figure 14.6-13). Make sure the heel does not hit; if it does, it will brake the turning momentum.

10. Watch the right foot during turns. It should appear to push the thrower leftward, into each turn.

11. Listen for the right foot as it alights. It should be silent. A thump means the thrower

is off balance, or the hammer is ahead of him.

12. Watch the left foot. It must not leave ground during winds or turns, even for an instant, until after hammer is released.

13. Watch the left foot track down circle. It should do so in a straight line across circle. Make sure none of the turns are undercompleted . . . each must be a full 360°, and only the last one may be a little over-completed.

14. Watch the hands during the winds. They must pass through a very wide radius.

15. . . .and watch the eyes and head during the winds. The head should remain facing the same direction, to the thrower's right (about 280°), throughout the winds. The head must not turn to the front as the hammer comes forward except during the sweep into the first turn.

16. Watch the sweep into first turn. Make sure thrower shifts his weight firmly on to his left foot just before the hammer passes its low point (Figure14.1-12), and holds it there throughout transition. Make sure he presses way left and turns "outside his left foot" with a well-executed outer-edge roll.

17. Watch the hammer's low point. With each wind and turn, it will creep to the thrower's left, but should remain within bounds indicated in Table 3 in section 5.0. In particular, watch low point during sweep into first turn (280-300°), and at start of final sweep (320-330°).

18. Watch the width of hammer's radius during winds and turns. When thrown correctly, one is impressed with the extremely wide radius hammer sweeps through (Figure14.1).

19. Watch the shoulders during turns. They should not be pulled back as indicated by dotted lines in Figure14.2. Sense that they are relatively relaxed and are pulled forward slightly in direction of hammer from instant hammer passes 10° until right foot alights, particularly during first two turns. Watch thrower's upper body. It should remain perpendicular to ground and should be arched toward the hammer as it sweeps from 10° to its high point.

20. During the back portion of each turn, watch the left knee to see if it "gives" or bends quickly, ahead of hammer, immediately after it passes its high point, and before right foot alights (Figure14.6-16).

21. Watch the legs between turns. They must be flexed deeply, in a strong lifting position before the hammer passes its low point (Figure14.6-9).

22. It is difficult to see where the thrower actually starts each turn, but it should start before the hammer passes the right knee (Figure14.6-9).

23. Watch the head position relative to hips. They should turn together, square to each other. The eyes should not turn ahead of hips by an appreciable amount during turns, particularly during back portion of last turn.

24. While watching to see if hips and head are turning together, watch the arms and hammer. With each turn, they must trail the head and hips/legs by a little more.

25. Also watch the eyes. They must not look down, particularly at completion of each turn.

26. Watch how high the hands are as hammer sweeps through its high point. In first turn, they should naturally rise to shoulder height, and in succeeding turns, a little more, to about eye level (Figure 14.6-12, 20). If this is done correctly, hammer will travel on a properly inclined plane, and release angle will be an optimum 41-45°.

27. Watch how far the hands are from the thrower's body. They must stretch way out, particularly as hammer sweeps up to its high point.

28. Watch for the "hip-angle" (Figure 14.2). It must not disappear, particularly during the last turn.

29. Watch to make sure the thrower does not pull his arms in during final sweep.

30. Watch the left foot during release. It must not break from the ground until after hammer is released (Figure 14.6-23).

31. Watch where hammer lands. It should land a little to the right of center line besecting foul sectors, as you look out in direction of throw.

NUMBER OF TURNS. A. Bondarchuk, former world-record holder and later, Master Coach Hammer Throw, Soviet Union, is a first-level authority on all aspects of the event,[1]

It is the opinion of the author that three turns are at the moment more efficient and still open for many avenues of improvement. The ability to change from the preliminary swings into the first turn, for example, can be developed. So can the delivery action at a higher velocity and the rhythm of the throw.

Four turns can be recommended only to athletes who are unable to reach maximum velocity with three turns, and are capable of controlling the extra speed by changing the throwing rhythm and developing specific speed.

Although the contemporary three-turn technique enables throwers to reach the 75-80 meter range without difficulty, it is possible that four or more turns will be used by future hammer throwers, provided they have considerably more specific speed than the top performers of today.

THE ORGANIZATION OF PRACTICE

The overall requirements of hammer throwing, including technique, are undoubtedly the most demanding of the four throwing events. Size and strength are at highest levels, comparable to the shot and discus. For example, research has placed the centrifugal pull of the hammer at a shocking 300kg (660#) for champion throwers. At the 1972 Olympic Games, finalists had an average height of 1.87m (6'1 5/8") and average weight of 106.1 kg (232.4#). Great speed and agility are pre-requisites. The explosive quickness with which the turns are taken is truly remarkable. And certainly, perfection of technique in turning, in maximizing contact with the ground, and in using full power in the final pull is essential.

It follows that both the process of selecting candidates and introduction to hammer throwing should occur carefully and gradually. As a first principle, both basic and related strength training should precede work with the hammer. But problems of eliciting interest in the event and motivating such strength training may allow early throwing with a lightweight head and, optionally, a short wire. The thrill of releasing the hammer and watching it fly far out is exciting and not easily forgotten.

Mark Erickson[2] suggests two basic drills that he found useful at Cal-State, Stanislaus,

(1) The first drill does not require the use of a hammer. A long, smooth surface is required for practicing concentration turns. The thrower begins with the right toe slightly behind the left toe, head up, chest out, hips forward and knees bent. From this position the thrower will progress from slow motion turns to quick turns. The athlete should concentrate on each turn, consciously thinking his way through each one.

In the first phase of this drill, the thrower completes slow motion turns in two stages. The first stage is to turn the left foot to the 180° position. The left foot should be placed on a line. With the left foot on the line, the right foot should step over the left. It is important that the right leg does not swing

---

[1]A. Bondarchuk, "Three or Four Turns?", *Track Technique*, #73, Fall 1978, p. 2339.

[2]Mark Erickson, "Drills for Hammer Throwers," *Track & Field Quarterly Review*, Vol. 80, #1, Spring 1980, p. 57.

around the left leg. The thrower's goal should be to get the right foot back on the ground as quickly as possible after lifting it. This is best accomplished by stepping over the left foot and keeping the knees close together during turns until the right foot is put down about shoulders-width. The knees should almost touch during the step over.

After 20 or 30 slow motion turns the thrower should do complete turns, slowly increasing the speed and number of turns.

(2) The second drill helps keep the arms out. A 16 pound hammer is used with a 2-1/2 or 5 pound plate slipped over the wire. The added weight makes it difficult for the thrower to pull his arms in. With the heavy hammer the thrower will perform three sets of 15 winds. The first and third set is to the left, and the second set is to the right. These sets are tiring, and the thrower will learn that to relax the arms and keep them out makes the drill easier.

These drills, performed three to six times a week for five to fifteen minutes each, provide excellent warm-up and technique training.

At the 1939 Congress of European Track and Field Coaches, Coach Bondarchuk (SU) stated that the unique actions of hammer throwing place special emphasis on "whole" learning methods (70-80% of training time) as compared with "part" methods (20-30%). Practice of throwing technique occurs, with constantly changing emphases, throughout the entire cycle of each year's training. During the early period of general preparation, heavy hammers (9-16kg) are thrown with average speed in the turns.

Training throws can be divided into three categories--easy, medium and maximal. Easy throws are 50-80% maximal; medium throws, 80-90%. Training sessions begin with easy throws, shift to maximal throws, and end with medium throws in which awareness can be on phases of technique within the wholeness of action. As maximal practice throws increase in distance, so should both easy and medium throws.

Throwing with eyes closed is widely used during this process of improving coordination and a creation of "hammer feeling" takes place. In the second half of the preparatory period, hammers are changed. The athletes use standard weight hammers instead of heavy hammers. Beginning March-April, there is a steep decrease in the volume of throwing with the standard hammer due to the introduction of light-weight implements. There is a relation of 60% of light-weight hammers to 40% normal.

At commencement of the competition period, the volume of throwing work with the normal hammer increases, the work with the light hammer decreases, and the heavy hammer is re-introduced. The relation of hammer of different weights is: 60%--Normal; 20%--Light; 15%--Heavy.

Training Exercises
1. USSR hammer throwers train with various weighted implements beginning from 1 to 16kg.
2. Many integrating exercises are used
    a. Many turns are performed (20 to 100) with the hammer.
    b. Special strength exercises with barbells are used for suppleness of the shoulders and for basic muscular groups
        --generally 40% of training:
        --lift the barbell to the chest and high in the air
        --pushing and pulling exercises from the shoulders
        --isometric exercises for pulling in specific poses and attitudes which imitate the final effort.
3. The number of throws per day can be up to 200 in the 50-60 range. However, research and practice have shown that the number of practice throws can be much less. Presently we throw 30-40 and sometimes 50-60 at most in one day. The number of days per week of actual throwing depends on the individual. Some throw 3 and some throw 6 times per week. The average would be 5-6 times per week and presently they throw the variously weighted hammers.
4. Bear in mind that incorrect methods will have a negative result in the humeral areas at the expense of imbalance for throwing where the athlete

cannot stretch muscles particularly in the right arm. Every attempt is made to have a strong back but with the arms and legs relaxed.[1]

HOW THEY TRAIN[2]
<u>Scott Neilson</u>, 1978, Age 21, 6'5"/245# (1.95m/111kg).
University of Washington--NCAA champion, 1976-77-78; native of Vancouver, B.C., Canadian champion, 1977-78. Best distance--238'8" (72.79m).

Scott estimates that 40% of his training time is devoted to weight work, with "not as much as I would like" to running. He sometimes throws all out for practice, with a best of 237-0. "In the early part of the year most of my training is devoted to getting better body positions. This is best done at speeds less than 100%. As these become good I concentrate on timing, and it involves throwing at speeds close to 100%. If hard throwing is done before good body positions are established, they will come a lot slower."

From December to March, Scott changes over to competitive season training by dropping one lower body lifting session and adding two, then three throwing workouts. He adds, "Every fourth week I take off, or what amounts to doing 20% of a normal week's work."

Non-Competitive Season
Mon--Lower body lifting: a) clean, 6 x 135, 235, 265, 295, 315. b) squat in rack, 6 x 135, 235, 325, 415, 455, 4 x 495, 525. c) dead lift in rack, set of 6 to 580.
Tues--Light upper body lifting and gut work.
Wed--Same as Monday, no dead lift.
Thurs--Same as Tuesday.
Fri--Same as Monday.
Sat-Sun--Rest.

Competitive Season
Mon--10 min. stretching, 800-yard jog, 10 min. stretching, 15 min. hammer drills (winds, right and left; alternating winds and spins; set of 10 spins). 30 throws, 6 x 80 yards striding, 20 min. stretching.
Tues--Rest.
Wed--Same as Monday, only 20 throws. Then weight work: a) dead lift from rack, 6 each x 135, 235, 325, 425; 4 each x 475, 525, 565, 595, 615. b) leg extensions, 6 x 10 with gradual buildup. c) 30-45 and 2 x 15-60. d) side bends, 2 sets of 10 x 90, each side. e) bench press, 3 sets of 6, no heavy weight. f) chin ups, 2 x 8. g) upright rowing from knees, 2 sets 10 x 150. h) 15 min. stretch.
Thurs--Same as Monday.
Fri--Rest.
Sat--Compete.
Sun--Same as Wednesday, except no hammer drills or throwing.

---

[1]A. Bondarchuk, "Modern Trends in Hammer Throwing," *Track & Field Quarterly Review*, Vol. 80 #1, Spring 1980, p. 40.

[2]Win Arnold, "Scott Neilson," *Track Technique*, #73, Fall 1978, p. 2328.

Chapter 15
THE DECATHLON

Of all Modern Olympic contests, the decathlon most clearly reflects the Ancient Greek Games ideal of all-round, balanced excellence in sports. A full track meet in miniature, it provides the most demanding test of the five "s" words:speed, stamina, strength, skill and self-discipline--ever devised in any sports competition.

The decathlon includes ten events: four track events--100m dash, 110m high hurdles, 400m dash, 1500m run; three jumping events--running high jump, pole vault, running long jump; three throwing events--16# shot, discus, javelin. Performance in these ten events is scored, not by comparison with those of other competitors, but by reference to a scoring table. Examples: on the 1962 tables, six feet (1.83m) in the high jump scores 743 points; 50 feet (15.26m) in the shot 804 points; 50 seconds in the 400m dash, 805 points. The man gaining the greatest number of points for ten events is the decathlon winner.

Five events are held during each of two days; the 400m dash completes the first; the 1500m run, the second. An impression is held generally, eagerly nourished by the media, that such a schedule is cruelly exhausting or grueling. But we need only to watch such Olympic champions as Bruce Jenner or Bill Toomey as they scamper joyously around the track immediately after finishing the last event, the 1500, to know they are far from utter exhaustion. Year-round, effective training has prepared them for such a high level of energy output; such words as "grueling" are valid only when preparation is inadequate for attempted performance.

Personally,[1] the decathlon--in competition and for the most part in training--was an exciting joy. It was fun to move from one event to another, not once or twice, but ten times--ten phases of a single competition. Of course, in the 1920s, the high tension that exists in today's attitude of win-or-nothing was absent. Few cared--nationally or locally, even in an Olympic year--if we won or lost.

Secondly, and most important, I have always rejected sport as a violent struggle against antagonistic opponents. In the decathlon, the struggle is against time, distance, fatigue, and one's inner fears of weakness or failure. Other decathletes are fellow-competitors, helpful motivators to doing one's best, often ignored, often good friends, never hostile. Each concentrates on doing his utmost, without concern for diminishing the efforts of others. Whoever scores the most points on the Tables is the victor.

In my years of decathlon competition--Olympic and National--I cannot remember a single incident of hostility--no attempts to intimidate or even belittle, no unsettling jibes at the start of a sprint or hurdle, no "hogging" of implements during warm-ups. But I do remember a

---

For this Chapter--its facts, its viewpoints, its enthusiasm for the decathlon--I am heavily indebted to Dr. Frank Zarnowski and his publications: *THE DECATHLON GUIDE* (1976), *THE DECATHLON BOOK* (published annually), and *DECA NEWSLETTER* (published monthly), all of which provide all the information any decathlete or coach could possibly need. They can be purchased from the author, Mt. St. Mary's College, Dept. of Business and Economics, Emmitsburg, Maryland, 21727.

[1]The author was U.S. decathlon champion, 1928 and 1929 (American record, 7784 pts., 1920 Tables) and bronze medallist, 1928 Olympic Games, Amsterdam.

TABLE 15.1

OUTSTANDING PERFORMANCES -- DECATHLON

OLYMPIC CHAMPIONS

Date	Record[1]	Name	Affiliation	Age	Hgt.	Wgt.	Y[2]	D[3]
1912	6161	Hugo Weislander	Swe					
1920	5970	Helge Lövland	Nor					
1924	6668	Harold Osborn	USA	22	5'11½"	170	6	6
1928	6774	Paavo Yrjöla	Fin	26	6'	185	11	14
1932	6896	James Bausch	USA	26	6'2"	210	2	5
1936	7421	Glenn Morris	USA	24	6'2"	185	1	3
1948	6826	Robert Mathias	USA	17	6'2½"	190		
1952	7731	Robert Mathias	USA	22	6'3"	199	5	10
1956	7708	Milton Campbell	USA	23	6'3"	208	3	5
1960	8001	Rafer Johnson	USA	25	6'4"	200	7	11
1964	7887	Willi Holdorf	W.Germ	24	5'11½"	198	6	10
1968	8193	William Toomey	USA	29	6'1½"	195	11	38
1972	8454	Nikolay Avilov	USSR	24	6'3"	192	5	17
1976	8618	Bruce Jenner	USA	26	6'2"	198	7	29
1980	8495	Daley Thompson	G.B.	21	6'	195	6	14

WORLD-RECORD PERFORMANCES OF SPECIAL INTEREST

Comment

1912	6756	Jim Thorpe	USA	24	6'0"	190	Olympic 1st but disqualified

| 1930 | 6867 | Paavo Yrjöla | Fin | 28 | 6'0" | 180 | |

1932   7038   Akilles Jarvinen   Fin   By 1962 tables would have won 1928 and 1932 OG

1952   7731   Robert Mathias   USA   7887 by 1920 T
10.9   22-11   50-2½   6-3   50.2   14.7   153-10   13-1½   194-3   4:50.8

1960   8063   Rafer Johnson   USA   At Final Olympic Trials
10.6   24-9½   52-0   5-10   48.6   14.5   170-6½   13-¼   233-3   5:09.9

1969   8417   Bill Toomey   USA   Won 5 AAU titles (1965-69)--most ever.
10.3   25-5½   47-2¼   6-4   47.1   14.3   152-6½   14-¼   215-8   4:39.4

1976   8618   Bruce Jenner   USA   26   6'2"   198   Set in winning Montreal OG
10.94   23-8½   50-4¼   6-8   47.5   14.8   164-2   15-9   224-10   4:12.6

1980   8622   Daley Thompson   G.Brit.   21   6'0"   195
10.55   25-4   47-5¼   6-11   48.1   14.4   141-0   16-1   214-3   4:25.5

1980   8649   Guido Kratschmer   W.Ger.   25   6'1½"   200
10.58   25-7   50-9   6-6 3/4   48.04   13.92   149-4   15-1¼   218-2½   4:24.15

---

[1]Converted to 1962 Tables   [2]Years of competition   [3]Total no. of decathlons

number of helpful acts--sharing a blanket in the cold or poncho in the rain, or loaning tape, a pair of spikes, even a vaulting pole. In fact, most decathlons bring forth such acts of helping each other, and may the best man win. More so, I think, than in single-events. Perhaps the long and varied competition tends to avoid concentrations of tensions and emotions that spill over into aggression against others. Perhaps it's the scoring Tables that intervene between potential adversaries and become the real enemy. But whatever the reason, the decathlon is great fun, and fair play is the very essence of its attitudes.

Sam Adams, decathlete, UCSB track coach and U. S. National Decathlon Coach, strongly supports these views,[1]

> *(The decathlon) is an event that gives you, not one, but ten chances. It is an event that takes all your skills, and all your strength, and all your heart if you are to excel. There are no short cuts. There are no tricks. There are no easy ways to achieve your potential in this event. There is intelligent, progressive training for achievable goals. When goals are grasped, higher goals are always there to be reached for.*
>
> *Take up the challenge. You will find a close knit group of decathletes with a common goal, and an understanding of what you are experiencing. You will find challenge, frustration and satisfaction, disappointment and achievement, woe and joy. But most of all, you will find the Decathlon is the best of Track and Field, and Sport itself.*

The Ancient Greeks Had No Decathlon. Though the word, "decathlon," is Greek in origin-- *deka* (ten) + *athlos* (contests)--its use is modern. The Ancient Greek Games included only a five-event all-around: a running long jump with weights (2½-10#); a javelin throw using a thong looped over one or two fingers and twisted several times around the javelin shaft; a discus throw of varying weight from three to as much as 49 pounds; a stade race (sprinting one length of the stadium); and, most admired by all, wrestling. As soon as any man won three events, as with sets in modern tennis, he became pentathlon champion.[2]

The Ancient Greek Olympics occurred during a thousand years (776 B.C.-384 A.D.), with an almost unchanged schedule of events. Surprisingly, the first three events listed above were never held as single events, only as related to the pentathlon. This gives us some awareness of the high regard the Greeks has for well-rounded development as contrasted with one-event specialization. A man could be the greatest long jumper, discus thrower or javelin thrower of his time but never win an Olympic victory other than in the pentathlon with its emphasis on a harmony of speed, power and beauty of style.

HISTORY OF DECATHLON DEVELOPMENT

The first scoring tables for a ten-event all-around were constructed in 1883 by W. B. Curtis, sometimes called "the father of United States track and field" because of his early and vigorous efforts in organization. As with all later systems, scoring occurred without reference to others' performances, only by reference to some arithmetical standard. Curtis allowed 1000 points for equalling the 1883 AAU record, then scaled points down with little beyond good judgment to guide him, and with almost no basis for balanced scoring among the events.

Since then, at least a dozen versions of the decathlon have been proposed; some with other events; most with a "new and better" method of scoring; almost all by one of the Scandinavian countries: Sweden (1902, 1906, 1909, 1912, 1952, 1962); Finland (1909, 1934); Denmark (1901, 1910); Norway (1909). The only other proposals were by Germany (1911) and that by the United States (1920) used in the Antwerp, Paris and Amsterdam Olympics. Sweden's 1962 Tables (modified, 1971, by conversion to 100ths) remained in use through the 1980 Moscow Games.

---

[1]Sam Adams, "Reflections on Decathlon," *Track & Field Quarterly Review*, Vol. 79 #2, Summer 1979, p. 5.

[2]The most authoritative and fascinating source for these statements is H. A. Harris, *GREEK ATHLETES AND ATHLETICS*, Hutchinson & Co., London, 1964, 242 pps.

Modern Scoring Tables. A number of factors have made new Scoring Tables inevitable:
(1) improved implements, techniques and training methods have upset balanced scoring in the
1962-71 Tables; (2) modern computers provide precise progressions; (3) accumulation of enough
decathlon performances to provide a valid and reliable sampling for scoring; (4) realization,
based on 18 years experience, of errors of judgment in the old Tables.

Drafts for such modernized tables were presented before the 1980 Moscow Congress with
statistics valid to December 1979. Requirements for these Tables were:

1. The tables must be based on reliable recorded performances of decathletes throughout
    the world.

2. Progressive and corresponding rate of change in scores in all events.

3. Parameters on which tables are prepared must take into account the spread of
    performances, not just one average value.

4. The form of the tables should give a fair distribution of scores between
    individual athletes in all the events in the competition.

5. Mathematical and statistical basis for preparation of the tables should be
    such that the tables can be updated at regular intervals.

GREAT OLYMPIC DECATHLETES

The first decathlon in the Olympic Games was in 1912 at Stockholm, Sweden. Events were
scheduled during two days in the same order as today's competitions. New scoring tables gave
fairer, better-balanced scoring. As today, only three attempts were allowed in the three
throws and the long jump.

Jim Thorpe, 1912 Olympic "Champion." This first Olympic decathlon was actually won by the
Carlisle Indian, Jim Thorpe, generally considered America's greatest all-time, all-sport
athlete. It was his first and only decathlon! But his total of 8412 points (1912 Tables) surpassed by almost 700 points that of the official winner (Hugo Weislander, Sweden, 7724 points),
a point difference exceeded only once in Olympic history (Mathias, 1952, 912 points).

Today, with our perfect conditions for performance, we find it hard to appreciate the amazing quality of his achievement (6756, 1962 Tables). In 1912, facilities, equipment, training
were all at lowest levels. Jumping pits were of turned-over earth; high jump and pole vault
standards were but eight feet apart; the pole vault runways were "as long as possible--say
50 feet;" poles were of spruce that, for a big man, weighed about eight pounds; hurdles were
heavy and, when hit, rose on their inverted-T-shaped bases; throwing surfaces were of dirt;
running tracks were soft. Even more astonishing, Thorpe also won the pentathlon (winning four
of five events by wide margins); and was among the finalists in three individual events--high
jump, long jump, shot.

But in 1913, a newspaper disclosed, and Thorpe naively confirmed in writing, that he had
accepted money (small even for those days) for playing semi-pro baseball during summer vacations prior to the Olympics. If we weight 1912 Olympic attitudes and rules of amateurism plus
Thorpe's written acknowledgement of payments, the U.S. Olympic Committee (the I.O.C. was not
involved) had no choice but to ask that Thorpe's name be erased from the official books and
his prizes returned. For a half century Thorpe's pre-eminence as an amateur athlete was un-
recognized. But amateurism gradually acquired a more relaxed code; by present-day Olympic
rules and practice, Thorpe's misconduct would be ignored. In 1976, he was inducted into the
National Track and Field Hall of Fame which recognizes only amateur performances.

Jim Thorpe's great achievement through natural, untrained talent set the pattern for decathletes in the United States for the next half-century, until about 1960. It was generally considered a noteworthy but freakish event for which interest of spectators, media and competitors
was almost nil for three years of each Olympiad, and rose but little during the Olympic year.
The National AAU Outdoor Championships was the only regular competition. For this meet, open
to all with no qualifying standards, a paltry score of men might enter and a dozen or so
actually compete. In addition, the Relay Meets at Pennsylvania, Drake and Kansas variably did
and did not hold the event. With such minimal competition, no one trained seriously for the

decathlon as a separate event; a few weeks usually sufficed.

Harold Osborn, 1924 Olympic Champion. Harold Osborn is the only man in Olympic Games history to win the decathlon (6668 pts., 1962 tables, a world record) and an individual event (high jump, 6'6", Olympic record). Unlike other decathletes, Osborn entered the decathlon very gradually and late in his career--just after graduation from the University of Illinois, 1922. As a freshman, he first signed up as a distance runner, but, discovering on his own initiative that he could outdo all others in the high jump, he shifted to that event.

During my sophomore year in the fall, I started to enlarge my field a little. I tried hurdling and also took up my old event, the broad jump. In addition I generally managed to put in a little time with the weight men [he weighed about 160# at the time---JKD] and shortly afterward I took up cross-country work and made the squad.[1]

Osborn's coach at Illinois was Harry Gill, former Canadian All-Around Champion, so we can assume he was encouraged in such experiments. In his junior year, he "put in too much time training for the Pennsylvania Relays pentathlon. It finally proved to my satisfaction that running and jumping do not mix." In his senior year, he tried the septathlon in the Illinois Indoor Relays. But he did not compete in any decathlon until after graduation--1922, National AAU, second place. He won the National AAU titles in 1923, 1925 and 1926, as well as the Olympic title in 1924.

In 1924, Osborn established a world-record 6'8¼" in the high jump with a self-created, controversial style that resulted in changes in both high jump rules and construction of the standards. Also, Osborn undoubtedly had the longest multi-event career at high-quality levels in all track and field history. During 20 years (1923-1943), he won 18 National AAU outdoor and indoor titles in six events (35 medals in nine events), including the standing high jump and triple jump; and at age 37, in an informal competition, cleared 6'8½" in the high jump, a personal record.

Paavo Yrjöla, Finland, 1928 Olympic Champion. Paavo Yrjöla fully deserved selection to the DECA Hall of Fame for Decathletes. He competed in three Olympics during ten years (1922-1932) with a total of 14 decathlons--the most ever until Toomey's 38 in 11 years (1959-1969). He set four world records, climaxed by his 8053 (1920T) at the Amsterdam Olympics, but he also took 6th place at Los Angeles, 1932, at age 30.

Perhaps most remarkable, Yrjöla was a farmer, living some distance away from a track and field, and even further from a coach. In a 1976 TV interview he told how he constructed his own throwing and jumping facilities and ran over his own fields and through his own woods. (I was the U.S. champion and third at Amsterdam, 347 points behind. I had often wondered if a better effort here or there--. But as I listened to Yrjöla on TV, I bowed low to a superior decathlete who had overcome more handicaps than any of us.)

Jim Bausch, 1932 Olympic Champion. As with Osborn, Jim Bausch had no decathlon competition while in college; in fact, showed almost no potential. Bausch was known primarily as "Jarring Jim," a football fullback and basketball star at Kansas University. His best in track was a sixth place in the 1930 NCAA shot put championships at about 48 feet. But in his first decathlon, he won the 1931 Kansas Relays with an American record 7847 points (6529, 1962 tables). In total he competed in but five decathlons in a two-year career, climaxed by his world-record 8462 points (6896, 1962 tables) in winning the 1932 Olympics.

Glenn Morris, 1936 Olympic Champion. Equally remarkable in terms of natural, untrained talent was Glenn Morris, 1936 Olympic champion--7900 points (7421, 1962 tables). Glenn was an outstanding three-sport athlete at Colorado Agricultural College but in college track and field he showed no potential for the decathlon: 24.7--220y low hurdles, 15.4s--120y highs, 54s--440y hurdles. Amazingly, two years later, in his first decathlon, he won the Kansas Relays

---

[1] R. L. Templeton, *THE HIGH JUMP*, New York: American Sports Publishing Co., 1926, p. 157.

with an American record 7576 points (7192, 1962 tables). He then set successive world records at the American trials and Olympic finals. That was his entire decathlon career, all in one year--three attempts--one American record, two world records, one Olympic gold. Morris worked in Denver, hardly a decathlete's paradise. How much and what quality decathlon training could he have gotten in Denver with limited indoor facilities and coaching?

Keep in mind that during these years endurance training was considered to have negative effects for decathlon performance. What it might gain for the low-scoring 1500 was more than lost through its disastrous effects on muscle quickness and skill. Also that strength training was not merely ignored but actually abhorred for similar reasons. It's not surprising that, when setting his world record of 8462 points, Bausch did poorly in the endurance events (400m-- 54.2s, 1500m--5:17); and all the more credit to him that he did so well in the throwing events (shot--50'3", discus--146'3", javelin--203'1"), each of which surpassed the performances of all previous world-record decathletes. Even more amazing, Morris ran his Olympic 1500 in 4:33.2, not surpassed until 1972 when Avilov ran 4:22.8. Could his living and training, however limited, at Denver's 5000-feet altitude have been a contributing factor? Incidentally, his 4:33.2 was 25 seconds faster than he had ever run before, and was essential to his victory. Apparently his will-to-win was also a factor.

Bob Mathias, 1948, 1952 Olympic Champion. In contrast to late-blooming Bausch and Morris, the next two Olympic champions and world-record holders, Bob Mathias and Milt Campbell, began their track careers as decathletes while still in high school. Mathias' first attempt was at age 17 on June 10-11, 1948, at the end of his senior year. He won with 6790 points (1962 tables).[1] On June 26-27, he won the Olympic Trials--6902 points; on August 5-6, the London Olympic Finals--6826 points under the handicaps of heavy rain, soft takeoffs and track, and long delays in competition. During the next two years (Kiski Prep and Stanford--freshmen not eligible), Mathias won four decathlons, including two National AAU championships and a world record of 7452 points. That totalled seven decathlons during three pre-college years. He did not compete again for two years, winning the 1952 Olympic Trials with a world-record 7690   · points, and the Olympic Finals with his third career world record of 7731 points.

But once into his college career of varsity track and football, Mathias insisted that his contribution to the Stanford team was primary. By competing in 4-5-6 events "wherever I could score a point or more," he somehow achieved a more balanced all-round performance, as evidenced by his amazing attainment of eight personal records in winning the 1952 Helsinki Olympics. But during these two college track seasons, "he works out on the track from three to five or six o'clock,"[2] hardly an adequate time for a ten-event specialist.

As with all previous decathletes, endurance training was ignored, even shunned. His biographer[2] states that his endurance training consisted of "jogging a couple of laps," or more rarely "running for ten minutes on the Stanford golf course." During his years of competition (1948-1952), power training was just beginning. Weightmen such as Parry O'Brien, USC, and Otis Chandler, at Bob's own University, both praised and practiced its values but weight lifting is not even mentioned in Mathias' biography. That, at Helsinki, he achieved 50'2" in the shot and 153'10" in the discus is all the more noteworthy.

Milt Campbell, 1956 Olympic Champion. Before entering Indiana University in 1954, Campbell competed in three decathlons: (1) At the end of his high school junior year (age 18), he qualified for the American Olympic team by taking second to Mathias, defeating Floyd Simmons, the 1948 bronze medallist. His total points (7176) are the highest ever recorded for a first decathlon. (2) He took the 1952 Olympic silver medal (7132 points). (3) In 1953, after high school graduation, he won the National AAU title (7253 points).

Add that at Plainfield, N.J. High school he was an all-state football fullback, a letter

---

[1]Throughout the remainder of this section, all points, unless stated otherwise, will be scored on the 1962 tables.

[2]Jim Scott, *BOB MATHIAS, CHAMPION OF CHAMPIONS,* Englewood Cliffs, N.J.: Prentice-Hall, Inc., 1952, pp. 189, 191.

winner in wrestling, and an All-American high school free-style swimmer. (In 1953, black swimmers were rarely welcomed in swimming pools.) All in all, perhaps the most remarkable high school career in all of sport.

But then, strangest of all, during two years at Indiana, Campbell specialized in one event, the 120y high hurdles. In 1955 he won the National AAU championships in the fast time of 13.9s, but won no important college competitions. Though in the 1956 Olympics, he put the shot 48-5, high jumped 6-2½, ran the 400m in 48.8, and threw the javelin 187-3, he placed in none of these events while in college. One explanation of this is that he went to Indiana on a football scholarship, and was required to take part in spring football training. Lacking proper training for track, his interest in dual and conference meets would undoubtedly be low. In football he was outstanding; in 1956 he was drafted and played briefly for the Chicago Bears.

But, however he perfected his skills or gained power and endurance, his performance in the 1956 Melbourne Games was superb--seven personal bests out of ten events, totalling 7708 points for a new Olympic record, only 48 points behind Rafer Johnson's world record. In summary, one more example of tremendous natural, all-round talent, supported by minimal conditions for development.

Rafer Johnson, 1960 Olympic Champion. If anyone has surpassed Milt Campbell's record as an all-sports performer while still in high school, it was Rafer Johnson. In fact, if injuries had not handicapped him, he might have been the greatest all-time all-arounder at any level. A four-sport star at Kingsburg (CA) High School, Rafer, in June 1954, first won two prep decathlons, using the high school shot, discus and hurdles; then, on July 2-3, took third in the AAU championships with 6329 points. As a freshman at UCLA, he won three decathlons: 7055 in the Pan-Am Qualifying Meet in February, 7144 in the Pan-Am Finals in March, and 7758 for a new world record in the Central California AAU meet in June. All this at age 19. But, in his sophomore year, 1956, he competed and trained only for regular varsity meets. In dual meets he would compete in five or six events, winning some and scoring in most. On June 15, in the NCAA championships, he took two seconds to two future Olympic champions: Lee Calhoun in the high hurdles (13.8s), and Greg Bell in the long jump (25'4"). A month later he won the U.S. Olympic decathlon trials (7591 points), but in December at Melbourne, handicapped by an injured knee, he took second (7568 points) to Campbell's Olympic Record 7708 points. Injuries continued to plague Johnson during the next three years. Throughout 1957, he competed once in the javelin and in but three events in a hometown decathlon. In 1959, leg injuries and a serious auto collision with back injuries kept him out of all activity until he started jogging in February, 1960. In 1958, his college senior year, a serious thigh pull eliminated all sprinting, hurdling, and jumping, but somehow he achieved a great triple in the weight events--54' 11½", 170' 9½", 237' 10". After graduation (June 1958) he recovered enough to win three decathlons, including (July 3-4) an AAU title and (July 27-28) a world record 7896 points against his repeated rival, Kuznyetsov of the USSR.

In 1960, Johnson took no sprint starts until April, nor long jumps until June, but July 8-9, in the U.S. Olympic Final Trials, he was able to gain his third world record (8063 points), the first-ever over 8000 points. Then, Sept. 5-6, Rome, he gained that all-important goal, the Olympic championships with 8001 points. With only the final event (1500m) remaining, Johnson held a lead of but 56 points (a ten-second differential). With a previous best time of 4:54.2, made four years earlier at Melbourne, this was Johnson's weakest event in both points and confidence. Yang had trained at UCLA under Johnson's coaches Ducky Drake and Jack Davis, so Johnson was well aware of his best time of 4:36.9. But by clinging adamantly to C. K.'s shoulder, he finished within one second of Yang's time with a P.R. of 4:49.7, a great victory over a most worthy opponent.

It must be added that Rafer Johnson was an all-round person as well as decathlete. He trained for government service and acting as a future career. He lettered in basketball (UCLA was a basketball power!), spoke often before Los Angeles youth groups, and in his senior year, 1958, was elected president of the student body. In the decathlon, he won two Olympic medals--one gold, one silver. During seven years (1954-1960), he broke the world record three times while winning nine of 11 competitions. In regular college meets, he recorded: 100m--10.3, HH--13.8, long jump--25' 5 3/4", shot--54' 11½", discus--172' 3", javelin--251' 9½". But during his college years, Johnson was a team competitor. Only after the team season was over (1956 and 1958) did he train specially for the decathlon. And even those brief periods were diminished seriously by repeated injuries. Certainly basic endurance work could have greatly improved the 47.9s and 4:54.2 he recorded with little training in 1956.

<u>Bill Toomey, 1968 Olympic Champion</u>. Bill Toomey was the first world-level decathlete that, on the crucial balance between natural talent and proper training, weighed heavily on the side of training. At the University of Colorado, Bill's range of events was less than promising-- 24'8½" in the long jump, 51.7 for 400m hurdles, and good times in the 440-600 indoors--far from a firm foundation for the decathlon. His physique (6'1", 172#, 1962) was ordinary. His first decathlon score (1959, age 20) was 5349, as compared with 6790 (Mathias, age 17) or 7176 (Campbell, age 18). His first official world record (8417, Dec. 1969) was not achieved until age 31, after 34 decathlon competitions and ten years of year-round training specifically pointed toward improving his score in the decathlon.

Not until he was 24 (1963, 7066 points) did he take the decathlon seriously. But once committed, it became a matter of supreme importance, for which he allowed no hindrances and few distractions. He sought competition everywhere, in the United States and in Europe, even urging new meets so that he might have one more try at the record or merely at improvement-- against the world's best performers or whatever local talent was available. He moved to California to earn an M.A. in Education at Stanford, 1963, and ensure better year-round train- ing conditions and coaching. At Santa Barbara he worked with Coach Sam Adams, a former decath- lete (1956--7106 points) and generally considered America's foremost coach of this event. There he found a group of dedicated decathletes, including such champions as Russ Hodge, and John Warkentin. This provided an excellent situation for mutual help and development.

But, seeking perfection, he also spent six months (1965) in West Germany where he discovered the decathlon to be an event of long-time national interest. Its advocates argued that the nature of the decathlon and its training was inherent in the character and tradition of the German people--a disciplined approach to life, a belief in versatility and balance as opposed to narrow specialization, and in the unity of mind-body.

Of more direct value, Toomey sought the help of Friedel Schirmer, National Decathlon Coach. Schirmer had competed with high scores in the decathlon, had coached many decathletes including Holdorf, Walde and Beyer who had taken first, third and sixth in the 1964 Tokyo Olympics, and had studied thoroughly the requirements of decathlon development. He organized a decathlon training camp in a suburb of Cologne where all prospects could come for help. He systematized all aspects of training. He organized decathlon teams of six and eight men that had regular dual meets with other teams--club, area, national in scope--so that there was no need for competition in individual events. He followed a sequence of training consistent with the order of events in the decathlon. Above all, he planned development years ahead--in terms of a career as well as of this year, month or week.

It was too late in Bill Toomey's career to make such radical changes in techniques and methods. That would risk complete failure. But the experience was most encouraging; he was more convinced of his potential, and even more determined to gain both the Olympic champion- ship and a world record. From July 1965--when his world-record 8234 points in winning the National AAU championships was disallowed for meet management errors--until December 1969, he competed in 23 decathlons (ten in 1969 alone) in an all-out drive for the record. He won five consecutive NAAU titles (1965-1969). He won the 1968 Olympic title with a new Olympic record of 8193 points. He scored over 8000 in 11 meets; over 8200 in four; but time and time again fell short in some small but crucial way, leaving the field frustrated, even disgusted, but also determined to try again. Finally, on Dec. 10-11, 1969, some three months after the track season is usually over, in a specially organized competition against three other decathletes (all over 7000 points), Toomey gained his goal--a world-record 8417 points, 98 points over Kurt Bendlin's (West Germany) record.

In summary, probably no decathlete ever achieved so much from such an unpromising begin- ning. With full commitment throughout an 11-year career, he depended primarily on himself, with only temporary help from coaches. Needing power and weight, he followed a power-training program and related diet, gaining a powerful body and 195# in weight. Needing endurance, he took basic mileage running during the early months of each year. Needing even greater speed, he took related speed-power exercises. From a beginning of 23'2" in his one high-school event, the long jump, he finally achieved: 1500m--4:12.7; 100m--10.3, 400m--45.6, 110m hurdles-- 14.2, long jump--26'¼", and most amazingly, discus--154'2" and javelin--225'8". During 11 years, he competed in 38 decathlons; his last was his best.

Bruce Jenner, 1976 Olympic Champion. Bruce Jenner was the first United States champion decathlete to combine great all-round talent with all-out training. He started pole vaulting in the 7th grade. While still in high school, he played football, was an expert competitive water skier, and in track, high jumped 6'2", vaulted 13', triple jumped and threw the javelin 180 feet.

At Graceland College, Iowa, Jenner's track coach was L. D. Weldon, a fine javelin thrower in college, a decathlon enthusiast and, most important, coach of Jack Parker, third in the 1936 Berlin Olympic decathlon. Weldon saw the great potential in Bruce and made sure that first impressions were positive. In his first decathlon (sophomore year, age 20), Bruce scored 6991 points and found "it was so much fun, such a challenge...something I wanted to do. I decided right then to run cross-country next fall."[1]

As for dedicated training, for three years (April 1973 to July 30, 1976 when he won the Olympic title at Montreal with a world-record 8618 points), Bruce and his wife Chrystie lived in an apartment across the street from the San Jose City College track and field. "I couldn't get away from my training if I wanted to. If I had trouble getting started in the morning, I just looked out of my bedroom window at the running track. There it was out there--my destiny."

At San Jose he made the shocking discovery that he was not really strong, nor had basic endurance, nor speed, nor even much skill. At Graceland college he had been the best in every-thing. Here everybody was bigger, faster, stronger, more skilled, and even more dedicated. In power training he worked with such experts as shot-putter Al Feuerbach and discus throwers Mac Wilkins and John Powell. They also coached him in their specialties on the field. He sprinted with Olympian John Carlos. In fact, in every event, he could work out with men super-ior in performance and knowledge. "With that atmosphere, training all the time, with all those specialists to help me, I just had to get better." In the fall of 1975 he undertook basic endurance training. "He ran 10 miles a day beginning in October." Somedays he went to the 11th green on the Stanford University golf course. "That long fairway is 300 yards long, and steep. Twenty times he sprints up the hill, then jogs down to the bottom."

His wife, Chrystie, was a strong help-mate in many ways. Her earnings as an airline stewardess was, at first, their only income. When things went wrong and Bruce was discouraged, she was strongly supportive. After the 1976 Olympic triumph, his first words were, "We did it; you and I did it together." And he repeatedly said he could never have achieved so much without her help. In 1975, Bruce sold life insurance with $700 a month guaranteed if he could sell a certain quota every three months. This he found he could do within a week or two, so the remaining weeks were free for full-time training.

During the six months prior to Montreal he did just that--on a 24-hour-a-day basis. In their apartment he had a hurdle, a vaulting pole, a shot, discus, javelin. Often he spent hours thinking-feeling in a muscle-nerve sense, just how it should be done, unknowingly con-sistent with the methods now advanced by psycho-cybernetics.

I might run through a whole decathlon in my mind, over and over again every day. I think about each event and the things I have to do to score high. Then, when I'm actually in competition, I find myself doing those things naturally. That's why I have a hurdle here in the living room. Just walking through the motions here, looking at the hurdle and knowing what it feels like, all helps me run the hurdles better in a race....What I see in my mind changes as I progress in the event....Over the years I've watched my mind and my body grow closer together.

In another interview[2] Chrystie added to this,

He even visualizes the events in his dreams. He runs in his sleep. He falls

---

[1]Bruce Jenner & Peter Finch, *DECATHLON CHALLENGE--BRUCE JENNER'S STORY*, Englewood Cliffs, N.J.: Prentice-Hall, Inc., 1977. Quotes from pps. 42, 72, 73, 94, 93.

[2]Frank Zarnowski, *THE DECATHLON GUIDE*, "Interview with the Jenners" by Jeannette & Bert Nelson, Emmitsburg, Md: *DECA*, 1976, pps. 37-41.

asleep in 20 to 30 seconds and then I can see his legs moving...for about ten seconds. I know he's doing the 100. Or he'll give a big grunt and move his arm and shoulder. He's putting the shot.

In his seven year career (1970-1976), Bruce Jenner completed 27 decathlons with 16 victories including 10 over 8000 points, seven over 8200 points, and a final 1976 Olympic win with 8618 points, a world record. His best-ever performances, metric system, were 10.7, 7.32, 15.35, 2.03, 47.5-14.3, 51.70, 4.80, 69.48, 4:12.6.[1]

In summary, Jenner's career evidenced most of the essentials for great performance in the decathlon. True, at age 20, he had not performed at such high levels as had Milt Campbell or Rafer Johnson. But on the training-development-competition side of performance, he surpassed them all. Only two essentials of highest achievement were lower level--a Master Coach and time for development. For example, consider that in West and East Germany, National Coaches give full-time attention to one event, such as the decathlon, and that those showing talent and interest are placed under their care at an early age. Great as were Jenner's achievements, even greater decathlon scores lay in the future.

Daley Thompson, Great Britain, 1980 world record--8622 points. On his first 1980 warm-up decathlon for the Moscow Olympics, Daley Thompson surpassed Jenner's world record (8617) by five points. His first-day total was 4486, within 63 of Joachim Kirst's best-ever (4549, 1969) but, as usual, he had been weak in the throwing events (shot, 47-5¼; discus, 141-0; javelin, 214-3). Before starting the 1500, he knew he must do 4:26 or better. His personal best in a decathlon was 4:20.3 (1976). He ran 4:25.5. Guido Kratschmer (WG), silver medallist at Montreal and his chief rival for the Moscow crown, was second with 8421.

All indicators tended to show this was well below Thompson's potential best. None of the ten individual-event marks were personal records, as compared with Jenner's Montreal performance--four PRs plus two that equalled previous bests; or Milt Campbell's seven PRs in winning at Melbourne.

Up to June 1980, Thompson had competed during six years in 13 decathlons. His first (1975, age 17) produced 6685, as compared with the first efforts of Jenner (6991) and Campbell (7176). On his third try (1976, age 18) he set a World Junior Record at 7905; on his 11th (1978) he won the British Commonwealth Games with 8467, second in history to Bruce Jenner's 8617. In summary, remarkably consistent improvement.

A New York Times article (9/9/79) stated he had been lifting weights for five years and had improved greatly in strength. But with his "perfect" physique (6-0, 195#) for the decathlon it seemed obvious that improvement could still be made. In 1976, age 18, with a personal best of 7684 points, he was asked to predict his potential for each of the decathlon events. They added up to 8852. In the light of 1980, that seemed entirely possible.

According to the New York Times article, Thompson was able to train full time for the decathlon:

He receives about $11,000 a year for training expenses through Olympic-sanctioned broken-time payments. And because the decathlon is such a grueling event.... Thompson trains 'from 10 or 10:30 in the morning until 7 or 8 at night, seven days a week'...Each week, Thompson works on at least seven of his 10 events, and three days a week he competes against British decathletes and track specialists in practice meets.

Guido Kratschmer, West Germany, 1980 world record--8649 points. Two weeks after Thompson's effort--too late for adequate treatment here--Guido Kratschmer, West Germany, silver medallist at Montreal--moved the world record ahead by 27 points. Kratschmer was favored to win at Moscow had not the Olympic boycott been in force. With almost identical performance in the last three events, what a battle it would have been between him and Thompson.

---

[1] Frank Zarnowski, ibid., p.4.

[2] Ibid., pps. 45-51, 53-54.

POTENTIAL TALENTS FOR THE DECATHLON

Whether or not an athlete, now scoring more than ten points in various dual-meet events, should concentrate all his efforts on one event, the decathlon, depends on several factors--individual attitudes, his obligations to the team and institution, and, of special import, his potential for success as a decathlete.

Up to 1970, the decathlon was an extramural event for college men. Only off-and-on did the Relay Carnivals include it in their schedule. During the team season, potential decathletes competed in a number of single events. Even high school Olympians such as Bob Mathias or Milt Campbell competed as regular members of their college teams. Decathlon competition occurred during the summer or after college graduation, as happened with Jim Bausch and Glenn Morris.

Today, all that is changed. For 1980, Frank Zarnowski listed 48 decathlon competitions open to college men--most in April-May, but extending from Feb. 1 to Dec. 4. Prospective decathletes and their coaches now face a serious dilemma. Is it worthwhile to give up sure points in a number of single events? Even more fundamental, is it worthwhile to give full time-energy to this demanding ten-eventer despite its probable interference with high-level academic work? Not to mention, normal college life.

An Exciting Challenge. The first question in assessing an athlete's potential for the decathlon should be whether or not it appeals to him as an exciting challenge. He may be dismayed by its awesome heights but should be assured by Bill Toomey's slow climb from two mediocre performances (long jump and 400m) to a world record score in ten events. He may be turned away by the all-too-common description of the event as "grueling," "agonizing," "a man-killer." But decathletes know these are the judgments of the untrained and untried, those who lack a valid basis for judgment.

Experienced decathletes become inured to the pains of fatigue and effort just as they do to the physical effects of oxygen debt or lactic acid. Sure they are aware of pain and exhaustion, but not as problems or fears. In short, if a man can accept the pain (often called loosely "agony" or "torture") of his first six-minute try at 1500m, he'll find no greater pain at five minutes or even four. Inurement to pain parallels performance.

Physique. Next to personal interest in the event, physique might be considered a basic approach to talent. McNab[1] surveyed 33 decathletes in the 1968 Olympic Games as follows: Average height--6'½"; average weight--186½#. Bill Toomey, the champion, was 6'1½" tall and weighed 195#. But the height of these 33 men ranged from 5'6¼" to 6'4 3/4"; their weight, from 148# to 207#. In Table 15.1 the 12 Olympic champions (1924-1976) averaged 6' 1.8" in height and 194# in weight, and that includes Osborn at only 170#.

These figures are supported by Zarnowski's report[2] of the opinions of national decathlon coaches as to optimal size. They averaged 1.88cm (6'2"), with a range from 1.85 to 1.95. But Zarnowski emphasizes that this is just an average. "Today's decathlete comes in all shapes and sizes...Any size will do!"

At one extreme, he cites the 1974 Soviet champion, Rudolph Zigert, 6'6", 235#, but able to high jump 6'10"; and Rick Wanamaker, 1971 AAU champion, 6'9", 210#, but able to pole vault 15'1"! At the other extreme was Jeff Bennett, "by far the smallest top-grade decathlete in history," two-time AAU champion, who was only 5'8" tall and weighed but 152#. With this physique, he scored 8121 points and had best performances of: high jump--6'4 3/4", pole vaule-- 16'7 3/4", long jump--25'3½", 100m--10.3, 400m--46.3, 1500m--4:08.9, and remarkably, shot put--42'6".

All of this discussion is based on scores drawn from the 1962 Scoring Tables. Change the Tables, and physique requirements will change to correspond.

---

[1]Tom McNab, *DECATHLON*, London: British Amateur Athletic Board, 1971, paperback, 68 pps., p. 21.

[2]Frank Zarnowski, *op. cit.*, p. 19.

Basic Talents. A third approach to potentials for the decathlon focuses on basic qualities: speed, spring power, endurance, facility in motor learning, and most important, basic stick-to-itiveness and competitiveness. The last three of these underlie performance in all events.

Such basic qualities can be judged by two criteria--decathlon events and decathlon scoring tables. The events selected by Curtis for the 1884 all-around placed great emphasis on power (shot, hammer, 56# weight throw) and endurance (880 walk and mile run), with lesser emphasis on speed (100, high hurdles, long jump).

I doubt that the makers of the modern decathlon approached the problem of selecting events in this formal way but, clearly, the full range of sports talent was planned. At least four events were chosen in which leg speed is essential: (100, high hurdles, long jump, 400); three events for power (shot, discus, javelin); two or more events for spring (high jump, pole vault, long jump); and but one for endurance (1500), plus of course the 400.

Talent as determined by the scoring tables will be analyzed in detail in the next section, but in summary, Table 15.2 makes clear that the 1962 Tables provided highest scoring for Olympic champions (1912-1972) for the speed events--long jump, high hurdles, 400 and 100, in that order of points scored; lowest scoring for endurance (1500-10th in scoring) and power (javelin, shot, discus--9th, 8th, and 7th in scoring); with spring in the middle (high jump and pole vault, 5th and 6th in scoring). Table 15.3, based on 1962 Tables, shows a different rank of events for scoring in the 1976 Olympic Decathlon, produced by modern improvements in implements and training methods. Surprisingly, such upgrading lowered scoring in the 100m dash from 4th down to 8th. Greatest increases occurred with the pole vault (6th to 1st) and javelin (9th to 5th).

In 1980, the IAAF was preparing new tables that seek better balance, with higher scoring for the 1500 and lower scoring in those events in which technology has provided unwarranted aids.

A Talent for Competitiveness. Highest scores in the decathlon demand great talent for competitiveness of a unique kind. First it is an inner struggle to do one's best, not against a human opponent as in such sports as football or boxing, but against such abstractions as time, distance, inertia, gravity; or such "mental" deterrents as fatigue, pain, impatience, tension, stress. All-out efforts are essential but always within the limitations of relaxation and control, what might be called controlled recklessness or cold fury.

More than this, such drives must be repeated not merely ten times, but a score or more--if we count the attempts within such events as the weights and jumps. Further, there are long delays between events and single efforts. I sometimes think that the old ten-events-in-one-day method was more an advantage than a handicap; one moved quickly to the next event without the long cooling of muscles and competitive fire. It takes a special person to do his best, sometimes under conditions of rain and wind and cold, again and again and again, in events of such varied requirements in body and mind.

To me, it is truly fantastic that such Greats as Jim Thorpe, Bob Mathias, Milt Campbell or Rafer Johnson, in their first try at the decathlon, should have reached some 7000 points of a "perfect" 10,000; or that Bruce Jenner could score 8618 points in ten separate and varied events. Just think, if, on decathlon tables, we score the performances of the 10 relevant single-event champions of the 1976 Olympics, they would average roughly 1097 points. That is, Jenner in ten events came within 79 percent of equalling the level achieved by ten champions competing in but one event each. Along with talent and training, that takes competitiveness.

BALANCE IN SCORING AND TRAINING
The concept of balanced scoring, so seemingly obvious, is actually defined and used in various ways. The simplest way is to assume equitable tables and equal potentials for scoring for all events. A 7000-point scorer would score 700 points in every event. A more realistic way uses the difference between highest and lowest event scores. Zarnowski[1] and Nelson used this method, but excluded the 1500 since scoring is so unduly low in this event. Their method gave best-balanced scores and lowest differences to Mathias (130) and Kuznyetsov (131), and poorly-

---

[1]Frank Zarnowski & Bert Nelson, op. cit., p. 32.

TABLE 15.2

SCORING[4] AND BALANCE IN OLYMPIC CHAMPIONS

Name & Yr.	Ave.[1] Sco	100	LJ	Sh	HJ	400	HH	Dis	PV	Jav	1500	Ave.[2] Dev.	Dev.[3] Rank
Thorpe '12	676	756	776	658	743	712	787	623	601	574	524		
Deviation		+80	+100	-18	+67	+36	+111	-53	-75	-102	-152	79.4	5
Osborn '24	667	756	804	561	831	712	749	574	672	588	464		
Deviation		+89	+137	-106	+164	+45	+ 82	-93	+5	-79	-203	90.3	8
Yrjola '28	677	622	761	735	743	671	694	727	615	708	500		
Deviation		-55	+84	+58	+66	-6	+17	+50	-62	+31	-177	60.6	1
Bausch '32	690	643	810	808	588	633	730	774	807	785	321		
Deviation		-47	+120	+118	-102	-57	+40	-16	+117	+95	-369	108.1	11
Morris '36	742	780	814	734	725	833	859	744	672	692	568		
Deviation		+38	+72	-8	-17	+91	+117	+4	-70	-50	-180	63.9	2
Mathias '52	773	828	816	806	769	797	881	816	807	751	460		
Deviation		+55	+43	+33	-4	+24	+108	+43	+34	-22	-313	67.9	3
Campbell '56	771	853	887	774	760	860	963	781	644	713	461		
Deviation		+82	+116	+3	-11	+89	+192	+10	-127	-58	-310	99.9	10
Johnson '60	800	828	891	837	725	854	817	845	832	877	466		
Deviation		+28	+91	+37	-75	+54	+17	+45	+32	+77	-334	82.0	6
Holdorf '64	788	879	820	786	716	889	848	801	859	729	561		
Deviation		+91	+32	-2	-72	+101	+60	+13	+71	-59	-228	72.9	4
Toomey '68	842	986	972	751	796	943	926	809	876	830	528		
Deviation		+144	+130	-91	-54	+101	+84	-33	+34	-12	-314	99.7	9
Avilov '72	845	804	957	750	959	875	926	818	945	781	639		
Deviation		-41	+112	-95	+114	+30	+81	-27	+100	-64	-206	87.0	7
Total Score		8735	9308	8200	8355	8779	9180	8312	8330	8028	5492		
Score Rank		4	1	8	5	3	2	7	6	9	10		

[1]Average score for all ten events.
[2]Average deviation of each event from average score.
[3]Decathlete rank compared with 10 others in average deviation.
[4]1962 Scoring Tables were used throughout.

TABLE 15.3

SCORING AND BALANCE IN SIX PLACE-WINNERS--1976 OLYMPICS

Name		Ave.[1] Sco.	100	LJ	Sh	HJ	400	HH	Dis	PV	Jav	1500	Ave.[2] Dev.	Dev.[3] Rank
1.Jenner	USA	862	819	865	810	882	923	866	882	1005	863	715		
			-43	+3	-52	+20	+61	+4	+20	+143	+1	-147	49.4	1
2.Kratschmer	WG	841	890	901	774	882	889	895	795	957	837	595		
			+49	+60	-67	+41	+48	+54	-46	+116	-4	-246	93.4	5
3.Avilov	SU	837	749	925	778	1017	891	939	793	920	798	614		
			-88	+88	-59	+180	+54	+102	-44	+83	-39	-223	96.0	6
4.Pihl	SW	822	822	820	825	857	900	767	769	909	961	597		
			0	-2	+3	+35	+78	-55	-53	+87	+139	-225	67.7	3
5.Skowronck	Pol	811	799	873	726	779	903	876	789	1005	789	590		
			-12	+62	-85	-32	+92	+65	-22	+194	-22	-221	80.7	4
6.Stark	EG	805	721	816	794	779	844	782	791	969	927	625		
			-84	+11	-11	-26	+39	-23	-13	+164	+122	-180	67.3	2
Total Score			4800	5200	4707	5196	5350	5125	4819	5765	5175	3736		
Score Rank			8	3	9	4	2	6	7	1	5	10		

321

balanced scores with highest differences to Yang (335) and Johnson (269). Zarnowski and Nelson also studied balances: (1) between group scores in the three throws, the three jumps and the three runs, again excluding the 1500; and (2) between total scores on the first day and the second.

In my judgment the most useful way to define balance in scoring is to compare an individual's score for each event with his average score for all events. Such deviations are not between the extremes of performance as when contrasting high and low scores. They do not exclude any event. Their sum provides a total deviation for all ten events. In Table 15.2 Jim Thorpe, for example, had a total deviation of 794 from his average score of 676 points (1962 Tables.)

In his 1979 analysis of elite decathlon performances, William H. Freeman[1] concluded that,

> *To develop the elite decathlete, attention must be paid to a balanced development of the athlete's abilities across all ten events until they reach an optimal level, after which the specialty events can be emphasized. This observation agrees with the so-called West German School of decathlon training, led by Friedel Schirmer, which prefers not to permit the decathlete to develop specialty events until he can achieve a balanced effort at the 7000 point level.*

Such may have been the plan and even the training. Actual performances, however, did not support either. Defining balance as the deviation of each event score from the average score for all ten events, we find that Holdorf had a deviation total of 729; Walde, of 934; and Bendlin, of 1581. Surprisingly, these are not an improvement over American college products: Morris--639, Mathias--679, Johnson--320, Toomey--997, Campbell--999, Bausch--1081, or even Thorpe--794.

The question arises as to what extent such deviations are produced by the natural inconsistencies in competitive performance found, not only in the decathlon, but in all single-events. The answer would require considerable study but a hint can be gained from Jenner's best decathlon scores in each of five years, 1972-1976, climaxed by his Olympic Games 8618 record. Not only did Bruce improve his total score each time, his total deviation decreased quite consistently--894, 593, 600, 487, 494.

<u>Scoring by Events--1976 versus 1912-72</u>. Tables 15.2 and 15.3 show there has been a gradual increase in total scores and average scores from 1912 to 1976 for all ten events. But Table 15.4 indicates a change in relative scoring by events. Scoring for the pole vault moved from a 6th place ranking to 1st place; that for the javelin, from 9th to 5th. Improvements in implements, facilities and techniques are probable causes. Relative scoring lowered for the hurdles (2nd to 6th) and 100 (4th to 8th). Speed has a lower range of possible improvement as compared with power or endurance or skill; as they improve, speed will tend to hold even.

TABLE 15.4
RELATIVE SCORING BY EVENTS--1976 versus 1912-1972

	PV	400	LJ	HJ	Jav	HH	Dis	100	Sh	1500
1976 Event Ranking	1	2	3	4	5	6	7	8	9	10
1912-1972 Event Ranking	6	3	1	5	9	2	7	4	8	10

<u>Balance in the Basic Elements</u>. Performance totals of the 17 decathletes listed in Tables 15.2 and 15.3 show decisively that the 1500 is by far the most difficult event in which to score points. In Table 15.2 the 11 decathletes scored a total of only 5492 points, as compared with the next lowest total 8028 in the shot. From such facts Bert Nelson[2] concludes

---

[1]William H. Freeman, "An Analysis of Elite Decathlon Performances," *Track and Field Quarterly Review*, Vol. 79, #2, 1979, p. 49.

[2]Frank Zarnowski and Bert Nelson, *op. cit.*, p. 8.

that scoring for the 1500 should be upgraded, that is, should be based on a different standard from that used for the other nine events.

In my judgment, such views ignore certain underlying principles of the decathlon. No scoring tables can provide equal opportunities for scoring for all individuals. All tables arbitrarily assume a certain kind of decathlete--somewhere between a distance runner and a shot putter or sprinter, between a high jumper and discus thrower. All tables must be based on compromise, and cannot provide allowances that equalize individual differences.

The originators of the decathlon gave a first priority to speed. The four highest-scoring events among these Olympic champions (long jump-9308, hurdles-9180, 400-8779, 100-8735) have a high-level requirement in speed. Second priority was given to power. Three events involving big-muscle power achieved closely grouped scoring: discus-8312, shot-8200, javelin-8028. We should note that scores in Table 15.3, made by place-winners in the 1976 Games, do not coincide with these figures. Recent improvements in discus technique and both technique and construction of the javelin account for such differences. As pointed out previously, shot performances in the decathlon over the past 50 years have held relatively steady because of decathlon size limitations. Scores for 1976 athletes averaged 784 points; for earlier athletes 745. Improvement has come primarily through basic strength training. For example, Jeff Bennett, only 5'8", 152# in size was still able to put the shot 42'6".

That leaves but one event, the 1500, as a test of what might be called slower-paced endurance. (The 400 has an important endurance factor, but it's what can be called speed-endurance in which scoring is much more closely correlated with speed in the 100 than with endurance in the 1500.) But this concentration of testing within a single event simply multiplies the importance of that event, and does not imply a lesser role for endurance. As a fundamental principle, the basis for scoring should be the same for all ten events. That principle forces decathletes to compromise, to make-do as between body-size and excellence in such other events as the 1500, pole vault, hurdles or high jump. We are unlikely to ever see a 1000-point (61'5½") scorer in the shot that will do well in those four events, especially in the 1500. The opposite is equally true. In 1971, Brian Oldfield (6'5", 275#) set a record 60'1½" for the shot within a decathlon, but scored less than 7000 points total. In contrast, in 1972, Jeff Bennett (5'8", 152#) ran the 1500 in 4:08.9 (744 points), and in 1973 scored 8121 points total, but his shot was usually under 42 feet.

It is clear that decathlon tables are not pointed toward achieving 10,000 points, with adjustment of scoring criteria for each event to ensure that possibility. Rather, they seek to ensure equality of opportunity for every decathlete to do what he can within both the positives and the negatives of the scoring system.

Summary. (1) To define balance in performance as the deviation of each event score from the average score for all ten events provides a useful and valid basis for analyzing and comparing point scores. (2) Even though the facts disclosed here are inconclusive, we are still justified in assuming that balanced performance, and so balance in training for the ten events, is an ideal to be carefully planned and diligently sought. (3) the inconsistency of performance inherent in any competition might outweigh the low deviations from the average score gained from balanced training. Bruce Jenner's scores during five years were remarkably low in such inconsistency. (4) Balanced training requires long-time and continuous planning by well-trained experts. For example, within the ten-event format, highest-level endurance (1500m) and power (shot) oppose each other, cannot occur together. To be world's best in either is to rule out balance in the decathlon. Balanced training must seek a compromise between the two, and that requires expert planning. (5) Balanced training can be achieved in the United States only when men specialize as decathletes throughout their sports careers--post-college, college and high school.

Scoring, not balance, is the goal. The concept of balance, like that of technique in single events, may contribute to performance but actually wins no competitions. Perfect balance, like perfect technique, may end up last. In Table 15.3, Jenner was first in total scoring and in balanced scoring. But Kratschmer was second in scoring though 5th in balance; Avilov third in scoring, sixth in balance; Stark sixth in scoring, second in balance. In summary, the correlation between total scoring and balance is not high.

College decathletes will tend to plan in terms of short-time goals--this year or, at most,

323

four years. Though working toward better balance, first time-energy will be given to those events in which progress will come quickest. Example: A beginner can now vault 3.60m (11'9 3/4" --700 points) and put the shot 10.55m (32'9 3/4"--500 points). The West German approach would advocate basic strength training and work on shot technique. But for various reasons of size and aptitude, an equal mount of time given to the pole vaule might easily add some 15 inches (100 points) as compared with almost five feet (100 points) in the shot, for this man a more slowly gained improvement.

As a second example in which balance is secondary, a beginner can be weak in technique and confidence, though not necessarily in performance, in those three critical events--pole vault, hurdles and discus. Time and again, talented competitors slip the discus outside the sector three times (no points), fall down and out in the hurdles (no points), or fail to clear the first height in the pole vault (no points). A first priority should be practice for con- sistency and sureness in these events, even though other events might be weaker.

This argument is not at all against the concept of balance; in the final tests at highest levels, the decathlete with even one weak event in which he scores 300 points under his average for the other nine, is certainly handicapped and not likely to win. But it does argue that the main goal is highest scoring for ten events in whatever competition, late or soon, is consid- ered important for this individual. First priorities in time-energy should be on whatever procedures best further that goal.

TABLE 15.5
SAMPLE DECATHLON SCORES[1]

Total	100m	LJ	Shot	HJ	400m	HH	Dis	PV	Jav	1500m
5000	12.4	5.54	10.55	1.61	57.9	19.2	31.14	2.91	40.66	4:44.0
5500	12.2	5.75	11.27	1.66	56.5	18.5	33.42	3.08	44.00	4:36.0
6000	11.9	5.98	12.01	1.71	55.1	17.8	35.77	3.25	47.56	4:28.4
6500	11.7	6.21	12.77	1.77	53.7	17.1	38.20	3.42	51.25	4:21.3
7000	11.5	6.44	13.55	1.82	52.5	16.5	40.72	3.60	55.09	4:14.5
7500	11.2	6.67	14.36	1.88	51.3	16.0	43.31	3.78	59.06	4:08.2
8000	11.0	6.90	15.19	1.93	50.1	15.5	45.99	3.97	63.17	4:02.0
8500	10.8	7.15	16.05	1.99	49.0	15.0	48.75	4.17	67.42	3:56.1
9000	10.6	7.40	16.92	2.05	48.0	14.5	51.58	4.36	71.81	3:50.6

[1]Scores are derived from 1962 Tables. To indicate approximate performance needed to ensure the projected total, all figures provide one-tenth of the total score; example, 12.4 for the 100 equals 500 points. Actual scores in competition would of course vary greatly.

THE DECATHLON COACH
Traditionally, the American track and field coach is just that--a multi-event coach whose primary responsibility is to the team and the team schedule. Until about 1950, the Olympic Games were relatively unimportant. College and high school events were selected and organized exclusively in terms of their own interests. Distances were not metric. Such events as the 400m hurdles, steeplechase, three-mile, six-mile, 440 relay and decathlon were not held.

But with the development of the two wars--the Cold War between the USSR and the USA, and that between the NCAA and AAU--all this changed. To substantiate its claim to international recognition, the NCAA pointed its program toward Olympic events and the development of Olympic competitors. The responsibility of the college coach became divided between local success in dual meets and Conference championships on the one hand, and making a direct contribution to United States success in the Olympics on the other.

This evolution is reflected clearly in the changing attitudes of college coaches toward the decathlon. In 1948, Tulare High School coach, Virgil Jackson, stimulated Bob Mathias to try the decathlon. Bob was Olympic decathlon champion (1948) before he enrolled at Stanford, and (1952) after graduation. But during his three varsity years, he concentrated in both training and competition on University team events, including a year of football.

From 1956 to 1964, Ducky Drake of UCLA, gave much time and personal concern to the development of Rafer Johnson and C. K. Yang, the great Taiwan athlete who came to this country primarily to develop as a decathlete. But even for them, University competitions came first. Decathlon preparation came indirectly and after the school year was over.

In 1968, Coach L. D. Weldon of Graceland College, Iowa, recruited Bruce Jenner, primarily as a decathlon prospect. Weldon was a decathlon enthusiast who, in 1936 had coached Jack Parker to an Olympic bronze medal in the decathlon. While in college, Bruce competed in nine decathlons during the college track season, with the direct help of Coach Weldon. But Graceland, Iowa, provided limited opportunities and insights as to what was possible. After graduation Jenner moved to San Jose where he found no coach, but all the other essentials for development--unlimited time, good climate, training facilities, and most important, expertise among such single-event champions as shot-putter Al Feuerbach, and discus-thrower Mac Wilkins. On a questionnaire from THE DECATHLON GUIDE, Jenner listed as his coach, "Bertha Lou Jenner," that being the name of his constant companion, a Labrador retriever. Clearly the burden of overall planning was on his own shoulders.

Now that, as of 1970, the decathlon has become an official responsibility of the college coach, we can assume most coaches will regard it as just one more event in a track and field program of 21 wide-ranging events--far more than they, even with one or more assistants, can handle adequately. Most will argue that points scored in several single events will total more than those scored in one event, the decathlon, and so will ignore, if not discourage, the latter. Even if the decathlon is chosen, most coaches will assume that their prior experience with single events will provide adequate knowledge. And if scoring in Conference Championships is the criterion for success, they might get by.

But the decathlon, if taken as more than a mere "fun" event with minimal training, is not "just one more event," comparable to the addition of the steeplechase or 400m hurdles. A Dwight Stones can break the world record in the high jump without the help of a coach or even regular practice of technique. A Dave Roberts can do the same in the pole vault, even though a serious fulltime student in medical school. But the decathlon is far too all-encompassing and demanding of time-energy-commitment for such methods; assuming of course that highest personal levels are desired.

Bill Toomey did not become active in the decathlon until after graduation from the University of Colorado. Desperate for specialized coaching, he went for six months, 1965, to Cologne, Germany, to train under National Decathlon Coach, Friedel Schirmer. There he found large numbers of decathlon prospects from Olympic champions to beginners, but even more important, systematized training in all its aspects. Decathlon teams of five or more men each of similar scoring potential competed with those of other clubs or other nations. Training was focused on development for the decathlon as one's only event. An optimal number of competitions each year were scheduled for each individual. Though much of all this came too late for Toomey's effective use, he came home convinced of the great superiority of such a system for maximum development.

In Europe and the USSR, track and field has always been organized through clubs not connected with educational institutions, clubs that are organized, coached and financed by the National Governing Body for Sports. Primary goals relate to national achievement in the Olympic Games and other international meets. Both coaches and athletes are selected and trained accordingly. With team dual-meets at minimal levels, the need for all-event coaches is low. Usually, their coaches are certified to be expert in but one or only a few related events. If long experienced and well trained, both practically and scientifically, a man may be certified as a Master Coach, or even a National Coach for a single event such as the decathlon. He then concentrates his energies toward becoming a true Master of that event and its athletes. Small wonder that the most knowledgeable and respected decathlon coaches have developed, not in America, but abroad.

All this makes clear the wide range of decathlon attitudes and action by coaches--from that in the United States up to about 1960 to that in West Germany today. Even now, the American college system and coach are strongly oriented toward local dual-meets and Conference competition. If, as of 1979, the Big Ten Conference still refused to give field space and coaching time to such events as the hammer and javelin, what better treatment can be expected for the decathlon?

A few exceptions are notable. At the University of California (SB), Coach Sam Adams has been of great help for many years to both on-campus and off-campus decathletes. Adams was 5th in the 1956 Olympic decathlon trials, as well as a contestant in the 1974 Masters' decathlon. He coached a half-dozen on-campus decathletes, as well as many graduates from other colleges, including John Warkentin. Because of his wide reputation as a coach of decathletes, his own University created a special post as Director of UCSB's Outreach Track and Field Program with special responsibility for the decathlon. He is also Official National Coach for decathletes competing in international meets, here and abroad.

Another decathlon stalwart is Frank Zarnowski, professor of economics at Mount St. Mary's, Maryland, and Master Guru for the event in the United States. Zarnowski has organized competitions, officiated, announced, and even paid out of his own pocket for dozens of decathlon meets at all levels of competence. He has acted as manager and coach-of-sorts for decathlon teams competing abroad. Importantly, he has edited and published a monthly *Deca Newsletter* and, with Bert Nelson, has an annual, *THE DECATHLON BOOK*; all of which have been an excellent source of information and inspiration for decathletes and their coaches.

In summary, future improvements in the decathlon, as well as in the other phases of track and field, require the following: (1) much more effective training of track and field coaches, with certification of expertise on a single-event basis. A recent NOVA TV program stated that such training in East Germany takes seven years and is at least as rigorous as that required for the M.D. degree. (2) establishment throughout the United States of college-school-oriented track and field clubs (TAFCLUBS), using facilities now in place, sponsored and financed by local booster clubs, industries, and the National Governing Body for Track and Field.

HOW TO ORGANIZE YOUR OWN TRAINING SYSTEMS

In the discussion of "Potential Talents" the point was emphasized that the vaguely interested decathlete should try it or some portion of it simply because it's fun. But even at that level, he'll derive more satisfaction and encouragement if first efforts are preceded by a little preparation. No fun in trying to vault if one doesn't know how to hold the pole or make a takeoff. No fun in hurdling if such problems as which leg goes first, or how many strides between have not been worked out. No fun in running 400m or 1500 m if one drops exhausted at the finish. The decathlon is like the marathon--no matter how slow the pace, just covering the distance demands planned preparation.

Basic Needs. Because of the decathlon's all-inclusive demands, planning should first clear away the possible negatives--the basic needs of the athlete--food, shelter, sleep, vocation or studies, finances, and the like. Read the biography of any decathlon champion. You will find that he has found a solution for these basic life problems. In the early years, of course, such concentration is relatively low. A college decathlete, training-competing at low levels of time-energy, can be an excellent student and take part in most phases of college life. But as with any art, and certainly with one so total in its requirements, highest achievement in the decathlon demands that what must be done is done and, equally important, whatever prevents or detracts is nullified.

Up to about 1960, even Olympic champions could win on talent only. But the use of sports as an instrument of governmental or institutional prestige changed such a dilettante approach. Full-time concentration became a necessity; not even such essentials as earning a living or, for college men, high-level academic work could be permitted to interfere. Stick-to-itiveness became as necessary as physical talent. During his decathlon years, Toomey was given financial support by his father. Bruce Jenner had a selling job with brief time requirements and a major portion of wife Chrystie's income as airline stewardess. Daley Thompson was given Olympic-sanctioned "broken-time" payments ($11,000).

Without some such provision of basic needs and time-energy commitment, performance will be limited. Doubt as to whether such concentration and restriction is really worth the cost in human terms is certain to arise. For most, the answer will be negative; other interests and activities will be judged more worthwhile. It's a serious problem for both athletes and coaches.

Technique is Primary. Not all coaches or athletes agree that technique should be given first emphasis in training. Bob Hayes, an all-time Great in sprinting, almost ignored technique. Neither Dick Fosbury nor Dwight Stones spent much time on high-jump technique in practice. Bob Beamon was not the long jump's greatest technician. Many great shot-putters give power a 70-80 percent emphasis; technique only 20-30. Such natural decathletes as Jim Thorpe, Bob Mathias or Rafer Johnson scored over 700 points in their first attempts in the technique events within a decathlon. Why then should technique be a primary concern in decathlon training?

First, because for most athletes, acquiring a dependable and effective skill is a long-time undertaking. By 1976 Dave Roberts had practiced vaulting technique for some ten years. But in the Montreal Olympics he lost the title through defective technique in one miss at a lower height--17'6 3/4". Many a decathlete has eliminated himself by missing low heights in the pole vault or high jump, heights he would usually clear easily; or by falling from a hurdle, or by throwing the discus outside the throwing sector--all for lack of control in technique. It is important to add that the techniques acquired so early--junior high school is not too soon--should be biomechanically sound. To unlearn an unsound skill is time consuming, often ineffective and always disrupting. Innumerable instances suggest that no-learning is far better than established learning of poor technique.

BASIC-RELATED TRAINING. A first emphasis on sound technique has just been made. On the other hand, experts have long agreed that prior development of the basic qualities of speed, strength and endurance facilitates both technique and performance. Greater leg-speed helps technique in the hurdles and long jump. Greater basic strength gained from the Olympic lifts helps technique in the throwing events and jumps. Greater basic endurance helps performance in the 1500, as well as "technique" in a special meaning of the word.

Training for Speed. Velocity of muscle action underlies performance in at least nine of the events--critically in four (100, hurdles, 400, long jump), as shown by the high correlations among their scores. No need to repeat here the various ways of increasing basic speed described in Chapter 27.

Training for Power. Training for power in all its phases--basic, related and imitative--presents a difficult and even unsolvable problem for the decathlete. Event movement patterns vary greatly; to organize all three phases of power exercises for each of eight events is impossible within the same time frame that the single-eventer uses for his one event. The decathlete can only seek to understand his complex problem, plan his time-energy carefully, and accept compromise. Basic strength training, well-planned, becomes all the more essential. Related power training should not be neglected, especially for the six field events. Though all such training is less than the maximums of single-event athletes, it can be entirely adequate, capable of producing a 9000-point decathlete.

A 1976 study by M. Letzelter[1] and E. Schubert of West Germany, supports this approach. They conclude: (1) Individuals differ widely. (2) General strength development through weight-training exercises is sufficient for the decathlon. (3) Using average values, an athlete whose decathlon score is about 7500 points can snatch 85 kg, clean and jerk 110 kg, bench press 120 kg, clean 115 kg and squat 140 kg. (4) Better decathletes have a higher maximum basic strength level. In summary, "the decathlete has to economize his strength development and therefore finds that a general all-round development is for him more valuable than a specific approach for each event."

Such conclusions are supported by those of Schirmer[2], based on his actual experiences with decathletes. "Training to increase muscle strength ensured the basic conditions that enabled an athlete to learn the technique of a particular event better and faster. On the other hand, I learned that too much training to increase muscle strength could impair the sense of movement in a specific event."

Training for Endurance. Though new scoring tables may upgrade scores for the 1500, the need for basic endurance training for the decathlete will not change. Tables 15.2, 15.3 show

[1]M. Letzelter & E. Schubert, "Strength Level in the Decathlon," reported in *Track Technique*, # 70, Dec. 1977, p. 2244.

[2]Friedel Schirmer, "Decathlon Training, West German Style," in Frank Zarnowski, *The Decathlon Guide*, Emmitsburg, Md., DECA, 1975, p. 46.

that Olympic champions have averaged only 517 points (4:41.3) in the 1500, 244 points less than their average for all events. But such failures were not necessary, even for men over six feet in height and 180# in weight. They were primarily the effects of a long-time misunderstanding, even a phobia against long-distance running, not unlike that against strength training prior to 1950. Some "authorities" argue that such running, even at the start of each year, slows the muscles; others that the time consumed is not warranted by the 300 or so points that can be gained in only one event.

With such attitudes, the very thought of that last "grueling" race exhausts many decathletes even before the gun is fired. Their complex fears of the pain-agony-failure syndrome dinimish performance more than does actual impairment from physical exhaustion. In contrast, those with a solid background of basic endurance training have no such handicapping fears. In the Fall of each year they'll run 5-10 miles away from the track, including some hill work. Most of this will be aerobic (pulse rates under 150). As Bill Bowerman used to say, "If you can't tell a few jokes while running, you're going too fast." But a change of pace, as of terrain, is refreshing. Include some anaerobic fast-slow running (pulse rates up to 180, then down to 110 or so during recovery jogs). Gradually, it becomes fun.

Finch[1] provides details of Bruce Jenner's workouts in October, 1975. Each morning, every day, rain or shine, he ran 10 miles, sometimes all-out as though he was actually in Olympic competition. Perhaps because of its location across the street from his apartment, such runs were on the track. Then twice a week, in the afternoon, he motored to the Stanford University golf course. "The 11th fairway is 300 yards long, and steep. Twenty times he sprints up that hill, jogging down to the bottom each time." On other afternoons he worked on field events and hurdles, primarily for technique.

How long should such basic running be continued? Lydiard's Marathon Training System advocates mileage work to within a few weeks of competition, with only a relatively brief period of sharpening speed work. This would be unwise for the decathlete, especially since endurance adds points in but one event, the 1500. Decathletes, properly trained, should be even more confident of their ability to run 1500 meters than for any other event, for that is the last and, often, the crucial event. Great championships have been won and lost there. In June 1980, after nine events, Daley Thompson knew he had to run 4:26 or better if he was to gain his first world record. His previous best was 4:20.3, giving very little margin for confidence. He ran 4:25.5. With maximal endurance training, both his confidence and his time would have improved.

At the 1976 Olympics, Bruce Jenner (6'2", 198#) ran 4:12.6 (715 points). In 1972, Horst Beyer, West Germany (6'5", 212#) ran 4:14.8; Leonid Litvinyenko, USSR (6'1", 192#), an excellent 4:05.9. The accepted world's best for the 1500 within a decathlon is 3:54.2 by Simo Salorana, Finland, 1965. We can be certain that, in the future, world-class decathletes will regularly go under four minutes (816 points). Not until then will their claim as "world's greatest all-round athletes," balancing speed-power-endurance-skill, be truly valid.

Training for Spring. I have intentionally left out "spring" as a basic quality for which specific training should be done. "Spring" is a less definable quality, related to muscle velocity or explosiveness, skeletal leverage, coordination, but always specific to a particular action. For example, we might assume that the vertical jump-and-reach is a valid test of spring, and that great high jumpers would score well. But in tests given at the 1975 Olympic Development Camp at Indiana University, Donald Chu found low correlations. Shot-putters had a higher average jump-and-reach than did high jumpers. (Al Feuerbach, 260# shot-putter, easily surpassed Dwight Stones, 7'7" high jumper.) Chu concluded that ability in the high jump is specific to the particular actions and demands of that event, including the run-conversion-spring-clearance, and that the Sargent Jump was of little value in diagnosing talent for the high jump.

If such specificity holds for the high jump, how much more so for the long jump, in which velocity is so much a factor, or for the pole vault in which velocity-technique plays a primary role. In summary, basic work in terms of "spring" seeks related power in the specific muscle groups and movements of each event.

---

[1]Bruce Jenner & Phillip Finch, *op. cit.* pp. 91-94.

Training by Event Relatedness. Decathletes usually practice two, three or even more events during a single workout. In what order of events should such practice occur? East German coaches have emphasized the values of sequence training--practicing events in the same order they occur within a decathlon. They argue that a major problem in decathlon competition lies in performing maximally while transferring from one event to another of a quite different character and challenge; example--from the long jump to the shot. After being totally concentrated in a 130-foot run-and-jump, the decathlete must relax briefly, then re-orient and re-focus his energies within a seven-foot circle and behind a 16# iron ball, with only three trials in which to do his best without fouling. It's a physical-mental problem that the German coaches think is best solved by sequence training.

While not denying the potential values of any training that simulates competitive conditions, it seems clear that other considerations (basic training, weakness in one or more events, a need for greater balance and consistency, training time) must also be given their share of emphasis. Take the last--training time. A full training session for three or four events in sequence requires up to three hours. But many times, a day's work is divided into two sessions: mileage running in the morning and a shorter workout (1-1½ hours) on technique in the afternoon.

Sequence training would seem most helpful when preparing for competitions with only a dozen or so decathletes. Each day's events are completed within five hours or less, so that there is little time between events. NCAA rules state, "Whenever advisable, at least a half hour's rest between events shall be allowed each competitor." But actually, it is not always advisable; groups in running events are drawn by lot, so that the last to high jump may be the first to run the 400. Knowing that one has practiced that sequence on many occasions could help mind and body. But even for such small meets, the assumption of carry-over from practice to competition seems very doubtful. Practice is one thing; competition is quite another. Of course, if you think it helps, it helps.

But in large competitions, ten or more hours are needed for each day, with long waits between trials within an event, as well as between different events. In such competitions there is plenty of time for adjustments and related energy build-up. Actually, the tensions of waiting are often more of a problem than are event sequences. In fact, careful thought suggests that the crux of the problem lies within multiple competitions rather than in event sequences. One learns to compete by competing, more than by practicing certain simulated aspects of competition. Bruce Jenner competed in 27 decathlons; Bill Toomey in 38; John Warkentin in 49. They undoubtedly felt each decathlon to be important for itself, but equally as training in the many ways and means of competition. How marvellous that Jenner in winning his 27th decathlon at the 1976 Olympics, should have brought forth five personal records: pole vault, 1500, and three that occurred in sequence at the end of the first day--shot, high jump, 400. Call it what you will--concentration, confidence, relaxation, snowball effect, will-to-excel--such a performance requires a specific talent developed to its ultimate by both related training and many competitions.

In keeping with such thinking, some decathletes have tried to score as many points as possible in ten events, all within the shortest possible total time. In 1978, Warkentin held an unofficial USA record of 6747 points for ten events within a total of 30 minutes! A miracle of concentration--ten times within 30 minutes in widely varied events.

A different approach to training by event relatedness is derived from the 100-year experience of multiple-event athletes in non-decathlon competition and training. Doublers in the shot-discus have always practiced the shot first. "It just feels better that way." Men high jump before they pole vault; take sprint starts before hurdling or long jumping. As a rule of thumb, technique events are practiced first, though often preceded by sprint starts for reasons of technique and warm-up. If three or more activities involving high speed, power and endurance occur in a single session, they are practiced in that order. Saying that differently, events requiring quickness and little fatigue are practiced first; events requiring great effort and strain, or overall exhaustion, are done last. (Often, special time is set aside for heavy basic work in strength or endurance--in the morning, on a weekend, on a change-of-pace day.) There's no set pattern or requirement in all this; each decathlete should follow his own judgment, unique time allotments, and preference. But such long-time experience should not be ignored.

These over-all views are in agreement with those of Fred Kudu, USSR Chief Decathlon Coach, in his 1975 book, *DECATHLON*,[1]

Each training session has to solve several different problems and usually includes development of technique in one or two events. As the decathlon has a competitive order of events, it is advisable to follow this order in training.

However, it is not necessary to be strict about it. Far more important is to perform technique training and speed exercises at the start, strength and jumping exercises in the middle, and endurance development at the end of a training session.

The Beginner. "Beginners" in the decathlon vary greatly in age and related experience. Contrast the problems of a 16-year old high school junior with those of a 22-year college graduate in his first decathlon but with seven years of track and field competition and training behind him. But the basic goal is the same: to complete all ten events with a sense of satisfaction and encouragement for future decathlons.

Obviously, careful planning and preparation must be made.

(1) Since skill is the most difficult and gradual of all basics to acquire, first emphasis should be on adequate skill in all eight events. Of special concern are the danger events (pole vault, hurdles, discus, long jump) in which skill consistency will ensure against no-points performances.

(2) Related power is basic to at least five events and enhances performance quite apart from skill. Safest and best when acquired gradually and so, when started early.

(3) Practice events in decathlon order (e.g., 100-SHOT-LJ).

(4) A few trial runs in the 400 and 1500 may prevent too fast a pace in the first competition, and so avoid the "agony" of exhaustion no one cares to repeat.

(5) Various triathlons can be attempted in which any three events are competed in the same sequence as in the decathlon: LJ-SHOT-HJ, or PV-JAV-1500. Later, add a fourth event in decathlon sequence: 100-LJ-SHOT-HJ, or HH-PV-JAV-1500.

(6) Some authorities suggest prior competition in the pentathlon (LJ-JT-200-DT-1500), using regular decathlon scoring tables. This has an undoubted value of open competition in a sequence of events, with little or no stigma of failure in terms of one's own event, the decathlon. Another device is to organize a competition using the five events of the first day. Then, some days or weeks later, after proper preparation, compete in the second day's events.

A 1976 study by R. Kuptschinov,[2] USSR, reported that 78% of 64 decathlon coaches recommended that decathlon training be started at the ages of 13-14. First year: four two-hour sessions with a 50-50 balance between technique (no throwing events), and general conditioning in endurance, flexibility, sprints, easy long runs. Second year: four three-hour sessions with a 70-30 distribution between technique (including shot, javelin, no discus), and general conditioning with emphasis on developing power and more intensive endurance training (including interval runs at 150-300m). Third year: five three-hour sessions with a 75-25 balance between technique (all events) and general conditioning work in which strength training, mileage running, and gradually more intensive anaerobic endurance are added to the work load. In this third year, an eight-event competition using a decathlon sequence of events is introduced--the first competition mentioned in the study.

---

[1]Quoted as a footnote in *TRACK AND FIELD QUARTERLY REVIEW*, Vol. 79, #2, 1979, p. 19.

[2]R. Kuptschinov, "Training of Young Decathletes," reported in *TRACK AND FIELD QUARTERLY REVIEW*, Vol. 79, #2, 1979, p. 18.

TRAINING FROM BEGINNER TO MASTER. By Vern Gambetta and Gord Stewart.[1]

The very nature of the decathlon suggests that training should be a slow, methodical process. Training can be likened to putting together a large mosaic. Each piece (event) must be carefully prepared for. After much effort the pieces come together in a good score.

A proper foundation must be carefully laid in the first years of training. Progress should not be hurried. One must not think in terms of days or months, but in years. Few decathletes have risen to national class in less than three years.

Generally, the development of the decathlete can be divided into two distinct stages: the *learning stage* and the *specificity stage*. The main objective in the learning stage is to balance performance by working on the weaker events. During this stage the decathlete should concentrate on good all-around physical training aimed at developing speed, general strength, and endurance. During this stage, the athlete should compete often in those events in which he has reached a reasonable level of proficiency. He should also try to compete as often as possible in the "key events": 100m, 400m, 110H, and PV. During this learning stage, it would be advisable to compete each season in the number of decathlons that allows adequate time to recover and train between each one. For most decathletes this learning stage lasts for three or four years until the weak events are brought up to a standard of good all-around performance.

The specificity stage of training should begin when the athlete achieves a certain amount of parity between the three groups of events, (i.e. when there are no apparent weaknesses). The emphasis in this stage of training is on giving reasonably equal attention to each event.

TRAINING COMPONENTS

A sound decathlon training program should include the following components:

1) Speed--The development of sprinting speed is an integral and important part of training from the very beginning. At least five events are directly related to speed. Speed training should be carried out year round, not just as pre-season and in-season activities. Methods used should be sprint form drills, starts, and sprinting over 30m, 60m, 100m, and 150m.

2) Speed Endurance--Essentially this is 400 meter training. The emphasis here is on carrying the speed developed in the speed component over longer distances. Training would consist of running 200m, 300m, 400m, 500 and 600m at various speeds and combinations.

3) Technique--The goal in technique training is...not to develop a flawless technique, but to find one that is simple, mechanically sound and suited to the individual athlete....The greatest emphasis on technique should be during the learning stage--a time when the fundamental concepts and sound motor patterns are developed...

4) Strength Training--This can be divided into two kinds. *General strength training* consists of the traditional weight training exercises including squats, snatch, clean and jerk and bench press. These exercises emphasize the development of total overall body strength. The younger or beginning decathlete may initially confine his general strength training to a circuit on a Universal Gym...

Specific strength training encompasses the more dynamic exercises to develop power for running, jumping and throwing. This includes bounding, hopping, jumping over hurdles, depth jumping and medicine ball exercises.

General strength training dominates the learning stage. Once the decathlete becomes more proficient and enters the specificity stage of training, strength training is divided almost equally between general and specific strength.

It is important that strength training parallels technique work (not taking precedence over it.

---

[1]Vern Gambetta and Gord Stewart, "Decathlon Training: From Beginner to Master," *Track Technique* #70, Dec. 1977, p. 2219. Gambetta and Stewart (7438 pts--Canadian record) were both decathletes. Gambetta is editor of *Track Technique* and women's track coach at the University of California, Berkeley.

5) <u>Endurance Training</u>--The purpose of endurance training is to develop the aerobic base to run a good 1500m and to provide the general endurance necessary to handle the long hours of competition. This running should be based on the need for general endurance while keeping in mind that the 1500m has a 50%-50% aerobic anaerobic split. This can be accomplished by an off-season 20-30 minute steady run every other morning and a 20-30 minute fartlek session once a week. During the season, several paced 800m or 1200m would be advisable.

6) <u>Mobility (flexibility) Training</u>--This area is often neglected or played down as an important component of training. However, it is important since it assists in injury prevention as well as aiding technique (by allowing larger range of movement and faster movement through a given range). A daily fifteen minute pre-workout stretching session will pay large dividends.

TRAINING ORGANIZATION

On any given training day one should do sprint and technique work before any speed endurance training. Endurance and strength or power training should be at the end of the session.

In a sequence of training days the same principle holds. Technique work should follow a rest or light training day. Speed and speed endurance should be in the middle part of a training cycle with endurance and strength work towards the end of the cycle.

Because of the sheer demands of the decathlon, the training load will be heavy. Workload should be evenly distributed over a period of time interspersed with an adequate number of rest days. Planned rest periods during a training cycle should help minimize on overuse injuries and ensure that a large buildup of fatigue does not occur.

TRAINING CYCLES

An early, training cycle could be broken down into four phases. (1) Total rest and active rest take up the month of October. (2) Off-season training (strength, speed endurance, endurance emphasis) occupy the months November through January. (3) The four-month February to May period takes in indoor and pre-season activities. Speed endurance and technique work dominate this phase. The work load should not be sacrificed for indoor competitive results. (4) The in-season activities June through September ensures sharpening of speed and speed endurance and refining of technique. These are obviously crucial during the competitive phase of the yearly cycle.

There are a variety of short-term cycles which can be split into the three longer training phases of each year's activity. The crucial element is the number of training days before a planned rest day is taken. Experience will dictate the right combination.

To provide more specific guidelines, three short-term training cycles are outlined: A preparation period (off-season or pre-season) 21-day cycle; an in-season, competitive, 14-day cycle and a 3-day competitive season cycle.

The <u>21-day cycle</u> is designed for a younger decathlete in his first two or three years of training. The emphasis is on weak events and development of the fitness component.

The <u>14-day cycle</u> is for the young or seasoned decathlete alike. Both athletes could pursue the same general plan with the seasoned athlete emphasizing a lighter but more intense work load.

The <u>3-day cycle</u> is meant for the mature athlete preparing for important competitions.

Off-Season or Pre-Season Preparation Period
21-day Cycle for the Younger Decathlete

Day 1--1st day events: Sprint, LJ, SP, strength training
Day 2--A.M. 20 min. steady run. P.M. 2nd day events:HH, Dis, (PV), 400m training
Day 3--Weak events, strength training

Day 4--A.M. 30 min. fartlek. P.M. 1st day: SP, HJ, 400m training
Day 5--2nd day: PV, Jav, 1500 training
Day 6--A.M. 20 min. steady run. P.M. Warm-up, strength training

Day 7--Rest
Day 8--Sprinting, SP, HJ, strength training
Day 9--A.M. 20 min. steady run. P.M. HH, (PV), Jam, 400m training
Day 10--Weak events, strength training
Day 11--A.M. 30 min. fartlek. P.M. LJ, SP, 400m training

Day 12--HH, Dis, PV
Day 13--Warmup, strength training. P.M. A.M. 20 min. steady run
Day 14--Rest
Day 15-21--Same as Day 1-7

In-Season Competitive Cycle
14-day Cycle for the Younger or Seasoned Decathlete

Day 1--Sprinting, LJ, SP. P.M. Special strength training
Day 2--HH, Dis, (PV), 400m training
Day 3--Weak events. P.M. strength training
Day 4--Sprinting (starts), SP, HJ. P.M. 400m training
Day 5--HH, PV, Jav, 400m training
Day 6--General strength training
Day 7--Rest

Day 8--Sprinting, SP, HJ. P.M. Special strength training
Day 9--HH, (PV), Jav, 400m training
Day 10--LJ, SP, 1500m training, strength training
Day 11--HH, PV, 400m training
Day 12--Warmup--General strength training
Day 13--Competition, 4 or 5 events
Day 14--Rest

Note: In preparation for a decathlon on the 13th or 14th day of the 14-day cycle, the overall volume of work is reduced on days 8 through 12. Technique work should be minimal. On day 8, a fast 300m; on day 10, 2 x 60m and 2 x 150m fast; day 11 should be off and day 12 should include warmup activities only.

3-day Competitive Season Cycle
for the Mature Decathlete

Day 1--A.M. SP, Dis. P.M. HJ, 6 x 50m, 4 x 150m
Day 2--A.M. HH, Jav. P.M. PV, 400m training (e.g., 150m, 300m, 200m--fast with full recovery)

Day 3--A.M. LJ, 1500m training (e.g., 800, 300, 200 at race pace). P.M. General strength training
Day 4--Rest

Note: Events not done or not emphasized in the cycle can be done in the next cycle. Sprint technique, suppleness, "light" special strength training and easy 1500m work can be incorporated into each day's warmup.

HOW THEY TRAIN
Bruce Jenner--1976 Olympic Champion (8618 points, world record).

This program[1] relates to the training year 1973-4, Jenner's fourth year of training and competition in the decathlon. He had graduated from college, had almost full time for training, and coached himself--other than getting advice from single-event experts such as Feuerbach in the shot and Powell in the discus.

Technique Training. Jenner works all year around on the shot, discus, hurdles; two months before first decathlon, he starts pole-vaulting; one month before, he works on the javelin, long jump, and high jump. At all-comers meets in December and January, works on technique in discus, shot and hurdles. During the competitive season, workouts are shorter. Twice per week, after a good warmup, Jenner takes 5 hard competitive throws in the discus, shot, or javelin.

Number of Competitions. Jenner competes in four or more decathlons per year, spacing them at least one month apart.

Pre-Competitive Season (September-December). Runs two workouts per day of all over-distance, with morning workouts of 4-5 miles, afternoon workouts of 5-7 miles ("just get it in").

---

[1]Tom Jordan, "Bruce Jenner," *Track Technique*, #57, Sept. 1974, p. 1820.

Weightlifting 3 times per week, all year round. Examples: Dumbbells on an incline, 50 lbs. each hand, set of 6 works up to set of 5 with 85 lbs. in each hand by the competitive season. (Next year, Bruce plans to start at 85 and end up at 105 lbs.) Jenner does some Olympic lifting: e.g., does clean and jerk once every two weeks, trying for a PR each time (presently at 230). Does full squats twice per week, 6 x 5 reps, starting at 135 and working up to 315 lbs. Every two weeks, Jenner goes for a PR in the squats to "keep it exciting." Weightlifting basically the same all year around.

Jenner does some technique work every day. Concentrates on the weight events, the shot and discus.

December 15-February. Moves to the track and does miles, halves, and quarters in a hard-easy pattern. Hard day: 5 x 440 in 65 with 65 second rest; two sets (down to 60 seconds by the competitive season). Bruce feels this is a "great 1500 workout to learn pace." Easy day: Runs on grass 4 x 880 in 2:45 with a quarter jog interval. Mile workout: 2 x 6:00 mile.

March-April. Shortens distance to 440s, 330s, 220s. Examples: 3 x 440 in 54, complete rest between. 4 x 330 in 38 with long rest between; 5 x 220 in 25-26 with 220 walk recovery. During this period Jenner works on relaxation.

Competitive Season--April 15-July. In a typical week in the last month before his first decathlon, Jenner does more actual sprinting (330s, 220s, 165s, 110s), with every other day being a hard running workout: Mon., 2 x 220 in 23 with complete rest. Tue., 110s on grass, working on technique in running (knee lift, arm motion). Wed., 330 in 35-36 all-out, with walking start. Thurs., 110s on the grass, technique work. Fri., 4 x 165 (18.0, 17.5, 16.8, 16.2). Sat., 110s on grass. Sun., 6 x 110 acceleration, untimed on the track.

One week before meet, runs 330 all-out (PR 35.2). Five days before meet, 2 x 165, and relax. Complete rest, one day before meet. Same the rest of the competitive season.

A PROPOSAL FOR IMPROVED SCORING TABLES

For three years, Frank Zarnowski and associates worked to remove the deficiencies of the 1962 Scoring Tables, following criteria similar to those given here on page 312. Their final proposal[1] was made to the technical committee of the IAAF in March 1980, by whom it was tabled for further study, but who seemed likely to recommend similar, if not identical, Tables in the near future. Table 15.6 provides actual performances and comparable scores on 1962 and 1980 Tables.

TABLE 15.6
COMPARABLE SCORES 1962 and PROPOSED 1980 TABLES

Name	100	LJ	Shot	HJ	400	HH	Dis	PV	Jav	1500	TOTAL
Kratschmer	10.58	7.80	15.47	2.00	48.04	13.92	45.52	4.60	66.50	4:24.2	
1962	911	980	816	857	896	972	791	957	839	630	8649
1980	915	911	873	811	850	919	818	830	875	844	8646
Green	11.3	6.34	12.42	1.80	51.3	15.9	40.24	3.70	56.52	4:28.5	
1962	733	680	628	680	749	757	690	728	718	600	6962
1980	740	614	687	637	711	709	729	610	752	815	7004
Bardales	11.8	5.87	12.52	1.65	53.8	19.1	40.13	4.00	44.84	4:42.0	
1962	622	575	634	540	648	506	688	807	562	512	6094
1980	620	520	693	508	583	387	727	683	610	725	6056
Lester	11.8	5.46	12.09	1.70	57.4	18.0	34.45	3.70	48.01	5:29.2	
1962	622	482	599	588	517	582	572	728	606	262	5559
1980	620	439	667	551	419	490	633	610	648	414	5491

In summary, it seems clear that these proposed Tables: (1) are consistent with the five criteria cited here; (2) provide total scores very similar to those given by the 1962 Tables; (3) upgrade scoring considerably for the 1500, and somewhat in the three throwing events; and (4) lower scoring considerably for the pole vault, and slightly for the high jump, hurdles, 400 and long jump.

---

[1]Frank Zarnowski, Ph.D., A *Proposal for a Decathlon Scoring Table*, presented to the Technical Committee, International Amateur Athletic Federation, 1980, for possible revision/acceptance.

Chapter 16
A MODERN SYSTEM FOR COACHING FIELD EVENTS

Sports, in both competitive performance and training, have an inherent tendency toward "more"--especially more analysis of the essentials of performance and more programs that train those essentials--all of which requires more time-energy-commitment. We were so aware of this in the early 1950s when weight-training was first organized for sports. Not only did training become more strenuous, it became much more complex. Then when relatively simple Olympic weight-lifting was augmented by related power training, resistance exercises that simulated event patterns of movement, and even velocity training, the need for a careful organization of training activities was obvious.

But in recent decades, this natural tendency has been greatly increased--perhaps to a level of excess--by the almost world-wide adoption of sports as an instrument of government policy--first by Communist countries but, in reaction, by the West as well. That decision affected all levels of sport, down to elementary school ages and including both sexes. In 1960, the NCAA men's track and field program comprised 16 events; by 1971 it included 21. All the new events--six mile, three mile, triple jump, decathlon, 400m hurdles, 400m relay--were added for the specific intent of increasing the college program's contribution to the United States Olympic program. Four of these new events required endurance beyond that formerly expected of college students, and that meant more time-energy-commitment for sports training--I repeat--by students for whom college was already supposed to be a full time program.

In addition, the late 1970s saw the start of college women's programs in track and field. Again we see the international influence, with growing pressures for more events, longer-distance races, a decathlon to replace the septathlon that replaced the pentathlon, and through it all more extensity and intensity of training.

In brief, "modern sports training" between, roughly, 1950 and 1975 has been focussed on higher levels of performance through greater demands on human energies, time, and personal commitment. We have assumed, "the greater the challenge the greater the response;" "the longer-harder the work, the better the performance;" with little understanding of the importance of recovery periods, rest intervals, enjoyment and play, and the many kinds of variety that are just as essential to sports development as are increments of work and higher levels of stress.

A modern program of sports training assumes year-round training with only a month or so of related active-rest. Its goal is maximal individual performance. But--and here is the lesson now being given much greater attention--maximal performance results, not from maximal training, but from optimal training; not from training as might be given mechanical robots, but from a sports version of Norbert Wiener's "cybernetics"--the human uses of sports training.

Planning. That calls for planning at all levels and of all phases, planning in terms of scientifically oriented training, but just as essential, planning in terms of this particular individual: his unique energies, needs for development, commitment to sports within his total program of study or work.

The case is clearly evident in endurance training where for years the concept of marathon training--100, 150 or even more miles per week--tended to be considered inviolate. But in 1979-80, Sebastian Coe, Great Britain, held world records in the 800, 1000, 1500, and mile on a mileage program of not more than 50 miles a week. Is greater mileage and more time for running really so essential? The question is equally valid for field-event training.

PERIODIZATION

It is now accepted practice for track and field coaches to "periodize" their year training programs, following the organizational system, "Periodization," introduced by L. P. Matveyev, USSR, in 1962. Part of the attraction-rejection of Matveyev system lies in its use of such terms as microcycles, mesocycles, macrocycles or "polyvalent programs," that some claim are but pseudo-scientific jargon for common-sense ideas.

TABLE 16.1[1]

PERIODIZATION OF TRAINING
FOR FIELD EVENTS

Period I--PREPARATION FOR COMPETITION

       Phase 1: (Sept-Dec, 4 months)--Gradual Training
           for Heavy Training.
        Gradually increasing practice of technique
        Gradual build-up of basic strength
        Gradually more stressful fartlek--enjoyable
           speed-play runs

       Phase 2: (Dec-Feb, 2 months)--Training for Competition
           (Heaviest loadings of entire year)
        Practice for better technique
        Maintenance of basic strength
        Increasing use of related power training

Period II--INDOOR COMPETITION (Feb-Mar, 2 months)

        Emphasis on technique
        Maintenance of basic strength
        Use of related and imitative power training
        Gradual use of velocity training

Period III--PREPARATION FOR OUTDOOR COMPETITION (Mar-Apr, 6 weeks)

        Practice for better technique
        Re-emphasis on basic strength
        Gradual use of related power and velocity training

Period IV--MAJOR COMPETITION (April-June or July, 2-3 months)

        Developmental meets preparing for Big Meets
        Technique practice
        Maintenance of basic strength
        Increased use of related power and velocity training

Within all time segments--Periods, Phases, Cycles and Sub-Cycles--high-level stress should be balanced by active-rest--physically recuperative, mentally enjoyable, emotionally relaxed, and the monotony of year-round training avoided by use of variety in every form.

---

[1]My own version of Matveyev's "Periodization System," fitted to the American college-school schedule, and intentionally avoiding the jargon of the usual translations into English.

But careful study of Matveyev's system, such as reported by Scottish National Coach, Frank Dick[1], makes clear a great improvement over past methods. (There have been no past methods that justified the term "system".) The main goal of "Periodization" is development to highest performance levels at the period when needed most--the major competitions. This is accomplished by systematic planning of all related essentials, with special concern for (1) gradual increments of loading-intensity, (2) a balance of work/rest as an indivisible training unit, (3) the importance of variety in kinds of work, degree of work, competitive stress and much more, (4) division of the year into Periods, Phases, and Cycles of varying purposes, lengths and loadings.

Matveyev divided the year into two main Periods--Preparation and Competition--with a third Transition Period in which active-rest allowed adjustments for the succeeding year. (Nothing complex in that.) But the Preparation Period was divided into three Phases: (1) a gradual build-up for heavily loaded training, (2) training for competition--the most heavily loaded phase of the entire year, (3) a recovery and redevelopment phase that follows the initial Competitive Period and leads toward the final Competitive Period in which the Big Meets will occur.

Such a Matveyev system seems perfectly fitted for the American college schedule of indoor and outdoor seasons. Phase I--from the opening of school until about December 1, 4 months or so; Phase II--December until the start of indoor competition, 2 months or so; Phase III--from the Big Meet indoors through the first month or so of the outdoor competitive season, 4 to 8 weeks, depending on the individual situation.

Frank Dick's detailed four-part article warrants careful study. Without question, Matveyev and his associates have made an exhaustive analysis of the related factors of development for all events, on the track as well as on the field. As usual, limited space does not permit adequate explanation here. But the following concepts and their uses are consistent with the views of this OMNIBOOK and of Matveyev's Periodization System. I leave it to the individual coach and athlete to coordinate them within his own situation and needs.

Planning. The concept of planning is so easily accepted but so adamantly resisted in terms of taking time--days, even weeks of time--to think through, weigh carefully, outline on paper the many factors of competitive performance and related training. We tend to rely on the sole factor of MORE WORK, but it is more and better organized work that is the key to development.

Goals. Goal-oriented training, so important in the careers of so many champions, is a problem of knowing precisely where and when you intend to go, and precisely how to get there. It's like an expedition to climb Mt. Everest, in which the Summit is clearly the goal; and increasingly stressful effort, the means. But it's a hard road to travel, arduous and long: gradual acclimatization during the long treks up the foothills, then Camp I, Camp II, Camp III, Camp IV, Camp V and finally, if you're lucky, the Summit, each goal to be gained or risk failure of the entire expedition, but all contributing to the main goal, the Top of the World.

The Multiple Factors of Training. Planning was simple when one factor, better technique, was thought to be the 90-percent element in better performance. But modern training systems must balance technique with basic strength, related power, imitative power, velocity training, along with experience through developmental competition. For example, it is generally agreed that, with changing emphases, technique training and the maintenance of basic strength are year-round concerns. But each of the other factors is essential and must be given its time and proper emphasis.

Gradualism. That early efforts in demanding work--strength, endurance, velocity--should incur gradual increments of stress is accepted by all. But gradualism also relates to the shifts from one training phase to another, or to the build-up of competitive stress. Strained muscles and tendons usually result from too much too soon during early efforts, but also in shifting from one kind of effort to another.

Work-Rest. Interval training for endurance was so called because its inventors, Gerschler and Reindell, found that heart development occurred primarily during the recovery interval

[1]Frank Dick, "Periodization: An Approach to the Training Year," _Track Technique_, #62, Dec. 1975, p. 1968; #63, March 1976, p. 2005; #64, June 1976, p. 2030; #65, Sept. 1976, p. 2068.

between bouts of work. They concluded that the primary developmental unit was work-rest--two phases of one indivisible function. In planning cycles--Cycles I, II, or III--this two-phased function is central; the degree of stress (physical-mental-emotional) must be balanced by a comparable measure of easier recuperative activity. If a training segment, or two successive segments, is heavily loaded, the succeeding segment should serve as a recovery cycle in which natural processes of overcompensation prepares the athlete for the next higher-level of work. As always, individual differences play a major role.

The Uses of Variety. To be most effective, a program of year-round, strenuous work must introduce variety into as many aspects as inventiveness will permit. Vary the sequence of light and heavy weeks or days. Vary the proportion of work on technique and on basic strength or related power. Vary the kind of implements that are used in related or imitative power or in velocity training. Vary the games and activities that are used during periods of active rest.

Training Units and Cycles. In Matveyev's system, a training unit is a single work session; if training occurs twice in one day, it would count as two units. The smallest cycle is a microcycle: a mini-series of training units organized, especially in loading and intensity, to produce an optimal training effect.

In past college-school training programs, such a cycle--call it Cycle-I, indicating a minimal group of training units--was one week of work; including one day of competition, one rest day before competition and one after, with the remaining four days divided between heavy and medium work. That fitted well the general student program. But with modern increases in training levels, such cycles may be patterned differently, especially during Phases I and II of the Preparatory period when competition is lacking. The precise number of units in a cycle is not critical, but that cycles should be organized, each containing a balance of training essentials for that period, is critical. Physiologist David Costill states that "most physiological systems require three to four weeks to show a (developmental) response to a given training stress." From this it can be argued that a larger training group--call it Cycle II--might well be organized covering three or four weeks; each containing 3-4-5 subgroups of Cycle I training units.

Each cycle, whether at the I or II level, will include high-stress, low-stress, medium-stress segments. Normally, technique practice is low-stress, but many throws made with high-level concentration could create high stress. In contrast, training sessions for basic strength or related power tend to be exhausting, and are usually followed by easier "recovery" segments. Usually a "segment" is considered as one day, but it could be several days, or a full week, or even more--whatever length of time is optimal in achieving the intended purpose, whether of work or developmental rest.

Active-Rest. The expression, "active-rest," came into use along with the idea of year-round training. Each year's schedule included a transition period between the Big Meet that closed the old and the beginning of the new year's training routine. But even during that period, condition should not be allowed to regress through riotous living or even by doing nothing. Enjoyable big-muscle activity of any kind that was safe from injury restored both body and mind, and zest to the zeal that everyone took for granted.

But the active-rest principle goes beyond the long transition period. In interval training for endurance, recovery occurs more rapidly and completely by jogging between work-bouts, not by walking or lying down. Similarly for field-event training, days of either complete or modified rest are assumed to be days of active enjoyment of whatever non-stressful games--swimming, volleyball, basketball, soccer--are fun for the athlete and, to emphasize the point, safe from injury.

This is a refreshing innovation, not unlike the introduction of speed-play to endurance training. In the past, coaches have warned against all such "playing around." Their fear of the negatives cut off all such nonsense. True, the potential negatives are there, but the restorative values, especially of the mind, are now realized to outweigh them.

Chapter 17
HINTS FOR COMPETITION IN FIELD EVENTS

HINTS FOR COMPETITION IN FIELD EVENTS

Competitiveness is a word. Like all such words, it has a dictionary or average meaning--ability to attain a desired response in a competitive situation. But such a definition has real meaning only as it relates to this unique individual in this particular situation in this competitive action--here and now.

Each athlete and coach approaches the problem of competitiveness in his own way. For some it seems to come naturally, along with a natural physical aptitude for sports; for others it requires gradual development through longtime practice, much the same as for developing skill or relaxation (See Chapters 18-19). Therefore I emphasize the word "hints" as providing ideas--no more than that--to be discarded if they fail to fit.

A Climate of Competitiveness. A man's competitiveness can be derived from his surround as well as from within himself. A team tradition, a coach's charisma, or even a firm friend can ensure a quiet expectation of maximal performance that can be unbeatable.

Over the past 50 years, the simple act of donning a track suit with the emblem USC (Southern Cal) or O (Oregon) tended to add inches and feet. Whatever the means, those institutions had gradually developed a tradition or climate of success in track and field competition.

Outstanding qualities of leadership by coaches can have a similar effect. Dean Cromwell, USC's longtime Master Coach, had a habit of greeting a new prospect with an enthusiastic "Hi Champ." A small thing. He did it with everyone. But the prospect was pleased and, strangely, believed. Cromwell--"Call a man a champion and he'll be the more likely to prove you a prophet." Over a 40-year career, Jumbo Elliott, Villanova, acquired a similar reputation for coaching competence and success. His athletes dressed the part, talked the part, felt the part, acted the part. It almost seemed they could do no other than perform well when the going was toughest--22 Olympic team members and over 225 IC4A individual champions. He recruited great talent of course, but also he created a climate of success that strengthened even the weakest competitor on his squad.

Of course, the competitive surround can have much smaller dimensions. Some Catholics place themselves at a higher level of confidence simply by making the sign of the cross before stepping into the circle or starting a run-up. I had the great privilege of coaching the Hume twins who held hands at the NCAA mile finish line to make certain they won together. Running separately they had less confidence; together they "knew" they would win.

Competitiveness has a thousand roots; the art of good coaching lies in creating a healthful soil and climate by which each root can thrive and bear fruit. Brutus Hamilton, a Master at developing young men, once wrote, "For the most part I coach by indirection. I like to coach men without their realizing they are being coached. A coach can only point the way; inspired performances must come from deep within the boy himself." Perhaps so, but by such attitudes Hamilton created a climate of mutual supportiveness within which individual inspiration was most likely to grow.

Planning for Competitiveness. Al Oerter was the only man ever to win four Olympic golds in a single event, a great record of competitiveness at the most crucial moment. But that record didn't happen by mere inspiration or chance. Oerter told Jeff Johnson,[1]

> *In the weeks before an Olympic competition, I mentally simulate every conceivable situation for each throw. For example, I imagine I'm in 8th place. It's my fifth throw and it's pouring rain. What do I do? An inexperienced thrower might panic, or be thinking, "Gees, I hope I don't fall down." I know ahead of time what I will do under every condition. In Tokyo I won on my 5th throw. I passed the 6th because of the pain in my ribs and because my position in the order was such that it was clear that I had won. But I know to this day that if I had had to take my final throw that it would have been further than the 5th. I'm not saying it would have been good enough to win. I can't control how far the others are going to throw. Only that it would have been further. I knew just how I was going to throw it.*

Clearly, such planning worked for Oerter. Parry O'Brien's methods were somewhat more esoteric, derived from a college course in yoga, the Indian mental discipline aimed at concentrating the self into "that special world."

> *Alongside the practical physics belongs Parry's fierce concentration. He spends as much time just thinking about his shot as fondling it in the putting circle. Parry spent many of his nights alone in his ascetic bedroom, the lights dim, his weighty frame slack on the bed. From his tape recorder trickled the soothing sound of his own voice: "Keep low, keep back, keep your movement fast across the circle. Fast now! Fast! Fast! And beat them! Beat them all!" Parry is convinced that this nocturnal rite adds inches to his toss.[2]*

Dwight Stones' inability to jump well at the Montreal Olympic Games under rainy conditions led to the only double flop in Olympic history. As early as March 1976, he had spoken of his lack of confidence when a wet runway forced him to slow his approach run. But apparently he did nothing in the way of preparation. In contrast, Rolf Beilschmidt, after clearing 7-6½ in the rain,

> *I remember my coach coming out sometimes with a watering can and saying, "Now we'll try such-and-such a height; it's raining cats and dogs." Then he'd cover the approach with water until it was nice and slippery.[3]*

Practicing Maximal Efforts. Whether or not to attempt maximal efforts in practice depends on the event and, certainly, on the individual athlete. Some do and some don't. Dave Roberts, former world-record pole vaulter, often vaulted for height in practice, explaining, "Vaulting is a 100 percent event; it takes 100 percent to even make it to the pit." In my judgment, he was saying that a vault at 18 feet or so is simply a different event from one at 15-16, requiring different velocity-timing-spring-power. Practice should be specific to the effort that highest heights require.

High jumpers such as Fosbury and Stones never jumped at highest heights in practice. For them, the excitements of competition were required to produce the adrenalin necessary for such attempts. However, there is a great difference between jumping for and jumping at highest heights. In the latter case, awareness is centered on "how," not on "how high." Technique determines success or failure, not clearance. In fact, clearance of maximal heights will almost never occur in practice, but practice of the effort is the best way to ensure clearance in competition.

One solution to this problem in all field events is to fix meet priorities. Now one can use meets of lesser importance as "practice" meets which prepare for the BIG meets. Each athlete and coach will need to analyze just what is needed in the way of preparation, and "practice" accordingly.

---

[1] Jeff Johnson, "Al Oerter: Olympic Spirit," *Track & Field News*, December 1968, 10.

[2] *Time Magazine*, December 3, 1956.

[3] *Track & Field News*, September 1979, p. 34.

For example, in such "practice" meets, former discus world-record holder Fortune Gordien[1] found it helpful to stop for a moment before stepping into the discus circle; to concentrate on ONE THING ONLY that is to be done correctly on the next throw; then, when ready, to step in and throw.

When I first started competing in the discus, I would step into the ring, and then try to think of what I had to work on, but because of the pressure of being in "the circle of attention," so to speak, I was unable to concentrate on my purpose.

Gordien also suggests that this routine be made habitual in practice--advice that is sound for all field events.

Develop a Pre-Competition Routine. Each event calls for a different approach, and each man will develop his own unique methods, but these procedures are basic:

1. Before dressing, check the general lay-out for competition. What about the weather? Number of competitors? Probable length of the competition? Opportunities for warm-up? Where and how can I get myself ready for each competitive effort? What is the condition of the run-up and take-off surfaces? In the shot put, is the toe-board firmly fastened? Is the concrete at the back of the throwing circle rough or slippery? In the discus what is the direction and velocity of the wind? There are many other details to check, any one of which may decide the winning.

2. Before dressing, check in your implements, if so required; or better, have someone dependable do it for you. The process of weighing and measuring can be long and irritating to nerves already edgy.

3. Before dressing, check your equipment--shoes and shoelaces, spikes, competitor's number, sun lotion, towel, letters from Henrietta--whatever ensures confidence and relaxation. Need I add--*leave your valuables at home or in the hotel safe.*

4. Be ready for competition ON TIME--certainly not too late when things get hectic; and better, not too soon when delay wears away the competitive edge. Allow plenty of time in which to follow a routine of warm-up. On the other hand, disruptions of such routine occur frequently in competitions, and should not be mentally upsetting.

The Power of Positive Thinking. The concept of positive thinking has had popular acceptance, especially in the areas of religion (Norman Vincent Peale) and public relations (Dale Carnegie). Certainly it has great usefulness in sports competition if based on more than mere faith in good luck or intervention "on my side" by Providence. Such faith may work, but it's weak-minded, to speak softly.

But positive thinking that evolves out of careful preparation and competence is unbeatable. Now things happen, not by thinking so much as by assumption and certainty. Yashchenko had these reactions to his world-record 7-8 high jump in June, 1978:

While I was jumping, I wasn't thinking of records, only of jumping. When I cleared the world record, I was thinking a bit to myself, "Be surprised." But I wasn't surprised; it was too familiar. It really was...What I did think was, I could have gone higher....And later-- It was not really a test as such. For me the height did not exist as a barrier, or as a limit.

That may not be positive thinking, nor even thinking at all, but it's a sense of certainty in one's own competence that's hard to beat.

Controlled Recklessness. Research has shown that inexperienced athletes have inhibitions

---

[1]Fortune Gordien,"Tips for Discus Throwers," *Track Technique*, #69, Sept. 1977, p. 2190.

[2]Jon Hendershott, "Vladimir Yashchenko," *Track & Field News*, Sept. 1978, p. 12.

or "fears" that prevent all-out effort. But experienced athletes learn to disinhibit, to set aside or go with such fears. Blowing up the flames of competitiveness has a strong element of recklessness in it, of letting oneself go--all-out, for broke, nothing held back. Though made 25 years ago, O'Brien's comments are still valid: "You've got to get keyed up to a point where everything about you is so taut it might break. You've got to be mentally ready to make the toss. You've got to be nervous, get your blood flowing, your metabolism working faster and faster. Your heart has got to beat like a trip hammer. When I'm ready for a toss I'm all wrapped up in myself. I'm in a different world."

To veer away from sports a moment, I enjoyed Cyril Ritchard's remark on the TV recently that, even after a thousand or more performances, "I always keep a bucket handy to be sick in just before I go on stage." That's the attitude of a real champion. Not that being sick is a requirement, but having butterflies is.

But recklessness must be controlled. When extreme emotional stress is present without the means for its control, its effects are dissipated, tend to discoordinate action, even block action. Somehow the nerve impulses must be insulated within those positively related to the desired action. Somehow the energies must be channeled within those muscle groups which contribute to the action and withheld from those which inhibit it. Here, as with skill and power, there's no short cut for practice-practice-practice, combined with competitive experience.

Self-Detachment. There's a converse approach to O'Brien's method, that of losing all self-awareness in the competitive situation and action. Yashchenko implied this in his remarks. But recently I read[1] the comments of the great golfer Tom Watson, on the eve of the U.S. Open, 1980, that there had been a handful of occasions when he found himself in the twilight zone, when he just knew he would win:

"There have been five times when I've felt I could beat anybody," he said. Four of those times, he added, he won.

But he also understands that you do not climb to this lofty plateau; rather, you just are deposited there. In fact, if you try to hypnotize yourself into that frame of mind, you'll probably miss the cut instead. It is something that cannot be made to happen. Like the appearance of the leaves on trees every spring, you awake one day and it is just there.

"You can't control it," Watson agreed. "It just comes when it wants to, I guess."

---

[1] Bill Lyon, *The Philadelphia Inquirer*, June 17, 1980, p. C-1.

PART 2B
Coaching Endurance
Running

Chapter 18
WHY MEN RUN

Why do men run? The wisest answer would undoubtedly be given by a child, or by a runner, or by a Zen Master; without saying a word, they each would start running. Men do run, and that is the most penetrating reason of all as to why they run. It tells us, beyond all words and abstractions, that men are made *for* running, and have been made as they are by running.

Unfortunately I am not so wise, and so must use mere words. Why do men run? If I were a physiologist I would answer that they run because they have running bodies: running hearts, running lungs, running muscles, running bones. Without a long racial history of running, these would not be what they are. Man is a land animal. His use of other land animals for transportation has been limited and part-time. His use of machines is a last-minute innovation. Throughout a long racial history, he has had to depend upon himself whenever he wanted to go, and sometimes he wanted to go in a hurry. He had to run and by running he became a man-that-runs. Had he stuck to walking, he would now be quite different physically. The maximum stroke volume of his heart would never have reached the 200cc of blood, nor the number of beats --180 or so per minute--that a trained runner's heart can put forth. His muscles would contain only a fraction of the 317 billion blood capillaries that are now present. Of course there have been other developmental activities, such as fighting or making love, but even in these a little running ability was helpful.

Why do men run? If one were a cardiologist with a strong bent toward religious philosophy, as is George Sheehan, M.D., one would seek spiritual reasons as he tends to do. Though well into his 40s, George still ran in the Boston Marathon but, in a strange way, for the fun of it quite apart from any hope of recognitions or even first-50 placements. His anxwer:[1]

For the runner, less is better. The life that is his work of art is understated. His needs and wants are few, he can be captured in a few strokes. One friend, a few clothes, a meal now and then, some change in his pocket, and for enjoyment, his thoughts and the elements....

I see this simplicity as my perfection. In the eyes of others, however, it appears completely different. My success in removing myself from things and people, from ordinary ambition and desires, is seen as lack of caring, proof of uninvolvement, and failure to contribute.

So be it. A larger view of the world might include the possibility that such people are necessary, that the runner burning with a tiny flame on some lonely road does somehow contribute.

Now if I were a historian, I would explain that men run because running is deep in our social history. We are all familiar with the glorious run of Pheidippides from the battle ground of Marathon to cry, "Victory!" in the market-place in Athens. But all peoples have such tales of great running. Students of the ancient Inca civilization have become aware that the

---

[1]George Sheehan, M.D., "On the Run But Not in a Hurry," *The Daily Register*, Red Bank, N.J., April 1975.

345

very extensive system of roads throughout the widespread Inca territory was entirely for foot travel, and more specifically, running. They had no horses or other animals for rapid transportation. Messages were sent by relay runners, each of whom ran about a mile in distance, carrying knotted ropes by which to refresh their memories of the details they were to transmit by word of mouth. Much of this running was done at 9000 feet or more over the Andes mountains, so that development through stress must have been to highest potentials.

Why do men run? If I were a sociologist I would try to explain man's running by way of society's basic need for self-fulfillment through the self-discipline of striving and struggle whatever its forms--in the arts, in exploration of the earth, of outer space, and the great inner space within the individual self, in meaningful work of all kinds. Every sound society must have a foundation of what can be called moral energy, of courage and will to begin and maintain the development of energies and talents toward their highest potentials, despite all fear of danger, exhaustion, ridicule and ultimate failure. Inconsequential as running may seem in our society, what more available, more healthful, more developmental, more satisfying activity do we have to meet this universal need for self-affirmation? Small wonder that endurance running is the foremost activity in the Modern Olympic Games. It attracts more spectators, more world-wide attention, and more representatives from more nations than any other. The rising new nations of the world are keenly aware of this showcase and of society's tendency to accept the victory of even one man as proof of the virility of an entire nation. It has not been by chance that the 1960 Olympic marathon was won by an unknown from Ethiopia, or that most of recent world-records in running have been made by men from Australia, New Zealand and Finland.

To understand why men run, a sociologist might well turn to Finland where, between 1912 and 1980, a mere four millions of people produced more Olympic champions in running than any other nation. There he would find a great social need and readiness, born out of Finland's struggle for independence from the heavy hand of Russia, but he would also find that it was individual achievement which turned this social readiness into widespread action. The victories of Kohlemainen and Stenroos over the 1912 Olympic world excited the Finnish people tremendously; they made heroes of their runners, and villages a 100 miles north of the Arctic Circle built excellent running tracks and organized long-distance-running clubs. The astounding victories of Vasala and Viren in the Munich Olympic 1500, 5000 and 10,000, individual triumphs as they were, should also be judged as the outcome of Finnish "sisu," of social hardihood and courage.

Why do men run? If I were a psychologist, I might answer that to run is satisfying, that it is a natural activity which provides a sense of achievement for its own sake. I would quote a great runner like Roger Bannister, "I find in running - win or lose - a deep satisfaction that I cannot express in any other way....I sometimes think that running has given me a glimpse of the greatest freedom that a man can ever know, because it results in the simultaneous liberation of both body and mind."[2] Or I might quote a great coach of runners, Arthur Lydiard of New Zealand, "It is a simple unalloyed joy to tackle yourself on the battlefield of your own physical well-being and come out the victor."[3]

A psychologist would find great resources for study in the small-group dynamics of running. England's former mile champion, Bill Nankeville, has written of the closely-knit group of non-school running enthusiasts who nourished each other toward international levels of performance. Such great Irish runners as E. M. N. Tisdall, Ron Delany, Noel Carroll and Eamonn Coghlan developed out of small running clubs and the energies of individuals such as Billy Morton of Dublin. The great Gunder Haegg of Sweden probably never would have run competitively if his own father and his friends had not had an enthusiasm for running. Eugene, Oregon, with its 10,000 run-for-fun enthusiasts, is widely known as "the running capitol of the world." But who would know of Eugene without Bill Bowerman, his jogging medics and his champions?

In summary, it is impractical, if not impossible, to try to comprehend the innumerable cross-currents of racial inheritance, social customs, institutional incentives, family expectations, friendly encouragements and personal aggressions, impulsions, insecurities, and frustrations that can and do motivate a boy to run. Actually, there is never a single motive that

---

[2]Roger Bannister, THE FOUR MINUTE MILE, New York: Dodd, Mead & Co., 1955, p. 229.

[3]Arthur Lydiard and Garth Gilmour, RUN TO THE TOP, London: Herbert Jenkins, Ltd.,1962, p. 46.

can be isolated as exclusively responsible. As with other basic activities, men run for a great complex of reasons, limited only by one's discernment in abstracting them.

One of the most discerning stories of long distance running is by Alan Sillitoe, "The Loneliness of the Long Distance Runner."[4] When the big race is about two-thirds over, the "hero's" impulsion to prove his worth forced him to pour it on - "so by the haystack I decided to leave it all behind and put on such a spurt, in spite of the nails in my guts, that before long I'd left both Gunthorpe and the birds a good way off." Yet his sense of what he called honesty and realness would not let him win; or rather, would not let his dishonest trainer-jailer win through his efforts. In full sight of the finish line and the crowd, he deliberately slowed down, waited for his opponent to break the tape, then finished with his back straight and his eyes looking disdainfully into those of his trainer.

Few readers will suffer the twisted life that produced such a twisted motivation, but many will run with a similar tangle of likes and dislikes, tenacity and weakness, of which they are quite unaware and certainly could never put into words.

When a boy first starts to run competitively, his motives tend to be of as low an order as are his performances: to win a medal or a varsity letter, to make the team, to be one of the gang, to get one's picture in the school paper or year-book. Such a boy is likely to understand verbal motives that are only a short step beyond what he has already experienced. The coach who emphasizes the deeply hidden satisfactions that lie in hard work and self-discipline will find his words wasted. Even such a sensitive person as Roger Bannister admitted that, as a boy, he took up running as an escape from the gibes of his school-mates so that he would be free to do what really interested him: to be active as a student, a musician, and an actor.

In each instance, some obstacle becomes a challenge to overcome, some disinterest becomes a hobby, some inspiration cries out, "Begin!" But inspiration produces only the first few steps. During early stages, the runner may need a sort of baby's walker to hold him erect, and a fatherly voice to give encouragement. Until he was sure Gunder could go it alone, Haegg's father devised endless ways, even falsifying times on one occasion, to develop his son's confidence and belief in his running future.

Later, running may become an inescapable way of life. In 1957, at the age of 68, Clarence DeMar competed in a 10-mile race, notwithstanding the presence of a surgical colostomy. In 1978, at age 58, George Sheehan, M.D., published RUNNING & BEING,[5] a record of his total experience--spiritual, mental, physical--during some 15 years, including about 50 marathons.

Of course, some men by body structure, energy, and chemistry are better made for running than others. For these men, distance running is a challenge even when it is a hardship; play even when they slave at it; fun, even when they hate it. Cerutty wrote, "Running at its best is an outpouring, a release from tensions....An hour, two hours of hard training slips away as so many minutes. We become tired, exhaustingly tired, but never unhappy. It is work but it seems only fun. Exhilarating, satisfying fun."

We understand this when we realize that such attitudes were developed at Camp Portsea, Australia, where men ran along the beautiful seacoast, up great sand dunes, across open country --sometimes nude--then back, following Cerutty's uninhibited methods, to plunge into the cold sea. It is much harder to understand the motivations of the Englishman, W. R. Loader, who described his early training experiences through the sooty brick and stone deserts of Clyneside, Tyneside, and Merseyside, with their coke ovens, foundries, ship yards, blast furnaces, and machine shops. In one instance he had to run through a certain tough district of his town where the handicaps of terrain were as nothing compared with the derisive jeers of the onlookers, especially of the girls,

"Yah, look at the runner coming!...Mary Ann, look, it's a runner! He's got nae claes

---

[4]Alan Sillitoe, THE LONELINESS OF THE LONG-DISTANCE RUNNER, New York: New American Library of World Literature, 1959, p. 34.

[5]Dr. George Sheehan, RUNNING & BEING, New York: Simon & Schuster, 1978, 256 pps.

on!" Faces rose up all around, derisive, jeering, insulting. A scabby mongrel dog snapped at the heels, delighted for once to discover that someone else's life was being made a misery. Urchins sprinted alongside, mocking the runner's strides with their own exaggerated movements. It was a torment of the soul far more bitter than any torture of the body. And through it all one had to run with measured step, eyes fixed ahead as if unaware of the tumult, trying to abolish it by ignoring it....But it is a hard thing for youth to set itself alone against spite and hostility. I did that run a number of times and never faced it without a premonitory chill of the spine. Having stood the jeers to the point where I could persuade myself I wasn't giving up through cowardice, I quietly abandoned the practice.[6]

Though Loader's experiences and his way of relating them are unusual, the hindrances and distractions of social environment are common deterrents to why men run, or better, why men continue to run. Lasse Viren: "Sometimes...I realize I am running because I want to know how good I can become...That is still the main motivation, but gradually running has also become a narcotic for me. It is a lure I can't resist."

Viren was 31 when he ran at the Moscow Games, about right for maximal performance. But the eight years between Munich and Moscow had been long and arduous--training, training and more training--enough miles between 1971 and 1980 to run twice around the world. Maintaining enthusiasm was a serious problem. Especially since his wife and child must not be neglected. Viren: "We have been discussing this problem. Paivi won't put me in chains. A marriage shouldn't be a prison. And, as Paivi says, four years is just a twinkle in a human life." Maybe so, but twinkles sometimes become frowns, and frowns diminish enthusiasm for training.

So also with George Young, the first American distance runner to compete in four Olympic Games. The Olympic gold was never his, but during some 15 years he defeated Olympic champions and set several world records. George once said, "If I didn't have to work and I didn't have a family to support and if I didn't have to worry about anything else than running, maybe I could work twice as hard. And if I could work out twice as hard, what kind of runner could I be? That's always in the back of my mind." But George failed to understand the value of such limitations. Amateur running is avocational; studies or some vocation other than sport has first priority on one's time-energy-devotion. Both training and competition for running must occur within what's left over. To ensure fair competition, rules and regulations as to conduct off the field must be established, rules that can be only partially enforced. Others will break the rules, gain some real or imagined advantage. And therein lies the great burden but also the means to deep self-respect, if not glory, of the long-distance runner. One of the better ways of judging any man--in or out of sports--is by the degree of his adherence to social agreements that are not fully enforceable. Integrity and personal honor are words of high value, whatever their import in today's society.

I began this chapter by saying that men, even modern men, are men-that-run; that their vital organs and systems and chemistry are as they are because of the eons of running, just as the salt content of our blood is that of the sea because of eons of sea-living. To say that running is socially recognized or personally satisfying cheapens the argument, makes running an artificial action that waits upon cultural whims. Running is not so much a tool of the "New Emerging Nations" as an inherent part of a man-society-nature interaction. Not to run is as unthinkable as not to eat, or not to sleep, or not to make love.

But try as I may, I shall never say it as well as did Brutus Hamilton, head coach of the University of California and the 1948 U. S. Olympic track team,

People may wonder why young men like to run distance races. What fun is it? Why all that hard, exhausting work? Where is the good of it? It is one of the strange ironies of this strange life that those who work the hardest, who subject themselves

---

[6]W. R. Loader, *TESTAMENT OF A RUNNER*, London: William Heinemann Ltd., 1960.

to the strictest discipline, who give up certain pleasureable things in order to achieve a goal, are the happiest of men. When you see 20 or 30 young men line up for a distance race in some meet, don't pity them, don't feel sorry for them. Better envy them instead. You are probably looking at the 20 or 30 best "bon vivants" in the world. They are completely and joyously happy in their simple tastes, their strong and well-conditioned bodies, and with the thrill of wholesome competition before them. These are the days of their youth, when they can run without weariness; these are their buoyant, golden days; and they are running because they love it. Their lives are fuller because of this competition and their memories will be far richer. That's why men love to run. That's why men do run. There is something clean and noble about it.

Fig. 18.1--Sebastian Coe, Great Britain, who, within a 41-day period in 1979, set three world records: 800m-1:42.4; mile-3:49; 1500m-3:32.1. But who may have made an even greater contribution to the training of runners by reducing the present-day commitment to mileage and training primarily in terms of sustaining speed over longer and longer distances.

Chapter 19
ESSENTIALS OF TRAINING FOR ENDURANCE RUNNING

The essentials of training for endurance running underlie and support all sound training programs. If they are truly essential, no sound system can ignore them. But what is an essential? Forty years ago we might have answered, "over-distance, under-distance and time trials, not much else." Today, we are much more aware of the multiplicity of forces that influence development. A great deal of trial-and-error experience, stimulated and supported by scientific research, has enabled us to differentiate the various aspects of endurance, to work in terms of each, and then to achieve just the right balance in our final preparations for competition.

In fact the scope of what we call essential is limited only by our powers of analysis and discrimination of meanings. We have listed some 28 essentials; the number could easily be doubled. But even more important than analysis is our ability to synthesize and balance these essentials. Keep in mind that some of these essentials have been emphasized by some coaches following certain systems, to the underestimation and even exclusion of other essentials. Fartlek was misused as merely enjoyment of running in the woods. Interval training was misused as intensive anaerobic training without a long background of cross-country running.

Obviously some of these essentials are more crucial than are others; some are important only at certain stages of training. The art of sound coaching lies in weighing and selecting, lies in the wise choice of precisely what, precisely how much, and precisely when is best for this uniquely different runner at this stage of his career.

It's somewhat like the art of good cooking. My wife now has a 24-volume *ENCYCLOPEDIA OF COOKING,* a bewildering wealth of possible recipes. But her high reputation in the dining room has grown out of her good judgment in selecting just the right items in the right combination for these special guests.

ENDURANCE TRAINING IS ORGANICALLY BENEFICIAL AND MENTALLY WHOLESOME
In a valid sense, endurance training is the development of our capacities into the higher levels of health and energy. For too long, we have thought of health in the medical sense as being freedom from disease and impairments. Actually the truly healthy man is free from such obstacles but also free to function at his highest potentials of energy. Our organs and systems have evolved for use within the entire range of action--for restful inaction, for slow, easy movements, but equally for the utmost demands of work and play. As between hard but reasonable training, on the one hand, and low level or complete inactivity, as in bed rest on the other, hard training is far the more healthful. When it comes to the furtherance of positive health, we in track coaching need make no apology to any profession.

This assumes of course that our training programs are sound, gradually developed, individualized. Such programs seek the conservation of energy. We spend energy today in order to build more energy for tomorrow. We undergo the arduousness of work today in order that tomorrow we can do that same work more easily and enjoyably or at a higher level. By wise use of our powers, both physical and mental, our nature rebuilds them in ever greater abundance.

Energy is present in each of us, not fixed at one level or another, but within a range of possible use and development. This range is both broad and flexible. Its upper limits are far beyond what seems humanly possible and healthful if one considers the limited demands for human energy made by our machine culture. Further, those who reach the upper levels of that range of energy can be active day after day, year after year with no ill effects to their health or longevity. Their organisms develop not only resistance to fatigue but also increase their rate of recovery. Few of these individuals need more sleep than the average; many need less. They have learned to increase their supply of energy, not by saving it, but by using it wisely--gradually building up their demands on it.

ENJOYMENT OF RUNNING IS ESSENTIAL

The word "essential" means absolutely necessary, and that is its use here as we speak of enjoyment of training. True, awareness of enjoyment is not always present but, if long neglected, what is essential exacts its measure of retribution. Without enjoyment, running becomes a task, even a drudgery, and development less certain. Of course enjoyment has a range of meaning. Hopefully, it has a connotation of fun, laughter, even joy in running--joy in the effort and pain of running. But its lesser meanings are also valid: satisfaction, the sense of being wholly absorbed in action, cleaness after a hot shower following a long run.

In our culture, professional attitudes tend to predominate. Professionals emphasize winning and extrinsic rewards. "Fun in sports is for children. It's a job; get it done right and you will get paid for it." But the fact is that in every undertaking that requires long time and hard effort, human beings demand a portion of play in their effort, of doing it because it's fun. The reward may shift the degree of demand; it never erases it. Modern coaching has emphasized goal-insight methods. The goal motivates the action. But absorbing action needs no goal other than itself. Every champion works hard, sometimes to the point of drudgery, but how often they say simply, "I enjoy running; when I no longer enjoy it, I'll quit."

We think of Lydiard's marathon training as being the most strenuous and agonizing of any system. But the published biographies of his runners emphasize the fun of training as much as its demands. Halberg (1963, 26) for example,

I never thought Arthur was going to burn me out. . . . And I learned the pleasures of running. The fun of long, easy running with friends and rivals, the inner glow of satisfaction when the run was over and the body was reacting to the new strength that was being built into it. . . . The days were great fun. Arthur is a marvellous entertainer and we could listen all day to him spinning yarns.

A growing emphasis in endurance training--in swimming as well as running--is what Joe Henderson (1969, 6) calls the "PTA school of running: pain-torture-agony." Certainly a gradual development in courage toward pain is necessary to great performance in running. But this must be balanced by the fun of running, not merely because boys tend to make fun out of everything they do, but because fun and enjoyment are planned, are a built-in approach to both training and racing.

Balance Zatopek's love of fun as told by Gordon Pirie (1961, 50) with his callousness toward fatigue in his training and racing,

He [Zatopek] would jog for hours on the same spot, doing an endless "Knees up, Mother Brown," while reading a book or listening to the radio. Everything was fun to him. On washdays at home he piled all the dirty clothes in the bath and then ran on them for hours. . . . I had the pleasure of meeting him not only on the track but in his home. This was the gayest and merriest home I have ever visited. . . . They [Emil and his wife] used to romp like children. . . . Once in fun he threw her into a stream. . . . Unfortunately her foot hit a rock and she broke an ankle. While she had her leg in plaster, Emil ran with her on his back through deep snow for training. . . . Zatopek's sense of fun turned not only his training but his races into a joy. He never seemed to feel the awful tension before a race which lesser mortals endure. His antics often helped to release this tension for others.

Balance the scufflings and mad dashes into the sea by Cerutty and his wild men with Cerutty's advocacy of Stotanism (Stoicism + Spartanism), medieval ascetisicm, and his pleas to seek suffering. Consider the title of Ibbotson's book, *THE 4-MINUTE SMILER*, and his light-hearted agreement to run in a tough competition just to get a banquet ticket for his fiancee's girlfriend with the toughness he showed later in driving himself "in a blurred agony of effort and pain" to equal Bannister's world record of 3:59.4.

No wonder Brutus Hamilton described distance runners as "the best bon vivants in the world." No wonder Arthur Lydiard, (1962, 48) that hardened "slave-driver," emphasized,

All my search for the perfect training system convinced me of something else: The essence of athletics is the pleasure you can get out of it. . . . I actually came to enjoy knocking myself about because I came to grips with myself so frequently and at such a challenging physical and mental level. . . . It is a simple unalloyed joy to tackle yourself on the battlefield of your own physical wellbeing and come out the victor. . . .

Run for fun and from the fun will come the will to excel. From the will to excel could come an Olympic champion. Once you have found the fun there is in running, the task of training to the limits I prescribe will be much easier for you. . . .

There are jokes and laughter in training with these boys [Halberg, Snell, Magee], *not a grim, grasping grind with an eye on the watch and the mind concentrating on forcing the body to do the mind's bidding.*

A MEDICAL EXAMINATION MUST PRECEDE EACH YEAR'S TRAINING

Training for endurance running should be preceded by a thorough medical examination of the related organs and systems. Findings should be interpreted by a medical doctor with special training in sports medicine. As Roger J. Williams (1956) has demonstrated beyond all doubt, normal men often have structures and functions that are outside the range of normality. To be sure, a weakness of a lung, a kidney, or even the heart can be compensated in various ways. Examinations of successful marathon runners have disclosed organ deficiencies that would normally rule out competitive running.

However, in addition to using good judgment as related to the physical and emotional stresses of both training and competition, the track coach should do all he can to ensure healthy and normal systems. By requiring a medical examination, he reduces the chances of such weaknesses, he puts such responsibility where it belongs--on the medical profession, and very importantly, he removes from the minds of his runners all doubt as to their own health status for running.

MORE RUNNING = BETTER RUNNING

The most crucial principle in training for endurance running is that development is primarily the effect of more running: more miles per day, more days per year, more years per running career. Underlying all the training systems of the past century, with their special emphases on this or that alluring secret of development is an increasing emphasis on mileage and time. In 1904 Alfred Shrubb (2-mile W.R. - 9:09.6) trained exclusively on steady running twice a day, five days a week. But his week's total mileage was only about 35 miles. In the 1930s-40s, the American system of alternating days of over- and under-distance usually totalled even fewer miles per week, and certainly fewer miles per year.

Swedish fartlek was sold on a slogan of "get tired but don't feel tired." Actually, since men didn't feel so tired, they worked longer--and more intensely. When we first heard of interval training, we were excited by the prospect that our school runners could spend less time do-more quality work. Only later did we realize that the real emphasis was on more work, not on less time, and that Harbig's interval training was based on months of cross-country running. Similarly, Cerutty intrigued us with: "We train as we feel. . . . Our training should be a thing of enthusiasm . . . to run with joy, sheer beauty and strength, to race down some declivity, to battle manfully to the top of another." We often failed to read his next sentence that "Elliott has run up to 30 miles before exhaustion set in. This was in the heat of our summer."

Costill (1968, 22) suggests that few world-class distance runners train at less than 70 to 80 miles per week, and cites a survey by Lumian and Krumdick of the 125 entries in the 1962 Western Hemisphere Marathon. Sixty percent of the runners trained 45-52 weeks of the year. Forty-five percent trained twice a day. Nearly 40 percent covered more than 100 miles a week. Those who finished among the leaders were high in all three procedures: year-round training, twice a day, and mileage in excess of 100 miles/week.

Though done about ten years ago, a study by *Track & Field News* of the training of 30 world-level runners is still valid: it can be summarized as follows:

<u>MORE YEARS</u>. The average number of years of serious training was 11.8. The average age of first competitive running was 14.5; that of best competitive performance, 25.2. The number of years of training between first and best competitive performance ranged from 4 years for Jim Ryun (assuming he did not improve on his 1966 world records) to 19 for George Young, America's greatest steeplechaser. Bolotnikov, USSR, and Young did their best running at age 31, while Jim Ryun, up to 1970, made his world records at age 19.

<u>MORE DAYS PER YEAR</u>. These same 30 champions averaged 6.2 days per week and 10.6 months per year during their years of best running. It should be added that such daily training undoubtedly developed as a guarantee that enough work of the right kind was being done. Research supports this. For example, Astrand (1970, 395) emphasizes that year-round training is especially important in development of the oxygen-transporting system. Such training also fixes the habit of training and thereby avoids the danger of other interests and activities which might detract.

Apparently a few great runners have been exceptions to this rule. Kip Keino (Noronha, 1970, 55) reported that, with the exception of a few high-stress training periods, he trained only three times a week throughout the three years (1965-1968) of his best running. True, he usually worked out three times a day (6AM, 12N, 5PM), and was vigorously active on three other days, carrying out his duties as a physical instructor of the Kenya police. But he claims he averaged only about 50 miles a week in this program.

But David Costill (1979, 85) concluded from available schedules "that only with 5 or 6 training days per week can a runner...achieve maximal benefits."

<u>MORE MILES PER DAY</u>. The most striking conclusion to be drawn from Greg Brock's survey[1] of the training of 67 high school runners is of the wide range of mileage within which they all do well. In speaking of his high school training, the 1972 Olympic marathon champion, Frank Shorter, emphasized that his coaches' first concern was that they enjoy their running. In the early spring he averaged about 25 miles per week, with 5 miles on Tuesday and Thursday, and 10 miles on Sunday (4m-AM, 6m-PM). In contrast, the diary that coach Bob Timmons kept on Jim Ryun showed that, during his junior year, he totaled 4380 miles. Assuming 330 days of running, that averages over 13 miles per day, 90 miles per week.

For all runners, there is a level of diminishing returns at which increased mileage will not produce comparable improvement in performance; in fact, may even have a negative effect. General stress may produce specific illnesses or injuries--from stomach ailments including ulcers to Achilles tendonitis, shin splints or stress fractures; perhaps from too much; more likely, from too much too soon.

<u>TRAINING TWICE A DAY</u>. A second training run, usually in the early morning when it's cool and traffic is minimal, is now generally accepted as a part of modern training, even at the high school level. For many the discipline of early rising is mentally stimulating, even toughening. Total mileage tends to increase. However, many variables make research on its values for performance very difficult and of doubtful significance.

Formichev[2] and Fruktov compared the effects of training twice and once a day. They concluded that (1) working twice a day was highly advantageous, (2) the 2-a-day group improved considerably more than the other in the speed at which the control distance was run, and (3) the recovery time, based on pulse rates, was from 2 to 5 minutes shorter in the 2-a-day group.

In contrast, Costill (1968,22) found no greater improvement among the 2-a-day runners (4.5-5 miles jogging each morning) than in those practicing once a day. His criteria included heart rates during and after a standard treadmill run, and time in both the mile and $\frac{1}{2}$ mile run. However, he did observe that the supplemental training did seem to benefit certain individuals. Whether this was the effect of individuality or of differences in degree of fitness was not indicated.

[1]Greg Brock, *HOW HIGH SCHOOL RUNNERS TRAIN*, Los Altos, Ca.; Tafnews Press, 1976, paperback, 95 pps.

[2]A. Formichev and A. Fruktov, "Effectiveness of twice-a-day training," *Track Technique*, Sept. 1964, 530.

We have already cited the experience of Kipchoge Keino in training three times a day, but only three days a week. His excellent performances indicate this was a very effective program for this particular individual. But there is also a sound reasoning behind it. It alternates days of high stress with days of active rest and enjoyment. This is in keeping with research on intermittent work in which the length of the recovery period tends to increase as the length and stress of the work period is increased.

MORE RUNNING IS UNECONOMICAL OF TRAINING TIME. The research of Åstrand (1970, 377) and others has made it clear that developmental effects diminish in degree as the length of training is increased:

For instance, 2 hour training per week may cause an increase in maximal O_2 uptake, say by 0.4 liter/min. If the training is twice as much, that is, 4 hours per week, the increase in O_2 uptake will not be twice as great, . . . possibly 0.5 to 0.6 liter/min.

This leads us to the next closely-related principle.

MORE RUNNING = BETTER RUNNING BUT ONLY WITHIN ITS STRESS LIMITS

We have emphasized the important values of mileage training, but these values are limited by the degree of stress produced during that mileage. In 1931 Christensen[1] studied the effects of continuous running on heart rates. He found that regular training at a fixed pace gradually lowered the heart rate for that load; for example, from 180 to 160 beats/min., but that eventually a sticking point was reached. *Continued training at that same intensity of work produced no further improvement.* After training with a more demanding load, the heart rate during the original work load gradually lowered again, perhaps to 150. Each intensity produced its own level of development, no more (Astrand, 1970, 377).

Two reservations must be made. First, that "intensity" should be interpreted in terms of stress, not merely running pace. True, most training systems increase intensity by increasing pace. But it is also increased by such methods as Lydiard's speed-hill training, Cerutty's driving runs up 80-foot sand dunes, Haegg's varied and hilly terrains during fartlek, running with weighted vests or belts, or climbing stadium steps. Such actions increase stress and so lower heart rates and allied effects below those of fixed-pace continuous running.

Second, we should keep in mind that Christensen's "continued training at that intensity of work" was probably not maintained nearly as long as do modern marathon and mileage trainers. Some time after the body has reached a steady state for a certain running pace, a secondary increase in heart rate and general sense of fatigue can be observed, and at later intervals, further changes in awareness of stress. De Vries (1966, 74) explains this "in terms of fatigue of the skeletal musculature, which results in the recruitment of larger numbers of motor units, which results in a greater metabolic demand for the same level of work load--and thus an increase in the heart rate." That is, continuous steady-pace running creates a series of step-ups in intensity as general fatigue develops. To this degree, greater mileage produces greater intensities.

It is also very important to understand that different-length periods of work and rest are critical in the effects of interval training on endurance. For example, Karrasch (see Åstrand, 1970, 382) compared the values of three training methods on total work and heart rate.

Method A. Two 5-minute bouts of work at 1200 kgm/m, with 7.5 minutes rest between, produced 12,000 kgm but left the subject "exhausted" with a heart rate of 165.
Method B. Twelve 2-minute bouts of work at 1200 kgm/m, with 3-minute rest periods, also left the subject "exhausted," but resulted in 28,800 kgm of work done, with a heart rate of 160.
Method C. Forty-eight 30-second bouts of work were done at 1200 kgm/m, with 45 seconds of rest between. This method also produced 28,800 kgm of work but now the heart rate stayed below 100 during and after the workout.

---

[1]E. H. Christensen, "Beitruge zur Physiologie Schwere Körperlicher Arbeit," *Arbeitsphysiologie,* 4:1, 1931.

Other approaches to this problem of an optimal stimulus for development have dealt with oxygen consumption values. For example, I. Åstrand[1] assumed that, to improve, a runner should train at work loads producing 50 percent or more of the maximum oxygen consumption value. Costill (1968, 20) found agreement between this formula and that of Karvonen. Karvonen's average critical threshold heart rate of 133 is comparable to Astrand's figure of 57.9 percent of maximal oxygen consumption. Costill warns that both are minimal values for relatively low conditioned men, and not necessarily valid for competitive runners.

Of greater significance for high-level endurance training is the work of Karlsson[2] and others, who found that optimal training required maximal loading of the oxygen transport systems. However, Karlsson emphasized that maximal oxygen uptakes can be attained at submaximal speeds and that this lesser speed may be adequate for optimal training. *Astrand (1970, 390) suggests that such submaximal speeds could be about 80 percent of the maximum speed that can be maintained for from 3 to 5 minutes.* For example, a distance that could be run in 3 minutes should be run in 3.5 minutes without lowering the demand on the aerobic processes. Further, Astrand states that heart rates can be used in judging maximum work loads, and recommends a rate about 10 beats below maximum as a top value for most of the year's training. Costill (1968, 21) suggests that an optimal training pace would be the slowest pace that would produce maximum oxygen consumption. [Note: This pace can be determined by use of the nomogram described by Astrand (1970, 356, 618)].

In commenting on Karlsson's research, Åstrand (1970, 384) emphasizes the critical importance of running pace on the oxygen transport systems, certainly in intermittent work using 20 seconds work, 10 seconds rest. A speed of 22.75 km/hr produced maximal oxygen uptake and exhausted the runner in about 16 minutes; that of 22.0 km/hr reduced the oxygen uptake to 90 percent of maximum and allowed training to continue for 40 minutes. Though Astrand concludes that "it is an important but unsolved question" as to which of these two types of training is more effective, we can assume that answers will be found in the complex problem of individual differences with which this discussion was started.

A DEVELOPMENTAL STIMULUS FOR ENDURANCE RUNNING

What is an optimal developmental stimulus for endurance running? What mileage? What pace? What balance of stress-recovery? Obviously, a valid answer must make allowances for individual differences. Rolf Haikkola coached only Lassie Viren, declaring, "I can no longer coach several runners simultaneously. Even if they run the same distances, each schedule should be different;...the smaller one's group of pupils, the better the results."

But it is helpful to understand the underlying principle. Experts agree that more running leads to better performance only within the limits of stress produced; each pace develops its own stress effects. Is there a basic training principle for both low-slow running and high-intensity running?

Related research tends to use two criteria--heart rates and oxygen uptakes. In their development of interval training, Reindell and Gerschler focussed on heart rates. They concluded that, during the work period, near-maximal rates were best for optimal development; at the end of the rest interval, rates of about 130 were best.

Others, such as Karlsson[1] used oxygen uptakes. They found that optimal training required maximal loading of the oxygen transport systems. However, Karlsson emphasized that maximal oxygen uptakes can be attained at submaximal speeds and that this lesser speed may be adequate for optimal training. *Astrand (1970, 390) suggests that such submaximal speeds could be about 80 percent of the maximum speed that can be maintained for from 3 to 5 minutes.* For example, a distance that could be run in 3 minutes should be run in 3.5 minutes without lowering the demand on the aerobic processes. Costill (1968, 21) suggested that an optimal training pace would be the slowest pace that would produce maximal oxygen consumption.

---

[1] J. Karlsson, P-) Astrand, and B. Ekblom, "Training of the Oxygen-Transport System in Man," *Journal of Appl. Physiol.*, 22: 1061-65, 1967.

To increase the work time @ 2160 kpm/min to 60 minutes, intermittent work methods were tried. If the subject did intermittent work-rest for 3 minutes each, the total work output was the same as in Experiment 1. The subject finished up exhausted; the blood lactate, heart rate, and oxygen uptake were all maximal. In contrast, when the subject did intermittent work-rest for 30 seconds each, though the total oxygen uptake during the 60 minutes was reduced very little, the awareness of stress was less severe, the heart rate did not rise above 150, and the blood lactate was only 20 mg/100 ml.

We conclude that the work load (running speed) and the precise length of the work-rest periods must be weighed very carefully if we are to ensure optimum endurance training.

RAISING THE LEVEL OF ONE'S STEADY STATE WHILE RUNNING

In setting goals and judging progress there are various aspects of development from training on which attention can be focussed. Interval training focussed on heart development. Research in physiology tends to focus on maximum oxygen uptakes (Astrand, 1970, 386). Apparently Lydiard[1] found support for his marathon training by focussing on raising the level of the steady state.

At the start of a run, the respiratory exchange (oxygen intake and carbon-dioxide output) rises rapidly during the first two or three minutes to a value characteristic of the severity of the pace. If the pace is slow enough so that its oxygen requirement does not exceed the maximum oxygen uptake, the runner is able to reach a "steady state" in which he is able to supply his oxygen needs from immediate oxygen uptake. Under these conditions that pace can be continued almost indefinitely; when fatigue does arise it is not due to oxygen deficiency or to the accumulation of lactic acid in the muscles, but to secondary factors such as depletion of the glycogen store.

A steady state condition, then, denotes a pace at which oxygen uptake equals the oxygen requirement, and thus such functions as breathing, heart rate and stroke/volume attain fairly constant levels.

The pace at which a man can run a long distance depends on his capacity for maximum oxygen consumption; if low, his pace must be slow; if high, the pace can be high. It follows as a valid and crucial principle that endurance training is a process of raising the level, that is, the pace-distance, at which a steady state can be maintained. A beginner can maintain a steady state at a pace, say, of 75 seconds per 440; later he can maintain a pace of 72 or 70 seconds without incurring oxygen debt.

The implications of research are that a steady state can occur within a range of stress, not merely at a single point of stress. That is, there is a lowest pace that will produce maximal oxygen uptake and the allied phenomena, and also a highest pace that still will not produce oxygen debt. Aerobic training can proceed in progressive step-ups of pace, somewhat as occurs in weight training for strength. Each pace has its own inherent maximum developmental value. As the maximums for a given pace are reached, the pace is increased slightly even though distance be reduced temporarily. Then a gradual process of adjustment ennables the runner to maintain that pace at a lower level of stress, though still within the range of maximum oxygen uptake. Once again a step-up occurs.

The crucial question arises as to just how men can best raise the level at which they can maintain a steady state. That's the gist of endurance training. The answers of interval training are well-known--by repeated short overloads of anaerobic work-rest. Fartlek does it by playing at speed but "playing" should be interpreted as progressively more demanding pace-distance. In contrast, Arthur Lydiard, in his marathon training, emphasizes continuous running at both the higher and lower levels of aerobic pace. If such pace were all slow and easy, development would stop at the slow-and-easy level of stress. But Lydiard also requires his men to run at their "best aerobic speed" and "maximum steady state,"

---

[1]Arthur Lydiard, "Marathon Training," USTCA *Track and Field Quarterly Review*, Vol. 70, No. 4, February 1971, 9.

I kept the pressure on my athletes all the time. . . . It was never slow running. It was hard, strong running. The pressure was always on. . . . It was aerobic because we could maintain it all the way . . . and gradually as we improved and the steady state got higher, we would go faster. But I always left it to the athlete to put more pressure on himself and we understood it this way.

In other portions of this same talk, he makes it clear that a major goal is to raise the steady state level as high as possible before shifting the emphasis to anaerobic training.

TRAINING AEROBIC POWER

The distinction between aerobic and anaerobic training is a crucial one in modern distance running. In brief, aerobic running is at a pace that can be maintained indefinitely, with an ample O_2 supply to oxidize the carbohydrate sources of energy completely to CO_2 and H_2O, and therefore with no accumulation of lactic acid. Such a balanced aerobic condition is often called a "steady state." Pulse rates may range between 130-160 b/p/m.

In contrast, anaerobic running is at a faster pace than can be maintained in a steady state. It requires more oxygen than can be supplied, an "oxygen debt" is incurred, and a high lactic acid condition is built up in the muscle tissues and blood stream which, eventually, ends in exhaustion. Pulse rates may rise to sub-maximal (180-190 b/p/m).

In everyday distance running terminology, we tend to equate aerobic running with long-slow continuous running, though, as we shall see, slower-paced interval training can also be aerobic. Anaerobic running tends to be related in both research and actual practice to repetitions of faster-paced distances, as in interval training or intermittent work, as the Scandinavian researchers call it. But fast-paced continuous running is equally anaerobic.

From related research, Åstrand (1970, 389) concludes that to develop maximum aerobic power, it is unnecessary to use anaerobic methods, though this depends on the pace-distance of the race for which training is done. He states (1970, 391), for example, that "the ability to work for prolonged periods of time utilizing the largest possible percentage of the maximal oxygen uptake may probably primarily be developed just by working continuously during long periods of time (endurance training.")

But interval training can also be used in the development of aerobic power. For example, Åstrand (1970, 390) recommends intermittent work with about an 80% workload for from three to five minutes, with easy jogging or walking between, as being an optimal stimulus for aerobic power. The heart rate during such runs usually will not exceed ten beats below the maximum heart rate.

In the case of healthy young persons the speed of running may be reduced to about 80 percent of the maximum which may be maintained for a period of 3 to 5 min. If, in other words, the distance that may be covered by running . . . in a matter of say 3.0 min. is covered instead in about 3.5 min., the demand on the aerobic processes remains the same. Thus the stopwatch in such cases should be used to maintain a reduced tempo, not to stimulate the trainee to attain a better achievement in terms of faster timing.

The last sentence is of special importance. Though applied to intermittent work (interval training), it is a key also to Lydiard's[1] training with continuous running,

I realized a long time ago that it was not speed that we wanted but the necessary stamina to maintain the necessary speed over the distance. . . . We would encourage him to go out and run aerobically as far as he could, not as fast as he could over any given distance. We began to see that if you start with young people and encourage them to do a lot of long running (seeing how far they could run, not how fast they could run), we were going to lay the foundations for greater future champions.

Such an approach is not opposed to that of interval training as advanced by the original workers--Reindell, Nocker, Roskamm, Gerschler. They warned repeatedly against over-intensities, and we know that the interval training of Harbig and others was preceded by months of aerobic

---

[1]Lydiard, *op.cit.*, p. 130.

cross-country running. But interval training, as generally practiced, has emphasized increasing intensities of training. To the extent that this has been done too soon and over too long a training period, interval training has been misused.

Åstrand (1970, 391) writes that the submaximal efforts of aerobic training, whether continuous or intermittent work, are far more pleasant and less likely to produce the psychological stresses of highest-effort training which mixes aerobic and anaerobic training indiscriminantly. The latter should therefore be postponed "until a few months prior to the start of the season, otherwise the athlete may be unable to keep up his training program for psychological reasons."

In his summary of research as related to distance running, Costill (1968, 21) goes so far as to suggest that the optimal training pace during early season should be the slowest pace that stimulates maximal oxygen uptakes. This is a very cogent idea that should be carried into practice. Actually it is consistent with the strong emphasis that Lydiard (1962, 86) made in his training book on his Tables of Effort (3/4, 1/2, 1/4). For example, during the first two months of Lydiard's training schedule for the mile, only two workouts (time trials) are at full effort; during the first six weeks, only three workouts are at as high as 3/4 effort.

We should be clear that, to be continuously developmental, aerobic training must progressively overload the endurance systems. When an optimum distance has been achieved, pace must be increased so that higher levels of stress will stimulate development to higher levels of energy. This will cut mileage temporarily while the organism adapts to the new challenge. Perhaps such a program may be understood more clearly if we think in terms of progressive overloads of work, and compare it with that followed in weight training. For example, Ryun (1970) suggests a weight-training program which alternates between eight and 12 repetition maximums (RM). He advocates first a maximum load that can be lifted only eight times. This is gradually increased in number to 12. But now the weight is increased and the number of reps is reduced to eight. And so on, repeatedly.

In our analogy, we should compare the 8RM with that of 20 PM (pace-maximum), the slowest running pace that will produce maximum oxygen uptakes, and mild fatigue in, say, 20 minutes. Now gradually increase the distance to, say, 30 minutes (at a later stage to 40 or even 60 minutes). Then again step up the pace to 20 PM, and repeat the entire process again and again, throughout the year and the athlete's career. Almost all of such workouts would be within the range limits of aerobic training.

We know of no research that answers the question as to whether it is more developmental to tax 90 percent of the maximal oxygen uptake for a longer time, or to tax 100 percent for a much shorter time. For example, Karlsson and others (reported in Costill, 1968, 21, and also Åstrand, 1970, 384) used the same work-rest periods of 20 and 10 seconds for two efforts of running on a treadmill. But in one instance, a speed of 22.0 km/hr was used; in the other, 22.6 km/hr. In the second case, 100 percent oxygen uptakes occurred for about 16 minutes, the total workout time was about 25 minutes, and the total distance, about 9½ km. In the first case, oxygen uptakes reached only 90 percent of maximum for 40 minutes; total workout time, an hour or more; the distance, 22 km. Does not the answer depend on the special needs of today's training: racing distance; early, middle, or late season; nearness to the BIG races; individual maturity in terms of endurance, and so forth?

But Åstrand is certain that in terms of training for aerobic power, the total amount of work done is far more crucial than is the intensity (speed) of the work load (distance-pace). This holds true whether the work be marathon running or three minutes each of work and rest or even 10 seconds each of work and rest. We should be clear that even such short-interval training can be aerobic training if its pace is low enough to allow a relatively steady state condition in which oxygen uptake tends to equal oxygen use, so that no accumulation of lactic acid occurs. Heart rates and cardiac outputs should fluctuate only mildly as between load and recovery periods. (Åstrand (1970, 288) states that a work load of 10 seconds running (5 seconds recovery) at a speed that will exhaust a man after about 4 minutes of continuous running, would allow a total of 20 minutes of running without undue fatigue and with a minimum of anaerobic work. However, longer periods (2-3 min) of slower intermittent running would allow a total of 30 minutes of running.

TRAINING ANAEROBIC POWER

For a relatively short period of time, the energy needs of high-intensity running can be met through physiological processes for which oxygen is lacking (anaerobic training). Astrand (1970, 17) explains,

> The anaerobic energy output is relatively modest compared with the aerobic energy output. Glucose can, for instance, provide almost 20 times more energy per gram mole aerobically than anaerobically. It is thus clear that oxygen is the key for unlocking the doors to the great energy stores of the living cells. It is therefore the availability of oxygen to the working muscle cells which, in the final analysis, determines endurance in prolonged physical work. On the other hand, the residual energy of lactic acid is by no means lost. The lactic acid diffuses into the interstitial fluid, enters the circulating blood, and primarily in the liver, is eventually synthesized to glycogen or completely oxidized, for example, in the heart muscle.

All racing distances from the marathon down to 400m make some demand on anaerobic power-- if not during the major portion of the race (400-800), then during the final drive for the finish line; or more rarely, during the increased-pace laps by which men try to break away from the field during later portions of longer races.

It follows that anaerobic training will comprise some portion of training for all distances, including the marathon. In brief, such training will be either continuous running at close to racing pace or intermittent (interval) running with repetitions of work-rest at faster than racing pace. Training effects relate to the ability to consume, transport, and utilize large volumes of oxygen (as with aerobic training), but also to the development of muscle power and effectiveness to sustain the faster pace of shorter races or of the finish in longer races (Costill, 1979, 26-27). Aerobic training alone fails to serve this latter need.

It may be helpful if we relate such two-phased training to modern training for field-event power. There we speak of strength training as being basic, of being long-time, even year-round, as establishing the foundation for field-event power. Related and imitative power training requires higher-velocities in patterns of movement that simulate those of the event being trained for. Such high-velocity training is relatively brief and during the competitive period.

So with aerobic training (basic) as compared with anaerobic training (more specifically related to racing distance/pace). Both are essential; each serves its peculiar function. As a rule of thumb, anaerobic training is used during the competitive season for purposes of sharpening or peaking. Coach Haikkola, Viren's coach, wrote, "I need about four weeks, no more, to get a runner into top condition--taking for granted good health and an adequate background. In itself, it is quite easy for a runner to reach the peak. All one needs is a faster pace in training, short enough intervals, and constant pressure in repetition training." (Raevuori, ibid., 100).

But in preparing Viren for the Munich Olympic 5000 and 10,000 Haikkola used anaerobic intermittent training as a test of running condition. In June, Viren ran 20 x 200m with 200m jogging between, in which the repetitions averaged 30 seconds. In July they averaged 29; on August 23, (8 days before his first race) they averaged 27.2. In each test, the plan was to maintain even pace for the first 19 repetitions, but to open up for the last. On Viren's last 200, he ran 25.8s; "yet his pulse was lower than it had been in June. He was in better shape: more speed, less fatigue." (Raevuori, ibid., 101).

Repeated work-loads of this kind combine anaerobic and aerobic phases. Immediately following the runs, pulse rates will rise gradually toward higher levels; but during the rest interval will drop to about 120-130.

INTER-RELATIONSHIPS BETWEEN ANAEROBIC ENDURANCE AND LEG SPEED. Up to this point we have been writing of the problem of anaerobic endurance as though it were related exclusively to the mechanisms of circulation and respiration. Read the absorbing biographies of Kipchoge Keino or Ron Clarke and you will be aware of how closely anaerobic endurance is intertwined with having the muscular power to run fast. Keino, who always considered himself a 5000-meter runner because of his inability to match the speeds of men like Jim Ryun or Michel Jazy, ended up as Olympic champion, 1968, at 1500 meters by means of his sustained finishing speed.

I emphasize the phrase, "sustained finishing speed." Races are won by taking the lead at the right instant and being able to sustain that lead to the finish line. That may involve a desperate gamble of ten yeards or even ten inches. But few men can wait so long; most try for the lead over a longer, surer distance--200-400-800, even 1200 meters.

In the Olympic 1500 at Montreal, John Walker (NZ) took the lead with 300m to go. He sprinted the backstretch 100 in 12.5; the curve in an incredible 12.2; the final 100 in 13.2. The sustained finishing drive was at least 300 meters, but it was his speed on the last curve that ensured his victory.

In the Munich 1500, the crucial kick came later. Keino (Kenya) had run a fast third lap (55.3 as compared with 61.3 for the second lap). Vasala (Fin) stayed on his shoulder with Boit (Kenya) and Dixon (NZ) close behind. Only on the homestretch was Vasala able to sprint past Keino to the finish line. In the Rome 5000m, Murray Halberg (NZ) broke contact with three laps (1200m) to go by sprinting a shocking 61.1 lap.

In summary, each race is different, depending on the relative finishing drives of oneself and one's competitors. A "sustained finishing drive" can be defined two ways: (1) begin the final drive as early as possible without losing the lead at the finish, or (2) begin the finish drive as late as one can be certain of reaching the finish line first. Training should be specific to each race.

ACHIEVING AN OPTIMUM RATIO OF AEROBIC/ANAEROBIC TRAINING

Scientists and modern coaches are in general agreement (1) that a sound endurance-training program should include both mileage training (aerobic) and speed-endurance training (anaerobic), and (2) that first and separate emphasis during one-half to three-fourths of the training year should be on aerobic training. Disagreements occur as to the time at which anaerobic training should be introduced, and as to the degree to which the two types of training should be intermixed.

In general, the proponents of interval training have used about two or more months for aerobic fartlek; the remaining nine months, for anaerobic interval work. In contrast, Lydiard, the chief advocate of aerobic training, more than reverses the ratio. He[1] suggests that about four weeks is sufficient to bring about the benefits of anaerobic work. This is borne out by his training of Snell who ran a marathon just 55 days before setting his world record of 3:54.4 in the mile and two weeks later in the 880 in 1:45.1, and who had only a few weeks of intensive anaerobic and speed work just prior to these races.

In his discussion[1] at the USTCA clinic at Washington, 1970, Lydiard suggests an 8-week "sharpening" period prior to the Big Race. The first four of these are "hard anaerobic work" consisting of repeated intervals at 400, 800, and 200 meters:

In this period, I had the athletes in good condition. They had a high steady state, had their speed back, and the capacity to run anaerobically.

During the second 4-week period, Lydiard tried to achieve several things along with the anaerobic interval work: (1) wind sprints for greater sprinting speed, (2) progressively faster trial runs at or near his racing distance, (3) under-distance competition, and (4) a conservation of energy by easier training.

This program is consistent with that suggested by Åstrand (1970, 389) based on related research,

A training of the anaerobic motor power is important for many groups of athletes. Since this form of training is psychologically very exhausting, it should preferably not be introduced until a month or two prior to the competitive season.

---

[1]Lydiard, *op.cit.*, p. 26.

On the other hand, Jim Ryun's world records at these same distances were preceded by a much longer period of mixed aerobic and anaerobic training. Coach Timmons'[1] report of his training during the 12-week period from May 1 to July 24 includes cross-country jogging, long, hard runs at 10 to 15 miles, and repeated intervals at various distances from 120 to 440 yards, with emphasis on the shorter distances.

Lydiard makes a strong point of separating aerobic and anaerobic training. That is,get all the value you can out of the first before adding the second. But Haikkola (ibid., 100) points out that a steady run of 30km "doesn't always develop one as much as it should. Include a four-minute acceleration--now it has quite another meaning. It is no longer just the cardiovascular system that is improved; some muscles...are also developed."

In trying to understand this important problem, the following tenets may be of help.

1. Individuals differ over a wide range of reaction to the many phases of training.

2. A clear understanding as to the differences in both procedures and training effects of aerobic and anaerobic training is necessary. Costill (1979, 115) recommends in non-competitive training periods about one day per week of intermittent speed work; in competitive periods, two or three per week.

3. Early season training tends to emphasize continuous, steady-pace running at gradually increased distances. Bill Bowerman, Oregon coach, suggests that during this stage, if you can't talk with ease while running, you're going too fast.

4. As adaptation to training occurs, and assuming an optimum distance has been achieved, increases in pace are needed to overload the tissues and systems. Without such overloading, development will stop at that stress-pace level.

5. In faster-pace aerobic work, the total work output, a crucial consideration, is greater with intermittent run-jog than with continuous, steady-pace running.

6. Very short, intermittent work periods (30 seconds or shorter) can impose a very severe load on both muscles and the oxygen-transport systems without engaging the anaerobic processes or producing any significant elevation in blood lactate (Åstrand, 1970, 387).

7. If the racing distance (400-800), or the present training emphasis, requires a very fast pace, then the shorter the run in intermittent work should be. Åstrand (1970, 288) states that repeated run-rest periods of 10-5 seconds can prolong the total running time to 20 minutes without undue fatigue, at a pace which normally would exhaust a man after about four minutes of continuous running.

8. If training of the oxygen-transport systems is a primary concern, Astrand (1970, 290) suggests runs from two to three minutes in length at a pace which produces a high-level oxygen debt. If total work output is crucial, then the rest periods should allow full recovery.

9. If acceleration of the rate of development is primary, then intermittent work at short distances (400 down to 80 yards) at progressively faster pace or/and with shorter recovery periods is effective. Such intensive speed training is more effective in speeding up developmental changes than is slow-pace continuous running (Costill, 1968, 13).

10. If greater strength-speed of the running muscles is the primary aim, then repeated distances should be only five to 10 seconds in length, with full recovery between. Speed should be 9/10th maximum, what might be called a relaxed full speed.

---

[1]Bob Timmons, "Jim Ryun--How He Trains," *Track Technique*, 31, March 1968, 963.

HURT-PAIN-AGONY

In recent years there has been growing acceptance of the hurt-pain-agony approach to training and competitive efforts. Unless you're willing to pay the price at the highest levels of discomfort from fatigue and all-out effort, you're not likely to reach the top in sports. Swimming seems to have adopted this as an essential tenet. For example, Counsilman (1968, 337) states

> *We try to build pride in the ability of the swimmers to push themselves hard in this manner (the agony phase of exertion) when it is requested of them. . . . Social pressure is thus imposed on him to produce in practice or be ostracized.*

By making it an everyday experience, shared by all members of the team, the aversion to suffering tends to subside. Sure it hurts; it hurts all of us, but so what? The more men talk about agony in an unemotional way, the more it takes on the connotation of acceptable discomfort. Men develop mental as well as physical callouses to pain. I am reminded of Zatopek's statement that he trained until the pains of fatigue were no longer a problem.

In our discussion of great coaches, we wrote of Cerutty's adoption of the word "Stotan," a combination of "stoic" and "spartan." The Stoics were Greek philosophers who submitted without complaint to unavoidable pain. We all remember the fable of the Spartan boy who let a fox inside his shirt tear out his flesh rather than evidence weakness before his elders. "Seek suffering," said Cerutty, "and it will purge and toughen you."

The biographies of running champions tell repeatedly of the hardening of attitudes as of muscles. Nelson (1967, 235) writes of Jim Ryun's 3:51.3 mile,

> *Into the last curve Jim maintained his pace, but it became more difficult with each stride. Now he had only one physical resource to keep him going. He had only his remarkable ability to sprint in the presence of extreme fatigue. This was his bank account of reserve strength, into which he had made deposits almost every day for four years, in the freezing early morning of Kansas winters and in the heat of summer when most other people were resting.*

Murray Halberg relates that when he first started training with Lydiard, he would always feel sick after a few miles. So he'd throw up and keep on running. As matter of fact as that. Similarly, Snell (1965, 31) writes that at his first workout at Rome where he won his first Olympic championship, Lydiard had scheduled six 300s. After the fifth,

> *I tottered to Arthur and said, 'Arthur, if I do another, I'll vomit.' I was rather staggered when Arthur replied crisply that I should still do it and that I would probably be all the better if I did vomit. . . . Obediently, I did as he said--and just made it to the dressing room in time to heave out the contents of my stomach.*

In 1952 the late Professor Bykov reported to the Montreal Physiological Congress that the skin can be made to react to hot water (62 C) as it normally does to warm water (42 C) if, after a period of conditioning to the feeling of "warm," the subject is told the water is warm when it is really hot. Words and the meanings that are given to them can change body chemistry, circulation of the blood, modify reactions to physical or mental stress. We have reason to believe that the psychological limits which often keep performance below physiological limits are due to inhibitions implanted by endless cultural influences: both the printed and spoken word, warnings and attitudes given by parents, teachers, peers--often early in life. One of the major goals of coaching is to remove those inhibitions.

But at the same time, we coaches should be aware that Stotanism is a two-edged sword. One edge can cut away the inhibitions against pain. But the other can cut through the very tenuous threads by which beginners and more sensitive athletes are attached to running. It could cause them to quit running altogether, or even to avoid turning out for it at all. Great prospects for running are sometimes very sensitive--sensitive to pain and stress. A dozen world-level runners come to mind who were far from being Stotans. A tough coach would have lost them before they had a chance to get started. Without gradual adaptation to its meaning, agony is something to shudder over and certainly to avoid. The "joy of suffering" may be sought by ascetic saints or masochists, but not by the average boy. The coach who promotes it as a basic tenet of his training is likely to be held suspect.

As a physical fact, men vary greatly in the sensitivity of their pain receptors. For example, Roger J. Williams (1956, 38) examined the hands of 21 "normal" persons. On one hand, a given area evidenced 25 spots that the subject described as "insensitive to pain," and none, "highly sensitive to pain." In contrast, another subject responded that in this same area only one spot was "insensitive to pain," whereas 19 spots were "highly sensitive to pain." Obviously the results of such a test would be influenced by psychic as well as physical differences. But other observations led Williams to the conclusion that pain spots on people's bodies "are widely unequal in number and are distributed differently in individual people."

True, the pain of a pin-prick is not at all the same as the pain of anaerobic effort in running, or as that of exploding all one's energies with nothing held back behind a shot or into the air in the high jump. But the research of such men as Williams leads us to assume that the general pattern of individual differences would be similar.

Intelligently used, the pain-suffering-agony concept can be of value in training for sports. But biochemical individuality should be a constant concern. Even though we accept the thesis of psychic control of pain, as occurs in hypnosis or with the fire-walkers of the East, it is certain that such control is quite a different problem for the no-pain-spot subject as contrasted with the 19-pain-spot subject.

All this assumes that we learn to rise above the pains of exertion in competition by doing so in practice. Any all-out race is a test of will over increasing pain. Each additional lap increases fatigue, a concept that implies discomfort as much as it does impairment (Bartley & Chute, 1947, 47). The greater the awareness of discomfort-hurt-pain-agony, the greater the sense of effort that must be made to overcome it.

The solution lies in dulling awareness, or better, in accepting some degree of pain as a natural and necessary part of competitive running. All sense of aversion gradually falls away. Self-control is certain. Effort is required but it is no longer a problem. The runner knows he can make that effort. It hurts but so what! Hurting is a part of running just as is high blood lactate or an oxygen debt (Counsilman, 1968, 337). Cerutty said, "Seek suffering." He was right. But when you seek it, it loses its terrors; and when you find it, what was described as suffering becomes an every-day sensation, and one adopts a so-what attitude.

All this requires practice, both in training and in competition.

TRAINING EMPHASIS ACCORDING TO RACING DISTANCE

During recent years, coaches have emphasized training for basic endurance by which men have been able to run almost any distance. They argue that a solid foundation of stamina is the best means to utilizing one's natural speed. Snell trained by running the marathon, then broke the world record for both the 880 and mile.

But maximal efforts in running different distances depend on different percentages of energy from aerobic and anaerobic processes, and this argues for training according to one's racing distance. For example, in the marathon, energies are derived almost entirely from aerobic processes; in the 200 meters, almost entirely from anaerobic processes; in the 800 meters, aerobic and anaerobic energy yields are approximately equal.

At least three researchers (Nett,[1] Robinson,[2] and Åstrand (1970, 303) have worked on the problem. Their figures, which should be considered only approximate, are in general agreement. In Table 19.1 I have adjusted their differences.

We should keep in mind that speed work to gain greater sprinting speed serves a special and different need. It of course should be done in accordance with that need. But the degree of emphasis on speed work to gain greater anaerobic power should be related to the percentage of anaerobic need in a runner's racing distance.

----

[1]Toni Nett, *DER LAUF* (Running), Berlin: Bartels & Wernitz, 1960.

[2]Sid Robinson, "Physiological Considerations of Pace in Running Middle-Distance Races," *International Track and Field Digest*, 1956, 219.

TABLE 19.1

AEROBIC-ANAEROBIC NEEDS BY RACING DISTANCE

DISTANCE	AEROBIC NEEDS (Percentages)	ANAEROBIC NEEDS (Percentages)
Marathon	99	1
10,000	95	5
5,000	90	10
2 miles	85	15
1 mile	70	30
880	50	50
440	25	75

On the other hand, degree of emphasis is not the same as number of months to be given to these two kinds of training. Our principle does not mean, for example, that training for the 440 should devote only 1/4th of the year to aerobic training. If we ignore the demands of scheduled competition, and train solely for the BIG races, aerobic training for the 440 might well dominate 1/2 to 2/3rds of the year. This would leave four to six months of anaerobic training mixed with the other needs of the event.

TESTS OF CAPACITY FOR ENDURANCE RUNNING.

Though much research still needs to be done before we have fully valid and reliable tests of capacity for running endurance, there are certain tests with sufficient validity to warrant their use in our training programs. Certainly there are important values to be gained from such use, though of course they should be only supplementary to actual performance. Among such values are: (1) Some tests measure physical responses to submaximal workloads, so that the old bugaboo, motivation, is not so likely to upset precise measurement. (2) Functional tests of heart-rate reactions or maximal oxygen uptakes measure basic endurance, much as weight-lifting measures basic strength; specific endurance as related to a particular distance-pace is not measured. Thereby, comparisons can be made between one's basic endurance today and at any past or future time. (3) The athlete tends to be impressed with scientific procedures; their results will give him greater confidence in his success and assurance of his condition.

Over the years there have been many evaluations of physical endurance capacity, including the Harvard step test, the pulse ratio test, and more recently, the I. Åstrand test of maximal aerobic power. None of these were devised for the purpose of giving precise measurements by which we can predict running condition. Per-Olaf Åstrand, for example, refers to their method as being "at best, a screening test." Costill (1979, 26) agrees that a high VO_2 max is "a crucial factor for distance running success...but in itself does not guarantee a fast performance in marathon competition." Oxygen use at high levels for prolonged periods is also critical.

Astrand (1970, 286) defines maximal oxygen uptake or maximal aerobic power as "the highest oxygen uptake the individual can attain during physical work breathing air at sea level." Such uptake is dependent on many factors including: (1) cardiac function (stroke/volume and heart-beat rate), (2) pulmonary ventilation and diffusion, (3) oxygen-carrying capacity of the circulatory system, (4) extent and efficiency of the blood capillary beds in the related muscle systems, and (5) the arteriovenous difference in oxygen saturation.

To test maximum aerobic power directly requires complex laboratory equipment (treadmill or bicycle ergometer, Douglas bag, air analysis devices, and others) and expert technicians not usually available to coaches or runners. But Irma and Per-Olaf Åstrand (1970, 344, 617) devised a nomogram[1] which (1) uses heart rate as a predictive index of maximal oxygen uptake, and (2) uses performance efforts that are submaximal. A treadmill would be best, as being most similar to outdoor running, but either a step test or bicycle ergometer can be used. The test is very simple, requiring only ten minutes or less. Heart rates are taken by use of a stop watch during a 6-minute submaximal work period. By drawing a line on the nomogram

---

[1]A nomogram is a graph usually containing three parallel scales graduated for different variables so that when a straight line connects values of any two, the related value may be read directly from the third.

between the maximum pulse rate, say 160, and the workload value, say 1200 kpm/min, an intersection is made at a point on the line of oxygen uptake. This point gives the predicted value for maximum oxygen uptake.

Though modest in their overall claims, the Åstrands do state that "it has been widely applied in top athletes," (1970, 359), and is "valuable in following the effect of a training program when the pulse response in the same individual is compared before and after a training program and the subject serves as his own control." (1970, 618) Those wishing to actually use the test should consult the references provided here, so as to obtain the detailed instructions for taking pulse rates and determining workloads. The reliability of measurements is crucial.

HEART RATE DURING AND AFTER EXERCISE. Heart rate is the most easily measured aspect of bodily response to a workload. It can be counted manually, though to do so during action requires special instruction (see Åstrand, 1970, 620) and experience. But the recent improvement of heart-rate meters and telemetry makes electronic counting increasingly feasible for everyday use.

As exercise begins, the pulse rate increases very rapidly. During a run at 9/10th speed, the rate will increase to 180 or more within 15 seconds; lesser speeds will induce slower rates of increase. Heart rate during prolonged work is proportional to the workload that is carried (in running, to pace or angle of incline or resistance of the running surface or extra weight carried). During continuous running at aerobic pace, heart rates tend to rise gradually (120-170 b/p/m). Consensus among researchers is that heart rates above 140 are needed for significant training effects. During fast work-recovery training, as occurs in fartlek, long repetitions and interval training, heart rates will approach maximal levels (180-200 or more). During recovery periods, the pattern of such lowering relates to the running-stress created-- accumulation of lactic acid and other fatigue effects--but also to the level of condition of the runner. When heart rates fail to lower to about 120 during the recovery period (1-5 mins. depending on stress of run) the following run will induce greater stress and higher heart rates. If total work output is the primary purpose of the workout, recovery periods should be lengthened. This applies to fartlek training as much as to interval training.

Normally, pulse rates fall rapidly following exertion, making it necessary to record rates within the first 10 to 20 seconds of the recovery period, if they are to provide an accurate measure of the rate while running. Such a method (rate for 10 seconds x 6) is the usual procedure in interval training, and will be discussed at greater length under that heading. But since increased rate of recovery is one of the criteria of improving condition, it is also worthwhile to take additional heart rates for 10 seconds at the end of each minute for five minutes following a measured work load of running. Comparison of these rates can give one more measure of training effectiveness.

THE USES OF VARIETY.
The emphasis in modern training on year-round running makes variety an essential factor--a Master Key to maintaining enthusiasm and purpose.

VARIETY IN TERRAINS. Every training system must include varied terrains in its year-round program. It is the heart of fartlek. Olander's Swedish training center, Volodalen, provided Gunder Haegg with curving paths through woods and around lakes, up-hill and down-dale, with sometimes marshy footing. Percy Cerutty's Australian topography included high sand dunes, long sea beaches, dirt roads, and runs over the plains "in any direction our whim took us, followed by a dip in the ocean." Oregon's excellent training program, as first organized by Bill Bowerman, used four terrains--the running track, a golf course, the seashore and nearby mountain paths. Even interval training, as invented by Germany's Woldemar Gerschler, included cross-country and road running in its total schedule of training. Lydiard (1962, 62) placed strong emphasis on variety of terrains.

The time training we have outlined includes running over country roads, hills, flats, everything, to accustom our learner to all conditions and running surfaces. He is not going to be a fair-weather, fine-track athlete. He runs on turf as much as possible and deliberately seeks out mud and slush as well as fast, hard surfaces. . . . He doesn't mind whether there is a blazing sun overhead or it is pouring rain--out he goes.

True, Lydiard is emphasizing toughness, but he makes it clear that variety helps to make the toughening process easier, without boredom.

VARIETY IN COMPETITIONS. Obviously the men against whom the team members compete will provide variety in pace, in length and speed of finish, in racing tactics generally, and in competitive challenge. But there must also be variety in degree of emphasis on competitions from week to week. There is agreement among the world's master coaches of running that the year's competitions must be classified into at least three groups: (1) Crucial, (2) Important, (3) Developmental. The words don't matter. Lydiard called the first, "Big Races"; Timmons, high-goal races. But for pacing one's energies and attitudes, such variety is necessary.

VARIETY IN PRACTICE RUNNING. It's very difficult for today's coaches to realize the great increase in the kind of things that can be done in training for running today as compared with early years. It's almost shocking to me to remember that in 1948 I tried to help Herb Barten on his way to a third place in the London Olympic 800 meters with only four or five workouts in my coaching bag: Monday--1½ x distance; Tuesday--time trials, 3/4 distance; Wednesday--2 x ½ distance; Thursday--4 x ¼ distance; Friday--rest. A few short-relay events, a little sprinting, that was about it. All on a cinder 440-yard track.

In contrast to such wearisome sameness, look through Greg Brock's *HOW HIGH SCHOOL RUNNERS TRAIN*.[1] Each man will have a dozen or more running patterns. A list of all the patterns might number a hundred or so. Another excellent example of variety is to be found in Coach Timmons'[2] account of Jim Ryun's workouts during the 12 weeks preceding his world-record mile and 880. The hard or easy workouts occur either AM or PM. Off-the track running is cross-country, steady-pace, fartlek, or even road running. No two interval workouts are the same. Any one workout is likely to contain 3 or more interval distances, with varying paces. Within each workout there are intervals requiring 9/10 effort; others, very relaxed, easy effort. Such variety helped greatly to hide the very demanding exertions of the training schedule.

It should be added that variety can become confusing and defeat its purpose if it fails to follow a sound plan of progression.

VARIETY IN COMPANIONSHIP. Most men like to vary their running mates. First, it is important, even essential, to do some running alone, especially when the conditions are difficult and discouraging. There's no better way to develop self-dependence and stick-to-it-iveness. But also, there's value in running with men you enjoy. There's value in running with men of greater competitive experience--as also, occasionally, with those of lesser experience. There is value in training with men of superior endurance, or of superior sprinting speed at the finish. Many a champion has progressed by working out with four or five groups in a single workout.

VARIETY IN ALTITUDE. Costill (1979, 99) concluded from related research that "sea-level performance is not improved by altitude (2300m) training in men who are already well trained." However, the psychological uses of varied altitudes make them a worthwhile adjunct to every training system.

VARIETY IN TEMPERATURE-HUMIDITY. For many years, Scandinavian runners have claimed that their custom of regular sauna baths has been beneficial in their adjustment to the variety of weather conditions they meet in competition. Certainly it has been proved time and time again that those who have acclimated themselves to high temperatures have a great advantage when such conditions prevail.

VARIETY IN DEGREE OF STRESS. The concept of work-rest has many implications. It contrasts the training season with the active-rest season, the periods of major competition with those of developmental competition, weeks of high-stress training with weeks of free running with enjoyment, and of course, days of maximum effort with days of conservation of energy. It should be clear that variety in degree of stress should be a constant goal in every phase of the developmental process. In his excellent chapter on "Physical Training," Åstrand (1970, 375-430) strongly recommends the values of submaximal aerobic training as compared with maximal anaerobic training, but to ensure maximum training effects he feels that both are necessary, and suggests

---

[1] Available from *Track & Field News*, P.O. Box 296, Los Altos, California, 94022.

[2] Bob Timmons, "Jim Ryun--How He Trains," *Track Technique*, 31 March, 1968, 963.

that training programs should provide a variation in intensities which covers the full range of running from long-slow to short-fast, with both continuous and intermittent run-rest. Just how much variation should depend on individual differences in both attitudes and physical reaction, not merely on the coach's planned program or on group preferences.

VARIETY IN THE COOLING-OFF PERIOD. Bob Timmons, Jim Ryun's coach, used the swimming pool for 15 minutes or so after cross-country practice (1) as a flexibility exercise, and (2) as a warm-down comparable to the whirlpool, but better since it involved relaxed active work. He used flutter-kicking drills and bobbing drills to aid breathing. He felt they helped to eliminate shin splints and tight leg muscles (Nelson, 1967, 35). Timmons said he would have continued these drills in the spring except that the pool was a quarter-mile away. Even then, he did a few.

INEXORABLE TRAINING

The word "inexorable" was chosen carefully as implying "relentless," "implacable," "unyielding." Such terms relate both to regular training according to plan regardless of weather conditions or personal convenience, and to an unflinching attitude toward arduous effort. Old-time distance buffs tend to think immediately of two persons—Emil Zatopek and coach Percy Cerutty. Zatopek was one of the first (1946-1956) to extend both mileage and intensity of training. His 40 x 400 that gradually increased to 60 x 400 were considered superhuman, especially since they occurred in the snow and cold, and with army boots on his feet. He wrote, "Is it raining? It doesn't matter. Am I tired? That doesn't matter either...I practiced regardless, until will power was no longer a problem."

Percy Cerutty, Australian coach of Herb Elliott, preached a creed of Stotanism—"seek suffering."

Confidence grows if we overcome our tired bodies, running harder when we want to slow down. With confidence comes character and strength of body, will, and soul. No man becomes a champion without training hard; one of the reasons there are so few champions is that when the going is tough the weaker men drop out.[1]

Haikkola, in training Lasse Viren, felt that schedules were made to be followed:

The schedule is cut into months, then weeks, and finally days. This kind of farsightedness makes sense. It eliminates drastic changes in the schedules. "This is too hard; this is too easy"—that is something Lasse has never had to tell me. And best of all, Lasse always carries out the plans. It is not his habit to change his mind...The amount and load of training must not be compromised. It is essential to follow the plans exactly. Changes make an athlete uncertain.[2]

In Jim Ryun's story, (Nelson, 1967, 72) coach Timmons recalled:

Jim worked for six weeks to do one thing—to learn to sprint when he was tired. The poor guy had a mean old coach who would get him out and work him until he was exhausted, and then say, "Okay, Jim, we're going to do a little work now. You're going to sprint... I've a surprise for you. Im going to open the gates and let you run a little outside." He pointed up Campanile Hill, rising at a 25 degree angle for 230 yards from the stadium. "Run up there and back four times." Wearily, Jim looked up the hill, then back at Timmons. "You'd better call your wife," he said, "and tell her we'll be home for dinner at 8:30 instead of 7:30 as you told her."

From such stories we derive meanings out of our own untrained sensitivities and lack of self-discipline. Endurance training develops the boy as a whole, not merely his legs and heart, but his will-to-succeed, his acceptance of hardship, his persistence in doing it now, whether he feels like doing it or not. Attitudes toughen just as muscles toughen. Ryun (Nelson, 1967, 44) once said,

---

[1]Herb Elliott, *THE GOLDEN MILE,* London: Cassell & Co., Ltd., 1961, p. 48.

[2]Raevuori, ibid., p. 98.

The most important thing is the mental discipline. If you think right and make up your mind to it, the physical part is secondary. I know that sounds funny but it's that way with me.

The meaning of hard work is always relative. It is just as hard work for Joe Public to jog one mile as for Jim Ryun to jog ten. As long as the increments of hard work and denial are gained gradually, there is relatively little awareness of pain or self-sacrifice. J. W. Alford[1] explained this very well in his comments on the training of Zatopek:

I am reminded of the early rather inaccurate accounts of Zatopek's training, and the awe that was felt for the gruelling work we were led to believe he undertook. Zatopek did, of course, train very hard, and nobody is going to become a champion at the distance runs without a great deal of hard work. But his training was not so 'inhuman' and 'man-killing' as many still believe. It was a build-up, and the intensity of the training increased only as he felt himself ready for it.

Ron Clarke worked "hard." At least, over a period of 15 years he averaged 100 miles or more per week for 52 weeks a year, along with his duties as a family man with three children, and as a successful accountant. Still, he wrote (1966, 22)

There is no sacrifice in it. I lead what I regard as a normal life. . . . In my family physical fitness has always been regarded as important. . . . In my case I thoroughly enjoy running 100-odd miles a week. If I didn't I wouldn't do it.

TRAINING SYSTEMS MUST ADAPT TO THE UNIQUE INDIVIDUALITY OF EACH RUNNER

This principle does not suggest that there should be as many training systems as there are individual athletes. That would be chaos. Despite wide variability, men are more similar than they are different. But training systems, as set down on paper, necessarily relate to groups or to the "normal" individual. The application of these systems must be individualized in every way practicable.

The Lydiard system called marathon training is based soundly on the essentials of training. Should you--or any coach--adopt therefore the Lydiard system intact? Lydiard would be the first to object! For example, he writes (Lydiard, 1962, 34),

Coaching distance runners is like assembling a jigsaw (puzzle). All the coaches know the different methods of training . . . they all have the parts of the puzzle, but they don't know how to put them together correctly. . . . Coaching is more than a science. It is an art, bringing the athlete right on the relevant day.

Lydiard trained four great runners at the same time--Peter Snell, Murray Halberg, Barry Magee and Bill Baillie. They often trained together, but Lydiard's program for each was carefully planned in terms of individual needs.

Rolf Haikkola admits his great indebtedness to Lydiard who spent two years as clinic-coach in Finland. But Haikkola insisted he could train only one runner (Lasse Viren) at one time. "Even if they run the same distances, each schedule should be different. You mustn't neglect individual differences."

Similarly, Sebastian Coe trained alone under his father's close supervision,

You see, the day I started running was the day he started coaching. After that it was bringing his science (his father was an engineer--KD) to bear, studying everything he could find. He's got rid of 95% of what he's learned. The 5% he's kept is very specific. He has no other runners. People ask if he will coach them, and he says, "I don't know enough about you. I'd have to move in with you"....That usually ends it.[2]

---

[1] J. W. Alford, "Farther and Faster," *Coaching Newsletter*, London, No. 2 July 1956, p. 5.

[2] Kenny Moore, "A Hard and Supple Man," *Sports Illustrated*, June 20, 1980, p. 78.

Ron Clarke probably maintained a higher-level condition for running over a greater number of years than any other modern champion. Should you seek out and follow his schedules? He says, "No!" (Clarke, 1966, 157).

The methods of the champions . . . ought not to be followed indiscriminately. It is useless for a boy in England to attempt Peter Snell's methods. Peter may be built differently. He may think differently and he may have more, or less, time at his disposal. . . . What the boy should do is analyze the champion's methods and then try to learn from them. . . . Investigate, absorb and then adapt.

This principle emphasizes individualized training. But such training should not be done in a way that estranges the individual from his group. If individualized training creates an impression that a certain boy is different, special, of greater personal concern to the coach, a potential hazard is being fostered. Somehow the squad must come to understand that though all members are alike in the coach's expectation of best efforts, each is different in innate talent and energy, and in the best means to their development. Even after Jim Ryun returned to his high school squad as an Olympian, and an under-four minutes miler, he followed the same general pattern of work as did the squad as a whole. He ran with them, though of course at times there were wide differences in both quantity and quality of running.

Surprisingly, this problem of human variability as it relates to endurance has not attracted much research. But this statement by Astrand[1] indicates its scope,

In our data on maximum oxygen uptake in a fairly homogenous group of individuals with similar degrees of training, the standard deviation was 13 percent. If the average level is 2.50 1/min, 95 percent of those individuals will have an oxygen consumption in the range of 1.85 to 3.15 1/min. An increase in maximum aerobic work power of 20 percent can be considered a good result of training. Thus the 1.85 1/min individual undergoing hard training can improve to about 2.2 1/min, but he will still be below the mean value.

In contrast, the individual with an oxygen consumption of 3.15 could increase by training to 3.78 1/min or higher. Note that these figures are based on an average Scandinavian population. Among champion runners, maximum oxygen uptakes as high as 5.35 1/min have been reported (Sid Robinson's study of Don Lash, 1937).

From a practical coaching standpoint, why are these figures, and others as related to heart rates, stroke-volumes, etc., significant? Assuming that Astrand's estimate of a possible 20 percent improvement is valid, use of his nomogram (Astrand, 1970, 356) would disclose the approximate limits of improvement in this specific function. Even keeping in mind that running is always holistic, and that other factors can compensate for specific weaknesses, such knowledge can still be of significance.

In summary of this principle, keep in mind that a valid training system must be based on both a norm and a standard deviation. It must be based on what is sound for the average running prospect, but it must have a flexibility, a range of specific application, which makes allowances for rather wide individual differences. These differences are physical (structure and function), but equally important, they are inter-actional as related to temperature, humidity, altitude, and certainly as related to inter-personal and individual-group problems.

Limited as this discussion is, every coach soon discovers that its implications are the most complex and troublesome in the entire range of coaching problems.

TRAINING DIARY

Maintaining a diary of training, including competition, is absolutely mandatory, both for the coach and for the individual runner. How else can one judge training progressions for the future other than by the individual's reactions to training in the past? How can a coach plan a boy's future training other than by the experiences of runners that have preceded him? I

---

[1] Per-Olaf Åstrand, "Commentary," *Canadian Med. Assoc. J.*, 96, 730, March 25, 1967.

once had the privilege of examining the notebooks of Mihaly Igloi and was amazed at the detail with which he kept the records of all his men--not just the champions but the duds as well.

Igloi coached runners only. How can the coach of runners and jumpers and throwers find time and paper for such record-keeping? If you realize its importance, you'll find a way. For years I maintained a business time-card rack in the locker room. Each boy kept his own record, but I checked regularly from my own notebook that I used on the field. One successful coach has his managers maintain a portable alphabetized file on the field. A regular manila file folder is kept for each varsity regular; all others have 8½ x 11 sheets.

These diary sheets or cards should be printed so as to require a minimum of writing. Fred Wilt suggests a check-off system. An individual runner's diary may be very detailed, but for most situations, these essentials would be recorded:

Date, including day of week	Race results and reactions	Weather conditions
Hour of day	Hours of sleep	Pulse rate, basal and reactive
Terrain	Weight before and after	to a fixed workload
Details of training	Fatigue index before and after (A 5-point scale is best)	Problems related to training

SPECIFICITY OF TRAINING

By-passing such special conditions as high altitude or high heat-humidity, what is the case for specificity training for each distance? In general modern training emphasizes basic endurance derived from heavy total workloads at varying speeds, over varying terrains, in varying conditions of weather. Lydiard argues that stamina gained from his "marathon training" is the foundation of training, and that specific training should comprise a relatively short period of time--four weeks or even less.

Peter Snell's marathon training was continued up to a few weeks before he broke the world record for the mile (3:54.4) and, only one week later, the 880 (1:45.1). In 1966, though Jim Ryun had been running 80-120 miles a week, he set two world records within three weeks--mile (3:51.3) and 880 (1:44.9). In 1979, Sebastian Coe said, "I wasn't more than 85% race fit," but within a 12-day period he ran a 1:42.4 800m world record and a 3:49.0 world-record mile.

Clearly, as between these two events, specificity of training has little relevance. But there is a mental-emotional approach to specific training. Herb Elliott made a practice of "feeling-through" a BIG race during the training runs that preceded it. His legs carried him over the approximate distance while his mind analyzed and his emotions tried to experience the various stages and crises of the race. "Here my body will cry, 'Take it easy, matey!' but here I shall go faster." Or, "at this point, Bill will be crowding my elbow, but this is how I'll keep control, and relaxed." That's also specific training of a most practical kind.

ENDURANCE TRAINING AND MUSCLE-FIBER TYPES

Experiments by Costill (1979, 16) suggest that slower-paced endurance running impairs leg speed and power. This follows the basic principle underlying all training that muscle development corresponds to the kind and amount of stress the muscles incur. But in recent years, research has disclosed just how such speed impairment takes place.

Muscles are composed of fibers, the number of which remains relatively unchanged through-out life regardless of training. Such fibers can be classified into two types--fast twitch (FT) fibers that relate to speed and power, and slow twitch (ST) fibers that relate to endur-ance. The number of fibers of each kind also remains relatively unchanged throughout life regardless of training--a fact that leads Costill to believe "it may be possible to identify individuals with endurance potential early in life. Fast-twitch fibers possess fast, more powerful contractile properties; slow-twitch are slower, more prolonged, and less susceptible to fatigue.

The muscles of individuals differ in the percentage of FT as compared with ST fibers. "Recent studies of top-flight U.S. distance runners revealed that some had greater than 90 percent of their gastrocnemius muscle composed of ST fibers (Costill, 1979, 27). In contrast the leg muscles of world-class sprinters are mainly of FT fibers.

Though the number of fibers of each type remain relatively unchanged, "it is well known that FT fibers begin to take on the endurance characteristics of ST fibers" (Costill, 1979, 28). Consensus is that hypertrophy of ST fibers is one important effect of endurance training.

GRADUALISM IN RATE OF DEVELOPMENT.   We have mentioned how Lydiard placed great emphasis on a gradual approach to development, and how he predicted when Halberg was 17 that he would be world's champion, not in three or four years, but in ten years' time. Lyd-iard knew by experience that he could increase the intensity of training and thus advance per-formance this year, but he patiently refrained.

But very few men are trained by one coach throughout their running careers. And each coach tends strongly to limit his vision and judgment to his own period of influence. In junior high school, in high school, in college, everyone involved to even a minor degree--the boy him-self, his girl friend, parents, the school principal and janitor, the local postman, and the coach--all recognize achievement now, not at some far-off and uncertain future. Not to mention the demands of the track team and of the adamant school competitive schedule.

Some State high school rules limit the date of first organized track practice, hoping there-by to lessen the pressures on high school boys. This was the case in Kansas when Jim Ryun was at Wichita East High School. The intention of such rules is good; the effect, a loss of the gradual approach, a great increase in intensity of training, and a strong tendency to do too much too soon.

In *The Jim Ryun Story*, Coach Bob Timmons presents a strong case for running at the early ages, for what is called the "Age-group" program,

I think track coaches could learn a great deal from swimming coaches who . . . have worked with the age group program. . . . It's almost commonplace that the quality age group swim-mer goes after national records in competition. With this obvious and forceful positive attitude toward maximum achievement, you can see how successful it is. When age group track and field hits the world as age group swimming has, performances that we now feel are really outstanding will be achieved by teen-agers in routine fashion.

From a physical standpoint, no facts can be presented to refute his argument. But one only needs to read the book itself to realize the tremendous pressures of many kinds that come from thousands of persons quite unrelated to the boy and his career. Even a boy of Ryun's emotional maturity should not be subjected to such pressures. Certain arts, such as music, have their boy prodigies, but the public attention they are given is nothing as compared to that in sports. Jim Ryun was the greatest 19-year-old middle-distance runner the world had even known. At 22, probably the age of greatest potential improvement, he seemed to have run his last race, ex-hausted by the social pressure and constant tension of his running schedule. But once again, Bob Timmons (Nelson, 1967, 21),

As coaches, I think what we all want is for each boy to achieve his maximum potential. That's our job. And it seems a little unfair that if a boy is highly talented you should have to apologize because he runs fast at a young age. You wind up making excuses for the quality of his performances, and I find it a little hard to do.

Haikkola states the opposite case,

There are many examples of little kids specializing...in early childhood... Proponents say, 'This way boys and girls build a solid base for their future running.' How shortsighted they are. A much better base is built by versatile training: skiing, swimming, jumping, throwing, running, playing team games.

The European sports system, including distance running, has been related, not to schools and colleges, but to clubs. Runners have therefore tended to be older men and women; those with families to support and jobs to maintain. That is, the end-point of running has been indefinite and not related to some particular event such as high school or college graduation in America.

In Europe and the USSR, when asked how long he intends to continue training and competing, a runner tends to answer, "As long as I enjoy it and can see some worthwhile goal ahead of me." He knows the wherewithal will be provided. Under such a program, a more gradual approach can be made. Coaches and runners can plan ahead over a span of 20 years instead of four (for high school), then four more (for college), with little certainty of a program or coach or proper facilities beyond. Costill (1979, 13) says there is little doubt that the distance runner is at his best between 27 and 32 years of age, with many doing well at 35 and even beyond.

PEAKING FOR MAJOR COMPETITION

The degree to which peaking or pointing for competition is emphasized tends to be related to the number of months of each year devoted to training, and to the soundness of one's endurance fitness. Those coaches and runners who make the greatest ado about being at a high point at just the right moment tend to be those who do too little too late. They tend to rely on high intensities of training and lack the bottom foundation of long mileage training. When the Big Races come around, they have two choices. One, they try to acquire some last-minute ergs of energy by running "just one more" to make sure they have enough. Or, if they're wiser, they take it very easy, even lay off for several days. As a rule of thumb, the poorer one's condition, the greater the need for rest prior to competition.

Normally, peaking calls for a reduction in training stress--physically and--most important, mentally-emotionally. Some reduce training and competition during some 2-3 weeks before the Big Race--easy longer runs at 60-70% VO_2 max; easy repeat runs a little faster than racing pace, with full recovery between. That is sound theory based on long experience.

On the other hand, greatest personal performance sometimes occurs when all such precepts are ignored. For example, prior to the 1968 Mexico City Olympics, Kip Keino had not been sure he could run at all because of a gall bladder infection. In the Games, he ran:

Oct. 13--10,000 final in which he staggered off the track (gall bladder), then struggled to the finish line, unplaced.

Oct. 15--5000 heat; Oct. 17--5000 final in which he placed 2nd (14:05.2) to Gammoudi by only one meter, despite a last lap in 55s.

Oct. 18--1500 heat; Oct. 19--1500 semi-final; Oct. 20--1500 final (1st place, 3:34.9-- Olympic and personal record). All this at an altitude of 7300 feet.

Just where in that schedule would we find the niceties of peaking? Three widely different distances; personal disability; six tough races within 8 days--and the last was the best.

MENTAL-EMOTIONAL COMMITMENT. The most critical aspect of peaking is related to mental-emotional commitment, the clear-headed certainty that a particular race is the Big Race, and that all prior races, even though important and satisfying to win, are but preparation for the One Race. One can't be careless about these early races. How they are run, and the confidence one gains does affect one's own attitudes as well as those of one's later opponents. On this point, study Bannister's (1955, 222) preparation for his world-shaking race with Landy in the Vancouver mile-of-the-century. He deliberately tried to influence Landy's peaking as well as his own.

Though this subject of peaking is given, unavoidably, little space here, it warrants serious study of the biographies of the great runners and of how they prepared themselves for the Big Races.

WEIGHT TRAINING FOR ENDURANCE RUNNING
The tremendous effectiveness of weight training in modern sports has quite naturally led to its use in all phases of sport, even when such phases are largely irrelevant to the uses of strength, that is, to strength as the ability to move a few times against a heavy resistance.

Coaches and others often speak of "strong" runners. For example, even such an astute and experienced worker as Woldemar Gerschler has stated, "The maximum development of strength must favor running performance . . . running demands strength and therefore a runner needs strength training." Similarly, John P. Jesse[1] advocates weight training "as the most effective method for the development of strength in runners." Or again, in a different context, de Vries (1966, 330) writes, "A maximal level of strength should be developed along with the endurance training program. This allows a muscle group to work at lower percentages of its all-out capacity, and thus significantly increases endurance."

What is the real meaning-in-action of these three statements? Both Gerschler and Jesse apparently equate weight lifting strength with that required in the sprinting muscles as they make a "strong" effort to finish fast at the finish of a distance race. But the two structures-functions are not at all the same, or even similar. De Vries was discussing the research of Royce with isometric contractions. We understand that, in this case, a stronger muscle would have greater endurance in maintaining an isometric contraction against any submaximal weight. But isometric contractions never occur in running, or in any sport for that matter, and once again the meanings of "stronger" and "endurance" are in a quite different frame of reference from that of endurance running.

Strength, as developed by weight training, enables a muscle group to move against heavy resistance once, or not more than a few times. Such increased strength activates muscle fibers not previously functional; it does not increase the capillary bed so essential to endurance. Such strength increases are specific to the actions of their training, to the actions of the clean and jerk, or of the press. These are not at all running actions, neither in the

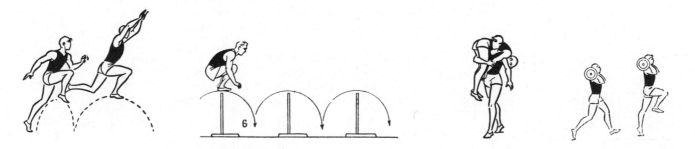

Fig. 21.3 -- Greater power as specifically related to the running muscles is what is needed; that is, power acquired through progressive resistance and many repetitions, not strength per se.

---

[1] John P. Jesse, "Weight Training for Runners," *The Royal Canadian Legion's Coaching Review*, Vol 7 No 1, June 1969.

Fig. 21.4[1] -- The comparative effects on muscles of strength training and of endurance training. Strength training causes a muscle to increase in size (top circles). Microscopic studies (middle circles) show that this increase in size is caused by an enlargement of individual muscle fibers. Blood capillaries are not developed at all by isometric strength training and very little by isotonic strength training (middle circles). Endurance, along with othereffects, increases both the number and the efficiency of blood capillaries within the muscle and thus improves its supply of oxygen and fuel (lowest circles).

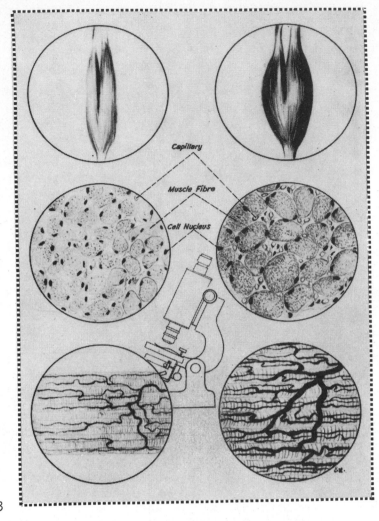

structures involved nor in their function.[2,3]

Greater sprinting speed, both in the 440 and in the final half-lap or so of a long distance race, can be improved by strengthening the muscle motor units involved in sprinting, but this is done best by sprinting against progressive increments of resistance: by repetitions at faster than racing pace, by gradual increases in sprint speed on straightaways, by endurance runs on varied terrains against resistances--sand beaches, sand dunes, long hill work.

De Vries (1966, 327) suggests that repeated isotonic contractions, as occur in running, require several groups of motor units for maximum endurance. As one group of muscle-fiber units fatigues, another group takes over the action. As general fatigue increases, each motor unit contributes less force, so that more and more units must be recruited to maintain pace. We

[1]Used with the kind permission of Ernst Jokl, M.D., from "Physique, Muscle Strength and Performance," *Amateur Athlete*, Vol. 33, No. 12, December, 1962, p. 14.

[2]Toni Nett, "Strength for Runners," *The Royal Canadian Legion's Coaching Review*, Vol 3 No 3, January 1966.

[3]Graham Adamson, "Some Misconceptions Concerning Strength and Endurance," *The Royal Canadian Legion's Coaching Review*, Vol 3 No 4, March 1966.

can conclude validly that some kind of power-endurance training is indicated. But again, such training should be specific to the desired action, training that develops the capillary beds along with the muscle fibers.

In summary, we agree with Åstrand's (1970, 81) statement, "When striving for muscle strength for a particular activity, the best training is that activity itself."

However, as we have said so many times, it is a man that runs, not a mere body. Whatever raises running morale, whatever helps the runner feel more capable, more fit, more competent to do the job, is of value and, other things being equal, should be done. Thus, weight lifting can be associated with effective results. A developing but skinny runner acquires several inches in upper-arm circumference or in the size of his shirt collar. Faster times in endurance running are made. Therefore post hoc ergo propter hoc, especially when he reads statements like those of de Vries and Gerschler, or when his coach tells him that strength is strength, that local muscle strength is cardiovascular strength.

We have no objections to weight lifting; in fact, we advocate it, as long as it does not interfere in time-energy with running. We believe in weight lifting for a general sense of well-being, for all-round physical development, for general self-confidence as well as competitive confidence. But weight lifting for physical endurance reasons? No! There are far more effective ways of acquiring this specific kind of running power.

DEVELOPMENTAL REST PERIODS.
For the purpose of great emphasis, this essential is placed last. There really are only two essentials of all endurance training--work and rest; the second is just as important as the first. Rest is a total-person concept. The athlete must be restored wholly if he is to continue on to higher levels of work.

This principle applies equally to the alternations of stress-days with rest-days, of stress periods with rest periods; and certainly it applies to mental-emotional stress as to physical stress.

The optimal ratio of work to rest is an individual problem solved only by trial-error-success. As running maturity increases, so does one's tolerance of work--within a single workout or in repeated days of high stress. Most non-beginners tolerate two days of hard work followed by a day of active rest. Some work best under alternate days of high stress and rest.

But for all--Olympic champion or beginner--an optimal ratio of stress/recovery is at the core of every sound training program.

Chapter 20
TRAINING SYSTEMS FOR ENDURANCE RUNNING

One might validly assume that a sound endurance-training system would encompass all the 28 essentials of training listed in the previous chapter. "Essential" implies absolutely necessary. Actually, in a practical sense, a sound system of training is an evaluation and adaptation of such "essentials" by one person, in a particular running environment, to the special abilities and needs of one unique runner.

This chapter will emphasize three of the most significant systems of endurance training-- fartlek, interval training and marathon training. All three are valid today; anyone of the three could be used today as a basis for training, and could develop Olympic champions and world records. But none could ignore the essentials of training.

Modern training systems tend to be eclectic, selecting and adapting from past systems what best seems to meet this individual's abilities and needs. Haikkola, coach of Lasse Viren, is frank in stating his indebtedness, "My coaching system is a mixture of Arthur Lydiard, Mihaly Igloi, Percy Cerutty, and Paavo Nurmi." But after telling the particulars of each man's contribution, he adds his own variations of their systems as they apply to the Finnish surround and Viren's unique needs.

In contrast, Kenny Moore saw little of such eclectic uses by Sebastian Coe's coach, his father. Peter Coe was an engineer, without personal experience or special training in distance running. He studied everything he could find on endurance running, then "got rid, he says, of 95% of what he learned." Sebastian explained, "Essentially it has been 100% quality, not quantity. It is speed endurance, that is, seeing how long you can endure speed. In the winters I very seldom have run more than 50 miles per week, less in the spring."

The direction of the Coe experiment thus far has been to train Sebastian as a sprinter, and, that done, turn his speed loose over longer and longer distances. "What we do are ranging shots, as I call them, running under and over distance races to bracket the target," says Peter. "In 1978, when Seb was aiming for the 800, we raced at 400 speed and 1500 for endurance. Last year the bracket was 400 and 3000 meters, and he got the records for three of the distances in between (800, 1500, mile--KD). This year the overdistance will be up to 5000 meters."[1]

Does such a system that ignores 95% of other's ideas, also ignore the essentials? Of course not. It can't. Careful analysis of the year's total program would disclose them, no matter how disguised or modified. For example, Moore tells of a workout at 14.4 miles ("a hard effort, a 5:30 pace in wet track suits and slickers--with wind and rain"); also a seven-mile race on the Sunday before Christmas ("It was cold, perhaps 36 degrees, and uphill into a headwind until the turnaround at halfway.")

The system may not emphasize mileage or long-slow-aerobic running, but clearly the essentials of endurance are there--must be there if maximal performances are to result.

---

[1]Kenny Moore, "A Hard and Supple Man," *Sports Illustrated,* June 20, 1980, p. 80.

FARTLEK

Fartlek is a system of endurance training for running which alternates strenuous and easy running over varied and interesting terrains. Both work distances and recovery times have been unmeasured. Interest in the terrain tends to pull attention away from the pains of fatigue; attitudes tend to reflect the zest of self-directed play.

Fartlek, in English, means "speed-play," which in itself is a happy contrast to our American term "workout." Play is activity for its own sake, activity in which awareness of exertion and even of oneself is lost in the action. The activity of play can be as exhausting as that of any work but the fun of playing absorbs the feelings of fatigue, if not its physical effects.

As Major Raoul Mollett (Wilt, 1959, 97) points out,

Fartlek was perhaps the most alluring discovery since the beginning of the century in the realm of training. . . . A window was opened on the forest, and at the same time an idea of training emerged which one would classify as "happy." Fartlek, with its walks, its runs at slow pace through the woods, its short sprints, was able to revolutionize the training of the track world. . . . There is without doubt not a single irreconcilable sedentary person who would not feel a twinge of nostalgia when faced with the thought of a man running barefoot on springy moss, in a setting of forests and lakes reflecting the sky. Faced with this picture, the track world felt an irresistible rise in spirits.

Fartlek is not merely an outworn training system of the past, suited only for Scandinavians. It can be made a sound modern system within which the essentials of endurance training can be effectively organized. Were this not so, fartlek would not be worth explanation here. True, its main tenet is get tired without feeling tired, on doing more work in less time without suffering the aversions of work.

HARDFARTLEK. But don't underestimate fartlek's total work output. In its own way, fartlek demands as much developmental work-rest as does any system; it must if it is to be effective. I've often thought that a better name would result by adding Gunder Haegg's concept of *hardfart*, which means hard fast running. It would then be *hardfartlek*, to make hardy with speed-play. As in interval training, fartlek increases the total amount of relatively fast running that is done by alternating recovery jogging with hardfartlek. The research of Åstrand (1970, 286) and others concludes that this permits faster-pace running with lower heart rates and related fatigue effects despite a much greater total work output. Fartlek could be defined as unsystemized interval training off the track. This opens up exciting possibilities to be discussed under "Modern Uses of Fartlek."

THE USES OF FARTLEK. Fartlek is a flexible and wide-ranging system which lends itself to a variety of needs and methods of organization. But we should be clear that fartlek requires specific purposes and precise organization as much as any system, including interval training. Fartlek is not a carefree "go-as-you-please" system as some have described it. Certainly it is not an escape from hard work. From a physical standpoint there is no more value in easy running on pine-needled paths than in easy running on a cinder track. To serve its goals, fartlek must be as physically demanding in both mileage and intensity as any system. There is no other way to development and great performance. To misunderstand this is to deny the system and follow a fool's path. Keeping all this in mind, we shall consider the various uses that past champions have made of fartlek.

GUNDER HAEGG. Though the word "fartlek" does not appear in Gunder Haegg's training diary, his methods were clearly a forerunner of the system. In the 5000-meter training course he laid out at Volodalen there were three places where he ran with bursts of energy ("*Ryck*"), four hills ("*Uppför*") including one steep hill, two bogs or marshy areas ("*Mry*") in which the footing was heavy, and at least one area of hard fast running (*Hårdfart*"). On this course and others of similar merit, Haegg trained for five years, 1940-1945. One need only read his carefully maintained training diary to understand the careful thought that went into planning the exact details of his program and the inexorable insistence upon doing what must be done whether one feels like doing it or not.

HERB ELLIOTT AND PERCY CERUTTY. Undoubtedly Cerutty's training methods were self-created out of his personal training experiences and his personal attitudes toward life. It was natural that his craving for self-sufficiency should have denied any indebtedness to others or being bound by others' systems. Actually, however, Cerutty's creed of stotanism (a union of sto-ic and spar-tan), with its insistence on hardihood and simple living was a variation of primitive camping at Volodalen, his sand dunes and surf-running a heightening of Haegg's steep hills and deep snow, his demands for repeated wild surges an outgrowth of the varying pace in competition and training by Zatopek and Kuts (Track & Field News, December, 1956, 10-12). This in no way belittles Cerutty's very important contribution to training for endurance running. It does emphasize that fartlek is inherent in his methods and attitudes. For example, this excerpt (Cerutty, 1959, 17) sounds much like the writings of Gosta Holmer,

> In his ordinary life he [man] has little chance to escape from the humdrum, the routine. Why then . . . add his exercise . . . to the list of compulsions? Athletics should be, and with me is, a prime means to escape from these imprisoning conditions to exult in our liberty, free movement, capacity to choose. Our training should be a thing of . . . enthusiasm . . . not a daily grind upon a grinding track, artificially hard. . . . How much better to run with joy, sheer beauty and strength, to race down some declivity, to battle manfully to the top of another.

Or better, here is a rather typical day for Herb Elliott at Cerutty's Camp Portsea, as described by the Australian track writer, Joe Galli,[1]

> Arrived Saturday afternoon. Elliott and two friends had just returned from a 30-mile hike over the rugged terrain, sleeping under the stars at night. A day previously Herb had run a mile in four minutes. We dived into bunks at Cerutty's headquarters and slept nine hours. At 5:00 A.M. we were up. We jogged half a mile to the beach, spent 30 minutes running along the hard sand and plunging into the surf, then back for breakfast. Soon we were off again, running over a sandy, bush track course of just over a mile with two killing climbs. I was proud to break ten minutes for the course. Herb ran it five times, never in more than 6:10. Next--weight lifting. Elliott lifted 200 pounds in the ordinary dead lift, and 125 in the press. Lunch was followed by a discussion of training. Then we tackled a giant 80-foot sandhill. One run up the hill finished me. I found it even hard to walk through its deep loose sand. Elliott scampers up as though it were a moderate grass slope.

Note that the word "fartlek" is not used here; nor is it used in any of Cerutty's writings. But the basic idea of fartlek (making hardy with speed-play) is definitely here.

TERRAINS. The essence of fartlek lies in distraction from awareness of fatigue. Part of such distraction comes from ever-changing speeds, but the major factor lies in ever-changing terrains. Choose fartlek as the core of your training program only if your locale affords at least one and preferably a number of challenging terrains. Train at racing altitude, but also at altitudes higher by a 1000 feet or more. Train in the cool woods and around cool lakes, but also under the hot sun and at high humidity. Train on the golf course or in the park. A hiking trail through the mountains or along a river might be ideal. Run under whatever conditions present a challenge: sand, mud, snow, rain, cold; what may seem a handicap can be a stimulus for developing what the Finns call "sisu," a hardiness of spirit and body that accepts no barriers.

EVALUATION OF FARTLEK

ADVANTAGES. 1. It develops self-dependent and resourceful runners. No coach is present; no measured distances exact effort; no watch forces the pace. For a mature runner, it affords freedom of self-development. He alone decides how far and fast he shall run, and when and where he shall run again.

2. It is mentally refreshing and invigorating. Its varied challenge makes work seem like play. Time-effort tend to slip away so that only after the workout is finished will the total

---

[1]Joe Galli, "Australian Report," Track & Field News, Box 296, Los Altos, Calif. 94022, February 1959, 13.

work output be realized. Runners cover more miles at greater and changing speeds; blood lactates and heart rates are lower; awareness of fatigue is less.

3. It provides a foundation of endurance for all running events from the marathon down to the 440. As Lydiard claims, rightly, for marathon training it provides the stamina by which to do more speed work when the training program calls for speed.

4. The daily training session tends to be run on a total time basis. This reduces the mental tension created by repetitions of measured distances, measured times, measured heart rates, measured recovery periods.

5. The softer running surfaces of field and woods paths result in greater relaxation of muscles and less muscle soreness.

6. The uncertain footing of open running tends to develop a shorter and more efficient stride, especially helpful in longer distance running.

7. Fartlek reduces track caretaking and the need for ever-open locker rooms. A man can roll out of bed at 6 AM, into his running togs, and out on whatever running area is near. Sometimes men spend more time travelling to a track than is spent running on it.

8. Fartlek encourages group running. That makes for more work and more fun.

WEAKNESSES. 1. The greatest strength of fartlek--free running in a low-tension situation-- is also its greatest weakness. Training must be relevant to the conditions of competition: measured distances, continuous and relatively steady pace, enurement to increasing discomfort and tension.

2. Free running means unmeasured work loads and work effects. One's training diary tends to show time and perhaps mileage of training, not much more. Comparison of performances-- today's with that of last month or year--is not measurably exact. Proof of progress is an important factor in any training system.

3. The advocates of fartlek tend to extol the glories of nature: soft pine-needled paths, sea-beaches, and the challenge of a wooded hill. But most of the runners of the world do not have such natural glories at hand. Rather, they have paved streets, reeking with exhaust fumes, concrete walks with strait-laced pedestrians who, as the Englishman Loader writes, are likely to jeer, "Mary Ann, look, it's a runner! He's got nae claes on!" But even the worst cities have cemeteries and river banks and zoos and golf courses which the determined will seek out, even though forced to do so at hours when decent folk--and the police--are indoors.

4. Group running has disadvantages as well as advantages. Beginners and those of lesser talent tend to be neglected and mis-used. They tend to do both too much and too little.

INTERVAL TRAINING

Interval training, as organized by Reindell, Roskamm and Gerschler (1962), is a training system for endurance running which alternates measured runs on a flat track at a measured pace with easy recovery jogs for a measured length of time. Precise measurement of all phases of work is essential to interval training; without it, the system becomes fartlek or some other form of fast-slow running.

Reindell and his associates centered their research on heart development. They chose the name "interval training" because the greatest stimulus for heart development occurs during the first ten seconds or so of the recovery interval. That is, the run provides the developmental challenge while the interval provides the developmental response. Immediately after completion of a run, the heart cavity is filled up suddenly, strongly, rhythmically to exert a very strong expansion stimulus on the walls of the heart.

From such findings, the German scientists drew certain important conclusions. The time for each run should not exceed 90 seconds. The intensity (distance x pace) should produce a heart rate of 170-180 during the first ten seconds of the recovery period, which should drop to about

130 within 30 seconds--and in all cases not more than 90 seconds--of the recovery period. For example, 10 x 440 @ 64 sec, alternated with 90 sec of recovery jogging. Should the pulse

Fig. 20.1 -- Ron Clarke, in 1966, held world records at seven distances from three miles through the one hour run, including a wonderful 13:25.8 for 5000 meters, and a fantastic 27:39.4 for 10,000 meters! For the most part he was self-coached and self-motivated. An Australian junior champion at 17 in 1955, a nonentity torch-bearer at the Melbourne Games, Clarke semi-retired for two years. Then, after a long training period that startled no one with either its inexorable mileage or inhuman intensity, he returned to dominate world distance running as had no one since Emil Zatopek.

at the end of 90 seconds be above 140, the pace should be slowed or the distance shortened.

It is commonly stated that there are four factors in interval training: (1) a measured distance to be run, (2) a pace that will produce a developmental heart stimulus, (3) an interval of easy jogging, and (4) the number of times the run is repeated. Depending on the precise purpose of a series of workouts, any three of these factors can be held constant while the fourth is gradually increased. Actually this is an oversimplification. In a single workout, the distance can be varied, as in one of Igloi's favorite methods (100y-200y-300y-400y-300y-200y-100y). Or the recovery interval can be varied: allow 30 seconds between efforts but 90 seconds between each set of efforts. The pace can be varied: slow the pace during the early and late efforts; increase the pace during the middle efforts when the body is most efficient. Or, other factors can be abstracted as our understanding of training becomes more clear. For example, to perform a given workout once is not enough; it should be repeated until mastery is certain. Mastery can be equated with degree of ease. A workout is truly mastered when it can be done free of physical and mental strain.

INTERMITTENT WORK. Interval training and intermittent-work training are basically the same in their repeated alternation of work and recovery. But they differ in that interval training emphasizes the number of recovery intervals--therefore many brief workloads--with their positive effects on heart development; whereas intermittent work emphasizes the stressful work period that tends to be longer--"60 seconds to five minutes" (Costill, 1979, 83). Both are anaerobic. Original researchers for interval training--Reindell, Gerschler, Roskamm--dealt primarily with heart effects; those for intermittent work--Scandinavians Christensen, Bóje, Anderson, Åstrand-- centered on oxygen uptakes out of which came the terms aerobic and anaerobic. A later section will explain intermittent work more completely.

MODERN INTERVAL TRAINING. Interval training is not a year-round, total-development program. Nor was it ever considered to be such by its originators. The training of Harbig, its first great champion, was preceded by several months of cross-country running, and during the racing season, included runs off the track. The research by Reindell and his associates was basically sound. However, it did occur within the limits of the heart-centered viewpoints these men held which had a tendency to ignore other considerations and thus to exaggerate anaerobic training, both in months of its use and the degree of its stresses.

As happens so often with every new idea or system, interval training was overused and misused by many coaches and runners who failed to understand its limitations. All too many prospective champions showed signs of overtraining, with limited energy reserves and enthusiasm for the Big Race. Most of these neglected to build a firm foundation of longer, less stressful work away from the track. Perhaps they lacked a suitable terrain. As a result, some coaches and runners today tend to reject both interval training and intermittent work.

This is a mistake. Such repeated-stress work is of great value. For example, Lasse Viren, in training for his great races at Montreal, used fartlek throughout the year with its unmeasured fast-slow alternations; intermittent work as early as February with 400-800m bursts; and interval training from June on--example, July 14, 20 x 200m average 28.8, pulse 172; after 2 minutes, 96. That is, he used his own versions of all systems--LSD work, (call it a Nurmi or Lydiard workout, as you prefer), fartlek, intermittent work and interval training. Note that the interval-training workout gave an excellent test of running condition, in some ways more informative than a trial race. The work load in distance-time was precisely measured, but also heart effects could be monitored.

THE FACTORS OF INTERVAL TRAINING
The following detailed discussion of the four factors of interval training assumes a separation of intermittent work from interval training, as explained above. The original research related to heart rates, not to oxygen uptakes. For example, for sound though arbitrary reasons, the greatest distance used--on rare occasions 500 or even 600m--is 400 meters; that is, a distance that can be covered within 90 seconds.

Important: each of these four factors has its own unique value for endurance. Full use of interval training will hold three factors constant, while using the fourth as a developmental variable that provides increments of stress.

THE DISTANCE OF EACH RUN. The word "distance" is used here as though it were a separate entity; actually, in running, such a factor is never separate from pace--is always a way of looking at distance-pace as one aspect of the workload.

The first researchers of the interval-training idea, with their focus on repeated heart effects, assumed distances of 400m or less--300m, 200m, 100m--distances that were long enough to push heart rates to near maximums (170-200 b/p/m), but short enough to allow many recovery intervals within a single workout--intervals in which heart rates dropped rapidly in the first ten seconds, then more slowly back to 120 or even lower.

As research shifts to maximal oxygen uptakes, distances tend to lengthen beyond 400 meters. But, as previously explained, the training system is now called "intermittent-work training"-- an arbitrary distinction but useful. Sebastian Coe called it "speed-endurance work"--increasing the distance over which you can run with speed, or in which you can endure speed. It's a different approach with special values and weaknesses.

The most commonly-used distance today, certainly for beginners, is 200 meters. There's no special developmental virtue in that exact distance, but as a half-lap or an eighth of a mile it is convenient. Indoors a single lap of about 160 yards, or two laps of 320 yards, would be both convenient and sound in their effects. All these distances satisfy the requirements of number of repetitions and cardiovascular development in general.

Another commonly-used distance is 400 meters. Such a distance is long enough to provide the benefits of more sustained running, with its steady rhythm and pace. If individual development is high enough, it permits many repetitions. Zatopek ran as many as 40 x 400 at about 65 seconds each. It is interesting that, at the age of 21, when Zatopek was training for the 1500 meters, he ran shorter distances. For example, 10 x 200m with 100m jog, or 2 x 100, 2 x 200, 1 x 300, 2 x 200, 2 x 100, with similar jogging distances--what has been called the funnel system.

Such a practice of increasing-decreasing the distance is consistent with Nocker's (1960, 81) conclusion that early and late efforts should be less stressful. Others argue that practice should simulate racing conditions in which stress is greatest at the end of the race. It was for this reason that Zatopek, and others, often reduced the recovery interval near the end of a day's practice, even though the pulse did not drop to the theoretically optimum 130 beats.

THE PACE OF EACH EFFORT. There are at least five criteria for judging the pace at which each effort should be run:

1. The distance of each run. As previously stated, pace cannot be separated from distance. But assuming equal pace, the greater the distance of each run, the greater the stress produced (Astrand, 1970, 382), even though the rest intervals are increased correspondingly: 3 x 400 @ 60s with 60s rest produces greater stress than 3 x 200 @ 30s with 30s rest. Ordinarily, the shorter the distance, the faster the pace, or the greater the number of repetitions.

2. Recovery heart rates. According to Reindell (1962) the intensity (distance x pace) of each effort should allow the pulse to drop to about 130 within not more than 90 seconds of the recovery interval. If the pulse is higher, the running pace should be reduced. However, he and his associates were working with older, more experienced runners. Most authorities today accept 120 b/p/m as an optimal figure.

Some workers make heart rate the criterion by which the length of the recovery interval is determined, prolonging it until the heart rate drops to 120. To count pulse rates, the athlete places his finger tips on the opposite wrist or on the carotid artery in the neck. When the count for ten seconds reaches 20, the next run can be started. Or to put it the other way, at the end of an optimal recovery interval, the heart rate should have dropped to 120.

3. Innate sprinting speed. A man with greater natural speed for sprinting can carry a given pace for a short distance with a relatively lower level of stress. Interval pace should be adjusted accordingly.

4. Competitive racing pace. Interval-training pace can be related to racing pace. A pace that is several seconds faster than racing pace not only achieves a developmental heart stress, it also develops a fast-twitch function in leg muscles so necessary for a sustained sprint at the finish.

On August 12, 1975, John Walker (NZ) set the world mile record at 3:49.4, an average 400 pace of 57.5s. Six weeks earlier, after running 8 miles steady in the morning, he completed an interval workout (PM)--8 x 300m @ 40.5 average, with a 300m jog between; fastest 300--39.8.[1] An equivalent 400m time would be 54s, 3.5s faster than racing pace. In various workouts during the preceding two months, Walker used these runs in his interval workouts--400, 300, 200, 150; on one occasion he ran 8 laps @ 69-70s, with four 50/60 yard dashes in each lap (50y sprint-- 60y float).

To use another example, British correspondent, Dave Cocksedge, gave this information to *Track & Field News*,[2]

> "Coach Harry Wilson gives him a killer session of 12 x 200m @ an average 26s, with 15-second rest intervals. This is done in three sets of four, with three minutes between each set. When he can manage this session comfortably, he knows he's ready."

The 200m average pace would be roughly three seconds under racing pace.

5. General feelings of fatigue. In interval training, the amount of work done, that is, the number of repetitions, is crucial in developing the cardiovascular and related systems (Åstrand, 1970, 382). Using this as your guide, set a pace-distance that produces relatively high feelings of fatigue at the end of the run, and relatively low feelings after a recovery interval of from 90 to 30 seconds--and which allows you to run at least six and up to about 20 repetitions. Equally important, you should no longer feel tired after about one hour following the total work- out. This method may not be technically precise, and may not be scientifically measureable in its effects, but it is both practical and sound. As training and maturity move upward, your feelings will become more objective and reliable.

THE RECOVERY INTERVAL. Though we use the adjective "recovery" to describe the time period between runs, Reindell (1962) emphasizes that, from a heart standpoint, the interval is as much a developmental period as a recovery period. During the first 30 seconds immediately following each run, the heart undergoes its greatest stress, and therefore its greatest stimulus for ex- pansion and development. Heart development can be judged in part by the greater volumes of blood delivered to the working muscles. Since maximum heart rates do not increase with train- ing, such greater blood volumes are achieved by heart hypertrophy through more complete filling and emptying of the heart cavities. Such hypertrophy is entirely normal and healthful, cer- tainly not harmful as was once implied by the term "athlete's heart."

Physical activity during intervals. Both research and practice have concluded that relaxed jogging, or at least fast walking, is most beneficial during recovery intervals. Such rhythmic movement of the large muscles has a massaging or pumping effect which ensures a full venous return of the blood to the heart. The heart can eject out to the lungs and muscle capillaries only as much blood as it receives. The full suffusion of blood to the heart cavities subsides rapidly (10-30 seconds) when the running stops. Mild activity helps to maintain it and its beneficial effects within the muscles.

For purposes of research, Gerschler asked his trainees to lie on a horizontal table immed- iately after running, with both the head and feet elevated. He found that their pulse rates

---

[1]"How They Train--John Walker," *Track Technique*, #64, June 1976, p. 2040.

[2]"Ovett: Changing Speeds," *Track & Field News*, November 1979, p. 47.

returned to normal by this method just about as quickly as they did when jogging. Gerschler followed this method while working with Gordon Pirie in June 1960, when the latter was training for the 5000-10,000-meter runs at the Rome Olympics. He found that 100 meters at three-quarters speed raised Pirie's heart rate (normal resting rate--38) to about 170, and that about 15 seconds of horizontal rest with feet and head raised brought the rate down to about 120; then, he would run again. But when Pirie was working away from Gerschler, he did the usual jogging between runs.

Length of recovery interval. From a cardio-vascular standpoint, the research of Reindell and his associates suggests an interval of less than 90 seconds. But later research (Astrand and others), based on oxygen uptakes, recommends a more flexible approach which tends to allow at least as much time for recovery as was needed for the run. For example, for the training of anaerobic power, Astrand (1970, 388) recommends alternating periods of maximal effort for 1 minute with rest periods of 4 to 5 minutes. Shorter rest periods would result in quick exhaustion and a decrease in the total work load. Even for the training of aerobic power, Astrand (1970, 391) suggests equal work and rest periods of from 3 to 5 minutes each.

On the other hand, the research of both Reindell and Åstrand (1970, 386) agrees that maximal oxygen uptakes and heart output can be attained by repeated work and rest periods of 10 to 15 seconds. Such a method can place great stress on both the muscles and the oxygen-transport systems without involving the anaerobic processes or producing high blood lactates.

The sport of swimming has adopted short-interval training as one of its most basic methods. For example, Counsilman[1] reports,

There has been a definite trend toward a shorter rest period between repeat swims when swimmers use interval training. Mike Burton, 1968 Olympic Champion for 400 and 1500-meter freestyle events, reports that one of his favorite workouts is 15 x 100 meters with 3 to 5 seconds rest between each 100. This would permit very little drop in pulse rate.

Counsilman then reports a workout by Fred Southward, National Four-Mile Champion, of 15 x 50-meter swims with 10 seconds rest, in which the mean heart rate after exertion was 185.9 and that before exertion, 180.1, an average drop of only 5.8 beats. When Fred took this same workout but with 50 seconds rest between, the work rate was 186.9; the rest rate was 149.8; difference--37.1. When emphasizing endurance, Fred kept the interval short; when speed was primary, the interval was lengthened. (Pulse rates were taken with a Gulton EKG telemeter.)

This points up the important suggestion that track coaches should keep in touch with modern trends in training for swimming. The problems are basically the same and we can learn much from them as they have learned from us. Counsilman's textbook, THE SCIENCE OF SWIMMING, contains much of value for training for running.

In summary, the length of the rest interval depends on the precise purpose of a workout. Interval training focusses on the number of times the heart is subjected to stress-recovery--any number from 6 to 60 (remember Zatopek's 60 x 400m?). Therefore, as a rule of thumb, the length of the recovery interval should be one that increases the number of repetitions within the total workout time. As another guideline, fit the time of the interval to that of the run--10s run, 10s rest; 60s run, 60s rest. Or let the heart rate be your guide--when the pulse drops to about 120, you are ready to run again.

It follows that modern interval training requires understanding of the many physiological effects of work stresses and intervals. Early users of interval training tended to follow certain very restrictive rules without understanding their special purposes. Today the rules are more permissive but, thereby, are more difficult to use properly. That is to say, modern research provides more and better information for making judgments, but this has the dual effect of making the art of good coaching more complex.

---

[1] James E. Counsilman, "Conditioning in Competitive Swimming." Paper presented at Symposium on Sports of the American Association for the Advancement of Science, Dallas, December 17, 1968.

THE NUMBER OF REPETITIONS. As a rule of thumb, the interval-training method emphasizes many repetitions; as said before, any number from 6 to 60, with 20 as a valid average figure.

The assumption here is that a sound foundation of endurance running has been laid, and that interval training is inserted into the schedule for some special purpose--speed-endurance training, speed under stress, repetitions at faster than racing pace, near-maximal sprint work; or even, as in Viren's example, to serve as a test of racing condition.

Rick Wohlhuter (1974, 880-1:44.1WR; mile-3:54.4) used intervals 3 or 4 times a week indoors, but limited pace to no-faster-than racing pace because of the danger of muscle injury on an unbanked 220 track. Since he took long runs in the morning, the number of these intervals was six or under, sometimes only two or three. When he moved outdoors, the number sometimes moved to 20 x 220 @ 29-30s with 60s rest; or 4 x 440 @ 60s with 60s rest, plus 4 x 330 @ 39s with 110 jogs, plus 4 x 220 @ 29s with 110 jogs between. The rest between sets was kept under 60s.[1]

In summary, the number of repetitions relates to workout purpose within the total context of training.

Working in sets. One way of maintaining a large number of repetitions along with a highly stressful pace is to work in sets. For example: 5 sets x (3 x 200 yards @ 7/8 speed) with 30 seconds between each 220 but 3 to 5 minutes between the sets.

MASTERY. Progressions in interval training can and should be based on the degree to which a given work load is mastered, that is, handled with full confidence and relative ease. All too often, coaches and runners feel they are ready for the next progression when they have achieved an interval workout once on the stop watch. This practice leads to a feeling of hurry and uncertainty, as well as to over-intensity of training.

Once a certain goal is achieved--say, 10 x 440 @ 70 with 90 sec rest between--it should be repeated several times during succeeding weeks, each time with greater relaxation and certainty of control. Now you have a fixed base of accomplishment from which you can move surely and safely upward to the next level. Each new level imposes more severe demands; a more gradual approach ensures that you are ready for those demands.

THE PROPER USE OF PROGRESSIONS

Traditionally, interval training has been organized by different progressions of stress factors (distance, pace, interval, etc.) within each of which there are gradual increments of stress. Study of Table 20.1 should make this clear. However, there is no necessary or even desirable

TABLE 20.1

CONSTANTS AND VARIABLES IN INTERVAL TRAINING

Method	Constant	Constant	Constant	Constant	Constant	Variable
A	Distance	Pace		Interval	Mastery	Repetitions
B	Distance	Pace	Repetitions		Mastery	Interval
C	Distance		Repetitions	Interval	Mastery	Pace
D	Distance	Pace	Repetitions	Interval		Mastery
E		Pace	Repetitions	Interval	Mastery	Distance

progression from Method A to B-C-D-E. So much depends on the inter-relationships between distance, pace, and rest interval. For example, in a study of Christensen (reported in Astrand, 1970, 383), when a subject alternated 10 sec of high-speed running with 5-sec rest intervals, he could do 120 repetitions without exhaustion and with a low blood lactate. If the rest pause was increased to 10 sec, the peak O_2 uptake was reduced from his maximum of 5.6 liters/min to 4.7 1/m. If the periods of rest and work were increased to 15 sec, the O_2 uptake was 5.3 liters/min, less than his maximum. Such knowledge is crucial in organizing progressions.

---

[1] "How They Train--Rick Wohlhuter," *Track Technique*, #58, December 1974, p. 1851.

   PROGRESSION BY NUMBER OF REPETITIONS. Having selected a fixed distance-pace-interval that meets the specific purpose of the workout--and the ability-condition of the runner--the number of repetitions is gradually increased from one workout to a later workout during the next week or so.

Examples:

Distance	Speed	Interval	Repetitions
400m	3/4th	90s	4 and progressively up to perhaps 10
300m	3/4th	60s	5 and progressively up to perhaps 10
200m	3/4th	30s	6 and progressively up to 10 or even 20
100m	3/4th	15s	10 and progressively up to perhaps 20

When the projected number of reps is reached, either the speed is increased or the interval time is decreased; reps drop back, and the cycle is repeated. The examples given can also be organized in sets. Example: 2 x (3 x 200m @ 30s) with 30s rest; allow 2-3 minutes between sets.

   PROGRESSION BY INCREASING THE PACE. The overall pattern follows that for number of repetitions, only now increasing stress is produced by gradually increasing the pace. This progression is perhaps the most developmental of all interval-training methods, for doing more work at faster-than-racing pace is a primary purpose of interval training. The number of reps is fixed arbitrarily to fit runner, distance and purpose.

   As a muscle-safety factor, do not increase pace more than 1-2 seconds faster than racing pace, but a later-season need to increase sprinting speeds (fast-twitch muscle fibers) may warrant 7/8th maximal pace.

   In an eclectic training system that emphasizes aerobic, steady paced LSD, along with an ample portion of playing at relaxed speeds (fartlek), this progression normally occurs late season, within the 4-6 week period before the Big Race. Since muscle stress is great, several days of full-recovery work should follow.

   PROGRESSION BY SHORTENING THE REST INTERVAL. Holding the other three factors constant, gradually decrease the length of the recovery interval. This is perhaps the most stressful way of developing anaerobic power. It should be used cautiously by even the more mature runners, with special emphasis on the principle of mastery discussed earlier. Move to the next level of work only when the present level can be done easily. Do not confuse this progression with the fully approved practice of using short work periods (10-15 seconds) of very fast running with rest periods of similar duration. See the discussion on short-interval training in swimming and also Åstrand (1970, 386).

   PROGRESSION BY LENGTHENING THE DISTANCE. The development of one's ability to run at slightly faster than racing pace over longer and longer distances could become the main focus of a training system, especially for shorter distances--400 to 1500 meters. Increasing distances by 50m increments from 200 to 300m would serve the needs of 400m; from 200 to 600m, the 800m; from 400 to 1000m, the 1500. As distances increase, it will be found necessary to increase the recovery interval.

INTERVAL TRAINING INTENSITIES

Lydiard very wisely warned against over-intensity of training, and devoted much time to organizing Tables of Effort by which runners could adjust their exertions to the needs of that particular day. Endurance energy is to be conserved, not merely burned up, by training.

   Interval training is inherently high-intensity training. But the principle of developmental load-rest applies here just as much, and even more than it does to marathon training. Reindell concluded that heart development occurred primarily during the recovery interval, hence the name of the system. That is, the rest period is crucial; without adequate rest, the endurance systems break down. This applies just as much to alternating days of work and rest as it does to alternating periods of work and rest in a single workout. Increments of intensity should be added gradually; that's why we train the year-round to gain time for the gradual approach.

<u>WAYS OF USING INTERVAL TRAINING.</u> One of the important assets of interval training lies in the great variety of workouts that can be devised. When I visited him at his home in Freiburg, Germany, Woldemar Gerschler made a strong point of this, and indicated how it had been carried out in the training of Harbig. He then suggested this basic approach as a guide:

1. Warm-up by jogging and repeated wind sprints to raise the heart rate to about 120.

2. Run a series of repetitions--for example, 6 x 220--at such a pace as brings the heart rate to about 170-180/min, that is, 10-15 beats below maximum rate.

3. During the recovery interval, walk or jog until the heart rate drops to 130-140. This length of time should not exceed 90 seconds; if it does, decrease the pace.

4. As physical condition improves, the number of repetitions can be increased to what is judged to be optimum, depending on the runner's maturity and condition, and on his racing distance.

5. When the number of repetitions is adequate, the time needed for recovery will gradually decrease. When this time drops down to that considered best for a given running distance-- in this example, about 30 seconds--the pace is increased to one that again requires a recovery period not exceeding 90 seconds. This sequence can be repeated several times this year and throughout the runner's years of training.

It hardly needs to be added that this approach is merely suggestive, and that Gerschler's actual methods were much more complex than this. We have related his schedule for Pirie of repeated 100-meter runs at 7/8 speed with only about 10 seconds recovery. For greater detail, see the training of Harbig in Wilt (1962, 5).

A second basic one-a-day schedule is outlined in Table 20.2. This schedule assumes that 12 x 440 @ 70s, for example, provides sufficient mileage. Beginning with the 9th week, pace is increased by 2-second increments. Obviously, these schedules are for beginners. They can be stepped up by adding miles of jogging either on or off the track, both before and after the main work, by increasing pace to higher levels of stress, by adding 10 x 100 yards of relaxation sprinting at the start and end of the workout, and other such methods. No man would be likely to follow this schedule exactly. It suggests trends, not actual workouts.

<u>BOB SCHUL, 1964 OLYMPIC 5000-METER CHAMPION.</u> Taken from diary kept by Mihaly Igloi.

AM--1200-meter warm-up run; 32 x 100m with 100m jog recoveries, some runs with finishing burst.
PM--4000-meter warm-up run; 15 x 100m relaxation runs; 3/4 mile in 3:00.9, 800m recovery jog;
    10 x 400m--average time, 62.3, with 200m recovery jogs between each, 400m jog; 16 x 150m
    fast sprints with 50m recovery jogs; 10 x 100m relaxation runs.

Note the long warm-up, with many relaxation runs at both the beginning and the end of the workout. These were an important part of Igloi's training. Igloi also made frequent use of the funnel system, as illustrated in the workouts by Jim Ryun under Coach Timmons.

<u>JIM RYUN'S TRAINING.</u> One of the most rewarding studies of interval training methods is Coach Timmon'[1] diary of Jim Ryun's training during the 12 weeks prior to his world-record performances in the mile and 880. The total mileage by weeks was 105 - 30 - 85 - 90 - 44 - 45 - 105 - 45 - 49 - 69 - 42. Workouts were 2-a-day, 7 days a week. Much cross-country work was done. The most outstanding feature of Ryun's training, other than quantity of work, was its variety, especially in the use of interval training methods. No two days were the same. The main workout could be in the morning or afternoon. Intervals were often of the funnel type advocated by Igloi. All interval distances were 440y or less; the shortest was 80y.

<u>Monday, May 2,</u> 12 weeks prior to running 3:51.3:

AM--jog mile; 16 x 100 with 100 jog; jog mile

---

[1] Bob Timmons, "Jim Ryun--How He Trains," *Track Technique*, 31, March, 1968, 963.

TABLE 20.2.

Examples of Development in Interval Training

About two months of conditioning in cross-country and fartlek are assumed.
Most sessions are preceded by 20-30 minutes of warm-up.

Weeks of Training

	1st	3rd	5th	7th
Mon.	Fartlek	3 x 3/4 @ 3:30	8 x 440 @ 70s	Fartlek
Tues.	3 x 880 @ 2:20	Fartlek	Fartlek	12 x 440 @ 70s
Wed.	Fartlek	6 x 440 @ 70s	10 x 440 @ 70s	Fartlek
Thurs.	6 x 440 @ 70s	4 x 880 @ 2:20	4 x 880 @ 2:20	6 x 880 @ 2:20
Fri.	2 x 3/4 @ 3:30	Fartlek	3 x 3/4 @ 3:30	8 x 440 @ 70s
Sat.	6-8x440 @ 70s	8 x 440 @ 70s	Fartlek	4 x 3/4 @ 3:30
Sun.	Rest	Easy Fartlek	Rest	Fartlek

	9th	13th	17th
Mon.	12x440 @ 68s	12x440 @ 66	12x440 @ 64
Tues.	4 x 880 @ 2:20	4 x 880 @ 2:15	4 x 880 @ 2:12
Wed.	12x440 @ 68s	3 x 4/4 @ 4:40	3 x 4/4 @ 4:35
Thurs.	Fartlek	Easy Fartlek	12x440 @ 64
Fri.	4 x 3/4 @ 3:28	12x440 @ 66	Fartlek
Sat.	Rest	6 x 330 @ 45s	6 x 330 @ 42s
Sun.	Fartlek	Fartlek	Fartlek

PM--warm-up; 6 x 150 @ :17, jog 150--jog 440--4 x 220 @ :26, jog 220--jog 440--2 x 330 @ :41.5, walk 110--jog 440--1 x 440 @ :56, jog 440--2 x 220 @ :26, jog 220--jog 440--6 x 150 @ :17, jog 150--warm down--followed by about ½ hour of light-weight training.

Friday, July 8, one week prior to running 3:51.3:

AM--warm-up; 4 x 440 (61-59.5-57.3-56) jog 220 between--jog 440--4 x 330 (41-41-41-42.5) walk 110--jog 440--4 x 220 (25.5-25.5-26-25) jog 220--jog 440--4 x 150, jog 150--jog 440-- 4 x 80, jog 80; warm down.

PM--cross-country, 5 miles.

These interval methods can be contrasted with those that occurred during the first week of the outdoor season of Ryun's junior year (age - 17):

AM--3 miles continuous running

PM--10 x 440 @ 71--interval of 3 min included 71-sec run--dumbbell work between sets; 10 x 440 @ 69--70# weights between sets; 10 x 440 @ 69--33# weights; 10 x 440 @ 67. Total--40 x 440 = 10 miles.

RALPH DOUBELL,[1] 1968 OLYMPIC 800-meter champion--1:44.3. Trained by Franz Stampfl, advisory coach to Roger Bannister.

A typical weekly schedule for Doubell would include 2 or 3 miles of jogging each morning. Afternoon sessions: All begin with 3 miles warm-up, then Monday, 20 x 440y; Tuesday, 30 x 220y; Wednesday, 10 x 880y; Thursday, 50 x 100y; Friday, rest; Saturday and Sunday, competition or time trials. The 30 x 220 series, for example, would be at 26-27 sec each, with a minute

---

[1] "Ralph Doubell--Assured Champion," *Track Technique*, 40, June, 1970, p. 1281.

or so between runs. In addition, there were 2-3 half-hour sessions weekly of weight training.

LONGER VERSUS SHORTER PERIODS OF WORK-REST. Tradition tends to advocate shorter and more intense work periods in late-season training. However, a strong case can be made for long intermittent-work periods closer to the event distance, so as to simulate the continuous running of competition. In such case, the interval should be long enough to ensure full recovery (Åstrand, 1970, 387). Sebastian Coe's training made use of this method.

THE VALUES OF INTERVAL TRAINING

Any sound evaluation of interval training must keep clearly in mind its intended use, not merely its misuse by those who have never taken time to study it. Certainly its creators, Gerschler and Reindell, never intended it to serve as a year-round, total program of running (Wilt, 1964, 229). Their greatest champions always engaged in several months of off-the-track running prior to the interval-training period. Again and again they have spoken out against the fanatic zeal toward ever-greater intensities of work. Such goals tend to destroy both physical and mental energies, not develop them.

In summary, the following values can be claimed for interval training when used intelligently:

1. By reason of the endless variety of its increasing challenges, interval training is interesting, satisfying, even enjoyable at times. Motivation is a built-in essential; ignore motivation and the system deteriorates.

2. It repeats measured dosages of stress-recovery many times in a single workout. In developing endurance, the number of times of stress is important, as well as the kind and degree of stress. In steady running, the condition of stress-recovery occurs but once.

3. Each stress-recovery period is a strong stimulus for development of the heart stroke-volume and allied effects. (Stroke volume = heart output ÷ heart beats).

4. At each stage of a workout, the heart effects of the work load can be accurately recorded, and the work adjusted accordingly. Heart rates can be taken by "feeling," by manually touching the wrist or carotid artery, by modern telemetering devices,[1] or by the heart-rate meters that are certain to be developed in the near future.

5. More high-quality work can be done. When the running pace is faster, the total work done is greater if periods of work and rest are alternated (Åstrand, 1970, 382).

6. More work is done with less awareness of fatigue (Åstrand, 1970, 287). Lower heart rates and related fatigue effects, the distraction of repeated changes in work-rest, awareness that this run-effort will soon be over, attention on the stopwatch--all combine to take awareness away from the discomforts of fatigue. Discomfort-pain-agony may still be there, but at a lesser level of awareness.

7. Interval training, properly used, tends to increase aerobic power and heart stroke-volume in a shorter training time than can other methods. Precise dosages of work provide an optimal stimulus for this particular runner. Other systems tend to use shotgun methods; interval training uses a scope rifle.

8. It is goal oriented. Each year, each season, each phase of training, each workout, each work effort--all have goals that can be clearly stated and accurately measured.

9. Its methods are so varied and flexible that each coach and each runner can have a personal approach to training. Apart from the physiological advantages, this gives a feeling of special personal meaning; I'm training my way. This adds zest to what might otherwise be only zeal.

---

[1] Kenneth D. Rose, M.D., "Telemeter Electrocardiography," USTCA *Quarterly Review*, February, 1965, 12.

THE WEAKNESSES OF INTERVAL TRAINING.

1. The main weakness of interval training lies in its greatest strength--in the fact that its work is necessarily discontinuous, in contrast to the relatively steady-pace, continuous stress of competitive racing. Mastery of discontinuous work does not ensure mastery of continuous work.

2. Interval training enthusiasts tend to concentrate on intensities of anaerobic running, before laying a firm foundation of aerobic running. Astrand's statement (1970, 389) is of crucial importance, "There is no evidence to support the assumption that it is of importance to engage the anaerobic processes to any extreme degree in order to train the aerobic power." Note: this weakness has a lesser application to training for the short-fast races from 220 yards to the mile.

3. Interval training, by its lowered fatigue, both physical and mental, deceives men into attempting too much, too fast, too soon. Even if we ignore possible dangers to the vital organs, muscles and tendons are strained and careers interrupted. Major Raoul Mollet (see Wilt, 1959, 97), in an excellent summary of endurance training systems, praised interval training highly, but also warned,

No doubt there will be more and more victims of the method, socially as well as physiologically, for such a way of life has great risks. For every experienced athlete, carefully observed and examined, aided in his training by blood analyses, electrocardiograms, etc., how many other athletes are there, dazzled by the thought of emulation and the spirit of imitation, but deprived of medical advantages and other paraphernalia of champions, who will suffer grave damage to their health?

4. Interval training is heart-centered. That is, its creators and users assume that the heart, as the most vital organ, is a sufficient criterion of training effects. But it is a person-situation that runs; the more a training program is founded in and simulates the whole person and the whole competitive situation, the more valid it becomes. No matter how vital the part, it is never a full substitute for the whole.

5. Interval training is monotonous in its terrain--a flat track. As practiced traditionally, it allows none of the varied and fatigue-distracting terrains so essential to fartlek, marathon training, and the like.

6. Interval training emphasizes analysis, and thereby awareness of all aspects of training. The runner is aware of each short run, its effort and possible failure in time; of the beating of his heart while running and during the interval; of the number of efforts still to be made; of the ever-present demanding coach; all of which taken day after day after day, tends to multiply tensions and fatigue. Fatigue lies in feeling as much as in physical impairment; there are few ways of avoiding the adamant demands of interval training.

7. In summary of these weaknesses, Toni Nett (see Wilt, 1964, 229), astute reporter of so many aspects of the track world, wrote,

Today interval training is no longer . . . the all-important and 'only' training method. It is one of many methods but it will continue to be used. . . . Today we use interval training for special purposes. For example, there is no better way than interval training to enlarge the heart in the shortest possible time, but this has its weaknesses too-- 'easy come, easy go.' The effect is not as stable as the enlarging processes of the heart by means of long-distance running.

DANGERS IN INTERVAL TRAINING

The basic assumption of this discussion is that the normal, healthy heart is immune to impairment from the stresses of cardiovascular training, but there are two reservations. First, we can never have absolute assurance that any given heart is completely normal and healthy. Weaknesses can be minutely specific and present in an otherwise highly functional organ. Also, infection or disease may produce weaknesses not previously present.

Second, excessive intensities of training without concern for immaturity or lack of condition have caused both scientists and coaches to withhold full approval. For example, Reindell, one of its founders, is quoted by Toni Nett (see Wilt, 1964, 200), "Interval training shows itself more and more to be a powerful means of stimulating the heart. It is therefore pure nonsense when I hear that some runners nowadays will do 50 to 100 x 100-meter runs in their interval training." Nett continues, "Anything in this world can be overdone; even this method of interval training, so beneficially effective in the development of running performance, can cause harm when used recklessly."

One hardly needs the research of Hans Selye (1956) to prove that adaptation energy is limited. In every field of human exertion: mountain climbing, starvation, cold, heart-humidity, fear of danger, there are limits of tolerance. Endurance running is no exception. Reckless efforts to do more and more high-intensity work can cause retrogression, and certainly will not produce highest-level performance.

In his discussions and reports of research related to anaerobic training, Astrand (1970, 391) is primarily concerned about the psychological stresses of such intensive work. But he does suggest a lowered developmental effect from extremely strenuous work (1970, 389). The cardiac output (stroke volume) is greatest when the workload produces maximum oxygen uptakes. As work stress increases, these values tend to diminish.

Lydiard[1] reports that East German research indicates that extremely heavy and prolonged interval work lowers the pH of the blood "even as low as 6.89 to 6.9." He states that this can upset the body metabolism.[2]

> For instance, we know that vitamins don't function properly in a low blood pH. So athletes are eating good food and not getting true value from it. We also understand that a low blood pH will upset the recovery rate of an athlete by interfering with enzyme functions. So our athletes aren't recovering as quickly. We also know that a low pH upsets the central nervous system. I think years ago we used to say he got stale. He was nervy, hard to live with, couldn't sleep. . . . We also know that low blood pH upsets neuromuscular coordinations. . . . And these are some of the reasons why I eliminate as much as possible the anaerobic training from the conditioning period.

But Lydiard states repeatedly that "I am not a physiologist." Obviously more research needs to be done on the problem.

---

[1]Arthur Lydiard, *ibid.*, 1971, 16.

[2]Herbert A. de Vries (1966, 131) states, "the extreme fluctuations of the pH of normal blood lie within pH values of 7.30 to 7.50. The extreme values in illness have been known to go as low as 6.95 and as high as 7.80."

THE LYDIARD SYSTEM OF ENDURANCE TRAINING

A careful analysis of the Arthur Lydiard[1] system of training for endurance running discloses a thoughtful and shrewd selection and balance of most of the essentials of training we have listed in this book. Among these important points of emphasis are the following:

1. Marathon training, the core of Lydiard's system, includes at least five basic endurance procedures: time running, cross-country, marathon training, road running, and speed-hill training. All but the last is at less than maximal steady state, but it is never slow running.

2. Zest in training should balance zeal.

3. On a year-round work schedule, aerobic/anaerobic training should be in a ratio of about 9/2. Usually sharpening for a Big Race can occur within about four weeks.

4. The development of steady-state endurance over long distances best ensures a solid foundation for sustained speed over shorter racing distances.

5. Planning of training and competitive schedules should be in terms of a runner's entire career--ten years or even more--not for just this one year, or for 3-4 school years.

6. Training stress as between work-rest should rise and fall from day to day, period to period, month to month. That development occurs during active-rest as during stressful work is as valid for marathon as for interval training.

7. Variety in all phases of training and competition is essential--variety of terains, of kinds of running, of kinds of running stress, and so much more.

8. A year's program should be pointed toward a few Big Races, for which all others are developmental.

9. Racing, especially over shorter distances, puts a premium on sustained maximal speed at the finish. The developmental of such sustained speed requires related speed-endurance training.

10. Prior to the Big Race, the conservation of endurance energy is a primary concern.

---

[1]This entire discussion is paraphrased from three sources:

Arthur Lydiard and Garth Gilmour, RUN TO THE TOP, London: Herbert Jenkins Ltd., 1962, 182 pages, hard cover.

Arthur Lydiard, "Arthur Lydiard's Running Training Schedules," Track and Field News, Box 296, Los Altos, California, 94022, 25 pages, 1970, paperback.

Arthur Lydiard, "Marathon Training," USTCA Quarterly Review, Vol. 70, No. 4, Feb. 1971, 9-29.

THE YEAR'S TRAINING SCHEDULE

Lydiard considered variety to be a crucial consideration in all aspects of training and competition: variety of terrains, of speeds, of challenges, of degrees of stress. He therefore developed, not two or three kinds of experience, as in our American system, but nine or ten kinds of running.

TIME RUNNING (For beginning runners). Begin by running steadily for a length of time that can be handled easily. Neither mileage nor pace are important. Gradually increase this time until you can run steadily and without severe stress for two hours.

CROSS-COUNTRY. Lydiard divides cross-country into two six-week periods. The first period includes time running and, later, mileage running up to 100 miles per week. The second period includes faster (what Lydiard calls "sharpening") running and time trials of various distances, paces and efforts. Competition should be delayed until needed as a developmental and motivational device. If a man is well prepared, competition is both fun and an aid to development; if not, it can be deadly.

THE GIST OF LYDIARD'S TRAINING SYSTEM

		New Zealand Time Schedule		Adapted to American Time Schedule	
Weeks	Date	Program		Date	Program
0	Mar. 26	Training-off period (3-4 weeks)		June 2	Training-off period (3-4 weeks)
4	Apr. 24	Cross-country (12-14 weeks) Time running Mileage running Marathon training		June 30 July 20 Aug. 15	Time running Mileage running Marathon training
				Sept. 10	Cross-country training
16	July 17	Cross-country BIG RACE		Nov. 15	Cross-country BIG RACE
17	July 19	Road-racing Road relay-racing (6-8 weeks)		Nov. 17 Dec. 15	Marathon training Speed hill-training
24	Sept. 15	Marathon training (8-10 weeks)		Feb. 1	Indoor track season
32	Nov. 10	Speed hill-training		Mar. 10	Indoor BIG RACE
40	Jan. 1	Track season (10-12 weeks) Repetition training Interval training Trials: over-and under-distance Development races		Mar. 12 Apr. 1 Apr. 20	Marathon training Speed hill-training Outdoor track season Interval training Repetition training Development races
52	Mar. 25	Outdoor BIG RACE		June 1	Outdoor BIG RACE

Note: Actual dates vary greatly; those given are merely suggestive.
The various types of training actually blend into one another and cannot be separated sharply as this Table seems to imply.

For explanation of the terms in this Table, see related article headings.

CROSS-COUNTRY RACING SCHEDULE (12 weeks). Train and compete on all kinds of surfaces and under all weather conditions. Alternate steady-pace running one day with repeated speed work at shorter distances the next, with the tempo of each gradually increased throughout the 12 weeks. As examples:

	First Week		Eighth Week
Mon:	15 miles (¼ effort)	Mon:	12 x 220 (½ effort)
Tues:	880 (¼ effort) mile (¼ effort) 880 (¼ effort)	Tues: Wed:	Six-mile time trial Three miles of 50-yard dashes

	First Week
Wed:	10 miles (½ effort)
Thur:	Mile (¼ effort)
	Mile (3/4 effort)
	3 x 100 (3/4 effort)
Fri:	6 x 220 (½ effort)
Sat:	Competition
Sun:	Jog 20 miles

	Eighth Week
Thur:	Three-mile time trial
Fri:	3 x 220 (full effort)
Sat:	Three-mile race
Sun:	Jog 20 miles

During the eighth week of this 12-week training schedule, Lydiard has placed two time-trials and one competition--a large number. But he interprets trials, as well as races, in terms of degree of effort, self-control, and improvement, NOT of all-out performance. In fact, he strongly holds back the latter until the few BIG RACES on which the entire year's program is based. On all other occasions, the man runs well within himself. He does his "best," but within the limits of control and of doing even better next week and next month.

MARATHON TRAINING. Lydiard states that 100 miles a week of marathon running is the key to his training system. On a basis of seven days each week, this averages 14 miles per day--or better, provides three days of 20 miles each, and four days of 10 miles each. If the 20-mile run is exhausting, an easier and shorter run the next day or even for two days, allows complete recovery before another strenuous run. In addition, for both physical and mental reasons, Lydiard varies his terrains and varies the degree of effort that goes into each run. Lydiard states that this marathon training is continued until 18 weeks before the first important track race, but in actual practice, the interval is sometimes less than this. On one occasion, Peter Snell broke the world-record for the half-mile less than six weeks after competing in a marathon race! Lydiard suggests this marathon schedule as having the necessary balance of essentials:

Monday: 10 miles (½ effort)--hilly course.
Tuesday: 15 miles (¼ effort)--easy undulating course.
Wednesday: 12 miles fartlek.
Thursday: 18 miles (¼ effort)--easy course.
Friday: 10 miles fast (3/4 effort)--flat course.
Saturday: 23-30 miles (¼ effort)--easy course.
Sunday: 15 miles (¼ effort)--easy course.

In his talk before the United States Track Coaches Association, January 1970, Lydiard stated that "my distance runners were actually running from up to 200-250 miles a week," counting all jogging and other easy running. He emphasized that the 100-miles-a-week was all "running just under the maximum steady state. It was hard, strong running. The pressure was always on; it was never slow running." He was referring to such men as Halberg, Snell and Magee whose ages were 26, 22, and 25 respectively, and who had a gradual build-up in stamina.

ROAD RACING. Lydiard undoubtedly adopted road running and racing because it was already well established in New Zealand. But he also argues its values as being a logical extension of the fence-climbing, changing terrain, and changing pace of cross-country. Road racing requires steady-pace running on firm surfaces. The races are strenuous, so that training is light and pleasant. Training should still be over all kinds of surfaces in order to maintain the flexible toughness of muscle and tendons gained in cross-country. But since Lydiard recommends the same training during this period that is followed for a two-mile track schedule, we can assume that the lack of this kind of program in our American system is not a critical loss.

SPEED-HILL TRAINING. This is the most strenuous part of Lydiard's entire year's program of training. He assigns about six weeks to it as compared with about ten weeks for marathon training and about 12 weeks for cross-country. A fairly steep hill (a one-in-three gradient is considered best) is found that is about one-half mile long. After a two-mile warm-up jog, the runner springs up this hill on his toes, exaggerating his knee lift. Lydiard emphasizes the springing action rather than speed of running. After about one-half mile of jogging, the man now sprints down hill, with full but relaxed strides. At the bottom he does repeated fast work: perhaps 3 x 220, then 6 x 50 on alternating runs. These are gradually increased in number and speed as condition improves. Each of these efforts totals about two miles of running; the four repetitions that Lydiard recommends, plus the preliminary jogging and warming-down afterwards, would total more than ten miles each day.

Lydiard cautions that this work must be done carefully and with just the right amount of emphasis on each phase, as this will affect later stages of the training program. He found that about one hour of this kind of springing up hill is enough. His experiments with longer periods brought diminishing and even negative returns.

TRACK TRAINING. Lydiard believes strongly in planning both competition and training. The relative importance of races must be clearly and adamantly established, and all phases of training, mental and physical, must build precisely toward the BIG RACES. He is highly critical of shot-gun systems that hope to be in shape for the BIG race by being in shape for all the races, as well as of the "peaking" systems that work at minimum levels, then by intensive work, bring the runner quickly and briefly to a peak performance--as was done so well by Roger Bannister. He therefore divides his track training into two periods of six weeks each.

First track-training period. The first period includes speed work but it is geared down to what the runner can handle easily and thus reserves the more-sharpening, faster runs for the later and more important period. Typical of these workouts are:

(a) over-distance at a steady, easy pace,
(b) under-distance at a faster but controlled pace,
(c) the actual racing distance but at a deliberately slower-than-racing pace,
(d) steady runs at from two to six miles,
(e) repetition running over distances between 220 yards to 880 yards,
(f) 15 or 20 x 440 yards,
(g) Two or three miles of alternating 50 yard dashes with 60 yards of recovery striding.

Second track-training period. The second six-week period continues the balance between repeated speed running and steady-pace running. Speed work is now "all-out" although even here Lydiard pushes or restrains according to how the boy seems to react. To the over-and under-distance work of the first six weeks, he adds time-trials. These trials do not attempt to see how fast the runner can cover a certain distance; rather they build on the experience of the first six weeks and provide a certainty of future improvement in time as well as of control over tension and fatigue. Improvement is planned so as to continue evenly from trial to trial. Lydiard thinks it is necessary to race twice a week during this last period, but these are mostly under- and over-distance races, so that effort and attitude is focussed strongly upon the BIG RACE coming later. One becomes racing fit by running races, not just by running.

THE BIG RACE. Before each crucial race--the one that has been planned for a full year ahead--Lydiard uses a full ten days for conserving energy. His men run every day, of course, but within easy effort. Steady-pace work, rather than repeated fast work, is best. If the year's schedule has been well planned, not even psychological conditioning should be a concern--though of course with some men it always is.

TRAINING-OFF PERIOD. Lydiard's "training-off" period is comparable to the "active-rest" of the Russian programs. The running continues but at an easier and more enjoyable level. He suggests, for example, 45 to 60 minutes each day of light jogging over varied surfaces PLUS,

Fig. 20.2. Peter Snell, 1960 Olympic 800-meter champion - 1:46.3, and 1964 Olympic champion in the 1500-meters - 3:38.1 and the 800-meters - 1:45.1. Despite his rather heavy musculature, Snell thrived on marathon training. At the age of 25, after about six years of strenuous training, he logged a total of 1012 miles over a ten-week period, his greatest total distance ever. He approached this distance build-up gradually and carefully, avoiding all speed running to avoid the leg injuries to which he was prone. He seldom ran two hard sessions on consecutive days.

once a week, a long run of 20 miles easy. Certainly, for Lydiard, running is a Way of life with a capital "W!" There's no other way to running supremacy!

SAMPLE 880 SCHEDULE

	First Week	Tenth Week
Mon:	Mile ($\frac{1}{2}$ effort) 6 starts at 30 yards	660 (3/4)
Tues:	6 x 880 ($\frac{1}{4}$ effort) 2 x 100 (3/4 effort)	880 time trials (improve without strain) 4 starts at 50 yards
Wed:	Competitive sprint 2 or 3 x 300 yards	4 x 440 at 880 racing speed 2 x 440 (full effort)
Thurs:	$\frac{1}{2}$ mile of repeated 50's 6 x 300 striding 1 x 200 (7/8 effort)	2 miles of repeated 50-yd. dashes 3 starts at 50 yards
Fri:	2 miles ($\frac{1}{2}$ effort)	6 x 220 ($\frac{1}{2}$ effort)
Sat:	6 starts at 50 yards 6 x 300 striding 1 x 300 full effort	Compete 880 yards
Sun:	Jog 10-14 miles	Long jog

SAMPLE MILE SCHEDULE

	First Week	Tenth Week
Mon:	Two miles ($\frac{1}{4}$ effort)	Mile of rep. 50's: 3 x 100 (full effort)
Tues:	4 x 880 ($\frac{1}{4}$ effort)	Mile time trial (improvement only)
Wed:	12 x 300 striding 1 x 880 ($\frac{1}{2}$ effort)	6 miles, sprint 100 yds. in each 440
Thur:	6 miles ($\frac{1}{4}$ effort)	Mile time trial (improve)
Fri:	6 x 440 ($\frac{1}{4}$ effort)	3 x 220 (full effort)
Sat:	One mile ($\frac{1}{4}$ effort) One mile ($\frac{1}{2}$ effort)	Mile competition
Sun:	Jog 15-20 miles	Jog over 20 miles

SAMPLE TWO-MILE SCHEDULE

	First Week	Tenth Week
Mon:	Two miles ($\frac{1}{4}$ effort)	15 x 200 ($\frac{1}{4}$ effort)
Tues:	10 x 300 ($\frac{1}{4}$ effort) 2 x 100 (3/4 effort)	2 mile time trial (improve)
Wed:	One mile ($\frac{1}{2}$ effort) 6 starts at 50	880-yard competition
Thur:	One mile ($\frac{1}{4}$ effort) 2 x 880 ($\frac{1}{2}$ effort)	2 miles of rep. 50-yd dashes
Fri:	6 x 200 ($\frac{1}{4}$ effort)	3 x 220 (full effort)
Sat:	3/4 mile ($\frac{1}{2}$ effort)	Jog 20 miles or more
Sun:	Jog 15-20 miles	

SAMPLE SIX-MILE SCHEDULE

	First Week	Tenth Week
Mon:	Two miles ($\frac{1}{4}$ effort)	One mile of 50-yd. dashes 3 x 100 (full effort) 3-mile time-trial (improve)
Tues:	4 x 880 ($\frac{1}{4}$ effort)	6 miles, 100-yd sprint in each 440
Wed:	12 x 300 striding 1 x 880 ($\frac{1}{2}$ effort)	
Thur:	6 miles ($\frac{1}{4}$ effort)	6-mile time trial
Fri:	6 x 440 ($\frac{1}{4}$ effort)	6 x 220 (3/4 effort)
Sat:	One mile ($\frac{1}{4}$ effort) One mile ($\frac{1}{2}$ effort)	Jog 20 or more miles
Sun:	Jog 15-20 miles	

Note: first week schedule for one mile and six miles is the same.

TABLES OF EFFORT

Graded effort, from the standpoint of both mental and physical stress, is a crucial part of the Lydiard system; another example of his studied attempt to achieve the freedom from tension which is so vital a part of Swedish "fartlek." In his book (1962, 87ff), he presents full tables of effort for each event from 220 yards to six miles. For the mile run, for example, he gives equivalent times for all best average times from 3 minutes 55 seconds to 5 minutes 30 seconds. The following incomplete tables indicate the method:

	880					One Mile		
Average Best Time	Effort 3/4	1/2	1/4		Average Best Time	Effort 3/4	1/2	1/4
1:52	1:58	2:03	2:08		4:15	4:21	4:28	4:38
1:55	2:01	2:06	2:11		4:20	4:26	4:33	4:44
1:58	2:04	2:09	2:14		4:25	4:31	4:38	4:50
2:01	2:07	2:12	2:17		4:30	4:36	4:43	4:56
2:04	2:10	2:15	2:20		4:35	4:41	4:48	5:02
2:07	2:13	2:18	2:23		4:40	4:46	4:53	5:08
2:10	2:16	2:21	2:26		4:45	4:51	4:58	5:14

TIME TRIALS

By "time trial" Lydiard does not mean to run a certain distance for best possible time. Rather he means a preparatory trial or rehearsal by which (1) the athlete can assess his weaknesses and so plan his future training, (2) he can accustom the body-mind to steady, hard running at an overload pace, which may be less than the projected racing pace, and (3) he can develop his courage and self-confidence. Successive trials should produce progressively better performance in which the time is but one factor.

OTHER IMPORTANT PROCEDURES

WEIGHT TRAINING. "I never allow my runners to use weights." (1971[1], 20)

AEROBIC-ANAEROBIC TRAINING. Develop aerobic power first and completely. "I never went on to another stage of training until I had developed the (aerobic) cardiac system first. . . . I never mix aerobic and anaerobic training." (1971[1], 10)

WEAKNESSES. "I was very careful to try to find the weaknesses of each athlete and through exercise evaluation, I would try to strengthen these weaknesses." (1971[1], 10)

STAMINA TO SUSTAIN SPEED OVER THE DISTANCE. "I used to try to get my athletes running a little slower in training rather than a little faster. . . . We would encourage him . . . to run aerobically as far as he could, not as fast as he could." (1971[1], 15). Running faster means a lesser total workload.

A HIGHER MAXIMUM STEADY STATE. Lydiard tried to increase maximum oxygen uptakes; that is, he gradually tried to raise the pace level at which a steady state could be maintained. (1971[1], 14).

ONE-A-DAY TRAINING. "We gained better results if an athlete ran two hours continuously than if he ran an hour in the morning and an hour in the evening." (1971[1], 13)

SPECIFICITY OF TRAINING. The athlete (body-mind) learns both basically and specifically what he does (1971[1], 24)

DEVELOPING SPRINTING ABILITY. Power for sprinting is developed by sprinting against resistance, either the resistance inherent in maximal speed work on the flat, or in such work as springing up hills. In doing the first, we use "typical American sprint training workouts."

---

[1]Arthur Lydiard, "Marathon Training," USTCA *Quarterly Review*, Vol. 70, No. 4, February 1971, 9-28.

The second has been explained under the head, "Speed-hill Training."

SHARPENING. Lydiard interprets the word "sharpening" as final preparation for important competition. The crucial question is "what does he need for this particular race." It does not necessarily mean either speed work or anaerobic work. Building absolute confidence is essential. Under-distance races may help the man who lags at the start of a race; over-distance races, the man who feels he lacks staying power. In summary, analyze weaknesses and strengthen them.

PEAK FITNESS. "Once you get a man to peak fitness, there is no more need for hard training. . . . It is hard racing that we want and very, very light training." (1971[1], 27)

SHOES. "I was a shoemaker and I got the shoes in good condition. I realized that the half inch or so of rubber under their feet was very, very important. . . . The skin underneath my foot is very soft because I always used well fitted shoes." (1971[1], 18)

EVALUATION: STRENGTHS

We have already emphasized the great strength of Lydiard's system that lies in its precisely balanced emphasis upon such related but contrasting factors as stamina and speed, and need not repeat it here. He claims that marathon training is the key to his system, in the sense that such "marathon" stamina provides a sound foundation for an even greater emphasis on speed than other systems can provide.

A second great strength of the Lydiard system lies in its variety. For example, it insists upon a variety of terrains--and by terrains we mean not only hills and woods paths and running tracks, but also deliberately selected mud and slush, soft sand, fences and stone walls, paved roads, uneven bush country--all for the purpose of establishing a wide and firm foundation of running fitness. On these varied running surfaces, Lydiard planned a variety of training methods: cross-country, road racing, marathon running, speed hill-training, and when he finally got on the flat running track, many of the devices of modern interval training and even of the old American over-and-under-distance training with its repeated time trials. I have often criticized the latter because of its over-emphasis upon all-out performance in each trial. Lydiard answers this by insisting upon planned increments of improvement: run what you can today, while being certain that you'll be able to improve upon it next week and six weeks from now. He even has gone so far as to provide detailed tables of effort on a time basis, as we have already described.

Another great advantage held by Lydiard does not lie so much within his system as in his location in New Zealand where he has almost complete freedom to fix his competitive schedule so as to further the development of the individual runner. He can decide what races a boy should enter so as to best prepare him for his BIG races of the year, regardless of the team situation. Competition, which we tend to rate as all-important, can be considered a motivator for training. In New Zealand, Lydiard can organize about eight months of training in which competition is secondary. In contrast, in the United States school program, there are about seven months in which team competition is crucial; individual development through daily training must often be a lesser concern.

This relative freedom meant that Lydiard could start beginning runners from where they were. They could then progress *gradually*--what a sound word that is!--*gradually* through the various steps of Lydiard's plan: through time training, mileage training, cross-country, road racing, and all the rest. Each new level could be attempted when the preceding level had been, not merely tried, but mastered to the point of certainty of control and ease of action.

This freedom from the burden of winning-them-all, which I have attributed to New Zealand, should also be credited to Lydiard's insistence upon first things first, then second things, then third--and so on. He is adamant in looking ahead twelve and fifteen months to THE BIG RACES and in planning the year's program in terms of them. Even more, he insists upon planning an entire career. For example, he wrote (1962, 29),

---

[1]*Ibid.*

So in 1953 I started these two nineteen-year-olds (Halberg and Magee) off together, although I still eased back on the work I gave Halberg because I still did not consider him strong enough for the full treatment. It was in the 1953 cross-country season--late in the year--before I finally got to work on him. In July that year I predicted publicly that Halberg would be the greatest middle-distance runner New Zealand had known and that he would start cracking world records at twenty-seven-- the year he actually won his Olympic title. . . .

EVALUATION: WEAKNESSES

As it is used in New Zealand, it is difficult to suggest important weaknesses in the Lydiard system. Unfortunately, it does present difficulties in its application to the American school-college program. Coaches are under pressure to win team victories, and such an emphasis is often opposed to individual development. School boys tend to judge their coach and his system-- as well as their personal success--on the basis of immediate results this year, this month, and even this week, rather than on gradual development toward some greater but doubtful goal far over the horizon and some ten years away.

Lydiard's system uses about six months of training with only minor competition prior to the track season; we now use only a few weeks. His system requires 52 weeks of some kind of running each year; our American school program, only about 40. His system calls for at least six different kinds of terrain and methods of running; ours, only two or three--and in most cities, only one! The relative disinterest of the New Zealand public allows Lydiard to evaluate the win-loss record of his team as his judgment may decide; ours tends to encourage individual development, of course, *but only as long as the team wins.*

But despite these and other difficulties, Lydiard's system can be of great help in our efforts to improve American running. Adopting its basic tenets will not require us to begin over again. We shall not need to abandon either fartlek or interval training. Actually, Lydiard uses his own versions of both, though he seldom uses the terms as such. But the clarity with which Lydiard has presented the major goals for training and the step-by-step methods by which those goals can be achieved provides us with a fresh and better way than we have ever had before.

A classic example of the problems and the benefits of attempting to transpose a coach-training system (no matter how effective in the home situation) to another different situation occurred when, between 1967-1969, Finland employed Arthur Lydiard as its chief national coach of distance running. Finland had a proud tradition, knowledgeable coaches who in their day had been champions, outstanding running talent. But Finnish distance running was in the doldrums; international success, certainty of training methods, confidence in coaches were all missing. With a sense of shame, Finland had to ask for help from outside.

Lydiard brought that help. His book, *RUN TO THE TOP*, was published in Finnish; for some runners and coaches it became a Bible to be followed precisely as done in New Zealand. A new national enthusiasm arose--not just for competitive running but equally for jogging for fun and fitness. But some coaches of high repute resented the outsider, and expressed their resentment publicly. Several national champions refused his coaching and system entirely. When Lydiard left Finland after only two years of trying, many considered him a complete failure. Matti Hannus wrote,[1]

Before leaving, Arthur wrote an article in which he said, 'Finnish runners are very talented--maybe the best in the world--but they are difficult to handle. It is hard to get them out to train. Results were expected too soon from me. I am sorry to notice I was given very little help but was needlessly criticized.'

But Lydiard had been both the stimulus to new efforts and the means to better training methods. His book became a guide that de-emphasized the earlier interval-training approach, and restored a more gradual and varied system that assimilated Lydiard within the Finnish tradition, climate and terrain, and time schedule. In 1972-1976 Finland enjoyed its greatest Olympic success in distance running since the 1920s, with five gold medals and one bronze. A Finnish triumph. I am reminded of Laotse's definition of the truly great departed leader of whom people say, "We did this thing ourselves."

---

[1] Matti Hannus, *FINNISH RUNNING SECRETS*, Mountain View, Cal.: *World Publications*, 1973, p. 31.

Chapter 21
HOW TO ORGANIZE YOUR OWN SYSTEM

In the light of all that has been said here up to this point, how would I proceed if I were given responsibility for a program of distance running in a school or college or club?

I'D START RUNNING

First, beyond all question, I'd begin with myself. Unless I have the feeling and spirit of running, the enthusiasm for running, the personal involvement in running, how could I be a sound coach of others? How would I acquire this? In three ways. First, I'd start jogging twice a week for five minutes - ten - twenty - thirty: then three times a week, then daily. I'd do it on a time and fun basis with no concern for the miles or the training effects. I'd try to find my first fun in the terrain. Wherever I could get away from people, from noise, from cars and trucks; wherever there was good footing, a hill or two, a few trees, a turn of path, there I'd run. If no such terrain was nearby, I'd run on the track week-days: change my pace, mark my distances, find my fun in measuring my progress; then run in the country on week-ends. In other words, I'd prefer a fartlek method, if the terrain made it possible; if not, I'd choose interval training.

A MAN RUNS WITH HIS HEART. But just to run wouldn't give me enough foundation for sound coaching. I'd want to know more and feel more about distance runners and running. I'd sub-scribe to *Track & Field News*[1] that tells of competition and "how they train," throughout the world and at home--amateur, college, high school. Then, to get the inside story of distance running champions, I'd send to *Track & Field News* for one, then three, then all the biographies listed at the end of this book. These are wonderful stories: true stories of challenge, toughness, heart-break, blisters, but, since they were world-champions, triump and self-realization.

START THE BOYS RUNNING

Distance runners develop primarily by a very simple process--progressive increments of enjoyable running. They don't need theories and systems and scientifically based essentials of training. Basically, more running = better running. So, before all else, start the boys running.

Where would I get the boys and how should they begin? First, I'd make my cornerstone the fact that all men--some more, some less--are made for running. Throughout a long history of racial development man has had to depend on his own body when he had to get somewhere in a hurry. He had to run, and by running, he acquired a running heart, running muscles, running bones. Running is doing what comes natural; though of course some, by excess weight, may have to find this out very gradually. Running is fun, as long as one runs within one's own capacity today.

For team members I'd start by organizing a time-running group. On a prominent bulletin board, I'd place the names of all those who can jog without walking for a given length of time: 20-minute joggers; 30- or 40- or even 60-minute joggers. I'd appoint leaders who would encourage beginners and laggards.

---
[1] *Track & Field News*, P.O. Box 296, Los Altos, CA 94022, published monthly.

STUDY TRAINING SYSTEMS

Of course, I'd want to understand all I could about the various training systems. As a starter, this book provides the gist of such systems, but I'd want to go also to the original sources. Certainly I'd acquire Fred Wilt's book, *RUN RUN RUN*, which summarizes the viewpoints and experiences of coaches and runners from all over the world--New Zealand, Germany, Australia, Russia, and the United States. But I know I'd have to dig deeper. I'd study *A SCIENTIFIC APPROACH TO DISTANCE RUNNING* by David L. Costill, a simplified but authoritative explanation of the physiology of running, including "training and preparation for Competition." But much good material is not in books. I'd subscribe to the various track journals, especially *Track Technique*, and the *USTCA Quarterly Review*. Now I'd have a background for making judgments, and a reference for every problem.

ANALYZE AND ORGANIZE THE ESSENTIALS OF TRAINING

It's not enough to know the various training systems. I'd want to understand them. This would come about by analyzing their essentials. What are the key ideas and actions that underlie all systems. The section on essentials in this book is the gist of some 20 years or more of study. Though far from being final or complete, it is a sound starting point. By re-reading and understanding, not their words, but the actions they demand, you can build the skeleton of your own training system. But to that skeleton you must add the flesh and blood of your own unique situation. Flesh and blood don't come cheaply; they demand effort--and time, years of time. You expect your runners to train year-round, five, six, even seven days a week. Do they deserve any less from you?

THE ACTION IS CRUCIAL, NOT THE NAME OF THE TRAINING SYSTEM. A man develops in running by what he does, not by the potency of the name that is given to what he does. Much as the name may impress the mind, and perhaps give a sense of assurance to the coach, it has absolutely no direct physical influence on the development of the body. Ron Clarke (1966, 158) makes a strong point of this in his chapter "The Secret of Training,"

The athlete who thinks for himself and works out his own methods is going to enjoy his sport all the more, as well as being a better athlete.

It follows that no individual type of training for distance racing, be it branded as interval, repetition or fartlek training, has any overwhelming advantage over another. The main essentials are that attention be paid to the athlete's weaknesses; that the training is not so intense that it unnecessarily exhausts; nor so easy as to be of no use; and, above all, that the training is consistent.

We repeat--don't allow another coach's winning record, or his winning personality, or his winning words to sell you on the merits of his system, then try to adapt your local situation to it. That's like buying a hat because of its appearance or low cost, then trying to re-shape your head to fit its size.

DEVELOP YOUR OWN ECLECTIC TRAINING SYSTEM

An eclectic system is one that analyzes the various training systems and selects from them the best, or the gist of their values, and then adapts those values to the unique situation (terrain, climate, training time available, age level, competitive schedule, and all the rest) that this coach and these boys find themselves in.

Yes, in the next few pages, we could outline what we believe is a sound training system. We do have certain viewpoints on the relative values of the systems and the so-called essentials. But for you to use our viewpoints is comparable to an expectation by your boys that you will do their training for them.

Instead, we suggest that you find your own answers. As a beginning, try answering the following questions in the light of your reading in this book and, hopefully, in the many references we have provided.

1. What is the broad spectrum of motivation that will support my system? Have I included the right proportions of community-institution-team enthusiasm, of work-play, of reward-intrinsic satisfaction, of self-dependence with followership, of hurt-pain-agony with the joy of running, of training-competition, of developmental races-BIG races?

2. Is my system based on the gradual approach to development? Gradual as related to this

year? to 3-4 years at this school? to the athlete's running career?

3. What terrains are available in our situation? How will they determine our training system? Is fartlek feasible?

What is meant by an eclectic training system? What are the criteria by which we can select our system? How distinguish between a "quantity" and a "quality" approach to training?

5. What is meant by "periodization of training"? By gradations of cycles? How do they affect outputs of energy?

6. Distinguish between LSD, marathon training, fartlek, interval training and intermittent work.

7. Consider Costill's remark, "We can only judge from current training methods which suggest that only with 5 or 6 training days per week can a runner perform sufficient work to enable him/her to achieve maximal benefits."

8. What is meant by developmental work-rest as two phases of one process? What is a developmental training stimulus? for heart development? for developing aerobic power? for developing anaerobic power? What is meant by "aerobic training is a process of gradually racing the pace at which a steady state can be maintained"?

9. What are the relative demands of the various racing distances for aerobic as compared with anaerobic power?

10. What are the implications of variety for the various aspects of distance running?

11. Discuss: individual variations--physical, biochemical, mental-emotional--make it *impossible* to design a single training system for everyone. Are training systems therefore invalid?

12. How does one peak for major competition?

13. What is the difference between a strong runner and a strong shotputter? Will strength training help develop a distance runner?

14. Why maintain a training diary? for the coach? for the individual runner?

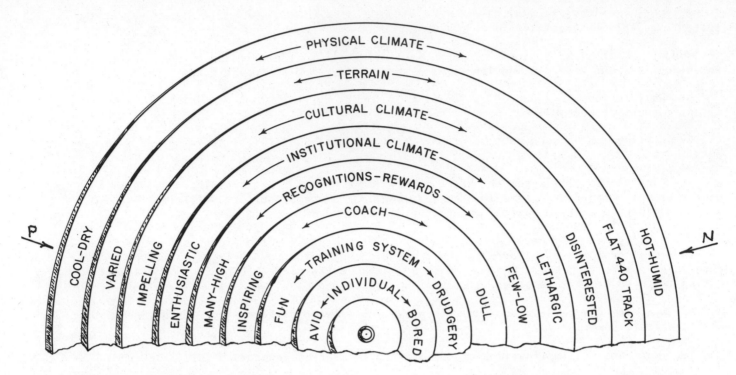

Fig. 21.1--A whole-part-whole approach to training for endurance running. Begin by seeing the chart as a whole; only as the overall system is supportive--point P on chart--can training be judged theoretically maximal. Now analyze the chart as though the disks could be rotated separately. Leave seven disks at point P, but rotate one--for example, terrain--so that the negative or non-supportive portion is at point P. With only a flat 400m track to run on, the entire training system is changed, along with each of the other six factors.

Or to take a different problem, leave the four outer disks at point N (Negative)--a difficult surround in which to train--but rotate the four inner disks--coach, training system, recognitions, individual--to activate their most positive aspects (now drawn at point P). Amazing what those four factors can accomplish, even though the other factors be non-supportive or even detrimental.

Note that the disk marked "individual" is analyzed in terms of only one factor: avid-bored. Actually, individuals differ in many ways--innate speed or endurance, time available for training, reaction to various stress factors, and a hundred more. That's what is meant when we say, "for 20 runners, there must be 20 training systems."

A wise coach will understand and use the fact that his real training system is not merely the running schedule, not merely what the runners' legs and bodies do, but rather is the sum-total of all related factors. This sum-total must be strongly positive if his system is to succeed. Such a wise coach will give as much thoughtful attention to these factors as a whole as is now commonly done for the running alone.

Cultural Climate. For example, take the problem of cultural climate (6th circle). I have written of the negative climate of W. R. Loader, training on the cobbled streets of shacktown London, reeking with exhaust fumes, frightened by barking and biting dogs, and jeered by the girls, "Mary Ann, look, it's a runner! He's got nae claes on!" Contrast this with the positive cultural environment of Lasse Viren, Finland's all-time great Olympic distance runner,

(Lasse) is not a lonely kid of the city without an identity of his own. He is a country boy, and his roots are strongly entwined with Myrskyla-- with its people, its soil, its values.[1]

Chris Brasher, 1956 Olympic steeplechase champion and now sports columnist for the London *Observer*, commented, "Lasse Viren is like a tree deeply rooted in Myrskyla. In this village lies his strength. He has not been torn away from his natural surroundings; that is why he is not overturned by storms of misfortune."

Terrain. In large measure, the terrains that are available will determine your system of training. Some make do with a kind of fartlek that is freely chosen, fast-slow running within whatever physical surroundings are available. But lacking the refreshing surround of Scandinavia's paths through the woods and around the lakes, fartlek is no longer speed-play (English translation). Zest may still be there but not derived from the terrain.

Take the hills or roads for running from Lydiard's system; the sand dunes, sea beaches and open country from Percy Cerutty's system, the varied terrains from Bowerman's Oregon system, the pine-needled paths of Myrskyla, Finland from Lasse Viren's system; in brief, change the terrain and you must necessarily organize a different program of training. That is to say, organize a training system that makes optimal use of whatever terrain--or multiple terrains-- is available to you. An effective training system can be devised using a grass or even macadamized field, or city streets if no park or golf course is available. It's not easy, but it has been done--many times.

Periodization. Perhaps the best example of this whole-part-whole approach to endurance training is the system called "Periodization," invented by L. P. Matveyev, USSR, and described in Chapter 16. In brief, it is an all-inclusive system of organizing time-effort-rest so as to ensure maximal workloads and optimal recovery. Periodization first views an athlete's entire career as a "macrocycle" of training, then focuses on smaller and smaller units of time-- mesocycles, microcycles, training units--so that each may be analyzed into its essentials-- work-rest, variety, and the like--and so contribute its values to the whole of training and competitive performance.

Four-Week Training Cycles. As David Costill points out (1979, 113) "most physiological systems require three or four weeks to show a response to a given training stress." It therefore seems good judgment to plan workouts in terms of four-week cycles--in terms of total mileage (preparatory season) or in terms of total intensity of work (winter and early competitive season). Figure 21.2 shows two four-week cycles in which total mileage gradually increases but with alternating weeks of heavier and lighter stress. In this way, the basic principle of work-rest=more vital to success than work alone--operates from month to month, from week to week, and from day to day. For example, the first week in Cycle A should alternate its days of heavy load and light load, thus ensuring both optimal work and adequate recovery.

I repeat, such cyclical time-segments relate to stress of all kinds--mileage, pace of intermittent work, length of recovery periods in interval work, but also to mental stress as occurs in competition or time trials--whatever challenges the adaptation energies. A chart similar to Figure 21.2 could be drawn for a single week in which days of heavy mileage (intensity-stress) are alternated with days of lighter work in which full recovery is gained.

---

[1]Antero Raevuori & Rolf Haikkola, *LASSE VIREN: OLYMPIC CHAMPION*, Portland, Oregon: Continental Publishing House, 1978, p. 3.

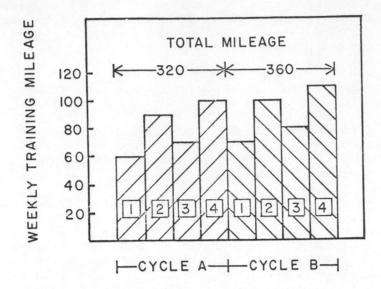

Fig. 21.2[1]--Two 4-week cycles of work-rest based only on total mileage by a mature runner. In general: (1) weeks of long mileage alternate with weeks of shorter mileage; (2) total mileage in any given week in Cycle B tends to be greater than that for the corresponding week in Cycle A; (3) within each week, days of high stress will be balanced by days of low stress-recovery.

The overall intention of such planning of year-round time-energy would be developmental--gradual increments of workloads and related rest, and from that, gradual improvements in performance.

Costill takes this method of 4-week cycles a step further by providing an example (Table 21.3) of how alternating LSD and faster-pace intermittent work can be gradually increased to ensure both a strong endurance base and the specific training (sharpening) needed for the Big Race. He warns, however, that this example seeks only to achieve a balance of such work, not recommended mileages. Beginning runners should attempt lesser work loads--only 30-40 miles per week, and at paces within the runner's present condition, not exceeding it.

For example, Costill recommends that each week should include days of LSD work of various kinds, but also "intermittent bouts of running at speeds equal to or faster than racing pace." During early preparatory phases, these would be limited to one day per week. During later preparatory phases or the early competitive period, they might well be increased to two days per week, or even three, though of course with varying distances-paces-recovery intervals. During competitive periods, such a faster-than-racing pace serves the dual role of increased developmental stress and of so-called sharpening--developing muscle speed-power through recruitment of the fast-twitch function in muscle fibers.

Intermittent Work. Like interval training, intermittent work implies alternating run-rest as a unified, inseparable concept. But it can be distinguished from Interval Training in these ways: (1) Interval Training is a year-round, total-training system that, for example, includes mileage running (LSD) in the Fall; a system devised by Reindell-Gerschler as "heart training" in which the number of times the "heart" was placed under stress was the main criterion of the system's effectiveness. To do this, work periods and recovery periods were relatively short--400 meters or less. Relatively high speeds over short distances forced muscles to work against heavy resistance without experiencing exhaustion: 30s work--30s rest, or even 10s work--5s rest.

---

[1]Adapted, with permission, from David L. Costill, A SCIENTIFIC APPROACH TO DISTANCE RUNNING, Los Altos, CA, Track & Field News, 1979, p. 114.

TABLE 21.3[1]

AN EXAMPLE OF DEVELOPMENTAL WORK SCHEDULES WITH INCREASING
WORK-REST CYCLES OF BOTH LSD AND INTERMITTENT WORK

NON-COMPETITIVE PHASE

Day of Week	WEEK 1	WEEK 2	WEEK 3	WEEK 4
1	10 miles	15 miles	15 miles	20 miles
2	5 "	5 "	5 "	5 "
3 a.m.	4 "	8 "	6 "	8 "
p.m.	4 x 800 m	4 x 1 mile	4 x 800 m	6 x 1 mile
4	10 miles	12 miles	10 miles	12 miles
5	8 "	10 "	8 "	10 "
6	10 "	12 "	10 "	15 "
7	6 "	10 "	6 "	8 "

Total Weekly Mileage

	55 miles	76 miles	62 miles	84 miles

COMPETITIVE PHASE

Day of Week	WEEK 1	WEEK 2	WEEK 3	WEEK 4
1	10 miles	10 miles	10 miles	10 miles
2 a.m.	8 miles	6 x 1 mile x 100%	8 miles	7 x 1 mile x 100%
p.m.	15 x 400m x 125%	8 miles	15 x 400m x 125%	8 miles
3	8 miles	10 miles	8 miles	10 miles
4 a.m.	6 miles	4 x 1.5 miles x 100%	6 miles	5 x 1.5 miles x 100%
p.m.	10 x 800m x 100%	6 miles	10 x 800m x 100%	6 miles
5	8 miles	6 miles	8 miles	6 miles
6	6 miles	4 miles	6 miles	4 miles
7	TIME TRIAL*	RACE	TIME TRIAL**	RACE

Total Weekly Mileage

	55-60 miles	55-60 miles	55-60 miles	55-60 miles

Note: During the non-competitive phase, all LSD running is performed at 60-70% of the runner's oxygen uptake capacity (% VO_2 max); all intermittent work at 85-90% VO_2 max, with rest intervals equal to the exercise periods.

During the competitive phase, LSD is at 70-80% VO_2 max; in intermittent work, rest intervals should be 1.5 to 2.0 times the duration of the run.

    * Time Trial = 75% of racing distance
    ** Time Trial = 1.0-1.25 times racing distance

In contrast, intermittent work has not been used as the focal point for planning a total training system. Instead, it is the term Scandinavian researchers used merely to distinguish it from continuous or steady work. It too can be used to include the short work-rest segments of interval training. But important values are derived from distinguishing it from Interval Training by extending its runs to 600 meters or more, and usually, its recovery segments to fit the specific goals of the workout. (2) The focus of intermittent work-rest is on maximal oxygen uptakes (VO_2 max) and transport, in contrast to heart rates and number of stress periods that concerned Interval Training researchers. For example, Astrand concludes from various experiments, "for the purposes of taxing the oxygen-transporting organs maximally, work periods of a few minutes duration represent an effective type of work." (3) Intermittent work-rest is done at relatively high-level speeds--little slower, but often faster than racing pace speeds that develop. The entire system adjusts itself to the demands of such pace--in particular the

---

[1]Used with permission of David L. Costill, ibid., p. 115.

faster-stronger FT muscles fibers and groups. (4) Intermittent work-rest develops efficient running by simulating the precise patterns-stresses of a projected racing distance--stride lengths and rhythms, arm-leg coordination and relaxation--in the sense of biomechanics and of the feel of action. To run a pace that "feels right" aids performance just as does "being right."

Overtraining. Near the end of his important book on a more scientific approach to the problems of endurance running, David Costill (1979, 116) emphasizes the dangers of excessive work--too much too soon:

> *"Overtraining" probably constitutes the greatest single error made in the management of the beginning runner. In light of the high rate of injury, emotional staleness and physical exhaustion which often accompany overtraining, the first principle to remember is to begin training at a very low level, estimated to be well within the runner's capacity. If after the first training sessions the runner develops muscle soreness, the work is too difficult. Should the runner find it impossible to complete the training distance or to maintain the training pace, the total training effort should be reduced. Symptoms of overtraining generally include restless sleep, loss of appetite, reduced performance, and elevated resting heart rate. These responses are applicable to runners with varied levels of experience, and generally demand several days to a week of reduced work or complete rest.*

For all runners, there is a level of diminishing returns at which increased volume will not produce comparable improvement in performance; in fact, may even have a negative effect. This raises the specter of Hans Selye's research on the limited adaptation energies of animals and men--as a General Stress Syndrome but also as a specific maladjustment of muscles-tendons to overwork.

Between February 8-21, 1976, five months prior to his great victories in the Montreal Olympic 5000 and 10,000, Lasse Viren logged a total of 332 miles in 14 days (no days of complete rest). That's an average of 24 miles per day. Viren was then 25 years of age and had been training for about ten years. His next three years were easier, but in 1980 he trained for the Moscow marathon, and once again, mileage was essential. After some 15 years of training, one might think boredom would be the main problem. But Viren said[1] his greatest worry was possible illness and injury--the result of "too much pressure." Tendonitis--especially of the Achilles, stomach ailments including ulcers, stress fractures, shin splints, heel bone spurs, sinuses, back problems--all upsetting to training schedules and mental poise. Causes are often specific, but more often seem related to overall stress that causes the weakest link to break down.

---

[1]Antero Raevuori & Rolf Haikkola, ibid., p. 113.

HOW THEY TRAIN[1]
Dave Wottle[2]-- 800-1500 meters.
   Born: August 7, 1950; Ht/Wt: 6-0/1.83, 138lb/64kg.
   Background: A 4:20.2 miler as a prep, Wottle improved to 4:06.8 as a college freshman.
As a sophomore he was an NCAA All-American in both track and cross country. Dave was a sur-
prise winner of the Final Olympic Trials in 1972, equalling the world record of 1:44.3. He
doubled back to qualify in the 1500, too. Then at Munich's 1972 Olympics he outkicked favorite
Yevgeniy Arzhanov of the Soviet Union for the 800 meter gold medal. In addition, he has picked
up four NCAA firsts: indoor 880 (1972) and mile (1973), and outdoor 1500 (1972) and mile (1973).
   Best Marks: 100, 10.8(e), 440, 50.2; 800m, 1:44.3; 880, 1:47.6; 1500, 3:36.2; mile,
3:53.3; two mile, 8:40.0i.

Fall Cross Country Training, 1968
Sun--10 mile run at 6:30 pace.
Mon--mile in 5:15, five minute rest; 880 in
   2:20; two minutes rest; 220 in 28 seconds,
   two minute rest; 440 in 70 seconds, three
   minute rest; 880 in 2:20, five minute rest;
   mile in 5:00, two mile jog.
Tue--20 x 440 in 70 with one minute interval,
   two mile jog.

Wed--20 minute calisthenics, four mile time
   trial, two mile jog.
Thu--eight mile fartlek averaging about 6:30
   per mile.
Fri--two to three miles easy running on golf
   course.
Sat--race.
No morning workouts during fall season.

Winter Training, 1969
Sun--12 miles.
Mon--four to five mile jog; 4 x 3/4 mile in
   3:20 with 440 walk-jog interval; four mile
   jog.
Tue--three to four miles, 20 x 220 in 32 seconds with 220 jog; five miles.
Wed--four miles, 6 x 880 in 2:05 with 440
   walk interval; four miles.

Thu--six mile fartlek, 4 x 440 in 70 seconds
   plus 60 at full speed at end; 4 x 440 increasing tempo each 50 with one minute rest
   after each; four to five miles.
Fri--five miles, 1½ miles of alternating hard
   and easy 110s; three to four miles.
Sat--12 mile jog.

Spring/Summer Training, 1969
Mon-Thu mornings: seven miles at 6:30 pace.
Sun--12 mile run at 6:30 pace.
Mon--four miles; 2 x two miles in 9:48 and
   9:30 with 20 minutes rest between; three
   mile jog.
Tue--three miles; 19 x 440 (6 in 70, 4 in 68,
   2 in 67, 2 in 66, and 1 each in 65, 64, 62,
   60) with 220 walk after each; two mile jog.

Wed--three miles; 1320 in 3:03, 880 in 2:03,
   440 in 69 with full recovery after each;
   three mile jog.
Thu--two mile jog.
Fri--AM, four miles at 7:00; PM, three to
   four miles at 7:30.
Sat--AM, two to three miles at 7:30; PM, race.

Eamonn Coghlan[3]-- 1500-5000 meters.
   Born: Nov. 21, 1952, in Dublin, Ireland. Ht/Wt: 5-10/139, 1.77/63.
   Background: One of the new breed of young, fast milers. After outdoor mile bests of only
4:04.0 in 1974, Coghlan became a disciplined trainer in '75 and reaped the benefits: IC4A
Champion, NCAA Champion, European Recordholder, and 8th fastest miler of all time. Attended
Villanova University.
   Best Marks: 880, 1:50.2; Mile, 3:53.3; 3M, 13:26.0.

   Coghlan trains year-round, beginning his season with cross country in the fall. Participation in the American outdoor and European outdoor seasons results in year-round racing as
well. Mileage during the winter months remains at between 70 and 95 miles per week; then

---

[1]These training schedules are for mature men of world rank, obviously too tough for less-ex-
perienced boys of high school or college age. But careful study will suggest patterns of
training that can be adjusted to the needs of any person, male or female, whatever the performance level.

[2]Fred Wilt, "Dave Wottle," *Track Technique*, 56, June 1974, p. 1790.

[3]Bob Daugherty, "Eamonn Coghlan," *Track Technique*, 61, September 1975, p. 1946.

during the outdoor season, interval work on the track replaces much of the overdistance work. Coghlan works very little with weights. He does do light bench pressing and curls 3 times a week for keeping the upper body in tone. A 5-mile run at 6:30-7:00 pace is done every morning, year-round. Coghlan's afternoon workouts:

Non-Competitive Season

Mon--9 mile run with several steep hills.
Tues-20 x 440 in 66 with 440 jog interval
  between.
Wed--10 miles easy.

Thu--9 miles of fartlek.
Fri--6½ miles of hills.
Sat--10 miles hard or race.
Sun--15-18 mile run.

Competitive Season

Mon--12 x 440, 3 sets of 4 with 1st set in 55,
  2nd in 58 and 3rd in 55 with a 440 jog in
  between.
Tues--9 miles easy.
Wed--6 x 440 in 57 with a 440 jog between.

Thu--12 x 330 in 39, 3 sets of 4, 440 jog
  between reps.
Fri--5 miles easy.
Sat--Race.

Lasse Viren[1] -- 5000-10,000 meters

Lasse Viren began systematic training when he was 16, and was then doing six to ten miles daily. In 1969, he ran 13:55.0 for 5000m (a Finnish junior record), and two years later this was down to 13:29.8 and alongside a 10,000m in 28:17.4. The training that was started in the winter of 1971-72 was planned to cover some 4500 miles and to take Viren to the Olympics; as is known, it brought him three world records and two gold medals.

With his coach, Rolf Haikkola (a former 14:14.2 runner), Viren plans about a year ahead, with four phases to the training--active rest (October), basic conditioning (November to April), hill/strength training (May) and competitive-season training (June to September). Within this pattern there is a cycle of two days with emphasis on long/easy and one day with emphasis on hard/fast; if the fast work proves to be particularly exhausting, then it will be followed by three days of the longer, easier work.

Winter training is done regardless of the weather, and Viren will run three times a day, covering 22-30 miles, with the longest single effort about 13½ miles of continuous running. If running just once or twice a day, this longest effort could be 22 miles. This running is at easy pace, though he might inject four minutes of good pace on occasion. The location of the training is changed regularly, so that there is no boredom. And Viren prefers to train alone.

As he moves towards the summer, the percentage of long, basic conditioning work is decreased, in favor of running that will develop speed, strength and rhythm. He does not lift weights, and his power/strength conditioning is done on an 800m hill; this hill is steep to begin with, then flattens a bit, then becomes steep again. Viren runs this at 3/4 speed, jogging down for recovery. He does not spring or jump as per Lydiard, finding that too rough on his tendons.

During the summer, Viren still avoids the track as a place for training (one Italian magazine actually records him as saying that his speed-training is never done on the track and that he has never done formal interval work)....But he does retain both the long/easy running and the deliberate speed work in his summer plan. The long runs will go to as much as 25 miles, or maybe 60-90 minutes of relaxed running. The fast stretches are part of his fartlek work, and can be either 50m sprint followed by 50m jog, or fast runs of 100m-400m inserted along the line; sometimes he does "rushes" of 1½ to 3 minutes. This speedplay is very flexible and often changed.

Injury-free (because, he says, of his avoidance of interval work), and with an unwavering confidence learned in racing, Viren has been able to increase his annual mileage from the 1250 figure of 1967-8 to the planned 5300 of 1972-73. He raced 48 times in 1971, including five ski races, though not so often in 1972. It is reported that, about five days before a big race, he will run a very hard 5000m, to force his heart-rate above 200. His warmup is 40 min jogging followed by five short sprints.

---

[1]Brian Mitchell, "Lasse Viren's Pre-Olympic Training," *Athletics Weekly*, 27, #42. Reprinted in *Track Technique*, 59, March 1975, p. 1876.

HOW THEY TRAIN

The following information on Steve Ovett and Sebastian Coe does not disclose their full year-round programs of training. It does, however, make clear contrasting approaches to training between two men whose records from 800m to one mile were almost identical. Such training contrasts were the result of innate individual differences--physique, body chemistry, whatever--but also the effect of different approaches to running and to the commitment of time-energy that can properly be given to running.

During 1977 and 1978, *Track & Field News* ranked Steve Ovett Number 1 in the world for the 1500m-mile distances. Earlier, he had concentrated on the 800m (5th place at Montreal), but under the guidance of Coach Harry Wilson, he extended his training mileage and moved up in racing distances. Given financial support--at some sacrifice--by his father, Ovett was free to train year-round seven days a week, two and even three times a day, with total weekly mileages beyond 100 miles, even throughout the winter. In brief, a life fully committed to running.

In contrast, when Sebastian Coe (age 22) set three world records within 41 days in 1979, his primary concern, expressed many times in many ways, was for completing his degree in social history and economics at Loughborough University. In fact, his record-breaking spree of just 41 days came a few weeks after he had completed his final examinations. He had studied many nights into the late hours and sometimes ran only twice a week. His weekly mileage was well under 50 miles. In brief, a life in which running was a part-time thing.

STEVE OVETT, Great Britain (Born Oct. 9, 1955; 6'0", 154#; 200m-21.7, 400m-47.9, 800-1:44.1, 1500-3:32.2, mile-4:48.8WR, 2 mile-8:13.5WR, 5000m-13:25.) Resting pulse, "around 37."

Ovett began as a quartermiler and then moved up--800m, mile, 2 mile, 5000m. At 13 he was Britain's fastest 400m runner; at 17 (1973), he was European Junior 800m champion. By the beginning of the 1980 track season (age 24), he had won 36 consecutive races at 1500m-mile--all leading up to his 1980 world-record 3:48.8. In these wins, Ovett usually followed the same pattern--stay out of trouble until the last 200m or so, then sprint all-out to the tape. But in his 3:48.8 race, Ovett had to carry pace over the final 600 yards with no one near. He slowed (56-57.5-57.5-57.8), in contrast to Coe's final 55.6 on his way to 3:49.

British correspondent, Dave Cocksedge, wrote *Track & Field News* in November 1978,

Training is tough. Two, sometimes three sessions a day, mainly on the roads and the lush green hills surrounding his hometown (Brighton, England). Together with constant training partner, Matt Patterson, a Scottish schoolteacher who lives nearby, Ovett pounds out more than 100M per week throughout the winter....Steve races often in different parts of the country, but has no interest in indoor racing.[1]

A year later, November 1979, Dave Cocksedge gave a few samples of Ovett's training,[2]

"(Coach) Harry Wilson's session with 1000m (run on sand dunes) is 4 x 1000 in 2:34, checking pulse rate throughout; e.g., 1 x 1000m in 2:35, pulse at end 156; 2 minutes rest, then pulse is 72. Another 1000 in 2:32, pulse is then 168; after 2 minutes rest, pulse is 98. A third 1000 in 2:28, pulse is 180; after 2 minutes rest, pulse 114. I've never seen Ovett do this on the track, however.

"Harry gives him a killer session of 12 x 200 in an average of 26 seconds with a 15 second rest interval. This is done in 3 sets of 4, with 3 minutes between each set. When he can manage this session comfortably, he knows he's ready.

"Harry talks about 'surging speed'; he says, 'It is obvious that ability to cruise is vital, but the athlete must be able to withstand oxygen debt during the race; then partially recover. Oxygen debt training is necessary, but also the ability to change running technique quickly.

"'Practice changing action, e.g., reps of 200-100 stride; 50 fast, 50 stride. Reps of 200-50 fast, 100 stride, 50 fast.'

"Harry says the key to Ovett's finishing kick is sprinting technique and leg strength plus mobility. He does a 12 x 60m session, usually indoors, and they average 6.8 seconds off a flying start. I've seen Steve blow away 47-second 400 men in a session of 60m sprints."

---

[1]Dave Cocksedge, "The Man They Love to Hate," *Track & Field News*, Nov., 1978, p. 7.
[2]Dave Cocksedge, "Ovett: Changing Speeds," *Track & Field News*, Nov. 1979, p. 47.

SEBASTIAN COE, Great Britain (Born Sept. 29, 1956, 5'9¼", 129#). 1979--400m-46.87; 7/5, Oslo, 800m-1:42.4WR; 7/17, Oslo, mile-3:49WR; 8/15, Zurich, 1500m-3:32.1WR. 1980--7/1, Oslo, 1000m-2:13.40WR; 5000m-14:06.2 ("slowed by strong, gusty winds and lack of competition.")

Coe provided the gist of his own training, "Essentially, it has been 100% quality, not quantity. It is speed-endurance; that is, seeing how long you can endure speed. In the winters, I very seldom have run more than 50 miles per week, less in the spring."

Kenny Moore explained,[1]

The direction of the Coe experiment thus far has been to train Sebastian as a sprinter and, that done, turn his speed loose over longer and longer distances. 'What we are doing are ranging shots, as I call them, running under and over racing distances to bracket the target,' said Peter (his trainer-father). In 1978, when Seb was aiming for the 800, we raced at 400 for speed and 1500 for endurance. Last year the bracket was 400 and 3000 meters, and he got the records for three of the distances in between. This year the overdistance will be up to 5000 meters. ...

According to Michael Coleman, *New York Times* London Correspondent, Coe began at age 16 as a cross country runner and English schools' 3000-meter champion. But he and his father-coach decided that if he was to attain his full potential as a runner, his basic speed would have to improve greatly.

"By trade, Peter Coe is an engineer, serving as production director of a cutlery firm. Never a runner himself, he was a keen club racing cyclist in younger days and from that sport is aware of the value of the sudden break-away sprint that catches opponents on the wrong wheel, or as is the case now, on the wrong foot. Track cyclists perfect that tactic, but runners rarely do.

"Certainly there are many middle-distance men who are as fast as Sebastian Coe. But what matters is where the sprint is released. A runner able to switch into overdrive at either the middle, end or beginning of a race--or any combination of those periods--can exert a paralyzing effect on victims waiting for the chop. To acquire this leg speed, father and son decided on a radical change in training methods. "Many people believe that to get results, you must run 75, 85 or even 100 miles a week," Sebastian said. "That's all wrong. For me only one thing counts: speed, speed, speed."

"The most mileage in a week for Coe was to be about 52 or 53 miles, with the longest run being about 11 miles. He worked out in the gym with light weights and ran around the track against the watch. But once the summer season started, he restricted his program to light morning running and then interval work on the track. The toughest part of the week is a series of six tempo-runs over 800 meters at about 80 percent of his capacity, trying for times between 1 minute 50 seconds and 1 minute 52 seconds, with a recovery interval of only one and a half minutes."[2]

In his *Sports Illustrated* article, Kenny Moore tells a similar story:

"When asked how he managed to stay fresh and strong on so little distance work, Coe said, 'My father says that you might not know the accepted lore of athletics, but if you know people and can sense the individual's needs, it can make all the difference.' 'Hear, hear,' said (former Oregon coach Bill) Bowerman. 'Yet I wouldn't know why some people can get away with less distance than others. I really haven't a clue.'

"In Coe's case, part of the reason has to do with the 10 and 11 hours every winter week that he spends in the Loughborough gym under the eye of George Gandy, a lecturer in biomechanics and the coordinator of his training program. 'It has been described as Coe's commando workout,' the runner said. 'In the fall, it's the use of everything you can think of in the gymnasium, lifting heavy weights twice a week, working every part of the body. After Christmas, we concentrate on every muscle from knees to sternum, using box-jumping, speed drills, repeatedly mounting a beam, high knee lifts, bounding on grass or a soft-sprung floor. All this was associated two and a half years ago with rapid improvement in my leg speed.

---

[1]Kenny Moore, "A Hard and Supple Man," *Sports Illustrated*, June 23, 1980, p. 74.

[2]*New York Times*, July 3, 1980.

"It must be that the strength and flexibility Coe brings to the track from such work supports him as well as would the result of interminable slow running. 'It was a happy accident that from the first, when I was 13, my father felt you ought not to smash a kid on the road, so he kept the distance low. As a junior in 1975, I averaged 28 miles per week and ran successfully--third in the European junior 1500--against those juniors who were running 80 or 90 miles.'"

And finally, to complete my effort to piece together the Sebastian Coe story, Amby Burfoot tells us that in 1977, age 20, Coe ran a 3:57 mile on an average of 28 miles a week; and in 1978 an 800 meters in 1:44.0 on 38 miles a week.

"During the worst of the exam period (Loughborough) Coe had worked out just twice a week-- one long run, one speed run. He resumed regular running only three weeks before the Bislett (Oslo) meet and had but one tune-up race, "an easy 800m in 1:46.6" the day before he left for Oslo.
"Two days later, running his first session on the Bislett track...Coe ran 2 x 400m in 52 seconds, 3 x 300 in 37, 3 x 200 in 23.5, 23.0 and 22.7--the last was a personal best for 200m. 'I realized immediately the special quality of the track,' Coe said, 'and knew that a good time was obviously on for the 800.'"[1]

Later in his article, Burfoot states that Seb Coe's favorite workout is repeat 880s, that usually occur at night "on dark, undulating roads outside the city limits, with his father driving a car to check mileage, time and possible accidents,

"Under these conditions, Seb has completed as many as eight repeat 880s in the 1:52 to 1:56 range. _He considers it the most important workout in his entire training program._

In summary, this story of contrasts--especially in training quantity-quality but also in commitment to running--is of great importance. In part, it can be explained on a basis of individual differences. But I'm inclined to view it as a shift in emphasis from an all-out belief in mileage and total commitment, as advanced by the theory of marathon training, toward a more effective use of less training time. Running should never be the whole of life, even during the few years of best running. The key question in training for running should be, "Within the limited time-energy available to me from my duties as a student or worker, how can I develop toward the highest levels of my potential"? Even accepting his uniqueness, Sebastian Coe and his father-trainer, Peter, have created a pattern of training that should and will influence future training systems, especially at college-school levels.

---

[1] Amby Burfoot, "Sebastian Coe," _Runner's World_, Sept. 1979, p. 70.

Chapter 22
RUNNING TECHNIQUE

Running technique is primarily an individual matter. It began when the athlete was two years or so of age, and over the course of a dozen or a score of years, it has become so "natural," or at least so firmly established, as not to be changed without disturbing a man's inner as well as his outer balance and relaxation. A sound rule-of-thumb, when it comes to running technique, is to leave it alone. All the other track and field events are learned later in life and are not practiced so constantly as is running. Their technique is much more susceptible to coaching. Again we remind you of the centipede who, when asked how his legs functioned, was unable to either speak or run.

However, the technique of some men can and should be improved, as long as we remember that improvement is related to a man's competitive performance, not to whether his technique is mechanically sound or aesthetically pleasing. One needs only to recall the awkward arms and strained face of Zatopek (Figure 18.1), or the swinging head of Jim Ryun to be certain that perfect technique is not essential to success.

Certainly the coach should understand the essentials of sound technique and be able to suggest changes when they will further running performance. In summary, the elements of technique can be logically considered under six headings: the overall action, body angle, length of stride, the recovery phase, foot placement, and use of the arms.

THE OVERALL ACTION
At the risk of repetition, coaching sound technique in running should focus on the overall action rather than the details of technique. Look for rhythm, smoothness, relaxation, ease of movement. If these are present, it means the runner has evolved during the years of his running a vital balance of the various factors of style. There is a "wisdom of the body," to use Walter B. Cannon's term, which compensates for this or that weakness and develops a technique which, taken overall, is sound. To focus attention on some one part is to upset the vital balance, and the man is not likely to run economically until that vital balance is restored.

BODY ANGLE
The degree of body lean tends to be adjusted naturally to the speed of running. During the early phase of acceleration, especially in the faster runs, there must be a pronounced forward lean in order for the runner to exert a forward-driving force against the ground. But during the later stages of running, the torso becomes almost erect.

Dyson (1967, 118) points out that the most commonly-selected pictures of runners show full extension of the driving foot. At that phase, an illusion of pronounced forward lean is shown. Actually, a more valid phase is at midstride, when it becomes clear how little lean is present.

Donald B. Slocum[1], M.D., an orthopedist of Eugene, Oregon with a long-time active interest in the mechanics of running, has emphasized the importance of maintaining this erect posture while running. He points out: (1) that the strong trunk (lower-back) muscles add greatly to

---

[1] Donald B. Slocum, M.D., "Biomechanics of Running," NCTCA *Clinic Notes*, 1963, 25.

the explosive thrust driving the body forward, which occurs between mid-stride and push-off; (2) that extension of the spine at push-off provides additional thrust; and (3) that forward lean decreases the amount of extension of the spine, shifts the center of gravity forward so that weight falls more heavily on the balls of the feet, and decreases the amount of thigh flexion in relation to the ground. The figures numbered 1 and 5 in Figure 22.2, as well as that of Snell (Figure 20.2),   all suggest the erect body angle that Slocum believes is optimum.

LENGTH OF STRIDE

Slocum[1] also points out that the length of stride depends on several variables, including (1) length of the legs in relation to the rest of the body, (2) the force exerted between mid-stride and push-off, (3) possible deceleration from forward extension of the foot, so that the angle of the lower leg is oblique to the ground, and so creates resistance to forward movement.

Similarly, Hopper[2] makes very clear that length of stride, as well as stride-rate, is determined mainly by the rate at which the grounded foot passes under the body from mid-stride to push-off; and rate is a function of force.

But from the athletes' point of view as well as of the coaching of athletes, stride length should be approached from the standpoints of naturalness, and of economy and ease of effort. Certainly to coach a change in length of stride is to risk disruption, not merely of the mechanics of running, but of the runner's self-confidence and poise. Such possible changes should be made early in the year's schedule of training, so that by much running, it becomes "natural" and beyond the need for conscious control.

REAR-LEG KICKUP

Probably because of America's more primary interest in sprinting during the first quarter of this century, coaches used to argue that the natural ballistic swing of the rear foot above the level of the knee (Figure 22.1-5),   as it pushed off and came forward for the next stride, was wasteful of energy and time spent in the air.

However, if the angle of the torso is optimum, and leg action is naturally relaxed, this kick-up is simply a follow-through action which shortens the weight arm of the leg lever as it swings forward.

For those specially interested in this leg-recovery phase of running, Dillman[3] has researched the precise patterns of leg movements and muscle forces involved.

FOOT PLACEMENT

In all human locomotion from walking to fastest sprinting, the placement of the foot is a function of the velocity of movement. We cannot assign one placement to long distance runners, for they pick up their pace at various stages of their race, and their foot placement necessarily changes. The same holds for half milers and milers. When sprinters jog, they place the foot as do the slower runners.

This was carefully researched by Toni Nett[4] when he took films of a score or more of world-ranked runners from sprinters to marathon runners. His conclusions seem unassailable:

---

[1]Donald B. Slocum, *ibid.*, 26.

[2]Bernard J. Hopper, "Characteristics of the Running Stride," *Track Technique*, 38, December 1969, 1205.

[3]Charles J. Dillman, "Muscular Torque Patterns of the Leg During the Recovery Phase of Sprint Running," an unpublished Ph.D. thesis, Pennsylvania State University, September 1969.

[4]Toni Nett, "Foot Plant in Running," *Track Technique*, 15, March 1964, 462.

1. All runners at all distances make first contact with the ground on the outside edge of the foot.

2. The precise point of contact varies with the speed of the running.

3. Sprinters contact the ground on the outside edge, high on the ball (joints of the little toe), as shown in A, Figure 22.1.

4. When running at an 800-1500 meter pace, the foot is planted on the outer edge of the sole (metatarsal arch)--B, Figure 22.1.

5. At a pace from the 1500 through the marathon, first contact is by the outside edge at the arch between the heel and the metatarsus--C, Figure 22.1.

6. In the follow-up action during a faster pace (including sprinters), the foot settles "heel on the ground"!

Nett concludes that the manner of foot placement is produced primarily by the mechanics of pace and not by differences in individual runners, though slight variations between men do exist.

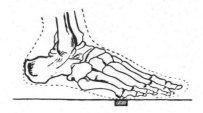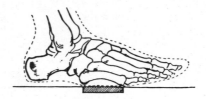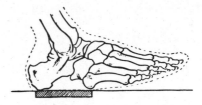

Figure 22.1   Placement of the foot in running. Figure A suggests the placement of a sprinter-440 man; B, that of an 880-man or miler; C that used for long distances. In actual running, no such clear-cut difference exists. In C there is a cushioned roll of the foot as the body moves lightly over it. In B, the heel drops buoyantly to the ground and cushions placement. In these three placements, note the difference in the angle of the fibula to that of a vertical to the ground, and the potential retarding effect if a forward reach of the foot on the heel were exaggerated.

SWING OF THE ARMS

The action of the arms should be a relaxed and rhythmic swing from a steady though free-moving shoulder girdle. Body balance and freedom from arm fatigue are the primary considerations. Both tend to come with uncoached running over long distances, from what I like to call "the wisdom of the body." Some runners are aware of fatigue first in the arms, perhaps from too much tension in the hands, or from carrying them too high. They gain recovery by lowering them, shaking them, or changing slightly the pattern of movement. Some men do special arm exercises with light weights and many reps, hoping this will prove helpful. In moderation, it certainly does no harm.

Only when pace picks up, usually near the finish, do the arms play a helping role in acceleration. Jokl[1] has presented evidence that greater power in the leg movements of running can be "triggered off" by emphasizing arm action. Certainly it is one way of shifting attention away from the dragging fatigue of the legs and into a slightly different and, hopefully, facilitating movement by the arms.

SUMMARY

In summary of this Chapter, I'm inclined to fall in line with such coaches as Arthur Lydiard (1962, 59) who says, "There is too much fuss and attention paid to style in a runner. Admittedly the runner looks nice, but it doesn't make him any faster." But in the very next paragraph, Lydiard warns, "Don't relax so much that an easy jog becomes a mere amble. While you are moving, keep a constant check on your stride, your balance, the movement of your arms. . . . You must still concentrate on what you are doing."

Well, there you have it. Do what comes "natcherly," as long as "natcherly" is mechanically sound; if it isn't, do what is mechanically sound until it comes "natcherly"! Therein lies the high art of sound coaching.

Fig. 22.2. Style in endurance running.

---

[1]Ernst Jokl, "Some Physiological Components of Modern Track Training," NCTCA *Clinic Notes*, 1956, 226.

Chapter 23
HINTS FOR COMPETITION IN ENDURANCE RUNNING

Winning a race is usually a problem of stamina and speed, but often, it is also one of careful planning ahead of time and of skillful tactics. The dozen or more biographies of great runners are filled with stories of the hardly perceptible maneuvers by which important races are won or lost. A moment's hesitancy here, a single step to the inside there, a slight miscalculation of the pace or of the degree of acceleration with which the final kick is started--any one of these can nullify all the months of inexorable training.

PLAN AND PREPARE AHEAD OF TIME

The tactical possibilities in endurance running are numerous. As in a game of checkers, for every move there is a countermove; for every attack there is a defense. But as in checkers, such counteractions are as much the product of prior study and careful preparation as they are of inspiration and skill. Weeks and possibly months before a BIG race, a number of questions need to be answered. What men will be in the race? How will each of them run in terms of position? Who will set pace and how fast? How even will the pace be? How and when will the various competitors try to break contact with the field? Finally, what should be my tactics?

The answers to such questions might well affect a runner's training for some weeks or even months prior to the BIG race. For example, Bannister (1955, 225) relates how, three weeks before meeting Landy at Vancouver, he tried to impress Landy with his great finishing speed by deliberately holding back in the British championship mile and then sprinting an amazing :53.8 last quarter, "almost as fast as I can run a flat 440 yards!" Apparently this bit of tactical showmanship reached Landy; at least he ran the first half at Vancouver in 1:57.2--too fast for either runner. At this point Bannister had lost the advantage of contact, but he had planned that this would happen and psychologically he was still "connected." He felt he had forced Landy to run too fast and in the last half held the upper hand. In races, a feeling such as this often makes the whole difference.

A second excellent example occurred in the 5000 and 10,000 at the Melbourne Olympics, when Kuts first broke contact with all but Gordon Pirie by setting too fast a pace at the start, then upset his arch rival by alternating wild bursts of speed with very slow jogging. At one point he almost stopped and waived to Pirie to take the lead. This was certainly a physical waste of energy as well as mentally disturbing to Kuts as well as to Pirie, but the difference lay in the fact that Kuts had planned such tactics for months and had inured both his body and his mind so they could maintain control. Without similar preparation, Pirie finally broke and finished third.

Four years later, at Rome, Murray Halberg won the 5000 by a tactic for which he had prepared himself by specific training. In his biography (Gilmour, 1963, 105) he said,

> In the eighth lap, I began working the plan. . . . Without being conscious of any extra effort, I improved my place to second in the field. I settled there momentarily, gathered my strength. Then, with all I had, I sprinted.

> I could almost sense the feelings of the other runners. "The fellow's mad. He can't sprint with three laps to go." But the break had its desired effect. They hesitated to follow; I got my big gap, and all I needed to do was to hang on.

Our real point here is not so much the tactic as the careful and specific planning and pre-

TABLE 23.1
OUTSTANDING PERFORMANCES -- 880y-800m RUNS
OLYMPIC CHAMPIONS

Date	Record 880y	Record 800m	Name	Affiliation	Time at 440	Age	Best 440 Time
1896		2:11	E. H. Flack	Australia			
1900		2:01.2	A. E. Tysoe	Gt. Britain			
1904		1:56	J. D. Lightbody	USA			
1908		1:52.8	Mel Sheppard	New York		25	
1912		1:51.9	Ted Meredith	Mercersburg	52.5	18	47.4
1920		1:53.4	A. G. Hill	Gt. Britain			
1924		1:52.4	D. G. A. Lowe	Gt. Britain			
1928		1:51.8	D. G. A. Lowe	Gt. Britain	55	26	
1932		1:49.8	Tom Hampson	Gt. Britain	55		
1936		1:52.9	John Woodruff	Pittsburgh	57	20	47
1948		1:49.2	Mal Whitfield	Ohio State	54	24	46.2
1952		1:49.2	Mal Whitfield	USA	54.2	28	
1956		1:47.7	Tom Courtney	Fordham	53	23	46.0
1960		1:46.3	Peter Snell	N. Zealand	52	21	
1964		1:45.1	Peter Snell	N. Zealand	52.4	25	
1968		1:44.3	Ralph Doubell	Australia	51.3	23	
1972		1:45.9	Dave Wottle	Bowling Green	53.3	22	
1976		1:43.50	A. Juantorena	Cuba	51.0	25	44.26
1980		1:45.4	Steve Ovett	Gt. Britain	54.5	24	

WORLD-RECORD HOLDERS OF SPECIAL INTEREST

Date	880y	800m	Name	Affiliation	Time at 440	Age	Best 440 Time
1884	1:55.4		Lon Myers	New York			
1916	1:52.2		Ted Meredith	Penna.	52.8	22	47.4
1932	1:50.9	1:50.0	Ben Eastman	Stanford	52.0		46.4
1936		1:49.7	Glen Cunningham	Kansas	54.0	27	
1938	1:49.2	1:48.4	Sidney Wooderson	England	52.7	24	
1939		1:46.6	Rudi Harbig	Germany	52.2	26	46.0
1957	1:46.8	1:45.8	Tom Courtney	Fordham	52.2	24	46.0
1962	1:45.1	1:44.3	Peter Snell	N. Zealand	51.0	23	
1966	1:44.9		Jim Ryun	Kansas	53.3	19	
1972		1:44.3	Dave Wottle	Bowling Green	52.8	22	
1973		1:43.7	M. Fiasconaro	Italy	51.2	24	45.5
1974	1:44.1		Rick Wohlhuter	U.Chgo.T.C.	51.0	26	
1977		1:43.4	A. Juantorena	Cuba			
1979		1:42.4	Sebastian Coe	Gt. Britain	24.6-26.0-24.8-27		46.8

BEST PERFORMANCES -- HIGH SCHOOL

BOYS
1969	1:49.4	Marcel Phillippe	Mater Christi HS, Astoria, N.Y.
1972	1:48.5	Dale Scott	El Cerrito, CA
1975	1:49.7	Dan Aldredge	Petaluma, CA
1979	1:48.2	Jeff West	Los Angeles, CA

GIRLS
1974	2:02.3	Mary Decker	Orange, CA

BEST PERFORMANCES -- WOMEN

1968	2:00.9[1]	Madeleine Manning	USA
1972	1:58.6[1]	H. Falck	W. Germany
1973	1:57.5[3]	Svetla Ztlateva	Bulgaria
1976	1:59.8[2]	Madeleine Jackson	Cleveland T.C.
1976	1:54.94[1,3]	Tatiana Kazankina	USSR
1980	1:53.5[3]	N. Olizarenko	USSR

[1]Olympic record   [2]American record   [3]World record

paration that was made for it. In the same Olympics, Herb Elliott won the 1500 meters. Perhaps he was the best man in the field and would have won whatever the tactic. But the fact is he won by an astonishing 20 yards in world record time by use of this tactic as told by Cordner Nelson (1970, 137),

> At 800 meters he was a close fourth behind Bernard's 1:57.8. He had wanted to make his break here, but now he felt too tired. Only his long practice at punishing himself enabled him to try. They had been averaging 14.7 seconds for each 100 meters. Suddenly he ran the next 100 in 13.2 seconds and he was ahead of a long line of discouraged runners.

Examples of the crucial importance of planning for tactics in the BIG races are countless. Every championship meeting affords new ones. Just one more--that of Kipchoge Keino against the field and especially Jim Ryun in the Mexico City Olympics, 1968. Handicapped by a gall bladder infection that caused him to collapse in the 10,000 on Monday of that week, Kipchoge was not at all sure he could complete the 1500 final. As told to us by Noronha (1970, 148), the medical doctor recommended that he not compete,

> Before we could say anything else on the matter, he bagan to discuss tactics for the big race. We realised that in his present condition he had not the slightest hope of out-kicking Jim Ryun at the end of a slow race and we would have to plan for a fast race. . . .

> From the gun, Ben Jipcho (Keino's fellow-countryman) shot away as if his life depended on it. . . . Ben Jipcho continued with unabated pace to reach the half-way mark in 1:53.3. At this point, Kip sprinted wide and took over the lead while Ryun started moving up from last place, obviously preparing for his dramatic final lap sprint. Suddenly, however, the American realized that the gap between him and Keino was widening. Kip was sprinting. He was now 40 yards in the lead and increasing speed. Ryun broke into his famous sprint, . . . but he had left it too late; Kip was far ahead, still going strongly at the tape. . . .

> Keino shared the credit for his convincing and glorious victory with Ben Jipcho, without whose invaluable pace-setting early in the race, it might have been quite a different story.

We have given four examples. In each, the crucial element was not so much that the tactic was clever or shrewd, as that these men had the toughness of spirit to make the tactic work under conditions of high stress. Such toughness isn't inborn; it arises out of repeated practice of just such toughness. Herb Elliott (1961, 169) tells of a practice just prior to the Olympics,

> I then started off from the 1500m. mark and ran the race I wanted to run in the final--only at half-pace. My concentration was as though I really were in the final. I cruised around for two laps and, with about 700 yards to go, I increased the pace, pretending that I was running at full gait as I wanted to in the race. I practiced passing a couple of blokes and imagined myself swooping to the front. From there I imagined the physical tiredness that would come in the last lap and how I would overcome it. With one lap to go I increased the effort a little more as I hoped to in the race.

We have already read how well he carried out this rehearsal in the Olympic final. But here we are emphasizing the importance of inuring oneself to the agony of effort. Again Elliott (1961, 160) writes, in his diary,

> I ran out at a reasonable pace, and set off back . . . determined to finish really tired and satisfied. I squibbed on it without realizing it and finished too fresh. It annoyed me. I began to think I had lost my capacity to hurt myself. I must be careful and see that I cultivate this capacity again. I mustn't become a sub-conscious squib. I was so annoyed that I did three laps of the Shrine hill to finish off.

Strategic moves are likely to be successful only after everyone, including yourself, is undergoing the agony of fatigue. The difference is that you know what you are doing, have learned how to come to terms with its agonies, and thus are able to drive on when the physical energy seems gone. It's as much a mental as a physical effort.

TABLE 23.2
OUTSTANDING PERFORMANCES -- MILE AND 1500m RUNS
OLYMPIC CHAMPIONS

Date	Record Mile	1500m	Name	Affiliation	Age	Quarter Times
1936		3:47.8	Jack Lovelock	N. Zealand	26	61.4-64.1-62.0-40.3
1948		3:49.8	H. Eriksson	Sweden		
1952		3:45.2	Josy Barthel	Luxembourg	25	58.2-63.6-61.7-41.7
1956		3:41.2	Ron Delany	Eire	21	60.0-61.4-61.0-38.8
1960		3:35.6	Herb Elliott	Australia	22	58.5-59.5-56.0-41.6
1964		3:38.1	Peter Snell	N. Zealand	24	58.3-61.5-58.7-38.6
1968		3:34.8	Kip Keino	Kenya	28	57.0-58.3-58.0-41.6
1972		3:36.3	Pekka Vasala	Finland	24	61.6-60.0-54.8-39.9
1976		3:39.17	John Walker	N. Zealand	24	
1980		3:38.4	Sebastian Coe	Gr. Britain		

WORLD-RECORD PERFORMANCES OF SPECIAL INTEREST

Date	Mile	1500m	Name	Affiliation	Age	Quarter Times
1886	4:12.8		W. G. George	England	28	58.5-63.3-67.0-65.0
1895	4:15.6		Thomas Conneff	New York		
1907		3:59.8	H. A. Wilson	England		
1913	4:14.4		John P. Jones	Cornell		61.8-67.6-66.8-58.2
1915	4:12.6		Norm S. Tabor	Brown		58.0-67.0-68.0-59.6
1924	4:10.4	3:52.6	Paavo Nurmi	Finland	26	58.6-63.2-64.9-63.7
1931	4:09.2	3:49.2	Jules Ladoumegue	France		60.8-63.4-63.8-61.2
1933	4:08.7	3:48.8	William Bonthron	Princeton	22	61.2-62.3-65.1-40.2
1934	4:06.8		Glen Cunningham	Kansas	25	61.8-64.0-61.8-59.2
1937	4:06.4		Sidney Wooderson	England	31	58.6-64.0-64.6-59.4
1944		3:43.0	Gunder Hagg	Sweden		56.7-59.8-61.5-45.0
1945	4:01.4		Gunder Hagg	Sweden	27	56.5-62.7-62.2-60.0
1954	3:59.4		Roger Bannister	Oxford	21	57.5-60.7-62.3-58.9
1954	3:58.0	3:41.8	John Landy	Australia	25	58.5-60.2-58.5-60.8
1958	3:54.5		Herb Elliott	Australia	20	58.2-59.9-60.9-55.5
1964	3:54.1		Peter Snell	N. Zealand	24	56.2-57.8-60.0-60.1
1967	3:51.1	3:33.1	Jim Ryun	Kansas	20	59.0-59.9-58.5-53.7
1974		3:32.2	Filbert Bayi	Tanzania	21	54.9-57.3-58.0-41.4
1975	3:49.4		John Walker	N. Zealand	23	55.9-59.2-57.0-57.3
1979		3:32.1	Sebastian Coe	Gt. Britain	22	
1979	3:49.0		Sebastian Coe	Gt. Britain	22	57.5-57.0-57.5-57.0
1980	3:48.8		Steve Ovett	Gt. Britain	25	56.0-57.5-57.5-57.8

BEST PERFORMANCES -- HIGH SCHOOL

BOYS
Date	Mile	1500m	Name	Affiliation
1965	3:55.3	3:39.0	Jim Ryun	East HS, Wichita, Kan.
1966	3:59.4		Tim Danielson	Chula Vista, CA
1967	3:59.8		Martin Liquori	Essex HS, Newark, N.J.

GIRLS
| 1969 | | 4:16.8 | Francie Larrieu | Svale, CA |
| 1973 | 4:40.7 | | Eileen Claugus | Sacto, CA |

BEST PERFORMANCES (1500m) -- WOMEN

Date	Time	Name	Affiliation	Age	Ht	
1972	4:01.4[1,3]	Lyudmila Bragina	USSR	19	5'5"	117
1975	4:08.5[2]	Francie Larrieu	PCC	24	5'4"	99
1976	4:07.3[2]	Cyndy Poor	SJ Cinder	23	5'4"	116
1976	4:02.61[2]	Jan Merrill	New London, Ct.	20	5'5"	110 (Olympic semi-final)
1976	3:56.0[3]	Tatiana Kazankina	USSR			
1976	4:05.48[1]	Tatiana Kazankina	USSR	25	5'4"	104
1980	3:56.6[1]	Tatiana Kazankina	USSR	29	5'4"	110

[1]Olympic champions   [2]American record   [3]World record

TACTICS CAN BE SELF-DEFEATING. We must distinguish between the strategy that develops out of a calm and reasoned assessment of the situation, and that which grows out of desperation and uncertainty. Hamlet would have made a poor distance runner. In contrast, a great one, Herb Elliott, (1961, 52) writes,

> [Fleming] was trying to anticipate everything that was going to happen in the mile, so that he could devise a counter. I told him that it was no wonder he vomited before most of his races; he was wasting all his nervous energy thinking about them. . . . Your mind is in such a jumble that it won't give your body a chance.

As to his own attitude toward tactics, Elliott (1961, 145) adds,

> I rarely go into a race with any preconceived tactics. If I do, it means I'm not particularly hopeful of my chances. Athletes who resort to tactics have no real confidence in themselves and lose as many races as they win. Dr. Roger Bannister apparently didn't train too well and needed tactics, as did Chris Chataway. If tactics are going to be used, they are best determined after the race starts, because no one can be sure how a race will be run. . . . The only tactics I admire are those of do-or-die.

Well, that's one side of the story, though it would not be difficult to refute Elliott's contention, even from among his own races. His point of a decisive determination to win in any event is well taken, however.

BE OPTIMISTIC BUT REALISTIC IN PLANNING. Of the six or more men in any race, only one can win. You know that's true. Come to terms with it as a fact. You can't always win. Planning always to win is unintelligent, blind, foolish. Plan to do even a little better than you and others think you can but plan in terms of the realities of the situation. Then execute that plan with fortitude. A win-or-nothing attitude often ends up with very, very little, and breaks a man's spirit for future races.

KEEP YOUR OPTIONS OPEN. One hardly needs to quote Robert Burns to remind you that the best laid plans of men, as of mice, often go awry. So--make your plans carefully and harden yourself to them, BUT keep your mind and your options open. Thus Bruce Tulloh (1968, 110) tells of his planning for the 1962 European Championship 5000 meters, with 11 outstanding runners including Bolotnikov of Russia, Zimny of Poland, and Bernard of France,

> My plans were therefore as follows: (1) If Bolotnikov set a fast pace I would just try to hang on. (2) If Bolotnikov did not get away I would have to watch the others for a break. (3) If no one did anything decisive, then I would go myself in the last 800 meters, as I did not want to risk all in a last lap sprint.

> As it turned out, the third plan worked without the front running expected of Bolotnikov, and nobody else seemed to have much idea as to what to do. I took off on the back straight of the 11th lap and . . . won easily from Zimny and Bolotnikov.

WHEN SHALL I TAKE THE LEAD? Often it is said that there are two kinds of runners--pace setters and those that sprint from behind at the finish. But this avoids the question as to just when the latter sprint from behind--during the last 100 yards? 300 yards? 600 yards? 1000 yards? In general, with certain exceptions, once a man has taken the lead, he should maintain that lead to the finish. The question then becomes "what is the least distance at which I can take the lead and hold it?" For Ron Delany in the Melbourne 1500 meters, the last 150 meters was the crucial distance. For Herb Elliott in the Rome 1500, he felt he could hold the lead for the last 600 meters, and did so. For Kipchoge Keino in the Mexico City 1500, if we except his pace-setting teammate, Ben Jipcho, he held the lead all the way. Any lesser distance would have given Jim Ryun the encouragement he needed. In this sense, there is but one basic question, "when shall I take the lead?"

STRATEGY SHOULD BE RELATIVE. The chosen tactics for any given race must depend on your own capabilities in stamina, toughness of will, and sprinting speed as related to these same qualities in your opponents. You might well be a front runner in this race, a sprinter from behind in the next. This of course means that "knowing your opponents" is almost as important as "knowing yourself."

TABLE 23.3
LONG DISTANCE RUNNING
OLYMPIC CHAMPIONS -- 5000m -- 10,000m RUNS

Date	5000m	10,000m	Name	Affiliation	Age
1912	14.36.6	31:20.8	H. Kolehmainen	Finland	
1920	15:55.6		J. Guillemot	France	
1920		31:45.8	Paavo Nurmi	Finland	26
1924	14:31.2		Paavo Nurmi	Finland	30
1924		30:23.2	V. J. Ritola	Finland	
1928	14:38.0		V. J. Ritola	Finland	
1928		30:18.8	Paavo Nurmi	Finland	34
1932	14:30.0		L. A. Lehtinen	Finland	
1932		30:11.4	J. Kusocinski	Poland	
1936	14:22.2		G. Hockert	Finland	
1936		30:15.4	I. Salminen	Finland	
1948	14:17.6		Gaston Reiff	Belgium	27
1948		29:59.6	Emil Zatopek	CSSR	26
1952	14:06.6	29:17.0	Emil Zatopek	CSSR	30
1956	13:39.6	28:45.6	Vladimir Kuts	USSR	29
1960	13:43.4		Murray Halberg	N. Zealand	27
1960		28:32.2	V. Bolotnikov	USSR	30
1964	13:48.8		Bob Schul	USA	27
1964		28:24.4	Billy Mills	USA	26
1968	14:05.0		M. Gammoudi	Tunisia	30
1968		29:27.4	Naftali Temu	Kenya	23
1972	13:26.4	27:38.4	Lasse Viren	Finland	23
1976	13:24.76	27:40.38	Lasse Viren	Finland	27
1980	13:21.0	27:42.7	Miruts Yifter	Ethiopa	33

WORLD RECORDS OF SPECIAL INTEREST

Date	2 mile	5000m		Name	Affiliation	Age
1904	9:09.6			Alfred Shrubb	England	26
1931	8:59.6			Paavo Nurmi	Finland	33
1936	8:58.4			Donald Lash	Indiana	23
1944	8:42.8			Gunder Hagg	Sweden	26
1961	8:30.0	13:10.0	(3mi)	Murray Halberg	N. Zealand	28
1966		13:16.6		Ron Clarke	Australia	29
1972		13:13.0		Emil Puttemans	Belgium	
1972	8:14.0	27:38.4	(10M)	Lasse Viren	Finland	
1973		27:30.8	(10M)	Dave Bedford	Gt. Britain	
1978	8:13.6			Steve Ovett	Gt. Britain	
1978		13:08.4	(5M)	Henry Rono	Kenya	
1978		27:22.4	(10M)	Henry Rono	Kenya	

BEST PERFORMANCES -- HIGH SCHOOL

BOYS

Date	2 mile	5000m		Name	Affiliation	
1964	8:53.6	13:44.0	(5M)	Gerry Lindgren	Rogers, Spokane, Wash.	
1966	8:48.4			Rick Riley	Ferris, Spokane, Wash.	
1969	8:41.6			Steve Prefontaine	Marshfield, Coos Bay, Ore.	
1974	8:41			Craig Virgin	Lebanon, Ill.	
1976		28:32.7	(10M)	Rudy Chapa	Hammond, Ind.	
1979	8:36.3			Jeff Nelson	Burbank, CA	

GIRLS

Date	2 mile	5000m		Name	Affiliation	
1979	10:03.5	16:13.7	(5M)	Mary Shea	Raleigh, N.C.	
1979		32:52.5	(10M)	Mary Shea	Raleigh, N.C.	

SELF-ASSURANCE. Once plans are made and supported by related experience in training or competition, there must be belief in their workability. Many a man has fussed and fumed over the possibility of a better plan, and so drained his nervous energy and will-to-win that an effective performance was impossible.

TACTICS WHEN SETTING PACE

EVEN PACE. Physiologically, even pace is considered most economical.[2] Thus, Morehouse (1963, 204) concludes,

> In distance races, whether running, swimming, rowing, or bicycling, energy must be conserved and a steady state established at a dangerously high level of energy expenditure. Under these conditions the race will be finished in the shortest time if the athlete has maintained a speed at which a maximum steady level has been established for the number of minutes required for the event. Then, at the proper distance before the end of the race, he increases the speed so that the maximum energy is expended in the most economical manner.

However, there is sound research backing for the view that in middle-distance races the pace should be slower than even during the first portion of the race. Sid Robinson[1] explains

> In recent treadmill experiments on a good runner we have found that the energy cost of running is greatly increased by fatigue in the late stages of an exhausting run. . . . Thus the energy cost of running at constant speed was smaller in the middle part of the run than in the first of it and increased greatly as he became fatigued in the last half minute. Associated with these changes in efficiency were increments of lactic acid of 52.7 mg. percent in the first minute, 40 mg. percent in the second minute, and 70 mg. percent per minute during the last 35 seconds. . . .

> From the data on hand we are able to make some very interesting deductions regarding the purely physical aspects of running middle distance races. It is obvious that the runner should pace himself so as to delay until near the end of the race the sudden increase in energy cost of running associated with great fatigue and high lactic acid concentration. If the first part of the race is run too fast the runner may acquire most of his oxygen debt and be forced to run the remainder of the race with a high lactic acid, with his efficiency greatly reduced, and at a much slower pace. . . .

PROGRESSIVE EFFORT. Ordinarily a front runner tries to maintain even pace. But mentally, this should be interpreted, not as shown on a watch, but as indicated by one's muscle and organ sense, by one's feelings of effort. Maintaining even pace is not at all to maintain an even effort. On the contrary, even pace requires a progressive increase of effort, certainly as the stage of steady state is passed and that of anaerobic running is reached. Ron Clarke (1967, 120) makes this very clear as he tells the story of the Landy-Bannister dual at Vancouver,

> His (Landy) approach was always logical; this time it was utterly rational. . . . So he would run it from in front. . . . He did not plan a schedule of times. The even-paced running with which he was so familiar was the most effective "schedule." But it had nothing to do with judgment of pace--it was judgment of progressive effort. An even-paced mile was achieved by running steadily through the first lap and then pushing a little harder every half-lap.

FASTER THAN EVEN PACE. If the early pace of a race is faster than even pace, the steady state condition of all competitors will have been lost too early, oxygen debts will have built up, and awareness of the discomforts of fatigue will be sharp. Assuming all men are of equal stamina, it will not now be the fastest man that wins the race, but the man who slows down the least. That is, the man who has so inured himself to fatigue, physically and mentally, that he can drive himself forward despite the dragging weights in his muscles and chest.

---

[1]Sid Robinson, "Physiological Considerations of Pace in Running Middle-Distance Races," *USTCA INTERNATIONAL TRACK & FIELD DIGEST*, 1956, 219-224.

[2]Brent MacFarlane, "The Chemistry for an Even-Paced 800 meters," *Track Technique*, 49, Sept. 1972, p. 1554.

BREAKING CONTACT. The runner who tends to set pace assumes that he cannot match the finishing speed of one or more of his competitors. Therefore, at some point in the race, he must break contact with them. The crucial questions are how and when. The gist of "how" lies in "getting the jump" on the field, either by suddenly sprinting from in front as did Herb Elliott at Rome, or by gradually pouring it on faster and faster until your opponents finally acknowledge your superior stamina and toughness and allow themselves to lose contact (Kipchoge at Mexico City).

Neither method will work unless accompanied by an inexorable determination, a bulldog tenacity to KEEP the lead. It's rather easy to pick up a few yards' lead; it's agonizingly hard to hold and increase that lead. We repeat with emphasis--a lead is something to be tenaciously maintained; that's the reason for taking it. If you don't intend to make the hard struggle to keep the lead, you're better off not taking it at all, assuming of course you plan to win. Sure you're tired, painfully tired. But everyone's at least equally tired; otherwise your tactic of breaking contact would never work at all. The success of your tactic lies in making them believe they are even more tired than they actually are, AND THAT YOU ARE MUCH LESS SO.

We are saying that awareness of fatigue is a prerequisite to success in this tactic, and therefore, as a rule of thumb, the effort should be made at a point least distant from the finish line. The more tired they AND YOU are, the better your chances. From the standpoint of preparation, it follows that it's not your sprinting ability that will assure success so much as your ability to speed up when utterly exhausted. Murray Halberg (1963, 105) had a 12-yard lead in the 5000 at the Rome Olympics,

One lap to go. I looked back. They seemed to be gaining. Already I felt as if I was at the end of my run. My whole body screamed to stop, to lie down. But only for an instant. It was this race or none. The hours and hours I had put into my training flashed through my mind. IT WAS MY DESTINY TO WIN, NOT TO QUIT.

Only 300 metres to go. From somewhere the strength returned to my aching body. Two hundred to go, and I knew I could not be caught. I threw in that last reserve of energy that always seemed to be there. . . . I reached the tape, relaxed completely--and hit the deck.

I am reminded of Herb Elliott's concern that "I had lost the capacity to hurt myself," and so at the end of a dispiriting workout, he forced himself to take three rounds of the heartbreaking Shrine hill to finish off, and so prove his mastery over his body.

THE SIZE OF THE FIELD. In a large field of runners, the man leading at the end of the first lap has usually gone faster than even pace, and may have paid a high price in energy for his position. Outdoors, such a position has little value, for the long straights allow a man to move up when he wishes. Usually, mature runners stay back for several laps, move up gradually and easily around the middle of the race, then pour it on for the later laps.

Indoors, this latter tactic does not work so well. Crowded conditions and the short straights often require a considerable expenditure of energy and even more frustration as the attempt to move up and into the lead is made. All runners tend to be worried and incautious; in one straight a hard-gained improvement of position may end up in last place again. Under such conditions, having and keeping the lead has definite advantages.

CHANGE OF PACE. To convince your opponent of your own stamina and determination to win, it is often wise to raise the pace when your lead is challenged. The challenger may feel he is at the end of his rope and must make one last effort; your pickup of pace will ensure his rope's end.

THE STRESS OF LEADING. Many coaches and runners feel that it is more fatiguing to lead than to follow. Certainly breaking the wind requires more physical energy. But the well-trained and mature runner who feels certain he is both physically and mentally more enduring than his opponents, relaxes in front. After all, that's his place; he belongs there. Why run behind men of less stamina than himself. Ron Clarke usually ran that way, won that way, set world's records that way. But sometimes, especially at the shorter distances, the result was less than his intent.

KEEPING AWAKE. Running in front tends to increase self-awareness, especially of one's feelings of lethargy, and all too often, of the rising tide of doubt. To avoid this, a runner should try to maintain awareness of his rivals, not out of worry, but to know where they are and thus keep one's mind off oneself. Murray Halberg (1963, 105), wrote that after taking the lead at Rome, "I kept looking back. As in Cardiff, I had to know where the others were. I wasn't going to be taken by surprise."

Fig. 23.1   The 800-meter final at the 1960 Rome Olympic Games -- about 150 meters from the tape. Peter Snell, 3rd from left here, was boxed in by Schmidt, but when Waegli, the leader here, moved out on the final straight, Snell came through fast to win in Olympic-record time-- 1:46.3. Running second here is Roger Moens, Belgium, 1955 world-record holder at 1:45.7. Third place, George Kerr, West Indies (5th here); fourth, Paul Schmidt, Germany; fifth, Christian Waegli, Switzerland.

TACTICS WHEN FOLLOWING PACE

As we have written, the key question for the follower, assuming his superior speed-stamina at the finish, is "What is the minimum distance within which I can take the lead and maintain it to the finish?" There is a second question, "How much of a lead can I get?

Assuming more or less equal abilities, the answer lies in surprising one's rivals. The sprint should come when they least expect it, they're absorbed in their own fatigue, or perhaps at some point in the curve "Where one should never attempt to pass," or immediately after dropping back from a fake attempt to pass. To move up, drop back, then surge suddenly forward has often gained the yard or two margin of victory.

Another tactic is to lay back, not in second, but in third or fourth position where the leader is not aware of your actions. Keep a half-lane to the outside. Then a fast acceleration will build up speed so that you're well past the leader before he knows what's happening.

BEING BOXED. Every coach and coaching book warns against being boxed in, and yet almost every championship race produces just such a situation, even with very experienced runners. In the Rome 800-meter final, had Waegli of Switzerland, the leader as they came into the final stretch, remained on the pole, Snell, boxed on the inside lane by Schmidt of Germany, would have undoubtedly finished up second or worse (See Figure 20.1). Some times, a man must allow the entire field to go by before he can break to the outside and make his try for the tape. Usually such an effort is too late.

When following, the more flexible position is a half-lane wide from the runner immediately in front of you. As you feel the challenge of a man on your right shoulder, you can now move up ahead of him, or by moving a few inches outward, discourage him from trying; this of course, without interfering with his progress.

EXPLODE INTO THE LEAD. When you have decided to take the lead all the way to the finish line, do it all-out, with as much shock to your opponent as possible. Thus Snell (1965, 53) tells the story of a race against the great West Indies 440 and 880 runner, George Kerr,

But in Napier, George taught me a sharp lesson in tactics which cost me the race. He used a stratagem which I promptly added to my repertoire and used successfully several times.

I was leading confidently along the back straight, second time around, when George (Kerr) unexpectedly sprinted past with an electrifying burst. He went past with such acceleration that I was partly demoralized. . . . This kind of lightning burst completely, if only momentarily, deflates the runner who is caught by it. Psychologically he is trapped into a feeling of hopelessness by the impression of sheer speed which his opponent's surge gives.

MAINTAINING CONTACT. Contact is as much a mental as a physical concept. A man must be adamant in his determination to never allow his rival(s) to achieve a lead that he cannot overcome. For the inexperienced, contact can be said to be present only when you can reach out and touch your opponent.

Once that distance widens to even four or five feet, it easily increases to four or five yards. Stay close so you can hear his labored breathing, so you can see his worried glances. It helps to keep your mind on him and off yourself; even more, it tends to keep him in doubt.

Actually, contact is a flexible thing that is measured by the toughness and self-control of the man maintaining it. In the 1954 Vancouver Mile, Bannister was 15 yards behind Landy at the half-mile mark. Landy was the world-record holder. Surely one would say that effective contact had been lost. But Bannister had planned it that way. He was prepared for the tough third quarter in which closer contact would have to be gained. As Bannister (1955, 235) tells it,

I quickened my stride, trying at the same time to keep relaxed. I won back the first yard, then each succeeding yard, until his lead was halved by the time we reached the back straight on the third lap. How I wished I had never allowed him to establish such a lead!

I had now "connected" myself to Landy again, though he was still five yards ahead. . . . I tried to imagine myself attached to him by some invisible cord. With each stride I drew the cord tighter and reduced his lead. . . . I fixed myself to Landy like a shadow.

This was truly an instance in which contact, and victory as well, were affairs of the mind as much as of the body.

PART 2C

Coaching Sprints, Hurdles, Relays

Chapter 24
THE 400-METER DASH

A SUMMARY HISTORY OF METHOD OF RUNNING

When track and field competition began in England in the early 1800s, men were not well trained either in terms of months of training or of intensity. It was obvious to such men that no one could sprint all-out for 440 yards, and that it was therefore a grueling endurance race which should be run with a good deal of speed held in reserve for the finish.

There were very few specialists in running. For example, in 1868, E. J. Colbeck won the English championships in 50.4, after having first taken a second place in the 100-yard dash and a first in the 880 in 2:02, for a new English record. A much more startling example was Lawrence "Lon" Myers, one of the all-time greats of track athletics. Myers held every American record, from the 50-yard dash to the mile. In 1880, he competed in seven races in a single afternoon and won four American championships in the 100, 220, 440 and 880. In 1881, he won the English 440 championship in a best time of 48.6. Unquestionably, Myers was capable of better time than this. He had been timed at 05.5 for 50 yards, 10.0 for 100 yards, and 20.2 for 200 yards, as well as 1:55.5 for the half mile. No times are available for the first 220 of his 48.6 race, a fact which in itself indicates that coaches and athletes were not then conscious of the importance of this knowledge.

However, we do know that in 1886, Wendell Baker, Harvard, set a 440-straightaway record of 47.6 on a track whose "loose upper surface was scraped" specially for the one-man race against time. His 220 was 23.2; the 350, 37.0; the 400, 42.9. That is, he "floated" the third 130 yards in 13.8, and the last 90 yards in a dying 10.6. By the way, he had torn a shoe in an attempt a half-hour earlier to break the 100-yard world record, lost it at 285 yards of the 440, but still "flashed a burst of speed to snap the tape in 47.6."[1]

The first official world's record for the 440 (47.4, 1916) was set by Ted Meredith, Pennsylvania, whose primary association with the 880 (he was the 1912 Olympic 800-meter champion), strongly influenced methods of training and competing in the 440 for several decades. All coaching books printed during this time include the 440 under middle-distance events and training.

However, between about 1920 and 1950, the exclusively American custom of running the first 220 on the straight gradually changed the event to an endurance sprint. There were no lanes and, since it was a distinct advantage to have the pole position around the curve and lead into the final straight, there was intense competition to be first at the 220 mark. This led to faster and faster times for the first 220, an increasing handicap for the half-miler type. I remember so well in 1940 how we shifted a fine junior 440 man, Breidenbach (47.0), to the 880 simply because he couldn't stay with the sprinters in National Championship competition. The great victory of Eric Liddell, of Scotland, in the 1924 Olympic 400-meter championships provided a clear example of the trend toward sprinters. Liddell was best known as a 100 and 220 sprinter, having best times of 09.7 and 21.4, but when religious scruples led him to refuse to

---

[1] "Wendell Baker--Record Breaker," *The Amateur Athlete*, July 1935, 7.

TABLE 24.1

OUTSTANDING PERFORMANCES -- 440y-400m DASH

OLYMPIC CHAMPIONS

Date	Record 440y	400m	Name	Affiliation	Age	Best 220 Time	1st 220 Time	2nd 220 Time
1896		54.2	Tom Burke	USA				
1900		49.4	Maxie Long	USA				
1904		49.2	Harry Hillman	NYAC	24			
1912		48.2	C.D.Reidpath	Syracuse				
1920		49.6	B.G.D.Rudd	S.Africa				
1924		47.6	Eric Liddell	Scotland	24	21.6	22.2	25.4
1928		47.8	Ray Barbuti	Syracuse	22			
1932		46.2	William Carr	Penna.	23	21.5	21.5	24.7
1936		46.5	Archie Williams	Calif.			21.6	24.5
1948		46.2	Arthur Wint	Jamaica	28	21.9	22.2	24.0
1952		45.9	George Rhoden	Jamaica	25	20.6	22.2	23.7
1956		46.7	Chas. Jenkins	Villanova	22	21.2	22.2	24.5
1960		44.9	Otis Davis	Oregon	28	21.1	21.8	23.1
1964		45.1	Mike Larrabee	Okla.	31	21.0	22.2	22.9
1968		43.86	Lee Evans	San Jose		20.7	21.4	22.4
1972		44.66	Vince Matthews	USA	25			
1976		44.26	A. Juantorena	Cuba	25			
1980		44.60	Victor Markin	USSR				

WORLD RECORDS OF SPECIAL INTEREST

Date	440y	400m	Name	Affiliation	Age	Best 220 Time	1st 220 Time	2nd 220 Time
1916	47.4	47.4	J.E.Meredith	Penna.	24			
1928		47.0	E. Spencer	Stanford	22	21.4	22.0	25.0
1932	46.4		Ben Eastman	Stanford	22	21.6	21.4	25.0
1939		46.0	Rudi Harbig	Germany	26	21.6	22.1	23.9
1948	46.0	45.9	Herb McKenley	Jamaica	26	20.4	21.0	24.9
1950		45.8	George Rhoden	Jamaica	23	20.6	20.9	24.9
1956		45.2	Lou Jones	Manhattan	25	20.9	21.3	23.9
1960		44.9	Carl Kauffman	Germany	24	20.9	21.8	23.1
1967	44.8	44.5	Tommie Smith	San Jose	23	20.0	21.7	22.8
1968		43.8	Lee Evans	San Jose	21	20.7	21.4	22.4

BEST PERFORMANCES -- HIGH SCHOOL

BOYS

Date	440y	400m	Name	Affiliation
1974		46.3	Ronnie Harris	Charlottesville, Va.
1975	46.5		Elrick Brown	Lufkin, Texas
1975		46.5	Tony Darden	Norristown, Pa.
1979		45.51	Bill Green	Palo Alto, CA.

GIRLS

Date	440y	400m	Name	Affiliation
1976		50.90	Sheila Ingram	Wash., D.C.

BEST PERFORMANCES -- WOMEN

Date	400m	Name	Affiliation	Age			
1972	51.08[1]	M. Zehrt	East Germany				
1974	50.14[3]	Riitta Salin	Finland				
1976	51.66	Debra Sapenter	Prairie View	24	5'7"	118	(8th O.G.)
1976	50.65[2]	Rosalyn Bryant	Chgo. TC	20			(5th O.G.)
1976	49.29[3]	Irena Szewinska	Poland	30	5'9"	132	
1979	48.60[3]	Marita Koch	E. Germany	22	5'7"	137	
1980	48.88[1]	Marita Koch	E. Germany	23	5'7"	137	

---

[1]Olympic champions   [2]American record   [3]World record

run the 100 trials on Sunday, he shifted his efforts to the 400. With almost no experience in the event, he sprinted all-out to a clear lead at the 200 post in 22.2, and ripped through the tape in 47.6 for a new Olympic record.

So two schools of coaching engaged in many an argument--the middle-distance group versus the sprint group. But it was often a confused argument. It was the sprinters that had speeded up times for the first 220, and yet logically, the 880 men should set a fast pace and run the sprint out of the less-well-trained dashmen.

The issue was well joined in 1932 through a series of duals in the ICAAAA and the Olympic Championships between Ben Eastman, Stanford, who had recently set a world-record 1:50.9 for the 880, and Bill Carr, Pennsylvania, a place-winner in the sprints and anchor man on Penn's sprint and mile relays. In a special record attempt at Palo Alto, Eastman had recently cut the world 440 record (two turns) down to 46.4.

Most American coaches, including Templeton, Eastman's tough-minded coach, believed that the half-miler should set a pace fast enough to kill off the sprinter. Apparently this was Eastman's plan for, though his best unofficial time for the 200m was 21.6, he ran 21.4 in the Olympic race, a "mad" pace for 1932 racing. (As a matter of interest, Lee Evans ran 21.4 on his way to a world-record 43.8 in 1968.) But Carr stayed right on Eastman's heels, was able to run faster down the finish stretch, and so to win. Perhaps the 440 was a race for sprinters, after all. Though a few die-hards argued that Templeton had used bad judgment in coaching his boy to set a 21.4-24.9 pace. If the pace had been slower, the half-miler would have won.

Both this judgment and the close relationship between the 440 and 880 was strongly supported some seven years later when Rudi Harbig of Germany shocked everyone by setting new world's records for the 400 meters (46.0) and 800 meters (1:46.6) within a period of three weeks. His splits for the 400m were 22.1--23.9, with a time difference of only 1.8 seconds as compared with Carr's 3.2 seconds. Harbig's best recorded time for the 200m curve was 21.6, so that he was running within 5/10th second of his best effort.

One of the greatest trios of all time, Herb McKenley, Arthur Wint, and George Rhoden, were all natives of the little island of Jamaica with a population of only 1 1/3 million people. McKenley first attracted world attention by running 46.2 for the 440 in May, 1946, a new world's record. The race started on the 220 straightaway and I, clocking the 220 times very carefully, was amazed to see 20.9 on my watch. Two weeks earlier, McKenley had made his best personal record for the 220 of 20.6, so that, like Harbig, he had run within 3/10th second of his maximum speed. Two years later, 1948, McKenley again ran 20.9 on the way to a new world record--46.0.

The 1952 Olympic final between Rhoden, McKenley, Wint, Whitfield, Matson of San Francisco, and Haas of Germany showed a different pattern. Following the general background as here related, one would have expected a blistering pace during the early stages of the race. However, Rhoden (22.2), McKenley (22.7), and Whitfield (22.9) were content to let 31-year old Wint set the pace at 21.7. This was the slowest pace ever run by either McKenley or Rhoden.   But Rhoden, by pouring it on during the third 110 yards, and McKenley by a tremendous spurt in the final straight, were able to come within 1/10 second of the best ever recorded, each with 45.9. Wint, the 1948 winner at London, was 5th in 47 flat. He said later that his 21.7 was 2/10 faster than he had ever run for 200 meters, and that he had made a great mistake in going out so fast.

The 1956 Olympic 400-meter final at Melbourne included Lou Jones of Manhattan, who had run 21.3 when he established his world record of 45.2 early that year, Karl Haas of Germany (best 400m--46.5, best 200m--20.7), A. Ignatyev of the USSR (best 400m--46.5, best 200m--20.7), Mal Spence of South Africa (best 400m--46.6), Voitto Hellsten of Finland (best 400m--46.5, best 200m--21.1) and Villanova junior, Charles Jenkins (best 400m--46.1 in winning the final Olympic tryout). The experts picked Lou Jones as a clear favorite; Jenkins as a possible place-winner.

In August, 1956, D. H. Potts,[1] an astute observer, wrote the following:

---

[1] D. H. Potts, *Track and Field News*, August 1956, 7.

I disagree with those who claim that Lou Jones has re-established the McKenley theory (1948) of how to run the 440. The secret of Jones' success is not running that first furlong at practically top speed as did Hustlin' Herb in the late 40s. What Lou has done is solve the problem of running his own race; that is to say, how to dole out his reserves so as to deplete them at the precise instant of finishing.

But in the Olympic final, Jones led by two meters at 200 meters in 21.8, with Spence and Ignatyev two meters back, held his lead by one meter at 300 meters (33.4), then slowed down rapidly to an inglorious fifth place (48.1). Ignatyev held the lead for a few meters, but Jenkins, strong and relaxed, soon took over and went on to win by a full meter in 46.7 (22.2--24.5, time difference--2.3 seconds).

Potts wrote in the December, 1956, issue of *Track and Field News*,

Afterwards Jones said he had no excuses. He felt he was physically in condition. . . . He said his defeat was due to the unexpected psychological shock of coming off the turn with Ignatyev practically even with him. He had run the first 300 meters hard and expected to emerge with at least a three or four meter lead. He was so unprepared for the possible failure of this strategy that he actually froze mentally. . . . Jenkins attributed his somewhat unexpected win to his coach's last letter, admonishing him to run relaxed, and to his Olympic roommate, Andy Stanfield, who kept him from getting nervous. Jenkins said he followed instructions and ran the first 300 relaxed. . . . I felt very strong after my semi-final, and I was confident I had a chance.

The 400-meter final at Rome, 1960, produced a photo-finish between Otis Davis, U.S.A. and Oregon, and Karl Kauffmann of Germany. Both men were credited with "a fantastic world record of 44.9!" Both men had identical 200-meter splits (21.8--23.1). The difference between them, and the key to success in the race, lay in their 300 meter time. Usually Davis started his finish as he came out of the final curve, but on this occasion he started earlier than ever before and thus picked up a full three meters at 300 meters (32.9) over Kauffmann (33.3). Kauffmann was gaining on Davis all the way to the tape but failed by two inches to catch him. Davis (lane 3) had men ahead of him at 200 meters and therefore a guide for his efforts. He was in front from about 290 meters to the finish. Kauffmann (lane 1) had Davis ahead of him all the way.

Four years later, at Tokyo, the 200 meters was 2/10th faster (21.6), and the race was won in quite different fashion. Syd DeRoner,[1] of *Track & Field News*, tells it this way:

Larrabee (the winner--45.1) had three of his top opponents on his outside with only Badenski of the contenders for the gold medal behind him in lane 2. Larrabee was off slowly and at the 200 meter mark was 6th. . . . Mottley, in 21.6 had a slight lead over Badenski, Williams, and Brightwell in that order. Larrabee started to move going into the turn but he caught only one man, Skinner, in the turn. Coming off the turn at the head of the straightaway it was Mottley, Badenski, Brightwell, Williams and Larrabee. Larrabee . . . was about 4 meters behind the leader, Mottley, as they started the final 100 meters. . . . Finally about 10 meters from the tape he caught Mottley and won going away in 45.1.

Cordner Nelson[2] tells the story of tactics at Mexico City, 1968:

Before 1968, 15 men had run under 45.5; at Mexico City it happened 18 times. . . . Personal records fell to at least 25 men. . . .

Evans ran hard from the start. He usually follows and comes from behind in the home-stretch, but he was in lane six with nobody to follow and he knew he would have to hurry

---

[1] Syd DeRoner, "Larrabee Wins in Stretch," *Track & Field News*, October/November 1964, 7.

[2] Cordner Nelson, "Evans 43.8 Stops James," *Track & Field News*, October/November 1968, 10.

to beat James. He made up the stagger on both Badenski and Omolo before the final turn.

"Art Simburg and Bud Winter helped me with my strategy," Lee said later. "The most important aspect was to run the first 100 hard, which I've never done before. In the back stretch I did my 'Winnipeg tip,'" which he explained was a tactic he learned from Vince Matthews at last year's Pan-Am Games. "Vince runs a great backstretch effort-lessly, but faster than anyone. I tried to run as fast as possible while staying relaxed."

His third 100-meters was the key, Evans said, "I took out my aggressions against the US Olympic Committee with a hard turn." Around the turn he tried to relax by picturing Tommie Smith's smooth stride, a sharp contrast with his own struggling lunges. Into the stretch he led by three yards and he seemed to have it won. "Anyone who has seen me run knows I can usually muster a kick after almost any pace," Lee said. But James in lane two ran beautifully down the long stretch. . . . But the tape appeared too soon and Larry's 43.9 was a yard short of winning.

The editors of *Olympic Track & Field* described the 1976 Olympic 400m at Montreal,

Newhouse led at 200m (21.5) with Frazier and Juantorena not far behind...Halfway through the turn, Juantorena made his move. He passed Frazier and reached the 300 in 32.3, just 0.2 back of Newhouse. It became a two-man race until the Cuban's pressure became inexorable. With 20 meters to go, he went into the lead and won going away (44.26); Newhouse (44.40). Frazier, struggling to hold form, managed to save the bronze from Brydenbach's late rush.

HOW TO RUN THE 440

This summary history of the various tactics used in running the 440 suggests at least two approaches to the problem--that of the physiology of efficient running at near-maximum pace, and that of know-how based on actual experience. The latter has many aspects, for each ath-lete-competition-situation is unique in certain details and each runner must handle a race in his own unique way. In summary, however, (1) a man must have a mental-muscle sense of know-ing-feeling pace when running in lanes all the way and there's no one in the outside lanes by which to guide, (2) he must be able on the backstretch to go "faster-looser" even though al-ready sprinting "all-out," and (3) he must be able to maintain control-tenacity-drive down the finishing stretch when there's nothing left to control nor energy with which to drive.

We shall discuss these two approaches in turn.

PHYSIOLOGICAL EFFICIENCY. From a related research standpoint, the work of Franklin Henry,[1] done in 1952, is still valid. Among his many conclusions, the following are relevant:

1. That men generally reached their top speed about 6 seconds after leaving the starting blocks.

2. That "it is physiologically impossible for the runner, after he has reached his peak velocity, to maintain it for more than about 15 or 20 yards."

3. That an earlier study by Sargent showed "that the energy cost of running in-creases as the 3.8th mathematical power of the speed."

4. That "it can be said with confidence that insofar as the physiological limit is involved in setting records, a steady pace will result in faster time for the 220 and 440 as well as the half, the mile, and the two-mile."

---

[1] Franklin M. Henry, "Research on Sprint Running," *The Athletic Journal*, February 1952, 30.

In 1960, Henry Taylor[2] reviewed related research on "The Oxygen Cost of Maximal Work," and concluded, "These data make it clear that athletes should conserve their anaerobic reserves until late in the contest." The answer to the question of how this can be done most effectively is--consider speed-endurance as a unity; each contributing its part to the whole. The greater one's sprinting speed, the easier one can run at a high-level speed; and the greater one's endurance, the easier and longer one can sustain speed at high levels.

This view is supported by an Estonian study[3] on 400-meter limits,

400 METER LIMITS, by J. Razumovski
Analyses of more than 1500 world-class quarter-milers indicate that basic speed is the most important single factor in 400 meters performances. There is a close correlation between 100 and 400 meter times, showing that a 56.6 second 400 meter clocking requires a 100 meter time not slower than 11.6 seconds. To reach 46.0 seconds one needs a minimum 100-meter speed of 10.6 seconds, while 10.3 seconds is the basic requirement for clocking 45.0 seconds.
Another important component for the 400 meter is a specific endurance. Research has shown that the relationship between aerobic and anaerobic processes in a 50.0 seconds performance is 1:6 and in a 46.0 seconds performance 1:8. In other words, a fast 400 meters is covered by using roughly 90 percent anaerobic energy production and 10 percent aerobic. From the anaerobic energy production 80 percent is made up from lactate processes. The lactate processes, which act unfavorably to fast and powerful muscle contractions, can be delayed when sufficient basic speed reserves are available. Consequently, the correct approach to 400 meter training is to develop muscular power and speed before attention shifts to specific endurance.

EXPERIENTIAL KNOW-HOW. A study of Table 26.1 discloses that in no instance of a world record or Olympic championship in the 440 has the time for the first 220 been slower than or equal to that for the second 220. That is, all such record runs have been in defiance of the findings of research as to economy of pace. The runs that came closest to even time were those by Jim Lea (45.0), time-difference--0.6 second; Mike Larrabee (45.1), time-difference--0.7 second; and Lee Evans (43.8), time difference--1.0 second. (Evans' splits were given me by his coach, Bud Winter.)

Near-maximum pace. Study of the right-hand column of Table 26.1 shows that all great 440s have been run at a near-maximum pace. Our figures are not entirely valid, for quartermilers do not train for or compete often enough in the 220 to disclose their true maximum for this distance. Note that Arthur Wint ran his 1952 Helsinki race at a faster pace by 2/10th second than he had ever run for the 200-meters alone. But for our purposes, they are acceptably valid.

When Tommie Smith ran 21.7 on the way to a 44.5 440, he was 1.7 seconds over his best time for the 220 of 20 seconds around one curve. This was the slowest relative time for any of the great 440s. In contrast, Lee Evans ran within 6 and 7/10ths of his maximum pace in his greatest 440s, as did Curtis Mills in running 44.7. Smith was primarily a 220 man. Had he trained fully for the 440, and run about 20.9, he might well have hung on for a 22.4 second 220 (a la Evans) and have achieved a 43.3 final time.

In summary, experience in competition suggests that a man can run the first 220 within less than one second of his 220 maximum without slowing down more than about one second in the second 220.

Minimum deceleration. This brings up the problem of sustaining minimum deceleration during the last 220 when lactic acid in the muscles is extremely high and the anaerobic mechanisms are

---

[1]Sid Robinson and others, "Fatigue and Efficiency of Men During Exhausting Runs," *Journal of Applied Physiology*, 1958, 12, 197.

[2]Henry Longstreet Taylor, "Exercise and Metabolism: in *Science and Medicine of Exercise and Sports*, edited by Warren R. Johnson, New York: Harper and Brothers, 1960, 155.

[3]J. Razumovski, "400-Meter Limits," *Track Technique*, #72, June 1978, p. 2308.

much less efficient. It seems that record performers have ignored Taylor's warning that anaerobic reserves should be conserved until late in the race.

The interview between Cordner Nelson and Lee Evans after his 43.8 race at Mexico City is of special significance. (1) Evans had to run the first 110 "hard, which I've never done before." (2) On the backstretch "I tried to run as fast as possible while staying relaxed." (3) Around the turn, he tried to relax, though without slowing down. (4) At the finish, he hung on, again with minimum slow-down. Of course, words are only a simulation of action, but Evans' words suggest a principle of very-close-to-maximum pace throughout with minimum deceleration at the finish.

Such a principle, based on actual experience but somewhat contrary to a sound body of related research, suggests that, if we ignore the competitive phase of racing, pace for the 440 should be based (1) on one's best time for the 220, (2) on sound and solid training for the 440, and (3) on extensive competitive experience by which a man learns how to sustain an all-out relaxed pace (what Winter called "faster-looser") for the full distance. Needless to say, without the latter two factors, pace would have to be much slower.

I am reminded of Dean Cromwell's response in 1941 to the statement of his star quartermiler, Cliff Bourland, that during his "float" on the backstretch, he dropped his arms and settled down in his striding. "In fact, Mr. Champion, you merely drop your tensions and everything else remains the same." To carry that thought farther, the whole problem of relaxation during maximum effort is one of the most fascinating in all of sport. It's what Alan Watts calls a double-bind action, an artless art in which true relaxation nullifies the very idea of effort or that a problem exists. The most interesting book I know on the subject is Herrigel's _Zen in the Art of Archery._[1] It may not be track and field but it points the way to greater self-control and greater performance.

SCIENCE AND EXPERIENCE. After decades of disagreement, the conclusions of science and experience are finally being resolved. On the one hand, the maximal sprinting speeds of 400-meter runners is increasing, making it easier to run faster. That is to say, though the first 200m in today's 400m races are faster, they are also slower--relative to the runners' maximal sprinting speeds. On the other hand, as science directs, anaerobic reserves are being conserved by more effective training, specifically related to the demands of the 400-meter distance. When science and experience coincide, human ultimates are being approached.

ORGANIZATION OF PRACTICE FOR THE 440

In terms of pace, the 440-yard race is certainly a sprint event. Training for it must therefore include the usual sprint work--starting practice, short sprints at 50 to 180 yards, and the like. We have therefore placed this chapter just before that on sprinting, and so provided easy access to the methods of practice described there.

But of at least equal import, the aerobic-anaerobic demands of the 440 are just as stressful as for any endurance event. Therefore this chapter follows immediately after those on training for endurance running. Chapter 21 on "How to Organize Your Own Training System" has direct application. Certainly training the year-round has as much validity for the 440 as for the 880 or mile. A modified Lydiard or Fartlek program would be entirely sound during the early months of each year. Variety of terrain, distance, and pace is just as essential for quarter-milers as for any distance men.

But the most related of all systems for 440 training is interval training that emphasizes repeated distances of 350 yards and under. The discussions in Chapter 20 on short-distance interval work should be of value.

Over the past 20 years, there has been a tremendous increase in the amount and intensity of

---

[1] Eugen Herrigel, ZEN IN THE ART OF ARCHERY, New York: Pantheon Books, Inc., 1953.

work done by quarter-milers. Formerly, they worked out with sprinters, and then finished with a few 220s or several 350s. Today they continue to work with sprinters about two days a week but on the other days they challenge the 880 men as to who can work the hardest. James Elliott,[1] coach of Olympic champion Charlie Jenkins and many other excellent quarter-milers, stated this point very concisely:

> *You have to sell quarter-milers on a program of hard work. The only way they can become great runners is by living track 12 months a year, 24 hours a day. How they live and what they do during that time determines the degree of greatness they a-chieve. . . . They must be convinced that there is no shortcut to success. . . . During the fall our quarter-milers jog a mile before practice and a mile after. We often run repeat 220s, concentrating on relaxation not speed, hitting them in about 28 seconds. . . . At first they can only do five or six 220s but they build up to where they are able to run 13 or 14 of them.*

During the competitive season, Elliott's men emphasized hard work during the early days of each week. They often ran repeat 660s on Mondays and repeat 300s on Tuesday.

SAMPLE TRAINING PROGRAM.--Curtis Mills, Texas A & M, world-record 440 yards--44.7, 1969. The following material has been re-arranged from a talk by Coach Charles Thomas,[2] Texas A & M. The actual workout schedule included a good deal of variety including road racing, sprint relay running, a little weight training, and repeat 150s which Mills considered his hardest workout but which he enjoyed. In this presentation, Coach Thomas emphasized what he called an up-and-down-the-ladder workout, but what is usually called the funnel system. Example: 220-220-660-440-220 (Mills' favorite workout).

Early Season (September-December inclusive). Four days a week (Monday-Thursday inclusive). The schedule for all weeks, including the first, tends to be the same.

Monday: 3¼-mile road race. On first Monday, run through without stopping. Improve time each week for 6-8 weeks. Mills ran about 21 minutes.
Tuesday: ladder workout emphasizing longer distances. Examples:

    220-220-660-220-220-440-220-220
    110-110-220-220-660 or 550-220-220-110-110
    110-110-330-330-550-330-110-110
    220-220-660-440-220
    220-220-660-220-220-330-110-110

Wednesday and Thursday: ladder workouts emphasizing short-fast distances. Examples:

    220-220-550-220-220
    110-110-220-330-220-110-110
    110-110-110-110-330-330-110-110
    330-220-110-110-220-330

Occasional time trials are held to select relay teams, to compare present conditions with that of last year, and to tune up for the early meets. For variety, continuous 7-man 880-yard relays are run, with each man running 7-10 x 220 and averaging about 28-30 seconds per 220. After about 8 weeks, the Monday 3¼-mile race is dropped, and the Tuesday schedule is then also used on Monday.

Middle Season (January-March inclusive). The ladder schedule is dropped in favor of work more specific to the 440. Emphasis is on speed over relatively longer distances (220-660 yards).

---

[1] Jim Elliott, "The Quarter Mile," in *CHAMPIONSHIP TRACK AND FIELD*, edited by Tom Ecker, Englewood Cliffs: Prentice-Hall, Inc., 1961, 30.

[2] Charles Thomas, "Training Schedule of Curtis Mills," USTCA *Quarterly Review*, Vol 71, No 1, 1971.

After warming up by repeating 6 or more 100-yard sprints, considerable time is given to baton work for the 440-880-mile relay teams. The fast relay runs often substitute for the sprinting that quarter-milers usually do.

Example of a week's work:

Monday: 2 x 500 (440 under 50), plenty of rest
Tuesday: 1 x 660 (about 1:21) or 2 x 660
Wednesday: 6 x 220 (easy pace around 30), an easy day to recover
Thursday: 4-5 x 300 or 6-7 x 220
Friday: 5 x 220 or 8 x 150 (5 medium, 3 fast)

Late Season (April-June inclusive). Emphasis on speedwork. The distance and number of repetitions of each interval workout are reduced; the speed is increased with full recovery between runs. Example of a week's work:

Monday: 1 x 500 (440 fast), then 2 x 150 fast
Tuesday: 3-4 x 300 (Mills averaged 31.5 for four)
Wednesday: 4 x 220 (22.0 average)
Thursday: 5-6 x 150 (increasing speed on each 150)
            or 5-6 x 100 (increasing speed on last three; Mills averaged 9.0 for each of
            the last three with a 10-yard flying start)
Friday: Rest
Saturday: Competition

Mills' Schedule (two weeks prior to his record 44.7 440).

Mon. AM: 6 x 150 fast; PM:6 x 110 fast   Sun: Rest
Tues. AM: 5 x 150 fast; PM: 5 x 220 (23 to 21 sec)   Mon: 4 x 150 fast
Wed. AM: 6 x 110 fast; PM: Easy warm-up only   Tues: 4 x 150 fast
Thur. AM: 4 x 150 fast; PM: Rest   Wed: Rest
Fri. Rest   Thur: Rest
Sat. Ran 46.2 in competition   Fri: 45.7 in NCAA trials
                                                 Sat: 44.7 in NCAA finals.

John Smith--How He Trains[1] (UCLA & So. California Striders TC)
Best Marks: 440y-44.5, world record, 1971; 100y-9.4; 220y-20.6; 660y-1:17.4.

Training: Smith's training from October through July is essentially the same, differing only in speed as the season progresses.
Monday: (a) 550-yards, start at 75.0 in October and gradually reduce the time to 63.0 in May; (b) 440-yards, start at 60.0 in October and gradually reduce the time to 48.0 in May; (c) 330-yards, start at 45.0 in October and gradually reduce the time to 35.0 in May. Walk as long as desired for recovery after each.
Tuesday & Thursday: sprints up a 508-yard grass hill, starting with one in October and increasing to five in January. Walk return recovery after each. After January, add 8 x 110-yards fast striding, jogging a 110 after each.
Wednesday: 3 x 330-yards, starting at 45.0 in October and gradually reducing the time to 32.0-34.0 in June. Walk as long as desired for recovery after each.
Thursday: After the competitive season starts in late February, the Thursday workout changes from repeating Tuesday's session to 3 x 165-yards in 15.0-16.0, starting on the curve of the track, followed by 3 x 150-yards in 13.0-14.0. Walk according to inclination for recovery.
Friday: 5-6 x 150-yards, starting at 15.0 in October and gradually reducing the time to 13.0 in May. Once or twice monthly, the Friday workout is changed to 4 x 220-yards, starting with 24.0, 23.0, 22.0 and 21.0 (with running start) in Feb. and gradually reducing the time to 22.0, 21.0, 20+ and 20+ in May. Walk according to inclination for recovery after each.
Saturday & Sunday: rest. During competitive season, race on Sat., rest Fri. and Sun. Smith lifts weights four times weekly, using 3 to 4 repetitions of the bench press (225-lbs), curl (95-100-lbs) and military press (140-lbs). He jogs an 880 warm-down after each workout. He attempts to run an even pace in competition. When he established his 440 world record, Smith ran the first 220 in 22.2 and the second in 22.3. He races about 20 times annually, and is coached by Jim Bush.
[1]Fred Wilt, "John Smith, How He Trains, *Track Technique*, #48, June 1972, p. 1513.

Chapter 25
THE SPRINTS

Racing short distances has been a part of the competitive play of every civilization and has been described in the literature of almost every people. We in Western civilization naturally turn to our own sources in Western literature. We refer to the foot races of the beautiful Atalanta whose love of the hunt and speed of foot were exceeded only by her love of beautiful apples or greed for gold, as you may prefer to look at it. Every schoolboy knows of Achilles, who held games as part of the funeral ceremonies for his friend Patroclus. One event of those games was a foot race, won by Ulysses, for which a great silver bowl, a huge ox, and half a talent of gold were offered as prizes.

But apart from legend, we have facts and artifacts to prove that sprinting was included in the ancient Greek Olympics. Excavations at Olympia, Delphi, Corinth, and other sites of the ancient games disclose well thought out devices for achieving a fair start--the toughest problem in sprinting. For example, at the Delphi stadium, 20 blocks of marble for starting are now in place. In each there are two grooves in which the racers set their feet, and adjacent to those grooves, a socket. Harris[1] explains both clearly and at length that a "husplex," that is, a post and arm, was set in this socket, that a string went from each arm through a groove (if rock surface) or a pipe (if earth surface) to the starter's pit. The few references to it in Greek literature indicate the husplex arm dropped, but it seems more effective to me if it lifted. By pulling all strings at once, the starter could lift the arms together and release the sprinters. (How Ben Ogden, of Temple University and Madison Square Garden starting-gate fame would take delight in these disclosures.)

Woe to him who sought a flying start. Not only would the rising arm catch him in the chin, the Greeks also had long forked sticks handy, and "Those who start too soon are beaten," said Andeimantus to Themistocles at the historic council before Salamis.

Incidentally, the threat of physical punishment is not entirely unknown in modern times. For instance, Webster[2] tells a story of how Arthur Duffey, the Georgetown champion, while touring England In 1902, had an even more threatening experience.

Duffey was a tremendously fast starter, and an amusing story is told of one experience with a North Country starter, who is said to have uttered a warning as he stood behind Duffey's curved end:

"Sitha, Duffey, lad," said the official, "Ah've brought shot gun for t'startin'. Ah've blank i't first barrel an't shot i't second. Tha canst guess where tha'l't get shot if tha tries any flyers."

---

[1] H. A. Harris, *GREEK ATHLETES AND ATHLETICS*, London: Hutchinson & Co., Ltd, 1964, 68. (Harris includes drawings of the husplex.)

[2] F. A. M. Webster, *ATHLETICS OF TO-DAY*. London: Frederick Warne & Co., Ltd., 1929, 46.

TABLE 25.1
OUTSTANDING PERFORMANCES -- SPRINTS

OLYMPIC CHAMPIONS

Date	Record		Name	Affiliation	Age	Hgt.	Wgt.
MEN	100m	200m					
1956	10.5	20.60R	Bobby Morrow	USA		6'1"	170
1960	10.20R		Armin Hary	Germany	23	6'	156
1960		20.5WR	Livio Berruti	Italy			
1964	10.0WR		Bob Hayes	USA	21	6'	189
1964		20.30R	Henry Carr	USA	22	6'3"	185
1968	9.95WR		Jim Hines	USA			
1968		19.8WR	Tommie Smith	USA	24	6'3"	173
1972	10.14	20.00	Valeriy Borzov	USSR	23	6'	174
1976	10.06		Haseley Crawford	Trinidad	26	6'1"	165
1976		20.23	Donald Quarrie	Jamaica	25	5'8"	155
1980	10.25		Allan Wells	Scotland	28	6'0"	168
1980		20.19	Pietro Mennea	Italy	28	5'10"	154
WOMEN							
1960	11.0	24.0	Wilma Rudolph	USA			
1964	11.4		Wyomia Tyus	USA			
1968	11.08WR		Wyomia Tyus	USA			
1968		22.58WR	I. Szewinska	Poland			
1972	11.07WR	22.40WR	Renate Stecher	E. Germany	22	5'6½"	145
1976	11.08		Annegret Richter	W. Germany	26	5'6"	115
1976		22.370R	Barbel Eckert	E. Germany			
1980	11.06		L.Kondratyeva	USSR	22	5'6¼"	132
1980		22.03	Barbel Woeckel	E. Germany			

WORLD-RECORD HOLDERS OF SPECIAL INTEREST

Date	100m	200m	Name	Affiliation	Age	Hgt.	Wgt.
1890	09.8y		John Owen	Detroit			
1896		21.2y	Bernie Wefers	NYAC			
1921	.09.5y	20.8y	Charles Paddock	USC	21	5'8"	160
1929	09.4y		George Simpson	Ohio State (With starting blocks)			
1935	09.4y	20.3y	Jesse Owens	Ohio State	20	5'10"	156
1967	09.21		Charles Greene	Nebraska			
1968	09.95		Jim Hines	USA			
1971		19.81	Don Quarrie	Jamaica	20	5'8"	155
1974	09.0y		Ivory Crockett	USA	26	5'8"	145
1975	09.9		Houston McTear	Baker HS, Fla.	18	5'7"	155
1979	10.01	19.72	Pietro Mennea	Italy	27	5'10"	154

SELECTED PERFORMANCES--HIGH SCHOOL

Date	100m	200m	Name	Affiliation	Age	Hgt.	Wgt.
BOYS	100m	200m					
1976	10.16		Houston McTear	Baker, Fla.			
1976		20.22	Dwayne Evans	Phoenix, Ariz.			
1978	10.39	20.90	Carlton Young	Central HS, Phila.			
1979	10.36	20.7	Calvin Smith	Clinton, Ms.			
1980	10.1		Bernie Jackson	Tempe, Ariz.			
GIRLS							
1976	11.13	22.77	C. Cheeseborough	Jacksonville, Fla.		5'6"	125
1976	11.24		Evelyn Ashford	Homestead, Fla.		5'5"	110
1979		23.42	Gwen Loud	Westchester, La.			
1979	11.47		Michelle Glover	Willingboro, N.J.			

Modern organized sprint races had their origin in professional racing, which was very prevalent in England during the entire 19th century and in much less organized fashion in this country until about 1910. The story of methods, stratagems, and gambling in professional racing forms is one of the most fascinating pages in all sports history. From the standpoint of techniques, one of the best of the scattered writings is that by William Curtis, written in 1899,[1]

During the early years of American amateur athletic sport, all the methods of management were naturally copied from the professionals. Running was limited almost entirely to matches, as there were no open competitions which athletes could enter, and the distances were in nine cases out of ten one of the two extremes--one hundred yards or ten miles. As there were but two starters in these match races, the methods of getting away were more primitive than at present and had been cunningly devised by veteran professionals to give the expert an advantage over the novice.

Several styles were in common use, the oldest being what was called the "break start." The judge stood on the starting line, the men went back fifteen or twenty paces, stood side by side, joined fingers lightly and trotted up to the judge. As they passed on either side of him, his body broke the touch of their fingers and they dashed away at full speed. If the judge thought the start fair, he said nothing, but if he thought either man had an unfair advantage they were recalled. . . .

However, the cunning of professional runners had devised methods of outwitting inexperienced opponents. A few steps from the judge the expert would slacken his trot and the other almost invariably would do the same. Just as he reached the judge the expert would suddenly quicken. As it required some fraction of a second for the other to follow this example, the men would pass the judge almost exactly abreast, the expert more than likely a few inches in the rear, but he would be running, while the other was only trotting. The advantage thus gained would amount to two or three yards in the first twenty-five yards of the race.

A more complicated style was the "mutual consent" start. A line was drawn across the track, fifteen or twenty feet behind the starting scratch. The men were placed between these lines and told to start by mutual consent, and whenever both men touched the ground in front of the starting scratch at the same time with any part of their persons it was considered a start.

A race of this kind between two experts was amusing. The men stood between the lines facing each other, pranced up to the starting mark sideways, and the one who was ahead would put his foot down over the mark, hoping that the other would follow. If he did, it would be a start, with the first man a foot or two in front; but if the second man did not like the start, he held back, did not put his foot over the mark, and the first man was ordered back for a fresh trial.

Starts of this style frequently lasted over an hour, especially if one of the runners was not extremely anxious for a race, and eventually this system was modified by inserting in the articles of agreement a clause substantially as follows: "Start by mutual consent; if not off inside an hour [or some other specified time], then to start by pistol." Resort to the pistol was necessary in so many cases that it gradually supplanted the mutual consent system, and became the customary way of starting sprints. . . .

These professional wolves usually traveled and prowled in pairs, one going first to a town, securing some employment, exhibiting his proficiency as a runner to a select few, and finally making a match and beating the local champion. Then the winner would explain that he knew a man in a neighboring town who thought he could run, and whose friends would back him heavily, but who really was several yards slower than championship speed and could be easily beaten. Negotiations would be opened with the stranger and a match arranged. All the men who had won on the first race wished to double their gains, while those who lost were anxious for a chance to get even, so the betting was heavy. The stranger won, of course; the town was pretty thoroughly cleaned of money, and the partners changed their names and moved to fresh harvest fields.

If, after beating the local champions in races on even terms and under ordinary conditions, any money still remained in sight, the professionals tried to secure it by offering contests on novel terms, and with such conditions as seemed to the uninitiated, foolhardy and sure to lose. One of these was called the "lying down start." The novice stood in his usual position, while the professional would lie flat on his back, with his head at the scratch and his feet pointing away from the finish, and the race started by pistol shot. To men unacquainted with this trick, it seemed as if the novice must win, and elderly know-it-alls, standing about, shifted their quids and wisely drawled out: "Why, Jimmy will be down to the other end before that fellow gets started."

But it did not work that way. When the pistol sounded, the professional turned on his face, rose to his hands and feet, and found himself in the attitude now universally adopted by present day sprinters (the crouch start), and which is much better than the old-fashioned erect position. This preliminary movement cost the professional about half a second, or five yards, and as this was about half the handicap, he could beat the novice in 100 yards. He usually caught his man near the seventy-fifth yard mark.

MODERN DEVELOPMENT OF STARTING TECHNIQUES

Such experiments in professional starting would naturally lead to the use of a crouch start in sprinting. Mike Murphy[2] the remarkable Pennsylvania, Yale, and Chief Olympic track coach, took credit in his book for inventing it,

The crouching start was introduced by me. This was in 1887, at Yale, and Charles H. Sherrill was the athlete who first demonstrated its superiority. When he used it in his first race, he was laughed at, and the starter, thinking that Sherrill did not know how to start, held up the race to give him instructions. Finally he was made to under-

---

[1] William Curtis, quoted in Archie Hahn, *HOW TO SPRINT*, New York: American Sports Publishing Company, 1925, 189.

[2] Michael C. Murphy, *ATHLETIC TRAINING*. New York: Charles Scribner's Sons, 1914, 32.

stand that Sherrill was using a new start. Sherrill immediately demonstrated how superior it was to the old standing start, which it displaced, and now the crouching start is used the world over for sprinters, hurdlers, and even quarter and half-milers.

Apparently, sound techniques as to foot placement in the starting holes, a high support on the fingers, and an effective "set" position, were all worked out in the first decade. A picture of Arthur Duffey, Georgetown champion, 1900-1903, shows him in a crouched "set" position very similar to that used today (Figure 25.1).

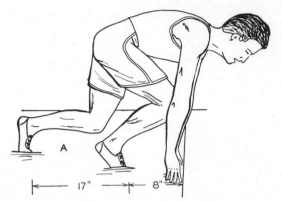

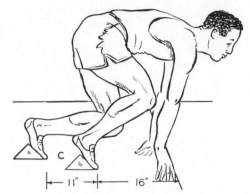

Fig. 25.1 -- Drawn from photo of Arthur Duffey (1902 - 09.6). For some 50 years or more (1880-1940) this was called the orthodox or regular block placement and set position.

Fig. 25.2 -- For many years this block placement was called the Australian or kangaroo start as used by Australian professional sprinters. Drawn from Golliday (1955 - 09.3)

Duffey's ideas[1] on getting out of the holes are sound. For example, he emphasizes that "often the arms are not used to full advantage"; that the primary push comes from the front leg although "both legs must be called into action at one moment"; that "at the report of the pistol, the left arm is swung directly ahead, flexed at the elbow, the right arm swinging directly backwards"; and, lastly, that there is "the necessity for forward action, by lifting the knees in a straight line and jabbing directly downward, without any of the side deviation which is such a common fault with the novice sprinter."

Around 1935 when Larry Snyder was coaching Jesse Owens and other fine sprinters, he believed a position which "crowded" the starting line was best. When starting from holes, "if the boy's foot is within 8 inches to a foot away from the starting line, never more than a foot, I feel that boy is ahead of the one whose front foot is 18 inches back." When starting from blocks, "he will probably have the front foot 2 or 3 inches from the starting line."[2] Snyder did not follow these instructions through the years, but they illustrate the trends of thinking and of trial-and-error efforts that coaches were making.

Early in the 1920s, a "Kangaroo" start (now commonly called the "bunch" start because the feet are close together) placed the front foot 17 to 19 inches back of the starting line and the back foot 10 to 12 inches behind the front one. This elongated position did not gain rapid favor for it seemed to put the sprinter that much farther from the starting line. However, the research studies of A. D. Dickinson in 1934 proved that this position was faster than any other in producing clearance of the starting blocks. This conclusion influenced increased use of the "bunch" start until by the 1950's it had become probably the most common of all.

However, in 1952, two pieces of research pointed out that a man might clear his blocks in a short time and yet not have either the momentum or the good balance to get him into fast

---

[1] Quoted by Archie Hahn, *op. cit.*, 65.

[2] Larry Snyder, an unpublished talk before the National College Track Coaches Association, June 1939.

action down the track. Both studies concluded that the "bunch" start was actually the least efficient. Henry[1] states:

> It is clear that the 16 and 21 inch toe-to-toe distance is the best. . . . The 11 inch "bunch" start is definitely the poorest of the four. While it is true that this position gets the runner off the blocks quickest, he is going slower as he leaves them and never recovers from this disadvantage.

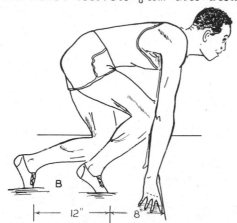

Fig. 25.3 -- Jesse Owens, 1935, "better than 09.4," crowded the starting line "to be nearer the finish line" - Coach Snyder.

Fig. 25.4 -- Bobby Morrow, 1956 Olympic champion. His block placement is close to Henry's "best possible".

DEVELOPMENT OF SPRINTING TECHNIQUES. A similar history of experimentation and development cannot be traced for the techniques of sprinting. After all, running, both fast and slow, is a part of man's evolution; its techniques grew with his bone structure and his way of living. The sprinting figures that circle the vases of ancient Greece give evidence of techniques of sprinting such as high knee action that would do credit to Jesse Owens or Tommie Smith.

DEVELOPMENT OF FINISH TECHNIQUES. Experimentation as to methods of finishing a race occurred early in modern sprinting. As far back as 1904, J. W. Morton[2] attempted a "throw" at the finish, which is still advocated by some good coaches today:

> At about twenty yards from the tape I take a long breath, quickly pulling myself together for a final effort. At this point a thrill seems to pass through my muscles; I travel much faster and, should it be a close finish, at about 8 feet from the tape I throw myself off the right leg, striking the tape with the left breast, and saving myself from collapsing by the left leg.

Charley Paddock, "world's fastest human" during the 1920's, made occasional and successful use (according to his coach, Dean Cromwell) of a full jump at the finish. Paddock frankly admitted that this leap "has been referred to as 'grand-stand play' and the 'freak finish of a freak performer,'" yet he firmly believed that "the jump has won so many more races for me than it lost that I can do no less than suggest it to the sprinter who runs high and has the patience to learn it, and the courage to use it."

Other methods of making the finish apparently also had an early origin. The lunge finish, which consisted of throwing the body well forward with the chest out and the arms far down and back, was originated by Arthur Duffey in 1900, according to Charley Paddock.[3]

---

[1] Franklin M. Henry, "Research on Sprint Running," *The Athletic Journal*, February 1952, 30.

[2] J. W. Morton, quoted by Archie Hahn, *op. cit.*, 70.

[3] Charles W. Paddock, *TRACK AND FIELD*, New York: A. S. Barnes & Co., 1933, 25.

Arthur Duffey was one of the first to scientifically use it. The Boston boy employed the lunge in a race against Bernie Wefers of the New York Athletic Club, who was American champion in 1895-96-97, and he won by the width of a hand. Wefers saw the advantage of the lunge, and at once set out to improve upon this method of finishing if possible. And his studies resulted in the introduction of a still better style.

This new finish was soon known as the "shrug," and it was accomplished by throwing the side of the body into the string with one hand held high, and the other held back behind the body. The forward lean of the "lunge" was maintained in the "shrug" but the tape could be broken 6 inches sooner, since the side of the body can be brought that much nearer the string than the chest....This "shrug" finish first perfected by Bernie Wefers had grown in popularity during the past thirty years until today it is in general use by a majority of the best sprinters throughout the world.

Fig. 25.5. Bob Hayes (Florida A & M, 6'0", 190#), 1964 Olympic 100-meters champion, 10.0 (timed electronically,) Olympic record and equalling world record. Also 1963 world-record 100 yards -- :09.1. An all-time great "natural" sprinter, he had only incidental coaching of technique by football coach, Jake Gaither. Three weeks after a strenuous college football season, he ran :09.2 for the 100. His style was rough but extremely powerful--and fast! In the Olympic final, he was even at the start (though with minimal arm action), one meter ahead at 40 meters, with an increasing margin of two meters at the finish-- this, over six excellent Olympic finalists!

FUNDAMENTALS OF SPRINTING

The Scope of the Problem. From the standpoint of time and action, any sprint begins in reaction to the sound of the starting gun and ends as the finish line on the ground is reached. This time-action period can be arbitrarily divided into five phases: (1) reaction time to the sound of the starting gun, (2) block-clearance time, (3) acceleration time, (4) velocity-maintenance time, and (5) the finish time.

1. Sprinter's Reaction Time (time lapse between sound of gun and first movement in response) is both inherited and improveable. The inborn tendency of some sprinters is to react to sound quickly; that of others, more slowly. Further, the consensus of related research is that reaction time is not correlated with speed, either out of the starting blocks or when sprinting. A great sprinter can have relatively slow reaction time; and an ordinary sprinter relatively fast reaction time. Further, Franklin Henry's research concluded that reaction time is uninfluenced by block spacing.

Ruddi Toomsalu[1] improved the average reaction time of 122 trainees from .139 seconds to .119 seconds. An insignificant improvement? In 1979, Pietro Mennea (Italy, 200m-19.72WR) won the European Cup 100-meters by only 1/100th of a second. But time-analysis found he reacted (0.13s) to the starting gun 2/100th faster than did 2nd-place winner Woronin (0.15s). Toomsalu does not state how he achieved this improvement in reaction time, but we can be certain that such improvements in sprinting would be specific to sprinting patterns of action.

It should be noted that these reaction times of over one-tenth second are consistent with those found by other investigators.[2] With such rare exceptions as Armin Hary, the 1960 100-meters Olympic winner, whose reaction time was reported to be .08 second, no man should be able to move a muscle until after one-tenth second has elapsed after the firing of the starting gun.

2. Block-Clearance Time requires a significant fraction of total sprint time. Dickinson[3] found that the average time required to get clear of the blocks (including reaction time) was 0.244 seconds for a 10.5-inch bunch start, 0.326 seconds for a 21-inch medium start and 0.387 seconds for a 26-inch elongated start. (Inches here refer to the distance between the two starting blocks.) But in later research, Franklin Henry[2] concluded that velocity out of the blocks is a greater concern than block-clearance time, and that in this respect, the longer 16- and 21-inch block placements were best. When the front block is moved forward, the front leg has a greater time in which to apply force against the block and thereby increase velocity. "Although the rear leg develops considerably more maximum force than the front, the latter contributes twice as much to block velocity because its impulse has a longer duration." Henry also reached another conclusion which I consider of even greater significance. "With block spacing held constant, speed in the sprint is significantly related to how close the individual approaches the ideal start." That is to say, is significantly related to the degree of perfection with which he has mastered the skills of starting.

3. Acceleration Time is the length of time-distance in which the sprinter accelerates his velocity. Earlier research had stated this length in terms of yards, but Franklin Henry found that time was a more valid measurement, and concluded that six seconds was the greatest time in which a man could continue to increase his velocity. We should keep in mind that Henry's subjects were experienced but not great sprinters, and should assume that highly skilled and talented sprinters can possibly shorten this time and certainly increase the number of yards covered.

4. Velocity-Maintenance Time is the length of time-distance in which a sprinter can

---

[1] Ruddi Toomsalu, "Sprint Start Speed Factors," *Track Technique*, No. 11, March, 1963, 325.

[2] Franklin M. Henry, "Force-Time Characteristics of the Sprint Start," *The Research Quarterly*, 23:3 (October, 1952).

[3] A. D. Dickinson, "The Effect of Foot-Spacing on the Starting Time and Speed in Sprinting," *The Research Quarterly*, 5:1 (February, 1934).

maintain maximum velocity. Though we may not accept at full value Franklin Henry's[1] conclusion that "it is physiologically impossible for the runner, after he has reached his peak velocity, to maintain it for more than about 15 or 20 yards," we should assume that he is not far wrong. Even in a 100-yard dash, the problem becomes one of minimum deceleration. Certainly, in the 220 and 440, other things being equal, the winner is the one that slows down the least.

5. The Finish Time is that small fraction of a second in which by some action such as forward lean or shoulder shrug, the sprinter can gain a difference in place in the eyes of the judges, and conceivably, a difference in time from the timers.

In summary of these five phases of the sprinting problem, it should be noted (1) that each phase requires learning and specific practice if mastery is to be attained, and (2) that the allocation of practice time should be in terms of all five phases, and not predominantly in terms of starting as has been so much the custom in the past.

SPRINTERS: BORN OR MADE?

A second fundamental of sprinting is that sprinters are made as well as born. Speed in running is present in each of us within a range of potential. In some, this range is at the higher levels of speed; in others, at the lower levels. But perfection can be acquired only through practice: year-round, precisely planned, and persistent. The right genes can make a boy run fast, but only proper training can make a boy run his best.

RELATED POWER

It is generally recognized today that fastest sprinting requires, not merely strength, but optimum power; that is, power in which the strength and velocity factors are developed in keeping with the needs of this specific sprinter. The overall method is explained in the section in this chapter on "Power Exercises." But there's a coaching art in applying that method to this particular athlete.

A MAN-SITUATION SPRINTS

This is probably the most important and difficult to coach of all the fundamentals. Good coaching must be in terms of men that sprint, of men that have many distractions, many deterrents, many frustrations, many fears, or at least doubts, that detract from sprinting. If these are not set aside, all the concentration on the mechanics of sprinting will come to nought. A sprinter must come to the starting line in competition with a feeling of high expectancy and confidence, with a mind that is tough and sure of its self-control and relaxation, and with emotions that are concentrated in terms of performance. But also we must be aware of the second portion of the expression, "man-situation." Coaching must always be in terms of the competitive situation a man will face on each unique occasion. True, wide experience enables a man to face almost any situation, but as competitive levels rise, so do emotions; and with them the disturbing effects of little delays and deterrents that would normally be brushed aside. This all applies to the situations of practice as well. Whether practice is boring or inspirational affects performance just as does its physiological soundness.

HOW TO BEGIN

A careful weighing of the various factors in sprinting will conclude that, assuming a year-round program of training as related to sprinting, one should begin with related fitness, related power, and related speed-endurance. Sprinting is an all-out action which places great stress on muscles and tendons. How often the year's best prospect views the championship race from the stands. We say in sympathy, "a pulled muscle"; but we should say in reproof, "careless early training."

Before any high-velocity sprinting is attempted, months should be spent in developing speed-endurance and the toughness of tendons and muscles that comes with resistance exercises. In the

---

[1] Franklin M. Henry, "Research in Sprint Running," *The Athletic Journal*, February 1952, 30.

Fall of the year, we tend to equate endurance training with competitive cross-country. And a case can be made for sprinters joining the team so as to enjoy group running. But long distances and slow pace are neither fun not effective for sprinters. Better to get a small group of sprinters, hurdlers, long and triple jumpers, and quarter-milers together. Then organize an interval-training program up and down hill, on a woods path, or an open field. Make sure there's safe footing.

For each schedule, have but one variable. For example, for some weeks hold the distance and the rest-interval constant, and increase gradually the number of times the run is made. When they can achieve a desired number, hold the distance and the number constant, and gradually decrease the length of the rest interval. Finally, make speed the variable, especially speed with bounce. Spring up the hill with long strides. Such a program will keep men interested for months. It has all the advantages of interval training on the track, plus the all-important one of challenge and change.

Fig. 25.6. Speed hill-sprinting. An excellent practice method of developing forward thrust, high knee lift, and a full length of stride.

Intermingled with the open-country running there should be related power training for sprinting, following the pattern outlined in the "Speed-Power Training" section of this chapter, and using the various exercises suggested there. As with interval training, organize a progressive-development program, so that progress can be measured. For example, the squat jump with weights, alternating the legs forward and back, would become a bore without some kind of progress. First, one can increase the weights by small increments up to perhaps 50 percent maximum, for our contention is that there are decreasing returns as the weights get very heavy. There is also a velocity factor for any given weight: (1) the height of each jump can be gradually increased, and (2) the cadence, or number of jumps per unit of time, can be gradually increased.

Follow some such process of analysis and emphasis on each of the factors for other exercises listed. In using the weighted drag, (1) use regular weight-lifting disks on the drag to measure progress, (2) lengthen the strides, and (3) increase cadence. Not all at once. Hold two factors constant, gradually increase the third.

SPEED-POWER TRAINING

Certain basic questions as to the relationship between strength and velocity in sprinting are still unanswered. Are we speaking of sheer strength as occurs in isometric exercises? If not, what is the optimum ratio of strength/velocity that will ensure maximum sprinting speed? That is, should the power training involve heavy resistances at necessarily slow speeds? Medium-heavy at medium speeds? Or light resistances at great speeds? What degree of relatedness is best in terms of sprinting movements? Is the squat exercise relevant? What are the implications of the fact that discus throwers do vertical heavy lifts for an event that is primarily rotational? How does this apply to sprinting? Most sprinters are well-muscled in their legs; their thighs tend to have a wide cross-section, one of the indications of a powerful muscle. But a few have relatively slender legs--Jesse Owens (5'10"--156#), or Pietro Mennea, Italy (5'10"--154#). What is the force factor in such legs, and would power exercises have aided them?

RELATED POWER EXERCISES

Exaggerated forward bound - knees high

Sprinting uphill or down a low grade

Use rubber cables or other "yielding" device; or attach to waist-shoulder belt.

SPRINTING — HURDLING

Stadium-steps
with weights or
bounding up
without weights

Drive against resistance --
weighted drag as shown or
or rubber cable held by
team-mate or ?

449

Despite the uncertainty of answers to such questions, both research and studies on the track with sprinters are gradually reaching sound conclusions, not colored by the recent over-enthusiasm which has tended to advance the values of any kind of heavy-weight lifting for any kind of sports activity from running the marathon to table tennis. At this point it would be well to read again Chapter 6, "The Dynamics of Human Power," especially the sections on the relationship between human power and speed, and on specificity in developing greater speed.

The following points will be of interest:

1. An increase in strength of a muscle produces an increase in the velocity with which that muscle can move against a similar degree of resistance.

2. A gain in speed results both from strength training in which movements simulate those of the activity being improved, and from training that improved strength without simulating the test activity.

3. However, higher positive correlations between the effects of strength training on speed are obtained when these are related in degree of emphasis on resistance and velocity; for example, between static strength and slow speeds in both the training and test activity, or between fast dynamic strength and fast speeds involving light resistances. The opposite is also true--low relationships between training and the test activity bring low correlations.

4. A report by Kruczalak[1], based on the admitted failure of Soviet coaches to develop sprinters by heavy-weight lifting as well as on Soviet research, concludes that intensive basic-strength training involving muscles and movements not related to sprinting can have a definitely negative effect on sprinting. He also reports that:

a. Increased power is most effective in developing speed when it produces a minimum increase in muscle mass (weight.) To develop such power without increasing muscle mass, fast exercises with light loads (20% of muscle strength) and high repetitions (8 to 15) are best.

b. Emphasis should be on muscle and movements that simulate those of sprinting: (1) fast sprints up small but steep hills, (2) running upstairs without weights or with small (10-20#) loads, (3) 60 to 100-meter accelerating sprints with small (10-20#) loads, (4) running with bounding strides with small (10-20#) loads, and (5) a very fast series of jumps without loading.

c. Overall strength and innate speed of muscle movement are not significantly related. Kruczalak reported a survey of leading Polish sprinters who on an average were well below the strength level of physical education students at Warsaw University.

d. Soviet physiologists studied the relative effects on sprinting of four training programs: (1) speed training only, (2) strength training only, (3) endurance training only, and (4) speed-strength-endurance training together without special emphasis. The fourth group made greatest gains; the speed group was next; the endurance group, third. Strength training had only limited influence on speed and had a negative influence on endurance.

RELATED POWER NEEDS. The greatest need for power is during the acceleration period out of the starting blocks--according to Franklin Henry[2], the first six seconds. His fastest sprinters exerted an average force of 157 foot-pounds of energy against the rear starting block, despite the decreasing resistance of the body in motion. This is the instant of greatest need. But such special need is continued throughout the first sixty yards or so of acceleration.

What are the power needs in terms of movements? First, there is the leg-foot extension as the body is pushed forward. Second, there is the upper-leg flexion as it is pulled forward for

---

[1]Eugeniusz Kruczalak, "Strength Training for Sprinters," *Track Technique*, 35, March 1969, 1106.

[2]Franklin M. Henry, "Force-Time Characteristics of the Sprint Start," *The Research Quarterly*, October 1952, 301-318.

the next stride. All other movements in sprinting, such as the drive of the arms, are second-ary and can be ignored from a physical power standpoint.

IMITATIVE POWER EXERCISES. Nothing in judgment, experience or research suggests a direct physical gain in sprinting speed from such basic weight-lifting exercises as squats, clean and press, bench press, or curls. Done in moderation, such exercises will do no physical harm, and may have certain mental benefits in terms of self-confidence. But that is the extent of their value.

In contrast, the exercises we have selected for pages 448-9 are closely related to sprint-ing in terms of the muscles involved, their movements, and, in some instances, can use progres-sive increments of resistance (overloading), one of the requirements for power development.

For example, Figure 25.6 (Speed Hill-Training), imitates the actions of sprinting, with exaggerations in terms of knee lift, forward propulsion by the back foot, arm drive, etc. By using a weighted vest with progressive overloads of weight, increasing power can be developed. Research by Milan Milakov[1] indicated that a combination of uphill and downhill training added to regular sprint training had a beneficial effect on sprinting speed. He used slopes that were lowgrade, less than five degrees to the horizontal.

STRENGTH FOR INDIVIDUAL SPRINTERS. Individuals differ in their need for greater strength in the formula: (power = strength x velocity). One would doubt the need for power training by such powerfully built sprinters as Bob Hayes or the shorter but well-muscled Ira Murchison. In contrast, first judgment suggests that taller and more slender sprinters such as Tommie Smith or Bobby Morrow might make good use of greater power. (Though we should not be deceived into accepting the over-simplified statement of physiologists that "other things being equal, strength is proportionate to muscle circumference.") Other things are never equal, so that specific testing plus judgment are necessary.

POWER TRAINING HELPS MAINTAIN ZEST. One of the strongest arguments for power training is that it has strong motivational value. When carefully organized within the total program by an enthusiastic coach, it gives the sprinter something more to do. Compared with the rela-tively complex programs of the pole vaulter or weight thrower, a sprinter has little to do to keep him zestful throughout about ten months of active training. These power training exer-cises, merely by being different, help to maintain zest.

In Milakov's study, the groups doing only uphill or downhill work did not improve as much as the group that combined this with regular sprint work. Power training should always be supplemental, not a substitute. As with other events, power training should be emphasized during the early months of each year, gradually diminishing during the competitive season, and maintained only as it proves or seems of value. It would certainly be at minimum levels and probably abandoned prior to the crucial competitions.

ESSENTIALS OF SOUND TECHNIQUE

Sound technique in sprint starting and running has two aspects: (1) soundness from the stand-point of generalized biomechanics, and (2) soundness for this particular sprinter in his mastery of all the related factors. In theory, the two should be in harmony, if not actually the same; or better, should differ only as the individual differs from the average. In practice the in-dividual sprinter's style may have significant "faults" even though his achievement is at world-record levels. Quick consideration of the world-record holders of the past thirty years will show that most had significant variances from what is generally considered to be sound technique. Consider Jesse Owens' crowded starting position, Ralph Metcalfe's patter-strides out of his blocks, Dave Sime's upward drive on his first three strides, Bob Hayes' off-line leg and arm action. But also consider that each of these champions had mastered his own form, whether or not it was theoretically and mechanically sound.

---

[1] Milan Milakov and Vernon Cox, "Improving Speed by Training on Sloping Surfaces," *Track Technique*, June 1962, 254.

Human beings are amazingly adept at adjusting to an imperfect method so as to produce an excellent result. This is the bane of so many research studies that assume "other things being equal"; they never are equal in human action. Whatever specific changes the researcher or the coach makes in technique are never performed in isolation. They always occur within a total pattern of response by the entire person; in fact, one can go further and say the entire person-situation. As one example, take the mechanically unsound "set" position of Jesse Owens: his feet 8 and 20 inches from the starting line; his head up and eyes focussed on the finish line--a position well designed to drive him straight up in the air. But Jesse's inner urge to go forward, not up, caused him to make the best of a bad position by adjusting his arm-leg actions and torso angles so as to gain an excellent start, at least by the standards of 1935, and even today. His total pattern of response was sound, despite the initial errors in starting position.

All this suggests that it is important that a sprinter's style be mechanically correct in all respects, but it is crucial that he master his own style, whatever it may be.

ON YOUR MARKS

Using the block placement previously suggested, back into your blocks: (1) place the back foot against its block first, with the toe just touching the ground as required by the rules; (2) place the front foot in its block; then (3) place the fingers just behind the starting line (Figures 25.9, 25.10). The weight is on the front knee and fingers, though there is pressure against the back block. The eyes are focussed on a spot three to five feet from the starting line; neck muscles are relaxed. The arms are straight down from the shoulders (Figure 25.9). Actually we are unsure of the value of being high on the finger tips, since today's starting direction is forward, not up, but custom has followed such a method for decades.

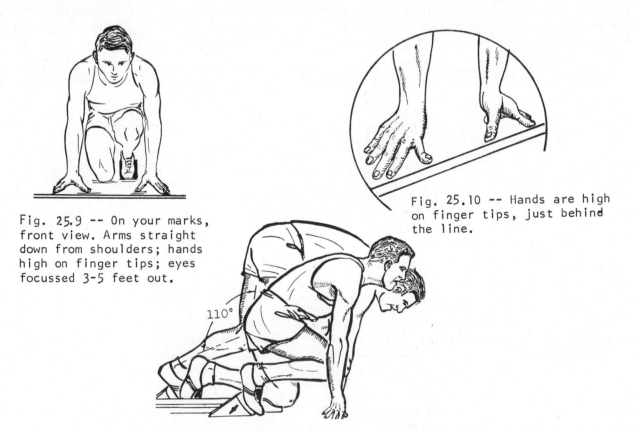

Fig. 25.9 -- On your marks, front view. Arms straight down from shoulders; hands high on finger tips; eyes focussed 3-5 feet out.

Fig. 25.10 -- Hands are high on finger tips, just behind the line.

Fig. 25.11 -- "On your marks" and "set". The angle at the knee joints when "set" are equally important with the distances between the hands and feet. That of about 110 degrees provides maximum initial drive.

PLACEMENT OF STARTING BLOCKS

Undoubtedly, in the United States since 1890, there have been more speeches, more arguments, more try-this-try-that, more research on the placement of starting blocks than on any other track or field problem. Up to 1930 there was a generally accepted "orthodox start" as shown in Figure 25.1. Jesse Owens moved both feet up as shown in Figure 25.3, on the theory of being closer to the finish line. In the 1920s, there was some use of a so-called "kangaroo" start with the front foot 17-19 inches from the starting line, and the back foot 10-12 inches further back (Figure 25.2). Research by Dickinson (1934) and Henry (1952) indicated that there should be a greater spread between the feet:

It is clear that the 16 to 21 inch toe to toe distance is the best. . . . The 11 inch "bunch" start is definitely the poorest of the four. While it is true that this position gets the runner off the blocks quickest, he is going slower as he leaves them and never recovers from this disadvantage.

This research assumed that first power came from the back foot; longer time of power application, from the front foot--an entirely sound assumption. But proof of the superiority of one placement over another is far from simple, for the many related factors can never be held constant. Change weight balance by changing block spacing and the sprinter naturally, without coaching, adapts his body balance, eye-focus, arm drive so as to compensate. In fact, the full merit of any block spacing can be judged only after long, thoughtful practice has enabled a sprinter to perfect that particular method; seldom possible in research.

Modern great sprinters tend to use the "kangaroo" spacing. Olympic champions (Hary, 1960; Borzov, 1972) and, according to Gabor Simonyi ("The Switch-Blade Start," *Track Technique*, 1978, p. 2350), all six finalists at Montreal used "kangaroo" block spacings--about a foot between blocks; about 2 feet from front block to starting line.

A RECOMMENDED METHOD. Place the back block first. Place it at such a distance from the starting line that, in the "set" position, when the high point of the back is about four inches above that of the neck, the angle at the back knee is close to 110 degrees (Figure 25.11). This angle of 110 degrees enables the back leg to apply maximum force immediately against the back block, and over a greater length of time than is possible if the knee angle were straighter.

Now place the front block. Here, according to research, the factor of duration of force is primary. Franklin Henry concluded, "Although the rear leg develops considerably more force than the front, the latter contributes twice as much to the block velocity because its impulse has a longer duration." Start with a 16-inch spacing between the blocks. However, the exact placement of this front block cannot be fixed, until the many other details of technique have been mastered.

Construct a style which emphasizes body forward, not up. Maximum acceleration requires forward lean. Keep the eyes and head down. Drive the arms forward, not up. You will tend to stumble, but learn to bring the knees up-and-under. Reach out with the feet; at this stage they will always be behind the center of gravity. Now that these phases of technique have been mastered, adjust and re-adjust your front block until you feel it gives you maximum force and duration of force. But once having established its place, keep it there. You're still in doubt? Don't fret about it! A half-century of experimenting still leaves us all in doubt. *The most important concern is to master your own method and have complete confidence in it.*

SET

At the command "set," the hips are pushed upward and forward until the desired angle of 110 degrees at the back knee is reached. Since the weight when "on your marks" is primarily on the front knee, the weight must roll up and forward. With a proper hold by the starter of about two seconds between the two commands, "set" and "go," there is plenty of time in which to do this; no need to pop up into the "set" position, then be forced to wait an unfair length of time before the gun. But the rules are clear that the set position must be gained "at once and without delay." Now the weight will be on the hands and on the front foot, in that order. Be sure that the back heel has settled back against its block so as to be ready for an instantaneous drive. (If only the toes are against the block, time is lost while the foot finds its firmest base for power action.)

GO!
The all-important goal of the actions that follow "go" is to achieve maximum acceleration and velocity as soon as possible. Henry has concluded that such maximum
velocity is achieved about six seconds after the start. In other words, the
sprinter is not *primarily* concerned about the shortness of time in which he can
clear the blocks, nor the velocity with which he leaves them, nor even his time
at 10 or 15 or 20 yards. Rather, it is the entire six seconds that concern him.
How often a man reacts first to the gun, then loses balance and drive about 10 or
15 yards out.

As long as acceleration continues (about 60 yards), body lean should be forward. To ensure this, the focus of the eyes should continue to be down, though
rising slowly from their focus when "set"; even at 40 yards out, they should focus
not more than 10 yards ahead.

Each stride out of the blocks will be longer than the preceding one, as a result of increasing velocity of course, but also as a result of training. Even
with the increasing cadence, a sprinter can train himself to push more forcefully
with each foot and pull each thigh forward more quickly, and so achieve greater
stride lengths. This is one of the important effects of uphill speed work in
which the sprinter bounds forward with high knee action so as to secure speed and
length of stride.

454

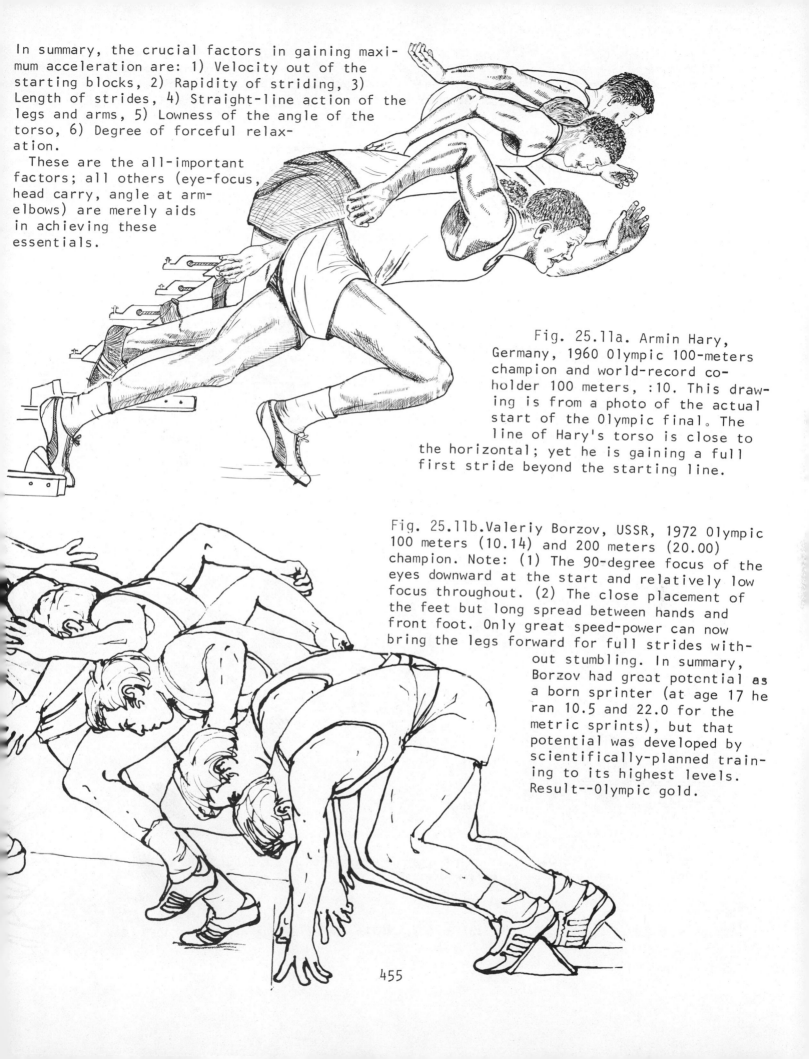

In summary, the crucial factors in gaining maximum acceleration are: 1) Velocity out of the
starting blocks, 2) Rapidity of striding, 3)
Length of strides, 4) Straight-line action of the
legs and arms, 5) Lowness of the angle of the
torso, 6) Degree of forceful relaxation.

These are the all-important
factors; all others (eye-focus,
head carry, angle at arm-
elbows) are merely aids
in achieving these
essentials.

Fig. 25.11a. Armin Hary,
Germany, 1960 Olympic 100-meters
champion and world-record co-
holder 100 meters, :10. This drawing is from a photo of the actual
start of the Olympic final. The
line of Hary's torso is close to
the horizontal; yet he is gaining a full
first stride beyond the starting line.

Fig. 25.11b.Valeriy Borzov, USSR, 1972 Olympic
100 meters (10.14) and 200 meters (20.00)
champion. Note: (1) The 90-degree focus of the
eyes downward at the start and relatively low
focus throughout. (2) The close placement of
the feet but long spread between hands and
front foot. Only great speed-power can now
bring the legs forward for full strides without stumbling. In summary,
Borzov had great potential as
a born sprinter (at age 17 he
ran 10.5 and 22.0 for the
metric sprints), but that
potential was developed by
scientifically-planned training to its highest levels.
Result--Olympic gold.

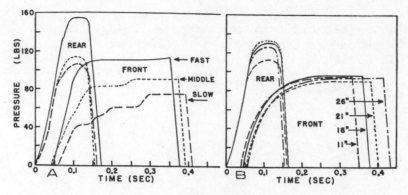

Fig. 25.12a. Pressures applied against the blocks by "fast," "middle" and "slow" sprinters. Note the quicker pressures, the higher pressures, and the more steady pressures applied by the faster sprinters. The back foot is off its block at about .17 seconds; the front, at about .37 seconds. Contrast the duration of force against the front block with that against the back block.

Fig. 25.12b. Comparison of average block pressures using four measurements between the blocks: 11, 16, 21, and 26 inches. On a basis of velocity out of the blocks, the 16- and 21- inch spacings were best *for these sprinters*. Both diagrams are from Franklin M. Henry, *op. cit.*

In the set position, the line of the back will be downward; that is, the hips will be above the shoulders. At first, this will cause stumbling. By lowering the hips, the stumbling may cease immediately, but this is a negative solution. Better to keep the hips high where maximum force can be applied; now practice, practice, PRACTICE! until you have learned to bring your knees and feet up, forward and out under the center of gravity, and so prevent stumbling this way, with no loss of force.

At "set" a full breath will usually be taken. This lifting and fixing of the chest is a normal and usually involuntary method of fixing attention and muscular readiness.

Fig. 25.13. Ira Murchison, 1958, 100 meters--:10.1. Murchison had an amazingly fast start. His starting style may well have been a function of his short, powerful legs. His height was 5'5". He emphasized a forward pull of the rear leg rather than the usual push against the back block. His coach, George Dales[1], wrote as follows:

---

[1] George G. Dales, "Coaching for the Sprint Start," *The Athletic Journal*, March, 1959, 24.

*Murchison's powerful arms permit him to exaggerate the forward lean. . . .
With his controversial, straight, but relaxed back leg barely in contact with the
rear block, he has eliminated one motion in the movement of his leg, that of straightening a conventional bent back leg before bending it again as some sprinters do. Murchison merely rests his back foot against the block and he is able to bring it up more
quickly to a bent position at the sound of the gun. He feels he can combine the
drive-off from the front block by the strong front leg with the running out of the
block by the relaxed back leg. . . .*

*(At "go") the relaxed (back) leg comes up from the rear block and drops just ahead
of the starting line where it now becomes the front and driving leg. . . . We found
no change in body angle at this point although Murchison's legs and arms have alternated positions a full stride. The only observeable change is a slight rise in the
focus of his eyes a bit farther down the track toward the finish line. Murchison's
ability to maintain his forward lean in the early stages of the sprint and his ability to combine this with a high knee lift give him a powerful thrust with each stride.*

    <u>Mind Set</u>. Throughout the entire starting process--just before and during--an increasing
focus of attention occurs. That means a shutting-out of all extraneous sounds-sights-thoughts
and a concentration on the going: on the forward drive of the off-arm and a reactive thrust of
the rear foot. The mind is not "on the gun," or "on the sound of the gun," as so many say.
The mind set is like a compressed spring that is released by the gun-sound. To fix the "mind"
on the gun is to focus it "there," but the action is "here." That's not quibbling with words;
such words make a significant difference.

SPRINTING ACTION

The dynamics of sprint action can be considered roughly as those of the legs and arms. These in turn can be analyzed exceedingly fine. I have at hand a 120-page doctoral thesis concerned only with the mechanics of the leg-recovery phase. But our treatment here of the problem must be brief and over-simplified.

LEG ACTION---DRIVING PHASE. Other things being equal (which, in human sprinting, they never are), speed in sprinting is the resultant of three interdependent variables--cadence or rate of striding, length of strides, and power of forward thrust.

Cadence is often called leg-speed. Innate muscle-fiber speed of action cannot be improved and will always set the limits of potential leg-speed. But other factors are variable and do allow a rather wide range of possible improvement in leg-speed--and by progressive overloads of work which bring more fibers into action, by a more effective use of the forward thrust of the legs, or by relaxation of all unrelated and opposing muscle groups. That is to say, leg-speed can definitely be improved by sound practice.

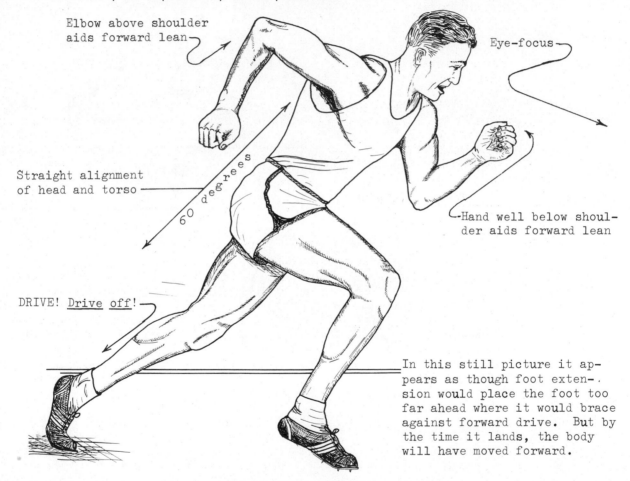

Elbow above shoulder aids forward lean

Eye-focus

Straight alignment of head and torso

60 degrees

Hand well below shoulder aids forward lean

DRIVE! Drive off!

In this still picture it appears as though foot exten-.sion would place the foot too far ahead where it would brace against forward drive. But by the time it lands, the body will have moved forward.

Fig. 25.14 -- Maintaining maximum velocity beyond 60-70 yards.

Ozolin's[1] summary of how to improve speed in any sports action is of great value, especially since he recognizes the uses of both physical and mental approaches to the problem. He mentions, for example, the tendency to level off at a certain speed of action; plateaus of speed are reached, just as in other human learning, which are fixed by following a set pattern of training in all its aspects. I am reminded of the weight-lifters "sticking points." Ozolin says that it requires a new and stronger stimulus and proportionately increased

---

[1]Nikolai Ozolin, "How to Improve Speed," *Track Technique*, 44, June 1971, 1400.

conditioning to move to a higher level of speed. For example, speed running against the resistance of a sandy surface, followed immediately by sprinting on a hard track. Competition in practice may lead the sprinter to ignore his built-up inhibitions and sprint faster than he thinks he can. As a third method, Ozolin mentions the research of A. V. Korobkov who found that the gradually accelerated rhythm of a metronome increased stride frequency in running in place by five to eight percent. This reminds me of the work of Ben Ogden, coach of Eulace Peacock, a 26-foot long jumper and one of the very few men ever to beat Jesse Owens, who coached his men to maintain cadence with the rapping of his cane on a board floor. Many hours were spent bouncing the feet in time with his stick: slowly, then faster-faster-faster. To work the knees and ankles, he'd then require them on each stride to touch a string stretched 24, 30 and even 36 inches high. Or, as a second variation, he'd hold the cadence even, and require them to bring their knees higher and higher.

Ozolin also suggests improving leg-speed by setting up conditions which overload the speed of action, as contrasted with the force of action--sprinting while attached by elastic cable to a motorcycle, or by sprinting on a down-hill track. Soviet researchers concluded that the motorcycle run gave "a feeling for a higher speed." One man improved his 50-yard time by 0.3 seconds after such a run. Other researchers found that down-hill sprinting, using a 2-3 percent decline, gave an average increase of "about 13 percent due to greater stride frequency." In his overall conclusions, Ozolin warns that development by such methods should be on a gradual step-by-step basis, that it takes three to four months to establish a new speed-level firmly, and that such work should be but one phase of the regular sprint-training program.

LENGTH OF STRIDE. A second variable in sprinting speed is the length of strides. Given a certain cadence, force, relaxation and other related factors, the longer a man's stride, the sooner he will reach the finish line. Stride length, in both the early acceleration and full-speed phases of sprinting, is highly trainable. I remember clearly how Coach Hoyt emphasized it greatly in the training of 1932 100-200 Olympic Champion, Eddie Tolan, and how such lack of stride length was a major factor in the failure of Ralph Metcalfe to be rated along with Jesse Owens as an all-time great sprinter. I can see Hoyt adding increments of distance as he marked each stride in the cinder track and required Eddie to reach out during the first 30 yards to the new and greater distances. In contrast, Metcalfe was coached that leg-speed was the crucial factor in the start so that his feet pattered out of the blocks.

Dyson (1967, 111) notes that in efficient running, the leading foot never reaches out "grotesquely" for a longer stride, and that "stride length is the product of a driving forward of the entire body." But the length of time in which the "driving forward" occurs is also a factor, especially during the acceleration phase. In running, the foot does land slightly in front of the center of body weight, though this distance does decrease with increased speed of running. There is also general agreement that if force can be exerted at all by the backward "pawing" action of the extended foot, that force is very slight and is mainly related to getting the foot down on the ground more quickly. But there is an optimum time-distance in which forward push or thrust should occur. Especially during the start, this time-distance tends to be cut short, so that special related practice is needed.

POWER OF FORWARD THRUST. Successful coaches of sprinting agree that forward thrust, or drive, or bounce as it is called variously, is essential and can be improved by training. Bud Winter, San Jose State, who probably developed more sprinters than any other coach, including Hal Davis, Ray Norton, and the great Tommie Smith, required practice of the forward drive from all his men. Time and time again, they drove up and down the grass infield--pushing, pushing, pushing more forcefully with each foot. This was also emphasized in gaining greater acceleration during starting practice.

Bill Marlow, coach of Peter Radford, one-time world-record holder in the 220 on the curve, called it "greater forward drive from the rear." He believed that putting first emphasis on a longer stride by way of a high knee lift and foot extension was "putting cart before the horse," and concentrated on "driving every time a foot contacts the ground."

Fig. 25.15. --Training for greater power for sprinting. The belt can be of any soft material: rubber, towel, or wide belt.

The word "bounce" also has its uses--"to leap or spring quickly." This suggests relaxation, resilience, quickness of force rather than hard effort. Coach Snyder used to speak of Jessie Owens as sprinting as though his feet were touching a hot stove. An exaggeration of course which denied Owens' full-stride action, but it does give a feeling of explosive ease of movement. As meet director, I watched Owens on that greatest-ever day in Ann Arbor, Michigan, and marvelled at his complete relaxation and seeming lack of effort. Many asked, "What will he do when he really tries to run?" But Charlie Hoyt, an astute observer, replied, "If he ever really tries, he'll never run as fast."

THE RECOVERY PHASE. Shortly after the toes of the driving foot leave the ground, the thigh begins an accelerating swing forward, then upward which Dyson (1967, 111) states "increases the forward force exerted by the ground, thus increasing the speed with which the Centre of Gravity is moved away from the supporting foot." Perhaps this is the source of the value which some coaches place on bringing the leg forward quickly and forcefully, with the thigh high and the foot reaching forward. Incidentally, still or sequence pictures which catch the forward foot off the ground and well ahead of the body are deceiving; in action, by the time the foot reaches the ground, the body has moved forward so that the center of body weight is above the foot and not behind it.

USE OF THE ARMS. Primarily, arm action achieves balance, offsets the twisting effect of the legs as they drive on each side of the body's centerline, and, according to some research, aids directly the straight-line thrust of the legs. Jokl[1] concluded from a study of the relative educability of the hands, arms and legs that "the complex flexion and extension pattern in hips, knees, feet, and toes, on which running and jumping are based, can be triggered off most effectively from the upper extremities." This is of great interest and possibly of real value to the mechanics of sprinting, but educability is not the same as actual use in action.

Dyson (1978, 117), however, supports Jokl's point,

. . .in sprinting, particularly, the arms may be used to spur on the legs, which speed up and consequently add to their horizontal component of drive; . . .

---

[1]Ernst Jokl, M.D., "Some Physiological Components of Modern Track Training," Clinic Notes, National College Track Coaches Association, 1956, 226.

Since both arms accelerate upwards and downwards simultaneously, . . . their upward movement adds to the vertical component of drive; and their downward acceleration coinciding with touch down, lessens the impact between the ground and front foot.

Moreover, by losing upward speed fractionally before the completion of leg drive, they ease the compression of the thrusting leg--and so permit more forceful and freer use of its foot and ankle.

In summary of the uses of the arms, they do aid greatly the steady straight-ahead posi-tion of the torso and shoulder girdle so important for balance, relaxation, and straight-line drive. They do, if properly used, help to ensure a sound body angle, especially during the start but also throughout the entire sprint. They do serve as a focal point for overall relaxation; if the hands are relaxed, the sprinter is more likely to be relaxed. And appar-ently, in the ways described by Jokl and Dyson, they can stimulate faster movements within the legs.

To best implement such uses, the angle at the elbows should remain the same throughout--about 90 degrees. Certainly there should be no increased flexion at the elbow and upthrust of the arm as it swings forward.

Fig. 25.16a. Valeriy Borzov, USSR, 1972 Olympic Champion on his marks. Borzov's block spacing would appear to be as little as ten inches between blocks and perhaps 25 inches to the starting line. Eyes-head are straight down. Hands are widely spread; arms at about 110 degrees. The overall effect of these positions would be to place the c.g. low and far ahead of the feet which would aid forward drive but cause imbalance, short strides and possible stumbling. To compen-sate, the feet are placed low in the block with the toes in full contact with the ground. This gives greater foot flexion-extension, a longer application of force, tends to drive the body upward, and so balances the excessive "falling" effect just cited. In summary, the effect would produce a start such as shown in Fig.25.16b. The result may well be an improvement over the "best possible" on-your-marks placements previously cited.

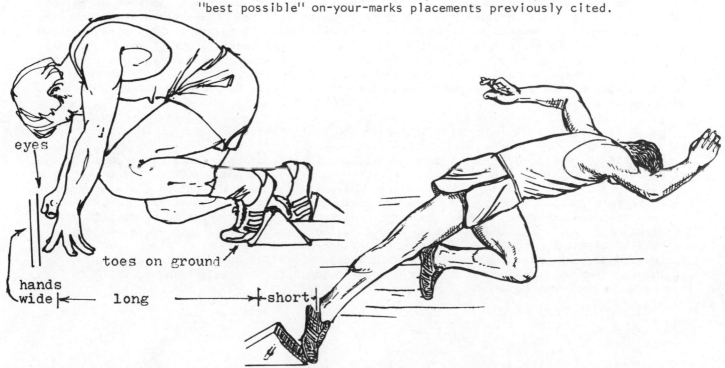

Fig. 25.16b.-- A remarkably powerful forward-thrust out of the blocks. Note how low the eyes-head are. During the early-learning period, this sprinter will have a tendency to chop his strides and may even stumble during the first ten yards. By developing powerful leg-foot thrusts, high knee action, a reaching out for six more inches on each stride, and a gradual lifting of the eyes and torso angle, he can gain perfect balance and maximum acceleration. This maximal forward drive would be a natural consequence of the on-your-mark positions of Figure 25.16a.

RELAXATION WHEN SPRINTING. Whatever one's degree of natural relaxation in sprinting, it can be improved by practice, both in competition and while training. In races, be aware of the looseness of your hands, of your arms, or of your neck and chin muscles. Always feel that you could have run just a little faster. A man's greatest races are "easy;" observers get an impression of "not trying," and wonder how much faster a man could do if his competition had forced him to go "all-out."

I hardly need repeat that relaxation is a whole-person concept--physical-mental-emotional. By-passing the book-length analysis of what might be meant by those three aspects, the sprinter experiences relaxation as an underloading of what we call "all-out" effort, or as a one percent reduction of tensions. Each athlete has a critical level of tension at which he performs best. If tension is lower, he is not properly "tuned up" for competition; if higher, he feels "tight," "lacking eagerness," "preoccupied as though in a trance."

In his research on weight-lifting, Arthur Steinhaus spoke of "disinhibiting the inhibitions," an awkward phrase, but it applies equally to relaxation in sprinting. The same impression of "taking it easy," of "sprinting as though on a red-hot stove" can be felt in the sprinting of Jesse Owens, Tommie Smith, Jim Hines, Valeriy Borzov or James Sanford. One is reminded of Coach Winter's admonition, "Think faster-looser, faster-looser; not harder but quicker." Anyone who questions that leg-speed is, in part, a function of the mind doesn't know sprinting.

Wysotschin's research[1] using a method of polimyography, concluded that, once beyond about 60 meters, relaxation plays an increasing role in sprint performances. Among a group of 50 sprinters, the relaxation factor had a value of 21.2% in improving 100-meter times; 48.32%, on 200-meter times. (No report was made of how relaxation was trained.)

In practice, run a series of 110-meter sprints, with full recovery between. From a running start, sprint at 98 percent speed for about 80 meters, preferably with a sprinter a meter or more ahead of you. Then sprint faster-looser; try to catch the man ahead over the last 20 meters. Impossible? But gradually you feel that you can run easier with no loss of velocity. Gradually you get a muscle-sense that to go faster, you let them flow--"faster-looser." You don't drop your arms; merely your tensions, or inhibitions. Of course you don't realize you have inhibitions until after you let them go. Gradually you learn to thrust more forcefully with each foot, not so much as an effort for power as a release of power. The power is there; you must, by repeated practice, get the knack of letting it go. It sounds like nonsense to make an effort not to make an effort, but great athletes learn to put into action what is non-sense in words.

Loader[2] puts all this into words that have the feel of action:

The sprinter knows when he (is running well). . . .The ease, the apparent lack of effort with which he moves, inform him. Conscious thought plays little part in his effort, for thinking did its work in the past, when the long routine of training had to be endured. . . . Motion is light and fluid, trammeled by no barriers. Limbs thrust, press, recover, thrust, in a cycle of movement so smooth as to be almost mechanical. . . . His body is being carried forward with a swift-sure speed so easy that he is hardly conscious of speed. The track does not seem to be traversed by individual, separate steps deliberately taken by flesh and blood but rather by a surging flow of spirit. . . . At such a moment there is no need for anyone to tell you. You know you can run. I mean, really run.

---

[1] Juri Wysotschin, "Relaxation in Sprinting," *Track Technique*, #68, June 1977, 2180.

[2] W. R. Loader, *THE TESTAMENT OF A RUNNER*, London: William Heinemann Ltd., 1960, p. 170. (This is a great book for sprinters--fascinating and helpful.)

THE FINISH

In the past, major concern in sprinting has been for the mechanics of starting. Today, without denying the importance of starting, emphasis is shifting to the problem of maintaining velocity and finishing. Franklin Henry's research concluded: (1) "That men generally reached their top speed about six seconds after leaving the starting blocks," (2) "That it is physiologically impossible for the runner, after he has reached his peak velocity, to maintain it for more than about 15 or 20 yards." Henry's subjects were not talented or highly-trained sprinters, so we should not interpret these conclusions exactly. But we should assume their approximate correctness. This means that all sprinters begin to slow down after about 80 yards, and that the man with the fastest finish is actually the man who slows down the least. If no one can maintain 100% velocity, what lesser percentage can be held? 99%? 98%? 97%?

Obviously, this is as much a mental-emotional problem as a physical one. In terms of action, what does it mean to maintain control? to relax? to hold your form? How does one run with "reckless abandon"? "controlled recklessness"? How does one "stay loose"? The important thing, of course, is the meaning of these terms *in action*. Actually, as Franklin Henry states, it may be "physiologically impossible" to sprint "top speed" at 80 yards, and then pick-up speed at the finish. But in terms of how a sprinter feels, it CAN be done.

Bud Winter, coach of Tommie Smith and many other great sprinters, believed in pick-up at the finish at any sprint distance--60 to 300 yards. He agreed it might be primarily "mental" but was sure there was also an actual physical acceleration. After Smith's record 220 on the straight in 19.5, they measured his stride-marks. From 120 to 200 yards, they measured 8'5"; in the next 12 yards, 8'7"; for the last three strides, 8'9".[1] Was Smith "coasting" between 120 and 200 yards? Coasting on a 19.5 220! But how else can this increase be explained? One answer is that pick-up and increased stride length was an inexorable requirement in Winter's schedule of practice for all his sprinters. He had an "ankle bounce" exercise, a "leg reach" exercise, a "bound forward" exercise, a "knees-up" exercise; and they all had to be done every practice. Pick-up may be "physiologically impossible," but it does seem to help get you there first, and that's what puts you on the top Olympic stand.

Fig. 25.17. The lunge--often the difference between victory and defeat. A marked forward lean on the last stride through the tape; head and eyes down more than is shown here; arms down to the side or even behind the torso. In the 1952 Olympic Games at Helsinki, the first four place-winners (Remigino, McKenley, Bailey and Smith) were all timed the same--10.4. But a yard from the tape, Remigino had mustered a desperate lunge, and thrust his right shoulder into the string. The Olympic champion--Lindy Remigino--by benefit of his finish style.

---

[1]Nordy Jensen, "Here's Tommie-Jet, Shades and All," *The Amateur Athlete*, September 1966, 17. (Jensen was sports information director at San Jose State, and should have the facts.) Also see Dick Drake, "That Tommie-Jet Gear," *Track & Field News*, May 1966, 1.

THE ORGANIZATION OF PRACTICE
Sprint training demands a year-round program of vigorous related activity which is just as carefully planned as for any other track or field event: a program of gradual development, first, in all-round endurance and physical condition; and later, toward specific sprinting skill and condition.

Modern training for sprinting emphasizes methods of gaining maximum velocity in the least possible time-distance, but equally important, emphasizes methods of maintaining maximum velocity through the finish line. In the past, such top speed began to diminish after about 80 yards. This is a serious problem in the 100; it is crucial in the 220. We tend to think of this maintenance of velocity as a problem in endurance, but it is equally a problem in relaxation, control, and skill. Call it what we may, the answer in terms of action lies in long-time related practice.

Perhaps toughness is the important word: toughness of muscle and tendon to withstand up-hill speed-training during the Fall of the year; toughness to practice day after day after day while following an interval-training schedule such as quarter-milers and half-milers might follow; toughness to work hard, but always within the limits of complete control and complete relaxation. Some call it will-power, and certainly that's part of the problem, but equally, it's a letting-go, a dropping of inhibitions against the pains of fatigue or against the dangers of all-out effort. We've used the term "controlled recklessness," as related to the field events, but it applies as well to sprinting.

By training the year-round, a man gradually learns to let himself go; he maintains control--in fact, his skill and control become automatic--but like the uninhibited madman, he throws away all restraint and releases his power. For the most part, a sprinter is unconscious of this release of power through daily practice. He may feel he's running faster and easier; that's about as far as his words will go. But release does come--through inexorable daily practice: tough, enjoyable, carefully planned, and reckless.

PRACTICE PROCEDURES
Each coach and each athlete must organize his own schedule, first on a year-round, then on a next-four-weeks basis. Judgment must consider ability, maturity, physical condition, season of competitive year, weather, interest, and personal problems. Thus to print a practice schedule here would be foolhardy.

Alternate days of hard work and easy work.

Injury and mental staleness do not result from too much work so much as doing too much work *too soon*. Use the gradual approach.

Light jogging for at least 20 minutes immediately following competition, or for an hour or more on the day after competition will ensure a better practice on the next day.

A proper workout requires about 90 minutes of continuous activity, divided into three equally important parts: (1) Twenty minutes of warm-up jogging and flexibility exercises; (2) Forty minutes of intensive work on endurance, speed, or skill; and (3) Twenty minutes of enjoyable relaxed jogging with other men regardless of their events. This last period is an excellent means of removing fatigue, preventing injury and muscle soreness, and building team morale.

WARM-UP AND PRE-SEASON PROCEDURES

1. Warm-up for 20 minutes with jogging, flexibility exercises, upper body strength exercises, and increasing-speed windsprints. Always finish up with easy jogging.

2. Fartlek. Get off the track to any varied terrain that is available. Enjoy getting tired while alternating repeated fast work (80% effort) with relaxed jogging.

3. If only a track is available, follow fartlek methods on the track. Devise methods that are enjoyable, that change speeds repeatedly, and that toughen.

AEROBIC SPEED-PLAY (Primarily Fall and early Spring running.) This should be thought of as a Run-for-Fun program to establish a base of general fitness for later training. Modern sprint-ers have banished the old fear that long running will slow muscle action. That's just not true! But such fartlek away from the track develops self-confidence if nothing else, and, lacking coercion from anyone, can be mighty satisfying.

TRAINING FOR GREATER SPEED-ENDURANCE

1. Repeated sprints with running start at from 60 to 120 yards, 80% speed, with short recovery jogging between. Build up gradually over several months to take three or more series of three or four sprints each. Get tired, rest by jogging, then get tired again. Do some curve sprinting.

2. Interval training on an organized basis. Use a fixed distance, 120 yards to 220 yards. (1) Use slower speed, set the rest interval at three minutes, then gradually increase the num-ber of sprints up to six. When this workout is mastered, that is, when it can be done with no muscle soreness or stiffness the next day, then (2) use slower speed, run six sprints, but gradually decrease the rest interval until the heart rate is reduced to about 110 beats within 60 seconds. Continue to full mastery. Finally, (3) gradually increase the speed of the sprints.

3. As condition improves, spring, that is, bound up low-grade hills, following the methods of Arthur Lydiard. The goal here is power and endurance. Spring forward with long strides, not short ones as is normal on hills. Warning: This is tough on the Achilles tendon. Use gradually and carefully.

4. Sprint 330 yards all-out *relaxed*. The emphasis here is on relaxation when tired. Try to maintain maximum velocity, but maintain control and relaxation. Repeat this workout until the problem of control is just no longer a problem.

5. Repetition relays--220 yards each leg. Use an odd number of men each team. Each man runs many times, from three to a dozen or more legs. Anchor man passes baton back to lead-off man. A valuable procedure with which to complete a day's work. Be sure opposing runners are paired for endurance and speed. First few legs are pace work; last legs are competitive.

TRAINING FOR GREATER RUNNING POWER

1. Take bouncing or leaping strides over various distances on track or grass. Drive force-fully forward with maximum-length strides, thrusting the ground backward in a "pawing" action as the free foot first touches the ground. High knee action is important, not in itself, but to ensure a full-length stride. Accentuate a forceful arm action. Variation 1--Same general procedure but emphasize quickness of foot-placement even though this decreases stride length. Variation 2--Same general procedure but wear weighted vest or belt. This is strenuous and in-jury-prone work; use gradual approach as to number of strides, rest between runs, number of repetitions, use of weights. Though greater force is the objective, emphasize quickness, an easy flowing of movement, rhythm and balance throughout. Variation 3--Take starts out of blocks, emphasizing explosive forward thrust for longer strides.

2. Organize a program of power exercises specifically related to the sprint muscles--the front thigh (quads), rear thigh (hamstrings), extensors and flexors of the lower leg-ankle-foot. Keep in mind the formula (power = strength x velocity) in which either strength or velo-city can be emphasized as is now done in training for javelin power. A heavy load with few repetitions develops $strength^{5x}$ x $velocity^{x}$; a light load develops $strength^{x}$ x $velocity^{5x}$. Both are essential, though as with the javelin, speed-power is prepotent over strength per se. Good judgment suggests that such power-exercise periods be followed by easy running and sprint-ing as fits within the schedule.

3. Wearing ankle weights between 1-2# each, gradually build up speed over about 50 yards--slowing down slowly. USSR research[1] found such resistances to be most effective; those above 2# changed the pattern of action and had a negative result. They also found that long jumpers gained more than sprinters by using such ankle weights, especially with those above 2#.

TRAINING FOR GREATER RUNNING SPEED. (Always run relaxed at 99 percent effort, especially when maximum speed is attempted.)

1. Starts at 20 yards. Take during middle of workout to ensure full warm-up and minimum fatigue. A dozen is not too many. Not merely quickness out of the blocks but quickness to 20

---

[1]N. Smirnov, "Ankle Weights in Training," *Track Technique*, #72, June 1978, p. 2308.

yards and beyond. On occasion, give team-mate one to three-foot handicap, then catch him before the tape--with a feeling of being relaxed, of releasing power, not forcing it.

2. With a running start, take repeated sprints (all-out but feeling 99 percent effort) at from 50 to 80 yards. Full rest (jogging-walking) between.

3. Sprint on downhill grade of 5 percent or less. Soviet research[1] found an increase of 17% in stride frequency on the flat immediately after downhill sprints on a 2 to 3-degree grade, but concluded the primary value of such work was to "give an extra little push that may dislodge the sprinter from his plateau." Consensus was that grades should not exceed 5 percent and such work should be light and increased carefully to avoid strains.

4. Run curves 95% effort-counter-clockwise and clockwise.

5. Competitive sprints at 3/4 competitive distance--75 or 180 yards. Variation--give team-mate of equal ability a one-yard handicap at start, maintain handicap for 50 yards, then catch him in the next 25.

TRAINING FOR VELOCITY OUT OF THE BLOCKS. Leroy Walker, 1976 U.S. Chief Olympic Track and Field Coach, an authority on sprinting, found these "tips"[2] helpful in the training of Olympians Edwin Roberts and Larry Black:

A prime prerequisite for a good start is "mental toughness" in approaching the starting line. This attitude is not suddenly generated as the sprinter waits for the gun. Roberts and Black developed their toughness through hours of practice as they gained confidence in their own ability to start. In each starting practice, attention is given to the following details:

1. Each gun start should approximate the conditions of an actual competitive start. No sloppy starts are permitted and recalls are made however slight the forward movement may be before the gun reports.

2. Concentrate on listening, not on thinking or anticipating.

3. Assume a "get-set" position which guarantees maximum momentum from the blocks--not just quickness of arms-legs coordinated action. Avoid too much pressure upon the hands or locking the elbows.

4. Guard against a "planting action" of the foot that leaves the rear block.

5. "Run-up" to the best running position. The exact distance from the blocks or exact number of strides before the desired body lean for efficient running will be achieved varies from runner to runner.

6. Achieve maximum momentum through effortless acceleration.

HOW THEY TRAIN
VALERIY BORZOV'S TRAINING (1972 Olympic Champion, 100m--10:14; 200m--20.00)
Borzov's overall training is consistent with the "Organization of Practice" presented here. His sprint-specialist coach Valentin Petrovski[3] analyzed with great thoroughness the factors of training and the means of optimal development. Space allows only two sample workouts from his beginning-competitive period:

Model A--the development of sprint endurance: Warmup, sprint with increasing speed 3-5 x 100-200m. (1st set). 30m sprint from a crouch start with medium speed, for the improvement of technique 4-5 x (2nd set). 30m sprint from a crouch start using starting commands at almost full speed 4-5 x recovery in between runs 1-2 minutes (3rd set). 60m sprint from a crouch start using starting commands 4-5 x with almost maximal speed, recovery in between runs 2-3 minutes (4th set). Repetition sprints from a crouch start or flying start over 60 or 100m with 70-90% of maximum speed 2-4 x recovery 1-2 minutes (5th set). After 4-6 minutes pause 400-600m easy run. The recovery between sets is regulated according to pulse rate, using 100-120 beats

---

[1]"There is Speed in Those Hills," *Track Technique*, #65, Sept. 1976, p. 2085.

[2]Leroy T. Walker, "Tips on Sprinting," *Track Technique*, #64, June 1976, p. 2036.

[3]Valentin Petrovski, "Synopsis of Borzov's Sprint Training and Coaching," *Track Technique*, #55, March 1974, p. 1950. (Translated by Gerald A. Carr, University of Victoria, B.C., Canada.) This article merits careful study.

Model B--the development of sprint speed: Warmup, sprint with increasing speed 3-4 x 80-100m (1st set). 30m sprint using a crouch start, medium intensity for improving technique 3-5 x (2nd set). 30m sprint from a crouch start with starting commands--almost flat out speed 3-5 x (3rd set). 60m sprint from a crouch start using starting commands with almost maximal speed 2-4 x (4th set). Sprint over 30m from a flying start at almost top speed 2-4 x (5th set). After 4-6 minutes, an easy run over 400m.

In relation to training goals in a weekly cycle, one cannot increase the number of sets in Model A or Model B further than 2-4 x a week with 5-6 sets.

PIETRO MENNEA (1979, 200m--19.72WR)
Coach Carlo Vittori said:[1]

"Mennea should get credit for demystifying the sprints. Perhaps one day the Americans will comprehend that natural talent isn't enough, and that work is always the ultimate key. With their bodies, what would a Riddick or a Steve Williams have done if they had the same determination as Mennea in training?
"One day I explained to Williams how Mennea trained. The American was startled--he was really terrified."

What kind of work does Mennea do? Some samples, according to Vittori:

Several days before his WR--5 x 80m in 8.3-8.5, with 2 minutes rest between. A 10-minute rest, then 5 x 100m ranging from 10.2 to 10.5 (average 10.4), with a 3 minute rest between. Then 20 minutes recuperation, followed by 300m in 33.1, run with progressive acceleration (12.3 for first 100, 20.8 for last 200).

Mennea had done the same workout at the Italian training camp in Formia, Italy, but with shorter recuperation times--his rest periods were naturally lengthened to accommodate for the high altitude at Mexico City.

Another day at Mexico included the following: 4 or 5 x 80m in 8.3, 3 minutes rest between; then 12-15 minutes rest, followed by 3-4 x 100m in 10.3-10.4, with a 3-4 minute rest; after a 15 minute rest, 2 x 150m in 15.2, 15.3.

Hurdler Harry Schulting reports in *Leichtathletik* that he saw Mennea run a fabulous 60m series last spring--6 x 60m in 6.5-6.6, followed by a rest period, then the whole process another 5 times for a total of 36 runs. "I wouldn't ever have believed it if I hadn't seen it myself," says the Dutchman. Someone asked Vittori, "How is this possible, unless Pietro's a robot?" Vittori replied, "We have the good fortune that he is indeed a robot!"

HOW THEY TRAIN[2] by Mel Rosen, Head Coach, Auburn University
FALL PROGRAM: We work five days a week in the Fall. We started with four days but found out everyone was staying in town on Friday so used Friday also. The second day of practice we have a 3½ mile cross country run to check on their condition, and then we get into the program. A typical one week workout is:
Mon--a long run of 3-5 miles plus weight training.
Tues--intervals on the track (6 x 440 in 90, 3 minutes rest).
Wed--long run of 3-5 miles plus weight training.
Thurs--4 x 660 in 2.05 on the track.
Fri--an optional long run and weight training.

Gradually we increase the work load and then cut down on rest periods. We run 3½ miles for time once every two weeks to check their progress.

Monday-Wednesday-Friday the sprinters lift weights. The weight program is set up to develop all-around body development with the following exercises: pull-ups, curls, military press,

[1]"Mennea: Made & Born," *Track & Field News*, November 1979, p. 47.
[2]Mel Rosen, "Developing Sprinters," *Track & Field Quarterly Review*, Vol.78 #3, Fall 1978, p.15. Mel Rosen, Auburn University has been most successful in developing such sprinting greats as Harvey Glance (NCAA champion, 60m-6.0s, 100m-9.9WR, 200m-20.1); Willie Smith (60y-5.9, 100m-10.1, 200m-20.5, 400m-45.3); or Stanley Floyd, 1980 NCAA & AAU 100m champion.

toe raises, bench press, sit-ups, leg curls.

They begin with light weights. They can do any other exercises they wish with the approval of the weight coach. The program is set up to do each exercise ten times and to move up to five pounds each workout till they can't do the exercise ten times. They stay at this level till they can do it ten times.

During the Fall we have three weight lifting contests mainly to check their progress in the weight room. The lifts we do are: bench press, military press, clean and jerk, curl. The contest is organized so that only three attempts are allowed on each exercise. They must lift the weights one time in good form; therefore, they are cautioned to try a weight they can handle the first time and then the next two times to try for their maximum effort.

Form running is done twice a week. We stride for ten minutes before the regular practice session during that day.

The interval running can be 220, 330, 440, 660 or 880; but mainly at a slow pace, trying to cut the rest interval down throughout the Fall. They do some starts in the Fall, mainly on their own with no competition, to check their style and to add variety to our training routine. We also do some baton handling to change the routine a little.

Early December: We have a 300 yard solo run for time to check their rank on the team; and during the following week we have an inter-squad meet to pick our lineup for our first meet in the middle of January.

January: We begin preparing for the indoor season. Our sprinters work on getting ready for the 60 yard dash, as we go from there to the 440 with no in between distances in our conference. We work Monday through Saturday and take Sunday off. A typical training schedule would be:
Mon--4 x 150 in 18 with a slow walk back.
Tues--6 x 30 yard starts, 6 x 50's in 6 flat.
Wed--6 x 30 yard starts, 6 laps of pick-ups on the straightaways, walking curves.
Thurs--2 easy 120's.
Fri--Rest.
Sat--Meet.

On Monday and Thursday we work outdoors, Tuesday and Wednesday we work indoors. On Monday and Wednesday we continue our weight training, after running practice, to maintain strength developed in the Fall. Some of the things we do which might be of interest is no long running except on Mondays. We feel this will help the sprinters when they change to the outdoor season as they move up to the 100 and 200 meters. We do as little running around curves as possible as we feel sprinters get hurt running sharp curves. We feel the sprinters should warm up well and cool down by jogging 880 after each workout. Weight training is not as intense as during the Fall, but is continued throughout the competitive season. If we have a sprinter who will also run the open 400 or mile relay, then we incorporate some 330's into his Monday workout and 200's in his Wednesday workout.

April: After the NCAA indoor meet we have only two weeks to get ready for our first big outdoor meet--the Florida Relays. Most of our time is spent on baton handling and some slow 150's, 220's or 330's to build up some stamina for the 100 and 200. Our typical workout after the Florida Relays is:
Mon--2 x 330's in 40 with 330 walk.
Tues--baton passes, 6 starts, 6 x 150's in 17, walk back.
Wed--baton passes, 6 starts, 6 x 100's in 10.8, walk back.
Thurs--2 easy 120's.
Fri--Rest.
Sat--Meet.

We feel sprinters need to be quick out of the blocks but they must also come out in good running position. Most of our sprinters use a medium start with the front foot 12 inches from the line and the back foot 22 inches from the line. We do not take more than six starts during each practice but those are quality starts. Some ideas: keep sprinters healthy--don't over-work in practice; ease them up at the end of the week; work on their skills each week; maintain their strength through weight training and quickness through starts; friendly competition in practice coming off blocks.

Chapter 26
COMPETITIVE HINTS FOR SPRINTS AND HURDLES

Competitive hints usually relate to the minutes and actions that immediately precede competition. These are crucial of course and must be carefully organized and carried out. But it would be fatal to think that they were the main part of developing a maximum competitive attitude and action. Actually, a competitive attitude in a mind-body sense is acquired primarily in the weeks and months and years before major competition. If a boy is careless in practice in the placement of his starting blocks; if he is discouraged by continually practicing against faster starters; if in practice or in minor competition, the starting gun is fired carelessly; if his track suit is sloppy or his spikes badly worn; if the institution he represents has little respect among track buffs; if any of these or a hundred other details are negative, or for that matter positive, in their effects, the athlete's competitive approach will be affected.

This holistic approach to competition is so crucial as to be explained in different ways. To a real degree, a man's total pattern of habitual response is sharply channeled or focussed within a single action. Because this action is so narrow in time and movement, we tend to isolate it, and minimize its backgrounds. But time and time again, I have watched great performers in competition, been amazed at their concentration and control, then later discovered a great breadth of preparation and thoughtful planning and wise counselling that lay behind their efforts. A man is born with a certain potential in terms of competitive spirit just as he is born with a certain potential for muscle velocity. But whether that potential is realized at maximum levels is determined by development through environment and experience and inspiration.

Since each athlete and his background are unique, it is difficult to prescribe specific measures that will ensure high competitive spirit as the man approaches the starting line. Some great champions tend to withdraw within themselves, to shut out the world, to concentrate their energies by eliminating the distractions of people and influences around them. Other equally great champions seem to expand under competition, seem to be unaware of the negatives, become talkative and cheerful and eager for the race to start. Only by knowing his man, can a coach give help that will be helpful.

However, a few suggestions may open possibilities. First, there should be a routine of action and attitude leading up to important competition. Whatever its details, they should develop confidence and a maximum of what we call nervous energy. The word, "routine" is crucial, a set pattern of action that one knows by past experience will lead to the single-mindedness needed at the start. Throughout the weeks before the BIG meet, a routine of practice, of eating and sleeping, of thinking and talking, should build the confidence and poise for this special competition and its special conditions.

I had the great privilege of coaching John Haines, National champion at 60 yards indoors for four straight years, 1953-1956. John was beaten occasionally in lesser meets. But during the week of the Championship, he was a different person. He spoke more confidently, laughed more, practiced with greater relaxation, started more sharply. Somehow, we all KNEW he was going to win. I repeat, WE ALL KNEW, and that's mighty important. The calm, undoubting attitude of high expectancy, whether created by the man himself, or his friends, or his coach and team-mates, is its own assurance of high performance.

The crucial time of course is during the last hour or so before the final race. During that brief period one's energies can build and build to the point of controlled but explosive tension. Or they can seep away, erg by erg, through distracted worry over one's opponents, through irritation with the starter and his uncertain way of handling men, through concern for one's shoe laces or spikes, or for the sudden awareness of an ache in the left knee, or--but the possible ways of escape are endless.

One of the best ways of finding concentration is to have a set pattern of things to do:

1. Report to the dressing room well ahead of time.

2. Dress steadily but leisurely.

3. Warm-up fully but gradually.

4. Go back to dressing room, towel off the sweat, check your shoes carefully: leather, spikes, laces, put on your number, etc., all ahead of time so that if something is wrong, there is plenty of time to fix it.

5. Back on the track, check the starter: his tone of voice in saying, "set," his steadiness and relaxation in holding men at "set," his gun reaction when several sprinters have false starts--whatever seems vital.

6. Ignore your opponents, or respond to them as you may prefer, but don't allow your contact with them to distract you or disrupt your concentration.

7. In all these actions, expect and welcome the nervousness, the dry mouth, the cold sweat, the stomach butterflies. They all signify the clearing of decks for action, for powerful action--just as long as you maintain control. This isn't self-hypnotism, or if it is, it is of the common-sense kind by which men rise in so many emergencies to their highest achievements. Call it what you will: competitive spirit, positive mental attitude, courage, willed control; the words mean little. But it is a range of quality that we all possess, and only needs careful and patient training to attain its full use.

8. Begin the actions of "go to your marks" early, and therefore calmly. Do it the same way every time (in practice as in the meets). In a very important sense, you're not thinking of anything. At this point thinking would be a distraction. It all becomes automatic. You're not attending to anything consciously. The world doesn't exist. Only afterward to you realize that there was "awareness" of many details; just as at this moment, by setting aside this page, you realize that you "heard" the noises in the next room, without really being conscious of them.

A sprinter or hurdler goes through the motions of starting, in somewhat the same manner as a pianist goes through the hand-finger motions of playing. In a sense, his fingers do the playing; through much practice, they have become "aware" of when to hit softly or when to slow the tempo. True, the player is conscious of how the playing is occurring, but it's a holistic consciousness. If the player thinks about it in a divisive way, in a way that analyzes how, that takes his technique apart, his playing will flounder. Or let his mind wander, and the music will suffer even though it's something he has played "perfectly" for years. So with starting, or, for that matter, with any competitive situation in sports. "Get with it, man!" may be jazz slang but it's also a sound attitude in competition.

Perhaps the best description ever written of both high and low competitive attitudes in sprinting is given by W. R. Loader[1] in TESTAMENT OF A RUNNER. His first story is of his great victory as a schoolboy at the English championships in 1935:

> Excitement was now working in me like yeast. Gone were all lethargy and detachment. . . . Coming second in both heat and semi-final had not taken undue toll of nervous energy. I was anxious for the start, desperate to go, knowing I had it in me to mount a desperate effort. . . . Previous doubts and anxieties now seemed ridiculous. Confidence burned like a flame.

---

[1] W. R. Loader, TESTAMENT OF A RUNNER, London: William Heinemann Ltd., 1960, 125-144.

The second description is of a similar situation a year later, in which, after a year of college where he met coldness and discouragement, he failed to even qualify for the final:

Suddenly it became desperately important to get into that final. . . . But through excessive brooding on mere part-success, the nerve had failed. The prospect of the contest did not induce a feeling of excitement so much as a feeling of dread. Even the most wishful thinking could not convince that this last chance was more than the slenderest. The finality of the affair turned the bowels to liquid. There was no spearhead of resolution, sharp and shining, but only a dull obstinacy. A year ago the White City had been warm and bright in the sunshine. This time it was grey and chill. Influenced by weather, the blood ran even cooler than before. Instead of creating confidence, memories of the other, triumphant occasion, merely deepened the sense of inadequacy. . . .

Apathetically I dug my holes. The other runners were jigging around, taking deep breaths, high-stepping, obviously keyed up at the prospect of the race. Beside them I felt heavy and lackadaisical. When we got down to our marks, my mind wouldn't concentrate. It wandered, thinking of Berlin, thinking of the season's mediocre efforts, thinking of how the promise had not been fulfilled. The gun took me by surprise.

In these two situations, the same individual was involved, but the dynamics in his life-situation had changed. If anything, desire was greater in the second race, but it had been dulled by discouragement and repeated defeat.

471

Chapter 27
THE HIGH HURDLES

A BRIEF HISTORY OF THE DEVELOPMENT OF TECHNIQUE

As with throwing the javelin, long jumping, or for that matter with any field or track event, technique cannot be separated from speed of action. In the final analysis, the best technique is the one that gets a man to the finish line first. But you wouldn't think so, if you listened to the endless controversies of the past 90 years between the advocates of hurdling technique and the get-there-first boys. I remember so well how the admirers of Herb Attlesey's beautiful style looked down their noses when Harrison Dillard, the 1948 Olympic 100-meters champion, won the 1952 Olympic hurdles. What lousy form! Notice how he sails over the hurdle! That controversy hasn't quieted down entirely even today, though 13-second times require hurdlers that are tall, fast, and in complete control.

As a sports event, hurdling goes back no further than the early 19th century in England. No mention of any such competition over obstacles has been found in ancient Greek or early European or Irish literature. Webster[1] states,

> There were hurdle races at the tutors' and dames' houses at Eton College as long ago as 1837, and that is the earliest reference to competition in this kind of sport that I have been able to find, but in BELL'S LIFE of 1853 mention is made of a match between two amateurs, one of the events included being a race with jumps over 50 hurdles each 3 feet 6 inches high. . . . The first authentic records of a hurdles time are supplied by A. W. T. Daniel, CUAC. He won the first Oxford and Cambridge 120 high hurdles event, 1864, in 17 3/4 seconds.

Similarly, Ross and Norris McWhirter[2] write:

> Ten flights, ten yards apart, seemed to be the accepted test from the earliest mentions but the height was merely that of the accepted sheep hurdle of the day, about 3½ feet. In 1866 there was some attempt to standardize the height, for a rule in the first Oxford minute book states "the hurdles shall be 3 feet 6 inches in [above-- J.K.D.] the ground." It is not recorded how many of the early pioneers were maimed by these crude jagged barriers, which were rigidly staked into the meadow, but it is at least certain that if any of them could now see six rows of zebra striped slats, with their 8 pounds toppling moment, they would wonder if it were the same event.

Although no mention of "sheep hurdles" has been found in American track literature, Comstock[3] suggests a similarly diabolical device--a single rope or pole all the way across the track

---

[1] F. A. M. Webster, ATHLETICS OF TO-DAY. London: Frederick Warne & Co., Ltd., 1929, 132.

[2] Ross and Norris McWhirter, GET TO YOUR MARKS. London: Nicholas Kaye, 1951, 135.

[3] Boyd Comstock, HOW TO HURDLE. New York: American Sports Publishing Co., 1924, 90.

TABLE 27.1

OUTSTANDING PERFORMANCES--HIGH HURDLES

OLYMPIC CHAMPIONS

Date	Record 110m.	Name	Affiliation	Hgt.	Wgt.	Time 100y	Est.HC[1]
1920	14.8	Earl Thomson	Canada	6'3"	180	10.3	
1924	15.0	Dan Kinsey	Illinois	6'	160	10.4	2.5
1928	14.8	S. J. Atkinson	So. Africa	6'3"	170		
1932	14.6	George Saling	Iowa	6'3"		9.8	2.9
1936	14.2	Forrest Towns	Georgia	6'2"	172	9.7	2.2
1948	13.9	William Porter	Northwestern	6'3"	160	9.6	2.5
1952	13.7	Harrison Dillard	Baldwin-Wallace	5'10"		9.4	
1956	13.5	Lee Calhoun	No.Caro. Col.	6'2"	165	9.7	
1960	13.8	Lee Calhoun	No.Caro. Col.				
1964	13.6	Hayes Jones	East. Mich.	5'10"	162	9.4	
1968	13.3	Willie Davenport	Southern U.	6'1"	175	9.4	
1972	13.24[2]	Rod Milburn	USA				
1976	13.30[2]	Guy Drut	France	6'2"	161		
1980	13.39	Thomas Munkelt	E. Germany	6'3/4"	172		

WORLD-RECORD PERFORMERS OF SPECIAL INTEREST

Date	Record 110m.	Name	Affiliation	Hgt.	Wgt.	Time 100y	Est.HC[1]
1898	15.2y	Alvin Kraenzlein	Pennsylvania	6'0"		10.0	3.3
1920	14.4y	Earl Thomson	Dartmouth	6'3"	180	10.3	2.0
1937	13.7y	Forrest Towns	Georgia	6'3"	172	9.7	2.2
1941	13.7y	Fred Wolcott	Rice	5'11½"		9.5	2.5
1948	13.6y	Harrison Dillard	Baldwin-Wallace	5'10"	155	9.4	2.6
1951	13.5y	Dick Attlesey	So. Calif.	6'3½"	178	9.6	2.0
1956	13.4	Jack Davis	So. Calif.	6'3"	178	9.6	2.0
1958	13.4	Elias Gilbert	Winst.-Salem	5'11"	155	9.7	2.0
1959	13.2	Martin Lauer	Germany	6'1½"	165	9.4	2.1
1960	13.2	Lee Calhoun	No.Caro. Col.	6'2"	170	9.5	1.8
1972	13.24m[2]	Rod Milburn	Southern U.	6'	175	9.4	1.96
1977	13.21	Alejandro Casanas	Cuba	6'½"	161		
1979	13.00[2]	Renaldo Nehemiah	Maryland U.	6'½"	170	10.1m	1.90

BEST PERFORMANCES--HIGH SCHOOL

BOYS   120y-39"   42"

Date	Record	Name	Affiliation			Time	
1975	13.74	Dedy Cooper	Ells. Richmond, CA				
1977	13.66	Philip Johnson	Gardena, CA				
1978	13.61	Dexter Hawkins	Atlanta, Ga.				
1977	12.90	Renaldo Nehemiah	Scotch Plains, N.J.			13.89	
1979	13.30	Rod Wilson	Bartram, Phila.			13.94	
1980	13.50	Jerome Wilson	Nashville, Tenn.				

GIRLS

Date	Record	Name	Affiliation				
1976	13.50	Sonya Hardy	Boulder, Colo.				
1979	12.95	Candy Young	Beaver Falls, Pa.	(100m H-33")			
1980	13.7	Carolyn Faison	Bay, Pan C., F.	(120y H-30")			

BEST PERFORMANCES--WOMEN

100m H-33"

Date	Record	Name	Affiliation	Age	Hgt.	Wgt.	
1972	12.59[3]	Annelie Ehrhardt	E. Germany	26	5'5½"	128	
1976	12.77[3]	Johanna Schaller	E. Germany	24	5'9"	143	
1979	12.86[4]	Deby LaPlante	Walnut, CA				
1979	12.48[5]	Grazyna Rabsztyn	Poland				
1980	12.56	Vera Komisova	USSR	27	5'6½"	132	

[1]Estimated Hurdle-Clearance Time. [2]Electronic timing. [3]Olympic champion. [4]American record [5]World record.

which undoubtedly evolved from the cross-country stone and rail fence-hopping in vogue at the time.

This, however, was found to be impractical for general usage, as one runner would gain an advantage over another by reason of the general hurdle being knocked down by the leading man. The installation of the individual hurdle was the result. This hurdle, made after the style of a sawbuck, was of substantial construction and being a dangerous piece of furniture to strike, the hurdler made an effort to clear it by a good margin.

But a picture I have of F. G. Maloney, Chicago, winning the 1901 Big Ten Conference hurdles in 16.2, shows every hurdle sawbuck of the first two men flat on the ground. No blood-spattered leg bones are apparent but that might be for lack of color photography.

Shortly after 1900, increasing interest in the low hurdles (in America only) created one that swung down in the middle to provide a low hurdle 2'6" high. The base of this hurdle was 24 inches wide, with the uprights placed in the middle to form an inverted-T shape. A man was disqualified if he knocked down three hurdles.

Not that a man would try to knock them down. For as they fell, they first had to rise on the 12-inch extension of the base, and that made clearance problems for a man's thigh or trail leg. To avoid this, Harry Hillman, 1904 Olympic 400-meters hurdles champion and coach at Dartmouth, invented the present L-type hurdle which swings down immediately on being hit. This hurdle greatly increased the confidence, hair-breadth clearance, and so the speed of hurdling, a factor to be kept in mind when comparing hurdlers before and after.

Of the many excellent hurdlers prior to the L-type hurdle (1935), only two warrant special mention in this recital of techniques development--Alvin Kraenzlein and Earl Thomson. Though actually he was not the first to do so, Kraenzlein is generally credited with originating the straight-forward, though bent, lead leg, and with sprinting over the hurdles instead of jumping them. He was a fine athlete, holding world records in the high and low hurdles as well as in the long jump. The unique contribution of Earl Thomson (Canada, Dartmouth, and long-time coach at Annapolis; 1920 Olympic champion and world-record holder--14.4) was a two-arms-forward drive "through" the hurdle that ensured forward lean and balance beyond the hurdle.

Fig. 27.1. Evolution of the high hurdle--a carpenter's horse with high-hurdle attachment, a T-type hurdle (about 1912), and an L-type hurdle (about 1942).

Up to about 1940, hurdling technique and size requirements seemed well established. Every record holder (Simpson, 1916-14.6; Thomson, 1920-14.4; Anderson, 1930-14.4; Beard, 1931-14.2; Saling, 1932-14.6; Keller, 1932-14.4; Towns, 1937-13.7) was 6'3" or taller, and followed about the same pattern of action over the hurdle.

But with the coming of Fred Wolcott, 1941, and Harrison Dillard (1946-1954), the shift toward sprinting ability was on. Wolcott did attempt both arms forward as did Thomson, but failed to lean into the hurdle or to cut down the lead leg beyond it. His clearance was high and a hurried trail leg straightened the torso prior to the landing. Coaches began to speak of a new style for shorter men who could sprint. Get those feet down fast--both off the hurdle and in between hurdles, and leave aesthetics to the Greeks and the tall boys.

Fig. 27.2 -- Jack Davis, USC, 1956 - 13.4, showing excellent straight-ahead action. The lead leg is coming straight through; hips are square to the hurdle; though the left arm-shoulder are out of line as the trail leg is brought through. See Davis' full forward lean in Figure 28.10.

Dillard's scant 5'10" and imperfect technique ruled out any chance of his becoming a great hurdler--they said! But after winning an NCAA hurdle trial (1947-13.9), he won 82 consecutive races, indoors and outdoors, and broke Towns' "human-ultimate" time of 13.7 by one-tenth second. Dillard's lead leg was locked at the knee, his torso somewhat twisted over the hurdle, his off-arm was wide and relatively uncontrolled, and his body lean upright on landing. But he ran 10.3 in winning the Olympic 100 meters in 1948, and that made the difference.

In the 1950's
Then a new trend began--height, technique, AND speed. Dick Attlesey was 6'3½" tall. He used a modified two-arms-forward style, an excellent forward lean into and through the hurdle, a relaxed lead leg which snapped down quickly, and a delayed trail leg which drove forward with remarkable speed. Add to this that he had been timed in 10.5 for 100 meters in official competition. Small wonder he was the first to record 13.5.

All this lead him to be?
Similarly, Jack Davis, the first (1956) to run 13.4, was 6'3" tall and had officially run 09.6 for the 100. On the other hand, Lee Calhoun won the 1956 Olympics in 13.5, despite a best time of only 09.9 for 100 yards and a height of 6'1". During the next four years, Calhoun concentrated on sprint work so that, prior to the 1960 Games, he had improved to 09.7. Undoubtedly this enabled him to win again at Rome, and, prior to the Games, to tie Martin Lauer's (Germany) world record of 13.2. Along with excellent technique over the hurdles, Calhoun had worked hard on perfecting a method of thrusting his head down and forward and so gaining an extreme forward lean at the tape. This gave him a number of important races, but especially, that over his teammate, Willie May, in the 1960 Olympic final.

But over the past decade, the sprinters have dominated the high hurdles competition. First came Hayes Jones, Eastern Michigan, 5'10", 162#, with many a win in the open 60 indoors and 100 outdoors, a best 100-yard time of 09.4, and the 1964 Olympic championship, 13.6. Then Willie Davenport, Southern U., 6'1", 175#, an official 10.3 for the 100 meters, the 1968 Olympic gold medal (13.3), a tie for the world record in 13.2, and in 1969 alone, the winner of 21 races under 14 flat. As to *the* technique, Jon Hendershott[1] describes *coaches* his style as "near-flawless", and quotes Berny Wagner, coach at Oregon State, *their*

Their
Davenport's excellent balance is maintained throughout, His fine lean into the hurdle, his lead with the knee, the flat action of his trailing leg with the knee barely clearing the hurdle, all give quickness and power over the barrier.

---

[1]Jon Hendershott, "Davenport Rare Master," *Track & Field News*, May 1970, 3.

His lead foot lands well under his body so that he is in a running position when he hits the track after clearing the hurdle. He doesn't let his trail leg rise as high as most other hurdlers...and this saves time in getting his first stride down fast.

Rod Millburn (Southern U., 1972 Olympic champion--13.24 WR). The first approved 13s time (hand-timed) for 120-yard high hurdles was made in the 1971 National AAU semi-finals by Rod Milburn. Millburn combined at highest levels the twin essentials of sprinting speed and technique. His arm action (two arms forward) was forceful and well balanced both over and between hurdles. His lead leg cut down quickly; his forward lean ennabled the rear leg to drive quickly to a full stride beyond. In 1971, he won 28 consecutive races; in 1972, his Olympic championship was preceded by 12 wins at 13.5 or faster, plus two windy 13.0s.

Hurdlers are Sprinters. By way of emphasizing the all-importance of sprinting speed for high-level hurdling, consider these facts: Harrison Dillard (HH-13.6y--100m-10.3); Hayes Jones (HH-13.6m--100y-09.4); Willie Davenport (HH-13.2y--100m-10.3); Rod Millburn (HH-13.0y--100y-09.3est). Dr. Dick Hill, coach of both Davenport and Millburn, stated that the latter was never timed for the 100 "but off the speed he showed in his 13-flat, I would equate it with 9.3 or better."

The next great hurdler was, apparently, even faster. Two weeks before setting a world hurdle record of 13 flat for 110 meters, Renaldo Nehemiah ran 100 meters in 10.1; 200 meters in 20.38--both in an Atlantic Coast Conference Championships.

Hurdle-Clearance Times. Judging the merits of hurdlers on the basis of the differences between their 120-yard sprint times (estimated from 100-yard times) and their 120-yard high-hurdle times is not a fully valid method. A hurdler's 100-yard speed is seldom tested and times given in papers and journals are as much hearsay as facts. Also a man's momentum over the 120-yard distance is continuous; his speed between the hurdles influences his speed over them. However, the attempt is interesting, if not of practical value.

Using this method, Table 27.1 discloses that, of earlier hurdlers, Lee Calhoun (1956-1960) was the most technically efficient with a time-difference of 1.8s. All others were estimated at two seconds flat, except for Millburn at 1.96s. In 1978, Nehemiah ran 13 flat which, off his 100-meter time of 10.1 gives him a 1.9s difference.

Fig. 27.3--Lee Calhoun, North Carolina State, 1956 and 1960 Olympic champion, 1960 world-record co-holder - 13.2, showing excellent forward lean into the hurdle. Note relaxed bent knee of lead leg. The lead foot has reached its greatest height in front of the hurdle and has now started to cut down to a quick landing. These men are sprinting "through" the hurdle.

HOW TO BEGIN

How to begin can be determined only by the local climate, adequacy of indoor facilities, extent of year-round practice, competitive schedule, and of course by the many individual considerations of both athlete and coach. However, there are certain guides to action.

BUILD A BACKGROUND OF FITNESS FOR HURDLING. The demands of hurdling for muscle-tendon toughness and flexibility, for high-speed action, for stamina in practice, all suggest a preliminary background of work before starting to hurdle. Cross-country running over varying terrain and at varying speeds and with other hurdlers and sprinters is both fun and helpful. Warm-up each day with flexibility exercises, stretching muscles and tendons carefully and gradually--GRADUALLY! A little more each week, not each day! Sprint up hills; recover on the way down, then repeat again and again.

BEGIN WITH VISUAL LEARNING. A hurdler's first concern is to acquire a feeling, or an impression of the wholeness of hurdling. Study other hurdlers in action, either directly or in movies. Get the feel of the action. Stay away from the coach at this point; you're not concerned now with details; just get a sense of the main movements and the flow of action.

BEGIN ACTION WITH THE LOW HURDLES. Most coaches prefer the low hurdles for beginners. The elements of fear and tension are not so likely to interfere with concentration on the techniques of hurdling. Begin with one hurdle, but move quickly to three. Place them nine or even less yards apart, or move them out to twelve yards and take five easy strides between. Make a take-off mark about six feet in front of the hurdle. Take several short strides, then as you feel ready, two driving strides at the hurdle. Don't be concerned with the details of technique. Just run over the hurdle. Hurdling style is merely modified sprinting style.

Persist with this kind of unanalyzed and unself-conscious activity. Run and run and run over those low hurdles, with little or even no coaching. The confidence and, yes, the courage you'll gain from working alone is even more crucial than the details of technique. Your tendency will be to rush through these preliminary workouts; you'll want to "know it all" NOW. But take it easy, relax, and enjoy your own way of hurdling.

WORK OVER THREE HURDLES. If you've secured a good background of low hurdling, you can begin with three high hurdles instead of the often recommended one hurdle. We like to place them about 11 yards apart on the grass and then use five strides between: three short and easy, two full length and driving. If five strides are used with the usual ten yards apart, the need to chop the first strides tends to straighten the body angle as you come down off the hurdle. Forward lean into and over the hurdle must be maintained in the strides between.

When ready--and don't hurry it--shift over to the cinder track and get your strides to the first hurdle. Move your starting blocks to the lane next to the hurdle. Now sprint beyond the hurdle and check your foot-marks in the cinders. (That's one advantage of cinders over the modern all-weather tracks!) You'll probably find that you made eight or nine footprints on the track. If eight seems feasible, place your take-off foot in the front starting block; if nine, the opposite.

Now read the section in this chapter on the hurdle start and the action to the first hurdle. Note that the hurdler comes up a stride sooner than the sprinter so he can be ready for the driving strides through the hurdle. Takeoff well back from the hurdle (champions use about 7 feet) so you'll have free space for the forward lean into the hurdle and the forward-upward thrust of the lead knee (study the forward 1½-arm thrust of the hurdler in Figure 27.9). This produces a wide split of the legs, with a delayed pull-over of the trail knee.

You're off to a good start. A few bruises here and there, but that's to be expected. A little confusion at times as to which arm goes with which leg, but that's natural. In general there hasn't been much surgical dissection of either you or the techniques of hurdling and, in the beginning, that's as it should be.

Renaldo Nehemiah (Scotch Plains HS, N.J., U. of Maryland; 1978--110m HH-13s flat, WR, electronically timed.) "The greatest natural athlete ever to concentrate on hurdling." "Always in control--off as well as on the track." "At age 20, the greatest hurdler ever." "At 6'½", 170#, a 37-inch inseam, and with the sleek lines of a greyhound...". "Superb fluidity and grace, no strain, smooth and easy like--well, like Jesse Owens."

These reactions by such hurdling experts as Wilbur Ross, Russ Rogers and his capable high school coach, Jean Poquette, provide a glimpse of the early career (1976-1980) of Renaldo "Skeets" Nehemiah. World politics eliminated the Moscow Olympics as a showcase for his talents; otherwise, he might have gained the renown of even the great Owens. An exaggeration? Perhaps. But I watched Jesse in 1935 on his greatest day ever--3 world records and a tie--and, in Nehemiah, I saw and felt the same fluid power, graceful ease, and complete control. Jesse, of course, went on to Berlin and to his media-invented "confrontation" with Hitler. It takes such headlines to make heroes, along with an ability to maintain personal poise and control within a climate of world adulation.

Coach Frank Costello once claimed Skeets had the ability to hold world records in five events--high hurdles, 400m hurdles, 200 and 400m dashes, and long jump. Then, to support his claim, mentioned 18-year-old performances of 09.4 for the 100y, 24'11½" for the long jump-- "just lifting his legs"; a 44.3 anchor leg on a 1600m relay; and this in practice--550y in 62s, walk 440; 440y in 47.1s,walk 440; 330y in 33.5. Some claim! Not bad support! At age 18, just out of high school, Skeets ran the 42-inch hurdles in 13.23s and the 39-inch in 12.9, surpassing all previous records.

In a 1979 *Track & Field News* interview[1], Jon Hendershott elicited these insights into Nehemiah's approach to hurdling:

T&FN: Why is running the highs well so important to you?
Nehemiah: I've never wanted to be a contender, just one of the crowd. I want to be someone who turns the event around, who goes out and explores new territory. But it's more than that ,too. It's so much a part of me. I'm learning each day what I can do and what I have to do.
T&FN: What factors make you the best high hurdler in the world?
Nehemiah: My consistency. In the few short years I've been running, I've learned that it isn't one fast time that's important. Consistency at a high level will make you the victor, rather than having to depend on catching one fast one.

Basically, last year for me was one of learning how to be in control at all times-- regardless of the meet, who was running, the conditions, what happened in my previous meet. Just establishing that consistency, both physically and mentally.

My biggest hang-up last year was the idea that, "It's a learning year. You have nothing to lose and everything to gain." Deep down inside, I just couldn't accept that. Or people would say, "You lost the race but set a new Junior Record." That was great to them, but to me it was a putdown. I was in there running against the big guys and I wanted to be considered as one of them.
T&FN: You obviously take running very seriously. It must play a major role in your life.
Nehemiah: It's very major and very serious. I'm totally serious about doing everything I possibly can to improve and I'm tuned in to finding any way possible to do that. No meet is insignificant or unimportant. I can't go halfway. I have to make a total effort.

That's why my high school coach, Jean Poquette, and I are so close. He has taught me never to rely on my natural ability, to always look for ways to improve. I'm never at perfection. There is always something I can work on to better my technique.
T&FN: You have mentioned competitive consistency frequently, but what do you really want to achieve in the highs?
Nehemiah: To be the best, from the time I start until the time I end. To do whatever I have to do to become the best.

---

[1]Jon Hendershott, "Renaldo Nehemiah," *Track & Field News*, February 1979, p. 10.

Like running under 13.20, breaking the World Record as many times as I can. These are goals of mine. It's all part of bringing out the best in me. I don't know what is my best, so the only way to find out is to try. I'm just not comfortable laying back. I want to go further.

T&FN: Does Renaldo Nehemiah, the man, apply those same powers of determination to other things in his life as Renaldo Nehemiah, the athlete does to the hurdles?

Nehemiah: Yes, in terms of total dedication to what he is doing. His sole purpose is to please himself and not deprive himself of the very best he can achieve. In anything, I always want to do the very best I can.

After running 12.9 in high school, I know a lot of people expected me to break the World Record right away. But last year, for me, was a transition year from high school to college--and more in academic and total environment than the height of the hurdles. I used last year as a time to really find out about myself. To decide what I really wanted, to see how I cope with pressure and to find out what kind of athlete I am. I wanted to put things into their proper perspective.

T&FN: Were there any races last year which turned out to be particularly valuable learning experiences?

Nehemiah: The NCAA Indoor was probably the biggest lesson I ever learned indoors. I took that race totally for granted. In the heats and semis, I was running very well: 7.11 and 7.13, no pressure and I was running fast.

But at the third hurdle in the final, I realized, "Hey, you're not only behind, but you're losing," and there were only two more to go. I snapped out of it, or I probably would have lost it. It was just a matter of realizing it at the right time, in time, and really wanting it. Ever since that day, I've never underestimated the field, regardless of how fast or slow they are capable of running. The hardest defeat to live with is your own. You can always push the blame off on someone else, but the hardest one to accept is when you know you were the total cause of it.

T&FN: Was any one race last year particularly satisfying?

Nehemiah: AAU semi-finals, not so much the final. Beating Greg Foster there. It was a stacked heat with Greg and Charlie Foster. I was coming off that NCAA defeat and pretty much automatically assuming I wouldn't face him in the semis. I just assumed it would be the finals.

It was a do-or-die situation; it was there whether I was ready to accept it or not, so I had to do it. If I were to beat him and be superior at that time, it was then and there. And I rose to the occasion. When I had to dig down

Fig. 27.4--Renaldo Nehemiah, 110m HH-13s even, WR. He here demonstrates perfect balance and control, forward alignment, and great sprinting speed.

and get it, I got it. I couldn't shortchange myself, even though the second of those two losses had been only a week before. I learned a lot from those losses. I was never convinced he could beat me. The thing that always kept me confident was that, at some point in both of those races, I was winning. Then I made a technical error and lost to him. I think if he had beaten me head up, no mistakes, then it might have been a different ball game. But I knew I was winning and he had to come get me and that helped keep me stable.

T&FN: After the AAU, you said a winner doesn't make mistakes. Do you mean mental or physical?

Nehemiah: I would say a winner doesn't make physical mistakes. He knows what it takes to be in top condition; he knows what he has to do in preparation of his body, the preparation for each race.

The mental mistakes are something that you have control over, depending on the situation. Of course, everyone is different; not everyone can endure pressure. That's where the fine line comes. With me, I would have to blame an error on a physical mistake, because I'm in control of my mind at all times when it comes to running. I know what I'm going to do throughout the race.

Because of the long season I had last year and the number of races I ran, and because of my lack of experience, I didn't know what to expect from myself in the big races. Then, too, I was running a lot of other races and I couldn't give my full concentration to the hurdles, which is what I obviously wanted to do. Now if anything is going to take away from my hurdles, I won't do it. I don't want to meet anybody, whether American or foreigner, unless I'm at full strength, so I must be.

T&FN: What former greats do you like?

Nehemiah: I base everything I've done, including my style, on Rod Milburn. Our forms are very similar. His strength was his technical ability off the hurdle; once he was over, getting on the ground as efficiently and quickly as possible.

I've compared our progressions at each age and what he did in certain meets: at the Junior nationals, his record was 13.7. I ran 13.89. He ran 13.24 as a best and I'm at twenty-three. I've used his progressions as a guide, not so much that I have to run better than his times, but because I want to better his standards. Those are my goals. People say he was one of the greatest, but I'm going to find out what I can do, too. I got a lot of confidence from Milburn because he was a small guy compared to the others, and I'm small compared to the others. There was something he had that the others didn't have, technically or physically. That's how I learned that size isn't the main thing; it's what you can do with what you have.

It was phenomenal how he could start out even and almost at will take control of the race. That's what I looked into the most. Not just to outlean someone at the tape or outsprint somebody off the last hurdle, but how was it that he could surge like that. That's what caused me to get into hurdling so deeply; I wanted to learn how to do it. The first race I ever did it was in high school when I ran 13.2 to tie the national record. All my others up to then I had just been stepping through, still running 13.5s, 13.6s. But this one was different--and I've felt that way only two other times, my World Record indoors in '78 and the 13.23 at Zurich.

T&FN: What was the feeling?

Nehemiah: An abnormal feeling, like I was running on the air. I almost had both feet on the ground before they touched. That's when I know I'm really running the hurdles. It was like a sprint; except for the long movement over the hurdle. I was sprinting. My legs had the chance to be in the sprint form.

I know the feeling when I get it. I was seeking that feeling all through my first year of college. But when I got it, I told my coach that something had been different in my rhythm and he said, "You have finally learned to run the hurdles."

T&FN: Is that the closest to "ideal" you have come?

Nehemiah: Yes, it is. I was never satisfied all last year because I wanted to find that feeling. When I did, I got a whole different attitude. When it came down to one-on-one hurdling, I had the right attitude. I was ready.

ESSENTIALS OF SOUND TECHNIQUE--THE START

Basically the techniques of the hurdle start are the same as for the sprint start. But specifically there are a few crucial differences. (1) Placement of the right and left blocks forward or back depends on which leg leads over the hurdle. (2) The location of each block relative to the starting line will depend on proper strides to the first hurdle as well as on quickness in starting. (3) The eyes in the set position will be a few degress higher to ensure the somewhat earlier rise in body angle during the first few strides. (4) The long-legged and very fast hurdler may find it best to reverse the blocks and take only seven strides to the first hurdle. He can then go all-out with no concern for over-running the hurdle. (5) If the takeoff foot is to be 7 feet from the hurdle (the usual "best" spot), strides may have to be adjusted; such adjustment must occur during the first four strides so as to free the action for all-out acceleration to and across the hurdle. (6) Arm action will be modified to make such changes effective.

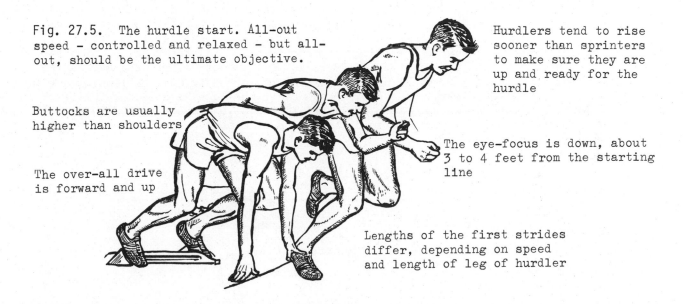

Fig. 27.5. The hurdle start. All-out speed - controlled and relaxed - but all-out, should be the ultimate objective.

Hurdlers tend to rise sooner than sprinters to make sure they are up and ready for the hurdle

Buttocks are usually higher than shoulders

The eye-focus is down, about 3 to 4 feet from the starting line

The over-all drive is forward and up

Lengths of the first strides differ, depending on speed and length of leg of hurdler

TO THE FIRST HURDLE

The approach to the first hurdle sets the pattern for the entire race. It must be at a maximal, controlled velocity that allows ample space for a full forward lean over-and-down from the hurdle, with no loss of forward velocity, balance or relaxation. The takeoff point before the hurdle is critical--too close is disastrous; too distant tends to diminish speed in the approach.

Fig. 27.6. Hurdle action, front view

Lead leg drives straight ahead

The head is lower in "b" than in "a"

When the trail foot (c) lands, it will be exactly in line with its take-off (a)

For the inexperienced hurdler, the approach must be more prudent, more concerned about tender skin and uncertain confidence. But gradually he must become aware that the real goal is speed, speed, more speed--not looking pretty or satisfying some ideally proper technique.

EFFECTIVE HURDLE CLEARANCE

The forward dip of the head along with a forward thrust of the arms initiate increased lean of the torso "through" the hurdle. An elongated sprinting stride of about 11 feet emphasizes an upward extension of the lead knee-foot that ensures a full split over the hurdle (Figure 27.7). The trail leg does push forward forcefully, but following the split so as not to move too soon in its clearance of the hurdle. Once started forward however, the trail knee--not the foot-- drives flatly through and on for a full stride to the next hurdle (Study Figure 27.9). Quickness in this action is essential.

Action of the Arms-Shoulders. The primary use of the arms during clearance is to ensure balance without reducing the pronounced forward lean of the torso or the square-to-the-hurdle line of the shoulders. As long as this is done effectively, the specific pattern of arm action is not of major concern. However this role is active throughout, not passive. Perfectly timed, their action can increase leg velocity. Perfectly executed, their action aids the forward dip of the head and shoulders (Figure 27.4--2-7). All effective hurdlers extend the lead hand close to the lead foot (Figure 27.7). Most extend the off hand only part way, then swing it in a short-radius motion close to the hip. A few great hurdlers have used a full two-arm extension (Figure 27.1) to accentuate forward lean into and beyond the hurdle. But in all methods, arm patterns should simulate those of sprinting as closely as is consistent with the 11-foot stride over the hurdle.

Fig. 27.7. A full split into the hurdle. Hurdling is a "dive" into or through the hurdle more than a jump over it. Forward lean is initiated by the head--down as close as feasible to the thigh-- and the forward extension of the lead shoulder-arm-hand. This ensures a full split at the crotch, delaying the trail leg but then aiding its forceful pull through and down to the ground.

POWER AND FLEXIBILITY IN HURDLING

In Chapter 25 on sprinting we have presented related power exercises that have direct application to hurdling. We repeat: high hurdling is sprinting--to, over, between and beyond ten obstacles. The required power is almost precisely the same. For example, Coach Maughan[1], Utah State, recommends a power exercise for both hurdlers and sprinters,

> *We call it plowing, a very familiar term with our farmboys. . . . We throw a strip of canvas around a boys' waist, and he tows another track man over a specified distance and number of times, just as if he were plowing the south forty. . . . (To do this) he must get up on his toes, pick up his knees, work his arms hard, and really lean into it. The boy holding the lines shouldn't put up too much resistance or he'll start wallowing like a football guard.*

To such exercises emphasizing the legs-ankles-feet, should be added two or three torso-power exercises such as sit-ups from an inclined bench, or the clean and press. Use lighter weights with greater velocities of movement.

But flexibility is also of great importance in hurdling, and special flexibility exercises such as those shown on pp. 484-5 should precede and become a regular part of practice throughout a man's career. Great hurdlers of a decade or so ago spent about one-fourth their total practice time in almost every practice on flexibility. Today, more time is given to power training, and speed training, and stamina training. But flexibility is absolutely essential; three sessions a week is a minimum and my judgment calls for more.

Flexibility requires stretching, a stretching of muscles and tendons beyond the requirements of ordinary sports activities. If we accept the word "overloading" as related to building strength in muscles, then "overstretching" should be acceptable in building flexibility. But therein lies its dangers as well as its benefits. Warm-up *very gradually* and *very carefully* for flexibility. Dick Attlesey, world-record holder, missed his chance to be Olympic champion through injury while warming up. He had been hurdling for some eight or more years but a high kick of the lead leg was too much too soon, and he lost months of crucial practice. Take it EASY! GRADUALLY! Stretch, don't strain.

The exercises illustrated on the following pages have been standard for a half-century or more. Organize a routine of exercises which you follow in practice and in meets. Begin with the larger muscle groups, as in trunk flexion (pp. 484-5 E, F or K). Move to the easier stretchers (pp. 484-5 A, C or L). Then end up with the crotch-stretchers (pages 484-5 D and J).

Fig. 27.8 -- Strides to and between the hurdles

---

[1] Ralph B. Maughan, "The 120-yard high hurdles," USTCA *Quarterly Review*, October 1966, 60.

FLEXIBILITY EXERCISES

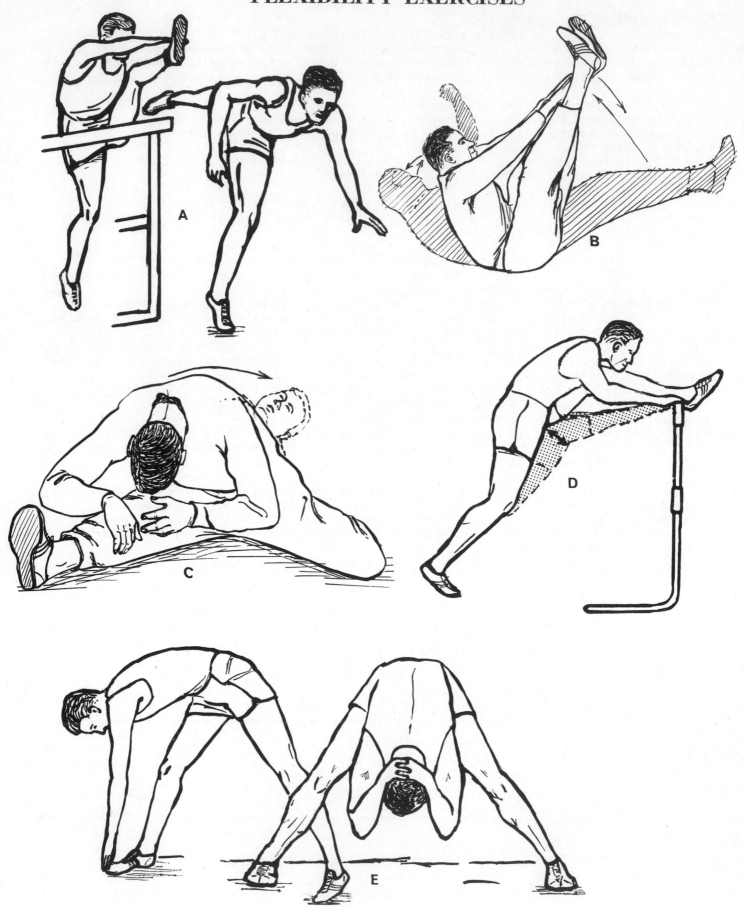

HURDLING

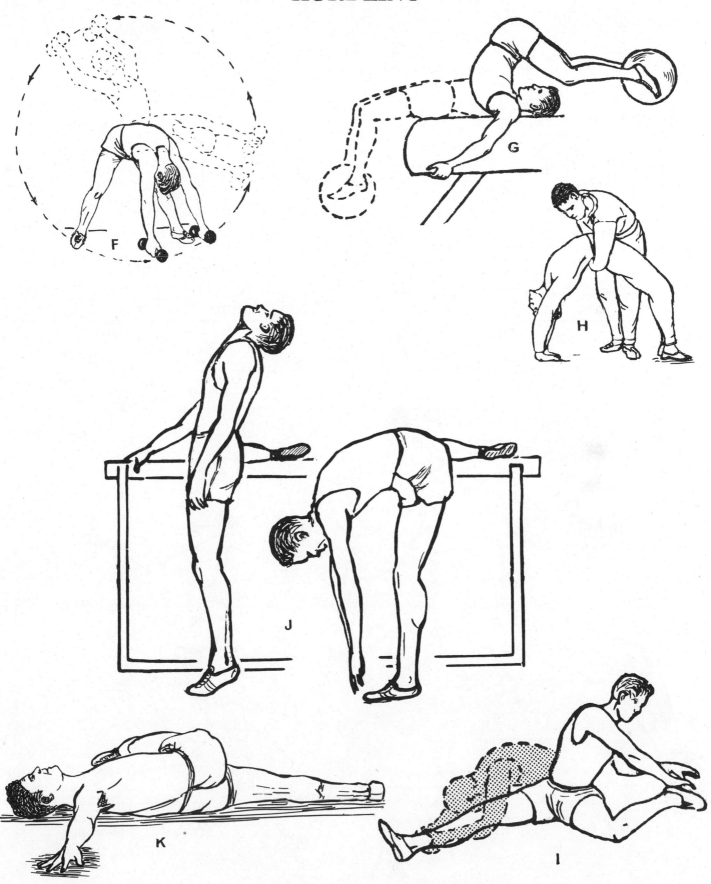

THE WHOLE ACTION

Figure 27.9. The whole action in hurdling. The first and all-important impression to be gained from this sequence is that of a sprinter taking an elongated stride over a low obstacle which requires only a minimum shift from sprinting style. After all a champion high hurdler requires only 2.0 seconds longer to clear ten hurdles than to sprint the same distance on the flat.

To take a high hurdle is not to take three sprinting strides and a jump; but rather four sprint strides, one of which--over the hurdle--is a little accentuated in its movements. Best form in hurdling is one that most nearly imitates sprinting form. Such details of form as distance of the take-off from the hurdle, whether one or two arms should be forward, or whether the lead leg should be snapped down or the trail leg be pulled rapidly through, must all be judged on how they affect the whole action back to the ground and into the sprinting.

The eyes are already focussed on the next hurdle

Excellent balance and forward lean into the next stride

The head rises very little above height when sprinting

The trail toe is kept high over and beyond the hurdle

The heel touches the ground but weight is forward on the toe

Landing distance - about 4 feet

HURDLING

To establish this part-in-whole awareness, try to get the feeling in your mind-muscles of the background pattern of this hurdling sequence. Now, on this background, follow the action of the lead leg in figures 2 through 8. Feel its relation to the forward lean of the body (figures 2-5) and the opening of the hip jackknife (figures 5-8). Now feel its relation to the trail leg. No, not just with your eye, feel it in the related muscle groups. Second, holding all this in your mind-muscles, feel through the action of the trail leg. Third, do the same for the left arm, and then for the right arm. All these aspects of hurdling inter-act with each other and with the whole of the action.

Done with concentrated and sharp imagery, you'll feel as though you were hurdling. And as a matter of fact, you are. When you feel through an action this way, nerve impulses of a low electrical potential are carried to the muscles, though of course not enough to activate them.

The lead foot points straight ahead with no inversion

The arm action leads back with the elbow

A 1½-arm forward style: lead arm forward and down; off arm ahead of hip

Flexible hips allow a full stretch in the crotch

The lead leg leads with the knee

The knee is bent throughout

A distant take-off (about 7½') permits a low-angle take-off and time for the lead foot to clear the hurdle

TOUCHDOWN TIMES FOR TEN HURDLES

A study[1] by Brent McFarlane, Ontario Provincial Coach, found that such Olympic hurdlers (men) as Guy Drut and Willie Davenport, and (women) Johanna Schaller and Grazyna Rabsztyn "had touchdown (TD) times of 2.4 and 2.5 off hurdle one, and maintained a consistent 1.0 to 1.1 throughout the race." Using these times as his base, McFarlane projected times for touchdown from each hurdle, using 10th seconds only. To smooth out his times, I have used 100th in estimating some figures.

TOUCHDOWN TIME CHART

MEN--110m Hurdles (42")

FT	H1	H2	H3	H4	H5	H6	H7	H8	H9	H10	Fin
13.0	2.4	3.4	4.4	5.4	6.4	7.4	8.4	9.4	10.5	11.6	13.0
14.0	2.5	3.55	4.6	5.65	6.7	7.8	8.9	10.05	11.2	12.4	14.0
15.0	2.6	3.75	4.9	6.05	7.2	8.35	9.5	10.7	12.0	13.3	15.0

WOMEN--100m Hurdles (33")

FT	H1	H2	H3	H4	H5	H6	H7	H8	H9	H10	Fin
12.8	2.4	3.4	4.4	5.4	6.4	7.4	8.4	9.5	10.6	11.7	12.8
14.0	2.5	3.6	4.7	5.8	6.9	8.05	9.3	10.45	11.6	12.8	14.0
15.0	2.6	3.75	4.9	6.05	7.3	8.5	9.75	11.0	12.3	13.6	15.0

Actual times for slower, less perfect hurdlers would not have such regular increments, but these figures indicate a loss of velocity after five or six hurdles.

RELAXATION IN HURDLING

All the experts say, "Hurdling is sprinting." But more precisely, they should speak of hurdling as sprinting as released by relaxation. In describing great hurdlers such as Renaldo Nehemiah or Greg Foster, we use words such as "poise," "control," "fluid grace," "smooth and easy like Jesse Owens"--all words implying relaxation.

Such relaxation --like speed--is a natural talent of the great hurdler, but it is also the effect of practice related to relaxation--maximal speed with a sense of letting things flow, or of holding back one erg of effort.

Most world records in the hurdles have been set under low-stress conditions--lesser meets or hurdlers--that provide challenge but relative ease of mind. Only that of Rod Millburn (1972-13.24) was made in the Olympic Games. Nehemiah's amazing 13s-even was made in a lesser invitational meet, but certainly did not lack highest quality competition (Casanas-13.21WR, Foster--13.22, Cooper 13.72). As Nehemiah put it, "The names got the adrenaline going...If we had gotten out even, it would have been even faster." Maybe that's the answer--enough adrenaline to make you try, not harder, but faster.

IAAF HURDLE SPACING

	Distance	H Hgt	To 1st H	Btwn Hs	To Finish
Men	110m	1.067m	13.72m	9.14	14.02
	120y	42"	15y	10y	15y
Women	100m	.84m	13m	8.5m	10.5m
	100m	33"	42'7 3/4"	27'10 5/8"	34'5 3/8"

---

[1] Brent McFarlane, "Touchdown Time Charts for the Hurdles," *Track Technique*, #67, March 1977, p. 2128.

THE TRAIL LEG

An effective trail leg: (1) is delayed to gain a full split of the legs and forward dive-in at the hurdle; (2) requires full extension in the crotch, and so, related flexibility exercises; (3) comes through flat or just above the horizontal as it crosses the hurdle; (4) lifts the toes high so as to avoid snagging the hurdle; (5) beyond the hurdle, brings the knee high with no loss of forward lean of the torso (Figure 27.10); and (6) reaches out for a full stride of about six feet toward the next hurdle (Figure 27.11).

Fig. 27.10. Hayes Jones, Eastern Michigan, 1964 Olympic champion - 13.4. Jones was winner of an amazing 56 straight races indoors at from 50 to 70 yards, 1960-1964. Often won both dash and hurdles.

Fig. 27.11. Two essentials of high hurdling technique are shown here -- (1) forward body lean so necessary for continuous velocity, and (2) a flat trail leg which is reaching out for a full stride to the next hurdle.

SPEED BETWEEN THE HURDLES

A slight decrease in body momentum occurs while sprinting over each hurdle, a decrease which, by expert hurdlers, totals about 2 seconds for 10 hurdles. These changes in speed are shown by the stride lengths which average about as follows: landing beyond hurdle--3'6"; 1st stride--6'; 2nd stride--6'10"; 3rd stride--6'6"; distance of takeoff foot from hurdle--7'2". This pattern is very important as suggesting a relatively even momentum. Many less expert hurdlers take 4' coming off the hurdle and only 5' on the first stride. This forces over-striding on the 2nd and 3rd strides, a broken rhythm, and unreadiness for the next hurdle.

The entire action over the hurdle affects these strides, but especially forward lean, balance off the hurdle, the full reach of the trail leg, and the use of the arms coming off, as well as between the hurdles. In the Sprint Chapter, we have discussed the energizing effect of vigorous arm action on the speed of the legs. Such action is even more effective in high hurdling.

But mental attitude is at least as critical as mechanics. Nehemiah told an interviewer, "I try to anticipate hurdle action--pull the rear leg through before the lead foot touches the ground; it can't be done but it does speed up the action." That is, he tries to move faster, not by thinking of mechanics, but by centering on the muscle-feel of actions before they occur.

FROM THE FIFTH HURDLE TO THE TAPE

Wilbur Ross[1], coach of Elias Gilbert and other fine hurdlers, has concentrated on this problem of maintaining velocity during the last five hurdles, and suggests this practice procedure. Set up two flights of five hurdles each, side by side but facing opposite directions. Using five strides between hurdles, run down and back with no rest between. Gradually increase the number of round trips, and that 40 or 50 is not impossible! This seems extreme but it does indicate the kind of emphasis that will develop hurdling stamina, relax-ation, and speed. With five strides, would not an 11-yard placement of the hurdles make for smoother striding?

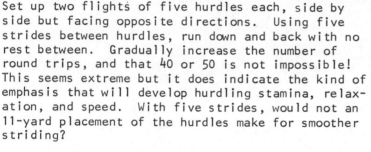

Fig. 27.12 -- Best clearance is gained by fol-lowing path A-A. The lead foot reaches its high-est point before the hurdle, then is thrust down.

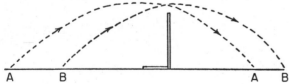

Fig. 27.13 -- Between the hurdles - sprint! Use the arms! Drive!

---

[1]Wilbur Ross, "From the Fifth Hurdle to the Tape," *The Athletic Journal*, March 1966, 55.

THE FINISH

Fig. 27.17a. The first and all-important
tenet for finishing a high hurdle race is
first clear the last hurdle. *How many a
champion, intent on the finish line, has
caught the hurdle with his lead or trail leg,
and lost -- sometimes the BIG race of his
entire career!* Assuming the hurdle has been
cleared, then the methods shown here are
valid. Both hurdlers are using a good body
lean--chin and eyes down, arms extended
down and back.

Fig. 27.17b. Two styles of finish. The white figure simply maintains good forward lean and
explodes through and beyond the finish line with no change in form. This style is conservative
but sound. Men can concentrate upon the total effort of the finish throughout the last 10
yards, rather than upon the actions of the last stride. The black figure shows clearly the
advantage of an exaggerated forward lean on the last stride. Many an Olympic decision has been
favorable to the athlete using this method, since men are picked "in the order in which any
part of their bodies (torso, as distinguished from head, neck, hands, feet) reach the finish
line."

THE ORGANIZATION OF PRACTICE

The high hurdles require at least as careful organization of a year-round program of training as does any track and field event. Consider their requirements: (1) skill, (2) speed, (3) flexibility, (4) endurance, and (5) power.

This all adds up to practice - PRACTICE - PRACTICE! There's just not enough hours in a day, or enough months in a year in which to master all the aspects of hurdling. Begin the year with these priorities of emphasis: (1) basic endurance and flexibility, (2) power exercises related to hurdling, (3) speed-endurance, (4) hurdling skill, (5) sprinting speed, and (6) hurdling speed.

BASIC ENDURANCE AND FLEXIBILITY. For basic endurance, run fartlek with the sprinters and 400-meter hurdlers and sprinters as suggested in Chapter 22. For basic flexibility, develop gradually a program of exercises from Chapter 6; later add the hurdle-flexibility exercises on pp. 484-5. It's a long year-round program; make it enjoyable!

RELATED POWER EXERCISES. It is sprinting power that is the goal, not weight-lifting power. Follow the power program of Chapter

SPEED-ENDURANCE. This phase emphasizes speed runs of off-the-track fartlek in which over a distance of about 300 meters, the heart rate rises to 160-170-180, then settles back to about 110 before anaerobic sprinting starts again. A small group makes it more fun. When on-the-track training seems best, such runs change to interval training at 300 meters or similar runs more related to hurdling--6 x 150m or 150-200-250-300-250-200-150, with only about 30 seconds between, enough time for the heart rate to drop to 120.

Sprinting. Just one more time--hurdling is sprinting. Throughout the year hurdlers should work out with sprinters--doing fartlek, intervals, starts out of the blocks. Potential hurdling time can be projected by adding about two seconds to 110m time. During the indoor season, Hayes Jones competed in both the sprint and hurdle. Many a hurdler has run on the 4 x 100m relay team.

HURDLING SKILL. Running over high hurdles for better technique can be introduced any time physical condition and good weather make it feasible. At first skill can be distinguished from speed--run the hurdles with attention concentrated on technique, keeping speed at easy levels. Warning! Skill and speed are actually indivisible, so that long before the season begins the hurdler must be challenged toward all-out, high-speed hurdling.

There are many variations of practice: (1) Run over 3 to 5 hurdles 11-12 yards apart, with five strides between. This reduces concern for striding between hurdles so that full concentration can be given to technique over them. (2) Run over 3 to 5 hurdles 9 yards apart. This also allows easy striding. (3) Sprint over 3 to 5 hurdles 10 yards apart, with the usual three strides between. (4) Sprint over eight hurdles with a 65 yard finish on the flat (150 yards total). (5) Sprint "all-out" over the first hurdle; continue at 98% velocity over next five hurdles, then pick up speed over last four hurdles (120 yards total).

HURDLING ENDURANCE. All hurdlers tend to slow down over the last 4-3-2 hurdles. To improve endurance, try Wilbur Ross' method: two flights of five hurdles each, side by side, with one flight reversed. Using five strides between, run down and back with no rest between. Run 2-3-4-5 circuits, or repeated sets of three circuits each set. With five strides, an 11-yard hurdle placement may be preferred.

WARMING UP. The wise hurdler will spend at least 20 minutes warming up with easy windsprints, with gradually more stressful flexibility exercises, and finally with faster windsprints.

HOW THEY TRAIN
Greg Foster (UCLA, 1977-1980, 6-3, 185#)
NCAA 110m HH Champion: 1978--13.22; 1979--13.28.
Best sprint times--100m-10.33; 200m-20.40.

Foster's time of 13.22, made at age 19, was the fastest ever except for Casanas' world record--13.21. After the race he commented,[1] "My start was lousy--about 3rd or 4th out of the blocks. Around the third hurdle I started moving my arms a lot more. I hit the 4th because I was close to it, and I hit the 5th, 6th and maybe the 7th. But I stayed up on my toes and cleared the last three, kept my quickness in between them and pulled it out in the end."

T&FN: You said you start hitting hurdles when you pump your arms harder.
Foster: My stride gets longer and I come too close to the hurdle...so close that it's hard to clear them.
T&FN: Do you hit the hurdles with your trailing knee because you try to hurry your trail leg?
Foster: That's part of it...I concentrate on pumping my arms harder instead of concentrating on clearing the hurdles. I have a tendency to snap my trail leg down quicker than I should, so I hit the hurdle.

(Foster was 6-3 tall, and fast. His comments are identical to those made by other tall-fast hurdlers--Calhoun, Davis, Attlesey, Keller, Saling--who had trouble hitting hurdles--KD).

Non-Competitive Season
Mon--550-440-330 at a fast but relaxed pace.
Tues--10 x 110, or sprints up a 550-yard hill.
Wed--3 x 330 in 36.0 or faster (last one close to all out but relaxed).
Thurs--Same as Tuesday.
Fri--165s with flying starts, "learning how to run the backstretch relaxed after coming off the turn very quick."
Sat--Jog.
Sun--Jog.

Competitive Season
Mon--Go over flights of 1, 2, and 3 hurdles 5 times each, ending with one fast 440 or 3 x 150.
Tues--10 x 110 or 3 x 220 (21.2 or faster), and "five-step" one flight of hurdles 2-3 times.
Wed--Go over five flights of hurdles (70 yards) 5 times. One mile warm down jog.
Thurs--3 x 75 with flying starts, 1 x 330 in 35.0.
Fri--Warm up only.
Sat--Compete.
Sun--Warm up only.

Greg feels that it is "good to know how your workouts are helping you," and will occasionally run at 100% effort. He feels that his technical strength is his ability to attack each hurdle, while his right arm action over the hurdle is his greatest liability. He notes, "I set up a flight of hurdles and five- or seven-step using only the trail leg on the first, the lead leg the second," finally going over the third hurdle in full form. "I do each of these three times, and this really helps my quickness between the hurdles."

Before a major meet, Greg tries to let his mind go blank and not think about his opponents. "I just do what I would normally do, on the day before a meet," he says. His pre-race warm-up consists of a mile jog followed by "a half hour of continuous stretching and 5-10 wind sprints to get the legs moving."

---

[1]Jon Hendershott, "Greg Foster," *Track & Field News*, August 1978, p. 16.

Chapter 28
THE 400-METER HURDLES

The 400-meter hurdles require toughness; not in some special awesome sense, as they have been viewed in the past through lack of familiarity, but toughness as is needed for the 880 or any speed-endurance distance. Of course it requires stamina, but that's a word to challenge men, not frighten them. On the contrary, this event, with its varied demand for speed, and endurance, and hurdling skill is the most exciting and challenging on the entire running program. No excuse for boredom here; every reason for trying to do one's best.

I'm reminded of the comments of Josh Culbreath (5'7" tall, but 1955 world-record holder at 50.4 and third at Melbourne): "What I lack in stature and speed, I make up in determination and endurance! . . . Lift your knees, pump those arms . . . lean forward and *drive, drive, drive!* Never give up; victory is always within your grasp--if you are a real fighter!" If you're looking for 440 hurdle prospects, look for such attitudes, as well as for height, speed, stamina, and hurdling skill.

As a matter of fact, the 400-meter hurdle event was not introduced into the college championship program until 1960 when concern for U. S. success in the Olympics took precedence over traditional college viewpoints. Prior to that time, in the Olympic years, high and low hurdlers merely added a little endurance training to their regular hurdle work. No wonder they thought it "an inhuman grueling event." A few men such as Roy Cochran (Indiana, 1948 Olympic champion) and Charlie Moore (Cornell, 1952 Olympic champion) ran on their college mile relay team and in the 600 in non-college indoor meets. But their viewpoints were still those of short-distance hurdling. Similarly, coach Larry Snyder[1] made it clear that Glenn Davis (Ohio State, 1956 and 1960 Olympic champion) never attained the maximum stamina of which he was capable, comparable to that of world-level 800m men for example. Davis had many outside distractions that reduced his training, and was accustomed to competing in six or seven events during the college season, so that there was no concentration on the intermediate hurdles.

True, the U. S. did win 11 Olympic 400m hurdle championships in the first 13 Games. But this merely indicated the rest of the world had taken the event even less seriously than we had. A partially valid indicator of low-level training is indicated by the time-differences between 400m flat and hurdling times. As a man's condition improves, he is better able to maintain pace and hurdling technique and so decrease his average time over the hurdles. In 1928, Lord Burghley had a time-difference of 6.7 seconds. Each Olympic champion thereafter decreased this time until in 1968 Hemery (Great Britain and Boston U.) achieved a difference of only 0.2 seconds, and in 1972, Akii-Bua, of 0.62. Such small differences cannot be fully valid. Hurdlers almost never run the 400m in competition often enough to provide maximum performances. Similar time differences in the 110m high hurdles rarely go under two seconds. In 1954 I made a related study of the 220y low hurdles and concluded that a minimum time difference of about one second was reasonably valid. (One man made better time in the lows than he had ever recorded in the flat distance!) The world record for the 400m-flat race is now under 44 seconds. A time-difference between ultimate flat-race time and ultimate hurdle time of about two seconds seems quite within reason, and we can assume an ultimate world record for the 400-meter hurdles close to 46 seconds even.

[1]Larry Snyder, "The 400-meter Hurdles," Clinic Notes, *National College Track Coaches Association*, 1960, 99.

TABLE 28..1

OUTSTANDING PERFORMANCES -- 400m AND 300m HURDLES

OLYMPIC CHAMPIONS

Date	Time 400m	Name	Affiliation	Best Time 400m	Time Diff.
1900	57.6	J. W. Tewksbury	Pennsylvania		
1904	53.0	Harry Hillman	Dartmouth		
1908	55.0	C. J. Bacon			
1920	54.0	Frank F. Loomis	Chicago		
1924	52.6	F. Morgan Taylor	Iowa		
1928	53.4	Lord Burghley	Grt. Britain	46.7	6.7
1932	51.7	R. M. N. Tisdall	Eire		
1936	52.4	Glenn Hardin	Louisiana	46.8	5.6
1948	51.1	Roy Cochran	Indiana	46.7	4.4
1952	50.8	Charles Moore	Cornell	47.0	3.8
1956	50.1	Glenn Davis	Ohio State	46.5	3.6
1960	49.3	Glenn Davis	Ohio State		
1964	49.6	Rex Cawley	So. Calif.	46.2	3.4
1968	48.1	Dave Hemery	Grt. Britain		
1972	47.82[1]	John Akii-Bua	Uganda		
1976	47.641	Edwin Moses	Morehouse St.	46.1	1.54
1980	48.70	Volker Beck	E. Germany		

WORLD-RECORD PERFORMANCES OF SPECIAL INTEREST

MEN

1934	50.6	Glenn Hardin	Louisiana	46.8	3.8
1958	49.2	Glenn Davis	Ohio State	45.7	3.5
1960	49.3y	Gert Potgeiter	So. Africa	46.3	3.0
1962	49.2	Salvatore Morale	Italy	47.6	1.6
1964	49.1	Rex Cawley	So. Calif.	45.7	3.4
1968	48.1	Dave Hemery	Gt. Britain	47.9	0.2
1970	48.8y	Ralph Mann	BYU	46.6	2.2
1972	47.82[1]	John Akii-Bua	Uganda	47.2	0.62
1974	48.7y	Jim Bolding	P.C.C.	45.3	3.4
1980	47.13	Edwin Moses	Morehouse St.	46.1	1.35

WOMEN

1979	54.78	Marina Makeyeva	SU		

BEST PERFORMANCES--HIGH SCHOOLS

BOYS--300H

1974	35.87y	Bill Blessing	Hillcrest, Dallas, Texas
1978	36.30y	Chris Person	Plainfield, N.J
1979	36.10m	Ken Scott	Beaverton, Or.

BOYS--400mH

1977	50.52m	Paul Lankford	Farmingdale, N.Y.
1978	51.00m	Chris Person	Plainfield, N.J.
1979	51.93	Ricky Griddine	Colum, S.C.

GIRLS--400mH

1979	58.31m	Sandra Farmer	Brooklyn, N.Y.

[1]Electronic timing

THE FIRST OLYMPIC 400-meter HURDLES

Though no history of technique for the 400-meter hurdles is given here, I can't resist including an excerpt from a 1965 letter to me from Walter Tewksbury, winner of the 1900 Olympic hurdles. At the time Mr. Tewksbury was the oldest living Olympian in the world.

I note in your chart the wide discrepancy in times from 57.6 in 1900 to under 50 seconds today. You will be interested in the following details of the 1900 race. Ten men ran in the final, starting on a curve. The hurdles were 10 telephone poles, 6 to 8 inches in diameter, 30 feet long, stretched across the track. They were one meter high with boxes of brush beneath the poles. A water jump 5 meters wide was across the track halfway between the last hurdle and the finish. Figure my long legs saved the day for me.

And to think that we consider our laned race on a Tartan surface over ten individual L-type hurdles a grueling challenge! Balderdash!

Edwin Moses (Morehouse College; 1976 Olympic IH Champion--47.64WR; Age 20, 6'1¼", 162#)
Apparently Edwin Moses was fashioned perfectly for running the 400m intermediate hurdles-- perfectly in terms of length of leg (37") and stride, of sprinting speed and endurance, of coordination and flexibility, and especially, of competitive temperament, and self control.

Consider the last, first. At Morehouse College, Georgia, Moses was an honors student in physics who regretted losing time from school because of track. That is, throughout his career, he kept his success in hurdling in perspective--delighted but restrained.

In an interview[1] by Jon Hendershott, Moses said he never ran the 400m hurdles until the Florida Relays, March 1976. In 1975, he usually ran the highs (13.9s), the quarter (46.1s), and the mile relay. Prior to the Florida meet "I had just been doing overdistance workouts-- 1000s and 600s, none of those special workouts for the IHs that coach came up with later... But once I started running them, I felt pretty comfortable. I ran 50.1 (2nd place) and I wasn't tired at all."

Fig. 28.1--Edwin Moses at Montreal, 1976-- 47.64WR. Note foot placement well outside lane line; forward body lean with trail leg moving to a full stride beyond.

He then went on to win the Penn Relays IH (49.8s), the Final Olympic Trials (48.3s), and a world-record 47.64s in the Olympic Championships--not bad for a first-year effort by a man who previously had never won a major championship in any event. In 1977-1980, he lost only one of some 50 races, was selected by T&FN as world's best for four years in succession, recorded the six best-ever times in track history, including four under 48 seconds; and, in 1977, a world-record 47.45.

T&FN: Does 46s seem formidable or just a natural progression?
Moses: It's a bit of both. I'm going to have to work at it, but I know I can do it. I know I can do 46.

In *Track & Field News*, March 1980, Hendershott wrote,

Moses learned early in his career to get along on his own, without the luxuries of training rooms or easily accessible facilities. He listened and learned, especially from his college coach, Lloyd Jackson..."Like training. You just have to get out there and do it. I mean, it hurts. I feel pain. But there are

---

[1]Jon Hendershott, "Edwin Moses," *Track & Field News*, Sept. 1976,, p. 33.

no secrets about the way I have run. Just a lot of hard work; more work than anybody realizes. Hard work plus talent, which is the same for any great athlete.

FINDING HURDLE CANDIDATES. Intermediate hurdlers are to be found among quartermilers, high hurdlers and sprinters, especially if they have a 35 to 37-inch crotch. In 1975, Ed Moses, 6'1¼"--165#, ran the high hurdles, 400 and 1600m relay, using all of his 37-inch inseam. Akii-Bua, 6'2"--170#, competed in various events including the decathlon (6900 pts). Such men make ideal prospects.

For the record, the heights-weights of the first four place winners at the Montreal and Munich Olympics were: 1976--Moses, 6-1¼, 165#; Shine, 6-0, 160#; Gavrilyenko, 6-1¼, 168#; Wheeler, 6-1, 165#; 1972--Akii-Bua, 6-1, 170#; Mann, 6-4, 185#; Hemery, 6-1½, 170#; Seymour, 6-1, 165#. If this is a reliable sampling, it does seem to show a pattern in physique.

A more valid method of selecting IH prospects is to add 3-4 seconds to a hurdler's best 400m time (actual if experienced; otherwise potential). I hardly need add--choose a man willing to work and undergo a little discomfort.

ESSENTIALS OF SOUND TECHNIQUE
The details of technical skill over the hurdles are adequately described in Chapter 27, the high hurdles. The three-inch difference in hurdle height does not make a significant difference. But the necessity of running counter-clockwise around two curves does give a definite advantage to those that lead with the inside (left) leg.

Measurements for Intermediate Hurdles. Distances are the same for men and women: 45m (147' 7 5/8") to the first hurdle, 35m (114' 10") between hurdles, 40m (131' 2 3/4") from last hurdle to finish line. For men, hurdle height is .914m (39"); for women, .762 (30").

SPRINTING TO THE FIRST HURDLE. Take a natural number of strides. Put the first hurdle in place at 49 yards 7.65 inches. Now sprint from starting blocks in the lane next to the hurdle; sprint past it at such a relaxed pace as can be maintained for 400 meters. The coach should mark your strides. The last mark should be six feet or more from the hurdle; if not, adjust your strides. After repeated efforts over several weeks, you may decide to reverse your feet in the blocks. How many strides? That's not the crucial question. Whatever number works best for you is best for you, regardless of the experts. However, as a matter of interest, experienced hurdlers take 21 strides; others, 22; some of lesser ability, 23. Moses used only 20.

How fast? As fast as you are likely to be able to maintain over the distance. You should be able to maintain a pace within five seconds of your best 440 time; Ralph Mann did within 2.2 seconds! As a matter of interest, times to the first hurdle among champions have varied from 5.9 to 6.2; among women, from 6.2 to 6.6.

STRIDES BETWEEN HURDLES. Most men with good hurdling technique and endurance can handle 15 strides throughout the full ten hurdles. (An even number forces a man to alternate the lead leg). Whether for lack of stride-length or of endurance, few men have been able to take 13 all the way. Charley Moore, 1952 Olympic winner, did it but he gave an impression of overstriding. In his first race, Ed Moses "ran 15 strides until the 6th hurdle, ran 14 strides for two because I wasn't sure of the pattern, and then 13 strides to the finish." But for the remainder of his career, he used 13 strides throughout. As a matter of interest, he experimented with 12 strides after the Games, and found he could do it comfortably.

Mike Shine, 2nd at Montreal, used 15 strides for all hurdles, in part because of an outside lead leg. Akii-Bua, winner at Munich, used 15 strides to H5; 14 to H9; then 15 from H9 to H10. John Le Masurier reports[1] that Tziortsis of Greece (finalist at Munich; semi-finalist at Montreal), only 175 Cms (5-9) tall, ran his early hurdles with 15 strides, then used 16 and finally 17 at the end. Clearly, stride patterns do vary.

Jon Hendershott[2] had an opportunity to interview a group of outstanding 400-meter hurdlers, and reported these comments on the matter of striding:

Paramount to faster times, either over meters or yards, is the number of strides between hurdles. "If the athlete can take 13 steps for five or six hurdles, this is a great advantage," Vanderstock feels. Dave Hemery goes even further. "To really get the record down where it belongs, a fellow should work on striding 13s all the way," he says.

Farmer pointed out some of the inherent advantages of "striding 13s," other than the speed factor. "At the start of any race, an athlete is a bundle of nervous energy, so why ask him to do anything but explode that energy at the very beginning of his race? Some people have said there is too much energy consumed in taking 13 strides for the first few hurdles, but there is even more energy used by putting on the brakes to chop stride. Competitively speaking, the most important reason for going 13s is that it applies pressure on the other hurdlers. Often you see a hurdler lose his concentration and rhythm as an opponent moves up on his inside after making up most of the original stagger.

On the other hand, Cawley doesn't see much difference in using 13 or 15 strides. "I don't believe either method is inherently faster than the other," he says. "It depends on the man using it. A tall man chopping to 15 steps would tire quickly and look as ridiculous as a short man bounding along stretching to make 13. Whichever method is most comfortable and efficient for the athlete should be used. Sometimes a mixture of the two is best."

Whitney adds another aspect to the stride controversy. "I used to think the 15-stride technique was the best," he comments. "With the advent of the Tartan track, though, I have to say 13 is the best. Just check the time differentials between dirt and Tartan. Hurdlers who have been no threat to us 15-striders on dirt turn around and run one or two seconds faster on Tartan. My difference is three-tenths.

"Tartan gives you an elongated stride," Whitney continues. "I found myself too close to the hurdles on Tartan, even at the end of a race."

Whitney brings up another requisite for faster times. "Left leg lead is essential," he says. "I am right, but I feel it makes at least a three to five-tenths difference. With a right leg lead you have to hurdle to the outside of the barrier, especially on the last turn when the staggers are being made up. I think every high school and college coach should demand that any hurdler with the slightest intention of becoming a medium hurdler use his left leg."

---

[1]John Le Masurier, "Olympic 400-Meter Hurdles (Men)--Mexico, Munich and Montreal," *Track & Field Quarterly Review*, Vol. 78 #4, Winter 1978, p. 39.

[2]Jon Hendershott, "Few US 440-Hurdle Specialists," *Track & Field News*, 1 May 1969, 16.

Oddly enough, Potgieter alternated lead legs, taking 14 steps between barriers. "I recommend every 440 hurdler learn to lead with either leg," he offers. "I found it very handy and I'm convinced that it is to every athlete's benefit in this race. I consider relaxation more important than speed in the intermediate hurdles, and alternating doesn't force the athlete to stretch for 13 steps or chop down to 15."

CHART 28.1[1]

TOUCHDOWN TIMES
MEN'S 400-METER HURDLES
1976, 1972, 1968 OLYMPIC FINALS

Athlete	Yr	To H1 lead leg	H1	H2	H3	H4	H5	1st 200	H6	H7	H8	H9	H10	H10 to fin	2nd 200	Diff	Time
Moses USA	'76	20(L)	6.0	9.8	13.5	17.4	21.4	23.1	25.4	29.6	33.9	38.2	42.6	5.04	24.54	1.44	47.64
				13(3.8)	13(3.7)	13(3.9)	13(4.0)		13(4.0)	13(4.2)	13(4.3)	13(4.3)	13(4.4)				
Akii-Bua UGA	'72	21(R)	6.1	9.8	13.6	17.4	21.3	23.0	25.4	29.5	33.7	38.1	42.6	5.2	24.8	1.8	47.82
				13(3.7)	13(3.8)	13(3.8)	13(3.9)		14.(4.1)	14(4.1)	14(4.2)	14(4.4)	15(4.5)				
Hemery GBR	'68	21(L)	6.1	9.8	13.6	17.5	21.5	23.3	25.4	29.6	33.9	38.3	42.8	5.3	24.8	1.5	48.1
				13(3.8)	13(3.8)	13(3.9)	13(4.0)		13(3.9)	15(4.2)	15(4.3)	15(4.4)	15(4.5)				
Hemery BGR	'72	21(L)	6.1	9.8	13.4	17.2	21.1	22.8	25.1	29.3	33.6	38.2	43.0	5.5	25.7	2.9	48.52
				13(3.7)	13(3.6)	13(3.8)	13(3.9)		13(4.0)	15(4.2)	15(4.3)	15(4.6)	15(4.8)				
Man USA	'72	22(L)	6.0	9.7	13.6	17.6	21.3	23.0	25.4	29.7	33.9	38.4	43.1	5.4	25.5	2.5	48.51
				(3.7)	(3.9)	(4.0)	(3.7)		(4.1)	(4.3)	(4.2)	(4.5)	(4.7)				
Seymour USA	'72	21(L)	6.1	9.9	13.8	17.7	21.7	23.4	25.9	30.2	34.5	39.1	43.5	5.1	25.2	1.8	48.64
				(3.8)	(3.9)	(3.9)	(4.0)		(4.2)	(4.3)	(4.3)	(4.6)	(4.4)				
Shine USA	'76	22	6.1	9.9	13.8	17.7	21.7	23.4	25.9	30.2	34.5	38.9	43.4	3.29	25.29	1.79	48.69
				15(3.8)	15(3.9)	15(3.9)	15(4.0)		15(4.2)	15(4.3)	15(4.3)	15(4.4)	15(4.5)				
Kennige GER	'68	21	6.0	9.9	13.8	17.8	21.9	23.8	26.1	30.5	34.9	39.4	44.0	5.0	25.2	1.4	49.0
				(3.9)	(3.9)	(4.0)	(4.1)		(4.2)	(4.4)	(4.4)	(4.5)	(4.6)				
Sherwood GBR	'68	21	6.0	9.8	13.7	17.7	21.8	23.7	26.4	30.2	34.7	39.4	43.9	5.1	25.3	1.6	49.0
				(3.8)	(3.9)	(4.0)	(4.1)		(4.2)	(4.2)	(4.5)	(4.7)	(4.5)				
Vanderstock USA	'68	22	5.9	9.7	13.8	17.8	21.8	23.7	25.9	30.2	34.5	38.9	43.5	5.5	25.3	1.6	49.0
				(3.8)	(4.1)	(4.0)	(4.0)		(4.1)	(4.3)	(4.3)	(4.4)	(4.6)				
Skomorokov USSR	'68	21	6.1	9.9	13.7	17.5	21.5	23.4	25.6	30.0	34.6	39.2	43.8	5.3	25.7	2.3	49.1
				(3.8)	(3.8)	(3.8)	(4.0)		(4.1)	(4.4)	(4.6)	(4.6)	(4.6)				
Whitney USA	'68	21	6.1	10.3	14.2	18.2	22.4	24.3	26.6	30.8	35.1	39.5	44.0	5.2	24.9	0.6	49.2
				(4.2)	(3.9)	(4.0)	(4.2)		(4.2)	(4.2)	(4.3)	(44)	(4.5)				
Schubert WG	'68	21(L)	6.0	9.8	13.7	17.7	21.8	23.7	25.9	30.3	34.8	39.3	44.0	5.2	25.5	1.8	49.2
				(3.8)	(3.9)	(4.0)	(4.1)		(4.1)	(4.4)	(4.5)	(4.5)	(4.7)				
Schubert WG	'72	21(L)	6.1	9.9	13.7	17.6	21.6	23.3	25.8	30.2	34.6	39.3	44.2	5.5	26.3	3.0	49.65
				(3.8)	(3.8)	(3.9)	(4.0)		(4.2)	(4.4)	(4.4)	(4.7)	(4.9)				
Tziortzis GR	'72	22(R)	6.2	9.9	13.8	17.7	21.8	23.5	26.1	30.3	34.8	39.4	44.2	5.5	26.2	2.7	49.66
				(3.7)	(3.9)	(3.9)	(4.1)		(4.3)	(4.2)	(4.5)	(4.6)	(4.8)				

TACTICS

In general, a man would do best to concentrate entirely on his own race and his own problems of proper stride, relaxation, and drive through to the finish. However, as experience and confidence are gained men learn to relax an infinitesimal degree "with their opponents" on the backstretch and going into the second durve. This is just enough to conserve their energies for the big drive to the tape. Glenn Davis was a master at this. He seldom had a lead until the seventh hurdle, but from then on he had his opponents "psyched out," for they knew how tough it would be to beat him over the last three.

It seems quite likely that Hemery established the pattern for the future in winning the 1968 Olympic final. Dick Drake[2] reported the race:

Schubert and Hemery were slightly ahead and Whitney already lagging by the

---

[1]This chart excerpted from John Le Masurier, ibid., p. 40.

[2]Dick Drake, "Hemery's 48.1 Cremates Field," *Track & Field News*, Oct/Nov, 1968, 23.

first hurdle. From there, Hemery pulled away startlingly--with remarkable technique that made the intermediates resemble low hurdles. Never have the first five hurdles been negotiated as quickly as Hemery was ripping over them. By the third, the 6' 1 1/2", 165-lb. Hemery had already made up the stagger on Whitney. He reached midway in the shocking 23.0, literally a half-flight ahead of his nearest competitors...

Powerfully but skillfully, Hemery left the field even further behind as he rounded the final curve and changed his steps from 13 to 15 after the sixth.

Hemery followed this same tactic at the 1972 Games, being timed by several observers in 20.8 at touchdown after the fifth hurdle (compared with 21.5 in 1968). At that point he had a yard or so lead over Ralph Mann, BYU 440y hurdle world-record holder, with Akii-Bua, in lane one, well under 21.5. Akii-Bua used 13 strides with an outside right leg lead for the first five hurdles, then shifted to 14 by alternating legs. (Six of the eight finalists led with the inside left leg.) The winner--Akii-Bua with a world-record time of 47.82, 1.2 seconds faster than his previous best but seemingly slower than his potential best. Ralph Mann was second in 48.51; Hemery third, in 48.52.

How did Akii-Bua win? By superior stamina, not tactics nor superior hurdling skill, though he was a 14.2 high hurdler before he turned to the intermediates. He reported that from December to May he did cross country running--8 to 12 miles a day--varied by runs up a 400-meter hill wearing a 25-pound vest. In May he moved to the track where his primary workout, often six times a week, was to run 1000 meters while striding over six intermediate hurdles on each lap. Hardly a model program designed to achieve optimal fitness for his event, but one that provided the basic toughness of body and spirit that he needed.

THE ORGANIZATION OF PRACTICE

Planning a program of year-round training for the 400m hurdles should place first emphasis on basic endurance as would any 400m or 800m runner. Throughout the early months train with such men in running fartlek on whatever interesting terrain is available. Ignore the hurdles altogether; develop speed-endurance as would any middle-distance man.

During the indoor season, train for and compete in the 400m or 600m runs as being more related to the event than would be the 60m hurdles. If hurdling seems necessary, then be sure to compete on the 1600m-relay team. It requires great skill to run 400m hurdles with a time difference of only two seconds. Such skill requires practice--much practice during months of time. But the more potential value lies in superior endurance, not in hurdling skill.

Acquiring Stride Rhythm and Certainty. (1) Keep a flight of 5 to 7 hurdles (men--39", women--30") on the outside lane of the track. Tape a starting line 45m to the first hurdle. Encourage informal practice to gain rhythm and confidence. For each hurdler, place tape 3 or 5 strides before each hurdle, from which point he is certain to reach the hurdle properly. (2) If necessary, place tape to mark all strides between two hurdles.

The precise number of strides--from 17 down to 13--is not nearly so important as is the sense of certainty that one can follow whatever stride pattern has been selected as optimal.

Time Trials and Endurance Workouts. Time trials over ten hurdles are seldom satisfactory. Most men need actual competition to do well in such a difficult event. Time trials over any lesser distance--5-6-7 hurdles--tend toward faster pace and different stride patterns; rhythm is upset and more may be lost than is gained.

One way to run trials is to combine an overdistance run with hurdles 35 meters apart and a 40-meter finish. Example: Run 300m on the flat to the 5th hurdle, and on to the finish line, a total of 515 meters. (Place tape 3-5 strides in front of 5th hurdle.)

Another method is to reverse the run and hurdles. Run the first five hurdles at competitive rhythm and speed--no faster; then run on the flat to a total distance of 500 or even 600 meters.

HOW THEY TRAIN

JIM BOLDING[1] was selected by T&FN as world's-best for 1974; won 14 of 15 races, mostly international; ran under 49 seconds ten times, with a world-record 48.7 for 440 yards, and 48.1 for 400 meters, a 1974 American record.

>   Age: 1974- 25; 6-1, 165#.
>   Best Marks: HH-13.7; 400m-45.3.

Non-Competitive Season (November-May. After graduating from Oklahoma State University, he had little competition indoors.)

Mon: 660-550-440-330-220 at 60-61 second pace with as short an interval between as possible. Weight training.
Tues: 4-6 mile run and strides.
Wed: 12 x 180 on hills with jog or rapid walk-down between. Weights.
Thurs: 8 x 440, 2 sets of 4 in 62-64 pace with a 65 second interval between reps and 440 walk rest between sets.
Fri: 4-6 mile run. Strides. Weights.
Sat: Interval work on golf course. 15 x 220 or 10-12 x 330, untimed with short interval between.
Sun: Rest.

Competitive Season (May and early June)

Mon: 3 x 440, 1st 440,220 flat then 220 hurdles; 2nd 440, 220 hurdles then 220 flat; 3rd same as first. 53 (!) seconds for each, with 440 jog between. Weights.
Tues: 10 x 180 on hills, same type as in non-competitive season, except faster.
Wed: 7-6-5-4- hurdles from blocks with interval-walk back to blocks the long way.
Thurs: 8 x 220 for an average, with 220 interval. Best average 24.3.
Fri: Jogging, stretching, strides.
Sat: Compete.
Sun: Rest or an easy run.

RICH GRAYBEHL, USC, finished 2nd 1978 NCAA Championships.
>   Age: 1978-22; 5-9, 155#
>   Best Marks: 400 IH-49.31; 100y--9.4.

Rich does weight training two days per week in the fall and winter (cuts down to one day per week in the spring), including bench press, curls and leg presses. His regular warmup consists of a half-mile jog, and then 20 minutes of hurdlers stretching: "A constant stretch, not with jerky motion."

Non-Competitive Season
Mon: 5 x 550.
Tues: 12 x 220; weights for 50 mins., including holding 10 lb. weights in each hand and doing running arm motion.
Wed: 10 x 330.
Thurs: 15 x 150; weights for 30 mins.
Fri: Jog 2M.
Sat: Run 5M.
Sun: Jog 2M.

Graybehl also finds running the 330 intermediates a useful training method, as they are "very effective for speed work on the 400 hurdles." Also, he runs the 330s as the first and last 3 hurdles of the full intermediates distance.

Competitive Season
Mon: 3 x 550; 5 x 110.
Tues: 1 x 330 with hurdles; 3 x 150; 20 mins. weights (mostly upper body).
Wed: 3 x 330, 220, 110.

---

[1]Roger Jennings, "Jim Bolding," *Track Technique*, #59 March 1975, p. 1877.

[2]Chris Rauch, "Rich Graybehl," *Track Technique*, #76 Summer 1979, p. 2423.

<u>Thurs.</u>: 3 x last six hurdles (330).
<u>Fri</u>: Jog mile.
<u>Sat</u>: Compete.
<u>Sun</u>: Jog 2M.

He considers his consistency to be his best aspect, and his lack of endurance his weakness.

Graybehl runs 14 steps for the first 5-7 hurdles and then switches to 15, but would like to run 13 for the first 5. He has found that when he runs "14 steps for 5 hurdles I run about 50.5 but when I run 14 steps for 7 hurdles, I run about 49.5"

Fig. 28.2--A left-leg lead enables the 400m hurdler to avoid being disqualified for running on the lane line, or for failing to bring the trail leg over the hurdle--a common fault with a right-leg lead.

Chapter 29
THE RELAYS

HISTORY OF DEVELOPMENT

Relay racing as a form of sports competition originated entirely in the United States. There were several background activities that might have germinated the idea. For example, there were the relays of horses by which stagecoaches went long distances and the Pony Express, by which news and mail were relayed to distant points in the country. Along more recreational lines, there were the old holiday competitions between firemen's cart-and-hose teams in which the fastest men "raised the alarm" by sprinting to and touching the cart so their teammates could start pulling it. The *Encyclopaedia Britannica*[1] credits the Massachusetts Firemen's "bean-pot" race as having been the model for relay racing:

> *The old method was for the men running the second quarter of the race each to take over a small flag from the first relay men as they arrived, before departing on their own stage of the race, at the end of which they, in turn, handed on their flags to the awaiting runners. The flags however were considered cumbersome, and for a time it was sufficient for the outgoing runner to touch or be touched by his predecessor.*

However, the origin of relay racing as a part of organized track and field athletics is clear, for no one questions that the University of Pennsylvania was the place, and Frank B. Ellis and H. L. Geyelin the "inventors" of the four-man race. Edward R. Bushnell, writing in the 50th- anniversary program of the Pennsylvania Relay Carnival, tells how these two men deliberately searched for something to make track sports draw more contestants and spectators. They conceived group effort as the solution:

> *The first experiment was made in 1893, with two teams of four men, each of whom ran a quarter mile. It worked so well in practice that it was decided to add the event to the spring track program and to invite Princeton to send a team. . . .*

> *The first race was such a success that it was repeated in 1894. . . . By this time the new event had aroused so much interest among coaches, athletes and the public that the Pennsylvania committee resolved to expand the idea and hold an invitation meet the following year with outside schools and colleges invited. Apparently the committee was not sure that a meet devoted entirely to relay racing would satisfy the track fans, because only nine races were scheduled for the first meet and they alternated with the events of the University's annual spring games. . . .*

> *In addition to Pennsylvania and Harvard, the other competing colleges in this first carnival were College of the City of New York vs. New York University, Rutgers vs. Swarthmore, Lafayette vs. Lehigh and Cornell vs. Columbia. The competing schools were Germantown Academy vs. Penn Charter, Cheltenham vs. Haverford, Episcopal vs. Delancey and Central High vs. Central Manual.*

---

[1] *Encyclopaedia Britannica*, 14th Edition, Vol. 19, p. 666.

It will be noted that this first carnival included races at all four levels: university, college, academy and preparatory school, and high school. The high schools were slow to organize and enter teams but soon they were sending the largest numbers of competitors. Estimates have been made that over 238,000 athletes competed in the Pennsylvania relays during its first 81 years, with average numbers in the past ten years exceeding 6,000. In 1976 over 500 high schools entered teams in one or more races.

THE EXPANSION OF RELAYS

The original Penn Relays program was expanded in 1897 to include the 2-mile and 4-mile relays; in 1915, the sprint medley and distance medley relays; in 1922, the 440 and 880 relays, and in 1926, the shuttle-hurdle relay.

From these experiences the relay idea has expanded rapidly in all phases of track and field. In 1910, the Drake relays were instituted by Drake University and the Greater Des Moines, Iowa, Relay Committee. These relays have been a distinctively community venture and, in addition to the competitive program, have made the relay weekend a time of city-wide holiday, pageantry, and hospitality. The program has been similar to that at Pennsylvania with its emphasis on numbers of competitors and on all levels of competition.

EMPHASIS ON NUMBERS. This emphasis has made these two great relay meets entirely unique in the sports world in terms of the soundness and the broadness of their base of competition. In a single afternoon, thousands of athletes compete on the same field and track, although the youngest is still in fifth grade of grammar school and running for the first time in a competitive track meet and the most experienced is several years beyond college and may have one or more world's records to his credit. It is difficult to conceive of an annual event occurring at a single place and time that is a more complete answer to those who accuse modern sports of encouraging only the few and the talented.

Relay meets have increased in number and influence quite consistently during the past 30 years. In 1930, the *National Collegiate Athletic Association Track and Field Guide* listed only four such meets: Pennsylvania, Drake, Kansas, and Ohio State. In 1971, 28 meets were considered large enough to be listed in detail. In addition, about a dozen lesser meets and indoor meets were sponsored by colleges across the country.

SPECTATOR INTEREST. The relay meet with its group competition has also increased spectator interest in track and field. Time schedules have become tight and precisely followed. For example, in 1970, during the first two hours of the Penn Relay Carnival, 30 relays @ 4 x 110 yards, with 8 teams in each relay, were run--an average of one race every four minutes! Consider that for each race, 32 competitors, often inexperienced, must be placed in their proper lanes, that eight leadoff men must be started together from staggered lanes, that all results must be recorded, violations reported--all within four minutes!

To add to all this, a so-called "Spectator Period" of three hours duration is scheduled at the end of the Carnival in which the Championship and Invitation events on the track and the field are presented. The spectators love it!

INDOOR RELAYS. During the indoor season, a large number of "Games" or "Invitation Meets" have been organized in large cities throughout the country under the sanction of the National AAU and more recently, the US Track and Field Federation. These meets tend to be pointed toward spectator interest and feature invitation events in which six or eight champions compete. But they also include a number of relay events for colleges, for clubs, and occasionally for high schools. Often the mile relay for colleges will climax the evening.

RELAYS IN THE OLYMPIC GAMES. Relays have gradually taken a more important role in the track and field portion of the Olympic Games. They were first included in the 1908 London Games with a medley (220-220-400-800). This was dropped in the 1912 Games at Stockholm but two relays were added--a 4 x 100m and a 4 x 400m. Because of its great wealth of sprinters and 440 men, the United States has dominated these relay events. Of the 24 competitions that have been run since 1912, the United States has won 19. But in almost all instances, the competition has been extremely close and exciting. As a matter of interest, the use of relay batons originated in the 1912 Stockholm Games.

ESSENTIALS OF TECHNIQUE IN RELAY RACING

We shall consider two aspects of technique in relay racing--the passing of batons, and the use of personnel, especially as to order of running.

PASSING THE BATON--THE VISUAL PASS. In all relays longer than 4 x 220 the outgoing runner (the receiver) takes primary responsibility for getting the baton by focussing his eyes on it until it is firmly grasped in his hand. This is commonly called the "sight" or "visual" pass (Figure 29.1).

Fig. 29.1 -- An inside (left-handed) sight or visual pass. The receiver focuses his eyes on the baton while at the same time attending to the entire situation which may change at the last instant. As he takes the baton, usually near the center of the zone, he accelerates quickly.

It is assumed that the incoming man will be fatigued from his endurance running, and so not in complete control of his efforts to transfer the baton. He simply does his best to stick the baton up in the air where his teammate can see it and grasp it. The three most common methods of accomplishing this are shown clearly in Figure 29.2

In the visual pass, the skill of getting a sure and effective pass, in terms of gaining time-distance, depends on the judgment of the receiver. There are no set marks on the track as occurs when using the blind pass. The receiver must judge, first, the lane in which he will get the baton (and sometimes the lanes are crowded and crossovers do occur at the last instant). Second, he must judge the speed of the incoming runner, and move out just fast enough to gain as much ground as he can, without running away from his man. Experienced runners are sometimes very adept in this, and can so time their pickup of acceleration at the last instant as to burst away from the field. This is especially important in the mile relay or sprint-medley relay in which incoming speeds are high. Such skilled receivers will often pick up three to five yards on their opponents. Method C in Figure29 .2 is usually used in shorter-faster relays in which the incoming man has good control. It may then become a semi-blind pass in which the receiver can, at the last instant, lose sight of the baton, glance ahead, and so orient himself to the difficulties of making his way through the pack. It has its advantages and its dangers!

PASSING THE BATON--THE BLIND PASS. The blind pass is used in those short-distance relays (440, 880 and sprint medleys) in which victory often depends on maintaining continuous maximum velocity of the baton throughout the exchange. Any deceleration for even a tenth of a second will lose a yard or more, and that may make the crucial difference in the final result.

In the Olympic Games, despite our great success, the precision of U. S. baton passing in the short relays has usually been something short of perfection. Of course, the team members have not practiced together until a few weeks before the Games, but also we've had such confidence in our superior sprinting ability as not to be impressed with the crucial importance of precision in baton-passing technique. A 1970 survey of U. S. college teams in major relay

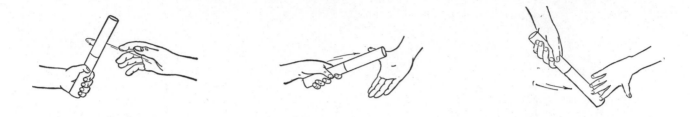

Fig. 29.2. Three accepted methods for the visual pass in longer relays.

meets indicated widely differing methods in all phases--an up-thrust (preferred) or a down-thrust of the baton into the receiving hand, taking the baton with the inside left hand or the outside right, switching the baton from one hand to the other while running, or starting position as related to the passing zone.

In contrast, a study by Dostal[1] of the 16 national teams that made the 1972 Olympic semi-finals showed a definite trend toward one overall method. Not being blessed with great sprinters as in the U. S., and so compelled to minimize time-loss in baton-passing, the national specialists of these countries have studied related techniques very carefully. Dostal's conclusions are therefore of special value. In summary, they were:

1. A strongly predominant use of the upward baton thrust (Figure 29.3).
2. No switching of the baton by a runner from one hand to the other.
3. Runners taking the baton on the curve receive with the inside left hand; those on the straight, with the outside right hand. That is, the baton is carried by successive runners in the right-left-right-left hands.
4. Baton exchange occurs in the last quarter or fifth of the passing zone (50-60 feet), the point of maximum speed for both runners (and the baton!). At the moment of exchange the torsos of the runners are about one meter apart.
5. The second and fourth runners started from a half-crouch position (sometimes called

---

[1]Emil Dostal, "400m Relay Exchange Techniques," *Track Technique*, #57, September 1974, p. 1802.

Fig. 29.3. Blind pass with upward thrust of the baton.

Fig. 29.4. Half-crouch starting position; better if left leg forward.

the Korobkov style after its originator, Gavriel Korobkov, former USSR National Coach), with one hand on the ground, and the inside left leg forward for better balance and support while waiting, and better arm-leg coordination on the first step (Figure 29.4). Some runners crouched with the right leg forward.

6. Some of the third runners also used the Korobkov method--head turned inwards--(and Dostal recommends it) though receiving on the straight and taking with the outside hand.

<u>Practicing technique</u>. As with any skill, perfect baton-exchange technique requires constant practice. The most obvious demonstration of this occurs every four years at the Olympic Games in which (1) the U.S. relay foursomes have only a half-dozen practice sessions prior to the Games--and show it; and (2) the relay teams of other countries are selected months ahead of time, practice baton exchanges thoroughly, with the same four men running in the same order--and show it by gaining ground on each exchange.

A second example occurred in the 1976 NCAA Championships on Franklin Field, Philadelphia, when Tennessee's superior passing brought them the title. Not only had these four men been together at Tennessee for four years, their coach Stan Huntsman had devised a warm-up and practice drill in which the four men, spaced within six feet of each other, circled the track at something less than a slow jog, while passing the baton forward, simulating race methods, then handing it overhead back to the first runner. The thrust-grasp of the baton was precise and crisp each time. <u>Practice</u>!

Fig. 29.5. When passing on a curve, the left-handed pass (outer land) has a definite advantage in visualizing the running situation.

<u>The 20-meter + 10-meter zones</u>. In 1962, the IAAF (International Amateur Athletic Federation) passed a rule which allows a man to take a position anywhere within a 10-meter zone and then run into the 20-meter passing zone as the baton is passed. Primarily this change cut down on the number of teams disqualified for passing outside the zone, but it has also produced faster baton velocities during the exchange.

Just where within the 10-meter zone an outgoing runner will start depends on several factors: (1) The degree of acceleration from the starting mark. Walker advocates a crouched-start

Fig. 29.6. Blind pass (20 meters plus 10 meters). Here the baton exchange is at 18 meters, a legal but unsafe area. Maximum baton speed can be attained and still pass at 12-15 meters.

position similar to that of "set" in sprint starting and urges an acceleration such as occurs in competitive sprinting.[1] (2) The spot at which the exchange of baton is to occur. If one man can maintain top momentum longer than the other, he should be asked to carry the baton a few yards further within the passing zone, and they will set up their method accordingly. Whitehead[2] made a careful study of movies of the excellent passing of the Russian team, 1964, and the British team (world record, 1963), and found that the first exchanged the baton at about six yards before the restraining line; the second, at about seven. These marks ensured high velocity of the baton and safety of passing within the zone.

Emplacement of Receiver's hand. It is crucial that the incoming runner have a clear and steady target, the hand, on which he can focus his actions. During the early acceleration period into the 20-meter zone, the receiver will drive both arms forcefully. But two strides (L-R-L or R-L-R) before the actual exchange point (C in Figure 29.6) is reached, the hand must be fixed at full though relaxed extension in receiving position. The shoulder girdle does not twist; eyes focus straight ahead; PMA (Positive Mental Attitude) is crucial; all-out velocity is not reduced as the critical last six yards are reached. *The baton will come when it is needed.*

Placement of the Baton. The incoming runner must grasp the baton near its lower end to expose a full six inches of its 11.81-inch length for a firm placement in the receiver's hand. The movement is not a hurried slapdash of the baton; rather, it is a careful press into the hand. Concentration is the key. *Keep your eye on that hand and see it grasp that baton.*

"Go!" Whatever the location of the starting point of the receiver within the 10-meter zone, he must have a marker by which to judge his "Go!" With the growing use of hard-surface tracks, a strip of tape is placed on the spot, its exact location being a matter of repeated trial in practice. Coach Walker[3], who has had many fine sprint relay teams, times his relay men to make certain they reach the 26-meter point in close to the same time they can achieve it in sprinting out of starting blocks.

Some coaches add sound to sight, and have the incoming runner call "Go!" or "Hike!" as he reaches a certain spot. In my judgment, it's better that a man depend on himself, and that his mind be pin-pointed in terms of the one sense, vision, rather than divided between eye and ear, especially when other disruptive sounds are certain to be present.

USE OF PERSONNEL--SPRINT RELAYS. In the sprint, blind-pass relays, the usual preference is to get a lead as soon as possible and keep it through the finish line. This would suggest that men run in order of 100-yard dash time. However, mental attitude is very important, and most coaches feel it helps confidence to have that best man running anchor. The others then rely on his ability to gain back what may have been lost. This then changes the order to 2-3-4-1 in order of merit. Some consideration should be given to fast and dependable starting out of the blocks, and most importantly, to the long-time pairing of men in perfecting the skill of passing. Some men have confidence in each other, practice a great deal together, take pride in their passing skill.

The all-important point is to make a decision as to the order of running early in the season, then have those combinations practice-practice-practice, until both their muscles and their minds know it will come off right! Such practice has its dangers. Men are going all-out (if the practice is to be effective); at times they may be off-balance in reaching forward; muscles may be contracting against resistance. Many a fine sprinter has lost weeks of competition through relay work. Precautions as to warming-up, overwork, or practice temperatures should be carefully taken.

---

[1] Leroy T. Walker, *CHAMPIONSHIP TECHNIQUES IN TRACK AND FIELD*, West Nyack, N.Y.: Parker Publishing Co., Inc., 1969, 56.
[2] See Nick Whitehead, *ibid.*, 5, for more detailed discussion.
[3] Leroy T. Walker, *ibid.*, 56.

USE OF PERSONNEL---LONGER-DISTANCE RELAYS. The use of personnel in longer-distance relays, including the mile relay, depends so much upon the competitive situation in a particular race, as well as on individual abilities and attitudes. How many teams in the race? What lane do you have and what chance of getting a sound position at the start? Even with a good start can and should the lead-off man spend his energies in holding that position? Some crazy running occurs during the first 200 yards or so, and a lead position can become a tail position within a distance of 20 yards, so that the job of passing has to be done all over again.

On the other hand, do the team members have the confidence and poise to take it easy at the start, then as the field thins out, move up with comparatively little interference to the position they want? In the meantime, what has happened to the leading contenders? Have they now built up such a lead that contact is lost and most difficult to regain? That is, your order of running depends somewhat on the order of running of your opponents.

When only two or three teams are competing, the main problems are first, to have the best anchor man, and second, to maintain contact. But when the field is crowded, the first leg is often the toughest. Some coaches decide in such a situation to run their strongest man first, then follow with numbers 3-4-2 in order of merit. The lead he may build up may hold through to the finish. But in many instances, the superiority of such a man is nullified in the frustrations of changing pace and place. It's a gamble!

No final conclusions can be reached here, other than the necessity of careful study by the coach of the competitive situation, of deciding as early as possible just what order to run, and then preparing the men, both physically and mentally for their task. Confidence and competence are two sides of one coin.

Indoor Relay Running. The usually crowded conditions of indoor running accentuate the problem of personnel use. Some coaches try to get a lead on the first legs so as to free the running of the later runners. Others use men of lesser ability first, wait for the field to spread out, then come from behind in the later stages. Each team and each situation has its own unique solutions.

In indoor relays there is a definite advantage in taking the baton with the inside left hand, especially when on the curve. Thereby the receiver can see the entire situation as it develops at the last instant, be aware of the lane line or curb, avoid fouling a competitor on an inner lane, and prevent both disqualification and injury.

HOW THEY TRAIN

Bill McClure has had great success for several decades with his relay teams at Abilene Christian and Louisiana State.[1] From his presentation at the 1978 U.S. Track Coaches Association Olympic Development Clinic, I have extracted only those portions that relate directly to exchanging the baton. In addition, McClure placed great emphasis on the importance of careful selection and use of personnel--relative sprinting speeds, endurance, curve-running abilities, etc.

The method we use at LSU is what I choose to call the "palm up" exchange. We have the lead-off man carry the baton in his right hand and exchange to the 2nd runner's left, and he retains the baton in his left hand exchanges to the 3rd runner's right, and he retains the baton in his right and exchanges to the 4th runner's left. We believe this gives us an advantage in allowing each runner to run the shortest distance to the exchange point...

In the lead-off position we would like to have our best man off the blocks and a good curve runner. He could be a high hurdler or the 2nd best sprinter. The second man is our best long-sprinter generally a quarter-miler or intermediate hurdler, someone who is big and strong and can fly on the straight-away. He will run, as will the anchor man, approximately 120 yards. The third man is generally either our second sprinter or a hurdler or quarter-miler who can really run the turn as

[1]Bill McClure, "Relays," USTCA Track & Field Quarterly Review, Vol. 78, #3, Fall 1978, p. 54.

his entire run is on the curve. The anchor man is our best sprint competitor-- the man who can reach down and get a little more when called on to perform. He (as the 2nd man) will run a bit farther than the 1st and 3rd men. Our 1st and 3rd men run the turns and the 2nd and 4th run the straights...

On the 1st and 3rd exchanges we want the outgoing runner to get the baton immediately after he crossed the near exchange zone mark. The 2nd exchange we want the outgoing runner to get the baton 15-17 yards into the exchange zone area. This enables us to run our strength on the straight and our weakness, the shorter distance, on the curve...

The responsibilities of the incoming and ougoing runner are specific and vital for the success of the team. For a successful exchange of the baton the incoming and outgoing runners need to make the pass while running an equal rate of speed, the rate being tops for each at the point of exchange.

1. Responsibility of the incoming Runner.
   a. Finish strong thru the exchange-run only on your 2/3 part of the lane (not behind the outgoing runner)
   b. Identify your teammate-check lane inside and outside yours as well as your own (colors, similar, etc.)
   c. Know where the exchange is to take place in the zone (early, middle, late)
   d. Know the emergency command and when to give it.
   e. Be Positive the outgoing runner takes the baton from you.
   f. Look the baton into the exchange.
   g. Stay in your lane after the pass. (Be sure you are clear before leaving track)

2. Responsibility of the Outgoing Runner.
   a. Locate your station 15 minutes prior to race.
   b. Make your check mark(s) as soon as permissible (consider weather, wind, etc.)
   c. Identify the team inside and outside of your lane. (Uniform color, etc.)
   d. Do not anticipate--rely on your practice and marks.
   e. Stay in your 1/3 part of the lane.
   f. Expect a good exchange.

3. The Lead-off Runner has other responsibilities concerning the race.
   a. The lead-off man is responsible for the baton.
   b. The grip on the baton for the start should be comfortable, legal and in the passing hand, with the grip being on the first 1/3 of the baton.

Believing practice makes for a better exchange we involve our relay units in baton work as part of their warm-up and warm-down, each man working with his partner(s) twice a week at their stations. As our exchange is from right to left, left to right, right to left, we do not have to worry about changing the baton from hand to hand. We work our alternates at all positions and if we have an injury we simply put the alternate in the injured man's position.

In the 4 x 200 relay we use the same personnel as our 4 x 100 unit. The only adjustment we make is in our marks. Each man divides his "go" mark in half and adds one foot, leaving the lean mark the same (if we have one). In the mile and other relays we use the visual exchange (right to left) or a combination of the sprint relay.

I do not look for "daylight" between the runners as criteria for a good exchange. I'm interested in the exchange being made at optimum speed. Once our athletes are settled on their distance for the "go" mark, most of our practice is done on the straight-away to prevent injuries. We also have a rule that a runner never tries to make an exchange if he has to stretch in a workout.

Confidence is the key to success and drill is the route to confidence.

Appendix A
DYNAMICS OF SKILL

INTRODUCTION

Any discussion of the dynamics of the skill events in track and field must focus on such fundamentals as "muscle sense," "whole-phase-whole learning," or "reinforcement," just as the dynamics of endurance must focus on such fundamentals as aerobic-anaerobic running, or those of power on overloading and relatedness. That is to say, in our modern and more scientific approach to coaching problems, we must understand and practice the basic knowledges that underlie our coaching of specific events. Such esoteric terms as "mental practice" or "feedback" may seem of little use when actually coaching a boy to throw the discus or hammer. But unless our modern coaching is consistent with the findings of related research, it will not be as effective and the athlete's performance will be decreased.

This is a hard fact which coaches of the pre-scientific decades find it agonizing if not impossible to swallow. As I write I just have to laugh a little as I think of the reaction to such gibberish by such excellent Olympic coaches as Lawson Robertson, Dean Cromwell, or Jim Kelley,--something comparable to "hogwash" or "horsefeathers"! And for their era, that's about what such an approach would have been, just as would heart-rate meters for coaching running or computers for coaching football. But today requires new and more scientific thinking and practice.

LEARNING A SKILL IS A HOLISTIC-DYNAMIC PROBLEM

In our introductory chapter we stated that the basic point of view of this book was "holistic-dynamic," a term coined by Abraham Maslow in his *MOTIVATION AND PERSONALITY*, 1970. By it, he emphasized wholes or systems in contrast to the separate elements of atomism.

The concept is of special value in coaching skills. Learning a skill is holistic in several ways. For example, the most valid unit of competitive performance is the whole person-situation in a time-place extensional sense. Skill is but one aspect of such performance and of the training behind it. Decades ago we assumed technique was a 90% factor in performance. If a man acquired proper technique, he needed only full motivation to achieve top performance. Thus, 90 percent of our practice time was devoted to improving technique. Today we recognize that high-level skill is based on a number of pre-requisites including related power, freedom from inhibitions, total mobilization of competitive energies, and others. Today, we know these basics of performance do not just happen; they must be practiced along with skill. Consequently, only a lesser portion of time-energy--say 50 percent or less--can be given to learning skill.

As a second example of holism, we begin a skill with a vaguely grasped whole. We make a simple analysis of it by which we realize the unreality of our first grasp of the skill and try to create a better and more complete whole. Again this whole is analyzed; again we sense the skill at a higher level of wholeness and effectiveness. This process continues endlessly--and holistically.

Learning a skill is also a dynamic problem in that the athlete-situation (including the coach) is never static, never identical from any point of view. We say this in the Heraclitus sense that no one of us is ever twice the same, and that "we can never step in the same river twice." Thus we can never coach the same boy or the same skill in successive practice sessions. Everything changes: the athlete, the coach, their inter-personal attitudes, their mastery of learning and teaching, their awareness of goals, the social and physical surround within which they live and work--nothing is ever identical.

This suggests chaos and total breakdown of the learning-teaching process, that is, until we remember that endless change and diversity is but one side of the coin. The other equally valid side is a basic unity of all things. Even though "never the same river twice," there's "always the river."

If this discussion confuses more than it clarifies, read again the introductory chapter of this book. Succeeding sections on skill learning, especially "whole-phase-whole learning," and "mental practice," should be helpful. If specially interested in the problem, be sure to read Maslow but perhaps even more crucial the delightful book by Wendell Johnson, *PEOPLE IN QUANDARIES,* the semantics of personal adjustment. I know of no better mind opener or tension dropper.

WHOLE-PHASE-WHOLE LEARNING IN FIELD EVENTS
Traditionally, the methods of motor learning as found in field events are presented from two points of view: that of "part learning" as developed by the "association" or stimulus-response schools of psychology, and that of whole-part-whole learning of the Gestalt or Organismic schools. These methods apply in our field as well.

PROGRESSIONS. By the stimulus-response theory of motor learning, the whole movement to be learned was divided into separate parts in a way that was meaningful logically (though not necessarily muscularly or organismically). Learning practice was then concentrated on each part in its logical order until each was learned well. Then the parts were re-joined as a basis for learning the whole movement.

Such coaching of parts has a definite validity in certain sports such as baseball, where for example the learning of batting skills has little relation to that of playing second base or pitching. But as a sport becomes less complex and more all-of-one-piece so to speak, such analysis and coaching of parts becomes less and less effective. I once observed an hour-long class in *discus throwing* (the italics are used with malice aforethought) in which the dozen or so prospects were taught: (1) to roll the discus around the first finger, (2) to toss it vertically while rolling it around the first finger, (3) to throw it from a standing position, and (4) to rotate the body without a discus. Considerable time and emphasis was given to perfecting each of these actions. These actions were called progressions, but progress occurred at such a slow rate and doubtful value as related to discus throwing that I wondered at the degree of acceptance by the students.

WHOLE-PART-WHOLE LEARNING. Effective coaching by whole-part-whole methods depends on a sound and precise understanding of the meaning of the concept. We do not wish to quibble over "mere words," as some might express it. But, as in every attempt at a more scientific approach, the precise meanings that are given to "whole" and "part" and their inter-relationships are basic to coaching that achieves a mastery of technique in the shortest possible time.

What degree of complexity should a teachable whole be? The most valid whole is the actual time-situation-action of the competition itself. And a strong case can be made for learning to perform in competition by performing in competition. At the other extreme, a coachable whole can be identified in almost any phase of movement, no matter how partial, as long as that phase is seen and used in its relationship to the whole movement of the event. Relatedness is the key to this method of motor learning.

Though such relatedness is implied by the hyphen in whole-part-whole, we prefer the word "phase" to that of "part." A part suggests a separate entity, as occurs in a machine such as a radio or automobile, in which the separate parts can be assembled to form the whole machine. This is never the case in human motor learning. In contrast, the word "phase" is always incomplete in its connotation, and always relative to its whole.

$WHOLE_1$-$PHASE_1$-$WHOLE_2$-$PHASE_2$-$WHOLE_3$ LEARNING. The wholes of a movement being learned are constantly changing. Only in the abstractions of our minds do they tend to remain the same. We can think of and speak of a movement such as high jumping as a fixed action. But each time we jump, that action changes--hopefully, it develops to a new and better whole (technique).

This is what is implied by the heading of this section. Think of $whole_1$ as a symbol for a first attempt to jump, in which we give special attention to $phase_1$, the upward thrust of the lead leg. Such attentive practice produces a change in skill, hopefully an improvement, so that we now have a new whole, as indicated by $whole_2$. Similarly, on our second effort, the action of the lead leg is not identical to that of the first effort, so we write it as $phase_2$.

This gives us the overall pattern of our preferred method of learning and coaching the skills of track and field. Each new phase emerges out of its precedent whole, and merges back into that whole at a different and, hopefully, more skilled level. At each new level of skill, the athlete feels, and may even yell, "I've got it!" He is experiencing what the Gestalt school calls a "perceptual reorganization" or insight that senses a closer approximation of the desired skill. "Closure" (Shaffer, 1956, 134) occurs, a restoration of equilibrium at a higher level. But the "it" that he feels probably recedes. He may even fall back to lower levels of skill for days or weeks. But with continued sound practice, there will come a new "I've got it!" at a new whole, and insight into a higher approximation of the goal. And so on, toward full mastery of "it."

The final goal is an all-out, uninhibited, perfect action. But with imperfect and finite men, such a goal, like that of Tennyson's Ulysses, "whose margin fades forever and forever as I move," constantly recedes with each new level of skill. After many years of striving, a Ralph Boston in the long jump or an Al Oerter in the discus feels that he is just beginning to grasp the real knack of his event. The only instance of perfect performance in motor learning is related by Eugen Herrigel (1953) in his autobiographical ZEN IN THE ART OF ARCHERY. The Zen Master is a coaching genius who demands, or better, assumes training and performance at the highest levels of non-effort. (If this is unclear, by all means read, or more likely, get lost in the book.)

USABLE WHOLES. Those who oppose the holistic approach to motor learning argue that sports are too complex to be learned as a whole, and must be divided into segments for separate practice. This certainly holds true for such actions as foul throwing in basketball or the backhand stroke in tennis. But it is our opinion that its application to field events should be limited as much as possible. As a rule of thumb, coach the largest whole, in terms of the event action, as can be used effectively. In most cases, this means the full action of the event performed at the highest usable speed.

When properly presented, field events are not so complex as to be unmanageable by the neophyte as a single undivided skill. The pole vault might be an exception, largely because of the danger of injury. But even in this event, once the beginner learns to grasp the pole firmly and swing into the air, we can take a "whole" though modified, approach. True the discus action is unique in sports, with its body rotation while holding the discus back in a power position, but boys well enough coordinated to be good prospects pick up the whole action quickly, even though imperfectly, of course.

Which reminds us to re-emphasize that holistic method does not require a perfect-or-not-at-all effort. It is enough that the learned whole (a) is acceptably satisfactory to the learner, and (b) is consistent with the whole skill that the coach is trying to teach.

In summary, learning by a whole-phase-whole method would proceed somewhat as follows:

a. A first emphasis upon the action as a whole, upon one thoughtless, unanalyzed, undivided movement. Such sense of the movement "as a whole" is initiated by watching and thus "getting the feel" of the action of expert throwers on the field, or on film, or by sequence drawings. Such a holistic feeling should precede all analytical coaching, and certainly, all teaching of so-called progressions in learning skills.

Some may prefer to reify this feeling of the whole action away from the coach, and even other throwers. Some coaches stay away from raw beginners on the first day or so. "You try it alone today, now that you've seen the champ in action; I'll see you tomorrow." This way the youngster gains a certain confidence, not in the sense of proper rhythm or skill, of course, but at least of having something positive, and of forming a base for interpreting the words of his coach.

Don't practice alone for long. It's amazing how the techniques of first learning tend to stay with a man; a wrong method learned early can be tough to break.

b. Now that you're back with the coach, relax, let yourself go, accept suggestions, ask questions. The coach isn't taking <u>you</u> apart; it's only your technique that concerns him. Naturally, you're going to feel unsure and off-balance when you try to focus your attention on holding your shoulder back while turning in the discus or shifting in the shot; everyone is--in the learning stage.

Gradually become aware of the parts of the whole event. For example, be conscious of the focus of your eyes while putting the shot. But maintain such awareness of parts as aspects of the whole, not as separate or unrelated entities. As separate entities, they disrupt what you are doing; they become a movement in themselves, rather than phases of the desired movement. For example, assume that your coach has called your attention to the focus of the eyes during the glide in the shot and then to their upward shift along a 75-degree plane during the final drive at the toeboard. Don't get into the circle yet. Take your time, think it through; or better, feel through the whole action of the put and the eye-focus as a phase of that action. Get the feel of it, out of the circle, not merely once but many times.

c. Now try it in the circle; try it as a whole but with an awareness of the phase, of the eye-focus. You did it!--or something like it. Now stop, and again think and feel through what you did, what you didn't do, and what you should have done. Now try it again, and again, and again. Not whole; then part; then whole as three distinct processes. But whole-phase-whole learning as one unified process.

MUSCLE SENSE IN LEARNING TRACK AND FIELD SKILLS

Muscle sense is the most crucial of all means to motor learning. In fact, Steinhaus[1] argues that it is man's most important sense organ, more vital to life than the eyes or the ears. This muscle sense, variously called the kinesthenic or proprioceptive sense, arises from stimulation of sensory organs by body movement, balance, and relation of the parts of the body.[2] Just as the eyes react only to light stimuli, and the ears only to sound stimuli, so the muscle-sense organs react only to sensory stimuli in the muscles and joints.

Movement, changes in muscle tension or stretch, changes in joint angles, pressures, resistances, all stimulate sense organs. These organs, including the muscle spindles, Golgi Tendon organ, Pacinian corpuscle, and Ruffini endings, give rise to sensations that report what the body is doing, and where it is as related to its parts, or to exterior objects where direct contact is made. Much of their effects helps to regulate movement and balance directly without reference to the cortex, but also there is a great deal of "feedback" into our consciousness. As Steinhaus tells us, "We can live without eyes, we can live without ears . . . but without the messages that come to us from our muscles and joint structures we could not talk, walk, breathe, find our mouth to feed it, or follow the printed line while reading--and probably we could not think."

Certainly, without these kinesthetic sense organs, the learning of track and field skills would be impossible, ignoring the fact that they would be meaningless as well.

Undoubtedly, men differ in their muscle-sense sensitivity, just as they do in the sensitivity of their eyes and ears and taste buds and olfactory organs. Some men are extremely high in their ability to discriminate sensations and interpret them muscularly, just as others have a similar ability in intellectual activities. Most men are predominantly "motor-minded," as related to motor learning. That is, they learn a movement best by doing that movement, or by simulating it at slower speeds or in related actions. But there is a wide range of difference among men in this respect. Some men seem to be visually-minded as related to motor learning. They are able to gain insights from watching others directly or in filmed action that are easily transmuted into the desired skill. Other men seem to be orally adept. They seem able to translate words into the action the words describe. Somehow they have trained themselves to

---

[1] Arthur H. Steinhaus, "Your Muscles See more Than Your Eyes," *Jour HPER,* September 1966, 38.

[2] E. A. Fleishman, "The Perception of Body Position in the Absence of Visual Cues," *J. Exp. Psychology,* 1953, 46, 261-270.

listen closely, feel the muscle-sense meanings of the words, then approximate the described skill quite closely. I've coached such men, and was often amazed at their ability to feel the meaning of my words, not merely as sound waves but as muscle movements.

Over 30 years of coaching have convinced me, though the related research is lacking, that this muscle sense or proprioception, to use the more scientific term, is present in each man within a range of potential use. Disregarding innate ability, a skilled performer is able to discriminate small differences between one effort and the next, differences that the unskilled does not detect. By intent awareness, the skilled performer feels such differences, much as the professional coffee or wine taster can, by both inborn talent and training, accept one product and reject another; or as the master violinist's muscle-sense organs detect infinitesimal differences in the movements of his bow.

It is also my experience that some so-called natural athletes, those that learn complex skills without apparent effort, sometimes have little conscious perception of how they do what they do. Skill seems to be acquired by muscle "insight," with little of the mental insight that the Gestaltists associate with learning. They seem to get "the feel" of action, with no conscious analysis on their part of how it is done. The ordinary athlete tends to repeat a movement many times, with awareness, before he learns it, so that there is a considerable involvement of the higher brain centers and therefore consciousness of the learned movements. In contrast, the natural athlete learns a new skill quickly, even at the first attempt, and the resultant skill becomes automatized within the cerebellum with comparatively little involvement of the cortex. In addition, this unawareness of the how of movement could be the effect of early coaching that seldom analyzed action, that instead emphasized doing the action without thought, imitating the techniques of others without taking them apart, so to speak.

Such men, highly effective as they may be as performers in competition, are likely to be less so as coaches. To be a competent teacher of techniques in sport, a man must have a highly developed awareness of the muscle senses. I emphasize the word "awareness." Muscle sense alone is not enough, for it functions primarily within the cerebellum. The effective coach needs the consciousness of the higher-brain centers if he is to have the feel of movement and be able to transmit that feel to others.

We accept the statement that one showing is worth a hundred sayings. It is equally true that one correct doing is worth a hundred showings. For example, it is very difficult to explain in words just how to tie a rather simple knot. It's far more effective to demonstrate how it is done. But one can teach even more quickly by helping the fingers manipulate the tieing. Once they get the feel of the action, learning is well under way. We hardly need to add that coaching requires a combination of all three methods (demonstration, active trying, and words) if it is to be most effective.

MENTAL PRACTICE

Mental practice, just as physical practice, is first of all a way of speaking. In reality there are not two separate practice methods--one physical, the other mental. Rather there are certain practices in which the physical is primary; others, in which the mental predominates. In both, there is a measurable flow of electrical impulses to the related muscles. In mental practice this flow is below the threshold of muscle sensitivity, so that no movement results. Actually I prefer not drawing even this sharp line of difference, for mental practice could also include a concentrated attention on the "how" of technique while moving very slowly through the action.

That there is such a measurable electrical flow was demonstrated by Jacobson (1932, 1934) who, studying relaxation, detected by very sensitive electromyography that mental states such as anxiety, fear, and tension do influence the muscle action potentials. Muscles are stimulated, even though below the threshold of movement. The converse of this was that complete muscle relaxation was achieved only when all such "mental" activity ceased.

Similarly, Shaw[1] measured muscle action potentials when weightlifters imagined, that is, concentrated attention on the simulation of the movements of lifting weights. The more

---

[1] W. A. Shaw, "The Distribution of Muscular Action Potentials during Imaging," *Psychological Record*, 1938, 2, 195.

concentrated the attention, the greater the electrical impulses. Lundervold[1] supported these findings when he reported increased electrical impulses to the muscles active in finger tapping, "when persons tested were sharply commanded to concentrate on the task," and conversely, fewer impulses when the subjects' thoughts were diverted from the tapping.

During my years of coaching, I have been impressed again and again by intelligent motor learners, notably Charles Fonville, former world-record holder in the shot. Sometimes he would come to me before starting a day's practice, saying "Coach, I think I've got it. I've been thinking about the action as the left foot hits the toeboard and I think I've got the hang of it." Then he'd go to the shot circle and immediately perform that phase of the action better than ever before. I asked Charlie several times just what he meant by "thinking." His answers were uncertain but tended to relate thought processes to action and the feel of action. He said that closing his eyes was helpful. He supposed that, even though he was lying in bed or sitting in a chair, his muscles did simulate the movements he was thinking about. Several times, sitting in the library, he found another student looking at him queerly and smiling, so he supposed that his "mental practice" was showing.

We must keep in mind that such men are highly talented, not merely in performing their events, but equally in their mind-muscle insight, their kinesthenic feeling of movement, and overall orientation to their events. Probably they can control their muscle action potentials, though well below the level of the threshold of muscle action, with much greater precision than can the beginner or the ordinary athlete. They're like the yogi who, according to recent observations by scientists, are able to control the autonomic nervous system including heart rate and blood pressure. Or, at a more feasible level, when in India in 1954 I observed and spoke at length with a man who had learned to make rippling movements of his pectorals and abdominals by just such concentrated mental practice.

In trying to decrease competitive tensions and improve skills in Olympic and University skiers, Richard Suinn[2] used a method he called "visuo-motor behavior rehearsal or VMBR" involving three steps: a version of Jacobsen's progressive relaxation, mental imagery as related to competitive performance, and mental imagery as related to improving skill. Results were strongly encouraging though of course still experimental and inconclusive.

MENTAL PRACTICE OFF AND ON THE FIELD. There is a tendency to assume that mental practice must occur away from the activity field, as when lying on one's bed, so that conscious perception and feeling of the desired movements can be undistracted and intently concentrated. Joel Sayre[3] reported that Parry O'Brien attempted such concentration in perfecting his style and his performances in meets,

> He [Parry] spends as much time just thinking about his shot as fondling it in the putting circle. Parry spent many of his nights alone in his ascetic bedroom, the lights dim, his weighty frame slack on the bed. From his tape recorder trickled the soothing sound of his own voice: "Keep low, keep back, keep your movement fast across the circle. Fast now! Fast! Fast! And beat them all! Beat them all!" Parry is convinced that this nocturnal rite adds inches to his toss.

But it is our view that mental practice is not an all-or-none method: all mental, no movement. Mental practice can occur also on the field when, between the regular practice efforts, the athlete reviews mentally what he has just done or is about to do. To refer again to O'Brien, he used to practice alone with but one shot. While walking slowly to and from the shot, he reviewed mentally and felt muscularly the many aspects of what he was doing. Call it thought-

---

[1]Arne Lundervold, "The Measurement of Human Reaction During Training," *Health and Fitness in the Modern World*, Chicago: The Athletic Institute, 1961, 125.

[2]Richard M. Suinn, "Body Thinking: Psychology for Olympic Champs," *Psychology Today*, July 1976, 38-43.

[3]Joel Sayre, "Parry's Power of Positive Thought," *Sports Illustrated*, March 21, 1955, 28.

ful practice if you prefer; the name is unimportant.

But it is important that the powers of the mind be added at their highest levels of concentration and reinforcement to the muscle senses of the body. A separate section emphasizes the crucial values of the muscle sense in motor learning. But to those values must be united the equally crucial values of conscious perception and control of movement.

MENTAL PRACTICE AND PHYSICAL SKILL RISE TOGETHER. The level of learning in mental practice is always proportioned to the level of skill in performing any given event. If performance is unskilled, the mental simulation of that action will be diffused, roughly approximate, vaguely related. That is, mental practice, as related to innervation of the related muscles (refer again to the research of Shaw and Lundervold), can be only slightly more skillful than actual performance. True, when watching a slow-motion movie of an expert performer, one may gain a mental concept of perfect skill, what might be called an eye-cortex concept in which the muscle sense would be at a minimum level. But to practice perfect skill mentally, so that a galvanometer would record electrical impulses to the related muscle groups, one's actual skill must be nearing perfection. Actually, mental practice and physical practice are verbal terms derived from the traditional dualism of mind and body; each focuses on only the extremes of the true range of action. In the human organism they are unified and cannot be separated.

MENTAL PRACTICE IS MORE THAN MENTAL INSIGHT. The concept of mental practice should not be confused with the Gestaltists' "insight," with its connotation of seeing or visualizing the solution of a problem. Kohler's (1925) ape saw the relationship between the stick and the previously unreachable banana. He learned the movement by visualizing relationships. Or to take a more recent example, yesterday I observed my eight-months old granddaughter as she watched her older brother spin a musical top by pumping its handle up and down. He then left the room. She crawled to the top, grasped the handle, dropped it; grasped the handle again, dropped it; then grasped the handle a third time and pumped it up and down in the correct way. I know she never had seen such a top before. There could have been no physical practice. By intent watching (mental practice?) she caught the idea. Gestaltists would call it insight, but such a term tends to ignore the crucial role of the muscle sense, and the unity of eye-cortex-muscle sense by which both Kohler's ape and my granddaughter achieved their goal.

But in the more complex movements of field and track events, mental practice does not produce immediate mastery of a skill, any more than does physical practice. We might gain a so-called mental insight of perfect skill, but actual insight in a mind-body sense can achieve only an approximation of such skill. At each stage, the learner feels again and again that he now has the knack of it, only to discover that the goal constantly recedes. This is so at even the highest levels, even at the level of a Warmerdam, a Brumel, or an O'Brien. Furthermore, one hardly needs the wisdom of a Zen Master to understand that, "he who has a 100 miles to walk should reckon ninety as but half the journey."

THE UNITY OF MENTAL-PHYSICAL PRACTICE. It may help to clarify our thinking if we consider sports practice as a parallelogram in which a diagonal line separates the physical aspect of practice from the mental (Figure A-1). No matter how automatized a skill may have become (AA), so that its actions are controlled entirely by the cerebellum, its improvement requires some degree of action in consciousness, that is, in the cortex. Similarly, no matter at how high a level of abstracting a certain insight of a skill might be, (CC), any attempt to "practice" that skill would result in low-level impulses to the muscles and stimulation of the muscle-spindle sensory organs.

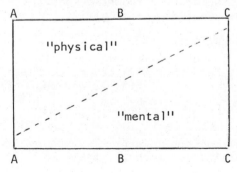

Fig. A.1 -- A crude representation of the mental-physical unity of sports action. Note that the dividing diagonal line never reaches zero -- all of one and none of the other.

Personally, I like much better the Chinese figure on the right, representing the yin-yang or unity-of-opposites principle.

HOW CLOSELY SHOULD MENTAL PRACTICE BE CONTROLLED BY THE COACH? A study by Jones[1] compared the values of two methods of mental practice in learning a new gymnastic skill: (1) controlled practice, and (2) individual freedom of practice. The first group had specific written instructions and close supervision of their mental practice. The second were free to discover their own insights and ways of procedure. Jones found that the undirected group learned more quickly, and reasoned that self-initiated methods led to better kinesthenic images and greater concentration in learning.

Such conclusions should not lead the coach to ignore mental practice altogether. They do caution us against over-coaching in all its forms, and suggest that the gist of coaching is to stimulate, encourage, and help the athlete to help himself.

TECHNIQUES OF MENTAL PRACTICE. Mental practice should not be thought of as some fanciful far-out method in which occult training of the mind produces some mysterious or magical effect on body training. Oxendine (1968, 238) states "there is research evidence to support the belief that a planned program of mental rehearsal might effectively supplement physical practice. . . . A planned program, and one in which some specific guidance is offered, seems more likely to result in useful conceptualization than will an informal or unstructured program." True, such research is scanty and its conclusions far from final, but it tends to support the basic tenets of mental practice. The following suggestions may be helpful in the development of method:

1. Mental Practice During Regular Practice on the Field. For example, in the high jump: (a) Think of the crossbar as at least six inches higher than your head; think-feel through in a mind-muscle sense the kind of run-jump that will clear such a bar--run velocity, rhythm, eye-head inclination, arm-leg actions, etc.--but emphasize the whole action, not its parts. (b) Think-feel through the particular phase of the jump you are now trying to improve; concentrate intently, so as to innervate the nerve-muscles of that phase. (c) Jump in terms of this phase-in-whole awareness, with special awareness of what happens during the phase being learned. (d) Immediately on landing, think-feel through the jump. What was the feeling of right action? Of wrong action? How will correct action feel on the next jump?

Repeat such a jump many times. Note that any one of these four steps can be emphasized by giving it more time and attention and concentration of awareness.

2.   Immediate Playback and Review of One's Own Performance, Using Special Movie or Graphic Sequence Cameras. Correct action can be reinforced and incorrect inhibited by immediate reactions of approval or disapproval. Repeat the correct action kinesthetically.

3. Mental Practice with Movies. Loop films of expert performers can be of great value for mental practice. Various methods can be devised: (a) Attentive awareness, in a mind-muscle sense, of the whole action at normal speed, emphasizing rhythm and the skill as a whole; (b) Attentive awareness of a phase of action at slow speed; (c) Immediately following either "a" or "b" use mental practice to reinforce the desired skill; for better concentration, try closing the eyes and attend to the muscle cues of correct action. A coach or other athlete might add his personal cues to correct action, but concentrated attention is done best when alone. (d) Immediately following such a "mental" session, go to the field and practice what was seen and felt.

4. Mental Practice with Sequence Pictures. Once the beginner has gained a feeling for the wholeness of action, sequence pictures with detailed comments provide cues to the details of action that might not be seen in movies or in watching experts on the field.

5. The Laws of Learning Apply to Mental Practice. Since the main difference between physical and mental practice is merely one of degree of nerve-muscle innervation, the accepted laws of motor learning have their applications for mental practice. What will be written here about reinforcement, length and distribution of practice, specificity of learning, and so forth,

---

[1] J. G. Jones, "Motor Learning without Demonstration of Physical Rehearsal, under Two Conditions of Mental Practice," Unpublished Master's Thesis, University of Oregon, 1963.

has implications, though not full application, for mental practice. Of special importance is the maintenance of a close relationship, especially in time, of these two kinds of practice.

SUMMARY. 1. Mental practice in its various forms can be of practical use in track and field. It should not be confused with the illusory mind training of the now discredited faculty psychology. Actually so-called mental practice is as much training of the muscle sense as of the mind, depending on the method and degree of emphasis.

2. Related research in motor learning tends to confirm such practical use.

3. Mental practice is not a new approach to motor learning, though its precise method might be so described. Human learning of physical skills always has had a "mental" aspect. Even inattentive drill has a "mental" accompaniment, though below the level of awareness.

4. Though no related research has been reported, we can assume that the closer the relationship between mental and physical practice in time, method, and action, the greater the reinforcement of learning.

5. Mental practice is helpful for all stages of learning from beginner to expert. As mastery of skill progresses, crude approximations become more and more precisely controlled "movements."

6. The techniques of mental practice that will be developed in the future will be increasingly consistent with those of physical practice. Some will develop a mid-point method in which it would be difficult to say whether the practice is mental or physical. (As illustration, see Herrigel, Eugen, ZEN IN THE ART OF ARCHERY.)

REINFORCEMENT IN LEARNING TRACK AND FIELD SKILLS

The concept of reinforcement has been of increasing value in the psychology of motor learning over the past half-century or more. It was basic to Thorndike's "Law of Effect" which, oversimplified, stated that a response that satisfies, strengthens a modifiable connection; a response that annoys, weakens it. It was inherent in Pavlov's experiments in conditioning in which a reward (food for the dog) tends to connect two stimuli (food and the sound of a tuning fork); that is, contiguity led to reinforcement. Hull related reinforcement to a reduction of need or drive; Skinner, to "operants," the memory of reward for certain behavior in past situations. Most other schools of learning, including the Gestalt school (Kohler, 1947), Field Theory (Lewin, 1935), Organismic (Goldstein, 1939), and the Holistic-dynamics theory of Maslow (1954) have used and contributed to a more effective use of the reinforcement concept. Unfortunately, the limited space of this book permits only a very brief summary of its more everyday uses for track coaching.

KNOWLEDGE OF RESULTS (FEEDBACK). If successful response is to be reinforced, the outcome must be satisfying, must follow the response quickly, and must be directly related to the specific response desired. Other things being equal, the greater the feeling of satisfaction, the sharper and more related the awareness of the desired action, and the more immediate the resulting satisfaction, the more likely that response is to be repeated.

In field events and in track events involving skill, there are many criteria by which an athlete can judge a response as successful. Of these, distance is the most obvious and, unfortunately, the most commonly used. How far did it go? How high was the bar? What does the watch show? But this is an indirect and often erroneous way of judging success as related to skill. Many factors other than skill may produce distance: effort, relaxation, balance, throwing angle, speed of preliminary movements, and many more.

It all seems simple to follow Skinner's admonition, "Elicit the response you want and reward it," especially when applied to Skinner's pigeons and rats. But such a formula becomes most complex when applied to the many aspects and attitudes of response that occur in track and field. Of course there are some coaches who keep their coaching very close to the simple level of Skinner's pigeons. In fact, I've worked with two assistant coaches who had just such a tendency. Their desired response was simple, "Clear the bar. Throw for distance, Win!" When these things happened, the athletes were rewarded. Admitted, they had fun practicing and competing, with little of the frustrations of precise techniques. The athletes were likely to be good competitors, for this is what they practiced. But maximum performance as related to potentials? Never! A few men did acquire surprisingly correct technique, perhaps by observing others at meets or by loop films. They certainly had excellent team spirit and they did have fun, perhaps more fun than do the more seriously and technically trained track team members. Make of that what you will.

However, the method of this book is to proceed through complexity by relatively arduous efforts to the simplicity of mastery of skill. The truly simple technique is not that of the novice or untrained natural athlete, but rather that of the master athlete who has struggled with technique for years until he has perfected it, and now performs so easily and "naturally" that all complexity is gone. The action is simple, even though at a very high level of skill.

REINFORCEMENT METHODS. First concern should be for wholeness, for getting the overall feel, balance, rhythm of the whole event. Reinforcement should be directed in terms of each of these phases of the whole action, one at a time. But always with part-in-whole awareness. And always with an immediate "Yes!" for the desired action; the more enthusiastic the "Yes!" the greater the reinforcement.

At first, only the coach--or another knowledgeable athlete can give such affirmation. Some signal: "Right! That's it! Good!"--if given immediately while the feel of the action is still keen--produces reinforcement, strengthens the nerve-muscle channels of action. At first, an athlete's concentration on one phase of action may result in a degree of paralysis by analysis as happened with the fabled centipede,

> A centipede was happy, quite,
>   Until a frog in fun said,
> "Pray tell, which leg goes after which?"
> This worked her mind to such a pitch,
> She lay distracted in the ditch,
> And knew not how to run.

As long as the athlete is thinking in terms of segments of action, the whole action will not be smooth and won't feel good. If that is all he experiences, a weakening of the desired response will occur; inhibition, not learning, is likely to take place. But the trained observer, the coach, overcomes this disturbed feeling by the strength of his affirmative "Right!" How fortunate the learner whose coach can say "Right!" with the strong conviction of personal bone-muscle experience.

Few athletes take an analytical view of their own efforts on their own initiative. Such an attitude must be learned, usually by way of the coach but also from fellow athletes, and even then it requires time, perhaps years of time. Quite often an athlete will go through four years of high school, and even four years more of college, accepting the reinforcing approval of his coach, but with only incidental awareness of the kinesthetic cues within his own muscles. Though some of the best talks to coaches on techniques have been given by athletes, some of the least analytical have also come from athletes, despite their record performances.

Perhaps the best example of strong reinforcement occurs when a group of athletes get together on the field, or in the locker room, and talk-feel their way through the details of their event. Listen to, or rather, watch such a group sometime. You'll see more of muscle movements than you'll hear of words, and the words will be more related to action and the feel of action than they are to the theory and science of action. "I was watching the champ and saw him do this--" (Simulated action by A that is repeated by the others, actually or by an inner simulation of the movement.) "Yes, I saw him do it just that way, but he did it because his balance was like this--" (Simulated action by B, repeated by the others.) And so on until the point was clear--in their muscles as well as in their heads. It's a wise coach that encourages such group discussions. I remember how we used to accuse Coach Cromwell of USC of shirking his coaching duties, and leaving the job to his champion athletes. Yet we rarely saw a poorly coached USC field event man.

Under such a system, the athlete does not have to translate--no, that's too easy a word--transmute the words of the coach into the muscle ac tions of the event. Transmute means to change from one kind of form or nature to another, and that's not at all a simple process. Now, his own cues or feelings of action are the reinforcing agent. He learns to interpret these cues so that "it feels right," or "it feels wrong." Some men develop an amazingly sensitive muscle-sense of proper technique, often more sensitive than the eye-sense of the coach. Since such cues are simultaneous with the action, they tend to give maximum reinforment from a time standpoint.

But it is a very rare athlete that doesn't need the additional reinforcement of confirmation of correct action from others, whether those others be a coach, a fellow-athlete, or a playback of his own performance by a sequence or movie camera. Even at the Olympic level, athletes need and seek such confirmation. It's a primary function of an Olympic Coach.

REINFORCING APPROXIMATIONS OF SKILL. A beginner's first efforts tend to be rough approximations of the desired skill, and his awareness of his actions is vague, out-of-focus, not mentally separable into parts. If the approximation is an improvement, the coach says, "Yes!" but the tyro is likely to ask, "What do you mean? What did I do?" Gradually, these approximations begin to narrow, are channeled into the precise nerve-muscle patterns that we call a skilled effort. Our main point here is that approval does not wait for some desired perfect effort, but is given for improvement, for a closer approximation of such an effort. This applies to the whole action of a jump or throw, but equally important, to each small phase of action as it becomes the focus of coaching attention. A coach may direct attention on the movements of the left arm during the high jump take-off. If the athlete approximates the desired action, even though very imprecisely, the effort should be reinforced.

REINFORCING SPECIFIC PHASES OF SKILL. This book emphasizes a holistic approach to coaching. Whenever feasible, perform the whole action in throwing or jumping, with attention focussed on the particular aspect that is being learned. For example, in the high jump though attention might be on gradual acceleration of speed in the run, total learning will occur more effectively if actual jumps are taken, rather than running without jumping. But since reinforcement is greater when the affirming response is close in time-action, it will help if the coach yells "O.K.!" at the crucial moment during the run, rather than after the jump is completed. Loud enough of course for the jumper to relate approval while in action to the muscle-sense cues of that precise moment. If such approval comes some 15 or more seconds later when the jumper has walked back to the start of another effort, it has a lesser potential for reinforcement. My own coaching experience suggests that men vary greatly in their sensitivity to such cues, and in their power to recall their relevance.

Usually, when concern is with technique rather than with clearing the bar, the attempt ends with the bar on the ground. Despite all the disclaimers of the coach, this is easily interpreted as failure, with a resulting inhibition of the technique that produced it. The immediate and loud approval of the coach during the action helps prevent such a misinterpretation.

EXTINCTION OF ERRORS IN TECHNIQUE. The problem of how to eliminate so-called errors in technique is one of the most difficult, and crucial, or all aspects of coaching. After all, we coach men, not techniques, and some men are mighty sensitive to being analyzed (taken apart), even if only in the mind of a coach.

To understand the problem of errors best, they should be seen holistically in terms of the athlete's total attitude. A coach's knowledge of mechanics may cause him to judge a certain action as an error in technique. To the athlete, regardless of theoretical mechanics, his habitual way of performing an event has produced greater performance, a degree of success, and feels right! But this coach says it's not right; it's an error. That's both disturbing and confusing, not merely to the related muscle-nerve patterns, but to the athlete as a person.

When the athlete first does the mechanically-right action, though the coach yells "Right!" it feels wrong. At that stage, the "right" action is not integrated into his habitual way of jumping or throwing. His well-learned muscle-nerve cues cry out "Wrong!" and tend to inhibit further actions of the same kind. A coach has to be respected if his "Right!" is to achieve the dual task of strengthening the desired bond to correct action, and also disinhibit the effect of the athlete's cues that tell him "Wrong!" As long as the athlete is unable to integrate the technically sound action into his own individual style, his performance will be uncoordinated, tense, unsatisfying, and probably disappointing in height or distance. To serve as a positive reinforcement, a coach's approving signals must over-balance these negatives. We should emphasize that if a coach is critical and expresses disapproval of errors, he piles negatives on negatives. Small wonder the athlete often rebels inwardly, sometimes outwardly, and even quits the sport.

There are many ways of trying to solve the problem of extinguishing errors in technique; every coach and athlete with imagination will devise their own. Here we shall suggest three methods, all positive in their approach:

(1) In practice, encourage and reward attention to technique and the feel of correct technique; ignore or "punish" all concern for performance in terms of distance. Get rid of all measuring tapes or markers in practice. Keep the bar high enough to challenge the jumper, encourage him to make full efforts toward clearance as long as attention is on method, and to ignore the bar that falls to the ground. Remind them that the golfer who keeps his inner eye on distance can never keep his outer eye on the ball.

(2) Devise a major change in method, an entirely new total technique. In the high jump, change from the roll to the straddle or to the flop; in the javelin, change from a side-facing to a front-facing style. Now the attitude is toward learning something new, not on getting rid of the old.

(3) Ignore all direct reference to the error. Shift attention to some quite different phase of action that the coach knows can correct the error. Don't mention that there is such a relationship. Example: in the shot put, correct an "in-the-bucket" left foot by emphasizing the flexion of the right hip and the clockwise turn to the right by the right foot, shoulder, head and eyes. Make no reference to the left foot, but the coach will note that the left foot does not now drop "in the bucket."

The relative effectiveness of these methods will vary greatly with the teachability of the learner, but also the teaching skill of the coach. The latter is definitely a fine art in which imagination and a delicate touch are essential. Sometimes the technique the athlete learns first is very hard to change. For four years I coached a college athlete in a new, mechanically more effective, and very different style of high jumping. We thought he had learned it well. The old style was gone. But today, some 40 years later, I can still feel the shock of watching him in his senior-year Big 10 Conference meet, revert to his old style and clear the bar at a new record height!

Did this prove the old style was more mechanically "natural" for him, and that we had made a mistake in trying to change him? It's hard to say. But it did prove that the old style was more deeply anchored in his system so that when he dropped all inhibitions and all awareness of how he was jumping, he reverted to the style that had been more deeply reinforced over more years. I am reminded of my own experience in driving cars. For 20 years or more I drove gear-shift models. Even after five years or so of driving cars with automatic shifts, I often felt a strong urge in moments of semi-emergency to lift the left foot to the non-existent clutch and my right hand to the non-existent shift rod.

Throughout this discussion we have emphasized a positive approach, "elicit the response you want and reward it." But sometimes a fourth, more negative method may be helpful, if only to help the athlete compare the feel of doing it wrong with that of doing it right. Direct attention to the feel of the old "wrong" technique until the athlete senses that feeling as "wrong." Now try to associate the feeling of "right" with the new "right" technique. Rebuke and thereby inhibit what is "wrong"; reward (encourage, praise) what is "right." But also remember that the sooner the whole movement is "out of mind" and automatic, the better.

All of this becomes more difficult of course when, as happens occasionally, an athlete confuses the coach's criticism of technique as being a criticism of themselves personally. This produces a resistance to teaching techniques that even the most artful coach will find hard to overcome. Lack of space prevents fuller discussion; the reader will do well to study the chapter, "The Athlete Who Resists Coaching," (Ogilvie and Tutko, 1966, 26-45).

But in all such coaching, the emphasis should be strongly positive. As the old song goes, eliminate the negative by accentuating the positive. One could very well evaluate coaching skill on the degree to which this is accomplished.

FREQUENCY OF INDIVIDUAL COACHING. Should a coach be present each time an athlete practices, and give reinforcing approval of every correct effort? Disregarding the problem of being five places at one time, would such coaching be best? Most research suggests that learning occurs faster when other-person reinforcement is frequent, but not ever-present. There should be some opportunity for isolated self-evaluation. In fact, some effective coaches allow beginners a week or so of practice without any coaching so they can orient themselves to the event without the confusion of coaching analysis. Other coaches argue that errors in technique become embedded during that first week, and are hard to erase later. Take your choice.

In general, reinforcement is stronger and retained longer when it comes from the athlete's own muscle or kinesthetic sense. "That felt good! Let's see, what did I do? How did it feel? That was great!" It would take most enthusiastic praise from a respected coach to equal the strengthening effect of such a personal experience--assuming, of course, that what was interpreted as "right" was really right.

In our opinion, the evidence for maximum speed of learning and retention of correct technique suggests frequent reinforcement from the coach for the beginner, with a gradual decrease in frequency as the learner becomes aware of his own kinesthetic cues to correct action. Once the feel of action is gained, and especially if a small group of knowledgeable athletes will appraise each other, the frequency of adult coaching can be diminished. Above all, as someone once warned me, be aware of KISS--Keep It Simple, Stupid."

Obviously, individual differences would produce a different pattern of coaching for Johnny Milquetoast from that of a self-sufficient Roger Bannister (1955, 245) who insisted that "self-discovery is most rapid if we set out on the early stages alone. . . . The things a man learns for himself he never forgets . . . the things a man does by himself, he does best." On the other hand, we must consider that Roger was a runner whose skill was learned at the age of four, not a field-event man whose skill is usually learned at the age of 16 or later. The two problems are quite different.

EXTRINSIC REWARDS AND PUNISHMENTS. Prizes, awards, scholarships, travel do engender great enthusiasm and do motivate effort in general. When Jim Ryun was asked if his sacrifice of a normal social life had been worthwhile, he inquired as to how many of those boys who attended parties and dances regularly had ever seen Moscow and Helsinki? Such extrinsic rewards do ensure regular practice, do heighten attention and effort, and do urge conformance with training rules off the field. They are often attended by social recognition and a sense of self-importance.

But such material rewards are of lesser direct value in reinforcing improvements in skill in practice. First, there is a long separation in time between doing it right in practice and the reward following a meet performance. It would be a most retentive kinesthetic sense indeed that could relate the two in a degree that would strengthen the bonds of learning. Second, such prizes are for clearing the bar or for throwing farther than anyone else, not for the degree of technical skill. In competition, it's what you do that counts, not how you do it.

Some coaches use rewards in practice, from milk shakes to an invitation to the coach's home for dinner, but these are for measured performance, rarely for skill. The latter tends to be too subjective and immeasureable. In summary, when coaching for skill, rely on the intrinsic reinforcements that lie in the feel of action performed well. The inherent safisfaction aroused directly and immediately by such an action is enough to ensure its repetition. There's no need to reach outside for more tangible reinforcement.

COACHING FUNDAMENTALS AND DETAILS

A sound coach always emphasizes fundamentals in teaching the techniques of field events. But don't let that unqualified statement deceive you. For what is fundamental varies with the learner's natural ability, his expertness in this particular event, his understanding of the principles of mechanics, and of course, the entire approach of the coach in dealing with the problem.

As a matter of fact, it can be said that, though none disagree with our statement of the principle, each coach has his own unique interpretation of its meaning. I have known some "coaches" who, pleading the dangers of over-coaching details, have walked away from the problem altogether by making fun and competition in practice the main path to development. At the other extreme, some technical experts seem more concerned about verbalizing the details of their own theories than about advancing the performances of their athletes.

A group of experts could undoubtedly agree on a few fundamentals for each of the field events. But they could never agree on what is a fundamental for this particular athlete at this stage of his career. For to do so would necessitate a long-time and intimate coaching relationship with the boy, as well as with the manner in which he had been coached.

What is fundamental changes constantly with the technical development of each athlete. What would have been a disrupting detail to a beginner can become an entirely acceptable fundamental at a later stage of his development (Oxendine, 1968, 97). This suggests that a detail or non-essential of technique can be defined validly as one that tends to disrupt development more than it helps. What the athlete can ingest and use may not be a fundamental but it is quickly assimilated with what is fundamental. O'Brien's yogic exercises would be likely to disrupt the practice of a beginning shot putter; to him they were fundamental and in accord with his drive for maximum performance.

But also, the difference between what is fundamental and what is a disrupting detail depends on the coaching method. If the coaching follows a holistic pattern in which details are never presented separately but rather as they emerge out of fundamentals, then disruption will be minimal. In my own coaching, the use of the eyes was a fundamental in many phases of field events. Change the eye direction or focus, and over-all balance or power will change with it. I've heard many coaches say that calling attention to the eye focus was disrupting, and in their experience, a non-essential detail. Of course I insisted on so-called mental practice during which one got the feel of the eye change before actually jumping or throwing, feeling it as inherent in the whole action. Disrupting? Oh, a little; all change is disrupting at first. But acceptably so, for it was soon integrated into the whole.

In other words, this problem is not so much one of distinguishing clearly between what is fundamental and what is a non-essential detail, as it is of coaching what is immediately relevant and in ways that make that relevancy clear to the learner. Elsewhere we have retold the story of the distracted centipede. The question of "which leg goes after which" just wasn't relevant to her continued smooth locomotion. A similar story is told by Charles Laughton about a fellow-actor, Charles Boyer, who had forgotten his lines--but good! What happened? "Suddenly, at the same moment I was saying it, I saw a certain word on the page. That word blanked me out on all the other words. It was as simple--and awful--as that!"

We began by advocating the coaching of fundamentals, but now there seems to be no clear distinction between fundamentals and details, at least in terms of what is essential to improvement, or of the size of the miscle groups involved. We tend to think of details as being related to fine muscle movements. But a fine muscle movement can be just as essential to improvement as a large one.

Whatever distinction is made between fundamentals and details should (1) be very flexible, and (2) be in terms of relevancy, especially in the learner's mind, to the particular phase of technique on which he is now centering his attention. Whatever is essential to mastery and relevant now can be viewed as fundamental. Whatever is essential to mastery but not now relevant to present practice can be viewed as a disruptive detail. Whatever seems non-essential at this moment should be ignored, but with an open mind that can accept it as a crucial coaching point next week or next year.

Coaching non-essential details is often associated with those who theorize or merely talk so much that their words distract from learning. Needless to say, words should be closely fitted to what is essential. Once an athlete closes his ears to the endless flow of words, even the most sound of coaching ideas will never gain acceptance. Coaching words should merge with movement, not distract from it.

Some coaches, whether from other busy-ness or merely laziness, never learn technique in full and detail. They then excuse their ignore-ance by claiming to coach only fundamentals. Their claimed fear of "overcoaching" leads them to underrate coaching. They give the boys a few "fundamentals," then allow them freedom to find their own way, to develop their own details of technique on a trial and--all too often--error basis.

In fact, some very successful coaches have followed this practice, have proclaimed its virtues at clinics and in journals. But somehow, at some time, by some one, the details must be taught--by an assistant coach, by a previous coach, by other athletes, by study of films and books. Details must be learned if mastery is to be gained. To be learned, they must be practiced. To be practiced, the learner must be aware of them--in specific detail. Such awareness comes best through sound coaching.

A RANGE OF TOLERABLE ERROR

Sound field event coaching recognizes that so-called perfect form cannot be described exactly and narrowly, but rather within a range of what industry calls "tolerance of error"--that is, within a range of error that does not make a significant difference. For example, in the shot put, the left foot at the toeboard should be placed with the toe in line with the heel of the right. But near-maximal puts can be made within a 3 to 4-inch range of this position. Any negative effect of an "error" at one extreme or the other can be balanced in various ways-- faster hip rotation and stretch reflex in related muscles, better bracing and upward thrust by the left leg, directing the put slightly to the left, and the like.

To use a different example, Charlie Dumas won the 1956 Olympic high jump (6-11½) after having jumped 7-½ in the Olympic Trials. In his approach run, he took five very slow and only three fast steps--an intolerable error if judged by the velocities gained by modern jumpers-- Yashchenko, Stones, Wszola. But for Dumas and his day, the error was quite tolerable--a world record and the first man ever over seven feet.

The first corollary to this principle is that one should select a style that is mechanically sound for the goal one has in mind. If the goal must be easily and quickly attained because of lack of time or low motivation then the style must be one that is quickly learned. For example one would select the hop style in throwing the javelin. But if one hopes to attain maximum performance, regardless of time and difficulty, then a more mechanically perfect style would be chosen.

The second corollary is that, having selected a style that can produce maximum performance, there should be perfection of the individual's variation of that style. For example, there is much discussion as to the merits of the longtime Feuerbach style of putting the shot as compared with the discus style with its faster hip rotation and shot momentum. Each method has certain strengths and weaknesses. This corollary assumes that the crucial factor is not so much the style in general as it is the degree to which the individual has perfected all phases of his own unique style.

As one more example, the question as to which starting block spacing is best in sprinting can be answered (1) by deciding whether the spacing is within the range of tolerable error, mechanically, and (2) whether this sprinter has perfected a total pattern of starting that is best adapted to his unique block spacing.

In summary, this concept that there is a range within which error can be tolerated has many and valuable uses. It applies to overall technique, as indicated by the accepted range of high jump styles--western, straddle, Fosbury flop--each with its variations of the run-up, transition, take-off, clearance, but all acceptable. It applies to individual differences in all related factors--height, weight, power, attitude, nutrition, you name it. It applies to the specifics of technique--angle of throw in the discus or javelin, speed in the high jump or long jump run-up, distance through which power is applied in the shot, and 101 other aspects. And always its significance depends on the level of excellence in performance; the closer performance is to human ultimates, the narrower the tolerance of error. To sharpen understanding, review the section in this book on "Coaching fundamentals and details."

ERRORS OF ANTICIPATION

Dyson (1962, 143) coined a most valuable phrase, "errors of anticipation," which is very useful in coaching field events, as well as the skill aspects of starting and hurdling on the track. Perhaps the most common example is the golfer who cannot keep his eye on the ball, in anticipation--or better, in apprehension--of its flight down the fairway. The same kind of error occurs in our sport. I've watched the great stylist, Al Feuerbach, anticipate the upward heave of the shot by rotating and lifting the eyes-shoulders-torso before landing his right foot at the center of the circle. I've watched Al Oerter, four-time Olympic discus champion, anticipate the final power drive by a too-early leading of the eyes-head-shoulders. I've observed Olympic pole vaulters, such as Dave Roberts or Earl Bell, anticipate the upward pull-push by turning their hips an instant too soon.

Almost no one is entirely free of this error; certainly not the beginner who anticipates the effects of action and so neglects the action itself. High jumpers anticipate the layout over the bar, and so neglect the takeoff actions that ensure full power upward. Long jumpers and triple jumpers lose running velocity just before the board as they anticipate too soon the upward leap.

The specific cause of such anticipation is specific to each individual and each situation, but in general it is a failure in proper concentration, or a failure to maintain the whole action when emphasizing a particular phase of that action. The solution lies in learning to inhibit the doubt or distraction, and in concentrating on how the action is done rather than on its effects.

Several decades ago, coaches tended to emphasize the importance of "follow-through" in field events. But later they found that such emphasis led to anticipation of the follow-through, that men were up-and-out before they had settled down and applied full force. Since then, follow-through has been taught as an inherent ballistic effect of proper precedent action, and so could be largely ignored as a coaching point.

A 1978 study by Gideon Ariel[1] compared the techniques of the top six shotputters at the Montreal Olympics with those of a group of national class U.S. putters. Among the latter, he found two examples of errors of anticipation.

> *Although the clinic throwers reached high accelerations in the stance phase, they attained these...too early...and were unable to maintain the high values. The Olympic throwers...started with lower accelerations and attained higher values in the middle of the stance phase....*
> *In most cases the clinic putters raised the body prematurely during the gliding and transitional phases. The most efficient technique maintained the center of gravity low during the push-off phase, then raised it as rapidly as possible.*

IMPROVEMENT IN CONSISTENCY OF SKILL AS WELL AS IN DISTANCE

In the throwing events, we usually judge improvement by distance. But exclusive concern for distance may lead to increased tension and defects in skill. Many sound coaches use a second criterion of improvement in the throwing events—a decrease in radius of the landing pattern of the implements. The pattern made by a beginner will be spread out over a relatively wide area. His distances will be both short and long, as well as wide to the left and to the right. This will be true even though some defect, such as a foot "in the bucket" may shift his pattern to the left. For example, after a large number of puts in the shot, the landing pattern may have a radius of six or more feet. There will be little centering of the pattern; many puts will lie near the circumference of the pattern.

In contrast, the pattern made by an expert will be much smaller. His skill will be channeled, will be in a certain groove as we say. Now, after a long workout in the shot, the landing pattern will tend to be along a single plane of power application. The distance may range widely, but because of differences in effort, not of skill.

This principle is of practical use. Sound coaching will encourage a man to make his throws in practice "for distance" but always within the pattern of consistent skill. How far the implement lands should be balanced with how skillfully it was thrown, that is, with how well it landed within the pattern of consistency. In my own coaching I used to place two lines on the ground. One was an arc at a distance less than maximum for the thrower; the other was a radius which set the line of throw. This radius varied with the event and with the athlete. Depending on various peculiarities of style, such as the placement of the left foot at the toeboard, a great putter might put just to the left or possibly to the right of the centerline.

Though not as obvious, this principle applies equally to the jumping events. Certainly it applies to the pattern of steps made in the run-up. But the discerning coaching eye can see it also in the various aspects of technique while airborne. The coaching method remains the same—practice at near-maximum heights, if that seems best, but always within the pattern of consistency in skill.

---

[1] Gideon B. Ariel, Ph.D., Biomechanical Analysis of Shotputting," *Track & Field Quarterly Review*, Vol. 79 #4, Winter 1979, p. 27.

PLATEAUS OF LEARNING MOTOR SKILLS. Learners are less apt to become discouraged if they know about plateaus. Otherwise they tend to feel they have reached their limit of achievement, when actually they've hardly begun. I've always been fascinated by the implications for motor learning of the saying, "He that has walked 90 miles of a 100-mile journey is but halfway there."

Such slowdowns, especially in learning sports skills, have many possible causes, too numerous and complex to more than suggest here. Perhaps the technique being used is the limiting factor. The scissors style in high jumping has a lower maximum than does the straddle style. Perhaps a detail of technique is the limiting factor. A slow, uncertain run in the high jump can outweigh excellent technique in clearing the bar. Perhaps certain basic training has been neglected. Lack of related strength training limits performance in the high jump.

But there are also mental-emotional causes of plateaus. Over-training can produce chronic fatigue and disinterest. Failure or success in some other "unrelated" activity can reduce motivation in this activity. The distraction of other interests or other requirements may lead to a lower level of effort.

Obviously the method of breaking through these plateaus must be fashioned to the cause, rather than merely to the symptom. The traditional lay-off from activity is seldom a direct solution. It may work, but only if it brings about a fresh analysis of the problem which discloses the specific cause. One must hasten to add that in dealing with humans, there are often multiple causes, as well as multiple reactions to what seems to be the same cause.

Weight lifters speak of reaching a "sticking point," a stage at which no greater weight can be lifted. Suggestions given by most experts is that the overall conditions be changed in some way significant to the learner. Active-rest may refresh the energies. A new training partner may stimulate new insights and energies. The poundage can be reduced significantly with greater emphasis on explosiveness, so that a sense of "new beginning" is experienced. All such suggestions have reference to development in the field events.

Appendix B
DYNAMICS OF RELAXATION

THE DYNAMICS OF RELAXATION IN TRACK AND FIELD

Agreement can be easily reached on the general meaning of relaxation as a loosening or release of tension, as a letting-go from contraction or anxiety or inhibition. But such "letting-go" can occur in a multitude of ways and at many degrees of release. Relaxation can be total when it seeks recovery from exertion or release from tension. Or it can relate to the short-time and limited area of the relaxation phase of repeated movement.

From a physical standpoint, a completely relaxed muscle is inert, electrically silent, with no muscle fibers in contraction. But in all live tissue, even though motionless, some electrical discharge is always present along with some degree of muscle tension (tonus), even though below the threshold of movement. Above this threshold there are gradations of muscle strength and speed of contraction. These gradations occur by varying the frequency of nerve excitation and thereby the number of muscle-fiber groups that are active. Each muscle-fiber group has its own precise threshold of excitation. At that precise level, the unit contracts and continues to contract until the excitation falls below its critical threshold (Astrand, 1970, 79ff.).

It follows that the sports meaning of the expression "a relaxed muscle" is always relative to the ongoing action, whatever its degree of strength or speed. In a voluntary, all-out, dynamic contraction, no motor units would be inhibited, all would be active to their fullest extent, even though the movement can be validly described as relaxed. In relatively slow, repetitive movements, as occurs in running, relaxation is related primarily to the antagonistic muscles. In 1889 the great English physiologist, Sir Charles Sherrington, demonstrated that stimulation of a single point in the motor cortex of the brain excites the motoneurons which innervate the flexor muscles, and at the same time inhibits the motoneurons to the antagonistic extensors. In this case, a relaxed running action would maintain a precise alternation of innervation-inhibition. It seems reasonable to assume that tieing up while running is related to a breakdown of this alternation, as well as to increased contracture of muscle-fiber units within the running muscles.

But there are other uses of the word "relaxation." Relaxation is one way of looking at skill, for example, or at coordination, or power, or at self-control during physical effort. In sports, relaxation is inherent in the problems of hypertension and emotional stress that develop during the days and hours before important competition. In some events, such as the pole vault or discus throw, maintaining mental and physical relaxation (imperturbability) during the long waits between trials is a major problem, especially just prior to the final crucial efforts. In other events, reciprocal contraction-relaxation must be optimum, not merely of the leg and arm muscles but of many muscles of the torso as well. In all field events, certain maximum contractions can result only by "inhibiting the inhibitions," to use the expression of Ikai and Steinhaus (1963, 137), that is, by relaxing all inhibiting fibers.

Such a wide range of meaning for a single word may confuse as much as it clarifies, and we should be wary as to just which aspect of relaxation is being discussed. Of course, all this becomes even more complicated when we realize that no two competitive situations are ever exactly the same. What is effective in the way of achieving relaxation in one competition may be quite ineffective in another. What the gestaltists call the figure-ground or surround is always changing.

This makes it clear that there can be no one definition of relaxation. The physiologist may argue that ultimately it all boils down to a nerve-muscle condition, but that over-simplifies the problem. Better understanding and use requires a multiple approach, both in definitions and methods of achievement. We shall suggest ten: (1) relaxation through skill learning, (2) differential relaxation, (3) holistic reorientation, (4) withdrawal and return, (5) progressive relaxation, (6) positive auto-suggestion, (7) relaxation by "emptying" the mind, (8) by repressing the negatives, (9) by underloading the action, and (10) by concentration on positive external factors. Actually there is an infinity of methods, limited only by our insights during analysis and abstraction. But these ten will suggest the range of possibility.

The first six of these methods tend to be related to general rest and recovery, and can be used throughout the year, though especially during the days and hours preceding competition. The last three methods seek to achieve relaxation while actually competing.

RELAXATION THROUGH SKILL LEARNING. First efforts at a skill, without spectators, coaching, or conscious analysis, tends to be relaxed. Later, coaching and attention to the "parts" of skill create uncertainty and self-doubt, and lead to tension and negative contractions. This is magnified when competition is impending and the learner is anxious about his lack of readiness. But as he masters skill and succeeds in competition, his inhibitions--in both a physical and mental sense--tend to fall away (Åstrand, 1970, 80). The useless, random, and counter movements cease; the positive movements become more deeply channeled. Somehow the muscles coordinate of themselves, without conscious direction. We can see this clearly in skilled piano playing, for example, in which any attempt at conscious control would be disruptive.

Progress will be facilitated if the beginner is made aware of this tendency of any new skill to be accompanied by both physical and emotional tensions, including wasteful efforts by unrelated and opposing muscles. If he feels certain that these negatives will disappear with practice, he'll relax much more quickly. For example, to tell beginners the story of Wendell Johnson's (1946) work with stutterers could be very helpful. Speech involves muscle control; stuttering is often the effects of psychic tension and uncertainty of control. When stutterers were asked to read in unison, they tended to drop their self-awareness and read quite normally. Whenever any stutterer was asked to read alone, he began to stutter again. Other methods, such as the use of headphones into which distracting noises could be directed, produced similar results. In summary, as the stutterers realized that their speech problems were quite ordinary, common, normal, they began to improve.

So with tension in field and track events. As long as the athlete is enmeshed in his own self-doubts, he cannot relax; as he realizes that early tension is normal to all athletes, he will begin to concentrate on the action rather than on himself.

DIFFERENTIAL RELAXATION. Relaxation through skill learning is really the same as that called "differential relaxation" by the foremost researcher in this field, Edmund Jacobson (1957, 124). By this method Jacobson taught his patients to differentiate between the muscles active in a given movement, and those unrelated or opposed to action. He did this by emphasizing pin-pointed awareness of each phase of movement, confirmed by sensitive voltmeters which recorded the tiny electric currents (.0000001 volt) produced in the muscles. With practice, his patients learned to detect even very slight muscle tensions that normally would be unnoticed.

Every athlete goes through some such re-learning process, though he tends to do it in terms of the event movement as a whole, and without the "abnormal" pin-pointed awareness of Jacobson's patients. For example, Nelson (1970, 124ff.) quotes Al Oerter, a true genius at achieving relaxation on crucial throws in crucial competition,

In the weeks before an Olympic competition, I mentally simulate every conceivable situation for each throw. For example, I imagine I'm in eighth place; it's my fifth throw, and it's pouring rain. What do I do? An inexperienced thrower might panic or be thinking, "Gees, I hope I don't fall down." I know ahead of time what I will do under every condition.

Faced with just such conditions at Mexico City, he knew just what to do. He kept on warming up in the rain; he eliminated certain preliminary movements in the throwing circle, started his spin slowly and carefully, and threw 212' 4½", a new personal record by almost five feet--and that after some 18 years of discus throwing.

Notice that Oerter said, "I mentally simulate--." The meaning of this in both a mind sense and a muscle sense may be clarified by reviewing the section in this book on "Mental Practice," or by reading Steinhaus's[1] article on the amazing "awareness" of the muscle spindles and the related organs. The words can never explain the action adequately, but they help.

But all great athletes learn to sense the effortless effort, are constantly practicing in terms of it, and learn ways of finding it in competition, not just in general but under the specific conditions that may arise in this particular competition. They may never be able to put it into words but they get the feel of it, and know it instantly when it happens. When Danielsen of Norway made his world-record throw (281' 2½") in the javelin at the Melbourne Olympics, he yelled excitedly while the javelin was still in the air. He <u>knew</u> that was it! His muscle spindles needed no steel tape. They sensed the ease, the rhythm, the relaxation of the throwing, and thus were their own accurate calculation of the distance.

<u>RELAXATION BY HOLISTIC REORIENTATION</u>. This third method, which I have called holistic reorientation, seeks to establish a sound relationship between the athlete and his total life situation, with emphasis of course on his competitive situation. Its full explanation would require a large volume, rather than a few paragraphs. In summary, until a sound relationship exists between the athlete and his surround, he is not likely to compete up to his potential. This surround has many aspects. It relates to his basic life needs (Maslow, 1954, 22-106): nutrition, activity, sex, safety, belongingness, etc. It relates to his culture. Yesterday I watched a basketball game between two teams with different life styles, so to speak--Pennsylvania with the traditional Establishment control, short haircuts, close discipline and all; and Harvard with its "mod" freedom as suggested by be-ribboned tresses. An athlete must achieve a relaxed attitude within the climate of his sports culture, whatever it may be.

Holistic re-orientation also relates to the conditions of practice and competition that are peculiar to each event and to each competitive situation. For example, this method seeks relaxation in endurance running by coming to terms with reality, by acceptance of hurt-pain-agony, to use Counsilman's term, as an inherent part of running that everyone must experience, and without the anxiety or fear with which our culture paralyzes such efforts. Similarly there must be realistic acceptance of victory and defeat, or of the facts of inequality among men. By such calm acceptance, a sense of holding oneself apart from the battle is gained, call it imperturbability, courage, fortitude, what you will. By such letting-go of self, both danger and the fear of danger lose much of their hindering power.

Emil Zatopek, the truly great Czech distance runner, has told of his habit in practice of holding his breath while walking or jogging from one tree to another. He did this so as to adjust to the feelings of low oxygen, not to build up his will power over such feelings, but to come to terms with them. He wrote, "I practiced holding my breath until will power was no longer a problem." This is quite a different approach from that of repressing them by power of will. By this approach, low oxygen held no dangers or fears for him. He could relax. Self-control was not an issue and "will power was no longer a problem."

To take a different example from Zatopek, his face in competition expressed the full gamut of fatigue from mere breathlessness to agony. Many criticized this as indicating a lack of self-control and relaxation. But Cerutty, Herb Elliott's coach, interpreted Zatopek's grimaces as a positive aid to effort with no inhibitions. He said that so-called relaxation by conscious control, by a determined maintenance of proper style or a certain decorum of facial expression is "a concept of weakly men and coaches." In his book, *RUNNING WILD*, Gordon Pirie (1961, 35) supported Cerutty in these views and accused British runners of keeping

> . . . *a stiff upper lip even in the agony of a race. They restrain their emotions not to show suffering. The free and relaxed runner shows in his face and gestures that it is torture and agony to give his last ounce of energy. How silly to pretend that it is not. . . . The restrained runner can never reach the greatest heights.*

Under this method of relaxation, we achieve ease of movement by coming to terms with the so-called negatives, whether physical or mental-emotional in nature, and so using them in every

---

[1] Arthur Steinhaus, "Your Muscles See More Than Your Eyes," *JOURNAL HPER*, September 1966, 38.

way possible. I think of the negative effects of lactic acid as an outcome of fatiguing activity and a deterrent to running, but also of its re-synthesis to glycogen for use again. True, the body does attempt to buffer against its negative acidity, but it also makes use of its positive values.

Herb Elliott (1961) wrote repeatedly of the two-phased need for tension-relaxation before a BIG race. "Better to be keyed up than relaxed before a race. . . . In races, I must let my body go--relax 100 percent. . . . Sometimes your mind is in such a jumble that it won't give your body a chance" (p. 51). "Sometimes we'd go to a quiet park a few hours before the race so that I could run spiritedly for twenty minutes or so and imagine myself winning. I became calm then and, back at the hotel, find no difficulty in sleeping for two hours before going to the stadium half an hour before the race" (p. 146). "Running should be free expression of the body; in the words of the song, ought to be doing what comes naturally" (p. 50).

Under holistic reorientation, every opposing force must be viewed as having a helpful quality also, even if it's only a challenge which draws forth a higher response. Endurance swimming affords an excellent illustration of this. Obviously water resistance to forward progress is an opposing force. But the expert swimmer uses that resistance in the actions of his legs and arms which push him forward. That is, instead of opposing force by greater force, he uses the water, merges himself within it, relaxes with it. Buoyancy aids relaxation of course, but that is not our point. The relaxation we are speaking of is that of a fish in his natural element, in contrast to that of a cat which, hating and fearing the water, fights its way out of it.

Another way of explaining this method is to emphasize the sheer joy of effort, of losing oneself in the fun of action, in the excitement of personal development and improving performance, in the anticipation of goals achieved. It's hard not to be relaxed when jumping or throwing or running because one enjoys it. Like so many other athletes, Jim Ryun quit track when endless pressures from others created inner tensions; he attempted a comeback when his reorientation to the sport allowed him to relax and enjoy his running.

RELAXATION BY WITHDRAWAL-AND-RETURN. There is another aspect of relaxation by holistic reorientation which is best explained by use of Toynbee's phrase, "withdrawal-and-return." Coaches and athletes have made use of the idea for decades, or even centuries. When the relationship between the athlete and his total life situation becomes over-filled with problems, tensions, anxieties, he should withdraw from that world for a time, then return to it, refreshed and eager.

The Greeks used this method, with or without awareness, when they required every Olympic prospect to spend ten months prior to the Games, away from the distractions and hindrances of the home situation, while concentrating on training in the gymnasium environment created for that purpose.

One of the happiest examples of modern times was the pioneer tourist camp established at Vålådalen, Sweden, by Gosta Olander. There, among the lakes and rivers and forests and hills, his guests from the city found quiet and slow-moving, and complete relaxation of the body and spirit. There, by following a training program called fartlek (speed-play), Gunder Haegg and many other Swedish runners found the ease of mind that could accompany even the most strenuous of physical exertions. Running became not so much a problem of will power over the pains of fatigue, as of the release of energy while enjoying the natural surroundings. Olander was once quoted[1] as saying,

Training is not only bodily exertion but mental preparation. The ultimate springs of physical performance are not in the muscles but in the mind. Exercise should be directed at helping nature. . . . Animals are always fit. The reason is that they stay relaxed-- except when there is need for exertion, as in killing or escape. Their nerves never fight their muscles.

This was also the purpose behind Cerutty's move out of the tensions of Melbourne into the relative peace of a home along the sea coast at Portsea, where Herb Elliott and many others

---

[1] James Stewart Gordon, "Relax--and Get Fit!" *Today's Health,* August, 1964.

enjoyed the challenges of great sand dunes, of running naked along the beach and through the Australian bush. For a long weekend they would withdraw from their home tensions, relax for a time even though training strenuously, then return to the city with renewed vigor.

Many of us have experienced the excitement and joy of training during Spring Vacation. True, we worked out two or even three times a day, but the work was fun because we had dropped the tensions of normal living, and could achieve what might be called dynamic relaxation, that is, relaxation within strenuous action but without the life tensions that so inhibit full expression of our energies.

PROGRESSIVE RELAXATION. The term "progressive relaxation" was the invention of Dr. Edmund Jacobson (1957) who for over 25 years conducted research on relaxation and sleep. His methods have gained wide acceptance among therapists, physicians, mental hygienists, and others concerned with the conservation and restoration of human energies. His book for laymen, YOU MUST RELAX, is worth careful study by coaches. In brief, his method has two phases. (1) A muscle is first contracted hard, then suddenly relaxed, so that sharp awareness is gained of the contrasting feelings of tension and relaxation. (2) The subject relaxes one muscle group at a time in a systematic order from feet to head and head to feet. Gradually what Jacobson called "progressive relaxation" occurs throughout the body, and one might add, the mind as well.

The value of this method is for rest, recovery from fatigue, and prevention of wasteful tension during the days preceding competition, or during the rest periods of competition. With repeated practice an athlete learns to let go, to drop his tensions, instantaneously, by the cue of feeling tension and relaxing. It is possible to become very sensitive to this muscle sense, somewhat as a blind man's finger tips become sensitive to the raised dots of a Braille reader. Or as the actions of undressing, cleaning one's teeth, setting the clock, or reading in bed all serve as cues for falling asleep.

There have been many variations of Jacobson's methods. Steinhaus (1963, 306) suggests the following for schoolchildren sitting at a desk:

Keep your heads down; let your arms hang over the sides of your desk. Now imagine you are a large sack of flour that lies slumped over your desk. There is a tiny hole in each corner of the sack. Slowly, very slowly, the flour is running out of each hole; smoothly, smoothly, it is running out.

Feel it--just as if your arms and legs were running out of the sack. Slowly, steadily your arms are getting longer and longer and longer. You are getting limper and limper. You are lying heavily on your desk--slumped down--just like the sack of flour--flatter and flatter and flatter.

It works. Try it yourself, now. Soon you've let yourself go--all of you. Eddie Rickenbacher is reported to have followed just such methods in seeking relief from tension, and renewed energy for his strenuous life as flyer, aviation executive, public relations expert, you name it. But he used different analogies: a jellyfish completely limp in every part, a large burlap bag of potatoes, with holes out of which the potatoes are slowly rolling. Feel yourself deflate as each potato rolls away.

RELAXATION BY POSITIVE AUTO-SUGGESTION. Auto-suggestion is no longer an "in" word. Self-suggestion is now more easily accepted. Or, more commonly, relaxation by positive thinking, to use Norman Vincent Peale's term,[1] or relaxation by PMA (positive mental attitude), to use Napoleon Hill's term.[2] But auto-suggestion was in vogue in 1942 when psychologist Dorothy Yates first taught its values to Bud Winter, track coach at San Jose State. Winter became sufficiently enthusiastic about its potential for his track men, especially his sprinters, so that later, when the War brought him into the Navy, he sought Dr. Yates' help with the excessive nervous tensions of the men in pre-flight training school. Eventually, the Navy accepted mental conditioning by auto-suggestion as a regular part of its flight training program.

---

[1] Norman Vincent Peale, THE POWER OF POSITIVE THINKING, Englewood Cliffs, N.J.: Prentice-Hall, Inc., 1952.

[2] Napoleon Hill, SUCCESS THROUGH A POSITIVE MENTAL ATTITUDE, Englewood Cliffs, N.J.: Prentice-Hall, Inc., 1960.

Hubbard[1] summarized Dr. Yates' methods as follows:

First, in preliminary discussion, the athlete must be convinced the plan can be of assistance to him. Examples of success in concrete situations . . . are very helpful. At the same time, a non-technical description of the physical disturbances caused by nervous tension should also be given. Once the athlete understands the tremendous energy waste brought on by excess tension, the necessity for relaxation will become clear. . . .

Next, the athlete must be taught to relax--to rid himself of nervous tension. Dr. Yates tells her subjects to concentrate on a word of their own choice, such as "calm"--a word that signifies the exact opposite of tension. She explains that this chosen word will become the means for bringing back a state of relaxation in the future. Then she uses this word, and thoughts connected with it, in relaxing the subject.

The athlete lies on a couch or sits in a chair with a back high enough to support his head. He closes his eyes, and concentrates on the word he has selected as meaning the opposite of tension.

Dr. Yates talks to him slowly, reassuringly, asking him to picture in his mind a place of peace and tranquillity. She tells him to imagine he is there, to picture the calmness and contentment of the scene.

After about ten minutes of relaxation talk, Dr. Yates suggests that the athlete remain relaxed and quiet for a while, letting the thoughts of calmness and peace sink in. She allows him to spend at least five minutes in reflection.

At the end of this period she dismisses the subject, directing him to fall asleep each night thinking of his relaxation word. By so doing he will be able more quickly to cement the relationship between his word and a calm mental attitude. . . .

Usually in a very short time--perhaps two or three discussion periods with the psychologist--the athlete is able to relax without her guidance merely by forming a mental association between his chosen word ("calm" for example) and a relaxed condition.

Then, the subject must be taught what is called "set." For, while relaxation conserves energy, the employment of "set" enables an athlete to release that energy to the fullest and most productive extent when it is most needed--in action on the field, or in the ring. . .

While in the relaxed state, which he has been taught to attain, he sets his mind on being cool, or aggressive, or confident during a coming athletic event. At this point the "set," instead of being used to awaken the athlete, is used to give him confidence or whatever attribute he desires.

"Set," to Dr. Yates, is even more important than relaxation, and "set" and relaxation complement each other. The athlete employs "set" in learning to relax, and he uses the relaxed state to firmly implant "set" in his mind.

For this reason she combines the teaching of the two. In teaching "set" the first step is to have the subject accurately analyze his main difficulty. Is it lack of confidence? Is it an inability to remember the athletic skills he has learned?

Once the difficulty has been brought to the surface it is handled in this way: A short slogan is agreed upon--a slogan such as "I will be confident"--emphasizing a positive rather than a negative point of view.

Dr. Yates helps the subject relax, and then she repeats the slogan, amplifying its meaning to avoid monotony, but continually repeating the main theme.

---

[1] John M. Hubbard, "Autosuggestion--A New Formula in Mental Conditioning," *Scholastic Coach*, February, 1947, 14.

The athlete is told to go over his "set" slogan each night before falling asleep, along with his relaxation procedure.

Finally, the subject must be afforded an early opportunity to "try his wings," in order to prove to himself that this method of mental conditioning does work. "Nothing succeeds like success."

After the first few sessions, the athlete makes the entire method his own--the presence of an instructor is no longer required. Notice that the word "instructor" is used here, and not "psychologist."

That is because, as Dr. Yates points out, it is not necessary to resort to a trained psychologist, in implementing the formula.

Any coach who has gained the respect and friendship of his student athletes can achieve the desired results. His tutelage can be every bit as effective as that of a psychologist-- and any small mistakes in technique will not have a hindering effect if there is a basis of friendly trust.

Those having a special interest in this method will find other papers[1] by Dorothy Yates of value, as well as an excellent history of the entire movement in positive thinking by Donald Meyer,[2] including the viewpoints of William James, Emile Coué, Dale Carnegie, Henry Link, Harry Emerson Fosdick, and many others. What has been found helpful in other areas of life can be effective in sports.

RELAXATION BY "EMPTYING THE MIND." This method of relaxation can be interpreted and used as simply or as deeply as your interest in the subject may suggest. Viewed simply, it is a natural mental effect of Jacobson's progressive relaxation. As the muscles relax throughout the body, those related to speech and thought tend to relax also. We can only think of one thing at a time. As our attention concentrates on relaxing a particular muscle group, it shifts away from the doubts and anxieties that produce tension. Gradually, mental activity grows quiet; the mind, as we say, becomes empty. You may even fall asleep.

In his chapter, "Relaxing the Mind," Jacobson (1957, 160ff.) explains that electromyography has confirmed the presence of electrical stimuli to the speech muscles when a subject is thinking or worrying over a problem. He teaches that by relaxing the specific muscles related to speech, including the entire region of the lips, cheeks, jaws, and especially the eyes, the nervous excitation drops below the threshold, not only of speech but of thought as well. All mental imagery ceases. In support of such practice, Steinhaus (1963, 318) tells of his own ability to shut off the tuneful jingles that sometimes persist in the mind "by relaxing the muscles of my tongue and voice. Try it sometime. You can absolutely make such inner voices disappear."

Articles and books on the conservation of executive energies give many examples of high-pressure operators who, trained in some such method, gain a few minutes of complete mental relaxation, then snap back quickly with minds rested and cleared. For example, for 20 years I was associated with a man of tremendous energy, Dr. Joseph Maddy of the National Music Camp at Interlochen, Michigan. He had this remarkable facility to relax into nothingness for a few minutes, then to rise bubbling with vital energy. Steinhaus[3] has explained that the muscle sense is at least as sensitive as the visual sense, and that such men distinguish certain muscle-sense cues by which they relax and let their minds go empty. They don't try to relax; that's self-defeating. They simply let it all seep away.

But "emptying the mind" has a broader and deeper meaning than this, a meaning inherent in the word "holistic" as we have defined it, and in the relationship between the individual and the surrounding world. How can we find imperturbability in a time of trouble--of widespread social unrest, of war and violence, of growing awareness of inequality of opportunity based on irrele-

---

[1] Dorothy Yates, *Journal of Applied Psychology*, December 1943.
Journal of General Psychology, April 1946.

[2] Donald Meyer, *THE POSITIVE THINKERS*, New York: Doubleday & Company, Inc., 1965, Paperback edition, 342 pages.

[3] Arthur H. Steinhaus, "Your Muscles See More Than Your Eyes," *Journal HPER*, September 1966, 38.

vant factors, of communication machines that bombard us with troubles even before they happen. I suddenly think of John Carlos at Mexico City who, at the potentially most happy moment of his life, carried his troubles with him on the victory stand, and raised his black-gloved fist. How could he have found inner relaxation?

Discussion of this difficult point is not within the scope of this book. In our Western culture it tends to be a religious problem, rather than a sports problem. Read Paul Tillich's THE COURAGE TO BE, or the writings of Kierkegaard. It creeps into the writings of psychologists, as in C. G. Jung's THE UNDISCOVERED SELF, or P. W. Martin's EXPERIMENT IN DEPTH, or Donald Meyer's THE POSITIVE THINKERS.

But for fuller understanding, we must turn to the East for enlightenment. There, anxiety is truly inherent, but men have learned to empty themselves of it. Read almost any of the books by Alan Watts, especially the chapters "Empty and Marvellous," and "Sitting Quietly, Doing Nothing," in THE MEANING OF ZEN, or his PSYCHOTHERAPY EAST AND WEST. But most fascinating of all such writings, as well as most relevant to sports, is Eugen Herrigel's ZEN IN THE ART OF ARCHERY. Even though the concept of competitiveness is unacceptable in Zen, the book describes relaxation-in-activity at a higher dimension than we can even dream of in sports. In teaching the artless art of archery, the Zen Master admonishes his pupil to stop thinking about the shot, to just let it happen (Herrigel, 1953, 71).

> You only feel it (tension) because you really haven't let go of yourself. It is all so simple. You can learn from an ordinary bamboo leaf what ought to happen. It bends lower and lower under the weight of snow. Suddenly the snow slips to the ground without the leaf having stirred. . . . So indeed it is: when the tension is fulfilled, the shot must fall . . . from the archer like snow from a bamboo leaf, before he even thinks of it.

Admit that releasing an arrow is not at all the same as the powerful efforts of putting a shot or jumping high. But we must also admit that the athlete who has learned to free himself from all inner tension, physical or mental, who has learned how to "inhibit his inhibitions," who can release his full powers recklessly, with nothing held back--all within the channels of skill of course--has a tremendous advantage over the man who carries his and the world's tensions with him into the throwing circle or jumping runway.

One valid definition of relaxation is "the art of releasing power," not that of striving to use it.

RELAXATION BY REPRESSING THE NEGATIVES. "Relax! Go get 'em! Move up now! Relax!" How often I've listened to coaches, myself among them, urging our charges to lift themselves by their own bootstraps, so to speak, to run faster but easier, while a sharper and higher awareness of the anguish of fatigue threatens to overwhelm them. All too often, the coach allows his own anxiety to raise the pitch of his voice, and this the runner hears, even though he may not hear the words themselves.

All such admonitions to deliberately repress our feelings actually tend to exaggerate the feelings, just as the old will-power psychology which sought to repress our lusts ended mainly in increasing them. It is hard to exaggerate the negative effects on young runners when writers, coaches, physicians, parents carelessly use such words as agony, suffering, torture, or man-killer as being related to endurance running. Young runners tend to look for such terrors, and find them even when they're really non-existent. After all, the process of training inhibits awareness of pain just as it reduces the negative physical effects of fatigue. The mind of an experienced runner becomes inured to what the layman calls "the agony of running" just as his body becomes inured to low oxygen and lactic acid.

This is the reasoning behind the "hurt-pain-agony concept" of training advanced by Jim Counsilman (1968, 338), Indiana swimming coach. By bringing such words into everyday parlance and using them as a natural and inevitable part of every swimmer's experience, they lose their power to paralyze action. They even become a stimulus to good-humored kidding within the team.

Without some such training of this kind, the mind of the young runner anticipates and exaggerates both pain and failure, becomes more sensitive to the dangers of pain and the competition than of its own power to control and repress them. At the first sense of uneasiness or mild ache while running, they tend to feel, "There it is!" and soon "THERE IT IS!" The expectation creates reality. The coach that expects such a mind to exert control when he yells

"Relax!" is certain to be frustrated. Unfortunately he tends to blame the boy rather than his own approach to the problem.

Related sciences use the term "psychoneurosis" to identify a fixation of attention on the possible negative aspects of action. The fear of failing to rise up to the expectations of others, or of undergoing the horrors of exhaustion overwhelms the mind. (Have you ever thought of the connotation of that word we use so casually, "exhaustion?" To exhaust anything is "to use up or consume completely." Such a term has no place in sports. Who can estimate its subconscious effects?) The runner feels that somehow he must try harder, while all the time convinced that it won't be hard enough. In the *NEUROTIC PERSONALITY OF OUR TIMES*, Karen Horney writes of the dangers of our competitive culture in creating "basic anxiety, the feeling of being isolated and helpless in a potentially hostile world." Such anxiety is inherent in our track and field world, whether we recognize it or not, and the concept of winning by will power and repression of the negatives increases its dangers.

<u>RELAXATION BY UNDERLOADING THE ACTION</u>. Underloading the action should be interpreted primarily in terms of speed more than of resistance or strength, especially the speed of the preliminary movements of each event. When Harold Connolly set his world record in the hammer throw in 1962, at 231' 10" he wrote that "People were beginning to think that I was all washed up. I had been experimenting with four turns. It worked well most of the time but it broke down under the pressure of the big meets. With three turns, I could just get in there and throw." Whether this meant lesser speed or lesser inner tension is not significant. It certainly meant an increase in throwing power by way of relaxation.

Jokl[1] explained Bob Beamon's superhuman long jump (29' 2½") at Mexico City, in part, by the "absence of the inhibitory component" of hitting the board without fouling, after a full-speed run. He spoke of Beamon as "an unsophisticated natural jumper who pays little attention to the organization of the run-up and its markings." He just ran-and-jumped with no inhibitions or reservations. He hit the board perfectly. "I was just lucky," Beamon remarked after the event.

To give a reverse example, John Thomas overloaded the action in 1963 when he attempted to match Brumel's speed in the early steps of his run-up. Lacking the strength-training work and the specific skill of so fast an approach, he was unable to relax, and slowed the last three steps as a matter of both physical and mental necessity.

A different kind of underloading occurs in baseball when the batter swings a weighted bat before stepping to the plate. The action of swinging the regular bat now seems underloaded, so that he swings easier, faster, more relaxed. He now has a muscle sense of quickness rather than of hard effort. For some reason this custom has not caught on in throwing events. It's altogether reasonable that a weighted shot, discus, hammer, or javelin, used just prior to performance, would aid relaxation.

Underloading can also occur by reducing the mental tensions during competition. Each athlete has a critical level of tension at which he performs best. If tension is lower, he is not properly "keyed up" for the competition; if higher, he is "tight," and unrelaxed. A precise optimum tension is what is needed. Such tension is sometimes gained by having an athlete compete against superior competition during the weeks preceding an all-important team meet. Superior competition serves the same purpose as the weighted bat.

In summary, the underloading to produce relaxation can be of many kinds, physical and mental: a slight slowing of velocity in the preliminary movements, a simplifying of technique in competition, an ignore-ance of technique, deliberate overloading prior to competition--anything to help the athlete drop his tensions just below the critical level of uninhibited action.

<u>RELAXATION BY CONCENTRATION ON POSITIVE EXTERNAL FACTORS</u>. Fatigue and hypertension have both mental and physical aspects. Without denying the physical brakes applied by fatigue, we emphasize that the greater danger lies in the mental awareness of the feelings of fatigue. It is doubt of success, distaste for the discomforts of fatigue, fear of all-out effort, that restrain

---

[1] Ernst Jokl, M.D., "A Report on Bob Beamon's World-Record Long Jump," *U.S.T.C.A. Quarterly Review*, October 1969, 39.

performance at least as much as physical inability.

Obviously then, relaxation-in-action is maintained by concentrating on the positive factors, especially those that are external to the athlete. He loses himself; he insulates his sensitivity to the negatives of action by attending to the more factual aspects of his surround. In endurance running, he concentrates on race tactics, on the changing positions of various runners, especially the main contenders, on pace and the voice of the timer.

Most runners would agree that their greatest performances came when they were least aware of their own feelings. When Bannister (1955, 213) wrote of his first-ever mile under four minutes, he said, "There was no pain, only a great unity of movement and purpose. The world seemed to stand still, or did not exist. The only reality was the next 100 yards of track under my feet."

Though fiction, Alan Sillitoe's excellent story "The Loneliness of the Long-Distance Runner" sticks to the facts of running. His main character says, "I put on a spurt, and such a fast spurt it is because I feel that up to then I haven't been running and that I've used up no energy at all. And I've been able to do this because I've been thinking; and I wonder if I'm the only one in the running business with this system of forgetting that I'm running because I'm too busy thinking." Every biography of great runners tells the same story, though of course, the kind of thinking will vary.

For example, when the New Zealand runner, Murray Halberg, (1963, 105) wrote about his Olympic race at Rome, he told of his difficulties in keeping relax ed before the race until finally he became aware of the strain on the faces of his competitors. Only then,"I began to enjoy myself and look forward to the race." As to the race itself, he wrote,

It wasn't like Melbourne. I wasn't running in a blur. I could see the distant faces of the crowd. I was aware of everything. . . .

In contrast to Melbourne, from the start of the race I ran dead last and let the rest of the field carry me around. I could see the fellows in the lead changing places, getting checked, striving for better pole positions. It was almost as though I was watching the race from a detached position on the terrace. . . . During the eighth lap I began working the plan Arthur (Lydiard) and I had talked over for so long before the race.

Here is a mind concentrated on the positives of action, on the problems of other runners, and on the positive plan.

RELAXATION THROUGH WHOLENESS. I have deliberately held back the surest and best way to relaxation--that of feeling and being whole, all of one piece, within oneself and among one's family and friends. If, as Erich Fromm contends in MAN AGAINST HIMSELF, individual isolation and separateness is the primary evil in modern society, it follows that a sense of unity, of mutual supportiveness, of wholeness within and without is our greatest need.

Only the rare individual has it. Among coaches I have known, I think of Brutus Hamilton, Bill Bowerman, Leroy Walker; among athletes, Roger Bannister, Brian Sternberg, Valeriy Brumel. There are others, but these indicate the type--men who are solid, inwardly relaxed, at home in their world.

Kenny Moore,[1] in an SI article on Sebastian Coe, portrayed him as such a person--self-possessed, natural in all sorts of situations, nerveless while racing, unimpressed by records or victory,

"How have you become so free of anxiety before competition?" Sebastian was asked. "In having to be awakened before the Oslo race (in which he set the 1500m world record--KD), I guess I gave the appearance of calm, but I get nervous....I don't know. I can't say I consciously mastered it. It's just something that evolved, being less and less nervous."
Sebastian glanced at his family. "Feeling I'd be well and truly supported in my efforts had to be a part of it."

---

[1] Kenny Moore, "A Hard and Supple Man," *Sports Illustrated*, June 20, 1980, p. 74ff.

BIBLIOGRAPHY

The text material makes specific references to all but a few of the following books. They include books in related fields that support the basic viewpoints of the author, as well as those directly related to track and field and to track and field coaching. Single references, especially to articles, are given at the bottom of each page.

Astrand, P. O. *Textbook of Work Physiology*. New York: McGraw-Hill, Inc., 1970, 669 pp.

Bannister, Roger. *The Four Minute Mile*. New York: Dodd, Mead & Co., 1955, 252 pp.

Blake, Robert R. & Jane S. Mouton. *The Managerial Grid*. Houston: Gulf Publishing Company, 1964, 338 pp.

Brock, Greg. *How High School Runners Train*, Los Altos, CA: *Tafnews Press*, 1976, paper, 96 pps.

Bullard, Ernie & Larry Knuth. *Discus--Wilkins vs Powell*, L. K. Publications, 1977, available from *Tafnews Press*, paper, 62 pps.

Cartwright, D. and A. Zander. *Group Dynamics*. Evanston, Ill.: Row Peterson & Co., 1953.

Cerutty, Percy Wells. *Athletics*. *How to Become a Champion*. London: Stanley Paul & Co., Ltd., 1960, 189 pp.

_____. *Running with Cerutty*. Los Altos, CA: *Track & Field News*, 1959, 29 pp., paperback.

Clarke, Ron, and Alan Trengove. *The Unforgiving Minute*. London: Pelham Books, Ltd., 1966 189 pp.

_____, and Norman Harris. *The Lonely Breed*. London: Pelham Books Ltd., 1968, 187 pp.

Costill, David L., PhD. *A Scientific Approach to Distance Running*. *Track & Field News*, P.O. Box 296, Los Altos, CA, 94022, 1979, paper, 128 pp.

Counsilman, James E. *The Science of Swimming*. Englewood Cliffs, N.J.: Prentice-Hall, Inc., 1968, 457 pp.

De Vries, Herbert A. *Physiology of Exercise*. Dubuque, Iowa: Wm. C. Brown Co., 1966, 422 pp.

Dewey, John. "The Unity of the Human Being," in *Intelligence in the Modern World*, ed. Joseph Ratner. New York: Random House, 1939, 1069 pp.

Doherty, J. Kenneth. *Modern Track and Field*. Englewood Cliffs, N.J.: Prentice-Hall, Inc., 1963, 558 pp.

_____. *Modern Training for Running*. Englewood Cliffs, N.J.: Prentice-Hall, Inc., 1964, 281 pp

_____. *Track and Field Movies on Paper*, 2nd edition, one set of 3 books, 248 pp. 1967, available from *Track & Field News*, P.O. Box 296, Los Altos, CA, 94022.

_____. "Relaxation in All-Out Running," in *Proceedings Track and Field Institute*, ed. Allan J. Ryan, M.D. Madison: University of Wisconsin Extension Service, 1966, 2-28.

_____. "Holism in Training for Sports," in *Anthology of Contemporary Readings*, ed. Howard S. Slusher and Aileene S. Lockhart. Dubuque, Iowa: Wm. C. Brown Co., 1966, paper, 324 pp.

Dolson, Frank. *Always Young*. Mountain View, CA: World Publications, 1975, paper, 209 pp.

Dubos, René. *So Human an Animal*. New York: Charles Scribner's Sons, 1968, paper, 267 pp.

Dyson Geoffrey. *The Mechanics of Athletics*. London: University of London Press, 6th edition, 1974, 229 pp.

Ecker, Tom. *Track and Field Dynamics*. Los Altos, CA: Tafnews Press, 1971, paper, 112 pp.

Elliott, Herb, and Alan Trengove. *The Golden Mile*. London: Cassell & Co., Ltd., 1961, 178 pp.

Falls, Harold B., ed. *Exercise Physiology*. New York: Academic Press, 1968, 471 pp.

Ferstle, Jim. *Dave Wottle Story*. Mountain View, CA: World Publications, 1973, paper, 44 pp.

Ganslen, Richard V., Ph.D. *Mechanics of the Pole Vault*. 1980 Olympic 9th edition, paper, 176 pp., available from author, 1204 Windsor Drive, Denton, Texas, 76201.

Gilmour, Garth H. *A Clean Pair of Heels: The Murray Halberg Story*. London: Herbert Jenkins Ltd., 1963, 212 pp.

Goldstein, Kurt, M.D. *The Organism*. Boston: Beacon Press, 1963, paper, 531 pp.

Hannus, Matti. *Finnish Running Secrets*. Mountain View, CA: World Publications, 1973, paper, 93 pp.

Harris, Norman. *The Legend of Lovelock*. New Zealand: A.H. & A.W.Reed, 1964, 180 pp.

Hemphill, John K. *Leadership Studies*. Columbus: Ohio State University, Personnel Research Board, 1949-1956.

Henderson, Joe. *Thoughts on the Run*. Published by The Runner's World, P.O.Box 366, Mountain View, CA, 94040, 1970, 110 pp., paper.

_____. *New Views of Speed Training*. Mountain View, CA: The Runner's World, 1971, 48 pp.

Henry, Bill. *An Approved History of the Olympic Games*. New York: G.P.Putnam's Sons, 1948, 368 pp.

Herrigel, Eugen. *Zen in the Art of Archery*. New York: Pantheon Books Inc., 1953, 109 pp.

Hewson, Brian and Peter Bird. *Flying Feet*. New York: Arco Publishing Co., Inc., 1962, 160 pp.

Hoffman, Bob. *Weight Training for Athletes*. New York: The Ronald Press, 1961, 216 pp.

Hollander, E. P. and Raymond G. Hunt. *Current Perspectives in Social Psychology*. Paperback edition, New York: Oxford University Press, 1963, 557 pp.

Hooks, Gene. *Application of Weight Training to Athletics*. Englewood Cliffs, N.J.: Prentice-Hall, Inc., 1962, 254 pp.

Horney, Karen. *The Neurotic Personality of Our Times*. New York: W.W. Norton & Co., Inc., 1937, 299 pp.

Ibbotson, Derek and Terry O'Connor. *The 4-Minute Smiler*. London: Stanley Paul & Co., Ltd., 1960, 175 pp.

Jacobson, Edmund. *Progressive Relaxation*. Chicago: University of Chicago Press, 1938.

_____. *You Must Relax*. New York: McGraw-Hill, Inc., 1957, 269 pp.

Jarver, Jess. *Sprints and Relays*. Los Altos, CA: Tafnews Press, 1978, paper, 128 pp.

BIBLIOGRAPHY

Jenner, Bruce & Phillip Finch. *Decathlon Challenge*. Englewood Cliffs, N.J.: Prentice-Hall, Inc., 1977, 210 pp.

Jesse, John. *Strength, Power and Muscular Endurance for Runners and Hurdlers*. Pasadena, CA: The Athletic Press, P.O. Box 2314-D, 91105, paper, 1971, 158 pp.

Johnson, Wendell. *People In Quandaries*. New York: Harper, 1946, 532 pp.

Jordan, Tom. *Pre!*. Los Altos, CA: Tafnews Press, 1977, paper, 128 pp.

Kelly, Graeme. *Mr. Controversial--The Story of Percy Wells Cerutty*. London: Stanley Paul & Co., Ltd., 1964, 168 pp.

Kobayashi, Shigeru. *Creative Management*. New York: American Management Association, Inc. 1971.

Kohler, Wolfgang. *Gestalt Psychology*. New York: Liveright, 1947.

Laird, Donald A. and Eleanor C. *New Psychology for Leadership*. New York: McGraw-Hill, Inc., 1956, 226 pp.

_____. *Psychology: Human Relations and Motivations*. 4th edition. New York: McGraw-Hill, Inc., 1967, 440 pp.

Lawther, John. *The Learning of Physical Skills*. Englewood Cliffs, N.J.: Prentice-Hall, Inc., 1968, 150 pp.

Leterman, Elmer G. *Personal Power Through Creative Selling*. New York: Crowell-Collier, 1955, 256 pp.

Lewin, Kurt. *A Dynamic Theory of Personality*. New York: McGraw-Hill, Inc., 1935, paper, 286 pp.

_____. *Field Theory in Social Science*. New York: Harper & Row, 1951, paper, 346 pp.

Likert, Rensis. *New Patterns of Management*. New York: McGraw-Hill Book Co., 1961, 278 pp.

Lippitt, Robert et al. "The Dynamics of Power," in *Human Relations*. New York: Hermitage House, 1952, Vol. 5, 37-64.

Loader, W. R. *Testament of a Runner*. London: William Heinemann Ltd., 1960, 170 pp.

Lydiard, Arthur and Garth Gilmour. *Run to the Top*. London: Herbert Jenkins Ltd., 1962, 182 pp.

_____. *Running Training Schedules*. 2nd edition. Track & Field News, Box 296, Los Altos, CA, 94022, 1970, 30 pp.

Maslow, A. H. *Motivation and Personality*. New York: Harper & Row, 1954, 408 pp.

Matthews, Vince, with Neil Amdur. *My Race Be Won*. New York: Charterhouse, 1974, 396 pp.

McGregor, Douglas. *The Human Side of Enterprise*. New York: McGraw-Hill, Inc., 1960.

Menninger, Karl, M.D. *The Vital Balance*. New York: The Viking Press, 1963, 531 pp.

Morehouse, Laurence E. and Philip J. Rasch. *Scientific Basis of Athletic Training*. Philadelphia: W. B. Saunders Co., 1958, 238 pp.

Murphy, Gardner. *Human Potentialities*. London: George Allen & Unwin Ltd., 1960, 340 pp.

Natan, Alex, ed. *Sport and Society*. London: Bowes and Bowes, Ltd., 1958, 208 pp.

Nelson, Cordner. *The Jim Ryun Story*. Los Altos, CA: Tafnews Press, 1967, 272 pp.

Nelson, Cordner. *The Miler.* New York: S. G. Phillips, 1969, 158 pp.

_____. *Track and Field--The Great Ones.* London: Pelham Books, Ltd., 1968, 224 pp.

Nöcker, Joseph. *The Biological Foundations of Improvement Through Training.* Don Igelrud, Lother Schweder and Dieter Reetz, trans. Schorndorf, Germany: Verlag Karl Hofmann, 1960.

Noronha, Francis. *Kipchoge of Kenya.* Elimu Publishers, 1970. Distributed in U.S. by Tafnews Press, P.O. Box 296, Los Altos, CA 94022, paper, 160 pp.

O'Connor, Terry. *The 4-Minute Smiler: The Derek Ibbotson Story.* London: Stanley Paul & Co., Ltd., 1960, 171 pp.

Ogilvie, Bruce C. and Thomas A. Tutko. *Problem Athletes and How to Handle Them.* London: Pelham Books Ltd., 1966, 195 pp.

Oxendine, Joseph B. *Psychology of Motor Learning.* New York: Appleton-Century-Crofts, Inc., 1968, 366 pp.

Peters, J. H. and Joseph Edmundson. *In the Long Run.* London: Cassell & Co. Ltd., 1955, 216 pp.

Pickering, Ron. *Strength Training for Athletics.* London: Amateur Athletic Association, 24 Park Crescent, W.1. 2nd edition, paper, 1968, 72 pp.

Pirie, Gordon. *Running Wild.* London: W. H. Allen & Co., Ltd., 1961.

Raevuori, Antero and Rolf Haikkola. *Lasse Viren--Olympic Champion.* Portland, Oregon: Continental Publishing House, 1978, paper, 118 pp.

Reindell, Herbert, Helmut Roskamm, and Woldemar Gerschler. *Das Intervall-training.* Munich: Barth Publisher, 1962.

Ryan, Frank, Ph.D. *Weight Training.* New York: The Viking Press, 1969, 84 pp.

Selye, Hans, M.D. *The Stress of Life.* New York: McGraw-Hill, Inc., 1956, 324 pp.

Slusher, Howard S. and Aileene S. Lockhart. *Anthology of Contemporary Readings.* Dubuque, Iowa: Wm. C. Brown Co., 1966, 324 pp.

Snell, Peter and Garth Gilmour. *No Bugles No Drums.* Auckland, N.Z.: Minerva Ltd., 1965, 239pp.

Spencer, Bud. *High Above the Olympians.* Los Altos, CA: Tafnews Press, 1966, 300pp.

Stampfl, Franz. *Franz Stampfl on Running.* London: Herbert Jenkins Ltd., 1955, 159 pp.

Steinhaus, Arthur H. *Toward an Understanding of Health and Physical Education.* Dubuque, Iowa: Wm. C. Brown Co., 1963, 376 pp.

Tead, Ordway. *The Art of Leadership.* New York: McGraw-Hill, Inc., 1935, 307 pp.

Tulloh, Bruce. *Tulloh on Running.* London: William Heinemann Ltd., 1968, 146 pp.

Tutko, Thomas A. and Jack W. Richards. *Psychology of Coaching.* Boston: Allyn and Bacon, Inc., 1971, 216 pp.

Walker, Leroy T. *Championship Techniques and Track and Field.* West Nyack, N.Y.: Parker Publishing Co., 1969, 206 pp.

Williams, Roger J. *Biochemical Individuality.* New York: John Wiley & Sons, Inc., 1956, 214 pp.

BIBLIOGRAPHY

Wilt, Fred. *How They Train.* 2nd edition, 1973: Vol. 1--Middle Distances, 124 pp.; Vol. 2--Long Distances, 124 pp.; Vol. 3--Sprinting and Hurdling, 96 pp. Tafnews Press, P.O. Box 296, Los Altos, CA, 94022. All paperback.

_____. *Run, Run, Run.* Los Altos, CA: Track & Field News, 1964, paper, 281 pp.

_____, and Tom Ecker. *International Track and Field Coaching Encyclopedia.* West Nyack, N.Y.: Parker Publishing Co., 1970, 350 pp.

Winter, Lloyd C. ("Bud"). *So You Want to be a Sprinter.* San Francisco: Fearon Publishers, 2450 Fillmore St., 1956, paper, 48 pp.

_____. *The Rocket Sprint Start.* San Francisco: Fearon Publishers, 1964, 22 pp.

Wortman, Max S. *Emerging Concepts in Management.* New York: The Macmillan Co., 1969, 452 pp.

Zarnowski, Frank. *The Decathlon Guide.* 1976. Can be purchased from author, Mt. St. Mary's College, Dept. of Business and Economics, Emmitsburg, Maryland.

NAME INDEX

SUBJECT INDEX